Selections from
THE COMPLETE WORKS OF SWAMI VIVEKANANDA

Selections from

THE COMPLETE WORKS OF SWAMI VIVEKANANDA

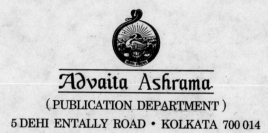

Advaita Ashrama
(PUBLICATION DEPARTMENT)
5 DEHI ENTALLY ROAD • KOLKATA 700 014

Published by
Swami Bodhasarananda
Adhyakṣha, Advaita Ashrama
Mayavati, Champawat, Uttarakhand, Himalayas
from its Publication Department, Kolkata
Email: mail@advaitaashrama.org
Website: www.advaitaashrama.org

Thirty-second Reprint, March 2013
20M5C

ISBN 978-81-85301-60-0 (Subsidized)
ISBN 978-81-7505-076-1 (Deluxe)

Printed in India at
Art Union Printing Works Private Ltd.
Kolkata 700 006

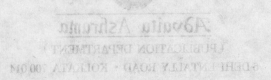

PUBLISHER'S NOTE TO THE ABRIDGED EDITION OF THE COMPLETE WORKS

The United Nations Organization has declared 1985 as the International Year of the Youth. In keeping with the spirit of this declaration, the Government of India announced that 12 January 1985 be observed as the National Youth Day all over the country — 12 January being the birthday of Swami Vivekananda in 1863 — and that 12 January shall be observed every year hereafter as the National Youth Day. In a communication, the Government of India mentioned the significance of the day: 'It was felt that the philosophy of Swamiji and the ideals for which he lived and worked could be a great source of inspiration to the Indian Youth'.

To the youth of India, there can be no better leader than Swami Vivekananda. Paying his tribute to Swamiji, the late Prime Minister Jawaharlal Nehru said: 'I do not know how many of the younger generation read the speeches and writings of Swami Vivekananda. But I can tell you that many of my generation were very powerfully influenced by him, and I think that it would do a great deal of good to the present generation if they also went through Swami Vivekananda's writings and speeches, and they would learn much from them. ... If you read Swami Vivekananda's writings and speeches, the curious thing you will find is that they are not old. ... He gave us something which brings us, if I may use the word, a certain pride in our inheritance. ... What Swamiji has written and said is of interest and must interest us and is likely to influence us for a long time to come. ... Directly or indirectly, he has powerfully influenced the India of today. And I think that our younger generation will take advantage of this fountain of wisdom, of spirit and fire, that flows through Swami Vivekananda.'

In this International Year of the Youth, we have great pleasure in placing this *Abridged Edition of the Complete Works of Swami Vivekananda*, which is a true mirror of Swamiji's literature, in the hands of the youthful world at a heavily subsidized price. This has been made possible thanks to the munificence of M/s. Hindustan Charity Trust 1959, Calcutta. We wish to take this opportunity to express our profound thanks to them for enabling us to spread Swamiji's literature at such a low price.

The Complete Works of Swami Vivekananda, in fact, is in eight volumes in English, published by us. They contain his original writings, inspiring lectures, exhorting epistles to his disciples and brother-disciples, conversations and dialogues, questions and answers, poetic compositions both in Sanskrit and English, four yogas, Inspired Talks, and several other items. There is hardly any problem affecting our motherland which has escaped his notice. Being a patriot of a high order, he lived and worked for the regeneration of India on national lines, in tune with her time-old genius and tradition.

The present book in your hands has been, in fact, published by us under the title *Selections from Swami Vivekananda* for nearly four decades. We hope and pray that this book in the present form will reach a wider circle of youth all over India and the world and inspire them to lead a purposeful life of thought and action, devotion and dedication.

Swamiji's message in brief was 'Be and Make'. In these pages, the reader will find ample inspiration to implement this simple message in his life. It is hoped that a thorough reading of this book will gradually lead the reader to go to the Complete Works in eight volumes and enable him to derive the full benefit of Swamiji's blessings and inspiration.

14 April 1985 PUBLISHER
Advaita Ashrama
Mayavati, Himalayas.

PUBLISHER'S NOTE

In this edition, the previous title *Abridged Edition of the Complete Works of Swami Vivekananda* is changed to *Selections from the Complete Works of Swami Vivekananda*. The 'Contents' remain the same.

1 February 1986 PUBLISHER
Advaita Ashrama
Mayavati, Himalayas.

PREFACE

The published writings and speeches of Swami Vivekananda cover nearly four thousand pages. Many do not have access to them, and others have not the time or patience to go through them all. The need for a selection from the Swamiji's writings and speeches has therefore long been felt. But to make a selection was not an easy task. For Swami Vivekananda was an inspired Seer, born with a mission. As such, everything that issued from his lips or pen has deep significance, and it is difficult to decide which to choose and which to leave out, particularly when the space at one's disposal is limited. And there will always be difference of opinion as to which writing or speech is more important and which less.

With these handicaps, we have ventured to bring out this volume of selections. We have tried to make them as representative as possible. Thus we have culled some of his Lectures, Discourses, Interviews, Answers to Questions, Inspired Talks, Conversations, Writings, Letters, Poems, and have also included translation[1] of some Bengali writings and utterances. These selections may not be universally accepted to be the best of what the Swami wrote and said, in spite of our earnest attempt to make them so, but they will at least give a glimpse of what a versatile genius Vivekananda was and how far-reaching and profound was his message. And we hope they will rouse a desire in some readers to study the Swami's thought more thoroughly.

PUBLISHER.

ADVAITA ASHRAMA
Mayavati, Himalayas
February 25, 1944.

[1] These pieces are marked in the book with asterisks.

Each soul is potentially divine.

The goal is to manifest this divinity within, by controlling nature, external and internal.

Do this either by work, or worship, or psychic control, or philosophy—by one, or more, or all of these—and be free.

This is the whole of religion. Doctrines, or dogmas, or rituals, or books, or temples, or forms, are but secondary details.

—*Swami Vivekananda*

CONTENTS

CONTENTS

SWAMI VIVEKANANDA

Now and then, at long intervals of time, a being finds his way to this planet who is unquestionably a wanderer from another sphere; who brings with him to this sorrowful world some of the glory, the power, the radiance of the far distant region from which he came. He walks among men but he is not at home here. He is a pilgrim, a stranger, he tarries but a night.

He shares the life of those about him, enters into their joys and sorrows, rejoices with them, mourns with them; but through it all, he never forgets who he is, whence he came, or what the purpose of his coming. He never forgets his divinity. He remembers that he is the great, the glorious, the majestic Self. He knows that he came from that ineffable, supernal region which has no need of the sun or moon, for it is illumined by the Light of lights. He knows that he *was*, long before the time when "all the sons of God sang together for joy".

Such a one, I have seen, I have heard, I have revered. At his feet I have laid my soul's devotion.

Such a being is beyond all comparison, for he transcends all ordinary standards and ideals. Others may be brilliant, his mind is luminous, for he had the power to put himself into immediate contact with the source of all knowledge. He is no longer limited to the slow processes to which ordinary human beings are confined. Others may be great, they are great only as compared with those in their own class. Others may be good, powerful, gifted, having more of goodness, more of power, more of genius than their fellow men. It is only a matter of comparison. A saint is more holy, more pure, more single-minded than ordinary men. But with Swami Vivekananda, there could be no comparison. He was in a class by himself. He belonged to another order. He was not of this world. He was a radiant being who had descended from another, from a higher sphere for a definite purpose. One might have known that he would not stay long.

Is it to be wondered at that nature itself rejoices in such a birth, that the heavens open and angels sing paeans of praise?

Blessed is the country in which he was born, blessed are they who lived on this earth at the same time, and blessed, thrice blessed are the few who sat at his feet.

—*Memoirs of Sister Christine*

LECTURES

ADDRESSES AT THE PARLIAMENT OF RELIGIONS

RESPONSE TO WELCOME

At the World's Parliament of Religions, Chicago, 11th September 1893

Sisters and Brothers of America,

It fills my heart with joy unspeakable to rise in response to the warm and cordial welcome which you have given us. I thank you in the name of the most ancient order of monks in the world; I thank you in the name of the mother of religions; and I thank you in the name of the millions and millions of Hindu people of all classes and sects.

My thanks, also, to some of the speakers on this platform who, referring to the delegates from the Orient, have told you that these men from far-off nations may well claim the honour of bearing to different lands the idea of toleration. I am proud to belong to a religion which has taught the world both tolerance and universal acceptance. We believe not only in universal toleration, but we accept all religions as true. I am proud to belong to a nation which has sheltered the persecuted and the refugees of all religions and all nations of the earth. I am proud to tell you that we have gathered in our bosom the purest remnant of the Israelites who came to Southern India and took refuge with us in the very year in which their holy temple was shattered to pieces by Roman tyranny. I am proud to belong to the religion which has sheltered and is still fostering the remnant of the grand Zoroastrian nation. I will quote to you, brethren, a few lines from a hymn which I remember to have repeated from my earliest boyhood, which is every day repeated by millions of human beings: *"As the different streams having their sources in different places all mingle their water in the sea, so, O Lord, the different paths which men take through different tendencies, various though they appear, crooked or straight, all lead to Thee."*

The present convention, which is one of the most august assemblies ever held, is in itself a vindication, a declaration to the world of the wonderful doctrine preached in the Gita: *"Whosoever comes to Me, through whatsoever form, I reach him; all men are struggling through paths which in the end lead to Me."* Sectarianism, bigotry, and its horrible descendant, fanaticism, have long possessed this beautiful earth. They have filled the earth with violence, drenched it often and often with human blood, destroyed civilisation, and sent whole nations to despair. Had it not been for these horrible demons, human society would be far more advanced than it is now. But their time is come; and I fervently hope that the bell that tolled this morning in honour of this convention may be the death-knell of all fanaticism, of all persecutions with the sword or with the pen, and of all uncharitable feelings between persons wending their way to the same goal.

WHY WE DISAGREE

15th September 1893

I will tell you a little story. You have heard the eloquent speaker who has just finished say, "Let us cease from abusing each other," and he was very sorry that there should be always so much variance.

But I think I should tell you a story which would illustrate the cause of this variance. A frog lived in a well. It had lived there for a long time. It was born there and brought up there, and yet was a little, small frog. Of course the evolutionists were not there then to tell us whether the frog lost its eyes or not, but, for our story's sake, we must take it for granted that it had its eyes, and that it every day cleansed the water of all the worms and bacilli that lived in it with an energy that would do credit to our modern bacteriologists. In this way it went on and became a little sleek and fat. Well, one day another frog that lived in the sea came and fell into the well.

"Where are you from?"

"I am from the sea."

"The sea! How big is that? Is it as big as my well?" and he took a leap from one side of the well to the other.

"My friend," said the frog of the sea, "how do you compare the sea with your little well?"

Then the frog took another leap and asked, "Is your sea so big?"

"What nonsense you speak, to compare the sea with your well!"

"Well, then," said the frog of the well, "nothing can be bigger than my well; there can be nothing bigger than this; this fellow is a liar, so turn him out."

That has been the difficulty all the while.

I am a Hindu. I am sitting in my own little well and thinking that the whole world is my little well. The Christian sits in his little well and thinks the whole world is his well. The Mohammedan sits in his little well and thinks that is the whole world. I have to thank you of America for the great attempt you are making to break down the barriers of this little world of ours, and hope that, in the future, the Lord will help you to accomplish your purpose.

PAPER ON HINDUISM

Read at the Parliament on 19th September 1893

Three religions now stand in the world which have come down to us from time prehistoric—Hinduism, Zoroastrianism and Judaism. They have all received tremendous shocks and all of them prove by their survival their internal strength. But while Judaism failed to absorb Christianity and was driven out of its place of birth by its all-conquering daughter, and a handful of Parsees is all that remains to tell the tale of their grand religion, sect after sect arose in India and seemed to shake the religion of the Vedas to its very foundations, but like the waters of the sea-shore in a tremendous earthquake it receded only for a while, only to return in an all-absorbing flood, a thousand times more vigorous, and when the tumult of the rush was over, these sects were all sucked in, absorbed and assimilated into the immense body of the mother faith.

From the high spiritual flights of the Vedanta philosophy, of which the latest discoveries of science seem like echoes, to the low ideas of idolatry with its multifarious mythology, the agnosticism of the Buddhists and the atheism of the Jains, each and all have a place in the Hindu's religion.

Where then, the question arises, where is the common centre to which all these widely diverging radii converge?

Where is the common basis upon which all these seemingly hopeless contradictions rest? And this is the question I shall attempt to answer.

The Hindus have received their religion through revelation, the Vedas. They hold that the Vedas are without beginning and without end. It may sound ludicrous to this audience, how a book can be without beginning or end. But by the Vedas no books are meant. They mean the accumulated treasury of spiritual laws discovered by different persons in different times. Just as the law of gravitation existed before its discovery, and would exist if all humanity forgot it, so is it with the laws that govern the spiritual world. The moral, ethical, and spiritual relations between soul and soul and between individual spirits and the Father of all spirits, were there before their discovery, and would remain even if we forgot them.

The discoverers of these laws are called Rishis, and we honour them as perfected beings. I am glad to tell this audience that some of the very greatest of them were women.

Here it may be said that these laws as laws may be without end, but they must have had a beginning. The Vedas teach us that creation is without beginning or end. Science is said to have proved that the sum total of cosmic energy is always the same. Then, if there was a time when nothing existed, where was all this manifested energy? Some say it was in a potential form in God. In that case God is sometimes potential and sometimes kinetic, which would make Him mutable. Everything mutable is a compound, and everything compound must undergo that change which is called destruction. So God would die, which is absurd. Therefore there never was a time when there was no creation.

If I may be allowed to use a simile, creation and creator are two lines, without beginning and without end, running parallel to each other. God is the ever-active providence, by whose power systems after systems are being evolved out of chaos, made to run for a time and again destroyed. This is what the Brahmin boy repeats every day: *"The sun and the moon, the Lord created like the suns and moons of previous cycles."* And this agrees with modern science.

Here I stand and if I shut my eyes, and try to conceive my existence, "I," "I," "I," what is the idea before me? The idea of a body. Am I, then, nothing but a combination of material substances? The Vedas declare "No". I am a spirit living in a body. I am not the body. The body will die, but I shall not die. Here am I in this body; it will fall, but I shall go on living. I had also a past. The soul was not created, for creation means a combination which means a certain future dissolution. If then the soul was created, it must die. Some are born happy, enjoy perfect health, with beautiful body, mental vigour, and all wants supplied. Others are born miserable; some are without hands or feet, others again are idiots, and only drag on a wretched existence. Why, if they are all created, why does a just and merciful God create one happy and another unhappy, why is He so partial? Nor would it mend matters in the least to hold that those who are miserable in this life will be happy in a future one. Why should a man be miserable even here in the reign of a just and merciful God?

In the second place, the idea of a creator God does not explain the anomaly, but simply expresses the cruel fiat of an all-powerful being. There must have been causes, then, before his birth, to make a man miserable or happy and those were his past actions.

Are not all the tendencies of the mind and the body accounted for by inherited aptitude? Here are two parallel lines of existence—one of the mind, the other of matter. If matter and its transformations answer for all that we have, there is no necessity for supposing the existence of a soul. But it cannot be proved that thought has been evolved out of matter; and if a philosophical monism is inevitable, spiritual monism is certainly logical and no less desirable than a materialistic monism; but neither of these is necessary here.

We cannot deny that bodies acquire certain tendencies from heredity, but those tendencies only mean the physical configuration through which a peculiar mind alone can act in a peculiar way. There are other tendencies peculiar to a soul caused by his past actions. And a soul with a certain tendency would by the laws of affinity take birth in a body which is the fittest instrument for the display of that tendency. This is in accord with science, for science wants to explain everything by habit, and habit is got through repetitions. So repetitions are necessary to explain the natural habits of a new-born soul.

And since they were not obtained in this present life, they must have come down from past lives.

There is another suggestion. Taking all these for granted, how is it that I do not remember anything of my past life? This can be easily explained. I am now speaking English. It is not my mother tongue, in fact no words of my mother tongue are now present in my consciousness, but let me try to bring them up, and they rush in. That shows that consciousness is only the surface of the mental ocean, and within its depths are stored up all our experiences. Try and struggle, they would come up and you would be conscious even of your past life.

This is direct and demonstrative evidence. Verification is the perfect proof of a theory, and here is the challenge thrown to the world by the Rishis. We have discovered the secret by which the very depths of the ocean of memory can be stirred up—try it and you would get a complete reminiscence of your past life.

So then the Hindu believes that he is spirit. Him the sword cannot pierce—him the fire cannot burn—him the water cannot melt—him the air cannot dry. The Hindu believes that every soul is a circle whose circumference is nowhere, but whose centre is located in the body, and that death means the change of this centre from body to body. Nor is the soul bound by the conditions of matter. In its very essence, it is free, unbounded, holy, pure, and perfect. But somehow or other it finds itself tied down to matter, and thinks of itself as matter.

Why should the free, perfect, and pure being be thus under the thraldom of matter, is the next question. How can the perfect soul be deluded into the belief that it is imperfect? We have been told that the Hindus shirk the question and say that no such question can be there. Some thinkers want to answer it by positing one or more quasi-perfect beings, and use big scientific names to fill up the gap. But naming is not explaining. The question remains the same. How can the perfect become the quasi-perfect; how can the pure, the absolute, change even a microscopic particle of its nature? But the Hindu is sincere. He does not want to take shelter under sophistry. He is brave enough to face the question in a manly fashion; and his answer is: "I do not know. I do not know how the perfect being, the soul, came to think of itself as imperfect, as joined to and conditioned by matter." But the fact is a fact for all that. It is a fact in everybody's consciousness that one thinks of oneself as the body. The Hindu does not attempt to explain why one thinks one is the body. The answer that it is the will of God is no explanation. This is nothing more than what the Hindu says, "I do not know."

Well, then, the human soul is eternal and immortal, perfect and infinite, and death means only a change of centre from one body to another. The present is determined by our past actions, and the future by the present. The soul will go on evolving up or reverting back from birth to birth and death to death. But here is another question: Is man a tiny boat in a tempest, raised one moment on the foamy crest of a billow and dashed down into a yawning chasm the next, rolling to and fro at the mercy of good and bad actions—a powerless, helpless wreck in an ever-raging, ever-rushing, uncompromising current of cause and effect; a little moth placed under the wheel of causation which rolls on crushing everything in its way and waits not for the widow's tears or the orphan's cry? The heart sinks at the idea, yet this is the law of Nature. Is there no hope? Is there no escape?—was the cry that went up from the bottom of the heart of despair. It reached the throne of mercy, and words of hope and consolation came down and inspired a Vedic sage, and he stood up before the world and in trumpet voice proclaimed the glad tidings: "Hear, ye children of immortal bliss! even ye that reside in higher spheres! I have found the Ancient One, who is beyond all darkness, all delusion: knowing Him alone you shall be saved from death over again." "Children of immortal bliss"—what a sweet, what a hopeful name! Allow me to call you, brethren, by that sweet name—heirs of immortal bliss—yea, the Hindu refuses to call you sinners. Ye are the Children of God, the sharers of immortal bliss, holy and perfect beings. Ye divinities on earth—sinners! It is a sin to call a man so; it is a standing libel on human nature. Come up, O lions, and shake off the delusion that you are sheep; you are souls immortal, spirits free, blest and eternal; ye are not matter, ye are not bodies; matter is your servant, not you the servant of matter.

Thus it is that the Vedas proclaim not a dreadful combination of unforgiving laws, not an endless prison of cause and effect, but that at the head of all these laws, in and through every particle of matter and force, stands one, "By whose command the wind blows, the fire burns, the clouds rain, and death stalks upon the earth."

And what is His nature?

He is everywhere, the pure and formless One, the Almighty and the All-merciful. "Thou art our father, Thou art our mother, Thou art our beloved friend, Thou art the source of all strength; give us strength. Thou art He that beareth the burdens of the universe; help me bear the little burden of this life." Thus sang the Rishis of the Veda. And how to worship Him? Through love. "He is to be worshiped as the one beloved, dearer than everything in this and the next life."

This is the doctrine of love declared in the Vedas, and let us see how it is fully developed and taught by Krishna, whom the Hindus believe to have been God incarnate on earth.

He taught that a man ought to live in this world like a lotus leaf, which grows in water but is never moistened by water; so a man ought to live in the world—his heart to God and his hands to work.

It is good to love God for hope of reward in this or the next world, but it is better to love God for love's sake, and the prayer goes: "Lord, I do not want wealth, nor children, nor learning. If it be Thy will, I shall go from birth to birth, but grant me this that I may love Thee without the hope of reward—love unselfishly for love's sake." One of the disciples of Krishna, the then Emperor of India, was driven from his kingdom by his enemies and had to take shelter with his queen, in a forest in the Himalayas, and there one day the queen asked him how it was that he, the most virtuous of men, should suffer so much misery. Yudhishthira answered: "Behold, my queen, the Himalayas, how grand and beautiful they are; I love them. They do not give me anything, but my nature is to love the grand, the beautiful, therefore I love them. Similarly, I love the Lord. He is the source of all beauty, of all sublimity. He is the only object to be loved; my nature is to love Him, and therefore I love. I do not pray for anything; I do not ask for anything. Let him place me wherever He likes. I must love Him for love's sake. I cannot trade in love."

The Vedas teach that the soul is divine, only held in the bondage of matter; perfection will be reached when this bond will burst, and the word they use for it is therefore Mukti—freedom, freedom from the bonds of imperfection, freedom from death and misery.

And this bondage can only fall off through the mercy of God, and this mercy comes on the pure. So purity is the condition of His mercy. How does that mercy act? He reveals Himself to the pure heart; the pure and the stainless see God, yea even in this life. Then and then only all the crookedness of the heart is made straight; then all doubt ceases. He is no more the freak of a terrible law of causation. This is the very centre, the very vital conception of Hinduism. The Hindu does not want to live upon words and theories. If there are existences beyond the ordinary sensuous existence, he wants to come face to face with them. If there is a soul in him which is not matter, if there is an all-merciful universal Soul, he will go to Him direct. He must see Him, and that alone can destroy all doubts. So the best proof a Hindu sage gives about the soul, about God, is—"I have seen the soul; I have seen God." And that is the only condition of perfection. The Hindu religion does not consist in struggles and attempts to believe a certain doctrine or dogma, but in realising—not in believing, but in being and becoming.

Thus the whole object of their system is by constant struggle to become perfect, to become divine, to reach God and see God, and this reaching God, seeing God, becoming perfect even as the Father in Heaven is perfect, constitutes the religion of the Hindus.

And what becomes of a man when he attains perfection? He lives a life of bliss infinite. He enjoys infinite and perfect bliss, having obtained the only thing in which man ought to have pleasure, namely God, and enjoys the bliss with God.

So far all the Hindus are agreed. This is the common religion of all the sects of India; but then perfection is absolute, and the absolute cannot be two or three. It cannot have any qualities. It cannot be an individual. And so when a soul becomes perfect and absolute, it must become one with Brahman, and it would only realise the Lord as the perfection, the reality, of its own nature and existence, the existence absolute, knowledge absolute, and bliss absolute. We have often and often read this called the losing of individuality and becoming a stock or a stone.

"He jests at scars that never felt a wound."

I tell you it is nothing of the kind. If it is happiness to enjoy the consciousness of this small body, it must be greater happiness to enjoy the consciousness of two bodies, the measure of happiness increasing with the consciousness of an increasing number of bodies, the aim, the ultimate of happiness being reached when it would become a universal consciousness.

Therefore, to gain this infinite universal individuality, this miserable little prison-individuality must go. Then alone can death cease when I am one with life, then alone can misery cease when I am one with happiness itself, then alone can all errors cease when I am one with knowledge itself; and this is the necessary scientific conclusion. Science has proved to me that physical individuality is a delusion, that really my body is one little continuously changing body in an unbroken ocean of matter, and Advaita (unity) is the necessary conclusion with my other counterpart, Soul.

Science is nothing but the finding of unity. As soon as science would reach perfect unity, it would stop from further progress, because it would reach the goal. Thus chemistry could not progress farther when it would discover one element out of which all others could be made. Physics would stop when it would be able to fulfil its services in discovering one energy of which all the others are but manifestations, and the science of religion become perfect when it would discover Him who is the one life in a universe of death. Him who is the constant basis of an ever-changing world, One who is the only Soul of which all souls are but delusive manifestations. Thus is it, through multiplicity and duality, the ultimate unity is reached. Religion can go no farther. This is the goal of all science.

All science is bound to come to this conclusion in the long run. Manifestation, and not creation, is the word of science today, and the Hindu is only glad that what he has been cherishing in his bosom for ages is going to be taught in more forcible language, and with further light from the latest conclusions of science.

Descend we now from the aspirations of philosophy to the religion of the ignorant. At the very outset, I may tell you that there is no *polytheism* in India. In every temple, if one stands by and listens, one will find the worshippers applying all the attributes of God, including omnipresence, to the images. It is not polytheism, nor would the name henotheism explain the situation. "The rose called by any other name would smell as sweet." Names are not explanations.

I remember, as a boy, hearing a Christian missionary preach to a crowd in India. Among other sweet things he was telling them was, that if he gave a blow to their idol with his stick, what could it do? One of his hearers sharply answered, "If I abuse your God, what can He do?" "You would be punished," said the preacher, "when you die." "So my idol will punish you when you die," retorted the Hindu.

The tree is known by its fruits. When I have seen amongst them that are called idolaters, men, the like of whom in morality and spirituality and love, I have never seen anywhere, I stop and ask myself, "Can sin beget holiness?"

Superstition is a great enemy of man, but bigotry is worse. Why does a Christian go to church? Why is the cross holy? Why is the face turned toward the sky in prayer? Why are there so many images in the Catholic Church? Why are there so many images in the minds of Protestants when they pray? My brethren, we can no more think about anything without a mental image than we can live without breathing. By the law of association the material image calls up the mental idea and vice versa. This is why the Hindu uses an external symbol when he worships. He will tell you, it helps to keep his mind fixed on the Being to whom he prays. He knows as well as you do that the image is not God, is not omnipresent. After all how much does omnipresence mean to almost the whole world? It stands merely as a word, a symbol. Has God superficial area? If not, when we repeat that word "omnipresent," we think of the extended sky or of space, that is all.

As we find that somehow or other, by the laws of our mental constitution, we have to associate our ideas of infinity with the image of the blue sky, or of the sea, so we naturally connect our idea of holiness with the image of a church, a mosque, or a cross. The Hindus have associated the ideas of holiness, purity, truth, omnipresence, and such other ideas with different images and forms. But with this difference that while some people devote their whole lives to their idol of a church and never rise higher because with them religion means an intellectual assent to certain doctrines and doing good to their fellows, the whole religion of the Hindu is centred in realisation. Man is to become divine by realising the divine. Idols or temples or churches or books are only the supports, the helps, of his spiritual childhood: but on and on he must progress.

He must not stop anywhere. *"External worship, material worship,"* say the scriptures, *"is the lowest stage; struggling to rise high, mental prayer is the next stage, but the highest stage is when the Lord has been realised."* Mark, the same earnest man who is kneeling before the idol tells you: *"Him the sun cannot express, nor the moon, nor the stars, the lightning cannot express Him, nor what we speak of as fire; through Him they shine."* But he does not abuse anyone's idol or call its worship sin. He recognises in it a necessary stage of life. *"The child is father of the man."* Would it be right for an old man to say that childhood is a sin or youth a sin?

If a man can realise his divine nature with the help of an image, would it be right to call that a sin? Nor, even when he has passed that stage, should he call it an error. To the Hindu, man is not travelling from error to truth, but from truth to truth, from lower to higher truth. To him all the religions, from the lowest fetishism to the highest absolutism, mean so many attempts of the human soul to grasp and realise the Infinite, each determined by the conditions of its birth and association, and each of these marks a stage of progress; and every soul is a young eagle soaring higher and higher, gathering more and more strength till it reaches the Glorious Sun.

Unity in variety is the plan of nature, and the Hindu has recognised it. Every other religion lays down certain fixed dogmas, and tries to force society to adopt them. It places before society only one coat which must fit Jack and John and Henry, all alike. If it does not fit John or Henry, he must go without a coat to cover his body. The Hindus have discovered that the absolute can only be realised, or thought of, or stated, through the relative, and the images, crosses, and crescents are simply so many symbols—so many pegs to hang the spiritual ideas on. It is not that this help is necessary for every one, but those that do not need it have no right to say that it is wrong. Nor is it compulsory in Hinduism.

One thing I must tell you. Idolatry in India does not mean anything horrible. It is not the mother of harlots. On the other hand, it is the attempt of undeveloped minds to grasp high spiritual truths. The Hindus have their faults, they sometimes have their exceptions; but mark this, they are always for punishing their own bodies, and never for cutting the throats of their neighbours. If the Hindu fanatic burns himself on the pyre, he never lights the fire of Inquisition. And even this cannot be laid at the door of his religion any more than the burning of witches can be laid at the door of Christianity.

To the Hindus, then, the whole world of religions is only a travelling, a coming up, of different men and women, through various conditions and circumstances, to the same goal. Every religion is only evolving a God out of the material man, and the same God is the inspirer of all of them. Why, then, are there so many contradictions? They are only apparent, says the Hindu. The contradictions come from the same truth adapting itself to the varying circumstances of different natures.

It is the same light coming through glasses of different colours. And these little variations are necessary for purposes of adaptation. But in the heart of everything the same truth reigns. The Lord has declared to the Hindu in His incarnation as Krishna: *"I am in every religion as the thread through a string of pearls. Wherever thou seest extraordinary holiness and extraordinary power raising and purifying humanity, know thou that I am there."* And what has been the result? I challenge the world to find, throughout the whole system of Sanskrit philosophy, any such expression as that the Hindu alone will be saved and not others. Says Vyasa, *"We find perfect men even beyond the pale of our caste and creed."* One thing more. How, then, can be Hindu, whose whole fabric of thought centres in God, believe in Buddhism which is agnostic, or in Jainism which is atheistic?

The Buddhists or the Jains do not depend upon God; but the whole force of their religion is directed to the great central truth in every religion, to evolve a God out of man. They have not seen the Father, but they have seen the Son. And he that hath seen the Son hath seen the Father also.

This, brethren, is a short sketch of the religious ideas of the Hindus. The Hindu may have failed to carry out all his plans, but if there is ever to be a universal religion, it must be one which will have no location in place or time; which will be infinite, like the God it will preach, and whose sun will shine upon the followers of Krishna and of Christ, on saints and sinners alike; which will not be Brahminic or Buddhistic, Christian or Mohammedan, but the sum total of all these and still have infinite space for development; which in its catholicity will embrace in its infinite arms, and find a place for, every human being, from the lowest grovelling savage not far removed from the brute, to the highest man towering by the virtues of his head and heart almost above humanity, making society stand in awe of him and doubt his human nature. It will be a religion which will have no place for persecution or intolerance in its polity, which will recognise divinity in every man and woman, and whose whole scope, whose whole force, will be centred in aiding humanity to realise its own true, divine nature.

Offer such a religion and all the nations will follow you. Asoka's council was a council of the Buddhist faith. Akbar's, though more to the purpose, was only a parlour-meeting. It was reserved for America to proclaim to all quarters of the globe that the Lord is in every religion.

May He who is the Brahman of the Hindus, the Ahura-Mazda of the Zoroastrians, the Buddha of the Buddhists, the Jehovah of the Jews, the Father in Heaven of the Christians, give strength to you to carry out your noble idea! The star arose in the East; it travelled steadily towards the West, sometimes dimmed and sometimes effulgent, till it made a circuit of the world, and now it is again rising on the very horizon of the East, the borders of the Sanpo, a thousandfold more effulgent than it ever was before.

Hail, Columbia, motherland of liberty! It has been given to thee, who never dipped her hand in her neighbour's blood, who never found out that the shortest way of becoming rich was by robbing one's neighbours, it has been given to thee to march at the vanguard of civilisation with the flag of harmony.

RELIGION NOT THE CRYING NEED OF INDIA

20th September 1893

Christians must always be ready for good criticism, and I hardly think that you will mind if I make a little criticism. You Christians, who are so fond of sending out missionaries to save the soul of the heathen—why do you not try to save their bodies from starvation? In India during the terrible famines, thousands died from hunger, yet you Christians did nothing. You erect churches all through India, but the crying evil in the East is not religion—they have religion enough—but it is bread that the suffering millions of burning India cry out for with parched throats. They ask us for bread but we give them stones. It is an insult to a starving people to offer them religion, it is an insult to a starving man to teach him metaphysics. In India a priest that preached for money would lose caste and be spat upon by the people. I came here to seek aid for my impoverished people, and I fully realised how difficult it was to get help for heathens from Christians in a Christian land.

BUDDHISM, THE FULFILMENT OF HINDUISM

26th September 1893

I am not a Buddhist, as you have heard, and yet I am. If China, or Japan, or Ceylon follow the teachings of the Great Master, India worships him as God incarnate on earth. You have just now heard that I am going to criticise Buddhism, but by that I wish you to understand only this. Far be it from me to criticise him whom I worship as God incarnate on earth. But our views about Buddha are that he was not understood properly by his disciples. The relation between Hinduism (by Hinduism, I mean the religion of the Vedas) and what is called Buddhism at the present day, is nearly the same as between Judaism and Christianity. Jesus Christ was a Jew. and Shâkya Muni was a Hindu. The Jews rejected Jesus Christ, nay, crucified him, and the Hindus have accepted Shakya Muni as God and worship him. But the real difference that we Hindus want to show between modern Buddhism and what we should understand as the teachings of Lord Buddha lies principally in this: Shakya Muni came to preach nothing new.

He also, like Jesus, came to fulfil and not to destroy. Only, in the case of Jesus, it was the old people, the Jews, who did not understand him, while in the case of Buddha, it was his own followers who did not realise the import of his teachings. As the Jew did not understand the fulfilment of the Old Testament, so the Buddhist did not understand the fulfilment of the truths of the Hindu religion. Again, I repeat, Shakya Muni came not to destroy, but he was the fulfilment, the logical conclusion, the logical development of the religion of the Hindus.

The religion of the Hindus is divided into two parts, the ceremonial and the spiritual. The spiritual portion is specially studied by the monks.

In that there is no caste. A man from the highest caste and a man from the lowest may become a monk in India and the two castes become equal. In religion there is no caste; caste is simply a social institution. Shakya Muni himself was a monk, and it was his glory that he had the large-heartedness to bring out the truths from the hidden Vedas and throw them broadcast all over the world. He was the first being in the world who brought missionarising into practice—nay, he was the first to conceive the idea of proselytising.

The great glory of the Master lay in his wonderful sympathy for everybody, especially for the ignorant and the poor. Some of his disciples were Brahmins. When Buddha was teaching, Sanskrit was no more the spoken language in India. It was then only in the books of the learned. Some of Buddha's Brahmin disciples wanted to translate his teachings into Sanskrit, but he distinctly told them, "I am for the poor, for the people; let me speak in the tongue of the people." And so to this day the great bulk of his teachings are in the vernacular of that day in India.

Whatever may be the position of philosophy, whatever may be the position of metaphysics, so long as there is such a thing as death in the world, so long as there is such a thing as weakness in the human heart, so long as there is a cry going out of the heart of man in his very weakness, there shall be faith in God.

On the philosophic side the disciples of the Great Master dashed themselves against the eternal rocks of the Vedas and could not crush them, and on the other side they took away from the nation that eternal God to which every one, man or woman, clings so fondly. And the result was that Buddhism had to die a natural death in India. At the present day there is not one who calls oneself a Buddhist in India, the land of its birth.

But at the same time, Brahminism lost something—that reforming zeal, that wonderful sympathy and charity for everybody, that wonderful leaven which Buddhism had brought to the masses and which had rendered Indian society so great that a Greek historian who wrote about India of that time was led to say that no Hindu was known to tell an untruth and no Hindu woman was known to be unchaste.

Hinduism cannot live without Buddhism, nor Buddhism without Hinduism. Then realise what the separation has shown to us, that the Buddhists cannot stand without the brain and philosophy of the Brahmins, nor the Brahmin without the heart of the Buddhist. The separation between the Buddhists and the Brahmins is the cause of the downfall of India. That is why India is populated by three hundred millions of beggars, and that is why India has been the slave of conquerors for the last thousand years. Let us then join the wonderful intellect of the Brahmin with the heart, the noble soul, the wonderful humanising power of the Great Master.

ADDRESS AT THE FINAL SESSION

27th September 1893

The World's Parliament of Religions has become an accomplished fact, and the merciful Father has helped those who laboured to bring it into existence, and crowned with success their most unselfish labour.

My thanks to those noble souls whose large hearts and love of truth first dreamed this wonderful dream and then realised it. My thanks to the shower of liberal sentiments that has overflowed this platform. My thanks to this enlightened audience for their uniform kindness to me and for their appreciation of every thought that tends to smooth the friction of religions. A few jarring notes were heard from time to time in this harmony. My special thanks to them, for they have, by their striking contrast, made general harmony the sweeter.

Much has been said of the common ground of religious unity. I am not going just now to venture my own theory.

But if any one here hopes that this unity will come by the triumph of any one of the religions and the destruction of the others, to him I say, "Brother, yours is an impossible hope." Do I wish that the Christian would become Hindu? God forbid. Do I wish that Hindu or Buddhist would become Christian? God forbid.

The seed is put in the ground, and earth and air and water are placed around it. Does the seed become the earth, or the air, or the water? No. It becomes a plant, it develops after the law of its own growth, assimilates the air, the earth, and the water, converts them into plant substance, and grows into a plant.

Similar is the case with religion. The Christian is not to become a Hindu or Buddhist, nor a Hindu or a Buddhist to become a Christian. But each must assimilate the spirit of the others and yet preserve his individuality and grow according to his own law of growth.

If the Parliament of Religions has shown anything to the world it is this: It has proved to the world that holiness, purity, and charity are not the exclusive possessions of any church in the world, and that every system has produced men and women of the most exalted character. In the face of this evidence, if anybody dreams of the exclusive survival of his own religion and the destruction of the others, I pity him from the bottom of my heart, and point out to him that upon the banner of every religion will soon be written, in spite of resistance: "Help and not Fight," "Assimilation and not Destruction," "Harmony and Peace and not Dissension."

THE SECRET OF WORK

Helping others physically, by removing their physical needs, is indeed great; but the help is greater according as the need is greater and according as the help is far-reaching. If a man's wants can be removed for an hour, it is helping him indeed; if his wants can be removed for a year, it will be more help to him; but if his wants can be removed for ever it is surely the greatest help that can be given to him. Spiritual knowledge is the only thing that can destroy our miseries for ever; any other knowledge satisfies wants only for a time. It is only with the knowledge of the spirit that the faculty of want is annihilated for ever; so helping man spiritually is the highest help that can be given to him. He who gives man spiritual knowledge is the greatest benefactor of mankind; and as such we always find that those were the most powerful of men who helped man in his spiritual needs, because spirituality is the true basis of all our activities in life. A spiritually strong and sound man will be strong in every other respect, if he so wishes. Until there is spiritual strength in man, even physical needs cannot be well satisfied. Next to spiritual comes intellectual help. The gift of knowledge is a far higher gift than that of food and clothes; it is even higher than giving life to a man, because the real life of man consists of knowledge. Ignorance is death, knowledge is life. Life is of very little value, if it is a life in the dark, groping through ignorance and misery. Next in order comes, of course, helping a man physically. Therefore, in considering the question of helping others, we must always strive not to commit the mistake of thinking that physical help is the only help that can be given. It is not only the last but the least, because it cannot bring about permanent satisfaction. The misery that I feel when I am hungry is satisfied by eating, but hunger returns; my misery can cease only when I am satisfied beyond all want. Then hunger will not make me miserable; no distress, no sorrow will be able to move me. So that help which tends to make us strong spiritually is the highest, next to it comes intellectual help, and after that physical help.

The miseries of the world cannot be cured by physical help only. Until man's nature changes these physical needs will always arise, and miseries will always be felt, and no amount of physical help will cure them completely. The only solution of this problem is to make mankind pure. Ignorance is the mother of all the evil and all the misery we see. Let men have light, let them be pure and spiritually strong and educated, then alone will misery cease in the world, not before. We may convert every house in the country into a charity asylum, we may fill the land with hospitals, but the misery of man will still continue to exist until man's character changes.

We read in the Bhagavad-Gita again and again that we must all work incessantly. All work is by nature composed of good and evil. We cannot do any work which will not do some good somewhere; there cannot be any work which will not cause some harm somewhere. Every work must necessarily be a mixture of good and evil; yet we are commanded to work incessantly. Good and evil will both have their results, will produce their Karma. Good action will entail upon us good effect; bad action, bad. But good and bad are both bondages of the soul. The solution reached in the Gita, in regard to this bondage-producing nature of work is, that if we do not attach ourselves to the work we do, it will not have any binding effect on our soul. We shall try to understand what is meant by this "non-attachment" to work.

This is the one central idea in the Gita; work incessantly, but be not attached to it. Samskâra can be translated very nearly by "inherent tendency". Using the simile of a lake for the mind, every ripple, every wave that rises in the mind, when it subsides, does not die out entirely, but leaves a mark and a future possibility of that wave coming out again. This mark, with the possibility of the wave reappearing, is what is called Samskara. Every work that we do, every movement of the body, every thought that we think, leaves such an impression on the mind stuff; and even when such impressions are not obvious on the surface, they are sufficiently strong to work beneath the surface, subconsciously. What we are every moment is determined by the sum total of these impressions on the mind. What I am just at this moment is the effect of the sum total of all the impressions of my past life. This is really what is meant by character; each man's character is determined by the sum total of these impressions. If good impressions prevail, the character becomes good; if bad, it becomes bad.

If a man continuously hears bad words, thinks bad thoughts, does bad actions, his mind will be full of bad impressions; and they will influence his thought and work without his being conscious of the fact. In fact, these bad impressions are always working, and their resultant must be evil, and that man will be a bad man; he cannot help it. The sum total of these impressions in him will create the strong motive power for doing bad actions. He will be like a machine in the hands of his impressions, and they will force him to do evil. Similarly, if a man thinks good thought and does good works, the sum total of these impressions will be good; and they, in a similar manner, will force him to do good even in spite of himself. When a man has done so much good work and thought so many good thoughts that there is an irresistible tendency in him to do good, in spite of himself and even if he wishes to do evil, his mind, as the sum total of his tendencies, will not allow him to do so; the tendencies will turn him back; he is completely under the influence of the good tendencies. When such is the case, a man's good character is said to be established.

As the tortoise tucks its feet and head inside the shell, and you may kill it and break it in pieces, and yet it will not come out, even so the character of that man who has control over his motives and organs is unchangeably established. He controls his own inner forces, and nothing can draw them out against his will. By this continuous reflex of good thoughts, good impressions moving over the surface of the mind, the tendency for doing good becomes strong and as the result we feel able to control the Indriyas (the sense-organs, the nerve-centres). Thus alone will character be established, then alone a man gets to truth. Such a man is safe for ever; he cannot do any evil. You may place him in any company, there will be no danger for him. There is a still higher state than having this good tendency, and that is the desire for liberation. You must remember that freedom of the soul is the goal of all Yogas, and each one equally leads to the same result. By work alone men may get to where Buddha got largely by meditation or Christ by prayer. Buddha was a working Jnâni, Christ was a Bhakta, but the same goal was reached by both of them. The difficulty is here. Liberation means entire freedom—freedom from the bondage of good, as well as from the bondage of evil. A golden chain is as much a chain as an iron one. There is a thorn in my finger, and I use another to take the first one out; and when I have taken it out, I throw both of them aside; I have no necessity for keeping the second thorn, because both are thorns after all. So the bad tendencies are to be counteracted by the good ones, and the bad impressions on the mind should be removed by the fresh waves of good ones, until all that is evil almost disappears, or is subdued and held in control in a corner of the mind; but after that the good tendencies have also to be conquered. Thus the "attached" becomes the "unattached". Work, but let not the action or the thought produce a deep impression on the mind. Let the ripples come and go, let huge actions proceed from the muscles and the brain, but let them not make any deep impression on the soul.

How can this be done? We see that the impression of any action to which we attach ourselves, remains. I may meet hundreds of persons during the day, and among them meet also one whom I love; and when I retire at night, I may try to think of all the faces I saw, but only that face comes before the mind—the face which I met perhaps only for one minute, and which I loved; all the others have vanished. My attachment to this particular person caused a deeper impression on my mind than all the other faces. Physiologically, the impressions have all been the same; every one of the faces that I saw pictured itself on the retina, and the brain took the pictures in, and yet there was no similarity of effect upon the mind. Most of the faces, perhaps, were entirely new faces, about which I had never thought before, but that one face of which I got only a glimpse found associations inside. Perhaps I had pictured him in my mind for years, knew hundreds of things about him, and this one new vision of him awakened hundreds of sleeping memories in my mind; and this one impression having been repeated perhaps a hundred times more than those of the different faces together, will produce a great effect on the mind.

Therefore, be "unattached"; let things work, let brain centres work; work incessantly, but let not a ripple conquer the mind. Work as if you were a stranger in this land, a sojourner; work incessantly, but do not bind yourselves; bondage is terrible. This world is not our habitation, it is only one of the many stages through which we are passing. Remember that great saying of the Sânkhya, "The whole of nature is for the soul, not the soul for nature." The very reason of nature's existence is for the education of the soul; it has no other meaning; it is there because the soul must have knowledge, and through knowledge free itself. If we remember this always, we shall never be attached to nature; we shall know that nature is a book which we are to read; and that when we have gained the required knowledge, the book is of no more value to us. Instead of that, however, we are identifying ourselves with nature; we are thinking that the soul is for nature, that the spirit is for the flesh, and, as the common saying has it, we think that man "lives to eat" and not "eats to live". We are continually making this mistake; we are regarding nature as ourselves and are becoming attached to it; and as soon as this attachment comes, there is the deep impression on the soul, which binds us down and makes us work not from freedom but like slaves.

The whole gist of this teaching is that you should work like a *master* and not as a *slave;* work incessantly, but do not do slave's work. Do you not see how everybody works? Nobody can be altogether at rest; ninety-nine per cent of mankind work like slaves, and the result is misery; it is all selfish work. Work though freedom! Work through love! The word "love" is very difficult to understand; love never comes until there is freedom. There is no true love possible in the slave. If you buy a slave and tie him down in chains and make him work for you, he will work like a drudge, but there will be no love in him. So when we ourselves work for the things of the world as slaves there can be no love in us, and our work is not true work. This is true of work done for relatives and friends and is true of work done for our own selves. Selfish work is slave's work; and here is a test. Every act of love brings happiness; there is no act of love which does not bring peace and blessedness as its reaction. Real existence, real knowledge, and real love are eternally connected with one another, the three in one; where one of them is, the others also must be; they are the three aspects of the One without a second—the Existence-Knowledge-Bliss. When that existence becomes relative, we see it as the world; that knowledge becomes in its turn modified into the knowledge of the things of the world; and that bliss forms the foundation of all true love known to the heart of man. Therefore true love can never react so as to cause pain either to the lover or to the beloved. Suppose a man loves a woman; he wishes to have her all to himself and feels extremely jealous about her every movement; he wants her to sit near him, to stand near him, and to eat and move at his bidding. He is a slave to her and wishes to have her as his slave. That is not love; it is a kind of morbid affection of the slave, insinuating itself as love. It cannot be love, because it is painful; if she does not do what he wants, it brings him pain. With love there is no painful reaction: love only brings a reaction of bliss; if it does not, it is not love, it is mistaking something else for love. When you have succeeded in loving your husband, your wife, your children, the whole world, the universe, in such a manner that there is no reaction of pain or jealousy, no selfish feeling, then you are in a fit state to be unattached.

Krishna says: "Look at Me, Arjuna! If I stop from work for one moment the whole universe will die. I have nothing to gain from work; I am the one Lord, but why do I work? Because I love the world." God is unattached because He loves; that real love makes us unattached. Wherever there is attachment, the clinging to the things of the world, you must know that it is all physical, attraction between sets of particles of matter; something that attracts two bodies nearer and nearer all the time, and if they cannot get near enough, produces pain; but where there is *real* love, it does not rest on physical attachment at all. Such lovers may be a thousand miles away from one another, but their love will be all the same; it does not die, and will never produce any painful reaction.

To attain this unattachment is almost a life-work, but as soon as we have reached this point, we have attained the goal of love and become free; the bondage of nature falls from us, and we see nature as she is; she forges no more chains for us; we stand entirely free and take not the results of work into consideration; who then cares for what the results may be?

Do you ask anything from your children in return for what you have given them? It is your duty to work for them, and there the matter ends. In whatever you do for a particular person, a city, or a state, assume the same attitude towards it as you have towards your children—expect nothing in return. If you can invariably take the position of a giver, in which everything given by you is a free offering to the world, without any thought of return, then will your work bring you no attachment. Attachment comes only where we expect a return.

If working like slaves results in selfishness and attachment, working as masters of our own mind gives rise to the bliss of non-attachment. We often talk of right and justice, but we find that in the world right and justice are mere baby's talk. There are two things which guide the conduct of men: might and mercy. The exercise of might is invariably the exercise of selfishness. All men and women try to make the most of whatever power or advantage they have. Mercy is heaven itself; to be good, we have all to be merciful. Even justice and right should stand on mercy. All thought of obtaining return for the work we do hinders our spiritual progress; nay, in the end it brings misery. There is another way in which this idea of mercy and selfless charity can be put into practice; that is, by looking upon work as "worship" in case we believe in a Personal God. Here we give up all the fruits of our work unto the Lord, and, worshipping Him thus, we have no right to expect anything from mankind for the work we do. The Lord Himself works incessantly and is ever without attachment. Just as water cannot wet the lotus leaf, so work cannot bind the unselfish man by giving rise to attachment to results. The selfless and unattached man may live in the very heart of a crowded and sinful city; he will not be touched by sin.

This idea of complete self-sacrifice is illustrated in the following story: After the battle of Kurukshetra, the five Pândava brothers performed a great sacrifice and made very large gifts to the poor. All people expressed amazement at the greatness and richness of the sacrifice and said that such a sacrifice the world had never seen before. But after the ceremony, there came a little mongoose, half of whose body was golden, and the other half brown, and he began to roll on the floor of the sacrificial hall. He said to those around, "You are all liars; this is no sacrifice." "What!" they exclaimed, "you say this is no sacrifice; do you not know how money and jewels were poured out to the poor and every one became rich and happy? This was the most wonderful sacrifice any man ever performed." But the mongoose said: "There was once a little village, and in there dwelt a poor Brahmin, with his wife, his son and his son's wife. They were very poor and lived on small gifts made to them for preaching and teaching. There came in that land a three years' famine, and the poor Brahmin suffered more than ever. At last when the family had starved for days, the father brought home one morning a little barley flour, which he had been fortunate enough to obtain, and he divided it into four parts, one for each member of the family. They prepared it for their meal, and just as they were about to eat there was a knock at the door. The father opened it, and there stood a guest. Now in India a guest is a sacred person, he is as a god for the time being, and must be treated as such. So the poor Brahmin said, 'Come in, sir; you are welcome.' He set before the guest his own portion of the food, which the guest quickly ate and said, 'Oh, sir, you have killed me; I have been starving for ten days, and this little bit has but increased my hunger. Then the wife said to her husband, 'Give him my share,' but the husband said, 'Not so'. The wife however insisted, saying, 'Here is a poor man, and it is our duty as householders to see that he is fed, and it is my duty as a wife to give him my portion, seeing that you have no more to offer him.' Then she gave her share to the guest, which he ate, and said he was still burning with hunger. So the son said, 'Take my portion also; it is the duty of a son to help his father to fulfil his obligations'. The guest ate that, but remained still unsatisfied; so the son's wife gave him her portion also. That was sufficient, and the guest departed, blessing them. That night those four people died of starvation. A few granules of that flour had fallen on the floor; and when I rolled my body on them, half of it became golden, as you see. Since then I have been travelling all over the world, hoping to find another sacrifice like that, but nowhere have I found one; nowhere else has the other half of my body been turned into gold. That is why I say this is no sacrifice."

This idea of charity is going out of India; great men are becoming fewer and fewer. When I was first learning English I read an English story book, in which there was a story about a dutiful boy who had gone out to work and had given some of his money to his old mother, and this was praised in three or four pages. What was that? No Hindu boy can ever understand the moral of that story. Now I understand it when I hear the Western idea—every man for himself. And some men take everything for themselves, and fathers and mothers and wives and children go to the wall. That should never and nowhere be the idea of the householder.

Now you see what Karma-Yoga means; even at the point of death to help any one, without asking questions. Be cheated millions of times and never ask a question, and never think of what you are doing. Never vaunt of your gifts to the poor or expect their gratitude, but rather be grateful to them for giving you the occasion of practising charity to them. Thus it is plain that to be an ideal householder is a much more difficult task than to be an ideal Sannyâsin; the true life of work is indeed as hard as, if not harder than, the equally true life of renunciation.

THE IDEAL OF KARMA-YOGA

The grandest idea in the religion of the Vedanta is that we may reach the same goal by different paths; and these paths I have generalised into four—viz those of work, love, psychology and knowledge. But you must, at the same time, remember that these divisions are not very marked and quite exclusive of each other. Each blends into the other. But according to the type which prevails, we name the divisions. It is not that you can find men who have no other faculty than that of work, nor that you can find men who are no more than devoted worshippers only, nor that there are men who have no more than mere knowledge. These divisions are made in accordance with the type or the tendency that may be seen to prevail in a man. We have found that, in the end, all these four paths converge and become one. All religions and all methods of work and worship lead us to one and the same goal.

I have already tried to point out that goal. It is freedom as I understand it. Everything that we perceive around us is struggling towards freedom, from the atom to the man, from the insentient, lifeless particle of matter to the highest existence on earth, the human soul. The whole universe is in fact the result of this struggle for freedom. In all combinations every particle is trying to go on its own way, to fly from the other particles; but the others are holding it in check. Our earth is trying to fly away from the sun, and the moon from the earth. Everything has a tendency to infinite dispersion. All that we see in the universe has for its basis this one struggle towards freedom; it is under the impulse of this tendency that the saint prays and the robber robs. When the line of action taken is not a proper one, we call it evil; and when the manifestation of it is proper and high, we call it good. But the impulse is the same, the struggle towards freedom. The saint is oppressed with the knowledge of his condition of bondage, and he wants to get rid of it; so he worships God. The thief is oppressed with the idea that he does not possess certain things, and he tries to get rid of that want, to obtain freedom from it; so he steals. Freedom is the one goal of all nature, sentient or insentient; and consciously or unconsciously, everything is struggling towards that goal. The freedom which the saint seeks is very different from that which the robber seeks; the freedom loved by the saint leads him to the enjoyment of infinite, unspeakable bliss, while that on which the robber has set his heart only forges other bonds for his soul.

There is to be found in every religion the manifestation of this struggle towards freedom. It is the groundwork of all morality, of unselfishness, which means getting rid of the idea that men are the same as their little body. When we see a man doing good work, helping others, it means that he cannot be confined within the limited circle of "me and mine". There is no limit to this getting out of selfishness. All the great systems of ethics preach absolute unselfishness as the goal. Supposing this absolute unselfishness can be reached by a man, what becomes of him? He is no more the little Mr. So-and-so; he has acquired infinite expansion. That little personality which he had before is now lost to him for ever; he has become infinite, and the attainment of this infinite expansion is indeed the goal of all religions and of all moral and philosophical teachings. The personalist, when he hears this idea philosophically put, gets frightened. At the same time, if he preaches morality, he after all teaches the very same idea himself. He puts no limit to the unselfishness of man. Suppose a man becomes perfectly unselfish under the personalistic system, how are we to distinguish him from the perfected ones in other systems? He has become one with the universe and to become that is the goal of all; only the poor personalist has not the courage to follow out his own reasoning to its right conclusion. Karma-Yoga is the attaining through unselfish work of that freedom which is the goal of all human nature. Every selfish action, therefore, retards our reaching the goal, and every unselfish action takes us towards the goal; that is why the only definition that can be given of morality is this: *That which is selfish is immoral, and that which is unselfish is moral.*

But, if you come to details, the matter will not be seen to be quite so simple. For instance, environment often makes the details different as I have already mentioned. The same action under one set of circumstances may be unselfish, and under another set quite selfish. So we can give only a general definition, and leave the details to be worked out by taking into consideration the differences in time, place, and circumstances. In one country one kind of conduct is considered moral, and in another the very same is immoral, because the circumstances differ. The goal of all nature is freedom, and freedom is to be attained only by perfect unselfishness; every thought, word, or deed that is unselfish takes us towards the goal, and, as such, is called moral. That definition, you will find, holds good in every religion and every system of ethics. In some systems of thought morality is derived from a Superior Being—God. If you ask why a man ought to do this and not that, their answer is: "Because such is the command of God." But whatever be the source from which it is derived, their code of ethics also has the same central idea—not to think of self but to give up self. And yet some persons, in spite of this high ethical idea, are frightened at the thought of having to give up their little personalities. We may ask the man who clings to the idea of little personalities to consider the case of a person who has become perfectly unselfish, who has no thought for himself, who does no deed for himself, who speaks no word for himself, and then say where his "himself" is. That "himself" is known to him only so long as he thinks, acts or speaks for himself. If he is only conscious of others, of the universe, and of the all, where is this "himself"? It is gone for ever.

Karma-Yoga, therefore, is a system of ethics and religion intended to attain freedom through unselfishness, and by good works. The Karma-Yogi need not believe in any doctrine whatever. He may not believe even in God, may not ask what his soul is, not think of any metaphysical speculation. He has got his own special aim of realising selflessness; and he has to work it out himself. Every moment of his life must be realisation because he has to solve by mere work, without the help of doctrine or theory, the very same problem to which the Jnâni applies his reason and inspiration and the Bhakta his love.

Now comes the next question: What is this work? What is this doing good to the world? Can we do good to the world? In an absolute sense, no; in a relative sense, yes. No permanent or everlasting good can be done to the world; if it could be done, the world would not be this world. We may satisfy the hunger of a man for five minutes, but he will be hungry again. Every pleasure with which we supply a man may be seen to be momentary. No one can permanently cure this ever-recurring fever of pleasure and pain. Can any permanent happiness be given to the world? In the ocean we cannot raise a wave without causing a hollow somewhere else. The sum total of the good things in the world has been the same throughout in its relation to man's need and greed. It cannot be increased or decreased. Take the history of the human race as we know it today. Do we not find the same miseries and the same happiness, the same pleasures and pains, the same differences in position? Are not some rich, some poor, some high, some low, some healthy, some unhealthy? All this was just the same with the Egyptians, the Greeks, and the Romans in ancient times as it is with the Americans today. So far as history is known, it has always been the same; yet at the same time we find that, running along with all these incurable differences of pleasure and pain, there has ever been the struggle to alleviate them. Every period of history has given birth to thousands of men and women who have worked hard to smooth the passage of life for others. And how far have they succeeded? We can only play at driving the ball from one place to another. We take away pain from the physical plane, and it goes to the mental one. It is like that picture in Dante's hell where the misers were given a mass of gold to roll up a hill. Every time they rolled it up a little, it again rolled down. All our talks about the millennium are very nice as school-boys' stories, but they are no better than that. All nations that dream of the millennium also think that, of all peoples in the world, they will have the best of it then for themselves. This is the wonderfully unselfish idea of the millennium!

We cannot add happiness to this world; similarly, we cannot add pain to it either. The sum total of the energies of pleasure and pain displayed here on earth will be the same throughout. We just push it from this side to the other side, and from that side to this, but it will remain the same, because to remain so is its very nature. This ebb and flow, this rising and falling, is in the world's very nature; it would be as logical to hold otherwise as to say that we may have life without death. This is complete nonsense, because the very idea of life implies death and the very idea of pleasure implies pain. The lamp is constantly burning out, and that is its life. If you want to have life you have to die every moment for it. Life and death are only different expressions of the same thing looked at from different standpoints; they are the falling and the rising of the same wave, and the two form one whole. One looks at the "fall" side and becomes a pessimist, another looks at the "rise" side and becomes an optimist. When a boy is going to school and his father and mother are taking care of him, everything seems blessed to him; his wants are simple, he is a great optimist. But the old man, with his varied experience, becomes calmer, and is sure to have his warmth considerably cooled down. So, old nations, with signs of decay all around them, are apt to be less hopeful than new nations. There is a proverb in India, "A thousand years a city, and a thousand years a forest." This change of city into forest and vice versa is going on everywhere, and it makes people optimists or pessimists according to the side they see of it.

The next idea we take up is the idea of equality. These millennium ideas have been great motive powers to work. Many religions preach this as an element in them—that God is coming to rule the universe, and that then there will be no difference at all in conditions. The people who preach this doctrine are mere fanatics, and fanatics are indeed the sincerest of mankind. Christianity was preached just on the basis of the fascination of this fanaticism, and that is what made it so attractive to the Greek and the Roman slaves. They believed that under the millennial religion there would be no more slavery, that there would be plenty to eat and drink; and, therefore, they flocked round the Christian standard. Those who preached the idea first were of course ignorant fanatics, but very sincere. In modern times this millennial aspiration takes the form of equality—of liberty, equality, and fraternity. This is also fanaticism. True equality has never been and never can be on earth. How can we all be equal here? This impossible kind of equality implies total death. What makes this world what it is? Lost balance. In the primal state, which is called chaos, there is perfect balance. How do all the formative forces of the universe come then? By struggling, competition, conflict. Suppose that all the particles of matter were held in equilibrium, would there be then any process of creation? We know from science that it is impossible. Disturb a sheet of water, and there you find every particle of the water trying to become calm again, one rushing against the other; and in the same way all the phenomena which we call the universe—all things therein—are struggling to get back to the state of perfect balance. Again a disturbance comes, and again we have combination and creation. Inequality is the very basis of creation. At the same time the forces struggling to obtain equality are as much a necessity of creation as those which destroy it.

Absolute equality, that which means a perfect balance of all the struggling forces in all the planes, can never be in this world. Before you attain that state, the world will have become quite unfit for any kind of life, and no one will be there. We find, therefore, that all these ideas of the millennium and of absolute equality are not only impossible but also that, if we try to carry them out, they will lead us surely enough to the day of destruction. What makes the difference between man and man? It is largely the difference in the brain. Nowadays no one but a lunatic will say that we are all born with the same brain power. We come into the world with unequal endowments; we come as greater men or as lesser men, and there is no getting away from that pre-natally determined condition. The American Indians were in this country for thousands of years, and a few handfuls of your ancestors came to their land. What difference have they caused in the appearance of the country! Why did not the Indians make improvements and build cities, if all were equal? With your ancestors a different sort of brain power came into the land, different bundles of past impressions came, and they worked out and manifested themselves. Absolute non-differentiation is death. So long as this world lasts, differentiation there will and must be, and the millennium of perfect equality will come only when a cycle of creation comes to its end. Before that, equality cannot be. Yet this idea of realising the millennium is a great motive power. Just as inequality is necessary for creation itself, so the struggle to limit it is also necessary. If there were no struggle to become free and get back to God, there would be no creation either. It is the difference between these two forces that determines the nature of the motives of men. There will always be these motives to work, some tending towards bondage and others towards freedom.

This world's wheel within wheel is a terrible mechanism; if we put our hands in it, as soon as we are caught we are gone. We all think that when we have done a certain duty, we shall be at rest; but before we have done a part of that duty, another is already in waiting. We are all being dragged along by this mighty, complex world-machine. There are only two ways out of it; one is to give up all concerns with the machine, to let it go and stand aside, to give up our desires. That is very easy to say, but is almost impossible to do. I do not know whether in twenty millions of men one can do that. The other way is to plunge into the world and learn the secret of work, and that is the way of Karma-Yoga. Do not fly away from the wheels of the world machine, but stand inside it and learn the secret of work. Through proper work done inside, it is also possible to come out. Through this machinery itself is the way out.

We have now seen what work is. It is a part of nature's foundation, and goes on always. Those that believe in God understand this better, because they know that God is not such an incapable being as will need our help. Although this universe will go on always, our goal is freedom, our goal is unselfishness; and according to Karma-Yoga that goal is to be reached through work. All ideas of making the world perfectly happy may be good as motive powers for fanatics; but we must know that fanaticism brings forth as much evil as good. The Karma-Yogi asks why you require any motive to work other than the inborn love of freedom. Be beyond the common worldly motives. "To work you have the right, but not to the fruits thereof." Man can train himself to know and to practise that, says the Karma-Yogi. When the idea of doing good becomes a part of his very being, then he will not seek for any motive outside. Let us do good because it is good to do good; he who does good work even in order to get to heaven binds himself down, says the Karma-Yogi. Any work that is done with any the least selfish motive, instead of making us free, forges one more chain for our feet.

So the only way is to give up all the fruits of work, to be unattached to them. Know that this world is not we, nor are we this world; that we are really not the body; that we really do not work. We are the Self, eternally at rest and at peace. Why should we be bound by anything? It is very good to say that we should be perfectly non-attached, but what is the way to do it? Every good work we do without any ulterior motive, instead of forging a new chain, will break one of the links in the existing chains. Every good thought that we send to the world without thinking of any return, will be stored up there and break one link in the chain, and make us purer and purer, until we become the purest of mortals. Yet all this may seem to be rather quixotic and too philosophical, more theoretical than practical. I have read many arguments against the Bhagavad-Gita, and many have said that without motives you cannot work. They have never seen unselfish work except under the influence of fanaticism, and, therefore, they speak in that way.

Let me tell you in conclusion a few words about one man who actually carried this teaching of Karma-Yoga into practice. That man is Buddha. He is the one man who ever carried this into perfect practice. All the prophets of the world, except Buddha, had external motives to move them to unselfish action. The prophets of the world, with this single exception, may be divided into two sets, one set holding that they are incarnations of God come down on earth, and the other holding that they are only messengers from God; and both draw their impetus for work from outside, expect reward from outside, however highly spiritual may be the language they use. But Buddha is the only prophet who said, "I do not care to know your various theories about God. What is the use of discussing all the subtle doctrines about the soul? Do good and be good. And this will take you to freedom and to whatever truth there is." He was, in the conduct of his life, absolutely without personal motives; and what man worked more than he? Show me in history one character who has soared so high above all. The whole human race has produced but one such character, such high philosophy, such wide sympathy. This great philosopher, preaching the highest philosophy, yet had the deepest sympathy for the lowest animals, and never put forth any claims for himself. He is the ideal Karma-Yogi, acting entirely without motive, and the history of humanity shows him to have been the greatest man ever born; beyond compare the greatest combination of heart and brain that ever existed, the greatest soul-power that has ever been manifested. He is the first great reformer the world has seen. He was the first who dared to say, "Believe not because some old manuscripts are produced, believe not because it is your national belief, because you have been made to believe it from your childhood; but reason it all out, and after you have analysed it, then, if you find that it will do good to one and all, believe it, live up to it, and help others to live up to it." He works best who works without any motive, neither for money, nor for fame, nor for anything else; and when a man can do that, he will be a Buddha, and out of him will come the power to work in such a manner as will transform the world. This man represents the very highest ideal of Karma-Yoga.

THE FIRST STEPS TO BHAKTI

The philosophers who wrote on Bhakti defined it as extreme love for God. Why a man should love God is the question to be solved; and until we understand that, we shall not be able to grasp the subject at all. There are two entirely different ideals of life. A man of any country who has any religion knows that he is a body and a spirit also. But there is a great deal of difference as to the goals of human life.

In Western countries, as a rule, people lay more stress on the body aspect of man; those philosophers who wrote on Bhakti in India laid stress on the spiritual side of man, and this difference seems to be typical of the Oriental and Occidental nations. It is so even in common language. In England, when speaking of death it is said, a man gave up his ghost; in India, a man gave up his body. The one idea is that man *is* a body and *has* a soul; the other, that man *is* a soul and *has* a body. More intricate problems arise out of this. It naturally follows that the ideal which holds that man is a body and has a soul, lays all the stress on the body. If you ask why man lives, you will be told it is to enjoy the senses, to enjoy possessions and wealth. He cannot dream of anything beyond, even if he is told of it; his idea of a future life would be a continuation of this enjoyment. He is very sorry that it cannot continue all the time here, but he has to depart, and he thinks that somehow or other he will go to some place where the same thing will be renewed. He will have the same enjoyments, the same senses, only heightened and strengthened. He wants to worship God, because God is the means to attain this end. The goal of his life is enjoyment of sense-objects, and he comes to know there is a Being who can give him a very long lease of these enjoyments, and that is why he worships God.

On the other hand the Indian idea is that God is the goal of life; there is nothing beyond God, and the sense-enjoyments are simply something through which we are passing now in the hope of getting better things. Not only so; it would be disastrous and terrible if man had nothing but sense-enjoyments. In our everyday life we find that the less the sense-enjoyments, the higher the life of the man. Look at the dog when he eats. No man ever ate with the same satisfaction.

Observe the pig, giving grunts of satisfaction as he eats; it is his heaven, and if the greatest archangel came and looked on, the pig would not even notice him. His whole existence is in his eating. No man was ever born who could eat that way. Think of the power of hearing in the lower animals, the power of seeing; all their senses are highly developed. Their enjoyment of the senses is extreme, they become simply mad with delight and pleasure. And the lower the man, also the more delight he finds in the senses. As he gets higher, the goal becomes reason and love. In proportion as these faculties develop, he loses the power of enjoying the senses.

For illustration's sake, if we take for granted that a certain amount of power is given to man, and that that can be spent either on the body, or the mind, or the spirit, then all the power spent on any one of these leaves just so much less to be expended on the others. The ignorant or savage races have much stronger sensual faculties than the civilised races, and this is, in fact, one of the lessons we learn from history, that as a nation becomes civilised the nerve organisation becomes finer, and they become physically weaker. Civilise a savage race and you will find the same thing, another barbarian race comes up and conquers it. It is nearly always the barbarian race that conquers. We see then that if we desire only to have sense-enjoyments all the time, we degrade ourselves to the brute state. A man does not know what he is asking for when he says he wants to go to a place where his sense-enjoyments will be intensified; that he can only have by going down to the brutes.

So with men desiring a heaven full of sense-pleasures. They are like swine wallowing in the mire of the senses, unable to see anything beyond. This sense-enjoyment is what they want, and the loss of it is the loss of heaven to them. These can never be Bhaktas in the highest sense of the word; they can never be true lovers of God. At the same time, though this lower ideal be followed for a time, it will also in course of time change, each man will find that there is something higher, of which he did not know, and so this clinging to life and to things of the senses will gradually die away. When I was a little boy at school, I had a fight with another school-fellow about some sweetmeats, and he being the stronger boy snatched them from my hand. I remember the feeling I had; I thought that boy was the most wicked boy ever born, and that as soon as I grew strong enough I would punish him, there was no punishment sufficient for his wickedness. We have both grown up now and we are fast friends. This world is full of babies to whom eating and drinking, and all these little cakes, are everything. They will dream of these cakes, and their idea of future life is where these cakes will be plentiful. Think of the American Indian who believes that his future life will be in a place which is a very good hunting ground. Each one of us has an idea of a heaven just as we want it to be, but in course of time, as we grow older, and see higher things, we catch higher glimpses beyond. But let us not dispense with our ideas of future life in the ordinary way of modern times, by not believing in anything—that is destruction. The agnostic who thus destroys everything is mistaken, the Bhakta sees higher. The agnostic does not want to go to heaven because he has none; while the Bhakta does not want to go to heaven because he thinks it is child's play.

What he wants is God. What can be a higher end than God? God himself is the highest goal of man; see Him, enjoy Him. We can never conceive anything higher, because God is perfection. We cannot conceive of any higher enjoyment than that of love, but this word love has different meanings. It does not mean the ordinary selfish love of the world; it is blasphemy to call that love. The love for our children and our wives is mere animal love; that love which is perfectly unselfish is the only love, and that is of God. It is a very difficult thing to attain to. We are passing through all these different loves, love of children, father, mother, and so forth. We slowly exercise the faculty of love, but in the majority of cases we never learn anything from it, we become bound to one step, to one person. In some cases men come out of this bondage. Men are ever running after wives, and wealth, and fame in this world, sometimes they are hit very hard on the head, and they find out what this world really is. No one in this world can really love anything but God. Man finds out that human love is all hollow. Men cannot love though they talk of it. The wife says she loves her husband, and kisses him; but as soon as he dies, the first thing she thinks about is the bank account, and what she shall do the next day. The husband loves the wife, but when she becomes sick, and loses her beauty, or becomes haggard, or makes a mistake, he ceases to care for her. All the love of the world is hypocrisy and hollowness.

A finite subject cannot love, nor a finite object be loved. When the object of the love of a man is dying every moment, and his mind also is constantly changing as he grows, what eternal love can you expect to find in the world? There cannot be any real love but in God, why then all these loves? These are mere stages. There is a power behind impelling us forward, we do not know where to seek for the real object, but this love is sending us forward in search of it. Again and again we find out our mistake. We grasp something, and find it slips through our fingers, and then we grasp something else. Thus on and on we go, till at last comes light; we come to God, the only One who loves. His love knows no change, and is ever ready to take us in. How long would any of you bear with me if I injured you? He in whose mind is no anger, hatred or envy, who never loses his balance, dies, or is born, who is he but God? But the path to God is long and difficult, and very few people attain Him. We are all babies struggling. Millions of people make a trade of religion. A few men in a century attain to that love of God, and the whole country becomes blessed and hallowed. When a son of God appears, a whole country becomes blessed. It is true that few such are born in any one century in the whole world, but all should strive to attain that love of God. Who knows but you or I may be the next to attain? Let us struggle, therefore.

We say that a wife loves her husband. She thinks that her whole soul is absorbed in him; a baby comes, and half of it goes out to the baby, or more. She herself will feel that the same love of husband does not exist now. So with the father. We always find that when more intense objects of love come to us the previous love slowly vanishes. Children at school think that some of their school-fellows are the dearest beings that they have in life, or their fathers or mothers are so; then comes the husband or wife, and immediately the old feeling disappears, and the new love becomes uppermost. One star arises, another bigger one comes, and then a still bigger one, and at last the sun comes, and all the lesser lights vanish. That sun is God. The stars are the smaller loves. When that Sun bursts upon him, a man becomes mad, what Emerson calls "a God-intoxicated man". Man becomes transfigured into God, everything is merged in that one ocean of love. Ordinary love is mere animal attraction. Otherwise why is the distinction between the sexes? If one kneels before an image, it is dreadful idolatry; but if one kneels before husband or wife, it is quite permissible!

The world presents to us manifold stages of love. We have first to clear the ground. Upon our view of life the whole theory of love will rest. To think that this world is the aim and end of life is brutal and degenerating. Any man who starts in life with that idea degenerates himself. He will never rise higher; he will never catch this glimpse from behind, he will always be a slave to the senses. He will struggle for the dollar that will get him a few cakes to eat. Better die than live that life. Slaves of this world, slaves of the senses, let us rouse ourselves; there is something higher than this sense-life. Do you think that man, the Infinite Spirit, was born to be a slave to his eyes, his nose and his ears? There is an Infinite, Omniscient Spirit behind that can do everything, break every bond; and that Spirit we are, and we get that power through love. This is the ideal we must remember. We cannot, of course, get it in a day. We may fancy that we have it, but it is a fancy after all; it is a long, long way off. We must take man where he stands, and help him upwards. Man stands in materialism; you and I are materialists. Our talking about God and Spirit is good, but it is simply the vogue in our society to talk thus; we have learnt it parrot-like and repeat it. So we have to take ourselves where we are as materialists, and must take the help of matter, and go on slowly, until we become real spiritualists, and feel ourselves spirits, understand the spirit, and find that this world which we call the infinite is but a gross external form of that world which is behind.

But something besides that is necessary. You read in the Sermon on the Mount, "Ask, and it shall be given you; seek, and you shall find; knock, and it shall be opened unto you." The difficulty is, who seeks, who wants? We all say we know God. One man writes a book to disprove God, another to prove Him. One man thinks it his duty to prove Him all his life; another, to disprove Him, and he goes about to teach man there is no God. What is the use of writing a book either to prove or disprove God? What does it matter to most people whether there is a God or not? The majority of men work just like a machine, with no thought of God, and feeling no need of Him. Then one day comes Death and says, "Come". The man says, "Wait a little, I want a little more time. I want to see my son grow a little bigger." But Death says, "Come at once." So it goes on. So goes poor John. What shall we say to poor John? He never found anything in which God was the highest; perhaps he was a pig in the past, and he is much better as a man. But there are some who get a little awakening. Some misery comes, someone whom we love most dies, that upon which we had bent our whole soul, that for which we had cheated the whole world, and perhaps our own brother, that vanishes, and a blow comes to us. Perhaps a voice comes in our soul and asks, "What after this?" Sometimes death comes without a blow, but such cases are few. Most of us when anything slips through our fingers say, "What next?" How we cling to the senses! You have heard of a drowning man clutching at a straw; a man will clutch at a straw first, and when it fails, he will say someone must help him. Still people must, as the English phrase goes, "sow their wild oats," before they can rise to higher things.

Bhakti is a religion. Religion is not for the many, that is impossible. A sort of knee-drill, standing up and sitting down, may be suited for the many, but religion is for the few. There are in every country only a few hundreds who can be, and will be, religious. The others cannot be religious because they will not be awakened, and they do not want to be. The chief thing is to *want* God. We want everything except God, because our ordinary wants are supplied by the external world; it is only when our necessities have gone beyond the external world that we want a supply from the internal, from God. So long as our needs are confined within the narrow limits of this physical universe, we cannot have any need for God; it is only when we have become satiated with everything here, that we look beyond for a supply. It is only when the need is there, that the demand will come. Have done with this child's play of the world as soon as you can, and then you will feel the necessity of something beyond the world, and the first step in religion will come.

There is a form of religion which is fashionable. My friend has much furniture in her parlour; it is the fashion to have a Japanese vase; so she must have one, even if it costs a thousand dollars. In the same way she will have a little religion, and join a church. Bhakti is not for such. That is not "want". Want is that without which we cannot live. We want breath, we want food, we want clothes; without them we cannot live. When a man loves a woman in this world, there are times when he feels that without her he cannot live, although that is a mistake. When a husband dies the wife thinks she cannot live without him; but she lives all the same. This is the secret of necessity; it is that without which we cannot live, either it must come to us or we die. When the time comes that we feel the same about God, or in other words, we want something beyond this world, something above all material forces, then we may become Bhaktas. What are our little lives when for a moment the cloud passes away, and we get one glimpse from beyond, and for that moment all these lower desires seem like a drop in the ocean? Then the soul grows, and feels the want of God, and must have Him.

The first step is, *what* do we want? Let us ask ourselves this question every day, do we want God? You may read all the books in the universe, but this love is not to be had by the power of speech, not by the highest intellect, not by the study of various sciences. He who desires God will get Love, unto him God gives Himself. Love is always mutual, reflective. You may hate me, and if I want to love you, you repulse me. But if I persist, in a month or a year you are bound to love me. It is a well-known psychological phenomenon. As the loving wife thinks of her departed husband, with the same love we must desire the Lord, and then we will find God, and all books, and the various sciences would not be able to teach us anything. By reading books, we become parrots; no one becomes learned by reading books. If a man reads but one word of love, he indeed becomes learned. So we want first to get that desire.

Let us ask ourselves each day, do we want God? When we begin to talk religion, and especially when we take a high position and begin to teach others, we must ask ourselves the same question. I find many times that I don't want God. I want bread more. I may go mad if I don't get a piece of bread; many ladies will go mad if they don't get a diamond pin, but they do not have the same desire for God; they do not know the only Reality that is in the universe. There is a proverb in our language—If I want to be hunter, I'll hunt the rhinoceros; if I want to be a robber, I'll rob the king's treasury. What is the use of robbing beggars or hunting ants? So if you want to love, love God. Who cares for these things of the world? This world is utterly false; all the great teachers of the world found that out; there is no way out of it but through God. He is the goal of our life, all ideas that the world is the goal of life are pernicious. This world and this body have their own value, a secondary value, as a means to an end, but the world should not be the end. Unfortunately, too often we make the world the end and God the means. We find people going to church and saying, God give me such and such, God heal my disease. They want nice healthy bodies, and because they hear that someone will do this work for them, they go and pray to Him. It is better to be an atheist than to have such an idea of religion. As I have told you, this Bhakti is the highest ideal; I don't know whether we shall reach it or not in millions of years to come, but we must make it our highest ideal, make our senses aim at the highest. If we cannot get to the end, we shall at least come nearer to it. We have slowly to work through the world and the senses, to reach God.

THE TEACHER OF SPIRITUALITY

Every soul is destined to be perfect, and every being, in the end, will attain to that state. Whatever we are now, is the result of whatever we have been, or thought, in the past, and whatever we shall be in the future will be the result of what we do or think now. But this does not preclude our receiving help from outside; the possibilities of the soul are always quickened by some help from outside, so much so, that in the vast majority of cases in the world, help from outside is almost absolutely necessary. Quickening influence comes from outside, and that works upon our own potentialities, and then the growth begins, spiritual life comes, and man becomes holy and perfect in the end. This quickening impulse, which comes from outside, cannot be received from books; the soul can receive impulse only from another soul, and from nothing else. We may study books all our lives, we may become very intellectual, but in the end we find we have not developed at all spiritually. It does not follow that a high order of intellectual development always shows an equivalent development of the spiritual side of man; on the other hand, we find cases almost every day where the intellect has become very highly developed at the expense of the spirit.

Now, in intellectual development we can get much help from books, but in spiritual development, almost nothing. In studying books, sometimes we are deluded into thinking that we are being spiritually helped; but if we analyse ourselves we shall find that only our intellect has been helped, and not the spirit. That is the reason why almost every one of us can *speak* most wonderfully on spiritual subjects, but when the time of action comes, we find ourselves so woefully deficient. It is because books cannot give us that impulse from outside. To quicken the spirit, that impulse must come from another soul.

That soul from which this impulse comes is called the Guru, the teacher, and the soul to which the impulse is conveyed is called the disciple, the student. In order to convey this impulse, in the first place, the soul from which it comes must possess the power of transmitting it, as it were, to another, and in the second place, the object to which it is transmitted must be fit to receive it. The seed must be a living seed, and the field must be ready ploughed, and when both these conditions are fulfilled, a wonderful growth of religion takes place. "The speaker of religion must be wonderful, so must the hearer be," and when both of these are really wonderful, extraordinary, then alone will splendid spiritual growth come, not otherwise. These are the real teachers, and these are the real students. Besides these, the others are playing with spirituality, just having a little intellectual struggle, just satisfying a little curiosity, but are standing only on the outward fringe of the horizon of religion. There is some value in that; real thirst for religion may thus be awakened; all comes in course of time. It is mysterious law of nature, that as soon as the field is ready, the seed *must* come, as soon as the soul *wants* religion, the transmitter of religious force *must* come. "The seeking sinner meeteth the seeking Saviour." When the power that attracts in the receiving soul is full and ripe, the power which answers to that attraction must come.

But there are great dangers in the way. There is the danger to the receiving soul of mistaking its momentary emotion for real religious yearning. We find that in ourselves. Many times in our lives, somebody dies whom we loved; we receive a blow; for a moment we think that this world is slipping between our fingers, and that we want something higher, and that we are going to be religious. In a few days that wave passes away, and we are left stranded where we were. We oft-times mistake such impulses for real thirst after religion, but so long as these momentary emotions are thus mistaken, that continuous, real want of the soul will not come, and we shall not find the "transmitter".

So, when we complain that we have not got the truth, and that we want it so much, instead of complaining, our first duty ought to be to look into our own souls, and find whether we *really* want it; in the vast majority of cases we shall find that we are not fit; we do not want; there was no thirst after the spiritual.

There are still more difficulties for the "transmitter". There are many who, though immersed in ignorance, yet, in the pride of their hearts, think they know everything, and not only do not stop there, but offer to take others on their shoulders, and thus "the blind leading the blind, they both fall into the ditch." The world is full of these; everyone wants to be a teacher, every beggar wants to make a gift of a million dollars. Just as the latter is ridiculous, so are these teachers.

How are we to know a teacher then? In the first place, the sun requires no torch to make it visible. We do not light a candle to see the sun. When the sun rises, we instinctively become aware of its rising, and when a teacher of men comes to help us, the soul will instinctively know that it has found the truth. Truth stands on its own evidences; it does not require any other testimony to attest it; it is self-effulgent. It penentrates into inmost recesses of our nature, and the whole universe stands up and says, "This is Truth". These are the very great teachers, but we can get help from the lesser ones also; and as we ourselves are not always sufficiently intuitive to be certain of our judgment of the man from whom we receive, there ought to be certain tests. There are certain conditions necessary in the taught, and also in the teacher.

The conditions necessary in the taught are purity, a real thirst after knowledge, and perseverance. No impure soul can be religious; that is one great condition; purity in every way is absolutely necessary. The other condition is, a real thirst after knowledge. Who *wants*? That is the question. We get whatever we want—that is an old, old law. He who wants, gets. To want religion is a very difficult thing, not so easy as we generally think. Then we always forget that religion does not consist in hearing talks, or in reading books, but it is a continuous struggle, a grappling with our own nature, a continuous fight, till the victory is achieved. It is not a question of one or two days, of years, or of lives, but it may be hundreds of lifetimes, and you must be ready for that. It may come immediately, or it may not come in hundreds of lifetimes, and we must be ready for that. The student who sets out with such a spirit finds success.

In the teacher we must first see that he knows the secret of the scriptures. The whole world reads scriptures, Bibles, Vedas, Korans, and others, but they are only words, external arrangement, syntax, the etymology, the philology, the dry bones of religion. The teacher may be able to find what is the age of any book, but words are only the external forms in which things come. Those who deal too much in words, and let the mind run always in the force of words, lose the spirit. So the teacher must be able to know the *spirit* of the scriptures. The network of words is like a huge forest in which the human mind loses itself and finds no way out. "The various methods of joining words, the various methods of speaking a beautiful language, the various methods of explaining the dicta of the scriptures," are only for the enjoyment of the learned. They do not attain perfection; they are simply desirous to show their learning, so that the world may praise them, and see that they are learned men. You will find that no one of the great teachers of the world went into these various explanations of texts; on their part there is no attempt at "text-torturing", no saying "this word means this, and this is the philological connection between this and that word". You study all the great teachers the world has produced, and you will see that no one of them goes that way. Yet *they* taught, while others, who have nothing to teach, will take up a word and write a three-volume book on its origin and use. As my Master used to say, what would you think of men who went into a mango orchard, and busied themselves in counting the leaves, and examining the colour of the leaves, the size of the twigs, the number of branches, and so forth, while only one of them had the sense to begin to eat the mangoes? So leave this counting of leaves and twigs, and this note-taking to others. That work has its own value in its proper place, but not here, in the spiritual realm. Men never become spiritual through such work; you have never once seen a strong spiritual man among these "leaf-counters". Religion is the highest aim of man, the highest glory, but it does not require "leaf-counting". If you want to be a Christian, it is not necessary to know whether Christ was born in Jerusalem or Bethlehem or just the exact date on which he pronounced the Sermon on the Mount; you only require to *feel* the Sermon on the Mount. It is not necessary to read two thousand words on when it was delivered. All that is for the enjoyment of the learned. Let them have it; say amen to that. Let *us* "eat the mangoes".

The second condition necessary in the teacher is that he must be sinless. The question was once asked me in England by a friend: "Why should we look to the personality of a teacher?—we have only to judge of what he says, and take that up." Not so. If a man wants to teach me something of dynamics or chemistry, or any other physical science, he may be of any character; he can still teach dynamics, or any other science. For the knowledge that the physical sciences require is simply intellectual and depends on intellectual strength; a man can have in such a case a gigantic intellectual power without the least development of his soul. But in the spiritual sciences it is impossible from first to last that there can be any spiritual light in that soul which is impure. What can such a soul teach? It knows nothing. Spiritual truth is purity. "Blessed are the pure in heart, for they shall see God." In that one sentence is the gist of all religions. If you have learnt that, all that has been said in the past, and all that it is possible to say in the future, you have known; you need not look into anything else, for you have all that is necessary in that one sentence; it could save the world were all the other scriptures lost. A vision of God, glimpse of the beyond, never comes until the soul is pure. Therefore in the teacher of spirituality, purity is the one thing indispensable; we must see *first* what he *is*, and *then* what he *says*. Not so with intellectual teachers; there we care more for what he says than what he is. With the teacher of religion we must first and foremost see what he is, and then alone comes the value of the words, because he is the transmitter. What will he transmit, if he has not that spiritual power in him? To give a simile—If this heater here is hot, it can convey heat vibrations, but if not, it is impossible to do so. Even so is the case with the mental vibrations of the religious teacher which he conveys to the mind of the taught. It is a question of transference, and not of stimulating only our intellectual faculties. Some power, real and tangible, goes out from the teacher and begins to grow in the mind of the taught. Therefore the necessary condition is that the teacher must be true.

The third condition is motive. We should see that he does not teach with any ulterior motive, for name, or fame, or anything else, but simply for love, pure love for you. When spiritual forces are transmitted from the teacher to the taught, they can only be conveyed through the medium of love; there is no other medium that can convey them. Any other motive, such as gain or name, would immediately destroy the conveying medium; therefore all must be done through love. One who has known God can alone be a teacher. When you see that in the teacher these conditions are fulfilled, you are safe; if they are not fulfilled, it is unwise to accept him. There is a great risk, if he cannot convey goodness; of his conveying wickedness, sometimes. This must be guarded against; therefore, it naturally follows that we cannot be taught by anybody and everybody.

The preaching of sermons by brooks and stones may be true as a poetical figure, but no one can preach a single grain of truth until he has it in himself. To whom do the brooks preach sermons? To that human soul only, whose lotus of life has already opened. When the heart has been opened, it can receive teaching from the brooks, or the stones, it can get some religious teaching from all these, but the unopened heart will see nothing but brooks and rolling stones. A blind man may come to a museum, but he comes and goes only; if he is to see, his eyes must first be opened. This eye-opener of religion is the teacher. With the teacher, therefore, our relationship is that of ancestor and descendant; the teacher is the spiritual ancestor, and the disciple is the spiritual descendant. It is all very well to talk of liberty and independence, but without humility, submission, veneration, and faith, there will not be any religion. It is a significant fact that where this relation still exists between the teacher and the taught, there alone gigantic spiritual souls grow, but in those who have thrown it off, religion is made into a diversion. In nations and churches where this relation between teacher and taught is not maintained, spirituality is almost an unknown quantity. It never comes without that feeling; there is no one to transmit, and no one to be transmitted to, because they are all independent. Of whom can they learn? And if they come to learn, they come to *buy* learning. Give me a dollar's worth of religion; cannot I pay a dollar for it? Religion cannot be got that way.

There is nothing higher and holier than the knowledge which comes to the soul transmitted by a spiritual teacher. If a man has become a perfect Yogi, it comes by itself, but it cannot be got in books. You may go and knock your head against the four corners of the world, seek in the Himalayas, the Alps, the Caucasus, the Desert of Gobi or Sahara, or the bottom of the sea, but it will not come, until you find a teacher. Find the teacher, serve him as a child, open your heart to his influence, see in him God manifested. Our attention should be fixed on the teacher as the highest manifestation of God, and as the power of attention concentrates there, the picture of the teacher as man will melt away, the frame will vanish, and the real God will be left there. Those that come to truth with such a spirit of veneration and love—for them, the Lord of truth speaks the most wonderful words. "Take thy shoes from off thy feet, for the place whereon thou standest is holy ground." Wherever His name is spoken that place is holy. How much more so is a man who speaks His name, and with what veneration ought we to approach a man out of whom come spiritual truths! This is the spirit in which we are to be taught. Such teachers are few in number, no doubt, in this world, but the world is never altogether without them. The moment it is absolutely bereft of these, it will cease to be, it will become a hideous hell, and will just drop. These teachers are the fair flowers of human life, and keep the world going; it is the strength that is manifested from these hearts of life that keeps the bonds of society intact.

Beyond these is another set of teachers, the Christs of the world. These Teachers of all teachers represent God Himself in the form of man. They are much higher; they can transmit spirituality with a touch, with a wish, which makes even the lowest and most degraded characters, saints in one second. Do you not read of how they used to do these things? They are not the teachers about whom I was speaking; they are the Teachers of all teachers, the greatest manifestations of God to man; we cannot see God except through them. We cannot help worshipping them, and they are the only beings we are bound to worship.

No man hath "seen" God, but as He is manifested in the Son. We cannot see God. If we try to see Him we make a hideous caricature of God. There is an Indian story that an ignorant man was asked to make an image of the God Shiva, and after days of struggle, he made an image of a monkey. So, whenever we attempt to make an image of God we make a caricature of Him, because we cannot understand Him as anything higher than man, so long as we are men. The time will come when we transcend our human nature, and know Him as He is; but so long as we are men, we must worship Him in man. Talk as we may, try as we may, we cannot see God except as a man. We may deliver great intellectual speeches, become very great rationalists, and prove that these tales of God are all nonsense, but let us come to practical common sense. What is behind this remarkable intellect? Zero, nothing, simply so much froth. When next you hear a man delivering great intellectual lectures against this worship of God, get hold of him and ask him what is his idea of God, what he means by "omnipotence", and "omniscience", and "omnipresent love," and so forth, beyond the spelling of the words. He means nothing, he cannot formulate an idea, he is no better than the man in the street who has not read a single book. That man in the street, however, is quiet and does not disturb the world, while the other man's arguments cause disturbance. He has no actual perception, and both are on the same plane. Religion is realisation, and you must make the sharpest distinction between talk and realisation. What you perceive in your soul is realisation. Man has no idea of the Spirit, he has to think of it with the forms he has before him. He has to think of the blue skies, or the expansive fields, or the sea, or something huge. How else can you think of God? So what are you doing, in reality? You are talking of omnipresence, and thinking of the sea. Is God the sea? A little more common sense is required. Nothing is so uncommon as common sense, the world is too full of talk. A truce to all this frothy argument of the world. We are by our present constitution limited and bound to see God as man. If the buffaloes want to worship God, they will see Him as a huge buffalo. If a fish wants to worship God, it will have to think of Him as a big fish. You and I, the buffalo, the fish, each represents so many different vessels. All these go to the sea to be filled with water according to the shape of each vessel. In each of these vessels is nothing but water. So with God. When men see Him, they see Him as man, and the animals as animal—each according to his ideal. That is the only way you can see Him; you have to worship Him as man, because there is no other way out of it.

Two classes of men do not worship God as man—the human brute who has no religion, and the Paramahamsa (highest Yogi), who has gone beyond humanity, who has thrown off his mind and body, and gone beyond the limits of nature. All nature has become his Self. He has neither mind nor body, and can worship God as God, as can a Jesus or a Buddha. They did not worship God as man. The other extreme is the human brute. You know how two extremes look alike. Similar is the case with the extreme of ignorance and the other extreme of knowledge; neither of these worships anybody. The extremely ignorant do not worship God, not being developed enough to feel the need for so doing. Those that has attained the highest knowledge also do not worship God—having realised and become one with God. God never worships God. Between these two poles of existence, if anyone tells you he is not going to worship God as man, take care of him. He is an irresponsible talker, he is mistaken; his religion is for frothy thinkers, it is intellectual nonsense.

Therefore, it is absolutely necessary to worship God as man, and blessed are those races which have such a "God-man" to worship. Christians have such a God-man in Christ; therefore, cling close to Christ; never give up Christ. That is the natural way to see God; see God in man. All our ideas of God are concentrated there. The great limitation Christians have is that they do not heed other manifestations of God besides Christ. He was a manifestation of God, so was Buddha, so were some others, and there will be hundreds of others. Do not limit God anywhere. Pay all the reverence that you think is due to God to Christ; that is the only worship we can have. God cannot be worshipped; He is the immanent Being of the universe. It is only to His manifestation as man that we can pray. It would be a very good plan, when Christians pray, to say, "In the name of Christ". It would be wise to stop praying to God, and only pray to Christ. God understands human failings and becomes a man to do good to humanity. "Whenever virtue subsides and immorality prevails, then I come to help mankind," says Krishna. He also says, "Fools, not knowing that I, the Omnipotent and Omnipresent God of the universe, have taken this human form, deride Me, and think that cannot be." Their minds have been clouded with demoniacal ignorance, so they cannot see in Him the Lord of the universe. These great Incarnations of God are to be worshipped. Not only so, they alone can be worshipped, and on the days of their birth, and on the days when they went out of this world, we ought to pay more particular reverence to them. In worshipping Christ I would rather worship Him just as He desires; on the day of His birth I would rather worship Him by fasting than by feasting—by praying. When these are thought of, these great ones, they manifest themselves in our souls, and they make us like unto them. Our whole nature changes, and we become like them.

But you must not mix up Christ or Buddha with hobgoblins flying through the air, and all that sort of nonsense. Sacrilege! Christ coming into a spiritualistic *seance* to dance! I have seen that pretence in this country. It is not in that way that these manifestations of God come. The very touch of one of them will be manifest upon a man; when Christ *touches,* the whole soul of man will change, that man will be transfigured just as He was. His whole life will be spiritualised; from every pore of his body spiritual power will emanate. What were the great powers of Christ in miracles, and healing, in one of His character? They were low, vulgar things that He could not help doing because He was among vulgar beings. Where was this miracle-making done? Among the Jews; and the Jews did not take Him. Where was it not done? In Europe. The miracle-making went to the Jews, who rejected Christ, and the Sermon on the Mount to Europe, which accepted Him. The human spirit took on what was true, and rejected what was spurious. The great strength of Christ is not in His miracles or His healing. Any fool could do those things, fools can heal others, devils can heal others. I have seen horrible demoniacal men do wonderful miracles. They seem to manufacture fruits out of the earth. I have known fools and diabolical men tell the past, present, and future. I have seen fools heal at a glance, by the will, the most horrible diseases. These are powers, truly, but often demoniacal powers. The other is the spiritual power of Christ, which will live, and always has lived, an almighty, gigantic love, and the words of truth which He preached. The action of healing men at a glance is forgotten, but His saying, "Blessed are the pure in heart," that lives today. These words are a gigantic magazine of power, inexhaustible, so long as the human mind lasts. So long as the name of God is not forgotten, these words will roll on and on, and never cease to be. These are the powers Jesus taught, and the powers He had. The power of purity; it is a definite power. So in worshipping Christ, in praying to Him, we must always remember what we are seeking. Not those foolish things of miraculous display, but the wonderful powers of the Spirit, which makes man free, gives him control over the whole of nature, takes from him the badge of slavery, and shows God unto him.

THE NEED OF SYMBOLS

Bhakti is divided into two portions. One is called Vaidhi, formal or ceremonial; the other portion is called Mukhyâ, supreme. The word Bhakti covers all the ground between the lowest form of worship and the highest form of life. All the worship that you have seen in any country in the world, or in any religion, is regulated by love. There is a good deal that is simple ceremony; there is also a good deal which, though not ceremony, is still not love, but a lower state. Yet these ceremonies are necessary. The external part of Bhakti is absolutely necessary to help the soul onward. Man makes a great mistake when he thinks that he can at once jump to the highest state. If a baby thinks he is going to be an old man in a day, he is mistaken, and I hope you will always bear in mind this one idea, that religion is neither in books nor in intellectual consent, nor in reasoning. Reason, theories, documents, doctrines, books, religious ceremonies are all *helps* to religion—religion itself consists of *realisation*. We all say, "There is a God." Have you seen God? That is the question. You hear a man say, "There is God in heaven". You ask him if he has seen Him, and if he says he has, you would laugh at him, and say he is a maniac. With most people religion is a sort of intellectual assent and goes no further than a document. I would not call it religion. It is better to be an atheist than to have that sort of religion. Religion does not depend on our intellectual assent, or dissent. You say there is a soul. Have you seen the soul? How is it we all have souls and do not see them? You have to answer the question, and find out the way to see the soul. If not, it is useless to talk of religion. If any religion is true, it must be able to show us the soul, to show us God and the truth in ourselves. If you and I fight for all eternity about one of these doctrines or documents, we shall never come to any conclusion. People have been fighting for ages, and what is the outcome? Intellect cannot reach there at all. We have to go beyond the intellect; the proof of religion is in direct perception. The proof of the existence of this wall is that we see it; if you sat down and argued about its existence or non-existence for ages, you could never come to any conclusion, but directly you see it, it is enough. If all the men in the world told you it did not exist, you would not believe them, because you know that the evidence of your own eyes is superior to that of all the doctrines and documents in the world.

To be religious, you have first to throw books overboard. The less you read of books, the better for you; do one thing at a time. It is a tendency in Western countries, in these modern times, to make a hotchpotch of the brain; all sorts of unassimilated ideas run riot in the brain, and form a chaos, without ever obtaining a chance to settle down and crystallise into a definite shape. In many cases it becomes a sort of disease, but this is not religion. Then some want a sensation. Tell them about ghosts, and people coming from the North Pole or any other remote place, with wings or in any other form, and that they are invisibly present and watching over them, and make them feel uncanny. Then they are satisfied and go home, but within twenty-four hours they are ready for a fresh sensation. This is what some call religion. This is the way to the lunatic asylum, and not to religion. The Lord is not to be reached by the weak, and all these weird things tend to weakness. Therefore go not near them; they only make people weak, bring disorder to the brain, weaken the mind, demoralise the soul, and a hopeless muddle is the result. You must bear in mind that religion does not consist in talk, or doctrines, or books, but in realisation; it is not learning, but *being*. Everybody knows, "Do not steal," but what of it? That man has really known, who has not stolen. Everybody knows, "Do not injure others," but of what value is it? Those who have not done so have realised it, they know it, and have built their character on it. Religion is realising, and I will call you a worshipper of God, when you have become able to realise the idea. Before that it is the spelling of the word, and no more. It is this power of realisation that makes religion. No amount of doctrines or philosophies or ethical books that you may have stuffed into your brain will matter much, only what you *are,* and what you have *realised.* So we have to realise religion, and this realisation of religion is a long process. When men hear of something very high and wonderful, they all think they will get that, and never stop for a moment to consider that they will have to work their way up to it; they all want to jump there. If it is the highest, we are for it. We never stop to consider whether we have the power, and the result is that we do not do anything. You cannot take a man with a pitchfork and push him up there; we all have to work up gradually. Therefore, the first part of religion is Vaidhi Bhakti; the lower phase of worship.

What are these lower phases of worship? They are various. In order to attain to the state where we can realise, we must pass through the concrete, just as you see children learn through the concrete first, and gradually come to the abstract. If you tell a baby that five times two is ten, it will not understand, but if you bring ten things and show how five times two is ten, it will understand. Religion is a long, slow process. We are all of us babies here; we may be old, and have studied all the books in the universe, but we are all spiritual babies. We have learnt the doctrines and dogmas, but realised nothing in our lives. We shall have to begin now in the concrete, through forms and words, prayers and ceremonies, and of these concrete forms there will be thousands; one form need not be for everybody. Some may be helped by images, some may not. Some require an image outside, others one inside the brain. The man who puts it inside says, "I am a superior man; when it is inside, it is all right; when it is outside, it is idolatry, I will fight it." When a man puts an image in the form of a church or temple, he thinks it is holy; but when it is in a human form, he objects to it!

So there are various forms through which the mind will take this concrete exercise, and then, step by step, we shall come to the abstract understanding, abstract realisation. Again, the same form is not for everyone; there is one form that will suit you, and another will suit somebody else, and so on. All forms, though leading to the same goal, may not be for all of us. Here is another mistake we generally make. My ideal does not suit you, and why should I force it on you? My fashion of building churches or reading hymns does not suit you; why should I force it on you? Go into the world and every fool will tell you that his form is the only right one, that every other form is diabolical, and he is only chosen man ever born in the universe. But in fact, all these forms are good and helpful. Just as there are certain varieties in human nature, so it is necessary that there should be an equal number of forms in religion, and the more there are, the better for the world. If there are twenty forms of religion in the world, it is very good; if there are four hundred, so much the better, there will be the more to choose from. So we should rather be glad when the number of religions and religious ideas increase and multiply, because they will then include every man, and help mankind more. Would to God that religions multiplied until every man had his own religion, quite separate from that of any other! This is the idea of the Bhakti-Yogi.

The final idea is that my religion cannot be yours, or yours mine. Although the goal and the aim are the same, yet each one has to take a different road, according to the tendencies of his mind; and although these roads are various, they must all be true, because they lead to the same goal. It cannot be that one is true and the rest not. The choosing of one's own road is called in the language of Bhakti, Ishta, the chosen way.

Then there are words. All of you have heard of the power of words, how wonderful they are! Every book—the Bible, the Koran, and the Vedas—is full of the power of words. Certain words have wonderful power over mankind. Again, there are other forms, known as symbols. Symbols have great influence on the human mind. But great symbols in religion were not created indefinitely. We find that they are the natural expressions of thought. We think symbolically. All our words are but symbols of the thought behind, and different people have come to use different symbols without knowing the reason why. It was all behind, and these symbols are associated with the thoughts, and as the thought brings the symbol outside, so the symbol, on the contrary, can bring the thought inside. So one portion of Bhakti tells about these various subjects of symbols and words and prayers. Every religion has prayers, but one thing you must bear in mind—praying for health or wealth is not Bhakti, it is all Karma, or meritorious action. Praying for any physical gain is simply Karma, such as a prayer for going to heaven and so forth. One that wants to love God, to be a Bhakta, must discard all such prayers. He who wants to enter the realms of light must first give up this buying and selling, this "shopkeeping" religion, and then enter the gates. It is not that you do not get what you pray for; you get everything, but such praying is a beggar's religion. "Foolish indeed is he who, living on the banks of the Ganga, digs a little well for water. A fool indeed is the man who, coming to a mine of diamonds, seeks for glass beads." This body will die some time, so what is the use of praying for its health again and again? What is there in health and wealth? The wealthiest man can use and enjoy only a little portion of his wealth. We can never get all the things of this world, and if not, who cares? This body will go, who cares for these things? If good things come, welcome; if they go away, welcome, let them go. Blessed are they when they come, and blessed are they when they go. We are striving to come into the presence of the King of kings. We cannot get there in a beggar's dress. Even if we wanted to enter the presence of an emperor, should we be admitted? Certainly not. We should be driven out. This is the Emperor of emperors, and in these beggar's rags we cannot enter. Shopkeepers never have admission there; buying and selling have no place there. As you read in the Bible, Jesus drove the buyers and sellers out of the Temple. Do not pray for little things. If you seek only bodily comforts, where is the difference between men and animals? Think yourselves a little higher than that.

So it goes without saying, that the first task in becoming a Bhakta is to give up all desires of heaven and other things. The question is how to get rid of these desires. What makes men miserable? Because they are slaves, bound by laws, puppets in the hand of nature, tumbled about like playthings. We are continually taking care of this body that anything can knock down, and so we are living in a constant state of fear. I have read that a deer has to run on the average sixty or seventy miles every day because it is frightened. We ought to know that we are in a worse plight than the deer. The deer has some rest, but we have none. If the deer gets grass enough, it is satisfied; but we are always multiplying our wants. It is a morbid desire with us to multiply our wants. We have become so unhinged and unnatural that nothing natural will satisfy us. We are always grasping after morbid things, must have unnatural excitement, unnatural food, drink, surroundings and life. As to fear, what are our lives but bundles of fears? The deer has only one class of fear, such as that from tigers, wolves, etc. Man has the whole universe to fear.

How are we to free ourselves from this is the question. Utilitarians say, "Don't talk of God and hereafter; we don't know anything of these things, let us live happily in this world."

I would be the first to do so if we could, but the world will not allow us. As long as you are a slave of nature, how can you? The more you struggle, the more enveloped you become. You have been devising plans to make you happy, I do not know for how many years, but each year things seem to grow worse. Two hundred years ago in the old world people had few wants, but if their knowledge increased in arithmetical progression, their wants increased in geometrical progression. We think that in salvation at least our desires will be fulfilled, so we desire to go to heaven. This eternal, unquenchable thirst! Always wanting something! When a man is a beggar, he wants money. When he has money, he wants other things, society, and after that, something else. Never at rest. How are we to quench this? If we get to heaven, it will only increase desire. If a poor man gets rich, it does not quench his desires, it is only like throwing butter on the fire, increasing its bright flames. Going to heaven means becoming intensely richer, and then desire comes more and more. We read of many human things in heaven in the different Bibles of the world; they are not always very good there, and after all, this desire to go to heaven is a desire after enjoyment. This has to be given up. It is too little, too vulgar a thing for you to think of going to heaven. It is just the same as thinking, "I will become a millionaire and lord it over people." There are many of these heavens, but through them you cannot gain the right to enter the gates of religion and love.

THE AIM OF RAJA-YOGA

All our knowledge is based upon experience. What we call inferential knowledge, in which we go from the less to the more general, or from the general to the particular, has experience as its basis. In what are called the exact sciences, people easily find the truth, because it appeals to the particular experiences of every human being. The scientist does not tell you to believe in anything, but he has certain results which come from his own experiences, and, reasoning on them, when he asks us to believe in his conclusions, he appeals to some universal experience of humanity. In every exact science there is a basis which is common to all humanity, so that we can at once see the truth or the fallacy of the conclusions drawn therefrom. Now, the question is, has religion any such basis or not? I shall have to answer the question both in the affirmative and in the negative.

Religion, as it is generally taught all over the world, is said to be based upon faith and belief, and, in most cases, consists only of different sets of theories, and that is the reason why we find all religions quarrelling with one another. These theories, again, are based upon belief. One man says there is a great Being sitting above the clouds and governing the whole universe, and he asks me to believe that solely on the authority of his assertion. In the same way, I may have my own ideas, which I am asking others to believe, and if they ask a reason, I cannot give them any. This is why religion and metaphysical philosophy have a bad name nowadays. Every educated man seems to say, "Oh, these religions are only bundles of theories without any standard to judge them by, each man preaching his own pet ideas." Nevertheless there is a basis of universal belief in religion, governing all the different theories, and all the varying ideas of different sects in different countries. Going to their basis we find that they also are based upon universal experiences.

In the first place, if you analyse all the various religions of the world, you will find that these are divided into two classes, those with a book, and those without a book. Those with book are the strongest, and have the largest number of followers. Those without books have mostly died out, and the few new ones have very small followings. Yet, in all of them we find one consensus of opinion, that the truths they teach, are the results of the experiences of particular persons. The Christian asks you to believe in his religion, to believe in Christ and to believe in him as the incarnation of God, to believe in a God, in a soul, and in a better state of that soul. If I ask him for reason, he says he believes in them. But if you go to the fountain-head of Christianity, you will find that it is based upon experience. Christ said he saw God; the disciples said they felt God; and so forth. Similarly, in Buddhism, it is Buddha's experience. He experienced certain truths, saw them, came in contact with them, and preached them to the world. So with the Hindus. In their books the writers, who are called Rishis, or sages, declare they experienced certain truths, and these they preach. Thus it is clear that all the religions of the world have been built upon that one universal and adamantine foundation of all our knowledge—direct experience. The teachers all saw God; they all saw their own souls, they saw their future, they saw their eternity, and what they saw they preached. Only there is this difference, that by most of these religions, especially in modern times, a peculiar claim is made, namely, that these experiences are impossible at the present day; they were only possible with a few men, who were the first founders of the religions that subsequently bore their names. At the present time these experiences have become obsolete, and therefore we have now to take religion on belief. This I entirely deny. If there has been one experience in this world in any particular branch of knowledge, it absolutely follows that that experience has been possible millions of times before, and will be repeated eternally. Uniformity is the rigorous law of nature; what once happened can happen always.

The teachers of the science of Yoga, therefore, declare that religion is not only based upon the experience of ancient times, but that no man can be religious until he has the same perceptions himself. Yoga is the science which teaches us how to get these perceptions. It is not much use to talk about religion until one has felt it. Why is there so much disturbance, so much fighting and quarrelling in the name of God? There has been more bloodshed in the name of God than for any other cause, because people never went to the fountain-head; they were content only to give a mental assent to the customs of their forefathers, and wanted others to do the same. What right has a man to say he has a soul if he does not feel it, or that there is a God if he does not see Him? If there is a God, we must see Him, if there is a soul, we must perceive it; otherwise it is better not to believe. It is better to be an outspoken atheist than a hypocrite. The modern idea, on the one hand, with the "learned," is that religion and metaphysics and all search after a Supreme Being are futile; on the other hand, with the semi-educated, the idea seems to be that these things really have no basis, their only value consists in the fact that they furnish strong motive powers for doing good to the world. If men believe in a God, they may become good and moral, and so make good citizens. We cannot blame them for holding such ideas, seeing that all the teaching these men get is simply to believe in an eternal rigmarole of words, without any substance behind them. They are asked to live upon words; can they do it? If they could, I should not have the least regard for human nature. Man wants truth, wants to experience truth for himself; when he has grasped it, realised it, felt it within his heart of hearts, then alone, declare the Vedas, would all doubts vanish, all darkness be scattered, and all crookedness be made straight. "Ye children of immortality, even those who live in the higher spheres, the way is found; there is a way out of all this darkness, and that is by perceiving Him who is beyond all darkness; there is no other way."

The science of Râja-Yoga proposes to put before humanity a practical and scientifically worked out method of reaching this truth. In the first place, every science must have its own method of investigation. If you want to become an astronomer, and sit down and cry, "Astronomy! Astronomy!" it will never come to you. The same with chemistry. A certain method must be followed. You must go to a laboratory, take different substances, mix them up, compound them, experiment with them, and out of that will come a knowledge of chemistry. If you want to be an astronomer, you must go to an observatory, take a telescope, study the stars and planets, and then you will become an astronomer. Each science must have its own methods. I could preach you thousands of sermons, but they would not make you religious, until you practised the method. These are the truths of the sages of all countries, of all ages, of men pure and unselfish, who had no motive but to do good to the world.

They all declare that they have found some truth higher than what the senses can bring to us, and they invite verification. They ask us to take up the method and practise honestly, and then, if we do not find this higher truth, we will have the right to say there is no truth in the claim, but before we have done that, we are not rational in denying the truth of their assertions. So we must work faithfully, using the prescribed methods, and light will come.

In acquiring knowledge we make use of generalisation, and generalisation is based upon observation. We first observe facts, then generalise, and then draw conclusions or principles. The knowledge of the mind, of the internal nature of man, of thought, can never be had until we have first the power of observing the facts that are going on within. It is comparatively easy to observe facts in the external world, for many instruments have been invented for the purpose, but in the internal world we have no instrument to help us. Yet we know we must observe in order to have a real science. Without a proper analysis, any science will be hopeless, mere theorising, and that is why all the psychologists have been quarrelling among themselves since the beginning of time, except those few who found out the means of observation.

The science of Raja-Yoga, in the first place, proposes to give us such a means of observing the internal states. The instrument is the mind itself. The power of attention, when properly guided, and directed towards the internal world, will analyse the mind, and illumine facts for us. The powers of the mind are like rays of light dissipated; when they are concentrated, they illumine. This is our only means of knowledge. Every one is using it, both in the external and the internal world; but, for the psychologist, the same minute observation has to be directed to the internal world, which the scientific man directs to the external; and this requires a great deal of practice. From our childhood upwards we have been taught only to pay attention to things external, but never to things internal, hence most of us have nearly lost the faculty of observing the internal mechanism. To turn the mind, as it were, inside, stop it from going outside, and then to concentrate all its powers, and throw them upon the mind itself, in order that it may know its own nature, analyse itself, is very hard work. Yet that is the only way to anything which will be a scientific approach to the subject.

What is the use of such knowledge? In the first place, knowledge itself is the highest reward of knowledge, and secondly, there is also utility in it. It will take away all our misery. When by analysing his own mind, man comes face to face, as it were, with something which is never destroyed, something which is, by its own nature, eternally pure and perfect, he will no more be miserable, no more unhappy. All misery comes from fear, from unsatisfied desire. Man will find that he never dies, and then he will have no more fear of death. When he knows that he is perfect, he will have no more vain desires, and both these causes being absent, there will be no more misery—there will be perfect bliss, even while in this body.

There is only one method by which to attain this knowledge, that which is called concentration. The chemist in his laboratory concentrates all the energies of his mind into one focus, and throws them upon the materials he is analysing, and so finds out their secrets. The astronomer concentrates all the energies of his mind and projects them through his telescope upon the skies; and the stars, the sun, and the moon, give up their secrets to him. The more I can concentrate my thoughts on the matter on which I am talking to you, the more light I can throw upon it. You are listening to me, and the more you concentrate your thoughts, the more clearly you will grasp what I have to say.

How has all the knowledge in the world been gained but by the concentration of the powers of the mind? The world is ready to give up its secrets if we only know how to knock, how to give it the necessary blow. The strength and force of the blow come through concentration. There is no limit to the power of the human mind. The more concentrated it is, the more power is brought to bear on one point; that is the secret.

It is easy to concentrate the mind on external things, the mind naturally goes outwards; but not so in the case of religion, or psychology, or metaphysics, where the subject and the object are one. The object is internal, the mind itself is the object, and it is necessary to study the mind itself, mind studying mind. We know that there is the power of the mind called reflection. I am talking to you. At the same time I am standing aside, as it were, a second person, and knowing and hearing what I am talking. You work and think at the same time, while a portion of your mind stands by and sees what you are thinking. The powers of the mind should be concentrated and turned back upon itself, and as the darkest places reveal their secrets before the penetrating rays of the sun, so will this concentrated mind penetrate its own innermost secrets. Thus will we come to the basis of belief, the real genuine religion. We will perceive for ourselves whether we have souls, whether life is of five minutes, or of eternity, whether there is a God in the universe or none. It will all be revealed to us This is what Raja-Yoga proposes to teach. The goal of all its teaching is how to concentrate the mind, then, how to discover the innermost recesses of our own minds, then, how to generalise their contents and form our own conclusions from them. It therefore never asks the question what our religion is, whether we are Deists, or Atheists, whether Christians, Jews, or Buddhists. We are human beings; that is sufficient. Every human being has the right and the power to seek for religion. Every human being has the right to ask the reason why, and to have his question answered by himself, if he only takes the trouble.

So far, then, we see that in the study of this Raja-Yoga no faith or belief is necessary. Believe nothing until you find it out for yourself; that is what it teaches us. Truth requires no prop to make it stand. Do you mean to say that the facts of our awakened state require any dreams or imaginings to prove them? Certainly not. This study of Raja-Yoga takes a long time and constant practice. A part of this practice is physical, but in the main it is mental. As we proceed we shall find how intimately the mind is connected with the body. If we believe that the mind is simply a finer part of the body, and that mind acts upon the body, then it stands to reason that the body must react upon the mind. If the body is sick, the mind becomes sick also. If the body is healthy, the mind remains healthy and strong. When one is angry, the mind becomes disturbed. Similarly when the mind is disturbed, the body also becomes disturbed. With the majority of mankind the mind is greatly under the control of the body, their mind being very little developed. The vast mass of humanity is very little removed from the animals. Not only so, but in many instances, the power of control in them is little higher than that of the lower animals. We have very little command of our minds. Therefore to bring that command about, to get that control over body and mind, we must take certain physical helps. When the body is sufficiently controlled, we can attempt the manipulation of the mind. By manipulating the mind, we shall be able to bring it under our control, make it work as we like, and compel it to concentrate its powers as we desire.

According to the Raja-Yoga, the external world is but the gross form of the internal, or subtle. The finer is always the cause, the grosser the effect. So the external world is the effect, the internal the cause. In the same way external forces are simply the grosser parts, of which the internal forces are the finer. The man who has discovered and learnt how to manipulate the internal forces will get the whole of nature under his control. The Yogi proposes to himself no less a task than to master the whole universe, to control the whole of nature. He wants to arrive at the point where what we call "nature's laws" will have no influence over him, where he will be able to get beyond them all. He will be master of the whole of nature, internal and external. The progress and civilisation of the human race simply mean controlling this nature.

Different races take to different processes of controlling nature. Just as in the same society some individuals want to control the external nature, and others the internal, so, among races, some want to control the external nature, and others the internal. Some say that by controlling internal nature we control everything. Others that by controlling external nature we control everything. Carried to the extreme, both are right, because in nature there is no such division as internal or external. These are fictitious limitations that never existed. The externalists and the internalists are destined to meet at the same point, when both reach the extreme of their knowledge. Just as a physicist, when he pushes his knowledge to its limits, finds it melting away into metaphysics, so a metaphysician will find that what he calls mind and matter are but apparent distinctions, the reality being One.

The end and aim of all science is to find the unity, the One out of which the manifold is being manufactured, that One existing as many. Raja-Yoga proposes to start from the internal world, to study internal nature, and, through that, control the whole—both internal and external. It is a very old attempt. India has been its special stronghold, but it was also attempted by other nations. In Western countries it was regarded as mysticism, and people who wanted to practise it were either burnt or killed as witches and sorcerers. In India, for various reasons, it fell into the hands of persons who destroyed ninety per cent of the knowledge, and tried to make a great secret of the remainder. In modern times many so-called teachers have arisen in the West worse than those of India, because the latter knew something, while these modern exponents know nothing.

Anything that is secret and mysterious in these systems of Yoga should be at once rejected. The best guide in life is strength. In religion, as in all other matters discard everything that weakens you, have nothing to do with it. Mystery-mongering weakens the human brain. It has wellnigh destroyed Yoga—one of the grandest of sciences. From the time it was discovered, more than four thousand years ago, Yoga was perfectly delineated, formulated and preached in India. It is a striking fact that the more modern the commentator the greater the mistakes he makes, while the more ancient the writer the more rational he is. Most of the modern writers talk of all sorts of mystery. Thus Yoga fell into the hands of a few persons who made it a secret, instead of letting the full blaze of daylight and reason fall upon it. They did so, that they might have the powers to themselves.

In the first place there is no mystery in what I teach. What little I know I will tell you. So far as I can reason it out I will do so, but as to what I do not know I will simply tell you what the books say. It is wrong to believe blindly. You must exercise your own reason and judgment; you must practise, and see whether these things happen or not. Just as you would take up any other science, exactly in the same manner you should take up this science for study. There is neither mystery nor danger in it. So far as it is true, it ought to be preached in the public streets, in broad daylight. Any attempt to mystify these things is productive of great danger.

Before proceeding further, I will tell you a little of the Sânkhya philosophy, upon which the whole of Raja-Yoga is based. According to the Sankhya philosophy the genesis of perception is as follows: the affections of external objects are carried by the outer instruments to their respective brain centres or organs, the organs carry the affections to the mind, the mind to the determinative faculty, from this the Purusha (the soul) receives them, when perception results. Next he gives the order back, as it were, to the motor centres to do the needful. With the exception of the Purusha all of these are material, but the mind is much finer matter than the external instruments. That material of which the mind is composed goes also to form the subtle matter called the Tanmâtras. These become gross and make the external matter. That is the psychology of the Sankhya. So that between the intellect and the grosser matter outside there is only a difference in degree. The Purusha is the only thing which is immaterial. The mind is an instrument, as it were, in the hands of the soul, through which the soul catches external objects. The mind is constantly changing and vacillating, and can, when perfected, either attach itself to several organs, to one, or to none. For instance, if I hear the clock with great attention, I will not, perhaps, see anything, although my eyes may be open, showing that the mind was not attached to the seeing organ, while it was to the hearing organ. But the perfected mind can be attached to all the organs simultaneously. It has the reflexive power of looking back into its own depths. This reflexive power is what the Yogi wants to attain; by concentrating the powers of the mind, and turning them inward he seeks to know what is happening inside. There is in this no question of mere belief; it is the analysis arrived at by certain philosophers. Modern physiologists tell us that the eyes are not the organ of vision, but that the organ is in one of the nerve centres of the brain, and so with all the senses; they also tell us that these centres are formed of the same material as the brain itself. The Sankhyas also tell us the same thing. The former is a statement on the physical side, and the latter on the psychological side; yet both are the same. Our field of research lies beyond this.

The Yogi proposes to attain that fine state of perception in which he can perceive all the different mental states. There must be mental perception of all of them. One can perceive how the sensation is travelling, how the mind is receiving it, how it is going to the determinative faculty, and how this gives it to the Purusha. As each science requires certain preparations, and has its own method, which must be followed before it could be understood, even so in Raja-Yoga.

Certain regulations as to food are necessary; we must use that food which brings us the purest mind. If you go into a menagerie you will find this demonstrated at once. You see the elephants, huge animals, but calm and gentle; and if you go towards the cages of the lions and tigers, you find them restless, showing how much difference has been made by food. All the forces that are working in this body have been produced out of food; we see that every day. If you begin to fast, first your body will get weak, the physical forces will suffer; then, after a few days, the mental forces will suffer also. First, memory will fail. Then comes a point, when you are not able to think, much less to pursue any course of reasoning. We have, therefore, to take care what sort of food we eat at the beginning and when we have got strength enough, when our practice is well advanced, we need not be so careful in this respect. While the plant is growing, it must be hedged round, lest it be injured; but when it becomes a tree, the hedges are taken away. It is strong enough to withstand all assaults.

A Yogi must avoid the two extremes of luxury and austerity. He must not fast, nor torture his flesh. He who does so, says the Gita, cannot be a Yogi: He who fasts, he who keeps awake, he who sleeps much, he who works too much, he who does no work, none of these can be a Yogi.

HINTS ON PRACTICAL SPIRITUALITY

(Delivered at the Home of Truth, Los Angeles, California)

This morning I shall try to present to you some ideas about breathing and other exercises. We have been discussing theories so long that now it will be well to have a little of the practical. A great many books have been written in India upon this subject. Just as your people are practical in many things, so it seems our people are practical in this line. Five persons in this country will join their heads together and say, "We will have a joint-stock company," and in five hours it is done; in India they could not do it in fifty years; they are so unpractical in matters like this. But, mark you, if a man starts a system of philosophy, however wild its theory may be, it will have followers. For instance, a sect is started to teach that if a man stands on one leg for twelve years, day and night, he will get salvation—there will be hundreds ready to stand on one leg. All the suffering will be quietly borne. There are people who keep their arms upraised for years to gain religious merit. I have seen hundreds of them. And, mind you, they are not always ignorant fools, but are men who will astonish you with the depth and breadth of their intellect. So, you see, the word practical is also relative.

We are always making this mistake in judging others; we are always inclined to think that our little mental universe is all that is; our ethics, our morality, our sense of duty, our sense of utility, are only things that are worth having. The other day when I was going to Europe, I was passing through Marseilles, where a bull-fight was being held. All the Englishmen in the steamer were mad with excitement, abusing and criticising the whole thing as cruel. When I reached England, I heard of a party of prize-fighters who had been to Paris, and were kicked out unceremoniously by the French, who thought prize-fighting very brutal. When I hear these things in various countries, I begin to understand the marvellous saying of Christ: "Judge not that ye be not judged." The more we learn, the more we find out how ignorant we are, how multiform and multi-sided is this mind of man. When I was a boy, I used to criticise the ascetic practices of my countrymen; great preachers in our own land have criticised them; the greatest man that was ever born, Buddha himself, criticised them. But all the same, as I am growing older, I feel that I have no right to judge. Sometimes I wish that, in spite of all their incongruities, I had one fragment of their power to do and suffer. Often I think that my judgment and my criticism do not proceed from any dislike of torture, but from sheer cowardice —because I cannot do it—I dare not do it.

Then, you see that strength, power, and courage are things which are very peculiar. We generally say a courageous man, a brave man, a daring man; but we must bear in mind that that courage or bravery or any other trait does not always characterise the man. The same man who would rush to the mouth of a cannon shrinks from the knife of the surgeon; and another man who never dares to face a gun, will calmly bear a severe surgical operation, if need be. Now, in judging others you must always define your terms of courage or greatness. The man whom I am criticising as not good may be wonderfully so in some points in which I am not.

Take another example: you often note, when people are discussing as to what man and woman can do, always the same mistake is made. They think they show man at his best because he can fight, for instance, and undergo tremendous physical exertion, and this is pitted against the physical weakness and the non-combating quality of woman. This is unjust. Woman is as courageous as man. Each is equally good in his or her way. What man can bring up a child with such patience, endurance, and love as the woman can? The one has developed the power of doing; the other, the power of suffering. If woman cannot act, neither can man suffer. The whole universe is one of perfect balance. I do not know, but some day we may wake up and find that the mere worm has something which balances our manhood. The most wicked person may have some good qualities that I entirely lack. I see that every day of my life. Look at the savage, I wish I had such a splendid physique. He eats, he drinks, to his heart's content, without knowing perhaps what sickness is, while I am suffering every minute. How many times would I have been glad to have changed my brain for his body! The whole universe is only a wave and a hollow; there can be no wave without a hollow. Balance, everywhere. You have one thing great, your neighbour has another thing great. When you are judging man and woman, judge them by the standard of their respective greatness. One cannot be in the other's shoes. The one has no right to say that the other is wicked. It is the same old superstition that says, "If this is done, the world will go to ruin." But in spite of this, the world has not yet come to ruin. It was said in this country that if the Negroes were freed, the country would go to ruin—but it was only made better. Several years ago a book came out depicting the worst thing that could happen to England. The writer showed that as workmen's wages were rising, English commerce was declining. A cry was raised that the workmen in England were exorbitant in their demands, and that the Germans worked for less wages. A commission was sent over to Germany to investigate this and it reported that the German labourers received higher wages. Why was it so? Because of the education of the masses. Then how about the world going to ruin if the masses are educated? In India, especially, we meet with old fogies all over the land. They want to keep everything secret from the masses. These people come to the very satisfying conclusion that they are the *créme de la créme* of this universe. They believe they cannot be hurt by these dangerous experiments. It is only the masses that can be hurt by them!

Now, coming back to the practical. The subject of the practical application of psychology has been taken up in India from very early times. About fourteen hundred years before Christ, there flourished in India a great philosopher, Patanjali by name. He collected all the facts, evidences, and researches in psychology and took advantage of all the experiences accumulated in the past. Remember, this world is very old; it was not created only two or three thousand years ago. It is taught here in the West that society began eighteen hundred years ago, with the New Testament. Before that there was no society. That may be true with regard to the West, but it is not true as regards the whole world. Often, while I was lecturing in London, a very intellectual and intelligent friend of mine would argue with me, and one day after using all his weapons against me, he suddenly exclaimed, "But why did not your Rishis come to England to teach us?" I replied, "Because there was no England to come to. Would they preach to the forests?"

"Fifty years ago," said Ingersol to me, "you would have

been hanged in this country if you had come to preach. You would have been burnt alive or you would have been stoned out of the villages."

So there is nothing unreasonable in the supposition that civilisation existed fourteen hundred years before Christ. It is not yet settled whether civilisation has always come from the lower to the higher. The same arguments and proofs that have been brought forward to prove this proposition can also be used to demonstrate that the savage is only a degraded civilised man. The people of China, for instance, can never believe that civilisation sprang from a savage state, because the contrary is within their experience. But when you talk of the civilisation of America, what you mean is the perpetuity and the growth of your own race.

It is very easy to believe that the Hindus, who have been declining for seven hundred years, were highly civilised in the past. We cannot prove that it is not so.

There is not one single instance of any civilisation being spontaneous. There was not a race in the world which became civilised unless another civilised race came and mingled with that race. The origin of civilisation must have belonged, so to say, to one or two races who went abroad, spread their ideas, and intermingled with other races; and thus civilisation spread.

For practical purposes, let us talk in the language of modern science. But I must ask you to bear in mind that, as there is religious superstition, so also there is a superstition in the matter of science. There are priests who take up the religious work as their speciality; so also there are priests of physical law, scientists. As soon as a great scientific name, like Darwin or Huxley, is cited, we follow blindly. It is the fashion of the day. Ninety-nine per cent of what we call scientific knowledge is mere theories. And many of them are no better than the old superstitions of ghosts with many heads and hands, but with this difference, that the latter differentiated man a little from stocks and stones. True science asks us to be cautious. Just as we should be careful with the priests, so we should be with the scientists. Begin with disbelief. Analyse, test, prove everything and then take it. Some of the most current beliefs of modern science have not been proved. Even in such a science as mathematics, the vast majority of its theories are only working hypotheses. With the advent of greater knowledge they will be thrown away.

In 1400 B.C. a great sage made an attempt to arrange, analyse, and generalise upon certain psychological facts. He was followed by many others who took up parts of what he had discovered and made a special study of them. The Hindus alone of all ancient races took up the study of this branch of knowledge in right earnest. I am teaching you now about it, but how many of you will practise it? How many days, how many months will it be before you give it up? You are impractical on this subject. In India, they will persevere for ages and ages. You will be astonished to hear that they have no churches, no Common Prayers, or anything of the kind; but they, every day, still practise the breathings and try to concentrate the mind; and that is the chief part of their devotion. These are the main points. Every Hindu must do these. It is the religion of the country. Only, each one may have a special method—a special form of breathing, a special form of concentration, and what is one's special method, even one's wife need not know; the father need not know the son's. But they all have to do these. And there is nothing occult about these things. The word "occult" has no bearing on them. Near the Ganga thousands and thousands of people may be seen daily sitting on its banks breathing and concentrating with closed eyes. There may be two reasons that make certain practices impracticable for the generality of mankind. One is: the teachers hold that the ordinary people are not fit for them. There may be some truth in this, but it is due more to pride. The second is the fear of persecution. A man, for instance, would not like to practise breathing publicly in this country, because he would be thought so queer; it is not the fashion here. On the other hand, in India, if a man prayed, "Give us this day our daily bread," people would laugh at him. Nothing could be more foolish to the Hindu mind than to say, "Our Father which art in Heaven." The Hindu, when he worships, thinks that God is within himself.

According to the Yogis, there are three principal nerve currents: one they call the Idâ, the other the Pingalâ, and the middle one the Sushumnâ, and all these are inside the spinal column. The Ida and the Pingala, the left and the right, are clusters of nerves, while the middle one, the Sushumna, is hollow and is not a cluster of nerves. This Sushumna is closed, and for the ordinary man is of no use, for he works through the Ida and the Pingala only. Currents are continually going down and coming up through these nerves, carrying orders all over the body through other nerves running to the different organs of the body.

It is the regulation and the bringing into rhythm of the Ida and Pingala that is the great object of breathing. But that itself is nothing—it is only so much air taken into the lungs; except for purifying the blood, it is of no more use. There is nothing occult in the air that we take in with our breath and assimilate to purify the blood; the action is merely a motion. This motion can be reduced to the unit movement we call Prâna; and everywhere, all movements are the various manifestations of this Prana. This Prana is electricity, it is magnetism; it is thrown out by the brain as thought. Everything is Prana; it is moving the sun, the moon, and the stars.

We say, whatever is in this universe, has been projected by the vibration of the Prana. The highest result of vibration is thought. If there be any higher, we cannot conceive of it. The nerves, Ida and Pingala, work through the Prana. It is the Prana that is moving every part of the body, becoming the different forces. Give up that old idea that God is something that produces the effect and sits on a throne dispensing justice. In working we become exhausted because we use up so much Prana.

The breathing exercises, called Prânâyama, bring about regulation of the breathing, rhythmic action of the Prana. When the Prana is working rhythmically, everything works properly. When the Yogis get control over their own bodies, if there is any disease in any part, they know that the Prana is not rhythmic there and they direct the Prana to the affected part until the rhythm is re-established.

Just as you can control the Prana in your own body, so, if you are powerful enough, you can control, even from here, another man's Prana in India. It is all one. There is no break; unity is the law Physically, psychically, mentally, morally, metaphysically, it is all one. Life is only a vibration. That which vibrates this ocean of ether, vibrates you. Just as in a lake, various strata of ice of various degrees of solidity are formed, or as in an ocean of vapour there are various degrees of density, so is this universe an ocean of matter. This is an ocean of ether, in which we find the sun, moon, stars, and ourselves—in different states of solidity; but the continuity is not broken; it is the same throughout.

Now, when we study metaphysics, we come to know the world is one, not that the spiritual, the material, the mental, and the world of energies are separate. It is all one, but seen from different planes of vision. When you think of yourself as a body, you forget that you are a mind, and when you think of yourself as a mind, you will forget the body. There is only one thing, that you are; you can see it either as matter or body—or you can see it as mind or spirit. Birth, life, and death are but old superstitions. None was ever born, none will ever die; one changes one's position—that is all. I am sorry to see in the West how much they make of death; always trying to catch a little life. "Give us life after death! Give us life!" They are so happy if anybody tells them that they are going to live afterwards! How can I ever doubt such a thing! How can I imagine that I am dead! Try to think of yourself as dead, and you will see that you are present to see your own dead body. Life is such a wonderful reality that you cannot for a moment forget it. You may as well doubt that you exist. This is the first fact of consciousness—I am. Who can imagine a state of things which never existed? It is the most self-evident of all truths. So, the idea of immortality is inherent in man. How can one discuss a subject that is unimaginable? Why should we want to discuss the *pros* and *cons* of a subject that is self-evident?

The whole universe, therefore, is a unit, from whatever standpoint you view it. Just now, to us, this universe is a unit of Prana and Âkâsha, force and matter. And mind you, like all other basic principles, that is also self-contradictory. For what is force?—that which moves matter. And what is matter?—that which is moved by force. It is a seesaw! Some of the fundamentals of our reasoning are most curious, in spite of our boast of science and knowledge. "It is a headache without a head," as the Sanskrit proverb says. This state of things has been called Mâyâ. It has neither existence nor non-existence. You cannot call it existence, because that only exists which is beyond time and space, which is self-existent. Yet this world satisfies to a certain degree our idea of existence. Therefore it has an apparent existence.

But there is the real existence in and through everything; and that reality, as it were, is caught in the meshes of time, space, and causation. There is real man, the infinite, the beginningless, the endless, the ever-blessed, the ever-free. He has been caught in the meshes of time, space, and causation. So has everything in this world. The reality of everything is the same infinite. This is not idealism; it is not that the world does not exist. It has a relative existence, and fulfils all its requirements. But it has no independent existence. It exists because of the Absolute Reality, beyond time, space, and causation.

I have made long digressions. Now, let us return to our main subject.

All the automatic movements and all the conscious movements are the working of Prana, through the nerves. Now, you see, it will be a very good thing to have control over the unconscious actions.

On some other occasion, I told you the definition of God and man. Man is an infinite circle whose circumference is nowhere, but the centre is located in one spot; and God is an infinite circle whose circumference is nowhere, but whose centre is everywhere. He works through all hands; sees through all eyes; walks on all feet; breathes through all bodies; lives in all life; speaks through every mouth; and thinks through every brain. Man can become like God and acquire control over the whole universe, if he multiplies infinitely his centre of self-consciousness. Consciousness, therefore, is the chief thing to understand. Let us say that here is an infinite line amid darkness. We do not see the line, but on it there is one luminous point which moves on. As it moves along the line, it lights up its different parts in succession, and all that is left behind becomes dark again. Our consciousness may well be likened to this luminous point. Its past experiences have been replaced by the present, or have become subconscious. We are not aware of their presence in us, but there they are, unconsciously influencing our body and mind. Every movement that is now being made without the help of consciousness was previously conscious. Sufficient impetus has been given to it to work of itself.

The great error in all ethical systems, without exception, has been the failure of teaching the means by which man could refrain from doing evil. All the systems of ethics teach, "Do not steal". Very good; but why does a man steal? Because all stealing, robbing, and other evil actions, as a rule, have become automatic. The systematic robber, thief, liar, unjust man and woman, are all these in spite of themselves! It is really a tremendous psychological problem. We should look upon man in the most charitable light. It is not so easy to be good. What are you but mere machines until you are free? Should you be proud because you are good? Certainly not. You are good because you cannot help it. Another is bad because he cannot help it. If you were in his position, who knows what you would have been? The woman in the street, or the thief in the jail, is the Christ that is being sacrificed that you may be a good man. Such is the law of balance. All the thieves and the murderers, all the unjust, the weakest, the wickedest, the devils, they all are my Christ! I owe a worship to the God Christ and to the demon Christ! That is my doctrine. I cannot help it. My salutation goes to the feet of the good, the saintly, and to the feet of the wicked and the devilish! They are all my teachers, all are my spiritual fathers, all are my Saviours. I may curse one and yet benefit by his failings; I may bless another and benefit by his good deeds. This is as true as that I stand here. I have to sneer at the woman walking in the street, because society wants it! She, my Saviour, she, whose streetwalking is the cause of the chastity of other women! Think of that. Think, men and women, of this question in your mind. It is a truth—a bare, bold truth! As I see more of the world, see more of men and women, this conviction grows stronger. Whom shall I blame? Whom shall I praise? Both sides of the shield must be seen.

The task before us is vast; and first and foremost, we must seek to control the vast mass of sunken thoughts which have become automatic with us. The evil deed is, no doubt, on the conscious plane, but the cause which produced the evil deed was far beyond in the realms of the unconscious, unseen and therefore, more potent.

Practical psychology directs first of all its energies in controlling the unconscious, and we know that we can do it. Why? Because we know the cause of the unconscious; the unconscious thoughts are the submerged millions of our old conscious thoughts, old conscious actions become petrified—we do not look at them, do not know them, have forgotten them. But, mind you, if the power of evil is in the unconscious, so also is the power of good. We have many things stored in us as in a pocket. We have forgotten them, do not even think of them, and there are many of them, rotting, becoming positively dangerous; they come forth, the unconscious causes which kill humanity. True psychology would therefore try to bring them under the control of the conscious. The great task is to revive the whole man, as it were, in order to make him the complete master of himself. Even what we call the automatic action of the organs within our bodies, such as the liver etc., can be made to obey our commands.

This is the first part of the study, the control of the unconscious. The next is to go beyond the conscious. Just as unconscious work is beneath consciousness, so there is another work which is above consciousness. When this superconscious state is reached, man becomes free and divine; death becomes immortality, weakness becomes infinite power, and iron bondage becomes liberty. That is the goal, the infinite realm of the superconscious.

So, therefore, we see now that there must be a twofold work. First, by the proper working of the Ida and the Pingala, which are the two existing ordinary currents, to control the subconscious action; and secondly, to go beyond even consciousness.

The books say that he alone is the Yogi who, after long practice in self-concentration, has attained to this truth. The Sushumna now opens and a current which never before entered into this new passage will find its way into it, and gradually ascend to (what we call in figurative language) the different lotus centres, till at last it reaches the brain. Then the Yogi becomes conscious of what he really is, God Himself.

Every one without exception, every one of us, can attain to this culmination of Yoga. But it is a terrible task. If a person wants to attain to this truth, he will have to do something more than listen to lectures and take a few breathing exercises. Everything lies in the preparation. How long does it take to strike a light? Only a second; but how long it takes to make the candle! How long does it take to eat a dinner?

Perhaps half an hour. But hours to prepare the food! We want to strike the light in a second, but we forget that the making of the candle is the chief thing.

But though it is so hard to reach the goal, yet even our smallest attempts are not in vain. We know that nothing is lost. In Gita, Arjuna asks Krishna: Those who fail in attaining perfection in Yoga in this life, are they destroyed like the clouds of summer? Krishna replies: Nothing, my friend, is lost in this world. Whatever one does, that remains as one's own, and if the fruition of Yoga does not come in this life, one takes it up again in the next birth. Otherwise, how do you explain the marvellous childhood of Jesus, Buddha, Shankara?

Breathing, posturing, etc. are no doubt helps in Yoga, but they are merely physical. The great preparations are mental. The first thing necessary is a quiet and peaceable life.

If you want to be a Yogi, you must be free, and place yourself in circumstances where you are alone and free from all anxiety. He who desires a comfortable and nice life and at the same time wants to realise the Self is like the fool who, wanting to cross the river, caught hold of a crocodile, mistaking it for a log of wood. "Seek ye first the kingdom of God, and everything shall be added unto you." This is one great duty, this is renunciation. Live for an ideal, and leave no place in the mind for anything else. Let us put forth all our energies to acquire that which never fails—our spiritual perfection. If we have true yearning for realisation, we must struggle, and through struggle growth will come. We shall make mistakes, but they may be angels unawares.

The greatest help to spiritual life is meditation (Dhyâna). In meditation we divest ourselves of all material conditions and feel our divine nature. We do not depend upon any external help in meditation. The touch of the soul can paint the brightest colour even in the dingiest places; it can cast a fragrance over the vilest thing; it can make the wicked divine —and all enmity, all selfishness is effaced. The less the thought of the body, the better. For it is the body that drags us down. It is attachment, identification, which makes us miserable That is the secret: to think that I am the Spirit and not the body, and that whole of this universe with all its relations, with all its good and all its evil, is but as a series of paintings, scenes on a canvas, of which I am the witness.

THE VEDANTA PHILOSOPHY

The Vedanta philosophy, as it is generally called at the present day, really comprises all the various sects that now exist in India. Thus there have been various interpretations, and to my mind they have been progressive, beginning with the dualistic or Dvaita and ending with the non-dualistic or Advaita. The word Vedanta literally means the end of the Vedas—the Vedas being the scriptures of the Hindus.[1] Sometimes in West, by the Vedas are meant only hymns and rituals of the Vedas. But at the present time these parts have almost gone out of use, and usually by the word Vedas, in India, the Vedanta is meant. All our commentators, when they want to quote a passage from the scriptures, as a rule, quote from the Vedanta, which has another technical name with the commentators—the Shrutis.[2] Now, all the books known by the name of the Vedanta were not entirely written after the ritualistic portions of the Vedas. For instance, one of them—the Ishâ Upanishad—forms the fortieth chapter of the Yajur-Veda, that being one of the oldest parts of the Vedas. There are other Upanishads[3] which form portions of the Brâhmanas or ritualistic writings; and the rest of the Upanishads are independent, not comprised in any of the Brahmanas or other parts

[1] The Vedas are divided mainly into two portions: the **Karma-kânda** and the Jnâna-kânda—the work-portion and the knowledge-portion. To the Karma-kanda belong the famous hymns and the rituals or **Brâhmanas.** Those books which treat of spiritual matters apart from ceremonials, are called Upanishads. The Upanishads belong to the Jnana-kanda, or knowledge-portion. It is not that all the Upanishads were composed as a separate portion of the Vedas. Some are interspersed among the rituals and at least one is in the Samhita, or hymn-portion. Sometimes the term Upanishad is applied to books which are not included in the Vedas—e.g. the Gitâ; but as a rule it is applied to the philosophical treatises scattered through the Vedas. These treatises have been collected and are called Vedanta.

[2] The term Shruti—meaning "that which is heard"—though including the whole of the Vedic literature, is chiefly applied by the commentators to the Upanishads.

[3] The Upanishads are said to be one hundred and eight in number. Their dates cannot be fixed with certainty—only it is certain that they are older than the Buddhistic movement. Though some of the minor Upanishads contain allusions indicating a later date, yet that does not

of the Vedas; but there is no reason to suppose that they were entirely independent of other parts, for, as we well know, many of these have been lost entirely, and many of the Brahmanas have become extinct. So, it is quite possible that the independent Upanishads belonged to some Brahmanas, which in course of time fell into disuse, while the Upanishads remained. These Upanishads are also called Forest Books or Aranyakas.

The Vedanta, then, practically forms the scriptures of the Hindus, and all systems of philosophy that are orthodox have to take it as their foundation. Even the Buddhists and Jains, when it suits their purpose, will quote a passage from the Vedanta as authority. All schools of philosophy in India, although they claim to have been based upon the Vedas, took different names for their systems. The last one, the system of Vyâsa, took its stand upon the doctrines of the Vedas more than the previous systems did, and made an attempt to harmonise the preceding philosophies such as the Sânkhya and the Nyâya, with the doctrines of the Vedanta. So it is especially called the Vedanta philosophy; and the Sutras or aphorisms of Vyasa are, in modern India, the basis of the Vedanta philosophy. Again, these Sutras of Vyasa have been variously explained by different commentators. In general there are three sorts of commentators[1] in India now; from their interpretations have arisen three systems of philosophy and sects. One is the dualistic, or Dvaita; a second is the qualified non-dualistic, or

prove the later date of the treatise, as in very many cases in Sanskrit literature, the substance of a book, though of very ancient date, receives a coating, as it were, of later events in the hands of the sectarians, to exalt their particular sect.

[1] The commentaries are of various sorts—such as the Bhâshya, Tikâ, Tippani, Churni etc.—of which all except the Bhashya are explanations of the text or difficult words in the text. The Bhashya is not properly a commentary, but the elucidation of a system of philosophy out of texts the object being not to explain the words, but to bring out a philosophy. So the writer of a Bhashya expands his own system, taking texts as authorities for his system.

There have been various commentaries on the Vedanta. Its doctrines found their final expression in the philosophical aphorisms of Vyasa. This treatise, called the Uttara Mimâmsa, is the standard authority of Vedantism—nay, is the most authoritative exposition of the Hindu scriptures. The most antagonistic sects have been compelled, as it were, to take up the texts of Vyasa, and harmonise them with their own philosophy.

Vishishtâdvaita, and a third is the non-dualistic, or Advaita. Of these the dualistic and the qualified non-dualistic include the largest number of the Indian people. The non-dualists are comparatively few in number. Now I will try to lay before you the ideas that are contained in all these three sects; but before going on, I will make one remark—that these different Vedanta systems have one common psychology, and that is the psychology of the Sânkhya system. The Sankhya psychology is very much like the psychologies of the Nyaya and Vaisheshika systems, differing only in minor particulars.

All the Vedantists agree on three points. They believe in God, in the Vedas as revealed, and in cycles. We have already considered the Vedas. The belief about cycles is as follows: All matter throughout the universe is the outcome of one primal matter called Akâsha; and all force, whether gravitation, attraction or repulsion, or life, is the outcome of one primal force called Prâna. Prana acting on Akasha is creating or projecting[1] the universe. At the beginning of a cycle, Akasha is motionless, unmanifested. Then Prana begins to act, more and more, creating grosser and grosser forms out of Akasha—plants, animals, men, stars, and so on. After an incalculable time this evolution ceases and involution begins, everything being resolved back through finer and finer forms into the original Akasha and Prana, when a new cycle follows. Now there is something beyond Akasha and Prana. Both can be resolved into a third thing called Mahat—the Cosmic Mind. This Cosmic Mind does not create Akasha and Prana, but changes itself into them.

We will now take up the beliefs about mind, soul, and God. According to the universally accepted Sankhya psycho-

Even in very ancient times the commentators on the Vedanta philosophy formed themselves into the three celebrated Hindu sects of dualists, qualified non-dualists, and non-dualists. The ancient commentaries are perhaps lost; but they have been revived in modern times by the post-Buddhistic commentators, Shankara, Râmânuja, and Madhva. Shankara revived the non-dualistic form, Ramanuja, the qualified non-dualistic form of the ancient commentator Bodhâyana, and Madhva the dualistic form. In India the sects differ mainly in their philosophy; the difference in rituals is slight, the basis of their philosophy and religion being the same.

[1] The word which is "creation" in the English language is in Sanskrit exactly "projection", because there is no sect in India which believes in creation as it is regarded in the West—a something coming out of nothing. What we mean by creation is projection of that which already existed.

logy, in perception—in the case of vision, for instance—there are, first of all, the instruments of vision—the eyes. Behind the instruments—the eyes—is the organ of vision or Indriya—the optic nerve and its centres—which is not the external instrument, but without which the eyes will not see. More still is needed for perception. The mind or Manas must come and attach itself to the organ. And besides this, the sensation must be carried to the intellect or Buddhi—the determinative, reactive state of the mind. When the reaction comes from Buddhi, along with it flashes the external world and egoism. Here then is the will; but everything is not complete. Just as every picture, being composed of successive impulses of light, must be united on something stationary to form a whole, so all the ideas in the mind must be gathered and projected on something that is stationary—relatively to the body and mind—that is, on what is called the Soul or Purusha or Atman.

According to the Sankhya philosophy, the reactive state of the mind called Buddhi or intellect is the outcome, the change, or a certain manifestation of the Mahat or Cosmic Mind. The Mahat becomes changed into vibrating thought; and that becomes in one part changed into the organs, and in the other part into the fine particles of matter. Out of the combination of all these, the whole of this universe is produced. Behind even Mahat, the Sankhya conceives of a certain state which is called Avyakta or unmanifested, where even the manifestation of mind is not present, but only the causes exist. It is also called Prakriti. Beyond this Prakriti, and eternally separate from it, is the Purusha, the soul of the Sankhya which is without attributes and omnipresent. The Purusha is not the doer but the witness. The illustration of the crystal is used to explain the Purusha. The latter is said to be like a crystal without any colour, before which different colours are placed, and then it seems to be coloured by the colours before it, but in reality it is not. The Vedantists reject the Sankhya ideas of the soul and nature. They claim that between them there is a huge gulf to be bridged over. On the one hand the Sankhya system comes to nature, and then at once it has to jump over to the other side and come to the soul, which is entirely separate from nature. How can these different colours, as the Sankhya calls them, be able to act on that soul which by its nature is colourless? So the Vedantists, from the very first affirm that this soul and this nature are one.[1] Even the dualistic Vedantists admit that the Atman or God is not only the efficient cause of this universe, but also the material cause. But they only say so in so many words. They do not really mean it, for they try to escape from their conclusions, in this way: They say there are three existences in this universe—God, soul, and nature. Nature and soul are, as it were, the body of God, and in this sense it may be said that God and the whole universe are one. But this nature and all these various souls remain different from each other through all eternity. Only at the beginning of a cycle do they become manifest; and when the cycle ends, they become fine, and remain in a fine state. The Advaita Vedantists—the non-dualists—reject this theory of the soul, and, having nearly the whole range of the Upanishads in their favour, build their philosophy entirely upon them. All the books contained in the Upanishads have one subject, one task before them—to prove the following theme: "Just as by the knowledge of one lump of clay we have the knowledge of all the clay in the universe, so what is that, knowing which we know everything in the universe?" The idea of the Advaitists is to generalise the whole universe into one—that something which is really the whole of this universe. And they claim that this whole universe is one, that it is one Being manifesting itself in all these various forms. They admit that what the Sankhya calls nature, exists, but say that nature is God. It is this Being, the Sat, which has become converted into all this—the universe, man, soul, and everything that exists. Mind and Mahat are but the manifestations of that one Sat. But then the difficulty arises that this would be pantheism. How came that Sat which is unchangeable, as they admit (for that which is absolute is unchangeable), to be changed into that which is changeable, and perishable? The Advaitists here have a theory which they call Vivarta Vâda or apparent manifestation. Ac-

[1] The Vedanta and the Sankhya philosophy are very little opposed to each other. The Vedanta God developed out of the Sankhya's Purusha. All the systems take up the psychology of the Sankhya. Both the Vedanta and the Sankhya believe in the infinite soul; only the Sankhya believes there are many souls. According to the Sankhya, this universe does not require any explanation from outside. The Vedanta believes that there is the one Soul, which appears as many; and we build on the Sankhya's analysis.

cording to the dualists and the Sankhyas, the whole of this universe is the evolution of primal nature. According to some of the Advaitists and some of the dualists, the whole of this universe is evolved from God. And according to the Advaitists proper, the followers of Shankarâchârya, the whole universe is the *apparent* evolution of God. God is the material cause of this universe, but not really, only apparently. The celebrated illustration used is that of the rope and the snake, where the rope appeared to be the snake, but was not really so. The rope did not really change into the snake. Even so this whole universe as it exists, is that Being. It is unchanged, and all the changes we see in it are only apparent. These changes are caused by Desha, Kâla, and Nimitta (space, time, and causation), or, according to a higher psychological generalisation, by Nâma and Rupa (name and form). It is by name and form that one thing is differentiated from another. The name and form alone cause the difference. In reality they are one and the same. Again, it is not, the Vedantists say, that there is something as phenomenon and something as noumenon. The rope is changed into the snake apparently only; and when the delusion ceases, the snake vanishes. When one is in ignorance, he sees the phenomenon and does not see God. When he sees God, this universe vanishes entirely for him. Ignorance or Maya, as it is called, is the cause of all this phenomenon—the Absolute, the Unchangeable, being taken as this manifested universe. This Maya is not absolute zero, nor non-existence. It is defined as neither existence nor non-existence. It is not existence, because that can be said only of the Absolute, the Unchangeable, and in this sense Maya is non-existence. Again, it cannot be said it is non-existence, for if it were, it could never produce the phenomenon. So it is something which is neither; and in the Vedanta philosophy it is called Anirvachaniya or inexpressible. Maya, then, is the real cause of this universe. Maya gives the name and form to what Brahman or God gives the material; and the latter seems to have been transformed into all this. The Advaitists, then, have no place for the individual soul. They say individual souls are created by Maya. In reality they cannot exist. If there were only one existence throughout, how could it be that I am one, and you are one, and so forth? We are all one, and the cause of evil is the perception of duality. As soon as I begin to feel that I am separate from this universe, then first comes fear, and then comes misery. "Where one hears another, one sees another, that is small. Where one does not see another, where one does not hear another, that is the greatest, that is God. In that greatest is perfect happiness. In small things there is no happiness."

According to the Advaita philosophy, then, this differentiation of matter, these phenomena, are, as it were, for a time, hiding the real nature of man; but the latter really has not been changed at all. In the lowest worm, as well as in the highest human being, the same divine nature is present. The worm form is the lower form in which the divinity has been more overshadowed by Maya; that is the highest form in which it has been least overshadowed. Behind everything the same divinity is existing, and out of this comes the basis of morality. Do not injure another. Love every one as your own self, because the whole universe is one. In injuring another, I am injuring myself; in loving another, I am loving myself. From this also springs that principle of Advaita morality which has been summed up in one word—self-abnegation. The Advaitist says, this little personalised self is the cause of all my misery. This individualised self, which makes me different from all other beings, brings hatred and jealousy and misery, struggles and all other evils. And when this idea has been got rid of, all struggle will cease, all misery vanish. So this is to be given up. We must always hold ourselves ready, even to give up our lives for the lowest beings. When a man has become ready even to give up his life for a little insect, he has reached the perfection which the Advaitist wants to attain; and at that moment when he has become thus ready, the veil of ignorance falls away from him, and he will feel his own nature. Even in this life, he will feel that he is one with the universe. For a time, as it were, the whole of this phenomenal world will disappear for him, and he will realise what he is. But so long as the Karma of this body remains, he will have to live. This state, when the veil has vanished and yet the body remains for some time, is what the Vedantists call the Jivanmukti, the living freedom. If a man is deluded by a mirage for some time, and one day the mirage disappears—if it comes back again the next day at some future time, he will not be deluded. Before the mirage first broke, the man could not distinguish between the reality and the deception. But when it has once broken, as long as he has organs and eyes to work with, he will see the image, but will no more be deluded. That fine distinction between the actual world and the mirage he has caught and the latter cannot delude him any more. So when the Vedantist has realised his own nature, the whole world has vanished for him. It will come back again, but no more the same world of misery. The prison of misery has become changed into Sat, Chit, Ananda—Existence Absolute, Knowledge Absolute, Bliss Absolute—and the attainment of this is the goal of the Advaita Philosophy.[1]

[1] The above address was delivered before the Graduate Philosophical Society of Harvard University, on March 25, 1896.

QUESTIONS AND ANSWERS
AT THE HARVARD UNIVERSITY DISCUSSION[1]

Q.—I should like to know something about the present activity of philosophic thought in India. To what extent are these questions discussed?

A.—As I have said, the majority of the Indian people are practically dualists, and the minority are monists. The main subject of discussion is Mâyâ and Jiva. When I came to this country, I found that the labourers were informed of the present condition of politics; but when I asked them—what is religion, and what are the doctrines of this and that particular sect, they said, "We do not know; we go to church". In India if I go to a peasant and ask him, "Who governs you?" he says, "I do not know; I pay my taxes." But if I ask him what is his religion, he says, "I am a dualist," and is ready to give you the details about Maya and Jiva. He cannot read or write, but he has learnt all this from the monks and is very fond of discussing it. After the day's work, the peasants sit under a tree and discuss these questions.

Q.—What does orthodoxy mean with the Hindus?

A.—In modern times it simply means obeying certain caste laws as to eating, drinking, and marriage. After that the Hindu can believe in any system he likes. There was never an organised church in India; so there was never a body of men to formulate doctrines of orthodoxy. In a general way, we say that those who believe in the Vedas are orthodox; but in reality we find that many of the dualistic sects believe more in the Puranas than in the Vedas alone.

Q.—What influence had your Hindu philosophy on the Stoic philosophy of the Greeks?

A.—It is very probable that it had some influence on it through the Alexandrians. There is some suspicion of Pithagoras' being influenced by the Sânkhya thought. Anyway, we think the Sankhya philosophy is the first attempt to harmonise

[1] This discussion followed the lecture on the Vedanta Philosophy delivered by the Swami at the Graduate Philosophical Society of Harvard University, U.S.A., March 25, 1896. (See p. 82, *ante*.)

the philosophy of the Vedas through reason. We find Kapila mentioned even in the Vedas: ऋषिं प्रसूतं कपिलं यस्तमग्रे —"He who (supports through knowledge) the first-born sage Kapila."

Q.—What is the antagonism of this thought with Western science?

A.—No antagonism at all. We are in harmony with it. Our theory of evolution and of Ākâsha and Prâna is exactly what your modern philosophies have. Your belief in evolution is among our Yogis and in the Sankhya philosophy. For instance, Patanjali speaks of one species being changed into another by the infilling of nature— "जात्यन्तरपरिणामः प्रकृत्यापूरात्" ; only he differs from you in the explanation. His explanation of this evolution is spiritual. He says that just as when a farmer wants to water his field from the canals that pass near, he has only to lift up his gate—निमित्तमप्रयोजकं प्रकृतीनां वरणभेदस्तु ततः क्षेत्रिकवत् । So each man is the Infinite already, only these bars and bolts and different circumstances shut him in, but as soon as they are removed, he rushes out and expresses himself. In the animal, the man was held in abeyance; but as soon as good circumstances came, he was manifested as man. And again, as soon as fitting circumstances came, the God in man manifested itself. So we have very little to quarrel with in the new theories. For instance, the theory of the Sankhya as to perception is very little different from modern physiology.

Q.—But your method is different?

A.—Yes. We claim that concentrating the powers of the mind is the only way to knowledge. In external science, concentration of mind is—putting it on something external; and in internal science, it is—drawing towards one's Self. We call this concentration of mind, Yoga.

Q.—In the state of concentration does the truth of these principles become evident?

A.—The Yogis claim a good deal. They claim that by concentration of the mind every truth in the universe becomes evident to the mind, both external and internal truth.

Q.—What does the Advaitist think of cosmology?

A.—The Advaitist would say that all this cosmology and everything else are only in Maya, in the phenomenal world. In truth they do not exist. But as long as we are bound, we have to see these visions. Within these visions things come in a certain regular order. Beyond them there is no law and order, but freedom.

Q.—Is the Advaita antagonistic to dualism?

A.—The Upanishads not being in a systematised form, it was easy for philosophers to take up texts where they liked to form a system. The Upanishads had always to be taken, else there would be no basis. Yet we find all the different schools of thought in the Upanishads. Our solution is that the Advaita is not antagonistic to the Dvaita. We say the latter is only one of three steps. Religion always takes three steps. The first is dualism. Then man gets to a higher state, partial non-dualism. And at last he finds he is one with the universe. Therefore, the three do not contradict but fulfil.

Q.—Why does Maya or ignorance exist?

A.—Why cannot be asked beyond the limit of causation. It can only be asked within Maya. We say we will answer the question when it is logically formulated. Before that we have no right to answer.

Q.—Does the Personal God belong to Maya?

A.—Yes; but the Personal God is the same Absolute seen through Maya. That Absolute under the control of nature is what is called the human soul; and that which is controlling nature is Ishvara, or the Personal God. If a man starts from here to see the sun, he will see at first a little sun; but as he proceeds he will see it bigger and bigger, until he reaches the real one. At each stage of his progress he was seeing apparently a different sun; yet we are sure it was the same sun he was seeing. So all these things are but visions of the Absolute, and as such they are true. Not one is a false vision, but we can only say they were lower stages.

Q.—What is the special process by which one will come to know the Absolute?

A.—We say there are two processes. One is the positive, and the other, the negative. The positive is that through which the whole universe is going—that of love. If this circle of love is increased indefinitely, we reach the one universal love. The other is the "Neti," "Neti"—"not this," "not this"—stopping every wave in the mind which tries to draw it out; and at last the mind dies, as it were, and the Real discloses Itself. We call that Samâdhi, or superconsciousness.

Q.—That would be, then, merging the subject in the object!

A.—Merging the object in the subject, not merging the subject in the object. Really, this world dies, and I remain. I am the only one that remains.

Q.—Some of our philosophers in Germany have thought that the whole doctrine of Bhakti (love for the Divine) in India was very likely the result of Occidental influence.

A.—I do not take any stock in that—the assumption was ephemeral. The Bhakti of India is not like the Western Bhakti. The central idea of ours is that there is no thought of fear. It is always, love God. There is no worship through fear, but always through love, from beginning to end. In the second place, the assumption is quite unnecessary. Bhakti is spoken of in the oldest of the Upanishads, which is much older than the Christian Bible. The germs of Bhakti are even in the Samhitâ (the Vedic hymns). The word Bhakti is not a Western word. It was suggested by the word Shraddhâ.

Q.—What is the Indian idea of the Christian faith?

A.—That it is very good. The Vedanta will take in every one. We have a peculiar idea in India. Suppose I had a child. I should not teach him any religion; I should teach him breathings—the practice of concentrating the mind, and just one line of prayer—not prayer in your sense, but simply something like this, "I meditate on Him who is the Creator of this universe: may He enlighten my mind!" That way he would be educated, and then go about hearing different philosophers and teachers. He would select one who, he thought, would suit him best; and this man would become his Guru, or teacher, and he would become a Shishya, or disciple. He would say to that man, "This form of philosophy which you preach is the best; so teach me." Our fundamental idea is that your doctrine cannot be mine, or mine yours. Each one must have his own way. My daughter may have one method, and my son another, and I, again, another. So each one has an Ishta, or chosen way, and we keep it to ourselves. It is between me and my teacher, because we do not want to create a fight. It will not help any one to tell it to others, because each one will have to find his own way. So only general philosophy and general methods can be taught universally. For instance, giving a ludicrous example, it may help me to stand on one leg. It would be ludicrous to you if I said every one must do that, but it may suit me. It is quite possible for me to be a dualist and for my wife to be a monist, and so on. One of my sons may worship Christ or Buddha or Mohammed, so long as he obeys the caste laws. That is his own Ishta.

Q.—Do all Hindus believe in caste?

A.—They are forced to. They may not believe, but they have to obey.

Q.—Are these exercises in breathing and concentration universally practised?

A.—Yes; only some practise only a little, just to satisfy the requirements of their religion. The temples in India are not like the churches here. They may all vanish to-morrow, and will not be missed. A temple is built by a man who wants to go to heaven, or to get a son or something of that sort. So he builds a large temple and employs a few priests to hold services there. I need not go there at all, because all my worship is in the home. In every house is a special room set apart, which is called the chapel. The first duty of the child, after his initiation, is to take a bath, and then to worship; and his worship consists of this breathing and meditating and repeating of a certain name. And another thing is to hold the body straight. We believe that the mind has every power over the body to keep it healthy. After one has done this, then another comes and takes his seat, and each one does it in silence. Sometimes there are three or four in the same room, but each one may have a different method. This worship is repeated at least twice a day.

Q.—This state of oneness that you speak of, is it an ideal or something actually attained?

A.—We say it is within actuality; we say we realise that state. If it were only in talk, it would be nothing. The Vedas teach three things: this Self is first to be heard, then to be reasoned, and then to be meditated upon. When a man first hears it, he must reason on it, so that he does not believe it ignorantly, but knowingly; and after reasoning what it is, he must meditate upon it, and then realise it. And that is religion. Belief is no part of religion. We say religion is a superconscious state.

Q.—If you ever reach that state of superconsciousness, can you ever tell about it?

A.—No; but we know it by its fruits. An idiot, when he goes to sleep, comes out of sleep an idiot or even worse. But another man goes into the state of meditation, and when he comes out he is a philosopher, a sage, a great man. That shows the difference between these two states.

Q.—I should like to ask, in continuation of Professor ——'s question, whether you know of any people who have made any study of the principles of self-hypnotism, which they undoubtedly practised to a great extent in ancient India, and what has been recently stated and practised in that thing. Of course you do not have it so much in modern India.

A.—What you call hypnotism in the West is only a part of the real thing. The Hindus call it self-hypnotisation. They say you are hypnotised already, and that you should get out of it and dehypnotise yourself. "There the sun cannot illume, nor the moon, nor the stars; the flash of lightning cannot illume that; what to speak of this mortal fire! That shining, everything else shines." That is not hypnotisation, but dehypnotisation. We say that every other religion that preaches these things as real is practising a form of hypnotism. It is the Advaitist alone that does not care to be hypnotised. His is the only system that more or less understands that hypnotism comes with every form of dualism. But the Advaitist says, throw away even the Vedas, throw away even the Personal God, throw away even the universe, throw away even your own body and mind, and let nothing remain, in order to get rid of hypnotism perfectly. "From where the mind comes back with speech, being unable to reach, knowing the Bliss of Brahman, no more is fear." That is dehypnotisation. "I have neither vice nor virtue, nor misery nor happiness; I care neither for the Vedas nor sacrifices nor ceremonies; I am neither food nor eating nor eater, for I am Existence Absolute, Knowledge Absolute, Bliss Absolute; I am He, I am He." We know all about hypnotism. We have a psychology which the West is just beginning to know, but not yet adequately, I am sorry to say.

Q.—What do you call the astral body?

A.—The astral body is what we call the Linga Sharira. When this body dies, how can it come to take another body? Force cannot remain without matter. So a little part of the fine matter remains, through which the internal organs make another body—for each one is making his own body; it is the mind that makes the body. If I become a sage, my brain gets changed into a sage's brain; and the Yogis say that even in this life a Yogi can change his body into a god-body.

The Yogis show many wonderful things. One ounce of practice is worth a thousand pounds of theory. So I have no right to say that because I have not seen this or that thing done, it is false. Their books say that with practice you can get all sorts of results that are most wonderful. Small results can be obtained in a short time by regular practice; so that one may know that there is no humbug about it, no charlatanism. And these Yogis explain the very wonderful things mentioned in all scriptures in a scientific way. The question is, how these records of miracles entered into every nation. The man who says that they are all false, and need no explanation, is not rational. You have no right to deny them until you can prove them false. You must prove that they are without any foundation, and only then have you the right to stand up and deny them. But you have not done that. On the other hand, the Yogis say they are not miracles, and they claim that they can do them even today. Many wonderful things are done in India today. But none of them are done by miracles. There are many books on the subject. Again, if nothing else has been done in that line except a scientific approach towards psychology, that credit must be given to the Yogis.

Q.—Can you say in the concrete what the manifestations are, which the Yogi can show?

A.—The Yogi wants no faith or belief in his science but that which is given to any other science, just enough gentlemanly faith to come and make the experiment. The ideal of the Yogi is tremendous. I have seen the lower things that can be done by the power of the mind, and therefore I have no right to disbelieve that the highest things can be done. The ideal of the Yogi is eternal peace and love through omniscience and omnipotence. I know a Yogi who was bitten by a cobra, and who fell down on the ground. In the evening he revived again, and when asked what happened, he said, "A messenger came from my Beloved". All hatred and anger and jealousy have been burnt out of this man. Nothing can make him react; he is infinite love all the time, and he is omnipotent in his power of love. That is the real Yogi. And this manifesting different things is accidental, on the way. That is not what he wants to attain. The Yogi says, every man is a slave except the Yogi. He is a slave to food, to air, to his wife, to his children, to a dollar, slave to a nation, slave to name and fame, and to a thousand things in this world. The man who is not controlled by any one of these bondages is alone a real man, a real Yogi. "They have conquered relative existence in this life who are firm-fixed in sameness. God is pure and the same to all. Therefore such are said to be living in God."

Q.—Do the Yogis attach any importance to caste?

A.—No; caste is only the training school for undeveloped minds.

Q.—Is there no connection between this idea of superconsciousness and the heat of India?

A.—I do not think so; because all this philosophy was thought out fifteen thousand feet above the level of the sea, among the Himalayas, in an almost Arctic temperature.

Q.—Is it practicable to attain success in a cold climate?

A.—It is practicable, and the only thing that is practicable in this world. We say you are a born Vedantist, each one of you. You are declaring your oneness with everything each moment you live. Every time that your heart goes out towards the world, you are a true Vedantist, only you do not know it. You are moral without knowing why; and the Vedanta is the philosophy which analysed and taught man to be moral consciously. It is the essence of all religions.

Q.—Should you say that there is an unsocial principle in our Western people, which makes us so pluralistic, and that Eastern people are more sympathetic than we are?

A.—I think the Western people are more cruel, and the Eastern people have more mercy towards all beings. But that is simply because your civilisation is very much more recent. It takes time to make a thing come under the influence of mercy. You have a great deal of power, and the power of control of the mind has especially been very little practised. It will take time to make you gentle and good. This feeling tingles in every drop of blood in India. If I go to the villages to teach the people politics, they will not understand; but if I go to teach them Vedanta, they will say: "Now, Swami, you are all right." That Vairâgya, non-attachment, is everywhere in India, even today. We are very much degenerated now; but kings will give up their thrones and go about the country without anything.

In some places the common village-girl with her spinning-wheel says, "Do not talk to me of dualism; my spinning-wheel says 'Soham, Soham,'—'I am He, I am He.'" Go and talk to these people, and ask them why it is that they speak so and yet kneel before that stone. They will say that with you religion means dogma, but with them realisation. "I will be a Vedantist," one of them will say, "only when all this has vanished, and I have seen the Reality. Until then there is no difference between me and the ignorant. So I am using these stones and am going to temples, and so on, to come to realisation. I have heard, but I want to see and realise." "Different methods of speech, different manners of explaining the methods of the scriptures—these are only for the enjoyment of the learned, not for freedom" (Shankara). It is realisation which leads us to that freedom.

Q.—Is this spiritual freedom among the people consistent with attention to caste?

A.—Certainly not. They say there should be no caste. Even those who are in caste say it is not a very perfect institution. But they say, when you find us another and a better one, we will give it up. They say, what will you give us instead? Where is there no caste? In your nation you are struggling all the time to make a caste. As soon as a man gets a bag of dollars, he says, "I am one of the Four Hundred". We alone have succeeded in making a permanent caste. Other nations are struggling and do not succeed. We have superstitions and evils enough. Would taking the superstitions and evils from your country mend matters? It is owing to caste that three hundred millions of people can find a piece of bread to eat yet. It is an imperfect institution, no doubt. But if it had not been for caste, you would have had no Sanskrit books to study. This caste made walls, around which all sorts of invasions rolled and surged, but found it impossible to break through. That necessity has not gone yet; so caste remains. The caste we have now is not that of seven hundred years ago. Every blow has riveted it. Do you realise that India is the only country that never went outside of itself to conquer? The great emperor Asoka insisted that none of his descendants should go to conquer. If people want to send us teachers, let them help, but not injure. Why should all these people come to conquer the Hindus? Did they do any injury to any nation? What little good they could do, they did for the world. They taught it science, philosophy, religion, and civilised the savage hordes of the earth. And this is the return —only murder and tyranny, and calling them heathen rascals. Look at the books written on India by Western people and at the stories of many travellers who go there; in retaliation for what injuries are these hurled at them?

Q.—What is the Vedantic idea of civilisation?

A.—You are philosophers, and you do not think that a bag of gold makes the difference between man and man. What is the value of all these machines and sciences? They have only one result; they spread knowledge. You have not solved the problem of want, but only made it keener. Machines do not solve the poverty question; they simply make men struggle the more. Competition gets keener. What value has Nature in itself? Why do you go and build a monument to a man who sends electricity through a wire? Does not Nature do that millions of times over? Is not everything already existing in Nature? What is the value of your getting it? It is already there. The only value is that it makes this development. This universe is simply a gymnasium in which the soul is taking exercise; and after these exercises we become gods. So the value of everything is to be decided by how far it is a manifestation of God. Civilisation is the manifestation of that divinity in man.

Q.—Have the Buddhists any caste laws?

A.—The Buddhists never had much caste, and there are very few Buddhists in India. Buddha was a social reformer. Yet in Buddhistic countries I find that there have been strong attempts to manufacture caste, only they have failed. The Buddhists' caste is practically nothing, but they take pride in it in their own minds.

Buddha was one of the Sannyâsins of the Vedanta. He started a new sect, just as others are started even today. The ideas which now are called Buddhism were not his. They were much more ancient. He was a great man who gave the ideas power. The unique element in Buddhism was its social element. Brahmins and Kshatriyas have always been our teachers, and most of the Upanishads were written by Kshatriyas, while the ritualistic portions of the Vedas came from the Brahmins. Most of our great teachers throughout India have been Kshatriyas, and were always universal in their teachings; whilst the Brahmin prophets with two exceptions were very exclusive. Râma, Krishna, and Buddha—worshipped as Incarnations of God—were Kshatriyas.

Q.—Are sects, ceremonies, and scriptures helps to realisation?

A.—When a man realises, he gives up everything. The various sects and ceremonies and books, so far as they are the means of arriving at that point, are all right. But when they fail in that, we must change them. "The knowing one must not despise the condition of those who are ignorant, nor should the knowing one destroy the faith of the ignorant in their own particular method, but by proper action lead them, and show them the path to come to where he stands."

Q.—How does the Vedanta explain individuality and ethics?

A.—The real individual is the Absolute; this personalisation is through Maya. It is only apparent; in reality it is always the Absolute. In reality there is one, but in Maya it is appearing as many. In Maya there is this variation. Yet even in this Maya there is always the tendency to get back to the One, as expressed in all ethics and all morality of every nation, because it is the constitutional necessity of the soul. It is finding its oneness; and this struggle to find this oneness is what we call ethics and morality. Therefore we must always practise them.

Q.—Is not the greater part of ethics taken up with the relation between individuals?

A.—That is all it is. The Absolute does not come within Maya.

Q.—You say the individual is the Absolute, and I was going to ask you whether the individual has knowledge.

A.—The state of manifestation is individuality, and the light in that state is what we call knowledge. To use, therefore, this term *knowledge* for the light of the Absolute is not precise, as the Absolute state transcends relative knowledge.

Q.—Does it include it?

A.—Yes, in this sense. Just as a piece of gold can be changed into all sorts of coins, so with this. The state can be broken up into all sorts of knowledge. It is the state of superconsciousness, and includes both consciousness and unconsciousness. The man who attains that state has all that we call knowledge. When he wants to realise that consciousness of knowledge, he has to go a step lower. Knowledge is a lower state; it is only in Maya that we can have knowledge.

MAYA AND ILLUSION

(Delivered in London)

Almost all of you have heard of the word Mâyâ. Generally it is used, though incorrectly, to denote illusion, or delusion, or some such thing. But the theory of Maya forms one of the pillars upon which the Vedanta rests; it is therefore necessary that it should be properly understood. I ask a little patience of you, for there is a great danger of its being misunderstood.

The oldest idea of Maya that we find in Vedic literature is the sense of delusion; but then the real theory had not been reached. We find such passages as, "Indra through his Maya assumed various forms." Here it is true the word Maya means something like magic, and we find various other passages, always taking the same meaning. The word Maya then dropped out of sight altogether. But in the meantime the idea was developing. Later, the question was raised, "Why can't we know this secret of the universe?"—and the answer given was very significant. "Because we talk in vain, and because we are satisfied with the things of the senses, and because we are running after desires; therefore, we, as it were, cover the Reality with a mist." Here the word Maya is not used at all, but we get the idea, that the cause of our ignorance is a kind of mist that has come between us and the Truth. Much later on, in one of the latest Upanishads, we find the word Maya reappearing, but this time, a transformation has taken place in it, and a mass of new meaning has attached itself to the word. Theories had been propounded and repeated, others had been taken up, until at last the idea of Maya became fixed. We read in the Shvetâshvatara Upanishad, "Know Nature to be Maya and the Ruler of this Maya is the Lord himself." Coming to our philosophers, we find that this word Maya has been manipulated in various fashions, until we come to the great Shankarâchârya. The theory of Maya was manipulated a little by the Buddhists too, but in the hands of the Buddhists it became very much like what is called Idealism, and that is the meaning that is now generally given to the word Maya. When the Hindu says the world is Maya, at once people get the idea that the world is an illusion. This interpretation has some basis, as coming through the Buddhistic philosophers, because there was one section of philosophers who did not believe in the external world at all. But the Maya of the Vedanta, in its last developed form, is neither Idealism nor Realism, nor is it a theory. It is a simple statement of facts—what we are, and what we see around us.

As I have told you before, the minds of the people from whom the Vedas came were intent upon following principles, discovering principles. They had no time to work upon details, or to wait for them; they wanted to go deep into the heart of things. Something beyond was calling them, as it were, and they could not wait. Scattered through the Upanishads, we find that the details of subjects which we now call modern sciences are often very erroneous, but, at the same time, their principles are correct. For instance the idea of ether, which is one of the latest theories of modern science, is to be found in our ancient literature in forms much more developed than is the modern scientific theory of ether today, but it was in principle. When they tried to demonstrate the workings of that principle, they made many mistakes. The theory of the all-pervading life principle, of which all life in this universe is but a differing manifestation, was understood in Vedic times; it is found in the Brâhmanas. There is a long hymn in the Samhitâs in praise of Prâna, of which all life is but a manifestation. By the by, it may interest some of you to know that there are theories in the Vedic philosophy about the origin of life on this earth very similar to those which have been advanced by some modern European scientists. You, of course, all know that there is a theory that life came from other planets. It is a settled doctrine with some Vedic philosophers that life comes in this way from the moon.

Coming to the principles, we find these Vedic thinkers very courageous and wonderfully bold in propounding large and generalised theories. Their solution of the mystery of the universe, from the external world, was as satisfactory as it could be. The detailed workings of modern science do not bring the question one step nearer to solution, because the principles have failed. If the theory of ether failed in ancient times to give a solution of the mystery of the universe, working out the details of that ether theory would not bring us much nearer to the truth. If the theory of all-pervading life failed as a theory of this universe, it would not mean anything more if worked out in detail, for the details do not change the principle of the universe. What I mean is, that in their inquiry into the principle, the Hindu thinkers were as bold, and in some cases, much bolder than the moderns. They made some of the grandest generalisations that have yet been reached, and some still remain as theories, which modern science has yet to get, even as theories. For instance, they not only arrived at the ether theory, but went beyond and classified mind also, as a still more rarefied ether. Beyond that again, they found a still more rarefied ether. Yet that was no solution, it did not solve the problem. No amount of knowledge of the external world could solve the problem. "But," says the scientist, "we are just beginning to know a little; wait a few thousand years and we shall get the solution." "No," says the Vedantist, for he has proved beyond all doubt that the mind is limited, that it cannot go beyond certain limits—beyond time, space, and causation. As no man can jump out of his own self, so no man can go beyond the limits that have been put upon him by the laws of time and space. Every attempt to solve the laws of causation, time, and space, would be futile, because the very attempt would have to be made by taking for granted the existence of these three. What does the statement of the existence of the world mean, then? "This world has no existence." What is meant by that? It means that it has no absolute existence. It exists only in relation to my mind, to your mind, and to the mind of everyone else. We see this world with the five senses, but if we had another sense, we would see in it something more. If we had yet another sense, it would appear as something still different. It has, therefore, no real existence; it has no unchangeable, immovable, infinite existence. Nor can it be called non-existence, seeing that it exists, and we have to work in and through it. It is a mixture of existence and non-existence.

Coming from abstractions to the common, everyday details of our lives, we find that our whole life is a contradiction, a mixture of existence and non-existence. There is this contradiction in knowledge. It seems that man can know everything, if he only wants to know; but before he has gone a few steps, he finds an adamantine wall which he cannot pass. All his work is in a circle, and he cannot go beyond that circle. The problems which are nearest and dearest to him are impelling him on and calling, day and night, for a solution, but he cannot solve them, because he cannot go beyond his intellect. And yet that desire is implanted strongly in him. Still, we know that the only good is to be obtained by controlling and checking it. With every breath, every impulse of our heart asks us to be selfish. At the same time, there is some power beyond us which says that it is unselfishness alone which is good. Every child is a born optimist; he dreams golden dreams. In youth he becomes still more optimistic. It is hard for a young man to believe that there is such a thing as death, such a thing as defeat or degradation. Old age comes, and life is a mass of ruins. Dreams have vanished into the air, and the man becomes a pessimist. Thus we go from one extreme to another, buffeted by nature, without knowing where we are going. It reminds me of a celebrated song in the *Lalita Vistara,* the biography of Buddha. Buddha was born, says the book, as the saviour of mankind, but he forgot himself in the luxuries of his palace. Some angels came and sang a song to rouse him. And the burden of the whole song is that we are floating down the river of life, which is continually changing, with no stop and no rest. So are our lives, going on and on, without knowing any rest. What are we to do? The man who has enough to eat and drink is an optimist, and he avoids all mention of misery, for it frightens him. Tell not to him of the sorrows and the sufferings of the world; go to him and tell that it is all good. "Yes, I am safe," says he. "Look at me, I have a nice house to live in. I do not fear cold and hunger; therefore do not bring these horrible pictures before me." But, on the other hand, there are others dying of cold and hunger. If you go and teach *them* that it is all good, they will not hear you. How can they wish others to be happy when they are miserable? Thus we are oscillating between optimism and pessimism.

Then, there is the tremendous fact of death. The whole world is going towards death; everything dies. All our progress, our vanities, our reforms, our luxuries, our wealth, our knowledge, have that one end—death. That is all that is certain. Cities come and go, empires rise and fall, planets break into pieces and crumble into dust, to be blown about by the atmospheres of other planets. Thus it has been going on from time without beginning. Death is the end of everything. Death is the end of life, of beauty, of wealth, of power, of virtue too. Saints die and sinners die, kings die and beggars die. They are all going to death, and yet this tremendous clinging on to life exists. Somehow, we do not know why, we cling to life; we cannot give it up. And this is Maya.

The mother is nursing a child with great care; all her soul, her life, is in that child. The child grows, becomes a man, and perchance becomes a blackguard and a brute, kicks her and beats her every day; and yet the mother clings to the child; and when her reason awakes, she covers it up with the idea of love. She little thinks that it is not love, that it is something which has got hold of her nerves, which she cannot shake off; however she may try, she cannot shake off the bondage she is in. And this is Maya.

We are all after the Golden Fleece. Everyone of us thinks that this will be his. Every reasonable man sees that his chance is perhaps one in twenty millions, yet everyone struggles for it. And this is Maya.

Death is stalking day and night over this earth of ours, but at the same time we think we shall live eternally. A question was once asked of King Yudhishthira, "What is the most wonderful thing on this earth?" And the king replied, "Every day people are dying around us, and yet men think they will never die." And this is Maya.

These tremendous contradictions in our intellects, in our knowledge, yea, in all the facts of our life, face us on all sides. A reformer arises and wants to remedy the evils that are existing in a certain nation; and before they have been remedied, a thousand other evils arise in another place. It is like an old house that is falling; you patch it up in one place and the ruin extends to another. In India, our reformers cry and preach against the evils of enforced widowhood. In the West, non-marriage is the great evil. Help the unmarried on one side; they are suffering. Help the widows on the other; they are suffering. It is like chronic rheumatism; you drive it from the head and it goes to the body, you drive it from there and it goes to the feet. Reformers arise and preach that learning, wealth, and culture should not be in the hands of a select few; and they do their best to make them accessible to all. These may bring more happiness to some, but, perhaps, as culture comes, physical happiness lessens. The knowledge of happiness brings the knowledge of unhappiness. Which way then shall we go? The least amount of material prosperity that we enjoy is elsewhere causing the same amount of misery. This is the law. The young, perhaps, do not see it clearly, but those who have lived long enough and those who have struggled enough, will understand it. And this is Maya. These things are going on, day and night, and to find a solution of this problem is impossible. Why should it be so? It is impossible to answer this, because the question cannot be logically formulated. There is neither *how* nor *why* in fact; we only know that it *is* and that we cannot help it. Even to grasp it, to draw an exact image of it in our own mind, is beyond our power. How can we solve it then?

Maya is a statement of the fact of this universe, of how it is going on. People generally get frightened when these things are told to them. But bold we must be. Hiding facts is not the way to find a remedy. As you all know, a hare hunted by dogs puts its head down and thinks itself safe; so when we run into optimism, we do just like the hare, but that is no remedy. There are objections against this, but you may remark that they are generally from people who possess many of the good things of life. In this country (England) it is very difficult to become a pessimist. Everyone tells me how wonderfully the world is going on, how progressive; but what he himself is, is his own world. Old questions arise. Christianity must be the only true religion of the world, because Christian nations are prosperous! But that assertion contradicts itself, because the prosperity of the Christian nation depends on the misfortune of non-Christian nations. There must be some to prey on. Suppose the whole world were to become Christian, then the Christian nations would become poor, because there would be no non-Christian nations for them to prey upon. Thus the argument kills itself. Animals are living upon plants, men upon animals and, worst of all, upon one another, the strong upon the weak. This is going on everywhere, and this is Maya. What solution do you find for this? We hear every day many explanations, and are told that in the long run all will be good. Taking it for granted that this is possible, why should there be this diabolical way of doing good? Why cannot good be done through good, instead of through these diabolical methods? The descendants of the human beings of today will be happy; but why must there be all this suffering now? There is no solution. This is Maya.

Again, we often hear that it is one of the features of evolution that it eliminates evil, and this evil being continually eliminated from the world, at last only good will remain. That is very nice to hear, and it panders to the vanity of those who have enough of this world's goods, who have not a hard struggle to face every day, and are not being crushed under the wheel of this so-called evolution. It is very good and comforting indeed to such fortunate ones. The common herd may suffer, but they do not care; let them die, they are of no consequence. Very good, yet this argument is fallacious from beginning to end. It takes for granted, in the first place, that manifested good and evil in this world are two absolute realities. In the second place, it makes a still worse assumption, that the amount of good is an increasing quantity, and the amount of evil is a decreasing quantity. So, if evil is being eliminated in this way, by what they call evolution, there will come a time when all this evil will be eliminated and what remains will be all good.

Very easy to say, but can it be proved that evil is a lessening quantity? Take, for instance, the man who lives in a forest, who does not know how to cultivate the mind, cannot read a book, has not heard of such a thing as writing. If he is severely wounded, he is soon all right again; while we die if we get a scratch. Machines are making things cheap, making for progress and evolution, but millions are crushed that one may become rich; while one becomes rich, thousands at the same time become poorer and poorer, and whole masses of human beings are made slaves. That way it is going on. The animal man lives in the senses. If he does not get enough to eat, he is miserable; or if something happens to his body, he is miserable. In the senses, both his misery and his happiness begin and end. As soon as this man progresses, as soon as his horizon of happiness increases, his horizon of unhappiness increases proportionately. The man in the forest does not know what it is to be jealous, to be in the law courts, to pay taxes, to be blamed by society, to be ruled over day and night by the most tremendous tyranny that human diabolism ever invented, which pries into secrets of every human heart. He does not know how man becomes a thousand times more diabolical than any other animal, with all his vain knowledge, and with all his pride. Thus it is that, as we emerge out of the senses, we develop higher powers of enjoyment, and at the same time, we have to develop higher powers of suffering too. The nerves become finer, and capable of more suffering. In every society, we often find that the ignorant, common man, when abused, does not feel much, but he feels a good thrashing. But the gentleman cannot bear a single word of abuse; he has become so finely nerved. Misery has increased with his susceptibility to happiness. This does not go much to prove the evolutionist's case. As we increase our power to be happy, we also increase our power to suffer, and sometimes I am inclined to think that if we increase our power to become happy in arithmetical progression, we shall increase, on the other hand, our power to become miserable in geometrical progression. We who are progressing know that the more we progress, the more avenues are opened to pain as well as to pleasure. And this is Maya.

Thus we find that Maya is not a theory for the explanation of the world: it is simply a statement of facts as they exist, that the very basis of our being is contradiction, that everywhere we have to move through this tremendous contradiction, that wherever there is good, there must also be evil, and wherever there is evil, there must be some good, wherever there is life, death must follow as its shadow, and every one who smiles will have to weep, and vice versa. Nor can this state of things be remedied. We may verily imagine that there will be a place where there will be only good, and no evil, where we shall only smile and never weep. This is impossible in the very nature of things; for the conditions will remain the same. Wherever there is the power of producing a smile in us, there lurks the power of producing tears. Wherever there is the power of producing happiness, there lurks somewhere the power of making us miserable.

Thus the Vedanta philosophy is neither optimistic nor pessimistic. It voices both these views and takes things as they are. It admits that this world is a mixture of good and evil, happiness and misery, and that to increase the one must of necessity increase the other. There will never be a perfectly good or bad world, because the very idea is a contradiction in terms. The great secret revealed by this analysis is that good and bad are not two cut and dried, separate existences. There is not one thing in this world of ours which you can label as good, and good alone, and there is not one thing in the universe which you can label as bad, and bad alone. The very same phenomenon which is appearing to be good now, may appear to be bad tomorrow. The same thing which is producing misery in one, may produce happiness in another. The fire that burns the child, may cook a good meal for a starving man. The same nerves that carry the sensations of misery carry also the sensations of happiness. The only way to stop evil, therefore, is to stop good also; there is no other way. To stop death, we shall have to stop life also. Life without death and happiness without misery are contradictions, and neither can be found alone, because each of them is but a different manifestation of the same thing. What I thought to be good yesterday, I do not think to be good now. When I look back upon my life and see what were my ideals at different times, I find this to be so. At one time, my ideal was to drive a strong pair of horses; at another time, I thought, if I could make a certain kind of sweetmeat, I should be perfectly happy; later I imagined that I should be entirely satisfied if I had a wife and children and plenty of money. Today I laugh at all these ideals as mere childish nonsense.

The Vedanta says there must come a time when we shall look back and laugh at the ideals which make us afraid of giving up our individuality. Each one of us wants to keep this body for an indefinite time, thinking we shall be very happy, but there will come a time when we shall laugh at this idea. Now, if such be the truth, we are in a state of hopeless contradiction—neither existence nor non-existence, neither misery nor happiness, but a mixture of them. What, then, is the use of Vedanta, and all other philosophies and religions? And, above all what is the use of doing good work? This is a question that comes to the mind. If it is true that you cannot do good without doing evil, and whenever you try to create happiness there will always be misery, people will ask you, "What is the use of doing good?" The answer is, in the first place, that we must work for lessening misery, for that is the only way to make ourselves happy. Every one of us finds it out sooner or later in our lives. The bright ones find it out a little earlier, and the dull ones a little later. The dull ones pay very dearly for the discovery and the bright ones less dearly. In the second place, we must do our part, because that is the only way of getting out of this life of contradiction. Both the forces of good and evil will keep the universe alive for us, until we awake from our dreams and give up this building of mud pies. That lesson we shall have to learn, and it will take a long, long time to learn it. Attempts have been made in Germany to build a system of philosophy on the basis that the Infinite has become the finite. Such attempts are also made in England, and the analysis of the position of these philosophers is this, that the Infinite is trying to express itself in this universe, and that there will come a time when the Infinite will succeed in doing so. It is all very well and we have used the words *Infinite* and *manifestation* and *expression,* and so on, but philosophers naturally ask for a logical fundamental basis for the statement that the finite can fully express the Infinite. The Absolute and the Infinite can become this universe only by limitation. Everything must be limited that comes through the senses, or through the mind, or through the intellect; and for the limited to be the unlimited is simply absurd, and can never be.

The Vedanta, on the other hand, says that it is true that the Absolute or the Infinite is trying to express itself in the finite, but there will come a time when it will find that it is impossible, and it will then have to beat a retreat, and this beating a retreat means renunciation which is the real beginning of religion. Nowadays it is very hard even to talk of renunciation. It was said of me in America that I was a man who came out of a land that had been dead and buried for five thousand years, and talked of renunciation. So says perhaps the English philosopher. Yet it is true that is the only path to religion. Renounce and give up. What did Christ say? "He that loseth his life for my sake shall find it." Again and again did he preach renunciation as the only way to perfection. There comes a time when the mind awakes from this long and dreary dream—the child gives up its play and wants to go back to its mother. It finds the truth of the statement, "Desire is never satisfied by the enjoyment of desire, it only increases the more, as fire when butter is poured upon it."

This is true of all sense-enjoyments, of all intellectual enjoyments, and of all the enjoyments of which the human mind is capable. They are nothing, they are within Maya, within this network beyond which we cannot go. We may run therein through infinite time and find no end, and whenever we struggle to get a little enjoyment, a mass of misery falls upon us. How awful is this! And when I think of it, I cannot but consider that this theory of Maya, this statement that it is all Maya, is the best and only explanation. What an amount of misery there is in this world, and if you travel among various nations you will find that one nation attempts to cure its evils by one means, and another, by another. The very same evil has been taken up by various races, and attempts have been made in various ways to check it, yet no nation has succeeded. If it has been minimised at one point, a mass of evil has been crowded at another point. Thus it goes. The Hindus, to keep up a high standard of chastity in the race, have sanctioned child-marriage, which in the long run has degraded the race. At the same time, I cannot deny that this child-marriage makes the race more chaste. What would you have? If you want the nation to be more chaste, you weaken men and women physically by child-marriage. On the other hand, are you in England any better off? No, because chastity is the life of a nation. Do you not find in history that the first death-sign of a nation has been unchastity? When that has entered, the end of the race is in sight. Where shall we get a solution of these miseries then? If parents select husbands and wives for their children, then this evil is minimised. The daughters of India are more practical than sentimental. But very little of poetry remains in their lives. Again, if people select their own husbands and wives, that does not seem to bring much happiness. The Indian woman is generally very happy; there are not many cases of quarrelling between husband and wife. On the other hand, in the United States, where the greatest liberty obtains, the number of unhappy homes and marriages is large. Unhappiness is here, there, and everywhere. What does it show? That, after all, not much happiness has been gained by all these ideals. We all struggle for happiness, and as soon as we get a little happiness on one side, on the other side there comes unhappiness.

Shall we not work to do good then? Yes, with more zest than ever, but what this knowledge will do for us is to break down our fanaticism. The Englishman will no more be a fanatic and curse the Hindu. He will learn to respect the customs of different nations. There will be less of fanaticism and more of real work. Fanatics cannot work, they waste three-fourths of their energy. It is the level-headed, calm, practical man who works. So, the power to work will increase from this idea Knowing that this is the state of things, there will be more patience. The sight of misery or of evil will not be able to throw us off our balance and make us run after shadows. Therefore, patience will come to us, knowing that the world will have to go on in its own way. If, for instance, all men have become good, the animals will have in the meantime evolved into men, and will have to pass through the same state, and so with the plants. But only one thing is certain; the mighty river is rushing towards the ocean, and all the drops that constitute the stream will in time be drawn into that boundless ocean. So, in this life, with all its miseries and sorrows, its joys and smiles and tears, one thing is certain, that all things are rushing towards their goal and it is only a question of time when you and I, and plants, and animals, and every particle of life that exists must reach the Infinite Ocean of Perfection, must attain to Freedom, to God.

Let me repeat, once more, that the Vedantic position is neither pessimism nor optimism. It does not say that this world is all evil or all good. It says that our evil is of no less value than our good, and our good of no more value than our evil. They are bound together. This is the world, and knowing this, you work with patience. What for? Why should we work? If this is the state of things, what shall we do? Why not become agnostics? The modern agnostics also know there is no solution of this problem, no getting out of this evil of Maya, as we say in our language; therefore they tell us to be satisfied and enjoy life. Here, again, is a mistake, a tremendous mistake, a most illogical mistake. And it is this. What do you mean by life? Do you mean only the life of the senses? In this, every one of us differs only slightly from the brutes. I am sure that no one is present here whose life is only in the senses. Then, this present life means something more than that. Our feelings, thoughts and aspirations are all part and parcel of our life; and is not the struggle towards the great ideal, towards perfection, one of the most important components of what we call life? According to the agnostics, we must enjoy life as it is. But this life means, above all, this search after the ideal; the essence of life is going towards perfection. We must have that, and, therefore, we cannot be agnostics, or take the world as it appears. The agnostic position takes this life, *minus* the ideal component, to be all that exists, and this, the agnostic claims, cannot be reached, therefore he must give up the search. This is what is called Maya, this nature, this universe.

All religions are more or less attempts to get beyond nature —the crudest or the most developed, expressed through mythology or symbology, stories of gods, angels or demons, or through stories of saints or seers, great men or prophets, or through the abstractions of philosophy—all have that one object, all are trying to get beyond these limitations. In one word, they are all struggling towards freedom. Man feels, consciously or unconsciously, that he is bound; he is not what he wants to be. It was taught to him at the very moment he began to look around. That very instant he learnt that he was bound, and he also found that there was something in him which wanted to fly beyond, where the body could not know, but which was as yet chained down by this limitation. Even in the lowest of religious ideas, where departed ancestors and other spirits, mostly violent and cruel, lurking about the houses of their friends, fond of bloodshed and strong drink, are worshipped, even there we find that one common factor, that of freedom. The man who wants to worship the gods sees in them, above all things, greater freedom than in himself. If a door is closed, he thinks the gods can get through it, and that walls have no limitations for them. This idea of freedom increases until it comes to the ideal of a Personal God, of which the central concept is that He is a Being beyond the limitation of nature, of Maya. I see before me, as it were, that in some of those forest retreats this question is being discussed by those ancient sages of India, and in one of them, where even the oldest and the holiest fail to reach the solution, a young man stands up in the midst of them, and declares: "Hear, ye children of immortality, hear, ye who live in the highest places. I have found the way. By knowing Him who is beyond darkness we can go beyond death."

This Maya is everywhere. It is terrible. Yet we have to work through it. The man who says that he will work when the world has become all good and then he will enjoy bliss, is as likely to succeed as the man who sits beside the Ganga and says, "I will ford the river when all the water has run into the ocean." The way is not with Maya, but against it. This is another fact to learn. We are not born as helpers of nature, but competitors with nature. We are its bond-masters, but we bind ourselves down. Why is this house here? Nature did not build it. Nature says, go and live in the forest. Man says, I will build a house and fight with nature, and he does so. The whole history of humanity is a continuous fight against the so-called laws of nature, and man gains in the end. Coming to the internal world, there too the same fight is going on, this fight between the animal man and the spiritual man, between light and darkness; and here too man becomes victorious. He, as it were, cuts his way out of nature to freedom. We see, then, that beyond this Maya the Vedantic philosophers find something which is not bound by Maya, and if we can get there, we shall not be bound by Maya. This idea is in some form or other the common property of all religions. But, with the Vedanta, it is only the beginning of religion and not the end. The idea of a Personal God, the Ruler and Creator of this universe, as He has been styled, the Ruler of Maya, or nature, is not the end of these Vedantic ideas; it is only the beginning. The idea grows and grows until the Vedantist finds that He who, he thought, was standing outside, is he himself and is in reality within. He is the one who is free, but who through limitation thought he was bound.

THE REAL AND THE APPARENT MAN

(Delivered in New York)

Here we stand, and our eyes look forward sometimes miles ahead. Man has been doing that since he began to think. He is always looking forward, looking ahead. He wants to know where he goes, even after the dissolution of his body. Various theories have been propounded, system after system has been brought forward, to suggest explanations. Some have been rejected, while others have been accepted, and thus it will go on, so long as man is here, so long as man thinks. There is some truth in each of these systems. There is a good deal of what is not truth in all of them. I shall try to place before you the sum and substance, the result, of the inquiries in this line that have been made in India. I shall try to harmonise the various thoughts on the subject, as they have come up from time to time among Indian philosophers. I shall try to harmonise the psychologists and the metaphysicians, and, if possible, I shall harmonise them with modern scientific thinkers also.

The one theme of the Vedanta philosophy is the search after unity. The Hindu mind does not care for the particular; it is always after the general, nay, the universal. "What is that, by knowing which everything else is to be known?" That is the one theme. "As through the knowledge of one lump of clay all that is of clay is known, so, what is that by knowing which this whole universe itself will be known?" That is the one search. The whole of this universe, according to the Hindu philosophers, can be resolved into one material, which they call Akâsha. Everything that we see around us, feel, touch, taste, is simply a differentiated manifestation of this Akasha. It is all-pervading, fine. All that we call solids, liquids, or gases, figures, forms, or bodies, the earth, sun, moon, and stars—everything is composed of this Akasha.

What force is it which acts upon this Akasha and manufactures this universe out of it? Along with Akasha exists universal power. All that is power in the universe, manifesting as force, or attraction—nay, even as thought—is but a different manifestation of that one power which the Hindus call Prâna. This Prana, acting on Akasha, is creating the whole of this universe. In the beginning of a cycle, this Prana, as it were, sleeps in the infinite ocean of Akasha. It existed motionless in the beginning. Then arises motion in this ocean of Akasha, by the action of this Prana and as this Prana begins to move, to vibrate, out of this ocean come the various celestial systems, suns, moons, stars, earth, human beings, animals, plants, and the manifestations of all the various forces and phenomena. Every manifestation of power, therefore, according to them, is this Prana. Every material manifestation is Akasha. When this cycle will end, all that we call solid will melt away into the next form, the next finer or the liquid form; that will melt into the gaseous, and that into finer and more uniform heat vibrations, and all will melt back into the original Akasha, and what we now call attraction, repulsion, and motion, will slowly resolve into the original Prana. Then this Prana is said to sleep for a period, again to emerge and to throw out all these forms; and when this period will end, the whole thing will subside again. Thus this process of creation is going down, and coming up, oscillating backwards and forwards. In the language of modern science, it is becoming static during one period, and during another period it is becoming dynamic. At one time it becomes potential, and at the next period it becomes active. This alteration has gone on through eternity.

Yet, this analysis is only partial. This much has been known even to modern physical science. Beyond that, the research of physical science cannot reach. But the inquiry does not stop in consequence. We have not yet found that one, by knowing which everything else will be known. We have resolved the whole universe into two components, into what are called matter and energy, or what the ancient philosophers of India called Akasha and Prana. The next step is to resolve this Akasha and the Prana into their origin. Both can be resolved into the still higher entity which is called mind. It is out of mind, the Mahat, the universally existing thought-power, that these two have been produced. Thought is a still finer manifestation of being than either Akasha or Prana. It is thought that splits itself into these two. The universal thought existed in the beginning, and that manifested, changed, evolved itself into these two Akasha and Prana; and by the combination of these two the whole universe has been produced.

We next come to psychology. I am looking at you. The

external sensations are brought to me by the eyes; they are carried by the sensory nerves to the brain. The eyes are not the organs of vision. They are but the external instruments, because if the real organ behind that which carries the sensation to the brain, is destroyed, I may have twenty eyes, yet I cannot see you. The picture on the retina may be as complete as possible, yet I shall not see you. Therefore, the organ is different from its instruments. Behind the instruments, the eyes, there must be the organ. So it is with all the sensations. The nose is not the sense of smell, it is but the instrument and behind it is the organ. With every sense we have, there is first the external instrument in the physical body, behind that, in the same physical body, there is the organ; yet, these are not sufficient. Suppose I am talking to you, and you are listening to me with close attention. Something happens, say, a bell rings; you will not, perhaps, hear the bell ring. The pulsations of that sound came to your ear, struck the tympanum, the impression was carried by the nerve into the brain; if the whole process was complete up to carrying the impulse to the brain, why did you not hear? Something else was wanting—the mind was not attached to the organ. When the mind detaches itself from the organ, the organ may bring any news to it, but the mind will not receive it. When it attaches itself to the organ, then alone is it possible for mind to receive the news. Yet, even that does not complete the whole. The instruments may bring the sensation from outside, the organs may carry it inside, the mind may attach itself to the organ, and yet the perception may not be complete. One more factor is necessary; there must be a reaction within. With this reaction comes knowledge. That which is outside sends, as it were, the current of news into my brain. My mind takes it up, and presents it to the intellect, which groups in relation to pre-received impressions, and sends a current of reaction, and with that reaction comes perception. Here, then, is the will. The state of mind which reacts is called Buddhi, the intellect.

Yet, even this does not complete the whole. One step more is required. Suppose here is a camera and there is a sheet of cloth, and I try to throw a picture on that sheet. What am I to do? I am to guide various rays of light through the camera to fall upon the sheet and become grouped there. Something is necessary to have the picture thrown upon, which does not move. I cannot form a picture upon something which is moving; that something must be stationary, because the rays of light which I throw on it are moving, and these moving rays of light must be gathered, unified, co-ordinated, and completed upon something which is stationary. Similar is the case with the sensations which these organs of ours are carrying inside and presenting to the mind, and which the mind in its turn is presenting to the intellect. This process will not be complete unless there is something permanent in the background upon which the picture, as it were, may be formed, upon which we may unify all the different impressions. What is it that gives unity to the changing whole of our being? What is it that keeps up the identity of the moving thing moment after moment? What is it upon which all our different impressions are pieced together, upon which the perceptions, as it were, come together, reside, and form a united whole? We have found that to serve this end there must be something, and we also see that that something must be, relatively to the body and mind, motionless. The sheet of cloth upon which the camera throws the picture is, relatively to the rays of light, motionless; else there will be no picture. That is to say, the perceiver must be an individual. This something upon which the mind is painting all these pictures, this something upon which our sensations, carried by the mind and intellect, are placed and grouped and formed into a unity, is what is called the soul of man.

We have seen that it is the universal cosmic mind that splits itself into the Akasha and Prana, and beyond mind we have found the soul in us. In the universe, behind the universal mind, there is a Soul that exists, and it is called God. In the individual it is the soul of man. In this universe, in the cosmos, just as the universal mind becomes evolved into Akasha and Prana, even so, we may find that the Universal Soul Itself becomes evolved as mind. Is it really so with the individual man? Is this mind the creator of his body, and his soul the creator of his mind? That is to say, are his body, his mind, and his soul three different existences, or are they three in one, or again, are they differrent states of existence of the same unit being? We shall gradually try to find an answer to this question. The first step that we have now gained is this: here is this external body, behind this external body are the organs, the mind, the intellect, and behind this is the soul. At the first step, we have found, as it were, that the soul is separate from the body, separate from the mind itself. Opinions in the religious world become divided at this point, and the departure is this. All those religious views which generally pass under the name of dualism hold that this soul is qualified, that it is of various qualities, that all feelings of enjoyment, pleasure, and pain really belong to the soul. The nondualists deny that the soul has any such qualities; they say it is unqualified.

Let me first take up the dualists, and try to present to you their position with regard to the soul and its destiny; next, the system that contradicts them; and lastly, let us try to find the harmony which non-dualism will bring to us. This soul of man, because it is separate from the mind and body, because it is not composed of Akasha and Prana, must be immortal. Why? What do we mean by mortality? Decomposition. And that is only possible for things that are the result of composition; anything that is made of two or three ingredients must become decomposed. That alone which is not the result of composition can never become decomposed, and therefore can never die. It is immortal. It has been existing throughout eternity; it is uncreate. Every item of creation is simply a composition; no one ever saw creation come out of nothing. All that we know of creation is the combination of already existing things into newer forms. That being so, this soul of man, being simple, must have been existing for ever, and it will exist for ever. When this body falls off, the soul lives on. According to the Vedantists, when this body dissolves, the vital forces of the man go back to his mind and the mind becomes dissolved, as it were, into the Prana, and that Prana enters into the soul of man, and the soul of man comes out, clothed, as it were, with what they call the fine body, the mental body, or spiritual body, as you may like to call it. In this body are the Samskâras of the man. What are the Samskaras? This mind is like a lake, and every thought is like a wave upon that lake. Just as in the lake waves rise, and then fall down and disappear, so these thought-waves are continually rising in the mind-stuff, and then disappearing, but they do not disappear for ever. They become finer and finer, but they are all there, ready to start up at another time, when called upon to do so. Memory is simply calling back into wave-form some of those thoughts which have gone into that finer state of existence. Thus, everything that we have thought, every action that we have done, is lodged in the mind; it is all there in fine form, and when a man dies, the sum total of the impressions is in the mind, which again works upon a little fine material as a medium. The soul, clothed, as it were, with these impressions and the fine body, passes out, and the destiny of the soul is guided by the resultant of all different forces represented by the different impressions. According to us there are three different goals for the soul.

Those that are very spiritual, when they die, follow the solar rays, and reach what is called the solar sphere, through which they reach what is called the lunar sphere, and through that they reach what is called the sphere of lightning, and there they meet with another soul who is already blessed, and he guides the new-comer forward to the highest of all spheres which is called the Brahmaloka, the sphere of Brahma. There these souls attain to omniscience and omnipotence, become almost as powerful and all-knowing as God Himself; and they reside there for ever, according to the dualists, or, according to the non-dualists, they become one with the Universal at the end of the cycle The next class of persons, who have been doing good works with selfish motives, are carried by the result of their good works, when they die, to what is called the lunar sphere, where there are various heavens, and there they acquire fine bodies, the bodies of gods. They become gods and live there, and enjoy the blessing of heaven for a long period and after that period is finished, the old Karma is again upon them and so they fall back again to the earth; they come down through the spheres of air and clouds, and all these various regions, and, at last, reach the earth through raindrops. There on the earth they attach themselves to some cereal which is eventually eaten by some man who is fit to supply them with material to make a new body. The last class, namely, the wicked, when they die, become ghosts or demons, and live somewhere midway between the lunar sphere and this earth. Some try to disturb mankind, some are friendly; and after living there for some time they also fall back to the earth and become animals. After living for some time in an animal body they get released, and come back, and become men again, and thus get another chance to work out their salvation. We see, then, that those who have nearly attained to perfection, in whom only very little impurity remains, go to the Brahmaloka through the rays of the sun; those who were a middling sort of people, who did some good work here with the idea of going to heaven, go to the heavens in the lunar sphere and there obtain god-bodies; but they have again to become men, and so have another chance to become perfect. Those that are very wicked become ghosts and demons, and then they may have to become animals; after that they become men again and get another chance to perfect themselves.

This earth is called the Karma-Bhumi, the sphere of Karma. Here alone man makes his good or bad Karma. When a man wants to go to heaven, and does good works for that purpose, he becomes a god, and does not as such store up any bad Karma. He just enjoys the effects of the good work he did on earth and when this good Karma is exhausted, there comes upon him the resultant force of all the evil Karma he had previously stored up in life, and that brings him down again to this earth. In the same way, those that become ghosts remain in that state, not giving rise to fresh Karma, but suffer the evil results of their past misdeeds, and later on remain for a time in an animal body without causing any fresh Karma. When that period is finished, they too become men again. The states of reward and punishment due to good and bad Karmas are devoid of the force of generating fresh Karma; they have only to be enjoyed or suffered. If there is an extraordinarily good or an extraordinarily evil Karma, it bears fruit very quickly. For instance, if a man has been doing many evil things all his life, but does one good act, the result of that good act will immediately appear, but when that result has been gone through, all the evil acts must produce their results also. All men who do certain good and great acts, but the general tenor of whose lives has not been correct, will become gods, and after living for some time in god-bodies, enjoying the powers of gods, they will have again to become men; when the power of the good acts is thus finished, the old evil comes up to be worked out. Those who do extraordinarily evil acts have to put on ghost and devil bodies, and when the effect of those evil actions is exhausted, the little good action which remains associated with them, makes them again become men. The way to Brahmaloka, from which there is no more fall or return, is called the Devayâna, i.e. the way to God: the way to heaven is known as Pitriyâna, i.e. the way to the fathers.

Man, therefore, according to the Vedanta Philosophy, is the greatest being that is in the universe, and this world of work the best place in it, because only herein is the greatest and the best chance for him to become perfect. Angels or gods, whatever you may call them, have all to become men, if they want to become perfect. This is the great centre, the wonderful poise, and the wonderful opportunity—this human life.

We come next to the other aspect of philosophy . There are Buddhists who deny the whole theory of the soul that I have just now been propounding. "What use is there," says the Buddhist, "to assume something as the substratum, as background of this body and mind? Why may we not allow thoughts to run on? Why admit a third substance beyond this organism, composed of mind and body, a third substance called the soul? What is its use? Is not this organism sufficient to explain itself? Why take anew a third something?" These arguments are very powerful. This reasoning is very strong. So far as outside research goes, we see that the organism is a sufficient explanation of itself—at least, many of us see it in that light. Why, then, need there be a soul as substratum, as a something which is neither mind nor body but stands as a background for both mind and body? Let there be only mind and body. Body is the name of a stream of matter continuously changing. Mind is the name of a stream of consciousness or thought continuously changing. What produces the apparent unity between these two? This unity does not really exist, let us say. Take, for instance, a lighted torch, and whirl it rapidly before you. You see a circle of fire. The circle does not really exist, but because the torch is continually moving, it leaves the appearance of a circle. So there is no unity in this life; it is a mass of matter continually rushing down, and the whole of this matter you may call one unity, but no more. So is mind; each thought is separate from every other thought. It is only the rushing current that leaves behind the illusion of unity, there is no need of a third substance. This universal phenomenon of body and mind is all that really is, do not posit something behind it.

You will find that this Buddhist thought has been taken

up by certain sects and schools in modern times, and all of them claim that it is new—their own invention. This has been the central idea of most of the Buddhistic philosophies, that this world is itself all-sufficient; that you need not ask for any background at all; all that is is this sense-universe; what is the use of thinking of something as a support to this universe? Everything is the aggregate of qualities; why should there be a hypothetical substance in which they should inhere? The idea of substance comes from the rapid interchanging of qualities, not from something unchangeable which exists behind them. We see how wonderful some of these arguments are, and they appeal easily to the ordinary experience of humanity—in fact, not one in a million can think of anything other than phenomena. To the vast majority of men nature appears to be only a changing, whirling, combining, mingling, mass of change. Few of us ever have a glimpse of the calm sea behind. For us it is always lashed into waves; this universe appears to us only as a tossing mass of waves. Thus we find these two opinions. One is, that there is something behind both body and mind, which is an unchangeable and immovable substance; and the other is, that there is no such thing as immovability or unchangeability in the universe, it is all change and nothing but change. The solution of this difference comes in the next step of thought, namely, the non-dualistic.

It says that the dualists are right in finding something behind all, as a background, which does not change; we cannot conceive change without there being something unchangeable. We can only conceive anything that is changeable, by knowing something which is less changeable, and this also must appear more changeable in comparison with something else which is less changeable, and so on and on, until we are bound to admit that there must be something which never changes at all. The whole of this manifestation must have been in a state of non-manifestation, calm and silent, being the balance of opposing forces, so to say, when no force operated, because force acts when a disturbance of the equilibrium comes in. This universe is ever hurrying on to return to that state of equilibrium again. If we are certain of any fact whatsoever, we are certain of this. When the dualists claim that there is a something which does not change, they are perfectly right, but their analysis that it is an underlying something which is neither the body nor the mind, a something separate from both, is wrong. So far as the Buddhists say that the whole universe is a mass of change, they are perfectly right; for, so long as I am separate from the universe, so long as I stand back and look at something before me, so long as there are two things—the looker-on and the thing looked upon—it will appear always that the universe is one of change, continuously changing all the time. But the reality is that there is both change and changelessness in this universe. It is not that the soul and the mind and the body are three separate existences, for this organism made of these three is really one. It is the same thing which appears as this body, as the mind, and as the thing beyond mind and body, but it is not at the same time all these. He who sees the body does not see the mind even, he who sees the mind does not see that which he calls the soul, and he who sees the soul—for him the body and mind have vanished. He who sees only motion never sees absolute calm, and he who sees absolute calm—for him motion has vanished. A rope is taken for a snake. He who sees the rope as the snake, for him the rope has vanished, and when the delusion ceases and he looks at the rope, the snake has vanished.

There is then but one all-comprehending existence, and that one appears as manifold. This Self, or Soul, or Substance, is all that exists in the universe. That Self, or Substance, or Soul, is, in the language of non-dualism, the Brahman, appearing to be manifold by the interposition of name and form. Look at the waves in the sea. Not one wave is really different from the sea, but what makes the wave apparently different? Name and form; the form of the wave, and the name which we give to it, "wave". That is what makes it different from the sea. When name and form go, it is the same sea. Who can make any real difference between the wave and the sea? So this whole universe is that One Unit Existence; name and form have created all these various differences. As when the sun shines upon millions of globules of water, upon each particle is seen a most perfect representation of the sun, so the one Soul, the one Self, the One Existence of the universe, being reflected on all these numerous globules of varying names and forms, appears to be various. But it is in reality only one. There is no "I" nor "you"; it is all One. It is either all "I" or all "you". This idea of duality, of two, is entirely false, and the whole universe, as we ordinarily know it, is the result of this false knowledge. When discrimination comes, and man finds there are not two but One, he finds that he is himself this universe. "It is I who am this universe as it now exists, a continuous mass of change. It is I who am beyond all changes, beyond all qualities, the eternally perfect, the eternally blessed."

There is, therefore, but one Atman, one Self, eternally pure, eternally perfect, unchangeable, unchanged. It has never changed, and all these various changes in the universe are but appearances in that one Self.

Upon it name and form have painted all these dreams; it is form that makes the wave different from the sea. Suppose the wave subsides; will the form remain? No, it will vanish. The existence of the wave was entirely dependent upon the existence of the sea, but the existence of the sea was not at all dependent upon the existence of the wave. The form remains so long as the wave remains, but as soon as the wave leaves, it vanishes, it cannot remain. This name and form is the outcome of what is called Mâyâ. It is this Maya that is making individuals, making one appear different from another. Yet it has no existence. Maya cannot be said to exist. Form cannot be said to exist, because it depends upon the existence of another thing. It cannot be said not to exist, seeing that it makes all this difference. According to the Advaita philosophy, then, this Maya, or ignorance—or name and form, or as it has been called in Europe, "time, space, and causality"—is out of this One Infinite Existence, showing us the manifoldness of the universe; in substance, this universe is One. So long as any one thinks that there are two ultimate realities, he is mistaken. When he has come to know that there is but One, he is right.

This is what is being proved to us every day, on the physical plane, on the mental plane, and also on the spiritual plane. Today it has been demonstrated that you and I, the sun, the moon, and the stars are but the different names of different spots in the same ocean of matter, and that this matter is continuously changing in its configuration. The particle of energy that was in the sun several months ago may be in the human being now; tomorrow it may be in an animal, the day after tomorrow it may be in a plant. It is ever coming and going. It is all one unbroken, infinite mass of matter, only differentiated by names and forms. One point is called the sun; another, the moon; another, the stars; another, the man; another, animal; another, plant; and so on. And all these names are fictitious; they have no reality, because the whole is a continuously changing mass of matter. This very same universe, from another standpoint, is an ocean of thought, where each one of us is a point called a particular mind. You are a mind, I am a mind, every one is a mind; and the very same universe viewed from the standpoint of knowledge, when the eyes have been cleared of delusions, when the mind has become pure, appears to be the Unbroken, Absolute Being, the ever pure, the unchangeable, the immortal.

What then becomes of all this threefold eschatology of the dualist, that when a man dies he goes to heaven, or goes to this or that sphere, and that the wicked persons become ghosts, and become animals, and so forth? None comes and none goes, says the non-dualist. How can you come and go? You are infinite, where is the place for you to go? In a certain school a number of little children were being examined. The examiner had foolishly put all sorts of difficult questions to the little children. Among others there was this question, "Why does not the earth fall?" His intention was to bring out the idea of gravitation or some other intricate scientific truth from these children. Most of them could not even understand the question, and so they gave all sorts of wrong answers. But one bright little girl answered it with another question: "Where shall it fall?" The very question of the examiner was nonsense on the face of it. There is no up and down in the universe; the idea is only relative. So it is with regard to the soul. The very question of birth and death in regard to it is utter nonsense. Who goes and who comes? Where are you not? Where is the heaven that you are not in already? Omnipresent is the Self of man. Where is it to go? Where is it not to go? It is everywhere. So all this childish dream, and puerile illusion of birth and death, of heavens and higher heavens and lower worlds, all vanish immediately for the perfect. For the nearly perfect it vanishes after showing them the several scenes up to Brahmaloka. It continues for the ignorant.

How is it that the whole world believes in going to heaven, and in dying and being born? I am studying a book, page after page is being read and turned over. Another page comes and is turned over. Who changes? Who comes and goes? Not I, but the book. This whole nature is a book before the soul, chapter after chapter is being read and turned over, and every now and then a scene opens. That is read and turned over. A fresh one comes, but the soul is ever the same—eternal. It is nature that is changing, not the soul of man. This never changes. Birth and death are in nature, not in you. Yet the ignorant are deluded; just as we under delusion think that the sun is moving, and not the earth, in exactly the same way we think that we are dying, and not nature. These are all, therefore, hallucinations. Just as it is a hallucination when we think that the fields are moving and not the railway train, exactly in the same manner is the hallucination of birth and death. When men are in a certain frame of mind, they see this very existence as the earth, as the sun, the moon, the stars; and all those who are in the same state of mind see the same things. Between you and me there may be millions of beings on different planes of existence. They will never see us, nor we them; we only see those who are in the same state of mind and on the same plane with us. Those musical instruments respond which have the same attunement of vibration, as it were; if the state of vibration which they call "man-vibration" should be changed, no longer would men be seen here. The whole "man-universe" would vanish, and instead of that, other scenery would come before us, perhaps gods and the god-universe, or perhaps, for the wicked man, devils and the diabolic world; but all would be only different views of the one universe.

It is this universe which, from the human plane, is seen as the earth, the sun, the moon, the stars, and all such things —it is this very universe which, seen from the plane of wickedness, appears as a place of punishment. And this very universe is seen as heaven by those who want to see it as heaven. Those who have been dreaming of going to a God who is sitting on a throne, and of standing there praising Him all their lives, when they die, will simply see a vision of what they have in their minds; this very universe will simply change into a vast heaven, with all sorts of winged beings flying about, and a God sitting on a throne. These heavens are all of man's own making. So what the dualist says is true, says the Advaitin, but it is all simply of his own making. These spheres and devils and gods, and reincarnations and transmigrations are all mythology; so also is this human life. The great mistake that men always make is to think that this life alone is true. They understand it well enough when other things are called mythologies, but are never willing to admit the same of their own position. The whole thing as it appears is mere mythology, and the greatest of all lies is that we are bodies, which we never were nor even can be. It is the greatest of all lies that we are mere men; we are the God of the universe. In worshipping God we have been always worshipping our own hidden Self.

The worst lie that you ever tell yourself is that you were born a sinner or a wicked man. He alone is a sinner who sees a sinner in another man. Suppose there is a baby here, and you place a bag of gold on the table. Suppose a robber comes and takes the gold away. To the baby it is all the same, because there is no robber inside, there is no robber outside. To sinners and vile men, there is vileness outside, but not to good men. So the wicked see this universe as a hell, and the partially good see it as heaven, while the perfect beings realise it as God Himself. Then alone the veil falls from the eyes, and the man, purified and cleansed, finds his whole vision changed. The bad dreams that have been torturing him for millions of years, all vanish, and he who was thinking of himself either as a man, or a god, or a demon, he who was thinking of himself as living in low places, in high places, on earth, in heaven, and so on, finds that he is really omnipresent, that all time is in him, and that he is not in time; that all the heavens are in him, that he is not in any heaven, and that all the gods that man ever worshipped are in him, and that he is not in any one of those gods. He was the manufacturer of gods and demons, of men and plants, and animals and stones, and the real nature of man now stands unfolded to him as being higher than heaven, more perfect than this universe of ours, more infinite than infinite time, more omnipresent than the omnipresent ether. Thus alone, man becomes fearless, and becomes free. Then all delusions cease, all miseries vanish, all fears come to an end for ever. Birth goes away, and with it death; pains fly, and with them fly away pleasures; earths vanish, and with them vanish heavens; bodies vanish, and with them vanishes the mind also. For that man the whole universe disappears, as it were. This searching, moving, continuous struggle of forces stops for ever, and that which was manifesting itself as force and matter, as struggles of nature, as nature itself, as heavens and earths and plants and animals and men and angels, and all that becomes transfigured into one infinite, unbreakable, unchangeable existence, and the knowing man finds that he is one with that existence. "Even as clouds of various colours come before the sky, remain there for a second and then vanish away," even so before this soul are all these visions coming, of earths and heavens, of the moon and the gods, of pleasures and pains; but they all pass away, leaving the one infinite, blue, unchangeable sky. The sky never changes; it is the clouds that change. It is a mistake to think that the sky is changed. It is a mistake to think that we are impure, that we are limited, that we are separate. The real man is the One Unit Existence.

Two questions now arise. The first is, "Is it possible to realise this? So far it is doctrine, philosophy, but is it possible to realise it?" It is. There are men living in this world for whom delusion has vanished for ever. Do they immediately die after such realisation? Not so soon as we should think. Two wheels joined by one pole are running together. If I get hold of one of the wheels and, with an axe, cut the pole asunder, the wheel, which I have got hold of stops, but upon the other wheel is its past momentum, so it runs on a little and then falls down. This pure and perfect being, the soul, is one wheel, and this external hallucination of body and mind is the other wheel, joined together by the pole of work, of Karma. Knowledge is the axe which will sever the bond between the two, and the wheel of the soul will stop—stop thinking that it is coming and going, living and dying, stop thinking that it is nature and has wants and desires, and will find that it is perfect, desireless. But upon the other wheel, that of the body and mind, will be the momentum of past acts, so it will live for some time, until that momentum of past work is exhausted, until that momentum is worked away, and then the body and mind fall, and the soul becomes free. No more is there any going to heaven and coming back, not even any going to the Brahmaloka, or to any of the highest of the spheres, for where is he to come from, or to go to? The man who has in this life attained to this state, for whom, for a minute at least, the ordinary vision of the world has changed and the reality has been apparent, he is called the "Living Free". This is the goal of the Vedantin, to attain freedom while living.

Once in Western India I was travelling in the desert country on the coast of the Indian Ocean. For days and days I used to travel on foot through the desert, but it was to my surprise that I saw every day beautiful lakes, with trees all round them, and the shadows of the trees upside down and vibrating there. "How wonderful it looks and they call this a desert country!" I said to myself. Nearly a month I travelled, seeing these wonderful lakes and trees and plants. One day I was very thirsty and wanted to have a drink of water, so I started to go to one of these clear, beautiful lakes, and as I approached, it vanished. And with a flash it came to my brain: "This is the mirage about which I have read all my life," and with that came also the idea that throughout the whole of this month, every day, I had been seeing the mirage and did not know it. The next morning I began my march. There was again the lake, but with it came also the idea that it was the mirage and not a true lake. So is it with this universe. We are all travelling in this mirage of the world day after day, month after month, year after year, not knowing that it is a mirage. One day it will break up, but it will come back again; the body has to remain under the power of past Karma, and so the mirage will come back. This world will come back upon us so long as we are bound by Karma: men, women, animals, plants, our attachments and duties, all will come back to us, but not with the same power. Under the influence of the new knowledge the strength of Karma will be broken, its poison will be lost. It becomes transformed, for along with it there comes the idea that we know it now, that the sharp distinction between the reality and the mirage has been known.

This world will not then be the same world as before. There is, however, a danger here. We see in every country people taking up this philosophy and saying, "I am beyond all virtue and vice, so I am not bound by any moral laws; I may do anything I like." You may find many fools in this country at the present time, saying, "I am not bound; I am God himself; let me do anything I like." This is not right, although it is true that the soul is beyond all laws, physical, mental, or moral. Within law is bondage; beyond law is freedom. It is also true that freedom is of the nature of the soul, it is its birthright; that real freedom of the soul shines through veils of matter in the form of the apparent freedom of man. Every moment of your life you feel that you are free. We cannot live, talk, or breathe for a moment without feeling that we are free, but, at the same time, a little thought shows us that we are like machines and not free. What is true then? Is this idea of freedom a delusion? One party holds that the idea of freedom is a delusion; another says that the idea of bondage is a delusion. How does this happen? Man is really free, the real man cannot but be free. It is when he comes into the world of Maya, into name and form, that he becomes bound. Free will is a misnomer. Will can never be free. How can it be? It is only when the real man has become bound that his will comes into existence, and not before. The will of man is bound, but that which is the foundation of that will is eternally free. So, even in the state of bondage which we call human life or god-life, on earth or in heaven, there yet remains to us that recollection of the freedom which is ours by divine right. And consciously or unconsciously we are all struggling towards it. When a man has attained his own freedom, how can he be bound by any law? No law in this universe can bind him, for this universe itself is his.

He is the whole universe. Either say he is the whole universe or say that to him there is no universe. How can he have then all these little ideas about sex, and about country? How can he say, I am a man, I am a woman, I am a child? Are they not lies? He knows that they are. How can he say that these are man's rights, and these others are woman's rights? Nobody has rights; nobody separately exists. There is neither man nor woman; the soul is sexless, eternally pure. It is a lie to say that I am a man or a woman, or to say that I belong to this country or that. All the world is my country, the whole universe is mine, because I have clothed myself with it as my body. Yet we see that there are people in this world who are ready to assert these doctrines, and at the same time do things which we should call filthy; and, if we ask them why they do so, they tell us that it is our delusion and that they can do nothing wrong. What is the test by which they are to be judged?

The test is here. Though evil and good are both conditioned manifestations of the soul, yet evil is the most external coating, and good is the nearer coating of the real man, the Self. And unless a man cuts through the layer of evil, he cannot reach the layer of good, and unless he has passed through both the layers of good and evil, he cannot reach the Self. He who reaches the Self, what remains attached to him? A little Karma, a little bit of the momentum of past life, but it is all good momentum. Until the bad momentum is entirely worked out and past impurities are entirely burnt, it is impossible for any man to see and realise truth. So, what is left attached to the man who has reached the Self and seen the truth, is the remnant of the good impressions of past life, the good momentum. Even if he lives in the body and works incessantly, he works only to do good; his lips speak only benediction to all; his hands do only good works; his mind can only think good thoughts; his presence is a blessing wherever he goes. He is himself a living blessing. Such a man will, by his very presence, change even the most wicked persons into saints. Even if he does not speak, his very presence will be a blessing to mankind. Can such men do any evil, can they do wicked deeds?

There is, you must remember, all the difference of pole to pole between realisation and mere talking. Any fool can talk. Even parrots talk. Talking is one thing, and realising is another. Philosophies, and doctrines, and arguments, and books, and theories, and churches, and sects, and all these things are good in their own way; but when that realisation comes these things drop away. For instance, maps are good, but when you see the country itself, and look again at the maps, what a great difference you find! So those that have realised truth do not require the ratiocinations of logic and all other gymnastics of the intellect to make them understand the truth, it is to them the life of their lives, concretised, made more than tangible. It is, as the sages of the Vedanta say, "even as a fruit in your hand"; you can stand up and say, it is here. So those that have realised the truth will stand up and say, "Here is the Self". You may argue with them by the year, but they will smile at you; they will regard it all as child's prattle; they will let the child prattle on. They have realised the truth and are full. Suppose you have seen a country and another man comes to you and tries to argue with you that that country never existed, he may go on arguing indefinitely, but your only attitude of mind towards him must be to hold that that man is fit for a lunatic asylum. So the man of realisation says, "All this talk in the world about its little religions is but prattle; realisation is the soul, the very essence of religion." Religion can be realised. Are you ready? Do you want it? You will get the realisation if you do, and then you will be truly religious. Until you have attained realisation there is no difference between you and atheists. The atheists are sincere but the man who says that he believes in religion and never attempts to realise it, is not sincere.

The next question is to know what comes after realisation. Suppose we have realised this oneness of the universe, that we are that One Infinite Being, and suppose we have realised that this Self is the Only Existence, and that it is the same Self which is manifesting in all these various phenomenal forms, what becomes of us after that? Shall we become inactive, get into a corner and sit down there and die away? "What good will it do to the world?" That old question! In the first place why should it do good to the world? Is there any reason why it should? What right has any one to ask the question, "What good will it do to the world?" What is meant by that? A baby likes candies. Suppose you are conducting investigations in connection with some subject of electricity and the baby asks you, "Does it buy candies?" "No," you answer. "Then what good will it do?" says the baby. So men stand up and say, "What good will this do to the world, will it give us money?" "No." "Then what good is there in it?" That is what men mean by doing good to the world.

Yet religious realisation does all the good to the world. People are afraid that when they attain to it, when they realise that there is but One, the fountains of love will be dried up, that everything in life will go away, and that all they love will vanish for them, as it were, in this life and in the life to come People never stop to think that those who bestowed the least thought on their own individualities have been the greatest workers in the world. Then alone a man loves when he finds that the object of his love is not any low, little, mortal thing. Then alone a man loves when he finds that the object of his love is not a clod of earth, but is the veritable God Himself. The wife will love the husband the more when she thinks that the husband is God Himself. The husband will love the wife the more when he knows that the wife is God Himself. That mother will love the children more, who thinks that the children are God Himself. That man will love his greatest enemy, who knows that that very enemy is God Himself. That man will love a holy man, who knows that the holy man is God Himself, and that very man will also love the unholiest of men because he knows the background of that unholiest of men is even He, the Lord. Such a man becomes a world-mover for whom his little self is dead and God stands in its place. The whole universe will become transfigured to him. That which is painful and miserable will all vanish; struggles will all depart and go. Instead of being a prison-house, where we every day struggle, and fight and compete for a morsel of bread, this universe will then be to us a playground. Beautiful will be this universe then! Such a man alone has the right to stand up and say, "How beautiful is this world!" He alone has the right to say that it is all good.

This will be the great good to the world resulting from such realisation, that instead of this world going on with all its friction and clashing, if all mankind today realise only a bit of that great truth, the aspect of the whole world will be changed, and, in place of fighting and quarrelling, there would be a reign of peace. This indecent and brutal hurry which forces us to go ahead of every one else will then vanish from the world. With it will vanish all struggle, with it will vanish all hate, with it will vanish all jealousy, and all evil will vanish away for ever. Gods will live then upon this earth. This very earth will then become heaven, and what evil can there be when gods are playing with gods, when gods are working with gods, and gods are loving gods? That is the great utility of divine realisation. Everything that you see in society will be changed and transfigured then. No more will you think of man as evil, and that is the first great gain. No more will you stand up and sneeringly cast a glance at a poor man or woman who has made a mistake. No more, ladies, will you look down with contempt upon the poor woman who walks the street in the night, because you will see even there God Himself. No more will you think of jealousy and punishments. They will all vanish, and love, the great ideal of love, will be so powerful that no whip and cord will be necessary to guide mankind aright.

If one-millionth part of the men and women who live in this world simply sit down and for a few minutes say, "You are all God, O ye men and O ye animals, and living beings, you are all the manifestations of the one living Deity;" the whole world will be changed in half an hour. Instead of throwing tremendous bomb-shells of hatred into every corner, instead of projecting currents of jealousy and of evil thought, in every country people will think that it is all He. He is all that you see and feel. How can you see evil until there is evil in you? How can you see the thief, unless he is there, sitting in the heart of your heart? How can you see the murderer until you are yourself the murderer? Be good, and evil will vanish for you. The whole universe will thus be changed. This is the greatest gain to society. This is the great gain to the human organism.

These thoughts were thought out, worked out amongst individuals in ancient times in India. For various reasons, such as the exclusiveness of the teachers and foreign conquest, those thoughts were not allowed to spread. Yet they are grand truths, and wherever they have been working man has become divine. My whole life has been changed by the touch of one of these divine men, about whom I am going to speak to you next Sunday; and the time is coming when these thoughts will be cast abroad over the whole world. Instead of living in monasteries, instead of being confined to books of philosophy to be studied only by the learned, instead of being the exclusive possession of sects and of a few of the learned, they will all be sown broadcast over the whole world, so that they may become the common property of the saint and the sinner, of men and women and children, of the learned and of the ignorant. They will then permeate the atmosphere of the world, and the very air that we breathe will say with every one of its pulsations, "Thou art That". And the whole universe with its myriads of suns and moons, through everything that speaks, with one voice will say, "Thou art That".

THE ATMAN

(*Delivered in America*)

Many of you have read Max Müller's celebrated book, *Three Lectures on the Vedanta Philosophy,* and some of you may, perhaps, have read, in German, Professor Deussen's book on the same philosophy. In what is being written and taught in the West about the religious thought of India, one school of Indian thought is principally represented, that which is called Advaitism, the monistic side of Indian religion; and sometimes it is thought that all the teachings of the Vedas are comprised in that one system of philosophy. There are, however, various phases of Indian thought; and, perhaps, this non-dualistic form is in the minority as compared with the other phases. From the most ancient times there have been various sects of thought in India, and as there never was a formulated or recognised church or any body of men to designate the doctrines which should be believed by each school, people were very free to choose their own form, make their own philosophy and establish their own sects. We, therefore, find that from the most ancient times India was full of religious sects. At the present time, I do not know how many hundreds of sects we have in India, and several fresh ones are coming into existence every year. It seems that the religious activity of that nation is simply inexhaustible.

Of these various sects, in the first place, there can be made two main divisions, the orthodox and the unorthodox. Those that believe in the Hindu scriptures, the Vedas, as eternal revelations of truth, are called orthodox, and those that stand on other authorities, rejecting the Vedas, are the heterodox in India. The chief modern unorthodox Hindu sects are the Jains and the Buddhists. Among the orthodox some declare that the scriptures are of much higher authority than reason; others again say that only that portion of the scriptures which is rational should be taken and the rest rejected.

Of the three orthodox divisions, the Sânkhyas, the Naiyâyikas, and the Mimâmsakas, the former two, although they existed as philosophical schools, failed to form any sect. The one sect that now really covers India is that of the later

Mimamsakas or the Vedantists. Their philosophy is called Vedantism. All the schools of Hindu philosophy start from the Vedanta or Upanishads, but the monists took the name to themselves as a speciality, because they wanted to base the whole of their theology and philosophy upon the Vedanta and nothing else. In the course of time the Vedanta prevailed, and all the various sects of India that now exist can be referred to one or other of its schools. Yet these schools are not unanimous in their opinions.

We find that there are three principal variations among the Vedantists. On one point they all agree, and that is that they all believe in God. All these Vedantists also believe the Vedas to be the revealed word of God, not exactly in the same sense, perhaps, as the Christians or the Mohammedans believe, but in a very peculiar sense. Their idea is that the Vedas are an expression of the knowledge of God; and as God is eternal, His knowledge is eternally with Him, and so are the Vedas eternal. There is another common ground of belief: that of creation in cycles, that the whole of creation appears and disappears; that it is projected and becomes grosser and grosser, and at the end of an incalculable period of time it becomes finer and finer, when it dissolves and subsides, and then comes a period of rest. Again it begins to appear and goes through the same process. They postulate the existence of a material which they call Âkâsha, which is something like the ether of the scientists, and a power which they call Prâna. About this Prana they declare that by its vibration the universe is produced. When a cycle ends, all this manifestation of nature becomes finer and finer and dissolves into that Akasha which cannot be seen or felt, yet out of which everything is manufactured. All the forces that we see in nature, such as gravitation, attraction, and repulsion, or as thought, feeling, and nervous motion—all these various forces resolve into that Prana, and the vibration of the Prana ceases. In that state it remains until the beginning of the next cycle. Prana then begins to vibrate, and that vibration acts upon the Akasha, and all these forms are thrown out in regular succession.

The first school I will tell you about is styled the dualistic school. The dualists believe that God, who is the creator of the universe and its ruler, is eternally separate from nature, eternally separate from the human soul. God is eternal; nature is eternal; so are all souls. Nature and the souls become manifested and change, but God remains the same. According to the dualists, again, this God is personal in that He has qualities, not that He has a body. He has human attributes; He is merciful, He is just, He is powerful, He is almighty, He can be approached, He can be prayed to, He can be loved, He loves in return, and so forth. In one word, He is a human God, only infinitely greater than man; He has none of the evil qualities which men have. "He is the repository of an infinite number of blessed qualities"—that is their definition. He cannot create without materials, and nature is the material out of which He creates the whole universe. There are some non-Vedantic dualists, called "Atomists", who believe that nature is nothing but an infinite number of atoms, and God's will, acting upon these atoms, creates. The Vedantists deny the atomic theory; they say it is perfectly illogical. The indivisible atoms are like geometrical points without parts or magnitude; but something without parts or magnitude, if multiplied an infinite number of times, will remain the same. Anything that has no parts will never make something that has parts; any number of zeros added together will not make one single whole number. So, if these atoms are such that they have no parts or magnitude, the creation of the universe is simply impossible out of such atoms. Therefore, according to the Vedantic dualists, there is what they call indiscrete or undifferentiated nature, and out of that God creates the universe. The vast mass of Indian people are dualists. Human nature ordinarily cannot conceive of anything higher. We find that ninety per cent of the population of the earth who believe in any religion are dualists. All the religions of Europe and Western Asia are dualistic; they have to be. The ordinary man cannot think of anything which is not concrete. He naturally likes to cling to that which his intellect can grasp. That is to say, he can only conceive of higher spiritual ideas by bringing them down to his own level. He can only grasp abstract thoughts by making them concrete. This is the religion of the masses all over the world. They believe in a God who is entirely separate from them, a great king, a high, mighty monarch, as it were. At the same time they make Him purer than the monarchs of the earth; they give Him all good qualities and remove the evil qualities from Him. As if it were ever possible for good to exist without evil; as if there could be any conception of light without a conception of darkness!

With all dualistic theories the first difficulty is, how is it possible that under the rule of a just and merciful God, the repository of an infinite number of good qualities, there can be so many evils in this world? This question arose in all dualistic religions, but the Hindus never invented a Satan as an answer to it. The Hindus with one accord laid the blame on man, and it was easy for them to do so. Why? Because, as I have just now told you, they did not believe that souls were created out of nothing. We see in this life that we can shape and form our future; every one of us, every day, is trying to shape the morrow. Today we fix the fate of the morrow; tomorrow we shall fix the fate of the day after, and so on. It is quite logical that this reasoning can be pushed backward too. If by our own deeds we shape our destiny in the future, why not apply the same rule to the past? If, in an infinite chain, a certain number of links are alternately repeated, then, if one of these groups of links be explained, we can explain the whole chain. So, in this infinite length of time, if we can cut off one portion and explain that portion and understand it, then, if it be true that nature is uniform, the same explanation must apply to the whole chain of time. If it be true that we are working out our own destiny here within this short space of time, if it be true that everything must have a cause as we see it now, it must also be true that that which we are now is the effect of the whole of our past; therefore, no other person is necessary to shape the destiny of mankind but man himself. The evils that are in the world are caused by none else but ourselves. We have caused all this evil; and just as we constantly see misery resulting from evil actions, so can we also see that much of the existing misery in the world is the effect of the past wickedness of man. Man alone, therefore, according to this theory, is responsible. God is not to blame. He, the eternally merciful Father, is not to blame at all. "We reap what we sow."

Another peculiar doctrine of the dualists is, that every soul must eventually come to salvation. No one will be left out. Through various vicissitudes, through various sufferings and enjoyments, each one of them will come out in the end. Come out of what? The one common idea of all Hindu sects is that all souls have to get out of this universe. Neither the universe which we see and feel, nor even an imaginary one, can be right, the real one, because both are mixed up with good and evil. According to the dualists, there is beyond this universe a place full of happiness and good only; and when that place is reached, there will be no more necessity of being born and reborn, of living and dying; and this idea is very dear to them. No more disease there, and no more death. There will be eternal happiness, and they will be in the presence of God for all time and enjoy Him for ever. They believe that all beings, from the lowest worm up to the highest angels and gods, will all, sooner or later, attain to that world where there will be no more misery. But our world will never end; it goes on infinitely, although moving in waves. Although moving in cycles it never ends. The number of souls that are to be saved, that are to be perfected, is infinite. Some are in plants, some are in the lower animals, some are in men, some are in gods, but all of them, even the highest gods, are imperfect, are in bondage. What is the bondage? The necessity of being born and the necessity of dying. Even the highest gods die. What are these gods? They mean certain states, certain offices. For instance, Indra the king of gods, means a certain office; some soul which was very high has gone to fill that post in this cycle, and after this cycle he will be born again as man and come down to this earth, and the man who is very good in this cycle will go and fill that post in the next cycle. So with all these gods; they are certain offices which have been filled alternately by millions and millions of souls, who, after filling those offices, came down and became men. Those who do good works in this world and help others, but with an eye to reward, hoping to reach heaven or to get the praise of their fellow-men, must when they die, reap the benefit of those good works—they become these gods. But that is not salvation; salvation never will come through hope of reward. Whatever man desires the Lord gives him. Men desire power, they desire prestige, they desire enjoyments as gods, and they get these desires fulfilled, but no effect of work can be eternal. The effect will be exhausted after a certain length of time; it may be aeons, but after that it will be gone, and these gods must come down again and become men and get another chance for liberation. The lower animals will come up and become men, become gods, perhaps, then become men again, or go back to animals, until the time when they will get rid of all desire for enjoyment, the thirst for life, this clinging on to the "me and mine". This "me and mine" is the very root of all the evil in the world. If you ask a dualist, "Is your child yours?" he will say, "It is God's. My property is not mine, it is God's." Everything should be held as God's.

Now, these dualistic sects in India are great vegetarians, great preachers of non-killing of animals. But their idea about it is quite different from that of the Buddhist. If you ask a Buddhist, "Why do you preach against killing any animal?" he will answer, "We have no right to take any life;" and if you ask a dualist, "Why do you not kill any animal?" he says, "Because it is the Lord's." So the dualist says that this "me and mine" is to be applied to God and God alone; He is the only "me" and everything is His. When a man has come to the state when he has no "me and mine," when everything is given up to the Lord, when he loves everybody and is ready even to give up his life for an animal, without any desire for reward, then his heart will be purified, and when the heart has been purified, into that heart will come the love of God. God is the centre of attraction for every soul, and the dualist says, "A needle covered up with clay will not be attracted by a magnet, but as soon as the clay is washed off, it will be attracted." God is the magnet and human soul is the needle, and its evil works, the dirt and dust that cover it. As soon as the soul is pure it will by natural attraction come to God and remain with Him for ever, but remain eternally separate. The perfected soul, if it wishes, can take any form; it is able to take a hundred bodies, if it wishes, or have none at all, if it so desires. It becomes almost almighty, except that it cannot create; that power belongs to God alone. None, however, perfect, can manage the affairs of the universe; that function belongs to God. But all souls, when they become perfect, become happy for ever and live eternally with God. This is the dualistic statement.

One other idea the dualists preach. They protest against the idea of praying to God, "Lord, give me this and give me that." They think that should not be done. If a man must ask some material gift, he should ask inferior beings for it; ask one of these gods, or angels or a perfected being for temporal things. God is only to be loved. It is almost a blasphemy to pray to God, "Lord, give me this, and give me that." According to the dualists, therefore, what a man wants, he will get sooner or later, by praying to one of the gods; but if he wants salvation, he must worship God. This is the religion of the masses of India.

The real Vedanta philosophy begins with those known as the qualified non-dualists. They make the statement that the effect is never different from the cause; the effect is but the cause reproduced in another form. If the universe is the effect and God the cause, it must be God Himself—it cannot be anything but that. They start with the assertion that God is both the efficient and the material cause of the universe; that He Himself is the creator, and He Himself is the material out of which the whole of nature is projected. The word "creation" in your language has no equivalent in Sanskrit, because there is no sect in India which believes in creation, as it is regarded in the West, as something coming out of nothing. It seems that at one time there were a few that had some such idea, but they were very quickly silenced. At the present time I do not know of any sect that believes this. What we mean by creation is projection of that which already existed. Now, the whole universe, according to this sect, is God Himself. He is the material of the universe. We read in the Vedas, "As the Urnanâbhi (spider) spins the thread out of its own body, even so the whole universe has come out of the Being."

If the effect is the cause reproduced, the question is: "How is it that we find this material, dull, unintelligent universe produced from a God, who is not material, but who is eternal intelligence? How, if the cause is pure and perfect, can the effect be quite different?" What do these qualified non-dualists say? Theirs is a very peculiar theory. They say that these three existences, God, nature, and the soul, are one. God is, as it were, the Soul, and nature and souls are the body of God. Just as I have a body and I have a soul, so the whole universe and all souls are the body of God, and God is the Soul of souls. Thus, God is the material cause of the universe. The body may be changed—may be young or old, strong or weak—but that does not affect the soul at all. It is the same eternal existence, manifesting through the body. Bodies come and go, but the soul does not change. Even so the whole universe is the body of God, and in that sense it is God. But the change in the universe does not affect God. Out of this material He creates the universe, and at the end of a cycle His body becomes finer, it contracts; at the beginning of another cycle it becomes expanded again, and out of it evolve all these different worlds.

Now both the dualists and the qualified non-dualists admit that the soul is by its nature pure, but through its own deeds it becomes impure. The qualified non-dualists express it more beautifully than the dualists, by saying that the soul's purity and perfection become contracted and again become manifest, and what we are now trying to do is to remanifest the intelligence, the purity, the power which is natural to the soul. Souls have a multitude of qualities, but not that of almightiness or all-knowingness. Every wicked deed contracts the nature of the soul, and every good deed expands it, and these souls, are all parts of God. "As from a blazing fire fly millions of sparks of the same nature, even so from this Infinite Being, God, these souls have come." Each has the same goal. The God of the qualified non-dualists is also a Personal God, the repository of an infinite number of blessed qualities, only He is interpenetrating everything in the universe. He is immanent in everything and everywhere; and when the scriptures say that God is everything, it means that God is interpenetrating everything, not that God has become the wall, but that God is in the wall. There is not a particle, not an atom in the universe where He is not. Souls are all limited; they are not omnipresent. When they get expansion of their powers and become perfect, there is no more birth and death for them; they live with God for ever.

Now we come to Advaitism, the last and, what we think, the fairest flower of philosophy and religion that any country in any age has produced, where human thought attains its highest expression and even goes beyond the mystery which seems to be impenetrable. This is the non-dualistic Vedantism. It is too abstruse, too elevated to be the religion of the masses. Even in India, its birth-place, where it has been ruling supreme for the last three thousand years, it has not been able to permeate the masses. As we go on we shall find that it is difficult for even the most thoughtful man and woman in any country to understand Advaitism. We have made ourselves so weak; we have made ourselves so low. We may make great claims, but naturally we want to lean on somebody else. We are like little, weak plants, always wanting a support. How many times I have been asked for a "comfortable religion!" Very few men ask for the truth, fewer still dare to learn the truth, and fewest of all dare to follow it in all its practical bearings. It is not their fault; it is all weakness of the brain. Any new thought, especially of a high kind, creates a disturbance, tries to make a new channel, as it were, in the brain matter, and that unhinges the system, throws men off their balance. They are used to certain surroundings, and have to overcome a huge mass of ancient superstition, ancestral superstition, class superstition, city superstition, country superstition, and behind all, the vast mass of superstition that is innate in every human being. Yet there are a few brave souls in the world who dare to conceive the truth, who dare to take it up, and who dare to follow it to the end.

What does the Advaitist declare? He says, if there is a God, that God must be both the material and the efficient cause of the universe. Not only is He the creator, but He is also the created. He Himself is this universe. How can that be? God, the pure, the spirit, has become the universe? Yes; apparently so. That which all ignorant people see as the universe does not really exist. What are you and I and all these things we see? Mere self-hypnotism; there is but one Existence, the Infinite, the Ever-blessed One. In that Existence we dream all these various dreams. It is the Atman, beyond all, the Infinite, beyond the known, beyond the knowable; in and through That we see the universe. It is the only Reality. It is this table; It is the audience before me; It is the wall; It is everything, minus the name and form. Take away the form of the table, take away the name; what remains is It. The Vedantist does not call It either He or She—these are fictions, delusions of the human brain—there is no sex in the soul. People who are under illusion, who have become like animals, see a woman or a man; living gods do not see men or women. How can they who are beyond everything have any sex idea? Everyone and everything is the Atman—the Self—the sexless, the pure, the ever-blessed. It is the name, the form, the body, which are material, and they make all this difference. If you take away these two differences of name and form, the whole universe is one; there are no two, but one everywhere. You and I are one. There is neither nature, nor God, nor the universe, only that one Infinite Existence, out of which, through name and form, all these are manufactured. How to know the Knower? It cannot be known. How can you see your own Self? You can only reflect yourself. So all this universe is the reflection of that One Eternal Being, the Atman, and as the reflection falls upon good or bad reflectors, so good or bad images are cast up. Thus in the murderer, the reflector is bad and not the Self. In the saint the reflector is pure. The Self —the Atman—is by Its own nature pure. It is the same, the one Existence of the universe that is reflecting Itself from the lowest worm to the highest and most perfect being. The whole of this universe is one Unity, one Existence, physically, mentally, morally and spiritually. We are looking upon this one Existence in different forms and creating all these images upon It. To the being who has limited himself to the condition of man, It appears as the world of man. To the being who is on a higher plane of existence, It may seem like heaven. There is but one Soul in the universe, not two. It neither comes nor goes. It is neither born, nor dies, nor reincarnates. How can It die? Where can It go? All these heavens, all these earths, and all these places are vain imaginations of the mind. They do not exist, never existed in the past, and never will exist in the future.

I am omnipresent, eternal. Where can I go? Where am I not already? I am reading this book of nature. Page after page I am finishing and turning over, and one dream of life after another goes away. Another page of life is turned over; another dream of life comes, and it goes away, rolling and rolling, and when I have finished my reading, I let it go and stand aside, I throw away the book, and the whole thing is finished. What does the Advaitist preach? He dethrones all the gods that ever existed, or ever will exist in the universe and places on that throne the Self of man, the Atman, higher than the sun and the moon, higher than the heavens, greater than this great universe itself. No books, no scriptures, no science can ever imagine the glory of the Self that appears as man, the most glorious God that ever was, the only God that ever existed, exists, or ever will exist. I am to worship, therefore, none but myself. "I worship my Self," says the Advaitist. To whom shall I bow down? I salute my Self. To whom shall I go for help? Who can help me, the Infinite Being of the universe? These are foolish dreams, hallucinations; who ever helped any one? None. Wherever you see a weak man, a dualist, weeping and wailing for help from somewhere above the skies, it is because he does not know that the skies also are in him. He wants help from the skies, and the help comes. We see that it comes; but it comes from within himself, and he mistakes it as coming from without. Sometimes a sick man lying on his bed may hear a tap on the door. He gets up and opens it and finds no one there. He goes back to bed, and again he hears a tap. He gets up and opens the door. Nobody is there. At last he finds that it was his own heartbeat which he fancied was a knock at the door. Thus man, after this vain search after various gods outside himself, completes the circle, and comes back to the point from which he started—the human soul, and he finds that the God whom he was searching in hill and dale, whom he was seeking in every brook, in every temple, in churches and heavens, that God whom he was even imagining as sitting in heaven and ruling the world, is his own Self. I am He, and He is I. None but I was God, and this little I never existed.

Yet, how could that perfect God have been deluded? He never was. How could a perfect God have been dreaming? He never dreamed. Truth never dreams. The very question as to whence this illusion arose is absurd. Illusion arises from illusion alone. There will be no illusion as soon as the truth is seen. Illusion always rests upon illusion; it never rests upon God, the Truth, the Atman. You are never in illusion; it is illusion that is in you, before you. A cloud is here; another comes and pushes it aside and takes its place. Still another comes and pushes that one away. As before the eternal blue sky, clouds of various hue and colour come, remain for a short time and disappear, leaving it the same eternal blue, even so are you, eternally pure, eternally perfect. You are the veritable Gods of the universe; nay, there are not two—there is but One. It is a mistake to say, "you and I"; say "I". It is I who am eating in millions of mouths; how can I be hungry? It is I who am working through an infinite number of hands; how can I be inactive? It is I who am living the life of the whole universe; where is death for me? I am beyond all life, beyond all death. Where shall I seek for freedom? I am free by my nature. Who can bind me—the God of this universe? The scriptures of the world are but little maps, wanting to delineate my glory, who am the existence of the universe. Then what are these books to me? Thus says the Advaitist.

"Know the truth and be free in a moment." All the darkness will then vanish. When man has seen himself as one with the Infinite Being of the universe, when all separateness has ceased, when all men and women, all gods and angels, all animals and plants, and the whole universe have melted into that Oneness, then all fear disappears. Can I hurt myself? Can I kill myself? Can I injure myself? Whom to fear? Can you fear yourself? Then will all sorrow disappear. What can cause me sorrow? I am the One Existence of the universe. Then all jealousies will disappear; of whom to be jealous? Of myself? Then all bad feelings disappear. Against whom can I have bad feeling? Against myself? There is none in the universe but I. And this is the one way, says the Vedantist, to Knowledge. Kill out this differentiation, kill out this superstition that there are many. "He who in this world of many sees that One, he who in this mass of insentiency sees that one Sentient Being, he who in this world of shadows catches that Reality, unto him belongs eternal peace, unto none else, unto none else."

These are the salient points of the three steps which Indian religious thought has taken in regard to God. We have seen that it began with the Personal, the extra-cosmic God. It went from the external to the internal cosmic body, God immanent in the universe, and ended in identifying the soul itself with that God, and making one Soul, a unit of all these various manifestations in the universe. This is the last word of the Vedas. It begins with dualism, goes through a qualified monism and ends in perfect monism. We know how very few in this world can come to the last, or even dare believe in it, and fewer still dare act according to it. Yet we know that therein lies the explanation of all ethics, of all morality and all spirituality in the universe. Why is it that every one says, "Do good to others?" Where is the explanation? Why is it that all great men have preached the brotherhood of mankind, and greater men the brotherhood of all lives? Because whether they were conscious of it or not, behind all that, through all their irrational and personal superstitions, was peering forth the eternal light of the Self denying all manifoldness, and asserting that the whole universe is but one.

Again, the last word gave us one universe, which through the senses we see as matter, through the intellect as souls, and through the spirit as God. To the man who throws upon himself veils, which the world calls wickedness and evil, this very universe will change and become a hideous place; to another man, who wants enjoyments, this very universe will change its appearance and become a heaven, and to the perfect man the whole thing will vanish and become his own Self.

Now, as society exists at the present time, all these three stages are necessary; the one does not deny the other, one is simply the fulfilment of the other. The Advaitist or the qualified Advaitist does not say that dualism is wrong; it is a right view, but a lower one. It is on the way to truth; therefore let everybody work out his own vision of this universe. according to his own ideas. Injure none, deny the position of none; take man where he stands and, if you can, lend him a helping hand and put him on a higher platform, but do not injure and do not destroy. All will come to truth in the long run. "When all the desires of the heart will be vanquished, then this very mortal will become immortal"—then the very man will become God.

THE ATMAN : ITS BONDAGE AND FREEDOM

(Delivered in America)

According to the Advaita philosophy, there is only one thing real in the universe, which it calls Brahman; everything else is unreal, manifested and manufactured out of Brahman by the power of Mâyâ. To reach back to that Brahman is our goal. We are, each one of us, that Brahman, that Reality, plus this Maya. If we can get rid of this Maya or ignorance, then we become what we really are. Accordingly to this philosophy, each man consists of three parts—the body, the internal organ or the mind, and behind that, what is called the Âtman, the Self. The body is the external coating and the mind is the internal coating of the Atman who is the real perceiver, the real enjoyer, the being in the body who is working the body by means of the internal organ or the mind.

The Âtman is the only existence in the human body which is immaterial. Because it is immaterial, it cannot be a compound, and because it is not a compound, it does not obey the law of cause and effect, and so it is immortal. That which is immortal can have no beginning because everything with a beginning must have an end. It also follows that it must be formless; there cannot be any form without matter. Everything that has form must have a beginning and an end. We have none of us seen a form which had not a beginning and will not have an end. A form comes out of a combination of force and matter. This chair has a peculiar form, that is to say a certain quantity of matter is acted upon by a certain amount of force and made to assume a particular shape. The shape is the result of a combination of matter and force. The combination cannot be eternal; there must come to every combination a time when it will dissolve. So all forms have a beginning and an end. We know our body will perish; it had a beginning and it will have an end. But the Self having no form, cannot be bound by the law of beginning and end. It is existing from infinite time; just as time is eternal, so is the Self of man eternal. Secondly, it must be all-pervading. It is only form that is conditioned and limited by space; that which is formless cannot be confined in space. So, according to Advaita Vedanta, the Self, the Atman, in you, in me, in every one, is omnipresent. You are as much in the sun now as in this earth, as much in England as in America. But the Self acts through the mind and the body, and where they are, its action is visible.

Each work we do, each thought we think, produces an impression, called in Sanskrit Samskâra, upon the mind and the sum total of these impressions becomes the tremendous force which is called "character". The character of a man is what he has created for himself; it is the result of the mental and physical actions that he has done in his life. The sum total of the Samskaras is the force which gives a man the next direction after death. A man dies; the body falls away and goes back to the elements; but the Samskaras remain, adhering to the mind which, being made of fine material, does not dissolve, because the finer the material, the more persistent it is. But the mind also dissolves in the long run, and that is what we are struggling for. In this connection, the best illustration that comes to my mind is that of the whirlwind. Different currents of air coming from different directions meet and at the meeting-point become united and go on rotating; as they rotate, they form a body of dust, drawing in bits of paper, straw, etc., at one place, only to drop them and go on to another, and so go on rotating, raising and forming bodies out of the materials which are before them. Even so the forces, called Prâna in Sanskrit, come together and form the body and the mind out of matter, and move on until the body falls down, when they raise other materials to make another body, and when this falls, another rises, and thus the process goes on. Force cannot travel without matter. So when the body falls down, the mind-stuff remains, Prana in the form of Samskaras acting on it; and then it goes on to another point, raises up another whirl from fresh materials, and begins another motion; and so it travels from place to place until the force is all spent; and then it falls down, ended. So when the mind will end, be broken to pieces entirely, without leaving any Samskara, we shall be entirely free, and until that time we are in bondage; until then the Atman is covered by the whirl of the mind, and imagines it is being taken from place to place. When the whirl falls down, the Atman finds that It is all-pervading. It can go where It likes, is entirely free, and is able to manufacture any number of minds or bodies It likes; but until then It can go only with the whirl. This freedom is the goal towards which we are all moving.

Suppose there is a ball in this room, and we each have a mallet in our hands and begin to strike the ball, giving it hundreds of blows, driving it from point to point, until at last it flies out of the room. With what force and in what direction will it go out? These will be determined by the forces that have been acting upon it all through the room. All the different blows that have been given will have their effects. Each one of our actions, mental and physical, is such a blow. The human mind is a ball which is being hit. We are being hit about this room of the world all the time, and our passage out of it is determined by the force of all these blows. In each case, the speed and direction of the ball is determined by the hits it has received; so all our actions in this world will determine our future birth. Our present birth, therefore, is the result of our past. This is one case: suppose I give you an endless chain, in which there is a black link and a white link alternately, without beginning and without end, and suppose I ask you the nature of the chain. At first you will find a difficulty in determining its nature, the chain being infinite at both ends, but slowly you find out it is a chain. You soon discover that this infinite chain is a repetition of the two links, black and white, and these multiplied infinitely become a whole chain. If you know the nature of one of these links, you know the nature of the whole chain, because it is a perfect repetition. All our lives, past, present, and future, form, as it were, an infinite chain, without beginning and without end, each link of which is one life, with two ends, birth and death. What we are and do here is being repeated again and again, with but little variation. So if we know these two links, we shall know all the passages we shall have to pass through in this world. We see, therefore, that our passage into this world has been exactly determined by our previous passages. Similarly we are in this world by our own actions. Just as we go out with the sum total of our present actions upon us, so we see that we come into it with the sum total of our past actions upon us; that which takes us out is the very same thing that brings us in. What brings us in? Our past deeds. What takes us out? Our own deeds *here,* and so on and on we go. Like the caterpillar that takes the thread from its own mouth and builds its cocoon and at last finds itself caught inside the cocoon, we have bound ourselves by our own actions, we have thrown the network of our actions around ourselves. We have set the law of causation in motion, and we find it hard to get ourselves out of it. We have set the wheel in motion, and we are being crushed under it. So this philosophy teaches us that we are uniformly being bound by our own actions, good or bad.

The Atman never comes nor goes, is never born nor dies. It is nature moving before the Atman, and the reflection of this motion is on the Atman; and the Atman ignorantly thinks it is moving, and not nature. When the Atman thinks that, it is in bondage; but when it comes to find it never moves, that it is omnipresent, then freedom comes. The Atman in bondage is called Jiva. Thus you see that when it is said that the Atman comes and goes, it is said only for facility of understanding, just as for convenience in studying astronomy you are asked to suppose that the sun moves round the earth, though such is not the case. So the Jiva, the soul, comes to higher or lower states. This is the well-known law of reincarnation; and this law binds all creation.

People in this country think it too horrible that man should come up from an animal. Why? What will be the end of these millions of animals? Are they nothing? If we have a soul, so have they, and if they have none, neither have we. It is absurd to say that man alone has a soul, and the animals none. I have seen men worse than animals.

The human soul has sojourned in lower and higher forms, migrating from one to another, according to the Samskaras or impressions, but it is only in the highest form as man that it attains to freedom. The man form is higher than even the angel form, and of all forms it is the highest; man is the highest being in creation, because he attains to freedom.

All this universe was in Brahman, and it was, as it were, projected out of Him, and has been moving on to go back to the source from which it was projected, like the electricity which comes out of the dynamo, completes the circuit, and returns to it. The same is the case with the soul. Projected from Brahman, it passed through all sorts of vegetable and animal forms, and at last it is in man, and man is the nearest approach to Brahman. To go back to Brahman from which we have been projected is the great struggle of life. Whether people know it or not does not matter. In the universe, whatever we see of motion, of struggles in minerals or plants or animals is an effect to come back to the centre and be at rest. There was an equilibrium, and that has been destroyed; and all parts and atoms and molecules are struggling to find their lost equilibrium again. In this struggle they are combining and re-forming, giving rise to all the wonderful phenomena of nature. All struggles and competitions in animal life, plant life, and everywhere else, all social struggles and wars are but expressions of that eternal struggle to get back to that equilibrium.

The going from birth to death, this travelling is what is called Samsâra in Sanskrit, the round of birth and death literally. All creation, passing through this round, will sooner or later become free. The question may be raised that if we all shall come to freedom, why should we *struggle* to attain it? If every one is going to be free, we will sit down and wait. It is true that every being will become free, sooner or later; no one can be lost. Nothing can come to destruction; everything must come up. If that is so, what is the use of our struggling? In the first place, the struggle is the only means that will bring us to the centre, and in the second place, we do not know why we struggle. We have to. "Of thousands of men some are awakened to the idea that they will become free." The vast masses of mankind are content with material things, but there are some who awake, and want to get back, who have had enough of this playing, down here. These struggle consciously, while the rest do it unconsciously.

The alpha and omega of Vedanta philosophy is to "give up the world," giving up the unreal and taking the real. Those who are enamoured of the world may ask, "Why should we attempt to get out of it, to go back to the centre? Suppose we have all come from God, but we find this world is pleasurable and nice; then why should we not rather try to get more and more of the world? Why should we try to get out of it?" They say, look at the wonderful improvements going on in the world every day, how much luxury is being manufactured for it. This is very enjoyable. Why should we go away, and strive for something which is not this? The answer is that the world is certain to die, to be broken into pieces and that many times we have had the same enjoyments. All the forms which we are seeing now have been manifested again and again, and the world in which we live has been here many times before. I have been here and talked to you many times before. You will know that it must be so, and the very words that you have been listening to now, you have heard many times before. And many times more it will be the same. Souls were never different, the bodies have been constantly dissolving and recurring. Secondly, these things periodically occur. Suppose here are three or four dice, and when we throw them, one comes up five, another four, another three, and another two. If you keep on throwing, there must come times when those very same numbers will recur. Go on throwing, and no matter how long may be the interval, those numbers must come again. It cannot be asserted in how many throws they will come again; this is the law of chance. So with souls and their associations. However distant may be the periods, the same combinations and dissolutions will happen again and again. The same birth, eating and drinking, and then death, come round again and again. Some never find anything higher than the enjoyments of the world, but those who want to soar higher find that these enjoyments are never final, are only by the way.

Every form, let us say, beginning from the little worm and ending in man, is like one of the cars of the Chicago Ferris Wheel which is in motion all the time, but the occupants change. A man goes into a car, moves with the wheel, and comes out. The wheel goes on and on. A soul enters one form, resides in it for a time, then leaves it and goes into another and quits that again for a third. Thus the round goes on till it comes out of the wheel and becomes free.

Astonishing powers of reading the past and the future of a man's life have been known in every country and every age. The explanation is that so long as the Atman is within the realm of causation—though its inherent freedom is not entirely lost and can assert itself, even to the extent of taking the soul out of the causal chain, as it does in the case of men who become free—its actions are greatly influenced by the causal law and thus make it possible for men, possessed with the insight to trace the sequence of effects, to tell the past and the future.

So long as there is desire or want, it is a sure sign that there is imperfection. A perfect, free being cannot have any desire. God cannot want anything. If He desires, He cannot be God. He will be imperfect. So all the talk about God desiring this and that, and becoming angry and pleased by turns is babies' talk, but means nothing. Therefore it has been taught by all teachers, "Desire nothing, give up all desires and be perfectly satisfied."

A child comes into the world crawling and without teeth, and the old man gets out without teeth and crawling. The extremes are alike, but the one has no experience of the life before him, while the other has gone through it all. When the vibrations of ether are very low, we do not see light, it is darkness; when very high, the result is also darkness. The extremes generally appear to be the same, though one is as distant from the other as the poles. The wall has no desires, so neither has the perfect man. But the wall is not sentient enough to desire, while for the perfect man there is nothing to desire. There are idiots who have no desires in this world, because their brain is imperfect. At the same time, the highest state is when we have no desires, but the two are opposite poles of the same existence. One is near the animal, and the other near to God.

THE IDEAL OF A UNIVERSAL RELIGION

How It Must Embrace Different Types Of Minds And Methods

Wheresoever our senses reach, or whatsoever our minds imagine, we find therein the action and reaction of two forces, the one counteracting the other and causing the constant play of the mixed phenomena that we see around us, and of those which we feel in our minds. In the external world, the action of these opposite forces is expressing itself as attraction and repulsion, or as centripetal and centrifugal forces, and in the internal, as love and hatred, good and evil. We repel some things, we attract others. We are attracted by one, we are repelled by another. Many times in our lives, we find that without any reason whatsoever, we are, as it were, attracted towards certain persons; at other times, similarly, we are repelled by others. This is patent to all, and the higher the field of action, the more potent, the more remarkable, are the influences of these opposite forces.

Religion is the highest plane of human thought and life, and herein we find that the workings of these two forces have been most marked. The intensest love that humanity has ever known has come from religion, and the most diabolical hatred that humanity has known has also come from religion. The noblest words of peace that the world has ever heard have come from men on the religious plane, and the bitterest denunciation that the world has ever known has been uttered by religious men. The higher the object of any religion and the finer its organisation, the more remarkable are its activities. No other human motive has deluged the world with blood so much as religion; at the same time, nothing has brought into existence so many hospitals and asylums for the poor; no other human influence has taken such care, not only of humanity, but also of the lowest of animals, as religion has done. Nothing makes us so cruel as religion, and nothing makes us so tender as religion. This has been so in the past, and will also, in all probability, be so in the future. Yet out of the midst of this din and turmoil, this strife and struggle, this hatred and jealousy of religions and sects, there have arisen, from time to time, potent voices, drowning all this noise—making themselves heard from pole to pole, as it were—proclaiming peace and harmony. Will it ever come?

Is it possible that there should ever reign unbroken harmony in this plane of mighty religious struggle? The world is exercised in the latter part of this century by the question of harmony; in society, various plans are being proposed, and attempts are made to carry them into practice; but we know how difficult it is to do so. People find that it is almost impossible to mitigate the fury of the struggle of life, to tone down the tremendous nervous tension that is in man. Now, if it is so difficult to bring harmony and peace to the physical plane of life—the external, gross, and outward side of it—then a thousand times more difficult is it to bring peace and harmony to rule over the internal nature of man. I would ask you for the time being to come out of the network of words. We have all been hearing from childhood of such things as love, peace, charity, equality, and universal brotherhood; but they have become to us mere words without meaning, words which we repeat like parrots, and it has become quite natural for us to do so. We cannot help it. Great souls, who first felt these great ideas in their hearts, manufactured these words; and at that time many understood their meaning. Later on, ignorant people have taken up those words to play with them, and made religion a mere play upon words, and not a thing to be carried into practice. It becomes "my father's religion," "our nation's religion," "our country's religion," and so forth. It becomes only a phase of patriotism to profess any religion, and patriotism is always partial. To bring harmony into religion must always be difficult. Yet we will consider this problem of the harmony of religions.

We see that in every religion there are three parts—I mean in every great and recognised religion. First, there is the philosophy which presents the whole scope of that religion, setting forth its basic principles, the goal, and the means of reaching it. The second part is mythology, which is philosophy made concrete. It consists of legends relating to the lives of men, or of supernatural beings, and so forth. It is the abstractions of philosophy concretised in the more or less imaginary lives of men and supernatural beings. The third part is the ritual. This is still more concrete, and is made up of forms and ceremonies, various physical attitudes, flowers and incense, and many other things that appeal to the senses. In these consists the ritual. You will find that all recognised religions have these three elements. Some lay more stress on one, some on another.

Let us now take into consideration the first part, philosophy. Is there one universal philosophy? Not yet. Each religion brings out its own doctrines, and insists upon them as being the only true ones. And not only does it do that, but it thinks that he who does not believe in them must go to some horrible place. Some will even draw the sword to compel others to believe as they do. This is not through wickedness, but through a particular disease of the human brain called fanaticism. They are very sincere, these fanatics, the most sincere of human beings; but they are quite as irresponsible as other lunatics in the world. This disease of fanaticism is one of the most dangerous of all diseases. All the wickedness of human nature is roused by it. Anger is stirred up, nerves are strung high, and human beings become like tigers.

Is there any mythological similarity, is there any mythological harmony, any universal mythology accepted by all religions? Certainly not. All religions have their own mythology, only each of them says, "My stories are not mere myths." Let us try to understand the question by illustration. I simply mean to illustrate, I do not mean criticism of any religion. The Christian believes that God took the shape of a dove, and came down to earth; to him this is history, and not mythology. The Hindu believes that God is manifested in the cow. Christians say that to believe so is mere mythology, and not history, that it is superstition. The Jews think that if an image be made in the form of a box, or a chest, with an angel on either side, then it may be placed in the Holy of Holies; it is sacred to Jehovah; but if the image be made in the form of a beautiful man or woman, they say, "This is a horrible idol; break it down!" This is our unity in mythology! If a man stands up and says, "My prophet did such and such a wonderful thing," others will say, "That is only superstition"; but at the same time they say that their own prophet did still more wonderful things, which they hold to be historical. Nobody in the world, as far as I have seen, is able to make out the fine distinction between history and mythology, as it exists in the brains of these persons. All such stories, to whatever religion they may belong, are really mythological, mixed up occasionally, it may be, with a little history.

Next come the rituals. One sect has one particular form of ritual, and thinks that that is holy, while the rituals of another sect are simply arrant superstition. If one sect worships a peculiar sort of symbol, another sect says, "Oh, it is horrible." Take for instance a general form of symbol. The phallus symbol is certainly a sexual symbol, but gradually that aspect of it has been forgotten, and it stands now as a symbol of the Creator. Those nations which have this as their symbol never think of it as the phallus; it is just a symbol, and there it ends. But a man from another race or creed sees in it nothing but the phallus, and begins to condemn it; yet at the same time he may be doing something which to the so-called phallic worshippers appears most horrible. Let me take two points for illustration, the phallus symbol and the sacrament of the Christians To the Christians the phallus is horrible, and to the Hindus the Christian sacrament is horrible. They say that the Christian sacrament, the killing of a man and the eating of his flesh and the drinking of his blood to get the good qualities of that man, is cannibalism. This is what some of the savage tribes do; if a man is brave, they kill him and eat his heart, because they think that it will give them the qualities of courage and bravery possessed by that man. Even such a devout Christian as Sir John Lubbock admits this, and says that the origin of this Christian symbol is in this savage idea. The Christians, of course, do not admit this view of its origin; and what it may imply never comes to their mind. It stands for a holy thing, and that is all they want to know. So even in rituals there is no universal symbol, which can command general recognition and acceptance. Where then is any universality? How is it possible then to have a universal form of religion? That, however, already exists. And let us see what it is.

We all hear about universal brotherhood, and how societies stand up especially to preach this. I remember an old story. In India, taking wine is considered very bad. There were two brothers who wished, one night, to drink wine secretly; and their uncle, who was a very orthodox man, was sleeping in a room quite close to theirs. So, before they began to drink, they said to each other, "We must be very silent, or uncle will wake up." When they were drinking, they continued repeating to each other, "Silence! Uncle will wake up," each trying to shout the other down. And, as the shouting increased, the uncle woke up, came into the room, and discovered the whole thing. Now, we all shout like these drunken men, "Universal brotherhood! We are all equal, therefore let us make a sect." As soon as you make a sect, you protest against equality, and equality is no more. Mohammedans talk of universal brotherhood, but what comes out of that in reality? Why, that anybody who is not a Mohammedan will not be admitted into the brotherhood; he will more likely have his throat cut. Christians talk of universal brotherhood; but anyone who is not a Christian must go to that place where he will be eternally barbecued.

And so we go on in this world in our search after universal brotherhood and equality. When you hear such talk in the world, I would ask you to be a little reticent, to take care of yourselves, for, behind all this talk is often the intensest selfishness. "In the winter sometimes a thunder-cloud comes up; it roars and roars, but it does not rain; but in the rainy season the clouds speak not, but deluge the world with water." So those who are *really* workers, and *really* feel at heart the universal brotherhood of man, do not talk much, do not make little sects for universal brotherhood, but their acts, their movements, their whole life, show out clearly that they in truth possess the feeling of brotherhood for mankind, that they have love and sympathy for all. They do not speak, they *do* and they *live*. This world is too full of blustering talk. We want a little more earnest work, and less talk.

So far we see that it is hard to find any universal features in regard to religion, and yet we know that they exist. We are all human beings, but are we all equal? Certainly not. Who says we are equal? Only the lunatic. Are we all equal in our brains, in our powers, in our bodies? One man is stronger than another, one man has more brain power than another. If we are all equal, why is there this inequality? Who made it? We. Because we have more or less powers, more or less brain, more or less physical strength, it must make a difference between us. Yet we know that the doctrine of equality appeals to our heart. We are all human beings; but some are men, and some are women. Here is a black man, there is a white man; but all are men, all belong to one humanity. Various are our faces; I see no two alike, yet we are all human beings. Where is this one humanity? I find a man or a woman, either dark or fair; and among all these faces, I know that there is an abstract humanity which is common to all. I may not find it when I try to grasp it, to sense it, and to actualise it, yet I know for certain that it is there. If I am sure of anything, it is of this humanity which is common to us all. It is through this generalised entity that I see you as a man or a woman. So it is with this universal religion, which runs through all the various religions of the world in the form of God; it must and does exist through eternity. "I am the thread that runs through all these pearls," and each pearl is a religion or even a sect thereof. Such are the different pearls, and the Lord is the thread that runs through all of them; only the majority of mankind are entirely unconscious of it.

Unity in variety is the plan of the universe. We are all men, and yet we are all distinct from one another. As a part of humanity, I am one with you, and as Mr. So-and-so I am different from you. As a man you are separate from the woman; as a human being you are one with the woman. As a man you are separate from the animal, but as living beings, man, woman, animal, and plant, are all one; and as existence, you are one with the whole universe. That universal existence is God, the ultimate Unity in the universe. In Him we are all one. At the same time, in manifestation, these differences must always remain. In our work, in our energies, as they are being manifested outside, these differences must always remain. We find then that if by the idea of a universal religion it is meant that one set of doctrines should be believed in by all mankind, it is wholly impossible. It can never be, there can never be a time when all faces will be the same. Again, if we expect that there will be one universal mythology, that is also impossible; it cannot be. Neither can there be one universal ritual. Such a state of things can never come into existence; if it ever did, the world would be destroyed, because variety is the first principle of life. What makes us formed beings? Differentiation. Perfect balance would be our destruction. Suppose the amount of heat in this room, the tendency of which is towards equal and perfect diffusion, gets that kind of diffusion, then for all practical purposes that heat will cease to be. What makes motion possible in this universe? Lost balance.

The unity of sameness can come only when this universe is destroyed, otherwise such a thing is impossible. Not only so, it would be dangerous to have it. We must not wish that all of us should think alike. There would then be no thought to think. We should be all alike, as the Egyptian mummies in a museum, looking at each other without a thought to think. It is this difference, this differentiation, this losing of the balance between us, which is the very soul of our progress, the soul of all our thought. This must always be.

What then do I mean by the ideal of a universal religion? I do not mean any one universal philosophy, or any one universal mythology, or any one universal ritual, held alike by all; for I know that this world must go on working, wheel within wheel, this intricate mass of machinery, most complex, most wonderful. What can *we* do then? We can make it run smoothly, we can lessen the friction, we can grease the wheels, as it were. How? By recognising the natural necessity of variation. Just as we have recognised unity by our very nature, so we must also recognise variation. We must learn that truth may be expressed in a hundred thousand ways, and that each of these ways is true as far as it goes. We must learn that the same thing can be viewed from a hundred different standpoints, and yet be the same thing. Take for instance the sun. Suppose a man standing on the earth looks at the sun when it rises in the morning; he sees a big ball. Suppose he starts on a journey towards the sun and takes a camera with him, taking photographs at every stage of his journey, until he reaches the sun. The photographs of each stage will be seen to be different from those of the other stages; in fact, when he gets back, he brings with him so many photographs of so many different suns, as it would appear; and yet we know that the same sun was photographed by the man at the different stages of his progress. Even so is it with the Lord. Through high philosophy or low, through the most exalted mythology or the grossest, through the most refined ritualism or arrant fetishism, every sect, every soul, every nation, every religion, consciously or unconsciously, is struggling upward, towards God; every vision of truth that man has, is a vision of Him and of none else. Suppose we all go with vessels in our hands to fetch water from a lake. One has a cup, another a jar, another a bucket, and so forth, and we all fill our vessels. The water in each case naturally takes the form of the vessel carried by each of us. He who brought the cup, has the water in the form of a cup; he who brought the jar—his water is in the shape of a jar, and so forth; but, in every case, water, and nothing but water, is in the vessel. So it is in the case of religion. Our minds are like these vessels, and each one of us is trying to arrive at the realisation of God. God is like that water filling these different vessels, and in each vessel, the vision of God comes in the form of the vessel. Yet He is One. He is God in every case. This is the only recognition of universality that we can get.

So far it is all right theoretically, but is there any way of practically working out this harmony in religions? We find that this recognition, that all the various views of religion are true, has been very very old. Hundreds of attempts have been made in India, in Alexandria, in Europe, in China, in Japan, in Tibet, and lastly in America, to formulate a harmonious religious creed, to make all religions come together in love. They have all failed, because they did not adopt any practical plan. Many have admitted that all the religions of the world are right, but they show no practical way of bringing them together, so as to enable each of them to maintain its own individuality in the conflux. That plan alone is practical which does not destroy the individuality of any man in religion, and at the same time shows him a point of union with all others. But so far, all the plans of religious harmony that have been tried, while proposing to take in all the various views of religion, have, in practice, tried to bind them all down to a few doctrines, and so have produced more new sects, fighting, struggling, and pushing against each other.

I have also my little plan. I do not know whether it will work or not, and I want to present it to you for discussion. What is my plan? In the first place I would ask mankind to recognise this maxim—"Do not destroy". Iconoclastic reformers do no good to the world. Break not, pull not anything down, but build. Help, if you can; if you cannot, fold your hands and stand by and see things go on. Do not injure, if you cannot render help. Say not a word against any man's convictions so far as they are sincere. Secondly, take man where he stands, and from there give him a lift. If it be true that God is the centre of all religions, and that each of us is moving towards Him along one of these radii, then it is certain that all of us *must* reach that centre. And at the centre, where all the radii meet, all our differences will cease; but until we reach there, differences there must be. All these radii converge to the same centre. One, according to his nature, travels along one of these lines, and another, along another; and if we all push onward along our own lines, we shall surely come to the centre, because, "All roads lead to Rome." Each of us is naturally growing and developing according to his own nature; each will in time come to know the highest truth, for after all, men must teach themselves. What can you and I do? Do you think you can teach even a child? You cannot. The child teaches himself. Your duty is to afford opportunities and to remove obstacles. A plant grows. Do *you* make the plant grow? Your duty is to put a hedge round it and see that no animal eats up the plant, and there your duty ends. The plant grows of itself. So is it in regard to the spiritual growth of every man. None can teach you; none can make a spiritual man of you. You have to teach yourself. Your growth must come from inside.

What can an external teacher do? He can remove the obstructions a little, and there his duty ends. Therefore help, if you can; but do not destroy. Give up all ideas that *you* can make men spiritual. It is impossible. There is no other teacher to you than your own soul. Recognise this. What comes of it? In society we see so many different natures. There are thousands and thousands of varieties of minds and inclinations. A thorough generalisation of them is impossible, but for our practical purpose it is sufficient to have them characterised into four classes. First, there is the active man, the worker; he wants to work, and there is tremendous energy in his muscles and his nerves. His aim is to work; to build hospitals, do charitable deeds, make streets, to plan and to organise. Then there is the emotional man, who loves the sublime and the beautiful to an excessive degree. He loves to think of the beautiful, to enjoy the aesthetic side of nature, and adore Love and the God of Love. He loves with his whole heart the great souls of all times, the prophets of religions, and the Incarnations of God on earth; he does not care whether reason can or cannot prove that Christ or Buddha existed; he does not care for the exact date when the Sermon on the

Mount was preached, or for the exact moment of Krishna's birth, what he cares for is their personalities, their lovable figures. Such is his ideal. This is the nature of the lover, the emotional man. Then, there is the mystic, whose mind wants to analyse its own self, to understand the workings of the human mind, what the forces are that are working inside, and how to know, manipulate, and obtain control over them. This is the mystical mind. Then, there is the philosopher, who wants to weigh everything and use his intellect even beyond the possibilities of all human philosophy.

Now a religion, to satisfy the largest portion of mankind, must be able to supply food for all these various types of minds; and where this capability is wanting, the existing sects all become one-sided. Suppose you go to a sect which preaches love and emotion. They sing and weep, and preach love. But as soon as you say, "My friend, that is all right, but I want something stronger than this; a little reason and philosophy; I want to understand things step by step and more rationally." "Get out," they say, and they not only ask you to get out but would send you to the other place, if they could. The result is that that sect can only help people of an emotional turn of mind. They not only do not help others, but try to destroy them; and the most wicked part of the whole thing is, that they will not only *not* help others, but do not believe in their sincerity. Again, there are philosophers, who talk of the wisdom of India and the East and use big psychological terms, fifty syllables long, but if an ordinary man like me goes to them and says, "Can you tell me anything to make me spiritual?", the first thing they would do would be to smile and say, "Oh, you are too far below us in your reason. What can you understand about spirituality?" These are high-up philosophers. They simply show you the door. Then there are the mystical sects, who speak all sorts of things about different planes of existence, different states of mind, and what the power of the mind can do, and so on; and if you are an ordinary man and say, "Show me anything good that I can do; I am not much given to speculation; can you give me anything that will suit me?" They will smile, and say, "Listen to that fool; he knows nothing, his existence is for nothing." And this is going on everywhere in the world. I would like to get extreme exponents of all these different sects, and shut them up in a room, and photograph their beautiful derisive smiles!

This is the existing condition of religion, the existing condition of things. What I want to propagate is a religion that will be equally acceptable to all minds; it must be equally philosophic, equally emotional, equally mystic, and equally conducive to action. If professors from the colleges come, scientific men and physicists, they will court reason. Let them have it as much as they want. There will be a point beyond which they will think they cannot go, without breaking with reason. They will say, "These ideas of God and salvation are superstitions, give them up!" I say, "Mr. Philosopher, this body of yours is a bigger superstition. Give *it* up, don't go home to dinner or to your philosophic chair. Give up the body, and if you cannot, cry quarter and sit down." For religion must be able to show how to realise the philosophy that teaches us that this world is one, that there is but One Existence in the universe. Similarly, if the mystic comes, we must welcome him, be ready to give him the science of mental analysis, and practically demonstrate it before him. And if emotional people come, we must sit, laugh, and weep with them in the name of the Lord; we must "drink the cup of love and become mad". If the energetic worker comes, we must work with him, with all the energy that we have. And this combination will be the ideal of the nearest approach to a universal religion. Would to God that all men were so constituted that in their minds *all* these elements of philosophy, mysticism, emotion, and of work were equally present in full! That is the ideal, my ideal of a perfect man. Everyone who has only one or two of these elements of character, I consider "one-sided"; and this world is almost full of such "one-sided" men, with knowledge of that one road only in which they move, and anything else is dangerous and horrible to them. To become harmoniously balanced in all these four directions is *my* ideal of religion.

And this religion is attained by what we, in India, call Yoga—union. To the worker, it is union between men and the whole of humanity; to the mystic, between his lower and Higher Self; to the lover, union between himself and the God of Love; and to the philosopher, it is the union of *all* existence. This is what is meant by Yoga. This is a Sanskrit term, and these four divisions of Yoga have in Sanskrit different names. The man who seeks after this kind of union is called a Yogi. The worker is called the Karma-Yogi. He who seeks the union through love is called the Bhakti-Yogi. He who seeks it through mysticism is called the Râja-Yogi. And he who seeks it through philosophy is called the Jnâna-Yogi. So this word Yogi comprises them all.

Now first of all let me take up Râja-Yoga. What is this Raja-Yoga, this controlling of the mind? In this country you are associating all sorts of hobgoblins with the word Yoga. I am afraid, therefore, I must start by telling you that it has nothing to do with such things. No one of these Yogas gives up reason, no one of them asks you to be hoodwinked, or to deliver your reason into the hands of priests of any type whatsoever. No one of them asks that you should give your allegiance to any superhuman messenger. Each one of them tells you to *cling* to your reason, to hold fast to it. We find in all beings three sorts of instruments of knowledge. The first is instinct, which you find most highly developed in animals; this is the lowest instrument of knowledge. What is the second instrument of knowledge? Reasoning. You find that most highly developed in man. Now in the first place, instinct is an inadequate instrument; to animals, the sphere of action is very limited, and within that limit, instinct acts. When you come to man, you see it is largely developed into reason. The sphere of action also has here become enlarged. Yet even reason is still very insufficient. Reason can go only a little way and then it stops, it cannot go any further; and if you try to push it, the result is helpless confusion, reason itself becomes unreasonable. Logic becomes argument in a circle. Take for instance the very basis of our perception—matter and force. What is matter? That which is acted upon by force. And force? That which acts upon matter. You see the complication, what the logicians call seesaw, one idea depending on the other, and this again depending on that. You find a mighty barrier before reason, beyond which reasoning cannot go; yet it always feels impatient to get into the region of the Infinite beyond. This world, this universe which our senses feel, or our mind thinks, is but one atom, so to say, of the Infinite, projected on to the plane of consciousness; and within that narrow limit, defined by the network of consciousness, works our reason, and not beyond. Therefore, there must be some other instrument to take us beyond, and that instrument is called inspiration. So instinct, reason, and inspiration are the three instruments of knowledge. Instinct belongs to animals, reason to men, and inspiration to God-men. But in all human beings are to be found, in a more or less developed condition, the germs of all these three instruments of knowledge. To have these mental instruments evolved, the germs must be there. And this must also be remembered that one instrument is a development of the other, and therefore does not contradict it. It is reason that develops into inspiration, and therefore inspiration does not contradict reason, but fulfils it. Things which reason cannot get at, are brought to light by inspiration; and they do not contradict reason. The old man does not contradict the child, but fulfils the child. Therefore you must always bear in mind that the great danger lies in mistaking the lower form of instrument to be the higher. Many times instinct is presented before the world as inspiration, and then come all the spurious claims for the gift of prophecy. A fool or a semi-lunatic thinks that the confusion going on in his brain is inspiration, and he wants men to follow him. The most contradictory, irrational nonsense that has been preached in the world, is simply the instinctive jargon of confused lunatic brains trying to pass for the language of inspiration.

The first test of true teaching must be, that the teaching should *not contradict reason.* And you may see that such is the basis of all these Yogas. We take the Raja-Yoga, the psychological Yoga, the psychological way to union. It is a vast subject, and I can only point out to you now the central idea of this Yoga. We have but one method of acquiring knowledge. From the lowest man to the highest Yogi, all have to use the same method; and that method is what is called concentration. The chemist who works in his laboratory concentrates all the powers of his mind, brings them into one focus, and throws them on the elements; and the elements stand analysed, and thus his knowledge comes. The astronomer has also concentrated the powers of his mind, and brought them into one focus; and he throws them on to objects, through his telescope; and stars and systems roll forward, and give up their secrets to him. So it is in every case; with the professor in his chair, the student with his books, with every man who is working to know. You are hearing me, and if my words interest you, your mind will become concentrated on them; and then suppose a clock strikes, you will not hear it, on account of this concentration; and the more you are able to concentrate your mind, the better you will understand me, and the more I concentrate my love and powers, the better I shall be able to give expression to what I convey to you. The more this power of concentration, the more knowledge is acquired, because this is the one and only method of acquiring knowledge. Even the lowest shoeblack, if he gives more concentration will black shoes better; the cook with concentration will cook a meal all the better. In making money, or in worshipping God, or in doing anything, the stronger the power of concentration, the better will that thing be done. This is the one call, the one knock, which opens the gates of nature, and lets out floods of light. This, the power of concentration, is the only key to the treasure-house of knowledge. The system of Raja-Yoga deals almost exclusively with this. In the present state of our body we are so much distracted, and the mind is frittering away its energies upon a hundred sorts of things. As soon as I try to calm my thoughts, and concentrate my mind upon any one object of knowledge, thousands of undesired impulses rush into the brain, thousands of thoughts rush into the mind and disturb it. How to check it and bring the mind under control is the whole subject of study in Raja-Yoga.

Now take Karma-Yoga, the attainment of God through work. It is evident that in society there are many persons who seem to be born for some sort of activity or other, whose minds cannot be concentrated on the plane of thought alone, and who have but one idea, concretised in work, visible and tangible. There must be a science for this kind of life too. Each one of us is engaged in some work, but the majority of us fritter away the greater portion of our energies, because we do not know the secret of work. Karma-Yoga explains this secret and teaches where and how to work, how to employ to the greatest advantage the largest part of our energies in the work that is before us. But with this secret we must take into consideration the great objection against work, namely, that it causes pain. All misery and pain come from attachment. I want to do work, I want to do good to a human being; and it is ninety to one that that human being whom I have helped will prove ungrateful, and go against me; and the result to me is pain. Such things deter mankind from working; and it spoils a good portion of the work and energy of mankind, this fear of pain and misery. Karma-Yoga teaches us how to work for work's sake, unattached, without caring who is helped, and what for. The Karma-Yogi works because it is his nature, because he *feels* that it is good for him to do so, and he has no object beyond that. His position in this world is that of a giver, and he never cares to receive anything. He knows that he is giving, and does not ask for anything in return and therefore he eludes the grasp of misery. The grasp of pain, whenever it comes, is the result of the reaction of "attachment".

There is then the Bhakti-Yoga for the man of emotional nature, the lover. He wants to love God, he relies upon and uses all sorts of rituals, flowers, incense, beautiful buildings, forms, and all such things. Do you mean to say, they are wrong? One fact I must tell you. It is good for you to remember, in this country especially, that the world's great spiritual giants have all been produced only by those religious sects which have been in possession of very rich mythology and ritual. All sects that have attempted to worship God without any form or ceremony have crushed without mercy everything that is beautiful and sublime in religion. Their religion is a fanaticism at best, a dry thing. The history of the world is a standing witness to this fact. Therefore do not decry these rituals and mythologies. Let people have them; let those who so desire have them. Do not exhibit that unworthy derisive smile and say, "They are fools; let them have it." Not so; the greatest men I have seen in my life, the most wonderfully developed in spirituality, have all come through the discipline of these rituals. I do not hold myself worthy to sit at their feet, and for *me* to criticise *them*! How do I know how these ideas act upon the human mind, which of them I am to accept and which to reject? We are apt to criticise everything in the world without sufficient warrant. Let people have all the mythology they want, with its beautiful inspirations; for you must always bear in mind that emotional natures do not care for abstract definitions of the truth. God to them is something tangible, the only thing that is real; they feel, hear, and see Him and love Him. Let them have their God. Your rationalist seems to them to be like the fool who, when he saw a beautiful statue, wanted to break it to find out of what material it was made. Bhakti-Yoga teaches them how to love, without any ulterior motives, loving God and loving the good because it is good to do so, not for going to heaven, nor to get children, wealth, or anything else. It teaches them that love itself is the highest recompense of love—that God Himself is love. It teaches them to pay all kinds of tribute to God as the Creator, the Omnipresent, Omniscient, Almighty Ruler, the Father and the Mother. The highest phrase that can express Him, the highest idea that the human mind can conceive of Him, is that He is the God of Love. Wherever there is love, it is He. "Wherever there is any love, it is He, the Lord is present there." Where the husband kisses the wife, He is there in the kiss; where the mother kisses the child, He is there in the kiss; where friends clasp hands, He, the Lord, is present as the God of Love. When a great man loves and wishes to help mankind, He is there giving freely His bounty out of His love to mankind. Wherever the heart expands, He is there manifested. This is what the Bhakti-Yoga teaches.

We lastly come to the Jnana-Yogi, the philosopher, the thinker, he who wants to go beyond the visible. He is the man who is not satisfied with the little things of this world. His idea is to go beyond the daily routine of eating, drinking, and so on; not even the teachings of thousands of books will satisfy him. Not even all the sciences will satisfy him; at the best, they only bring this little world before him. What else will give him satisfaction? Not even myriads of systems of worlds will satisfy him; they are to him but a drop in the ocean of existence. His soul wants to go beyond all that into the very heart of being, by seeing Reality as It is; by realising It, by being It, by becoming one with that Universal Being. That is the philosopher. To say that God is the Father or the Mother, the Creator of this universe, its Protector, and Guide, is to him quite inadequate to express Him. To him, God is the life of his life, the soul of his soul. God is his own Self. Nothing else remains which is other than God. All the mortal parts of him become pounded by the weighty strokes of philosophy, and are brushed away. What at last truly remains is God Himself.

Upon the same tree there are two birds, one on the top,

the other below. The one on the top is calm, silent and majestic, immersed in his own glory; the one on the lower branches, eating sweet and bitter fruits by turns, hopping from branch to branch, is becoming happy and miserable by turns. After a time the lower bird eats an exceptionally bitter fruit, and gets disgusted and looks up and sees the other bird, that wondrous one of golden plumage, who eats neither sweet nor bitter fruit, who is neither happy nor miserable, but calm, Self-centred and sees nothing beyond his Self. The lower bird longs for this condition but soon forgets it, and again begins to eat the fruit. In a little while, he eats another exceptionally bitter fruit, which makes him feel miserable, and he again looks up, and tries to get nearer to the upper bird. Once more he forgets and after a time he looks up, and so on he goes again and again, until he comes very near to the beautiful bird and sees the reflection of light from his plumage playing around his own body, and he feels a change and seems to melt away. Still nearer he comes, and everything about him melts away, and at last he understands this wonderful change. The lower bird was, as it were, only the substantial-looking shadow, the reflection of the higher: he himself was in essence the upper bird all the time. This eating of fruits, sweet and bitter, this lower, little bird, weeping and happy by turns, was a vain chimera, a dream: all along, the real bird was there above, calm and silent, glorious and majestic, beyond grief, beyond sorrow.

The upper bird is God, the Lord of this universe; and the lower bird is the human soul, eating the sweet and bitter fruits of this world. Now and then comes a heavy blow to the soul. For a time, he stops the eating and goes towards the unknown God, and a flood of light comes. He thinks that this world is a vain show. Yet again the senses drag him down, and he begins as before to eat the sweet and bitter fruits of the world. Again an exceptionally hard blow comes. His heart becomes open again to divine light; thus gradually he approaches God, and as he gets nearer and nearer, he finds his old self melting away. When he has come near enough he sees that he is no other than God, and he exclaims: "He whom I have described to you as the Life of this universe, as present in the atom, and in suns and moons—He is the basis of our own life, the Soul of our soul. Nay, thou art That." This is what this Jnana-Yoga teaches. It tells man that he is essentially divine. It shows to mankind the real unity of being and that each one of us is the Lord God Himself, manifested on earth. All of us, from the lowest worm that crawls under our feet to the highest being to whom we look up with wonder and awe—all are manifestations of the same Lord.

Lastly, it is imperative that all these various Yogas should be carried out in practice; mere theories about them will not do any good. First we have to hear about them, then we have to think about them. We have to reason the thoughts out, impress them on our minds, and we have to meditate on them, realise them, until at last they become our whole life. No longer will religion remain a bundle of ideas or theories, nor an intellectual assent; it will enter into our very self. By means of intellectual assent we may today subscribe to many foolish things, and change our minds altogether tomorrow. But true religion never changes. Religion is realisation; not talk, nor doctrine, nor theories, however beautiful they may be. It is being and becoming, not hearing or acknowledging; it is the whole soul becoming changed into what it believes. That is religion.

FIRST PUBLIC LECTURE IN THE EAST

(Delivered in Colombo)

After his memorable work in the West, Swami Vivekananda landed at Colombo on the afternoon of January 15, 1897, and was given a right royal reception by the Hindu community there. The following address of welcome was then presented to him:

SRIMAT VIVEKANANDA SWAMI

REVERED SIR,

In pursuance of a resolution passed at a public meeting of the Hindus of the city of Colombo, we beg to offer you a hearty welcome to this Island. We deem it a privilege to be the first to welcome you on your return home from your great mission in the West.

We have watched with joy and thankfulness the success with which the mission has, under God's blessing, been crowned. You have proclaimed to the nations of Europe and America the Hindu ideal of a universal religion, harmonising all creeds, providing spiritual food for each soul according to its needs, and lovingly drawing it unto God. You have preached the Truth and the Way, taught from remote ages by a succession of Masters whose blessed feet have walked and sanctified the soil of India, and whose gracious presence and inspiration have made her, through all her vicissitudes, the Light of the World.

To the inspiration of such a Master, Shri Ramakrishna Paramahamsa Deva, and to your self-sacrificing zeal, Western nations owe the priceless boon of being placed in living contact with the spiritual genius of India, while to many of our own countrymen, delivered from the glamour of Western civilisation, the value of our glorious heritage has been brought home.

By your noble work and example you have laid humanity under an obligation difficult to repay, and you have shed fresh lustre upon our Motherland. We pray that the grace of God may continue to prosper you and your work, and

We remain, Revered Sir,
Yours faithfully,
for and on behalf of the Hindus of Colombo,
P. Coomara Swamy,
Member of the Legislative Council of Ceylon,
Chairman of the Meeting.
A. Kulaveerasingham, *Secretary.*

Colombo, January, 1897

The Swami gave a brief reply, expressing his appreciation of the kind welcome he had received. He took advantage of the opportunity to point out that the demonstration had not been made in honour of a great politician, or a great soldier, or a millionaire, but of a begging Sannyâsin, showing the tendency of the Hindu mind towards religion. He urged the necessity of keeping religion as the backbone of the national life if the nation were to live, and disclaimed any personal character for the welcome he had received, but insisted upon its being the recognition of a principle.

On the evening of the 16th the Swami gave the following public lecture in the Floral Hall:

What little work has been done by me has not been from any inherent power that resides in me, but from the cheers, the goodwill, the blessings that have followed my path in the West from this our very beloved, most sacred, dear Motherland. Some good has been done, no doubt, in the West, but specially to myself; for what before was the result of an emotional nature, perhaps, has gained the certainty of conviction and attained the power and strength of demonstration. Formerly I thought as every Hindu thinks, and as the Hon. President has just pointed out to you, that this is the Punya Bhumi, the land of Karma. Today I stand here and say, with the conviction of truth, that it is so. If there is any land on this earth that can lay claim to be the blessed Punya Bhumi, to be the land to which soul on this earth must come to account for Karma, the land to which every soul that is wending its way Godward must come to attain its last home, the land where humanity has attained its highest towards gentleness, towards generosity, towards purity, towards calmness, above all, the land of introspection and of spirituality—it is India. Hence have started the founders of religions from the most ancient times, deluging the earth again and again with the pure and perennial waters of spiritual truth. Hence have proceeded the tidal waves of philosophy that have covered the earth, East or West, North or South, and hence again must start the wave which is going to spiritualise the material civilisation of the world. Here is the life-giving water with which must be quenched the burning fire of materialism which is burning the core of the hearts of millions in other lands. Believe me, my friends, this is going to be.

So much I have seen, and so far those of you who are students of the history of races are already aware of this fact. The debt which the world owes to our Motherland is immense. Taking country with country, there is not one race on this earth to which the world owes so much as to the patient Hindu, the mild Hindu. "The mild Hindu" sometimes is used as an expression of reproach; but if ever a reproach concealed a wonderful truth, it is in the term, "the mild Hindu", who has always been the blessed child of God. Civilisations have arisen in other parts of the world. In ancient times and in modern times, great ideas have emanated from strong and great races. In ancient and in modern times, wonderful ideas have been carried forward from one race to another. In ancient and in modern times, seeds of great truth and power have been cast abroad by the advancing tides of national life; but mark you, my friends, it has been always with the blast of war trumpets and with the march of embattled cohorts. Each idea had to be soaked in a deluge of blood. Each idea had to wade through the blood of millions of our fellow-beings. Each word of power had to be followed by the groans of millions, by the wails of orphans, by the tears of widows. This, in the main, other nations have taught; but India has for thousands of years peacefully existed. Here activity prevailed when even Greece did not exist, when Rome was not thought of, when the very fathers of the modern Europeans lived in the forests and painted themselves blue. Even earlier, when history has no record, and tradition dares not peer into the gloom of that intense past, even from then until now, ideas after ideas have marched out from her, but every word has been spoken with a blessing behind it and peace before it. We, of all nations of the world, have never been a conquering race, and that blessing is on our head, and therefore we live.

There was a time when at the sound of the march of big

Greek battalions the earth trembled. Vanished from off the face of the earth, with not even a tale left behind to tell, gone is that ancient land of the Greeks. There was a time when the Roman Eagle floated over everything worth having in this world; everywhere Rome's power was felt and pressed on the head of humanity; the earth trembled at the name of Rome. But the Capitoline Hill is a mass of ruins, the spider weaves its web where the Caesars ruled. There have been other nations equally glorious that have come and gone, living a few hours of exultant and exuberant dominance and of a wicked national life, and then vanishing like ripples on the face of the waters. Thus have these nations made their mark on the face of humanity. But we live, and if Manu came back today he would not be bewildered, and would not find himself in a foreign land. The same laws are here, laws adjusted and thought out through thousands and thousands of years; customs, the outcome of the acumen of ages and the experience of centuries, that seem to be eternal; and as the days go by, as blow after blow of misfortune has been delivered upon them, such blows seem to have served one purpose only, that of making them stronger and more constant. And to find the centre of all this, the heart from which the blood flows, the mainspring of the national life, believe me when I say after my experience of the world, that it is here.

To the other nations of the world, religion is one among the many occupations of life. There is politics, there are the enjoyments of social life, there is all that wealth can buy or power can bring, there is all that the senses can enjoy; and among all these various occupations of life and all this searching after something which can give yet a little more whetting to the cloyed senses—among all these, there is perhaps a little bit of religion. But here, in India, religion is the one and the only occupation of life. How many of you know that there has been a Sino-Japanese War? Very few of you, if any. That there are tremendous political movements and socialistic movements trying to transform Western society, how many of you know? Very few indeed, if any. But that there was a Parliament of Religions in America, and that there was a Hindu Sannyâsin sent over there, I am astonished to find that even the cooly knows of it. That shows the way the wind blows, where the national life is. I used to read books written by globe-trotting travellers, especially foreigners, who deplored the ignorance of the Eastern masses, but I found out that it was partly true and at the same time partly untrue. If you ask a ploughman in England, or America, or France, or Germany to what party he belongs, he can tell you whether he belongs to the Radicals or the Conservatives, and for whom he is going to vote. In America he will say whether he is Republican or Democrat, and he even knows something about the silver question. But if you ask him about his religion, he will tell you that he goes to church and belongs to a certain denomination. That is all he knows, and he thinks it is sufficient.

Now, when we come to India, if you ask one of our ploughmen, "Do you know anything about politics?" He will reply, "What is that?" He does not understand the socialistic movements, the relation between capital and labour, and all that; he has never heard of such things in his life, he works hard and earns his bread. But you ask, "What is your religion?" he replies, "Look here, my friend, I have marked it on my forehead." He can give you a good hint or two on questions of religion. That has been my experience. That is our nation's life.

Individuals have each their own peculiarities, and each man has his own method of growth, his own life marked out for him by the infinite past life, by all his past Karma as we Hindus say. Into this world he comes with all the past on him, the infinite past ushers the present, and the way in which we use the present is going to make the future. Thus everyone born into this world has a bent, a directon towards which he must go, through which he must live, and what is true of the individual is equally true of the race. Each race, similarly, has a peculiar bent, each race has a peculiar *raison d'être,* each race has a peculiar misson to fulfil in the life of the world. Each race has to make its own result, to fulfil its own mission. Political greatness or military power is never the mission of our race; it never was, and, mark my words, it never will be. But there has been the other mission given to us, which is to conserve, to preserve, to accumulate, as it were, into a dynamo, all the spiritual energy of the race, and that concentrated energy is to pour forth in a deluge on the world whenever circumstances are propitious. Let the Persian or the Greek, the Roman, the Arab, or the Englishman march his battalions, conquer the world, and link the different nations together, and the philosophy and spirituality of India is ever ready to flow along the new-made channels into the veins of the nations of the world. The Hindu's calm brain must pour out its own quota to give to the sum total of human progress. India's gift to the world is the light spiritual.

Thus, in the past, we read in history that whenever there arose a great conquering nation uniting the different races of the world, binding India with the other races, taking her out, as it were, from her loneliness and from her aloofness from the rest of the world into which she again and again cast herself, that whenever such a state has been brought about, the result has been the flooding of the world with Indian spiritual ideas. At the beginning of this century, Schopenhauer, the great German philosopher, studying from a not very clear translation of the Vedas made from an old translation into Persian and thence by a young Frenchman into Latin, says, "In the whole world there is no study so beneficial and so elevating as that of the Upanishads. It has been the solace of my life, it will be the solace of my death." This great German sage foretold that "The world is about to see a revolution in thought more extensive and more powerful than that which was witnessed by the Renaissance of Greek Literature", and today his predictions are coming to pass. Those who keep their eyes open, those who understand the workings in the minds of different nations of the West, those who are thinkers and study the different nations, will find the immense change that has been produced in the tone, the procedure, in the methods, and in the literature of the world by this slow, never-ceasing permeation of Indian thought.

But there is another peculiarity, as I have already hinted to you. We never preached our thoughts with fire and sword. If there is one word in the English language to represent the gift of India to the world, if there is one word in the English language to express the effect which the literature of India produces upon mankind, it is this one word, "fascination". It is the opposite of anything that takes you suddenly; it throws on you, as it were, a charm imperceptibly. To many, Indian thought, Indian manners, Indian customs, Indian philosophy, Indian literature are repulsive at the first sight; but let them persevere, let them read, let them become familiar with the great principles underlying these ideas, and it is ninety-nine to one that the charm will come over them, and fascination will be the result. Slow and silent, as the gentle dew that falls in the morning, unseen and unheard yet producing a most tremendous result, has been the work of the calm, patient, all-suffering spiritual race upon the world of thought.

Once more history is going to repeat itself. For today, under the blasting light of modern science, when old and apparently strong and invulnerable beliefs have been shattered to their very foundations, when special claims laid to the allegiance of mankind by different sects have been all blown into atoms and have vanished into air, when the sledge-hammer blows of modern antiquarian researches are pulverising like masses of porcelain all sorts of antiquated orthodoxies, when religion in the West is only in the hands of the ignorant and the knowing ones look down with scorn upon anything belonging to religion, here comes to the fore the philosophy of India, which displays the highest religious aspirations of the Indian mind, where the grandest philosophical facts have been the practical spirituality of the people. This naturally is coming to the rescue, the idea of the oneness of all, the Infinite, the idea of the Impersonal, the wonderful idea of the eternal soul of man, of the unbroken continuity in the march of beings, and the infinity of the universe. The old sects looked upon the world as a little mud-puddle and thought that time began but the other day. It was there in our old books, and only there that the grand idea of the infinite range of time, space, and causation, and above all, the infinite glory of the spirit of man governed all the search for religion. When the modern tremendous theories of evolution and conservation of energy and so forth are dealing death blows to all sorts of crude theologies, what can hold any more the allegiance of cultured humanity but the most wonderful, convincing, broadening, and ennobling ideas that can be found only in that most marvellous product of the soul of man, the wonderful voice of God, the Vedanta?

At the same time, I must remark that what I mean by our religion working upon the nations outside of India comprises only the principles, the backgound, the foundation upon which that religion is built. The detailed workings, the minute points which have been worked out through centuries of social necessity, little ratiocinations about manners and customs and social well-being, do not rightly find a place in the category of religion. We know that in our books a clear distinction is made between two sets of truths. The one set is that which abides for ever, being built upon the nature of man, the nature of the soul, the soul's relation to God, the nature of God, perfection, and so on; there are also the principles of cosmology, of the infinitude of creation, or more correctly speaking—projection, the wonderful law of cyclical procession, and so on—these are the eternal principles founded upon the universal laws in nature. The other set comprises the minor laws which guided the working of our everyday life. They belong more properly to the Purânas, to the Smritis, and not to the Shrutis. These have nothing to do with the other principles. Even in our own nation these minor laws have been changing all the time. Customs of one age, of one Yuga, have not been the customs of another, and as Yuga comes after Yuga, they will still have to change. Great Rishis will appear and lead us to customs and manners that are suited to new environments.

The great principles underlying all this wonderful, infinite, ennobling, expansive view of man and God and the world have been produced in India. In India alone man has not stood up to fight for a little tribal God, saying "My God is true and yours is not true; let us have a good fight over it." It was only here that such ideas did not occur as fighting for little gods. These great underlying principles, being based upon the eternal nature of man, are as potent today for working for the good of the human race as they were thousands of years ago, and they will remain so, so long as this earth remains, so long as the law of Karma remains, so long as we are born as individuals and have to work out our own destiny by our individual power.

And above all, what India has to give to the world is this. If we watch the growth and development of religions in different races, we shall aways find this that each tribe at the beginning has a god of its own. If the tribes are allied to each other, these gods will have a generic name, as for example, all the Babylonian gods had. When the Babylonians were divided into many races, they had the generic name of Baal, just as the Jewish races had different gods with the common name of Moloch; and at the same time you will find that one of these tribes becomes superior to the rest, and lays claim to its own king as the king over all. Therefrom it naturally follows that it also wants to preserve its own god as the god of all the races. Baal-Merodach, said the Babylonians, was the greatest god; all the others were inferior. Moloch-Yahveh was the superior over all other Molochs. And these questions had to be decided by the fortunes of battle. The same struggle was here also. In India the same competing gods had been struggling with each other for supremacy, but the great good fortune of this country and of the world was that there came out in the midst of the din and confusion a voice which declared एकं सद्विप्रा बहुधा वदन्ति—"That which exists is One; sages call It by various names." It is not that Shiva is superior to Vishnu, not that Vishnu is everything and Shiva is nothing, but it is the same one whom you call either Shiva, or Vishnu, or by a hundred other names. The names are different, but it is the same one. The whole history of India you may read in these few words. The whole history has been a repetition in massive language, with tremendous power, of that one central doctrine. It was repeated in the land till it had entered into the blood of the nation, till it began to tingle with every drop of blood that flowed in its veins, till it became one with the life, part and parcel of the material of which it was composed; and thus the land was transmuted into the most wonderful land of toleration, giving the right to welcome the various religions as well as all sects into the old mother-country.

And herein is the explanation of the most remarkable phenomenon that is only witnessed here—all the various sects, apparently hopelessly contradictory, yet living in such harmony. You may be a dualist, and I may be a monist. You may believe that you are the eternal servant of God, and I may declare that I am one with God Himself; yet both of us are good Hindus. How is that possible? Read then एकं सद्विप्रा बहुधा वदन्ति—"That which exists is One; sages call It by various names." Above all others, my countrymen, this is the one grand truth that we have to teach to the world. Even the most educated people of other countries turn up their noses at an angle of forty-five degrees and call our religion idolatry. I have seen that; and they never stopped to think what a mass of superstition there was in their own heads. It is still so everywhere, this tremendous sectarianism, the low narrowness of the mind. The thing which a man has is the only thing worth having;

the only life worth living is his own little life of dollar-worship and mammon-worship; the only little possession worth having is his own property, and nothing else. If he can manufacture a little clay nonsense or invent a machine, that is to be admired beyond the greatest possessions. That is the case over the whole world in spite of education and learning. But education has yet to be in the world, and civilisation—civilisation has begun nowhere yet. Ninety-nine decimal nine per cent of the human race are more or less savages even now. We may read of these things in books, and we hear of toleration in religion and all that, but very little of it is there yet in the world; take my experience for that. Ninety-nine per cent do not even think of it. There is tremendous religious persecution yet in every country in which I have been, and the same old objections are raised against learning anything new. The little toleration that is in the world, the little sympathy that is yet in the world for religious thought, is practically here in the land of the Aryas, and nowhere else. It is here that Indians build temples for Muhammedans and Christians; nowhere else. If you go to other countries and ask Mohammedans or people of other religions to build a temple for you, see how they will help. They will instead try to break down your temple and you too if they can. The one great lesson, therefore, that the world wants most, that the world has yet to learn from India, is the idea not only of toleration, but of sympathy. Well has it been said in the *Mahimanah-stotra*: "As the different rivers, taking their start from different mountains, running straight or crooked, at last come unto the ocean, so, O Shiva, the different paths which men take through different tendencies, various though they appear, crooked or straight, all lead unto Thee." Though they may take various roads, all are on the way. Some may run a little crooked, others may run straight, but at last they will all come unto the Lord, the One. Then and then alone, is your Bhakti of Shiva complete when you not only see Him in the Linga, but you see Him everywhere. He is the sage, he is the lover of Hari who sees Hari in everything and in everyone. If you are a real lover of Shiva, you must see Him in everything and in everyone. You must see that every worship is given unto Him whatever may be the name or the form; that all knees bending towards the Caaba, or kneeling in a Christian church, or in a Buddhist temple are kneeling to Him whether they know it or not, whether they are conscious of it or not; that in whatever name or form they are offered, all these flowers are laid at His feet; for He is the one Lord of all, the one Soul of all souls. He knows infinitely better what this world wants than you or I. It is impossible that all difference can cease; it must exist; without variation life must cease. It is this clash, the differentiation of thought that makes for light, for motion, for everything. Differentiation, infinitely contradictory, must remain, but it is not necessary that we should hate each other therefore; it is not necessary therefore that we should fight each other.

Therefore we have again to learn the one central truth that was preached only here in our Motherland, and that has to be preached once more from India. Why? Because not only is it in our books, but it runs through every phase of our national literature and is in the national life. Here and here alone is it practised every day, and any man whose eyes are open can see that it is practised here and here alone. Thus we have to teach religion. There are other and higher lessons that India can teach, but they are only for the learned. The lessons of mildness, gentleness, forbearance, toleration, sympathy, and brotherhood, everyone may learn, whether man, woman, or child, learned or unlearned, without respect of race, caste, or creed. "They call Thee by various names; Thou art One."

REPLY TO THE ADDRESS OF WELCOME AT RAMNAD

At Ramnad the following address was presented to Swami Vivekananda by the Raja:

His Most Holiness,

Sri Paramahamsa, Yati-Râja, Digvijaya-Kolâhala, Sarvamata-Sampratipanna, Parama-Yogeswara, Srimat Bhagavân Sree Ramakrishna Paramahamsa Karakamala-Sanjâta, Râjâdhirâja-Sevita, SREE VIVEKANANDA SWAMI, MAY IT PLEASE YOUR HOLINESS,

We, the inhabitants of this ancient and historic Samasthânam of Sethu Bandha Rameswaram, otherwise known as Râmanâthapuram or Ramnad, beg, most cordially, to welcome you to this, our motherland. We deem it a very rare privilege to be the first to pay your Holiness our heartfelt homage on your landing in India, and that, on the shores sanctified by the footsteps of that great Hero and our revered Lord—Sree Bhagavân Râmachandra.

We have watched with feelings of genuine pride and pleasure the unprecedented success which has crowned your laudable efforts in bringing home to the master-minds of the West the intrinsic merits and excellence of our time-honoured and noble religion. You have with an eloquence that is unsurpassed and in language plain and unmistakable, proclaimed to and convinced the cultured audiences in Europe and America that Hinduism fulfils all the requirements of the ideal of a universal religion and adapts itself to the temperament and needs of men and women of all races and creeds. Animated purely by a disinterested impulse, influenced by the best of motives and at considerable self-sacrifice, Your Holiness has crossed boundless seas and oceans to convey the message of truth and peace, and to plant the flag of India's spiritual triumph and glory in the rich soil of Europe and America. Your Holiness has, both by precept and practice, shown the feasibility and importance of universal brotherhood. Above all, your labours in the West have indirectly and to a great extent tended to awaken the apathetic sons and daughters of India to a sense of the greatness and glory of their ancestral faith, and to create in them a genuine interest in the study and observance of their dear and priceless religion.

We feel we cannot adequately convey in words our feelings of gratitude and thankfulness to your Holiness for your philanthropic labours towards the spiritual regeneration of the East and the West. We cannot close this address without referring to the great kindness which your Holiness has always extended to our Raja, who is one of your devoted disciples, and the honour and pride he feels by this gracious act of your Holiness in landing first on his territory is indescribable.

In conclusion, we pray to the Almighty to bless your Holiness with long life, and health, and strength to enable you to carry on the good work that has been so ably inaugurated by you.

With respects and love,
We beg to subscribe ourselves,
Your Holiness' most devoted and obedient
DISCIPLES and SERVANTS.

RAMNAD,
25th January, 1897.

The Swami's reply follows *in extenso*:

The longest night seems to be passing away, the sorest trouble seems to be coming to an end at last, the seeming corpse appears to be awaking and a voice is coming to us—away back where history and even tradition fails to peep into the gloom of the past, coming down from there, reflected as it were from peak to peak of the infinite Himalaya of knowledge, and of love, and of work, India, this motherland of ours—a voice is coming unto us, gentle, firm, and yet unmistakable in its utterances, and is gaining volume as days pass by, and behold, the sleeper is awakening! Like a breeze from the Himalayas, it is bringing life into the almost dead bones and muscles, the lethargy is passing away, and only the blind cannot see, or the perverted will not see, that she is awakening, this motherland of ours, from her deep long sleep. None can resist her any more; never is she going to sleep any more; no outward powers can hold her back any more; for the infinite giant is rising to her feet.

Your Highness and gentlemen of Ramnad, accept my heartfelt thanks for the cordiality and kindness with which you have received me. I feel that you are cordial and kind, for heart speaks unto heart better than any language of the mouth; spirit speaks unto spirit in silence, and yet in most unmistakable language, and I feel it in my heart of hearts. Your Highness of Ramnad, if there has been any work done by my humble self in the cause of our religion and our motherland in the Western countries, if any little work has been done in rousing the sympathies of our own people by drawing their attention to the inestimable jewels that, they know not, are lying deep buried about their own home—if, instead of dying of thirst and drinking dirty ditch water elsewhere out of the blindness of ignorance, they are being called to go and drink from the eternal fountain which is flowing perennially by their own home—if anything has been done to rouse our people towards action, to make them understand that in everything, religion and religion alone is the life of India, and when that goes India will die, in spite of politics, in spite of social reforms, in spite of Kubera's wealth poured upon the head of every one of her children—if anything has been done towards this end, India and every country where any work has been done owe much of it to you, Raja of Ramnad. For it was you who gave me the idea first, and it was you who persistently urged me on towards the work. You, as it were, intuitively understood what was going to be, and took me by the hand, helped me all along, and have never ceased to encourage me. Well is it, therefore, that you should be the first to rejoice at my success, and meet it is that I should first land in your territory on my return to India.

Great works are to be done, wonderful powers have to be worked out, we have to teach other nations many things, as has been said already by your Highness. This is the motherland of philosophy, of spirituality, and of ethics, of sweetness, gentleness, and love. These still exist, and my experience of the world leads me to stand on firm ground and make the bold statement that India is still the first and foremost of all the nations of the world in these respects. Look at this little phenomenon. There have been immense political changes within the last four or five years. Gigantic organisations undertaking to subvert the whole of existing institutions in different countries and meeting with a certain amount of success have been working all over the Western world. Ask our people if they have heard anything about them. They have heard not a word about them. But that there was a Parliament of Religions in Chicago, and that there was a Sannyâsin sent over from India to that Parliament, and that he was very well received and since that time has been working in the West, the poorest beggar has known. I have heard it said that our masses are dense, that they do not want any education, and that they do not care for any information. I had at one time a foolish leaning towards that opinion myself, but I find experience is a far more glorious teacher than any amount of speculation, or any amount of books written by globe-trotters and hasty observers. This experience teaches me that they are not dense, that they are not slow, that they are as eager and thirsty for information as any race under the sun; but then each nation has its own part to play, and naturally, each nation has its own peculiarity and individuality with which it is born. Each represents, as it were, one peculiar note in this harmony of nations, and this is its very life, its vitality. In it is the backbone, the foundation, and the bed-rock of the national life, and here in this blessed land, the foundation, the backbone, the life-centre is religion and religion alone. Let others talk of politics, of the glory of acquisition of immense wealth poured in by trade, of the power and spread of commercialism, of the glorious fountain of physical liberty; but these the Hindu mind does not understand and does not want to understand. Touch him on spirituality, on religion, on God, on the soul, on the Infinite, on spiritual freedom, and I assure you, the lowest peasant in India is better informed on these subjects than many a so-called philosopher in other lands. I have said, gentlemen, that we have yet something to teach to the world. This is the very reason, the *raison d'être,* that this nation has lived on, in spite of hundreds of years of persecution, in spite of nearly a thousand year of foreign rule and foreign oppression. This nation still lives; the *raison d'être* is it still holds to God, to the treasure-house of religion and spirituality.

In this land are, still, religion and spirituality, the fountains which will have to overflow and flood the world to bring in new life and new vitality to the Western and other nations, which are now almost borne down, half-killed, and degraded by political ambitions and social scheming. From out of many voices, consonant and dissentient, from out of the medley of sounds filling the Indian atmosphere, rises up supreme, striking, and full, one note, and that is renunciation. Give up! That is the watchword of the Indian religions. This world is a delusion of two days. The present life is of five minutes. Beyond is the Infinite, beyond this world of delusion; let us seek that. This continent is illumined with brave and gigantic minds and intelligences which even think of this so-called infinite universe as only a mud-puddle; beyond and still beyond they go. Time, even infinite time, is to them but non-existence. Beyond and beyond time they go. Space is nothing to them; beyond that they want to go, and this going beyond the phenomenal is the very soul of religion. The characteristic of my nation is this transcendentalism, this struggle to go beyond, this daring to tear the veil off the face of nature and have at any risk, at any price, a glimpse of the beyond. That is our ideal, but of course all the people in a country cannot give up entirely. Do you want to enthuse them, then here is the way to do so. Your talks of politics, of social regeneration, your talks of money-making and commercialism—all these will roll off like water from a duck's back. This spirituality, then, is what you have to teach the world. Have we to learn anything else, have we to learn anything from the world? We have, perhaps, to gain a little in material knowledge, in the power of organisation, in the ability to handle powers, organising powers, in bringing the best results out of the smallest of causes. This perhaps to a certain extent we may learn from the West. But if any one preaches in India the ideal of eating and drinking and making merry, if any one wants to apotheosise the material world into a God, that man is a liar; he has no place in this holy land, the Indian mind does not want to listen to him. Ay, in spite of the sparkle and glitter of Western civilisation, in spite of all its polish and its marvellous manifestation of power, standing upon this platform, I tell them to their face that it is all vain. It is vanity of vanities. God alone lives. The soul alone lives. Spirituality alone lives. Hold on to that.

Yet, perhaps, some sort of materialism, toned down to our own requirements, would be a blessing to many of our brothers who are not yet ripe for the highest truths. This is the mistake made in every country and in every society, and it is a greatly regrettable thing that in India, where it was always understood, the same mistake of forcing the highest truths on people who are not ready for them has been made of late. My method need not be yours. The Sannyasin, as you all know, is the ideal of the Hindu's life, and every one by our Shâstras is compelled to give up. Every Hindu who has tasted the fruits of this world must give up in the latter part of his life, and he who does not is not a Hindu and has no more right to call himself a Hindu. We know that this is the ideal—to give up after seeing and experiencing the vanity of things. Having found out that the heart of the material world is a mere hollow, containing only ashes, give it up and go back. The mind is circling forward, as it were, towards the senses, and that mind has to circle backwards; the Pravritti has to stop and the Nivritti has to begin. That is the ideal. But that ideal can only be realised after a certain amount of experience. We cannot teach the child the truth of renunciation; the child is a born optimist; his whole life is in his senses; his whole life is one mass of sense-enjoyment. So there are childlike men in every society who require a certain amount of experience, of enjoyment, to see through the vanity of it, and then renunciation will come to them. There has been ample provision made for them in our Books; but unfortunately, in later times, there has been a tendency to bind every one down by the same laws as those by which the Sannyasin is bound, and that is a great mistake. But for that a good deal of the poverty and the misery that you see in India need not have been. A poor man's life is hemmed in and bound down by tremendous spiritual and ethical laws for which he has no use. Hands off! Let the poor fellow enjoy himself a little, and then he will raise himself up, and renunciation will come to him of itself. Perhaps in this line, we can be taught something by the Western people; but we must be very cautious in learning these things. I am sorry to say that most of the examples one meets nowadays of men who have imbibed the Western ideas are more or less failures.

There are two great obstacles on our path in India, the Scylla of old orthodoxy and the Charybdis of modern European civilisation. Of these two, I vote for the old orthodoxy, and not for the Europeanised system; for the old orthodox man may be ignorant, he may be crude, but he is a man, he has a faith, he has strength, he stands on his own feet; while the Europeanised man has no backbone, he is a mass of heterogeneous ideas picked up at random from every source—and these ideas are unassimilated, undigested, unharmonised. He does not stand on his own feet, and his head is turning round and round. Where is the motive power of his work?—in a few patronising pats from the English people. His schemes of reforms, his vehement vituperations against the evils of certain social customs, have, as the mainspring, some European patronage. Why are some of our customs called evils? Because the Europeans say so. That is about the reason he gives. I would not submit to that. Stand and die in your own strength; if there is any sin in the world, it is weakness; avoid all weakness, for weakness is sin, weakness is death. These unbalanced creatures are not yet formed into distinct personalities; what are we to call them—men, women, or animals? While those old orthodox people were staunch and were men. There are still some excellent examples, and the one I want to present before you now is your Raja of Ramnad. Here you have a man than whom there is no more zealous a Hindu throughout the length and breadth of this land; here you have a prince than whom there is no prince in this land better informed in all affairs, both oriental and occidental, who takes from every nation whatever he can that is good. "Learn good knowledge with all devotion from the lowest caste. Learn the way to freedom, even if it comes from a Pariah, by serving him. If a woman is a jewel, take her in marriage even if she comes from a low family of the lowest caste." Such is the law laid down by our great and peerless legislator, the divine Manu. This is true. Stand on your own feet, and assimilate what you can; learn from every nation, take what is of use to you. But remember that as Hindus everything else must be subordinated to our own national ideals. Each man has a mission in life, which is the result of all his infinite past Karma. Each of you was born with a splendid heritage, which is the whole of the infinite past life of your glorious nation. Millions of your ancestors are watching, at it were, every action of yours, so be alert. And what is the mission with which every Hindu child is born? Have you not read the proud declaration of Manu regarding the Brâhmin where he says that the birth of the Brahmin is "for the protection of the treasury of religion"? I should say that *that* is the mission not only of the Brahmin, but of every child, whether boy or girl, who is born in this blessed land "for the protection of the treasury of religion". And every other problem in life must be subordinated to that one principal theme. That is also the law of harmony in music. There may be a nation whose theme of life is political supremacy; religion and everything else must become subordinate to that one great theme of its life. But here is another nation whose great theme of life is spirituality and renunciation, whose one watchword is that this world is all vanity and a delusion of three days, and everything else, whether science or knowledge, enjoyment or powers, wealth, name, or fame, must be subordinated to that one theme. The secret of a true Hindu's character lies in the subordination of his knowledge of European sciences and learning, of his wealth, position, and name, to that one principal theme which is inborn in every Hindu child—the spirituality and purity of the race. Therefore between these two, the case of the orthodox man who has the whole of that life-spring of the race, spirituality, and the other man whose hands are full of Western imitation-jewels but has no hold on the life-giving principle, spirituality—of these, I do not doubt that every one here will agree that we should choose the first, the orthodox, because there is some hope in him—he has the national theme, something to hold to; so he will live, but the other will die. Just as in the case of individuals, if the principle of life is undisturbed, if the principal function of that individual life is present, any injuries received as regards other functions are not serious, do not kill the individual, so, as long as this principal function of our life is not disturbed, nothing can destroy our nation. But mark you, if you give up that spirituality, leaving it aside to go after the materialising civilisation of the West, the result will be that in three generations you will be an extinct race; because the backbone of the nation will be broken, the foundation upon which the national edifice has been built will be undermined, and the result will be annihilation all round.

Therefore, my friends, the way out is that first and foremost we must keep a firm hold on spirituality—that inestimable gift handed down to us by our ancient forefathers. Did you ever hear of a country where the greatest kings tried to trace their descent not to kings, not to robber-barons living in old castles who plundered poor travellers, but to semi-naked sages who lived in the forest? Did you ever hear of such a land? This is the land. In other countries great priests try to trace their descent to some king, but here the greatest kings would trace their descent to some ancient priest. Therefore, whether you believe in spirituality or not, for the sake of the national life, you have to get a hold on spirituality and keep to it. Then stretch the other hand out and gain all you can from other races, but everything must be subordinated to that one ideal of life; and out of that a wonderful, glorious, future India will come—I am sure it is coming—a greater India than ever was. Sages will spring up greater than all the ancient sages; and your ancestors will not only be satisfied, but I am sure, they will be proud from their positions in other worlds to look down upon their descendants, so glorious, and so great.

Let us all work hard, my brethren; this is no time for sleep. On our work depends the coming of the India of the future. She is there ready waiting. She is only sleeping. Arise and awake and see her seated here on her eternal throne, rejuvenated, more glorious than she ever was—this motherland of ours. The idea of God was nowhere else ever so fully developed as in this motherland of ours, for the same idea of God never existed anywhere else. Perhaps you are astonished at my assertion; but show me any idea of God from any other scripture equal to ours; they have only clan-Gods, the God of the Jews, the God of the Arabs, and of such and such a race, and their God is fighting the Gods of the other races. But the idea of that beneficent, most merciful God, our father, our mother, our friend, the friend of our friends, the soul of our souls, is here and here alone. And may He who is the Shiva of the Shaivites, the Vishnu of the Vaishnavites, the Karma of the Karmis, the Buddha of the Buddhists, the Jina of the Jains, the Jehovah of the Christians and the Jews, the Allah of the Mohammedans, the Lord of every sect, the Brahman of the Vedantists, He the all-pervading, whose glory has been known only in this land—may He bless us, may He help us, may He give strength unto us, energy unto us, to carry this idea into practice. May that which we have listened to and studied become food to us, may it become strength in us, may it become energy in us to help each other; may we, the teacher and the taught, not be jealous of each other! Peace, peace, peace, in the name of Hari!

THE MISSION OF THE VEDANTA

On the occasion of his visit to Kumbakonam, the Swamiji was presented with the following address by the local Hindu community:

REVERED SWAMIN,

On behalf of the Hindu inhabitants of this ancient and religiously important town of Kumbakonam, we request permission to offer you a most hearty welcome on your return from the Western World to our own holy land of great temples and famous saints and sages. We are highly thankful to God for the remarkable success of your religious mission in America and in Europe, and for His having enabled you to impress upon the choicest representatives of the world's great religions assembled at Chicago that both the Hindu philosophy and religion are so broad and so rationally catholic as to have in them the power to exalt and to harmonise all ideas of God and of human spirituality.

The conviction that the cause of Truth is always safe in the hands of Him who is the life and soul of the universe has been for thousands of years part of our living faith; and if today we rejoice at the results of your holy work in Christian lands, it is because the eyes of men in and outside of India are thereby being opened to the inestimable value of the *spiritual* heritage of the *pre-eminently religious* Hindu nation. The success of your work has naturally added great lustre to the already renowned name of your great Guru; it has also raised us in the estimation of the civilised world; more than all, it has made us feel that we too, as a people, have reason to be proud of the achievements of our past, and that the absence of telling aggressiveness in our civilisation is in no way a sign of its exhausted or decaying condition. With clear-sighted, devoted, and altogether unselfish workers like you in our midst, the future of the Hindu nation cannot but be bright and hopeful. May the God of the universe who is also the great God of all nations bestow on you health and long life, and make you increasingly strong and wise in the discharge of your high and noble function as a worthy teacher of Hindu religion and philosophy.

A second address was also presented by the Hindu students of the town.

The Swami then delivered the following address on the Mission of the Vedanta:

A very small amount of religious work performed brings a large amount of result. If this statement of the Gitâ wanted an illustration, I am finding every day the truth of that great saying in my humble life. My work has been very insignificant indeed, but the kindness and the cordiality of welcome that have met me at every step of my journey from Colombo to this city are simply beyond all expectation. Yet, at the same time, it is worthy of our traditions as Hindus, it is worthy of our race; for here we are, the Hindu race, whose vitality, whose life-principle, whose very soul, as it were, is in religion. I have seen a little of the world, travelling among the races of the East and the West; and everywhere I find among nations one great ideal which forms the backbone, so to speak, of that race. With some it is politics, with others it is social culture; others again may have intellectual culture and so on for their national background. But this, our motherland, has religion and religion alone for its basis, for its backbone, for the bed-rock upon which the whole building of its life has been based. Some of you may remember that in my reply to the kind address which the people of Madras sent over to me in America, I pointed out the fact that a peasant in India has, in many respects, a better religious education than many a gentleman in the West, and today, beyond all doubt, I myself am verifying my own words. There was a time when I did feel rather discontented at the want of information among the masses of India and the lack of thirst among them for information, but now I understand it. Where their interest lies, there they are more eager for information than the masses of any other race that I have seen or have travelled among. Ask our peasants about the momentous political changes in Europe, the upheavals that are going on in European society—they do not know anything of them, nor do they care to know; but the peasants, even in Ceylon, detached from India in many ways, cut off from a living interest in India—I found the very peasants working in the fields there were already acquainted with the fact that there had been a Parliament of Religions in America, that an Indian Sannyâsin had gone over there, and that he had had some success.

Where, therefore, their interest is, there they are as eager for information as any other race; and religion is the one and sole interest of the people of India. I am not just now discussing whether it is good to have the vitality of the race in religious ideals or in political ideals, but so far it is clear to us that, for good or for evil, our vitality is concentrated in our religion. You cannot change it. You cannot destroy it and put in its place another. You cannot transplant a large growing tree from one soil to another and make it immediately take root there. For good or for evil, the religious ideal has been flowing into India for thousands of years; for good or for evil, the Indian atmosphere has been filled with ideals of religion for shining scores of centuries; for good or for evil, we have been born and brought up in the very midst of these ideas of religion, till it has entered into our very blood and tingled with every drop in our veins, and has become one with our constitution, become the very vitality of our lives. Can you give such religion up without the rousing of the same energy in reaction, without filling the channel which that mighty river has cut out for itself in the course of thousands of years? Do you want that the Gangâ should go back to its icy bed and begin a new course? Even if that were possible, it would be impossible for this country to give up her characteristic course of religious life and take up for herself a new career of politics or something else. You can work only under the law of least resistance, and this religious line is the line of least resistance in India. This is the line of life, this is the line of growth, and this is the line of well-being in India—to follow the track of religion.

Ay, in other countries religion is only one of the many necessities in life. To use a common illustration which I am in the habit of using, my lady has many things in her parlour, and it is the fashion nowadays to have a Japanese vase, and she must procure it; it does not look well to be without it. So my lady, or my gentleman, has many other occupations in life, and also a little bit of religion must come in to complete it. Consequently he or she has a little religion. Politics, social improvement, in one word, this world, is the goal of mankind in the West, and God and religion come in quietly as helpers to attain that goal. Their God is, so to speak, the Being who helps to cleanse and to furnish this world for them; that is apparently all the value of God for them. Do you not know how for the last hundred or two hundred years you have been hearing again and again out of the lips of men who ought to have known better, from the mouths of those who pretend at least to know better, that all the arguments they produce against the Indian religion is this—that our religion does not conduce to well-being in this world, that it does not bring gold to us, that it does not make us robbers of nations, that it does not make the strong stand upon the bodies of the weak and feed themselves with the life-blood of the weak. Certainly our religion does not do that. It cannot send cohorts, under whose feet the earth trembles, for the purpose of destruction and pillage and the ruination of races. Therefore they say—what is there in this religion? It does not bring any grist to the grinding mill, any strength to the muscles; what is there in such a religion?

They little dream that that is the very argument with which we prove our religion, because it does not make for this world. Ours is the only true religion because, according to it, this little sense-world of three days' duration is not to be made the end and aim of all, is not to be our great goal. This little earthly horizon of a few feet is not that which bounds the view of our religion. Ours is away beyond, and still beyond; beyond the senses, beyond space, and beyond time, away, away beyond, till nothing of this world is left and the universe itself becomes like a drop in the transcendent ocean of the glory of the soul. Ours is the true religion because it teaches that God alone is true, that this world is false and fleeting, that all your gold is but as dust, that all your power is finite, and that life itself is oftentimes an evil; therefore it is, that ours is the true religion. Ours is the true religion because, above all, it teaches renunciation and stands up with the wisdom of ages to tell and to declare to the nations who are mere children of yesterday in comparison with us Hindus—who own the hoary antiquity of the wisdom, discovered by our ancestors here in India—to tell them in plain words: "Children, you are slaves of the senses; there is only finiteness in the senses, there is only ruination in the senses; the three short days of luxury here bring only ruin at last. Give it all up, renounce the love of the senses and of the world; that is the way of religion." Through renunciation is the way to the goal and not through enjoyment. Therefore ours is the only true religion.

Ay, it is a curious fact that while nations after nations have come upon the stage of the world, played their parts vigorously for a few moments, and died almost without leaving a mark or a ripple on the ocean of time, here we are living, as it were, an eternal life. They talk a great deal of the new theories about the survival of the fittest, and they think that it is the strength of the muscles which is the fittest to survive. If that were true, any one of the aggressively known old world nations would have lived in glory today, and we, the weak Hindus, who never conquered even one other race or nation, ought to have died out; yet we live here three hundred million strong! (A young English lady once told me: What have the Hindus done? They never even conquered a single race!) And it is not at all true that all its energies are spent, that atrophy has overtaken its body: that is not true. There is vitality enough, and it comes out in torrents and deluges the world when the time is ripe and requires it.

We have, as it were, thrown a challenge to the whole world from the most ancient times. In the West, they are trying to solve the problem how much a man can possess, and we are trying here to solve the problem on how little a man can live. This struggle and this difference will still go on for some centuries. But if history has any truth in it and if prognostications ever prove true, it must be that those who train themselves to live on the least and control themselves well will in the end gain the battle, and that those who run after enjoyment and luxury, however vigorous they may seem for the moment, will have to die and become annihilated. There are times in the history of a man's life, nay, in the history of the lives of nations, when a sort of world-weariness becomes painfully predominant. It seems that such a tide of world-weariness has come upon the Western world. There, too, they have their thinkers, great men; and they are already finding out that this race after gold and power is all vanity of vanities; many, nay, most of the cultured men and women there, are already weary of this competition, this struggle, this brutality of their commercial civilisation, and they are looking forward towards something better. There is a class which still clings on to political and social changes as the only panacea for the evils in Europe, but among the great thinkers there, other ideals are growing. They have found out that no amount of political or social manipulation of human conditions can cure the evils of life. It is a change of the soul itself for the better that alone will cure the evils of life. No amount of force, or government, or legislative cruelty will change the conditions of a race, but it is spiritual culture and ethical culture alone that can change wrong racial tendencies for the better. Thus these races of the West are eager for some new thought, for some new philosophy; the religion they have had, Christianity, although good and glorious in many respects, has been imperfectly understood, and is, as understood hitherto, found to be insufficient. The thoughtful men of the West find in our ancient philosophy, especially in the Vedanta, the new impulse of thought they are seeking, the very spiritual food and drink for which they are hungering and thirsting. And it is no wonder that this is so.

I have become used to hear all sorts of wonderful claims put forward in favour of every religion under the sun. You have also heard, quite within recent times, the claims put forward by Dr. Barrows, a great friend of mine, that Christianity is the only universal religion. Let me consider this question awhile and lay before you my reasons why I think that it is Vedanta, and Vedanta alone that can become the universal religion of man, and that no other is fitted for the role. Excepting our own almost all the other great religions in the world are inevitably connected with the life or lives of one or more of their founders. All their theories, their teachings, their doctrines, and their ethics are built round the life of a personal founder, from whom they get their sanction, their authority, and their power; and strangely enough, upon the historicity of the founder's life is built, as it were, all the fabric of such religions. If there is one blow dealt to the historicity of that life, as has been the case in modern times with the lives of almost all the so-called founders of religion—we know that half of the details of such lives is not now seriously believed in, and that the other half is seriously doubted—if this becomes the case, if that rock of historicity, as they pretend to call it, is shaken and shattered, the whole building tumbles down, broken absolutely, never to regain its lost status.

Every one of the great religions in the world excepting our own, is built upon such historical characters; but ours rests upon principles. There is no man or woman who can claim to have created the Vedas. They are the embodiment of eternal principles; sages discovered them; and now and then the names of these sages are mentioned—just their names; we do not even know who or what they were. In many cases we do not know who their fathers were, and almost in every case we do not know when and where they were born. But what cared they, these sages, for their names? They were the preachers of principles, and they themselves, so far as they went, tried to become illustrations of the principles they preached. At the same time, just as our God is an Impersonal and yet a Personal God, so is our religion a most intensely impersonal one—a religion based upon principles—and yet with an infinite scope for the play of persons; for what religion gives you more Incarnations, more prophets and seers, and still waits for infinitely more? The *Bhâgavata* says that Incarnations are infinite, leaving ample scope for as many as you like to come. Therefore if any one or more of these persons in India's religious history, any one or more of these Incarnations, and any one or more of our prophets are proved not to have been historical, it does not injure our religion at all; even then it remains firm as ever, because it is based upon principles, and not upon persons. It is in vain we try to gather all the peoples of the world around a single personality. It is difficult to make them gather together even round eternal and universal principles. If it ever becomes possible to bring the largest portion of humanity to one way of thinking in regard to religion, mark you, it must be always through principles and not through persons. Yet as I have said, our religion has ample scope for the authority and influence of persons. There is that most wonderful theory of Ishta which gives you the fullest and the freest choice possible among these great religious personalities. You may take up any one of the prophets or teachers as your guide and the object of your special adoration; you are even allowed to think that he whom you have chosen is the greatest of the prophets, greatest of all the Avatâras; there is no harm in that, but you must keep to a firm background of eternally true principles. The strange fact here is that the power of our Incarnations has been holding good with us only so far as they are illustrations of the principles in the Vedas. The glory of Shri Krishna is that he has been the best preacher of our eternal religion of principles and the best commentator on the Vedanta that ever lived in India.

The second claim of the Vedanta upon the attention of the world is that, of all the scriptures in the world, it is the one scripture the teaching of which is in entire harmony with the results that have been attained by the modern scientific investigations of external nature. Two minds in the dim past of history, cognate to each other in form and kinship and sympathy, started, being placed in different routes. The one was the ancient Hindu mind, and the other the ancient Greek mind. The former started by analysing the internal world. The latter started in search of that goal beyond by analysing the external world. And even through the various vicissitudes of their history, it is easy to make out these two vibrations of thought as tending to produce similar echoes of the goal beyond. It seems clear that the conclusions of modern materialistic science can be acceptable, harmoniously with their religion, only to the Vedantins or Hindus as they are called. It seems clear that modern materialism can hold its own and at the same time approach spirituality by taking up the conclusions of the Vedanta. It seems to us, and to all who care to know, that the conclusions of modern science are the very conclusions the Vedanta reached ages ago; only, in modern science they are written in the language of matter. This then is another claim of the Vedanta upon modern Western minds, its rationality, the wonderful rationalism of the Vedanta. I have myself been told by some of the best Western scientific minds of the day, how wonderfully rational the conclusions of the Vedanta are. I know one of them personally who scarcely has time to eat his meal or go out of his laboratory, but who yet would stand by the hour to attend my lectures on the Vedanta; for, as he expresses it, they are so scientific, they so exactly harmonise with the aspirations of the age and with the conclusions to which modern science is coming at the present time.

Two such scientific conclusions drawn from comparative religion, I would specially like to draw your attention to: the one bears upon the idea of the universality of religions, and the other on the idea of the oneness of things. We observe in the histories of Babylon and among the Jews an interesting religious phenomenon happening. We find that each of these Babylonian and Jewish peoples was divided into so many tribes, each tribe having a god of its own, and that these little tribal gods had often a generic name. The gods among the

Babylonians were all called Baals, and among them Baal Merodach was the chief. In course of time one of these many tribes would conquer and assimilate the other racially allied tribes, and the natural result would be that the god of the conquering tribe would be placed at the head of all the gods of the other tribes. Thus the so-called boasted monotheism of the Semites was created. Among the Jews the gods went by the name of Molochs. Of these there was one Moloch who belonged to the tribe called Israel, and he was called the Moloch-Yahveh or Moloch-Yava. In time, this tribe of Israel slowly conquered some of the other tribes of the same race, destroyed their Molochs, and declared its own Moloch to be the Supreme Moloch of all the Molochs. And I am sure, most of you know the amount of bloodshed, of tyranny, and of brutal savagery that this religious conquest entailed. Later on, the Babylonians tried to destroy this supremacy of Moloch-Yahveh, but could not succeed in doing so.

It seems to me, that such an attempt at tribal self-assertion in religious matters might have taken place on the frontiers and India also. Here, too, all the various tribes of the Aryans might have come into conflict with one another for declaring the supremacy of their several tribal gods; but India's history was to be otherwise, was to be different from that of the Jews. India alone was to be, of all lands, the land of toleration and of spirituality; and therefore the fight between tribes and their gods did not long take place here. For one of the greatest sages that was ever born found out here in India even at that distant time, which history cannot reach, and into whose gloom even tradition itself dares not peep—in that distant time the sage arose and declared, एकं सद्व विप्रा बहुधा वदन्ति—"He who exists is one; the sages call Him variously." This is one of the most memorable sentences that was ever uttered, one of the grandest truths that was ever discovered. And for us Hindus this truth has been the very backbone of our national existence. For throughout the vistas of the centuries of our national life, this one idea—एकं सद्व विप्रा बहुधा वदन्ति—comes down, gaining in volume and in fullness till it has permeated the whole of our national existence, till it has mingled in our blood, and has become one with us. We live that grand truth in every vein, and our country has become the glorious land of religious toleration. It is here and here alone that they build temples and churches for the religions which have come with the object of condemning our own religion. This is one very great principle that the world is waiting to learn from us. Ay, you little know how much of intolerance is yet abroad. It struck me more than once that I should have to leave my bones on foreign shores owing to the prevalence of religious intolerance. Killing a man is nothing for religion's sake; tomorrow they may do it in the very heart of the boasted civilisation of the West, if today they are not really doing so. Outcasting in its most horrible forms would often come down upon the head of a man in the West if he dared to say a word against his country's accepted religion. They talk glibly and smoothly here in criticism of our caste laws. If you go to the West and live there as I have done, you will know that even some of the biggest professors you hear of are arrant cowards and dare not say, for fear of public opinion, a hundredth part of what they hold to be really true in religious matters.

Therefore the world is waiting for this grand idea of universal toleration. It will be a great acquisition to civilisation. Nay, no civilisation can long exist unless this idea enters into it. No civilisation can grow unless fanaticism, bloodshed, and brutality stop. No civilisation can begin to lift up its head until we look charitably upon one another; and the first step towards that much-needed charity is to look charitably and kindly upon the religious convictions of others. Nay more, to understand that not only should we be charitable, but positively helpful to each other, however different our religious ideas and convictions may be. And that is exactly what we do in India as I have just related to you. It is here in India that Hindus have built and are still building churches for Christians and mosques for Mohammedans. That is the thing to do. In spite of their hatred, in spite of their brutality, in spite of their cruelty, in spite of their tyranny, and in spite of the vile language they are given to uttering, we will and must go on building churches for the Christians and mosques for the Mohammedans until we conquer through love, until we have demonstrated to the world that love alone is the fittest thing to survive and not hatred, that it is gentleness that has the strength to live on and to fructify, and not mere brutality and physical force.

The other great idea that the world wants from us today,

the thinking part of Europe, nay, the whole world—more, perhaps, the lower classes than the higher, more the masses than the cultured, more the ignorant than the educated, more the weak than the strong—is that eternal grand idea of the spiritual oneness of the whole universe. I need not tell you today, men from Madras University, how the modern researches of the West have demonstrated through physical means the oneness and the solidarity of the whole universe; how, physically speaking, you and I, the sun, moon, and stars are but little waves or wavelets in the midst of an infinite ocean of matter; how Indian psychology demonstrated ages ago that, similarly, both body and mind are but mere names or little wavelets in the ocean of matter, the Samasthi; and how, going one step further, it is also shown in the Vedanta that behind that idea of the unity of the whole show, the real Soul is one. There is but one Soul throughout the universe, all is but one Existence. This great idea of the real and basic solidarity of the whole universe has frightened many, even in this country. It even now finds sometimes more opponents than adherents. I tell you, nevertheless, that it is the one great life-giving idea which the world wants from us today, and which the mute masses of India want for their uplifting, for none can regenerate this land of ours without the practical application and effective operation of this ideal of the oneness of things.

The rational West is earnestly bent upon seeking out the rationality, the *raison d' être* of all its philosophy and its ethics; and you all know well that ethics cannot be derived from the mere sanction of any personage, however great and divine he may have been. Such an explanation of the authority of ethics appeals no more to the highest of the world's thinkers; they want something more than human sanction for ethical and moral codes to be binding, they want some eternal principle of truth as the sanction of ethics. And where is that eternal sanction to be found except in the only Infinite Reality that exists in you and in me and in all, in the Self, in the Soul? The infinite oneness of the Soul is the eternal sanction of all morality, that you and I are not only brothers—every literature voicing man's struggle towards freedom has preached that for you—but that you and I are really one. This is the dictate of Indian philosophy. This oneness is the rationale of all ethics and all spirituality. Europe wants it today just as much as our downtrodden masses do, and this great principle is even now unconsciously forming the basis of all the latest political and social aspirations that are coming up in England, in Germany, in France, and in America. And mark it, my friends, that in and through all the literature voicing man's struggle towards freedom, towards universal freedom, again and again you find the Indian Vedantic ideals coming out prominently. In some cases the writers do not know the source of their inspiration, in some cases they try to appear very original, and a few there are, bold and grateful enough to mention the source and acknowledge their indebtedness to it.

When I was in America, I heard once the complaint made that I was preaching too much of Advaita, and too little of dualism. Ay, I know what grandeur, what oceans of love, what infinite, ecstatic blessings and joy there are in the dualistic love-theories of worship and religion. I know it all. But this is not the time with us to weep even in joy; we have had weeping enough; no more is this the time for us to become soft. This softness has been with us till we have become like masses of cotton and are dead. What our country now wants are muscles of iron and nerves of steel, gigantic wills which nothing can resist, which can penetrate into the mysteries and the secrets of the universe, and will accomplish their purpose in any fashion even if it meant going down to the bottom of the ocean and meeting death face to face. That is what we want, and that can only be created, established, and strengthened by understanding and realising the ideal of the Advaita, that ideal of the oneness of all. Faith, faith, faith in ourselves, faith, faith in God—this is the secret of greatness. If you have faith in all the three hundred and thirty millions of your mythological gods, and in all the gods which foreigners have now and again introduced into your midst, and still have no faith in yourselves, there is no salvation for you. Have faith in yourselves, and stand up on that faith and be strong; that is what we need. Why is it that we three hundred and thirty millions of people have been ruled for the last one thousand years by any and every handful of foreigners who chose to walk over our prostrate bodies? Because they had faith in themselves and we had not. What did I learn in the West, and what did I see behind those frothy sayings of the Christian sects repeating that man was a fallen and hopelessly fallen sinner? There

I saw that inside the national hearts of both Europe and America reside the tremendous power of the men's faith in themselves. An English boy will tell you, "I am an Englishman, and I can do anything." The American boy will tell you the same thing, and so will any European boy. Can our boys say the same thing here? No, nor even the boy's fathers. We have lost faith in ourselves. Therefore to preach the Advaita aspect of the Vedanta is necessary to rouse up the hearts of men, to show them the glory of their souls. It is, therefore, that I preach this Advaita; and I do so not as a sectarian, but upon universal and widely acceptable grounds.

It is easy to find out the way of reconciliation that will not hurt the dualist or the qualified monist. There is not one system in India which does not hold the doctrine that God is within, that Divinity resides within all things. Every one of our Vedantic systems admits that all purity and perfection and strength are in the soul already. According to some, this perfection sometimes becomes, as it were, contracted, and at other times it becomes expanded again. Yet it is there. According to the Advaita, it neither contracts nor expands, but becomes hidden and uncovered now and again. Pretty much the same thing in effect. The one may be a more logical statement than the other, but as to the result, the practical conclusions, both are about the same; and this is the one central idea which the world stands in need of, and nowhere is the want more felt than in this, our own motherland.

Ay, my friends, I must tell you a few harsh truths. I read in the newspaper how, when one of our fellows is murdered or ill-treated by an Englishman, howls go up all over the country; I read and I weep, and the next moment comes to my mind the question: Who is responsible for it all? As a Vedantist I cannot but put that question to myself. The Hindu is a man of introspection; he wants to see things in and through himself, through the subjective vision. I, therefore, ask myself: Who is responsible? And the answer comes every time: Not the English; no, they are not responsible; it is we who are responsible for all our misery and all our degradation, and we alone are responsible. Our aristocratic ancestors went on treading the common masses of our country underfoot, till they became helpless, till under this torment the poor, poor people nearly forgot that they were human beings. They have been compelled to be merely hewers of wood and drawers of water for centuries, so much so, that they are made to believe that they are born as slaves, born as hewers of wood and drawers of water. With all our boasted education of modern times, if anybody says a kind word for them, I often find our men shrink at once from the duty of lifting them up, these poor down-trodden people. Not only so, but I also find that all sorts of most demoniacal and brutal arguments, culled from the crude ideas of hereditary transmission and other such gibberish from the Western world, are brought forward in order to brutalise and tyrannise over the poor all the more. At the Parliament of Religions in America, there came among others a young man, a born Negro, a real African Negro, and he made a beautiful speech. I became interested in the young man and now and then talked to him, but could learn nothing about him. But one day in England, I met some Americans; and this is what they told me. This boy was the son of a Negro chief who lived in the heart of Africa, and that one day another chief became angry with the father of this boy and murdered him and murdered the mother also, and they were cooked and eaten; he ordered the child to be killed also and cooked and eaten; but the boy fled, and after passing through great hardships and having travelled a distance of several hundreds of miles, he reached the sea-shore, and there he was taken into an American vessel and brought over to America. And this boy made that speech! After that, what was I to think of your doctrine of heredity!

Ay, Brâhmins, if the Brahmin has more aptitude for learning on the ground of heredity than the Pariah, spend no more money on the Brahmin's education, but spend all on the Pariah. Give to the weak, for there all the gift is needed. If the Brahmin is born clever, he can educate himself without help. If the others are not born clever, let them have all the teaching and the teachers they want. This is justice and reason as I understand it. Our poor people, these downtrodden masses of India, therefore, require to hear and to know what they really are. Ay, let every man and woman and child, without respect of caste or birth, weakness or strength, hear and learn that behind the strong and the weak, behind the high and the low, behind every one, there is that Infinite Soul, assuring the infinite possibility and the infinite capacity of all to become great and good. Let us proclaim to every soul: उत्तिष्ठत जाग्रत

प्राप्य वरान्निबोधत—Arise, awake, and stop not till the goal is reached. Arise, awake! Awake from this hypnotism of weakness. *None* is really weak; the soul is infinite, omnipotent, and omniscient. Stand up, assert yourself, proclaim the God within you, do not deny Him! Too much of inactivity, too much of weakness, too much of hypnotism has been and is upon our race. O ye modern Hindus, de-hypnotise yourselves. The way to do that is found in your own sacred books. Teach yourselves, teach every one his real nature, call upon the sleeping soul and see how it awakes. Power will come, glory will come, goodness will come, purity will come, and everything that is excellent will come when this sleeping soul is roused to self-conscious activity. Ay, if there is anything in the Gita that I like, it is these two verses, coming out strong as the very gist, the very essence, of Krishna's teaching—"He who sees the Supreme Lord dwelling alike in all beings, the Imperishable in things that perish, he sees indeed. For seeing the Lord as the same, everywhere present, he does not destroy the Self by the Self, and thus he goes to the highest goal."

Thus there is a great opening for the Vedanta to do beneficent work both here and elsewhere. This wonderful idea of the sameness and omnipresence of the Supreme Soul has to be preached for the amelioration and elevation of the human race here as elsewhere. Wherever there is evil and wherever there is ignorance and want of knowledge, I have found out by experience that all evil comes, as our scriptures say, relying upon differences, and that all good comes from faith in equality, in the underlying sameness and oneness of things. This is the great Vedantic ideal. To have the ideal is one thing, and to apply it practically to the details of daily life is quite another thing. It is very good to point out an ideal, but where is the practical way to reach it?

Here naturally comes the difficult and the vexed question of caste and of social reformation, which has been uppermost for centuries in the minds of our people. I must frankly tell you that I am neither a caste-breaker nor a mere social reformer. I have nothing to do directly with your castes or with your social reformation. Live in any caste you like, but that is no reason why you should hate another man or another caste. It is love and love alone that I preach, and I base my teaching on the great Vedantic truth of the sameness and omnipresence of the Soul of the Universe. For nearly the past one hundred years, our country has been flooded with social reformers and various social reform proposals. Personally, I have no fault to find with these reformers. Most of them are good, well-meaning men, and their aims too are very laudable on certain points; but it is quite a patent fact that this one hundred years of social reform has produced no permanent and valuable result appreciable throughout the country. Platform speeches have been made by the thousand, denunciations in volumes after volumes have been hurled upon the devoted head of the Hindu race and its civilisation, and yet no good practical result has been achieved; and where is the reason for that? The reason is not hard to find. It is in the denunciation itself. As I told you before, in the first place, we must try to keep our historically acquired character as a people. I grant that we have to take a great many things from other nations, that we have to learn many lessons from outside; but I am sorry to say that most of our modern reform movements have been inconsiderate imitations of Western means and methods of work; and that surely will not do for India; therefore, it is that all our recent reform movements have had no result.

In the second place, denunciation is not at all the way to do good. That there are evils in our society even a child can see; and in what society are there no evils? And let me take this opportunity, my countrymen, of telling you that in comparing the different races and nations of the world I have been among, I have come to the conclusion that our people are on the whole the most moral and the most godly, and our institutions are, in their plan and purpose, best suited to make mankind happy. I do not, therefore, want any reformation. My ideal is growth, expansion, development on national lines. As I look back upon the history of my country, I do not find in the whole world another country which has done quite so much for the improvement of the human mind. Therefore I have no words of condemnation for my nation. I tell them, "You have done well; only try to do better." Great things have been done in the past in this land, and there is both time and room for greater things to be done yet. I am sure you know that we cannot stand still. If we stand still, we die. We have either to go forward or to go backward. We have either to progress or to degenerate. Our ancestors did great things in the past, but we have to grow into a fuller life and march beyond even their great achievements. How can we now go back and degenerate ourselves? That cannot be; that must not be; going back will lead to national decay and death. Therefore let us go forward and do yet greater things; that is what I have to tell you.

I am no preacher of any momentary social reform. I am not trying to remedy evils, I only ask you to go forward and to complete the practical realisation of the scheme of human progress that has been laid out in the most perfect order by our ancestors. I only ask you to work to realise more and more the Vedantic ideal of the solidarity of man and his inborn divine nature. Had I the time, I would gladly show you how everything we have now to do was laid out years ago by our ancient law-givers, and how they actually anticipated all the different changes that have taken place and are still to take place in our national institutions. They also were breakers of caste, but they were not like our modern men. They did not mean by the breaking of caste that all the people in a city should sit down together to a dinner of beef-steak and champagne, nor that all fools and lunatics in the country should marry when, where, and whom they chose and reduce the country to a lunatic asylum, nor did they believe that the prosperity of a nation is to be gauged by the number of husbands its widows get. I have yet to see such a prosperous nation.

The ideal man of our ancestors was the Brahmin. In all our books stands out prominently this ideal of the Brahmin. In Europe there is my Lord the Cardinal, who is struggling hard and spending thousands of pounds to prove the nobility of his ancestors, and he will not be satisfied until he has traced his ancestry to some dreadful tyrant who lived on a hill and watched the people passing by, and whenever he had the opportunity, sprang out on them and robbed them. That was the business of these nobility-bestowing ancestors, and my Lord Cardinal is not satisfied until he can trace his ancestry to one of these. In India, on the other hand, the greatest princes seek to trace their descent to some ancient sage who dressed in a bit of loin-cloth, lived in a forest, eating roots and studying the Vedas. It is there that the Indian prince goes to trace his ancestry. You are of the high caste when you can trace your ancestry to a Rishi, and not otherwise.

Our ideal of high birth, therefore, is different from that of others. Our ideal is the Brahmin of spiritual culture and renunciation. By the Brahmin ideal what do I mean? I mean the ideal Brahmin-ness in which worldliness is altogether absent and true wisdom is abundantly present. That is the ideal of the Hindu race. Have you not heard how it is declared that he, the Brahmin, is not amenable to law, that he has no law, that he is not governed by kings, and that his body cannot be hurt? That is perfectly true. Do not understand it in the light thrown upon it by interested and ignorant fools, but understand it in the light of the true and original Vedantic conception. If the Brahmin is he who has killed all selfishness and who lives and works to acquire and propagate wisdom and the power of love—if a country is altogether inhabited by such Brahmins, by men and women who are spiritual and moral and good, is it strange to think of that country as being above and beyond all law? What police, what military are necessary to govern them? Why should any one govern them at all? Why should they live under a government? They are good and noble, and they are the men of God; these are our ideal Brahmins, and we read that in the Satya Yuga there was only one caste, and that was the Brahmin. We read in the Mahâbhârata that the whole world was in the beginning peopled with Brahmins, and that as they began to degenerate, they became divided into different castes, and that when the cycle turns round, they will all go back to that Brahminical origin. This cycle is turning round now, and I draw your attention to this fact. Therefore our solution of the caste question is not degrading those who are already high up, is not running amuck through food and drink, is not jumping out of our own limits in order to have more enjoyment, but it comes by every one of us, fulfilling the dictates of our Vedantic religion, by our attaining spirituality, and by our becoming the ideal Brahmin. There is a law laid on each one of you in this land by your ancestors, whether you are Aryans or non-Aryans, Rishis or Brahmins, or the very lowest outcasts. The command is the same to you all, that you must make progress without stopping, and that from the highest man to the lowest Pariah, every one in this country has to try and become the ideal

Brahmin. This Vedantic idea is applicable not only here but over the whole world. Such is our ideal of caste as meant for raising all humanity slowly and gently towards the realisation of that great ideal of the spiritual man who is non-resisting, calm, steady, worshipful, pure, and meditative. In that ideal there is God.

How are these things to be brought about? I must again draw your attention to the fact that cursing and vilifying and abusing do not and cannot produce anything good. They have been tried for years and years, and no valuable result has been obtained. Good results can be produced only through love, through sympathy. It is a great subject, and it requires several lectures to elucidate all the plans that I have in view, and all the ideas that are, in this connection, coming to my mind day after day. I must, therefore, conclude, only reminding you of this fact that this ship of our nation, O Hindus, has been usefully plying here for ages. Today, perhaps, it has sprung a leak; today, perhaps, it has become a little worn out. And if such is the case, it behoves you and me to try our best to stop the leak and holes. Let us tell our countrymen of the danger, let them awake and help us. I will cry at the top of my voice from one part of this country to the other, to awaken the people to the situation and their duty. Suppose they do not hear me, still I shall not have one word of abuse for them, not one word of cursing. Great has been our nation's work in the past; and if we cannot do greater things in the future, let us have this consolation that we can sink and die together in peace. Be patriots, love the race which has done such great things for us in the past. Ay, the more I compare notes, the more I love you, my fellow-countrymen; you are good and pure and gentle. You have been always tyrannised over, and such is the irony of this material world of Mâyâ. Never mind that; the Spirit will triumph in the long run. In the meanwhile let us work and let us not abuse our country, let us not curse and abuse the weather-beaten and work-worn institutions of our thrice-holy motherland. Have no word of condemnation even for the most superstitious and the most irrational of its institutions, for they also must have served some good in the past. Remember always that there is not in the world any other country whose institutions are really better in their aims and objects than the institutions of this land. I have seen castes in almost every country in the world, but nowhere is their plan and purpose so glorious as here. If caste is thus unavoidable, I would rather have a caste of purity and culture and self-sacrifice, than a caste of dollars. Therefore utter no words of condemnation. Close your lips and let your hearts open. Work out the salvation of this land and of the whole world, each of you thinking that the entire burden is on your shoulders. Carry the light and the life of the Vedanta to every door, and rouse up the divinity that is hidden within every soul. Then, whatever may be the measure of your success, you will have this satisfaction that you have lived, worked, and died for a great cause. In the success of this cause, howsoever brought about, is centred the salvation of humanity here and hereafter.

VEDANTA AND ITS APPLICATION TO INDIAN LIFE

There is a word which has become very common as an appellation of our race and our religion. The word "Hindu" requires a little explanation in connection with what I mean by Vedantism. This word "Hindu" was the name that the ancient Persians used to apply to the river Sindhu. Whenever in Sanskrit there is an "s", in ancient Persian it changes into "h", so that "Sindhu" became "Hindu"; and you are all aware how the Greeks found it hard to pronounce "h" and dropped it altogether, so that we became known as Indians. Now this word "Hindu" as applied to the inhabitants of the other side of the Indus, whatever might have been its meaning in ancient times, has lost all its force in modern times; for all the people that live on this side of the Indus no longer belong to one religion. There are the Hindus proper, the Mohammedans, the Parsees, the Christians, the Buddhists, and Jains. The word "Hindu" in its literal sense ought to include all these; but as signifying the religion, it would not be proper to call all these Hindus. It is very hard, therefore, to find any common name for our religion, seeing that this religion is a collection, so to speak, of various religions, of various ideas, of various ceremonials and forms, all gathered together almost without a name, and without a church, and without an organisation. The only point where, perhaps, all our sects agree is that we all believe in the scriptures—the Vedas. This perhaps is certain that no man can have a right to be called a Hindu who does not admit the supreme authority of the Vedas. All these Vedas, as you are aware, are divided into two portions—the Karma Kânda and the Jnâna Kânda. The Karma Kanda includes various sacrifices and ceremonials, of which the larger part has fallen into disuse in the present age. The Jnana Kanda, as embodying the spiritual teachings of the Vedas known as the Upanishads and the Vedanta, has always been cited as the highest authority by all our teachers, philosophers, and writers, whether dualist, or qualified monist, or monist. Whatever be his philosophy or sect, every one in India has to find his authority in the Upanishads. If he cannot, his sect would be heterodox. Therefore, perhaps the one name in modern times which would designate every Hindu throughout the land would be "Vedantist" or "Vaidika", as you may put it; and in that sense I always use the words "Vedantism" and "Vedanta". I want to make it a little clearer, for of late it has become the custom of most people to identify the word Vedanta with the Advaitic system of the Vedanta philosophy. We all know that Advaitism is only one branch of the various philosophic systems that have been founded on the Upanishads. The followers of the Vishishtâdvaitic system have as much reverence for the Upanishads as the followers of the Advaita, and the Vishishtadvaitists claim as much authority for the Vedanta as the Advaitist. So do the dualists; so does every other sect in India. But the word Vedantist has become somewhat identified in the popular mind with the word Advaitist, and perhaps with some reason, because, although we have the Vedas for our scriptures, we have Smritis and Purânas—subsequent writings—to illustrate the doctrines of the Vedas; these of course have not the same weight as the Vedas. And the law is that wherever these Puranas and Smritis differ from any part of the Shruti, the Shruti must be followed and the Smriti rejected. Now in the expositions of the great Advaitic philosopher Shankara, and the school founded by him, we find most of the authorities cited are from the Upanishads, very rarely is an authority cited from the Smritis, except, perhaps, to elucidate a point which could hardly be found in the Shrutis. On the other hand, other schools take refuge more and more in the Smritis and less and less in the Shrutis; and as we go to the more and more dualistic sects, we find a proportionate quantity of the Smritis quoted, which is out of all proportion to what we should expect from a Vedantist. It is, perhaps, because these gave such predominance to the Paurânika authorities that the Advaitist came to be considered as the Vedantist *par excellence,* if I may say so.

However it might have been, the word Vedanta must cover the whole ground of Indian religious life, and being part of the Vedas, by all acceptance it is the most ancient literature that we have; for whatever might be the idea of modern scholars, the Hindus are not ready to admit that parts of the Vedas were written at one time and parts were written at another time. They of course still hold on to their belief that the Vedas as a whole were produced at the same time, rather if I may say so, that they were never produced, but that they always existed in the mind of the Lord. This is what I mean by the word Vedanta, that it covers the ground of dualism, of qualified monism, and Advaitism in India. Perhaps we may even take in parts of Buddhism, and of Jainism too, if they would come in—for our hearts are sufficiently large. But it is they that will not come in, we are ready for upon severe analysis you will always find that the essence of Buddhism was all borrowed from the same Upanishads; even the ethics, the so-called great and wonderful ethics of Buddhism, were there word for word, in some one or other of the Upanishads; and so all the good doctrines of the Jains were there, minus their vagaries. In the Upanishads, also, we find the germs of all the subsequent development of Indian religious thought. Sometimes it has been urged without any ground whatsoever that there is no ideal of Bhakti in the Upanishads. Those that have been students of the Upanishads know that that is not true at all. There is enough of Bhakti in every Upanishad if you will only seek for it; but many of these ideas which are found so fully developed in later times in the Puranas and other Smritis are only in the germ in the Upanishads. The sketch, the skeleton, was there as it were. It was filled in in some of the Puranas. But there is not one full-grown Indian ideal that cannot be traced back to the same source—the Upanishads. Certain ludicrous attempts have been made by persons without much Upanishadic scholarship to trace Bhakti to some foreign source; but as you know, these have all been proved to be failures, and all that you want of Bhakti is there, even in the Samhitâs, not to speak of the Upanishads—it is there, worship and love and all the rest of it; only the ideals of Bhakti are becoming higher and higher. In the Samhita portions, now and then, you find traces of a religion of fear and tribulation; in the Samhitas now and then you find a worshipper quaking before a Varuna, or some other god. Now and then you will find they are very much tortured by the idea of sin, but the Upanishads have no place for the delineation of these things. There is no religion of fear in the Upanishads; it is one of Love and one of Knowledge.

These Upanishads are our scriptures. They have been differently explained, and, as I have told you already, whenever there is a difference between subsequent Pauranika literature and the Vedas, the Puranas must give way. But it is at the same time true that, as a practical result, we find ourselves ninety per cent Pauranika and ten per cent Vaidika—even if so much as that. And we all find the most contradictory usages prevailing in our midst and also religious opinions prevailing in our society which scarcely have any authority in the scriptures of the Hindus; and in many cases we read in books, and see with astonishment, customs of the country that neither have their authority in the Vedas nor in the Smritis or Puranas, but are simply local. And yet each ignorant villager thinks that if that little local custom dies out, he will no more remain a Hindu. In his mind Vedantism and these little local customs have been indissolubly identified. In reading the scriptures it is hard for him to understand that what he is doing has not the sanction of the scriptures, and that the giving up of them will not hurt him at all, but on the other hand will make him a better man. Secondly, there is the other difficulty. These scriptures of ours have been very vast. We read in the *Mahâbhâshya* of Patanjali, that great philological work, that the Sâma-Veda had one thousand branches. Where are they all? Nobody knows. So with each of the Vedas; the major portion of these books has disappeared, and it is only the minor portion that remains to us. They were all taken charge of by particular families; and either these families died out, or were killed under foreign persecution, or somehow became extinct; and with them, that branch of the learning of the Vedas they took charge of became extinct also. This fact we ought to remember, as it always forms the sheet-anchor in the hands of those who want to preach anything new or to defend anything even against the Vedas. Wherever in India there is a discussion between local custom and the Shrutis, and whenever it is pointed out that the local custom is against the scriptures, the argument that is forwarded is that it is not, that the customs existed in the branch of the Shrutis which has become extinct and so has been a recognised one. In the midst of all these varying methods of reading and commenting on our scriptures, it is very difficult indeed to find the thread that runs through all of them; for we become convinced at once that there must be some common ground underlying all these varying divisions and subdivisions. There must be harmony, a common plan, upon which all these little bits of buildings have been constructed, some basis common to this apparently hopeless mass of confusion which we call our religion. Otherwise it could not have stood so long, it could not have endured so long.

Coming to our commentators again, we find another difficulty. The Advaitic commentator, whenever an Advaitic text comes, preserves it just as it is; but the same commentator, as soon as a dualistic text presents itself, tortures it if he can, and brings the most queer meaning out of it. Sometimes the "Unborn" becomes a "goat", such are the wonderful changes effected. To suit the commentator, "Aja" the Unborn is explained as "Ajâ" a she-goat. In the same way, if not in a still worse fashion, the texts are handled by the dualistic commentator. Every dualistic text is preserved, and every text that speaks of non-dualistic philosophy is tortured in any fashion he likes. This Sanskrit language is so intricate, the Sanskrit of the Vedas is so ancient, and the Sanskrit philology so perfect, that any amount of discussion can be carried on for ages in regard to the meaning of one word. If a Pandit takes it into his head, he can render anybody's prattle into correct Sanskrit by force of argument and quotation of texts and rules. These are the difficulties in our way of understanding the Upanishads. It was given to me to live with a man who was as ardent a dualist, as ardent an Advaitist, as ardent a Bhakta, as a Jnani. And living with this man first put it into my head to understand the Upanishads and the texts of the scriptures from an independent and better basis than by blindly following the commentators; and in my opinion and in my researches, I came to the conclusion that these texts are not at all contradictory. So we need have no fear of text-torturing at all! The texts are beautiful, ay, they are most wonderful; and they are not contradictory, but wonderfully harmonious, one idea leading up to the other. But the one fact I found is that in all the Upanishads, they begin with dualistic ideas, with worship and all that, and end with a grand flourish of Advaitic ideas.

Therefore I now find in the light of this man's life that the dualist and the Advaitist need not fight each other. Each has a place, and a great place in the national life. The dualist must remain, for he is as much part and parcel of the national religious life as the Advaitist. One cannot exist without the other; one is the fulfilment of the other; one is the building, the other is the top; the one the root, the other the fruit, and so on. Therefore any attempt to torture the texts of the Upanishads appears to me very ridiculous. I begin to find out that the language is wonderful. Apart from all its merits as the greatest philosophy, apart from its wonderful merit as theology, as showing the path of salvation to mankind, the Upanishadic literature is the most wonderful painting of sublimity that the world has. Here comes out in full force that individuality of the human mind, that introspective, intuitive Hindu mind. We have paintings of sublimity elsewhere in all nations, but almost without exception you will find that their ideal is to grasp the sublime in the muscles. Take for instance, Milton, Dante, Homer, or any of the Western poets. There are wonderfully sublime passages in them; but there it is always a grasping at infinity through the senses, the muscles, getting the ideal of infinite expansion, the infinite of space. We find the same attempts made in the Samhita portion. You know some of those wonderful Riks where creation is described; the very heights of expression of the sublime in expansion and the infinite in space are attained. But they found out very soon that the Infinite cannot be reached in that way, that even infinite space, and expansion, and infinite external nature could not express the ideas that were struggling to find expression in their minds, and so they fell back upon other explanations. The language became new in the Upanishads; it is almost negative, it is sometimes, chaotic, sometimes taking you beyond the senses, pointing out to you something which you cannot grasp, which you cannot sense, and at the same time you feel certain that it is there. What passage in the world can compare with this?—

न तत्र सूर्यों भाति न चन्द्रतारकं नेमा विद्युतो भान्ति कुतोऽयमग्निः।—"There the sun cannot illumine, nor the moon nor the stars, the flash of lightning cannot illumine the place, what to speak of this mortal fire." Again, where can you find a more perfect expression of the whole philosophy of the world, the gist of what the Hindus ever thought, the whole dream of human salvation, painted in language more wonderful, in figure more marvellous than this?

द्वा सुपर्णा सयुजा सखाया समानं वृक्षं परिषस्वजाते ।
तयोरन्यः पिप्पलं स्वाद्वत्त्यनश्नन्नन्यो अभिचाकशीति ॥
समाने वृक्षे पुरुषो निमग्नोऽनीशया शोचति मुह्यमानः ।
जुष्टं यदा पश्यत्यन्यमीशमस्य महिमानमिति वीतशोकः ॥

Upon the same tree there are two birds of beautiful plumage, most friendly to each other, one eating the fruits, the other sitting there calm and silent without eating—the one on the lower branch eating sweet and bitter fruits in turn and becoming happy and unhappy, but the other one on the top, calm and majestic; he eats neither sweet nor bitter fruits, cares neither for happiness nor misery, immersed in his own glory. This is the picture of the human soul. Man is eating the sweet and bitter fruits of this life, pursuing gold, pursuing his senses, pursuing the vanities of life—hopelessly, madly careering he goes. In other places the Upanishads have compared the human soul to the charioteer, and the senses to the mad horses unrestrained. Such is the career of men pursuing the vanities of life, children dreaming golden dreams only to find that they are but vain, and old men chewing the cud of their past deeds, and yet not knowing how to get out of this network. This is the world. Yet in the life of every one there come golden moments; in the midst of the deepest sorrows, nay, of the deepest joys, there come moments when a part of the cloud that hides the sunlight moves away as it were, and we catch a glimpse, in spite of ourselves of something beyond—away, away beyond the life of the senses; away, away beyond its vanities, its joys, and its sorrows; away, away beyond nature, or our imaginations of happiness here or hereafter; away beyond all thirst for gold, or for fame, or for name, or for posterity. Man stops for a moment at this glimpse and sees the other bird calm and majestic, eating neither sweet nor bitter fruits, but immersed in his own glory, Self-content, Self-satisfied. As the Gita says, यस्त्वात्मरतिरेव स्यादात्मतृप्तश्च मानवः आत्मन्येव च संतुष्टस्तस्य कार्यं न विद्यते ॥—"He whose devotion is to the Atman, he who does not want anything beyond Atman, he who has become satisfied in the Atman, what work is there for him to do?" Why should he drudge? Man catches a glimpse, then again he forgets and goes on eating the sweet and bitter fruits of life; perhaps after a time he catches another glimpse, and the lower bird goes nearer and nearer to the higher bird as blows after blows are received. If he be fortunate to receive hard knocks, then he comes nearer and nearer to his companion, the other bird, his life, his friend; and as he approaches him, he finds that the light from the higher bird is playing round his own plumage; and as he comes nearer and nearer, lo! the transformation is going on. The nearer and nearer he comes, he finds himself melting away, as it were, until he has entirely disappeared. He did not really exist; it was but the reflection of the other bird who was there calm and majestic amidst the moving leaves. It was all his glory, that upper bird's. He then becomes fearless, perfectly satisfied, calmly serene. In this figure, the Upanishads take you from the dualistic to the utmost Advaitic conception.

Endless examples can be cited, but we have no time in this lecture to do that or to show the marvellous poetry of the Upanishads, the painting of the sublime, the grand conceptions. But one other idea I must note, that the language and the thought and everything come direct, they fall upon you like a sword-blade, strong as the blows of a hammer they come. There is no mistaking their meanings. Every tone of that music is firm and produces its full effect; no gyrations, no mad words, no intricacies in which the brain is lost. No signs of degradation are there—no attempts at too much allegorising, too much piling of adjectives after adjectives, making it more and more intricate, till the whole of the sense is lost, and the brain becomes giddy, and man does not know his way out from the maze of that literature. There was none of that yet. If it be human literature, it must be the production of a race which had not yet lost any of its national vigour.

Strength, strength is what the Upanishads speak to me from every page. This is the one great thing to remember, it has been the one great lesson I have been taught in my life; strength, it says, strength, O man, be not weak. Are there no human weaknesses?—says man. There are, say the Upanishads, but will more weakness heal them, would you try to wash dirt with dirt? Will sin cure sin, weakness cure weakness? Strength, O man, strength, say the Upanishads, stand up and be strong. Ay, it is the only literature in the world where you find the word "Abhih", "fearless", used again and again; in no other scripture in the world is this adjective applied either to God or to man. Abhih, fearless! And in my mind rises from the past the vision of the great Emperor of the West, Alexander the Great, and I see, as it were in a picture, the great monarch standing on the bank of the Indus, talking to one of our Sannyâsins in the forest; the old man he was talking to, perhaps naked, stark naked, sitting upon a block of stone, and the Emperor, astonished at his wisdom, tempting him with gold and honour to come over to Greece. And this man smiles at his gold, and smiles at his temptations, and refuses; and then the Emperor standing on his authority as an Emperor, says, "I will kill you if you do not come", and the man bursts into a laugh and says, "You never told such a falsehood in your life, as you tell just now. Who can kill me? Me you kill, Emperor of the material world! Never! For I am Spirit unborn and undecaying: never was I born and never do I die; I am the Infinite, the Omnipresent, the Omniscient; and you kill me, child that you are!" That is strength, that is strength! And the more I read the Upanishads, my friends, my countrymen, the more I weep for you, for therein is the great practical application. Strength, strength for us. What we need is strength, who will give us strength? There are thousands to weaken us, and of stories we have had enough. Every one of our Puranas, if you press it, gives out stories enough to fill three-fourths of the libraries of the world. Everything that can weaken us as a race we have had for the last thousand years. It seems as if during that period the national life had this one end in view, viz how to make us weaker and weaker till we have become real earth-worms, crawling at the feet of every one who dares to put his foot on us. Therefore, my friends, as one of your blood, as one that lives and dies with you, let me tell you that we want strength, strength, and every time strength. And the Upanishads are the great mine of strength. Therein lies strength enough to invigorate the whole world; the whole world can be vivified, made strong, energised through them. They will call with trumpet voice upon the weak, the miserable, and the downtrodden of all races, all creeds, and all sects to stand on their feet and be free. Freedom, physical freedom, mental freedom, and spiritual freedom are the watchwords of the Upanishads.

Ay, this is the one scripture in the world, of all others, that does not talk of salvation, but of freedom. Be free from the bonds of nature, be free from weakness! And it shows to you that you have this freedom already in you. That is another peculiarity of its teachings. You are a Dvaitist; never mind, you have got to admit that by its very nature the soul is perfect; only by certain actions of the soul has it become contracted. Indeed, Râmânuja's theory of contraction and expansion is exactly what the modern evolutionists call evolution and atavism. The soul goes back, becomes contracted as it were, its powers become potential; and by good deeds and good thoughts it expands again and reveals its natural perfection. With the Advaitist the one difference is that he admits evolution in nature and not in the soul. Suppose there is a screen, and there is a small hole in the screen. I am a man standing behind the screen and looking at this grand assembly. I can see only very few faces here. Suppose the hole increases; as it increases, more and more of this assembly is revealed to me, and in full when the hole has become identified with the screen —there is nothing between you and me in this case. Neither you changed nor I changed; all the change was in the screen. You were the same from first to last; only the screen changed. This is the Advaitist's position with regard to evolution—evolution of nature and manifestation of the Self within. Not that the Self can by any means be made to contract. It is unchangeable, the Infinite One. It was covered, as it were, with a veil, the veil of Mâyâ, and as this Maya veil becomes thinner and thinner, the inborn, natural glory of the soul comes out and becomes more manifest. This is the one great doctrine which the world is waiting to learn from India. Whatever they may talk, however they may try to boast, they will find out day after day that no society can stand without admitting this. Do you not find how everything is being revolutionised? Do you not see how it was the custom to take for granted that everything was wicked until it proved itself good? In education, in punishing criminals, in treating lunatics, in the treatment of common diseases even, that was the old law. What is the modern law? The modern law says, the body itself is healthy; it cures diseases of its own nature. Medicine can at the best but help the storing up of the best in the body. What says it of criminals? It takes for granted that however low a criminal may be, there is still the divinity within, which does not change, and we must treat criminals accordingly. All these things are now changing, and reformatories and penitentiaries are established. So with everything. Consciously or unconsciously that Indian idea of the divinity within every one is expressing itself even in other countries. And in your books is the explanation which other nations have to accept. The treatment of one man to another will be entirely revolutionised, and these old, old ideas of pointing to the weakness of mankind will have to go. They will have received their death-blow within this century. Now people may stand up and criticise us. I have been criticised, from one end of the world to the other, as one who preaches the diabolical idea that there is no sin! Very good. The descendants of these very men will bless me as the preacher of virtue, and not of sin. I am the teacher of virtue, not of sin. I glory in being the preacher of light, and not of darkness.

The second great idea which the world is waiting to receive from our Upanishads is the solidarity of this universe. The old lines of demarcation and differentiation are vanishing rapidly. Electricity and steam-power are placing the different parts of the world in intercommunication with each other, and, as a result, we Hindus no longer say that every country beyond our own land is peopled with demons and hobgoblins, nor do the people of Christian countries say that India is only peopled by cannibals and savages. When we go out of our country, we find the same brother-man, with the same strong hand to help, with the same lips to say godspeed; and sometimes they are better than in the country in which we are born. When they come here, they find the same brotherhood, the same cheer, the same godspeed. Our Upanishads say that the cause of all misery is ignorance; and that is perfectly true when applied to every state of life, either social or spiritual. It is ignorance that makes us hate each other, it is through ignorance that we do not know and do not love each other. As soon as we come to know each other, love comes, must come, for are we not one? Thus we find solidarity coming in spite of itself. Even in politics and sociology, problems that were only national twenty years ago can no more be solved on national grounds only. They are assuming huge proportions, gigantic shapes. They can only be solved when looked at in the broader light of international grounds. International organisations, international combinations, international laws are the cry of the day. That shows the solidarity. In science, every day they are coming to a similar broad view of matter. You speak of matter, the whole universe as one mass, one ocean of matter, in which you and I, the sun and the moon, and everything else are but the names of different little whirlpools and nothing more. Mentally speaking, it is one universal ocean of thought in which you and I are similar little whirlpools; and as spirit it moveth not, it changeth not. It is the One Unchangeable, Unbroken, Homogeneous Atman. The cry for morality is coming also, and that is to be found in our books. The explanation of morality, the fountain of ethics, that also the world wants; and that it will get here.

What do we want in India? If foreigners want these things, we want them twenty times more. Because, in spite of the greatness of the Upanishads, in spite of our boasted ancestry of sages, compared to many other races, I must tell you that we are weak, very weak. First of all is our physical weakness. That physical weakness is the cause of at least one-third of our miseries. We are lazy, we cannot work; we cannot combine, we do not love each other; we are intensely selfish, not three of us can come together without hating each other, without being jealous of each other. That is the state in which we are —hopelessly disorganised mobs, immensely selfish, fighting each other for centuries as to whether a certain mark is to be put on our forehead this way or that way, writing volumes and volumes upon such momentous questions as to whether the look of a man spoils my food or not! This we have been doing for the past few centuries. We cannot expect anything high from a race whose whole brain energy has been occupied in such wonderfully beautiful problems and researches! And are we not ashamed of ourselves? Ay, sometimes we are; but though we think these things frivolous, we cannot give them up. We speak of many things parrot-like, but never do them; speaking and not doing has become a habit with us. What is the cause of that? Physical weakness. This sort of weak brain is not able to do anything; we must strengthen it. First of all, our young men must be strong. Religion will come afterwards. Be strong, my young friends; that is my advice to you. You will be nearer to Heaven through football than through the study of the Gita. These are bold words; but I have to say them, for I love you. I know where the shoe pinches. I have gained a little experience. You will understand the Gita better with your biceps, your muscles, a little stronger. You will understand the mightly genius and the mighty strength of Krishna better with a little of strong blood in you. You will understand the Upanishads better and the glory of the Atman when your body stands firm upon your feet, and you feel yourselves as men. Thus we have to apply these to our needs.

People get disgusted many times at my preaching Advaitism. I do not mean to preach Advaitism, or Dvaitism, or any *ism* in the world. The only *ism* that we require now is this wonderful idea of the soul—its eternal might, its eternal strength, its eternal purity, and its eternal perfection. If I had a child I would from its very birth begin to tell it, "Thou art the Pure One". You have read in one of the Puranas that beautiful story of queen Madâlasâ, how as soon as she has a child she puts her baby with her own hands in the cradle, and how as the cradle rocks to and fro, she begins to sing, "Thou art the Pure One, the Stainless, the Sinless, the Mighty One, the Great One." Ay, there is much in that. Feel that you are great and you become great. What did I get as my experience all over the world, is the question. They may talk about sinners—and if all Englishmen really believed that they were sinners, Englishmen would be no better than the negroes in Central Africa. God bless them that they do not believe it! On the other hand, the Englishman believes he is born the lord of the world. He believes he is great and can do anything in the world; if he wants to go to the sun or the moon, he believes he can; and that makes him great. If he had believed his priests that he was a poor miserable sinner, going to be barbecued through all eternity, he would not be the same Englishman that he is today. So I find in every nation that, in spite of priests and superstition, the divine within lives and asserts itself. We have lost faith. Would you believe me, we have less faith than the Englishman and woman—a thousand times less faith! These are plain words; but I say these, I cannot help it. Don't you see how Englishmen and women, when they catch our ideals, become mad as it were; and although they are the ruling class, they come to India to preach our own religion notwithstanding the jeers and ridicule of their own countrymen? How many of you could do that? And why cannot you do that? Do you not know it? You know more than they do; you are more wise than is good for you, that is your difficulty! Simply because your blood is only like water, your brain is sloughing, your body is weak! You must change the body. Physical weakness is the cause and nothing else. You have talked of reforms, of ideals, and all these things for the past hundred years; but when it comes to practice, you are not to be found anywhere—till you have disgusted the whole world, and the very name of reform is a thing of ridicule! And what is the cause? Do you not know? You know too well. The only cause is that you are weak, weak, weak; your body is weak, your mind is weak, you have no faith in yourselves! Centuries and centuries, a thousand years of crushing tyranny of castes and kings and foreigners and your own people have taken out all your strength, my brethren. Your backbone is broken, you are like downtrodden worms. Who will give you strength? Let me tell you, strength, strength is what we want. And the first step in getting strength is to uphold the Upanishads, and believe—"I am the Soul", "Me the sword cannot cut; nor weapons pierce; me the fire cannot burn; me the air cannot dry; I am the Omnipotent, I am the Omniscient." So repeat these blessed, saving words. Do not say we are weak; we can do anything and everything. What can we not do? Everything can be done by us; we all have the same glorious soul, let us believe in it. Have faith, as Nachiketâ. At the time of his father's sacrifice, faith came unto Nachiketa; ay, I wish that faith would come to each of you; and every one of you would stand up a giant, a world-mover with a gigantic intellect—an infinite God in every respect. That is what I want you to become. This is the strength that you get from the Upanishads, this is the faith that you get from there.

Ay, but it was only for the Sannyâsin! Rahasya (esoteric)! The Upanishads were in the hands of the Sannyasin; he went into the forest! Shankara was a little kind and said even Grihasthas (householders) may study the Upanishads, it will do them good; it will not hurt them. But still the idea is that the Upanishads talked only of the forest life of the recluse. As I told you the other day, the only commentary, the authoritative commentary on the Vedas, has been made once and for all by Him who inspired the Vedas—by Krishna in the Gita. It is there for every one in every occupation of life. These conceptions of the Vedanta must come out, must remain not only in the forest, not only in the cave, but they must come out to work at the bar and the bench, in the pulpit, and in the cottage of the poor man, with the fishermen that are catching fish, and with the students that are studying. They call to every man, woman, and child whatever be their occupation, wherever they may be. And what is there to fear! How can the fishermen and all these carry out the ideals of the Upanishads? The way has been shown. It is infinite; religion is infinite, none can go beyond it; and whatever you do sincerely is good for you. Even the least thing well done brings marvellous results; therefore let every one do what little he can. If the fisherman thinks that he is the Spirit, he will be a better fisherman; if the student thinks he is the Spirit, he will be a better student. If the lawyer thinks that he is the Spirit, he will be a better lawyer, and so on, and the result will be that the castes will remain for ever. It is the nature of society to form itself into groups; and what will go will be these privileges. Caste is a natural order; I can perform one duty in social life, and you another; you can govern a country, and I can mend a pair of old shoes, but that is no reason why you are greater than I, for can you mend my shoes? Can I govern the country? I am clever in mending shoes, you are clever in reading Vedas, but that is no reason why you should trample on my head. Why if one commits murder should he be praised, and if another steals an apple why should he be hanged? This will have to go. Caste is good. That is the only natural way of solving life. Men must form themselves into groups, and you cannot get rid of that. Wherever you go, there will be caste. But that does not mean that there should be these privileges. They should be knocked on the head. If you teach Vedanta to the fisherman, he will say, I am as good a man as you; I am a fisherman, you are a philosopher, but I have the same God in me as you have in you. And that is what we want, no privilege for any one, equal chances for all; let every one be taught that the divine is within, and every one will work out his own salvation.

Liberty is the first condition of growth. It is wrong, a thousand times wrong, if any of you dares to say, "I will work out the salvation of this woman or child." I am asked again and again, what I think of the widow problem and what I think of the woman question. Let me answer once for all—am I a widow that you ask me that nonsense? Am I a woman that you ask me that question again and again? Who are you to solve women's problems? Are you the Lord God that you should rule over every widow and every woman? Hands off! They will solve their own problems. O tyrants, attempting to think that you can do anything for any one! Hands off! The

Divine will look after all. Who are you to assume that you know everything? How dare you think, O blasphemers, that you have the right over God? For don't you know that every soul is the Soul of God? Mind your own Karma; a load of Karma is there in you to work out. Your nation may put you upon a pedestal, your society may cheer you up to the skies, and fools may praise you: but He sleeps not, and retribution will be sure to follow, here or hereafter.

Look upon every man, woman, and every one as God. You cannot help anyone, you can only serve: serve the children of the Lord, serve the Lord Himself, if you have the privilege. If the Lord grants that you can help any one of His children, blessed you are; do not think too much of yourselves. Blessed you are that that privilege was given to you when others had it not. Do it only as a worship. I should see God in the poor, and it is for my salvation that I go and worship them. The poor and the miserable are for our salvation, so that we may serve the Lord, coming in the shape of the diseased, coming in the shape of the lunatic, the leper, and the sinner! Bold are my words; and let me repeat that it is the greatest privilege in our life that we are allowed to serve the Lord in all these shapes Give up the idea that by ruling over others you can do any good to them. But you can do just as much as you can in the case of the plant; you can supply the growing seed with the materials for the making up of its body, bringing to it the earth, the water, the air, that it wants. It will take all that it wants by its own nature, it will assimilate and grow by its own nature.

Bring all light into the world. Light, bring light! Let light come unto every one; the task will not be finished till every one has reached the Lord. Bring light to the poor; and bring more light to the rich, for they require it more than the poor. Bring light to the ignorant, and more light to the educated, for the vanities of the education of our time are tremendous! Thus bring light to all and leave the rest unto the Lord, for in the words of the same Lord, "To work you have the right and not to the fruits thereof." "Let not your work produce results for *you,* and at the same time may you never be without work."

May He who taught such grand ideas to our forefathers ages ago help us to get strength to carry into practice His commands!

THE WORK BEFORE US

(Delivered at the Triplicane Literary Society, Madras)

The problem of life is becoming deeper and broader every day as the world moves on. The watchword and the essence have been preached in the days of yore when the Vedantic truth was first discovered, the solidarity of all life. One atom in this universe cannot move without dragging the whole world along with it. There cannot be any progress without the whole world following in the wake, and it is becoming every day clearer that the solution of any problem can never be attained on racial, or national, or narrow grounds. Every idea has to become broad till it covers the whole of this world, every aspiration must go on increasing till it has engulfed the whole of humanity, nay, the whole of life, within its scope. This will explain why our country for the last few centuries has not been what she was in the past. We find that one of the causes which led to this degeneration was the narrowing of our view, narrowing the scope of our actions.

Two curious nations there have been—sprung of the same race, but placed in different circumstances and environments, working out the problems of life each in its own particular way. I mean the ancient Hindu and the ancient Greek. The Indian Aryan—bounded on the north by the snow-caps of the Himalayas, with fresh-water rivers like rolling oceans surrounding him in the plains, with eternal forests which, to him, seemed to be the end of the world—turned his vision inward; and given the natural instinct, the superfine brain of the Aryan, with this sublime scenery surrounding him, the natural result was that he became introspective. The analysis of his own mind was the great theme of the Indo-Aryan. With the Greek, on the other hand, who arrived at a part of the earth which was more beautiful than sublime, the beautiful islands of the Grecian Archipelago, nature all around him generous yet simple—his mind naturally went outside. It wanted to analyse the external world. And as a result we find that from India have sprung all the analytical sciences, and from Greece all the sciences of generalisation. The Hindu mind went on in its own direction and produced the most marvellous results. Even at the present day, the logical capacity of the Hindus, and the tremendous power which the Indian brain still possesses, is beyond compare. We all know that our boys pitched against the boys of any other country triumph always. At the same time when the national vigour went, perhaps one or two centuries before the Mohammedan conquest of India, this national faculty became so much exaggerated that it degraded itself, and we find some of this degradation in everything in India, in art, in music, in sciences, in everything. In art, no more was there a broad conception, no more the symmetry of form and sublimity of conception, but the tremendous attempt at the ornate and florid style had arisen. The originality of the race seemed to have been lost. In music no more were there the soul-stirring ideas of the ancient Sanskrit music, no more did each note stand, as it were, on its own feet, and produce the marvellous harmony, but each note had lost its individuality. The whole of modern music is a jumble of notes, a confused mass of curves. That is a sign of degradation in music. So, if you analyse your idealistic conceptions, you will find the same attempt at ornate figures, and loss of originality. And even in religion, your special field, there came the most horrible degradations. What can you expect of a race which for hundreds of years has been busy in discussing such momentous problems as whether we should drink a glass of water with the right hand or the left? What more degradation can there be than that the greatest minds of a country have been discussing about the kitchen for several hundreds of years, discussing whether I may touch you or you touch me, and what is the penance for this touching! The themes of the Vedanta, the sublimest and the most glorious conceptions of God and soul ever preached on earth, were half-lost, buried in the forests, preserved by a few Sannyâsins, while the rest of the nation discussed the momentous questions of touching each other, and dress, and food. The Mohammedan conquest gave us many good things, no doubt; even the lowest man in the world can teach something to the highest; at the same time it could not bring vigour into the race. Then for good or evil, the English conquest of India took place. Of course every conquest is bad, for conquest is an evil, foreign government is an evil, no doubt; but even through evil comes good sometimes, and the great good of the English conquest is this: England.

nay the whole of Europe, has to thank Greece for its civilisation. It is Greece that speaks through everything in Europe. Every building, every piece of furniture has the impress of Greece upon it; European science and art are nothing but Grecian. Today the ancient Greek is meeting the ancient Hindu on the soil of India. Thus slowly and silently the leaven has come; the broadening, the life-giving and the revivalist movement that we see all around us has been worked out by these forces together. A broader and more generous conception of life is before us; and although at first we have been deluded a little and wanted to narrow things down, we are finding out today that these generous impulses which are at work, these broader conceptions of life, are the logical interpretation of what is in our ancient books. They are the carrying out, to the rigorously logical effect, of the primary conceptions of our own ancestors. To become broad, to go out, to amalgamate, to universalise, is the end of our aims. And all the time we have been making ourselves smaller and smaller, and dissociating ourselves, contrary to the plans laid down in our scriptures.

Several dangers are in the way, and one is that of the extreme conception that we are *the* people in the world. With all my love for India, and with all my patriotism and veneration for the ancients, I cannot but think that we have to learn many things from other nations. We must be always ready to sit at the feet of all, for, mark you, every one can teach us great lessons. Says our great law-giver, Manu: "Receive some good knowledge even from the low-born, and even from the man of lowest birth learn by service the road to heaven." We, therefore, as true children of Manu, must obey his commands and be ready to learn the lessons of this life or the life hereafter from any one who can teach us. At the same time we must not forget that we have also to teach a great lesson to the world. We cannot do without the world outside India; it was our foolishness that we thought we could, and we have paid the penalty by about a thousand years of slavery. That we did not go out to compare things with other nations, did not mark the workings that have been all around us, has been the one great cause of this degradation of the Indian mind. We have paid the penalty; let us do it no more. All such foolish ideas that Indians must not go out of India are childish.

They must be knocked on the head; the more you go out and travel among the nations of the world, the better for you and for your country. If you had done that for hundreds of years past, you would not be here today at the feet of every nation that wants to rule India. The first manifest effect of life is expansion. You must expand if you want to live. The moment you have ceased to expand, death is upon you, danger is ahead. I went to America and Europe, to which you so kindly allude; I have to, because that is the first sign of the revival of national life, expansion. This reviving national life, expanding inside, threw me off, and thousands will be thrown off in that way. Mark my words, it has got to come if this nation lives at all. This question, therefore, is the greatest of the signs of the revival of national life, and through this expansion our quota of offering to the general mass of human knowledge, our contribution to the general upheaval of the world, is going out to the external world.

Again, this is not a new thing. Those of you who think that the Hindus have been always confined within the four walls of their country through all ages, are entirely mistaken; you have not studied the old books, you have not studied the history of the race aright if you think so. Each nation must give in order to live. When you give life, you will have life; when you receive, you must pay for it by giving to all others; and that we have been living for so many thousands of years is a fact that stares us in the face, and the solution that remains is that we have been always giving to the outside world, whatever the ignorant may think. But the gift of India is the gift of religion and philosophy, and wisdom and spirituality. And religion does not want cohorts to march before its path and clear its way. Wisdom and philosophy do not want to be carried on floods of blood. Wisdom and philosophy do not march upon bleeding human bodies, do not march with violence but come on the wings of peace and love, and that has always been so. Therefore we had to give. I was asked by a young lady in London, "What have you Hindus done? You have never even conquered a single nation." That is true from the point of view of the Englishman, the brave, the heroic, the Kshatriya—conquest is the greatest glory that one man can have over another. That is true from his point of view, but from ours it is quite the opposite. If I ask myself what has been the cause of India's greatness, I answer, because we have never conquered. That is our glory. You are hearing every day, and sometimes, I am sorry to say, from men who ought to know better, denunciations of our religion, because it is not at all a conquering religion. To my mind that is the argument why our religion is truer than any other religion, because it never conquered, because it never shed blood, because its mouth always shed on all, words of blessing, of peace, words of love and sympathy. It is here and here alone that the ideals of toleration were first preached. And it is here and here alone that toleration and sympathy have become practical; it is theoretical in every other country; it is here and here alone, that the Hindu builds mosques for the Mohammedans and churches for the Christians.

So, you see, our message has gone out to the world many a time, but slowly, silently, unperceived. It is on a par with everything in India. The one characteristic of Indian thought is its silence, its calmness. At the same time the tremendous power that is behind it is never expressed by violence. It is always the silent mesmerism of Indian thought. If a foreigner takes up our literature to study, at first it is disgusting to him; there is not the same stir, perhaps, the same amount of go that rouses him instantly. Compare the tragedies of Europe with our tragedies. The one is full of action, that rouses you for the moment, but when it is over there comes the reaction, and everything is gone, washed off as it were from your brains. Indian tragedies are like the mesmerist's power, quiet, silent, but as you go on studying them they fascinate you; you cannot move; you are bound; and whoever has dared to touch our literature has felt the bondage, and is there bound for ever. Like the gentle dew that falls unseen and unheard, and yet brings into blossom the fairest of roses, has been the contribution of India to the thought of the world. Silent, unperceived, yet omnipotent in its effect, it has revolutionised the thought of the world, yet nobody knows when it did so. It was once remarked to me, "How difficult it is to ascertain the name of any writer in India", to which I replied, "That is the Indian idea." Indian writers are not like modern writers who steal ninety per cent of their ideas from other authors, while only ten per cent is their own, and they take care to write a preface in which they say, "For these ideas I am responsible". Those great master minds producing momentous results in the hearts of mankind were content to write their books without even putting their names, and to die quietly, leaving the books to posterity. Who knows the writers of our philosophy, who knows the writers of our Purânas? They all pass under the generic name of Vyâsa, and Kapila, and so on. They have been true children of Shri Krishna. They have been true followers of the Gita; they practically carried out the great mandate, "To work you have the right, but not to the fruits thereof."

Thus India is working upon the world, but one condition is necessary. Thoughts like merchandise can only run through channels made by somebody. Roads have to be made before even thought can travel from one place to another, and whenever in the history of the world a great conquering nation has arisen, linking the different parts of the world together, then has poured through these channels the thought of India and thus entered into the veins of every race. Before even the Buddhists were born, there are evidences accumulating every day that Indian thought penetrated the world. Before Buddhism, Vedanta had penetrated into China, into Persia, and the Islands of the Eastern Archipelago. Again when the mighty mind of the Greek had linked the different parts of the Eastern world together there came Indian thought; and Christianity with all its boasted civilisation is but a collection of little bits of Indian thought. Ours is the religion of which Buddhism with all its greatness is a rebel child, and of which Christianity is a very patchy imitation. One of these cycles has again arrived. There is the tremendous power of England which has linked the different parts of the world together. English roads no more are content like Roman roads to run over lands, but they have also ploughed the deep in all directions. From ocean to ocean run the roads of England. Every part of the world has been linked to every other part, and electricity plays a most marvellous part as the new messenger. Under all these circumstances we find again India reviving and ready to give her own quota to the progress and civilisation of the world. And that I have been forced, as it were, by nature, to go over and preach to America and England is the result. Every one of us ought to have seen that the time had arrived. Everything looks propitious, and Indian thought, philosophical and spiritual, must once more go over and conquer the world. The problem before us, therefore, is assuming larger proportions every day It is not only that we must revive our own country —that is a small matter; I am an imaginative man—and my idea is the conquest of the whole world by the Hindu race.

There have been great conquering races in the world. We also have been great conquerors. The story of our conquest has been described by that noble Emperor of India, Asoka, as the conquest of religion and of spirituality. Once more the world must be conquered by India. This is the dream of my life, and I wish that each one of you who hear me today will have the same dream in your minds, and stop not till you have realised the dream. They will tell you every day that we had better look to our own homes first and then go to work outside. But I will tell you in plain language that you work best when you work for others. The best work that you ever did for yourselves was when you worked for others, trying to disseminate your ideas in foreign languages beyond the seas, and this very meeting is proof how the attempt to enlighten other countries with your thoughts is helping your own country. One-fourth of the effect that has been produced in this country by my going to England and America would not have been brought about, had I confined my ideas only to India. This is the great ideal before us, and every one must be ready for it—the conquest of the whole world by India—nothing less than that, and we must all get ready for it, strain every nerve for it. Let foreigners come and flood the land with their armies, never mind. Up, India, and conquer the world with your spirituality! Ay, as has been declared on this soil first, love must conquer hatred, hatred cannot conquer itself. Materialism and all its miseries can never be conquered by materialism. Armies when they attempt to conquer armies only multiply and make brutes of humanity. Spirituality must conquer the West. Slowly they are finding out that what they want is spirituality to preserve them as nations. They are waiting for it, they are eager for it. Where is the supply to come from? Where are the men ready to go out to every country in the world with the messages of the great sages of India? Where are the men who are ready to sacrifice everything, so that this message shall reach every corner of the world? Such heroic souls are wanted to help the spread of truth. Such heroic workers are wanted to go abroad and help to disseminate the great truths of the

Vedanta. The world wants it; without it the world will be destroyed. The whole of the Western world is on a volcano which may burst tomorrow, go to pieces tomorrow. They have searched every corner of the world and have found no respite. They have drunk deep of the cup of pleasure and found it vanity. Now is the time to work so that India's spiritual ideas may penetrate deep into the West. Therefore young men of Madras, I specially ask you to remember this. We must go out, we must conquer the world through our spirituality and philosophy. There is no other alternative, we must do it or die. The only condition of national life, of awakened and vigorous national life, is the conquest of the world by Indian thought.

At the same time we must not forget that what I mean by the conquest of the world by spiritual thought is the sending out of the life-giving principles, not the hundreds of superstitions that we have been hugging to our breasts for centuries. These have to be weeded out even on this soil, and thrown aside, so that they may die for ever. These are the causes of the degradation of the race and will lead to softening of the brain. That brain which cannot think high and noble thoughts, which has lost all power of originality, which has lost all vigour, that brain which is always poisoning itself with all sorts of little superstitions passing under the name of religion, we must beware of. In our sight, here in India, there are several dangers. Of these, the two, Scylla and Charybdis, rank materialism and its opposite arrant superstition, must be avoided. There is the man today who after drinking the cup of Western wisdom, thinks that he knows everything. He laughs at the ancient sages. All Hindu thought to him is arrant trash—philosophy mere child's prattle, and religion the superstition of fools. On the other hand, there is the man educated, but a sort of monomaniac, who runs to the other extreme and wants to explain the omen of this and that. He has philosophical and metaphysical, and Lord knows what other puerile explanations for every superstition that belongs to his peculiar race, or his peculiar gods, or his peculiar village. Every little village superstition is to him a mandate of the Vedas, and upon the carrying out of it, according to him, depends the national life. You must beware of this. I would rather see every one of you rank atheists than superstitious fools, for the atheist is alive and you can make something out of him. But if superstition enters, the brain is gone, the brain is softening, degradation has seized upon the life. Avoid these two. Brave, bold men, these are what we want. What we want is vigour in the blood, strength in the nerves, iron muscles and nerves of steel, not softening namby-pamby ideas. Avoid all these. Avoid all mystery. There is no mystery in religion. Is there any mystery in the Vedanta, or in the Vedas, or in the Samhitâs, or in the Puranas? What secret societies did the sages of yore establish to preach their religion? What sleight-of-hand tricks are there recorded as used by them to bring their grand truths to humanity? Mystery mongering and superstition are always signs of weakness. These are always signs of degradation and of death. Therefore beware of them; be strong, and stand on your own feet. Great things are there, most marvellous things. We may call them supernatural things so far as our ideas of nature go, but not one of these things is a mystery. It was never preached on this soil that the truths of religion were mysteries or that they were the property of secret societies sitting on the snow-caps of the Himalayas. I have been in the Himalayas. You have not been there; it is several hundreds of miles from your homes. I am a Sannyâsin, and I have been for the last fourteen years on my feet. These mysterious societies do not exist anywhere. Do not run after these superstitions. Better for you and for the race that you become rank atheists, because you would have strength, but these are degradation and death. Shame on humanity that strong men should spend their time on these superstitions, spend all their time in inventing allegories to explain the most rotten superstitions of the world. Be bold; do not try to explain everything that way. The fact is that we have many superstitions, many bad spots and sores on our body—these have to be exercised, cut off, and destroyed—but these do not destroy our religion, our national life, our spirituality. Every principle of religion is safe, and the sooner these black spots are purged away, the better the principles will shine, the more gloriously. Stick to them.

You hear claims made by every religion as being the universal religion of the world. Let me tell you in the first place that perhaps there never will be such a thing, but if there is a religion which can lay claim to be that, it is only our religion and no other, because every other religion depends on some person or persons. All the other religions have been built round the life of what they think a historical man; and what they think the strength of religion is really the weakness, for disprove the historicity of the man and the whole fabric tumbles to the ground. Half the lives of these great founders of religions have been broken into pieces, and the other half doubted very seriously. As such, every truth that had its sanction only in their words vanishes into air. But the truths of our religion, although we have persons by the score, do not depend upon them. The glory of Krishna is not that he was Krishna, but that he was the great teacher of Vedanta. If he had not been so, his name would have died out of India in the same way as the name of Buddha has done. Thus our allegiance is to the principles always, and not to the persons. Persons are but the embodiments, the illustrations of the principles. If the principles are there, the persons will come by the thousands and millions. If the principle is safe, persons like Buddha will be born by the hundreds and thousands. But if the principle is lost and forgotten and the whole of national life tries to cling round a so-called historical person, woe unto that religion, danger unto that religion! Ours is the only religion that does not depend on a person or persons; it is based upon principles. At the same time there is room for millions of persons. There is ample ground for introducing persons, but each one of them must be an illustration of the principles. We must not forget that. These principles of our religion are all safe and it should be the life-work of every one of us to keep them safe, and to keep them free from the accumulating dirt and dust of ages. It is strange that in spite of the degradation that seized upon the race again and again, these principles of the Vedanta were never tarnished. No one, however wicked, ever dared to throw dirt upon them. Our scriptures are the best preserved scriptures in the world. Compared to other books there have been no interpolations, no text-torturing, no destroying of the essence of the thought in them. It is there just as it was first, directing the human mind towards the ideal, the goal.

You find that these texts have been commented upon by different commentators, preached by great teachers, and sects founded upon them; and you find that in these books of the Vedas there are various apparently contradictory ideas. There are certain texts which are entirely dualistic, others are entirely monistic. The dualistic commentator, knowing no better, wishes to knock the monistic texts on the head. Preachers and priests want to explain them in the dualistic meaning. The monistic commentator serves the dualistic texts in a similar fashion. Now this is not the fault of the Vedas. It is foolish to attempt to prove that the whole of the Vedas is dualistic. It is equally foolish to attempt to prove that the whole of the Vedas is non-dualistic. They are dualistic and non-dualistic both. We understand them better today in the light of newer ideas. These are but different conceptions leading to the final conclusion that both dualistic and monistic conceptions are necessary for the evolution of the mind, and therefore the Vedas preach them. In mercy to the human race the Vedas show the various steps to the higher goal. Not that they are contradictory, vain words used by the Vedas to delude children; they are necessary not only for children, but for many a grown-up man. So long as we have a body and so long as we are deluded by the idea of our identity with the body, so long as we have five senses and see the external world, we must have a Personal God. For if we have all these ideas, we must take, as the great Râmânuja has proved, all the ideas about God and nature and the individualised soul; when you take the one you have to take the whole triangle—we cannot avoid it. Therefore as long as you see the external world, to avoid a Personal God and a personal soul is arrant lunacy. But there may be times in the lives of sages when the human mind transcends as it were its own limitations, when man goes even beyond nature, to the realm of which the Shruti declares, "whence words fall back with the mind without reaching it"; "There the eyes cannot reach nor speech nor mind"; "We cannot say that we know it, we cannot say that we do not know it". There the human soul transcends all limitations, and then and then alone flashes into the human soul the conception of monism: I and the whole universe are one; I and Brahman are one. And this conclusion you will find has not only been reached through knowledge and philosophy, but parts of it through the power of love. You read in the *Bhâgavata,* when Krishna disappeared and the Gopis bewailed his disappearance that at last the thought of Krishna became so prominent in their minds that each one forgot her own body and thought she was Krishna, and began to decorate herself and to play as he did. We understand, therefore, that this identity comes even through love. There was an ancient Persian Sufi poet, and one of his poems says, "I came to the Beloved and beheld the door was closed; I knocked at the door and from inside a voice came, 'Who is there?' I replied, 'I am'. The door did not open. A second time I came and knocked at the door and the same voice asked, 'Who is there?' 'I am so-and-so.' The door did not open. A third time I came and the same voice asked, 'Who is there?' 'I am Thyself, my Love', and the door opened."

There are, therefore, many stages, and we need not quarrel about them even if there have been quarrels among the ancient commentators, whom all of us ought to revere; for there is no limitation to knowledge, there is no omniscience exclusively the property of any one in ancient or modern times. If there have been sages and Rishis in the past, be sure that there will be many now. If there have been Vyâsas and Vâlmikis and Shankarâchâryas in ancient times, why may not each one of you become a Shankaracharya? This is another point of our religion that you must always remember, that in all other scriptures inspiration is quoted as their authority, but this inspiration is limited to a very few persons, and through them the truth came to the masses, and we have all to obey them. Truth came to Jesus of Nazareth, and we must all obey him. But the truth came to the Rishis of India—the Mantra-drashtâs, the seers of thought—and will come to all Rishis in the future, not to talkers, not to bookswallowers, not to scholars, not to philologists, but to seers of thought. The Self is not to be reached by too much talking, not even by the highest intellects, not even by the study of the scriptures. The scriptures themselves say so. Do you find in any other scripture such a bold assertion as that—not even by the study of the Vedas will you reach the Âtman, You must open your heart. Religion is not going to church, or putting marks on the forehead, or dressing in a peculiar fashion: you may paint yourselves in all the colours of the rainbow, but if the heart has not been opened, if you have not realised God, it is all vain. If one has the colour of the heart, he does not want any external colour. That is the true religious realisation. We must not forget that colours and all these things are good so far as they help; so far they are all welcome. But they are apt to degenerate and instead of helping they retard, and a man identifies religion with externalities. Going to the temple becomes tantamount to spiritual life. Giving something to a priest becomes tantamount to religious life. These are dangerous and pernicious, and should be at once checked. Our scriptures declare again and again that even the knowledge of the external senses is not religion. That is religion which makes us realise the Unchangeable One, and that is the religion for every one. He who realises transcendental truth, he who realises the Atman in his own nature, he who comes face to face with God, sees God alone in everything, has become a Rishi. And there is not religious life for you until you have become a Rishi. Then alone religion begins for you, now is only the preparation. Then religion dawns upon you, now you are only undergoing intellectual gymnastics and physical tortures.

We must, therefore, remember that our religion lays down distinctly and clearly that every one who wants salvation must pass through the stage of Rishihood—must become a Mantradrashta, must see God. That is salvation; that is the law laid down by our scriptures. Then it becomes easy to look into the scripture with our own eyes, understand the meaning for ourselves, to analyse just what we want, and to understand the truth for ourselves. This is what has to be done. At the same time we must pay all reverence to the ancient sages for their work. They were great, these ancients, but we want to be greater. They did great work in the past, but we must do greater work than they. They had hundreds of Rishis in ancient India. We will have millions—we are going to have, and the sooner every one of you believes in this, the better for India and the better for the world. Whatever you believe, that you will be. If you believe yourselves to be sages, sages you will be tomorrow. There is nothing to obstruct you. For if there is one common doctrine that runs through all our apparently fighting and contradictory sects, it is that all glory, power, and purity are within the soul already; only according to Ramanuja, the soul contracts and expands at times, and according to Shankara, it comes under a delusion. Never mind these differences. All admit the truth that the power is there—potential or manifest it is there—and the sooner you believe that, the better for you. All power is within you; you can do anything and everything. Believe in that, do not believe that you are weak; do not believe that you are half-crazy lunatics, as most of us do nowadays. You can do anything and everything without even the guidance of any one. All power is there. Stand up and express the divinity within you.

THE VEDANTA

(*Delivered at Lahore on the 12th November 1897*)

Two worlds there are in which we live, one the external, the other internal. Human progress has been made, from days of yore, almost in parallel lines along both these worlds.

The search began in the external, and man at first wanted to get answers for all the deep problems from outside nature. Man wanted to satisfy his thirst for the beautiful and the sublime from all that surrounded him; he wanted to express himself and all that was within him in the language of the concrete; and grand indeed were the answers he got, most marvellous ideas of God and worship, and most rapturous expressions of the beautiful. Sublime ideas came from the external world indeed. But the other, opening out for humanity later, laid out before him a universe yet sublimer, yet more beautiful, and infinitely more expansive. In the Karma-kânda portion of the Vedas, we find the most wonderful ideas of religion inculcated, we find the most wonderful ideas about an overruling Creator, Preserver, and Destroyer of the universe presented before us, in language sometimes the most soul-stirring. Most of you perhaps remember that most wonderful Shloka in the Rig-Veda Samhitâ where you get the description of chaos, perhaps the sublimest that has ever been attempted yet. In spite of all this, we find it is only a painting of the sublime outside, we find that yet it is gross, that something of matter yet clings to it. Yet we find that it is only the expression of the Infinite in the language of matter, in the language of the finite, it is the infinite of the muscles and not of the mind; it is the infinite of space, and not of thought.

Therefore in the second portion or Jnâna-kânda, we find there is altogether a different procedure. The first was a search in external nature for the truths of the universe; it was an attempt to get the solution of the deep problems of life from the material world. यस्यैते हिमवन्तो महित्वा—"Whose glory these Himalayas declare." This is a grand idea, but yet it was not grand enough for India. The Indian mind had to fall back, and the research took a different direction altogether; from the external the search came to the internal, from matter to mind.

There arose the cry. "When a man dies, what becomes of him?" अस्तीत्येके नायमस्तीति चैके etc. "Some say that he exists, others, that he is gone; say, O king of Death, what is the truth?" An entirely different procedure we find here. The Indian mind got all that could be had from the external world, but it did not feel satisfied with that. It wanted to search further, to dive into its own soul, and the final answer came.

The Upanishads, or the Vedanta, or the Aranyakas, or Rahasya, is the name of this portion of the Vedas. Here we find at once that religion has got rid of all external formalities. Here we find at once that spiritual things are told not in the language of matter, but in the language of the spirit, the superfine, in the language of the superfine. No more any grossness attaches to it, no more is there any compromise with things of worldly concern. Bold, brave, beyond the conception of the present day, stand the giant minds of the sages of the Upanishads, declaring the noblest truths that have ever been preached to humanity, without any compromise, without any fear. This, my countrymen, I want to lay before you. Even the Jnana-kanda of the Vedas is a vast ocean; many lives are necessary to understand even a little of it. Truly has it been said of the Upanishads by Râmânuja that they form the head, the shoulders, the crest of the Vedas, and surely enough the Upanishads have become the Bible of modern India. The Hindus have the greatest respect for the Karma-kanda of the Vedas, but, for all practical purposes, we know that for ages by Shruti have been meant the Upanishads, and the Upanishads alone. We know that all our great philosophers, whether Vyâsa, Patanjali, or Gautama, and even the father of all philosophy, the great Kapila himself, whenever they wanted an authority for what they wrote, everyone of them found it in the Upanishads, and nowhere else, for therein are the truths that remain for ever.

There are truths that are true only in a certain line, in a certain direction, under certain circumstances, and for certain times—those that are founded on the institutions of the times. There are other truths which are based on the nature of man himself, and which must endure so long as man himself endures. These are the truths that alone can be universal, and in spite of all the changes that have come to India, as to our social surroundings, our methods of dress, our manner of eating, our modes of worship—these universal truths of the Shrutis, the marvellous Vedantic ideas, stand out in their own sublimity, immovable, unvanquishable, deathless, and immortal. Yet the germs of all the ideas that were developed in the Upanishads had been taught already in the Karma-kanda. The idea of the cosmos, which all sects of Vedantists had to take for granted, the psychology which has formed the common basis of all the Indian schools of thought, had there been worked out already and presented before the world. A few words, therefore, about the Karma-kanda are necessary before we begin the spiritual portion, the Vedanta; and first of all I should like to explain the sense in which I use the word Vedanta.

Unfortunately there is the mistaken notion in modern India, that the word Vedanta has reference only to the Advaita system, but you must always remember that in modern India, the three Prasthânas are considered equally important in the study of all the systems of religion. First of all there are the Revelations, the Shrutis, by which I mean the Upanishads. Secondly, among our philosophies, the Sutras of Vyasa have the greatest prominence, on account of their being the consummation of all preceding systems of philosophy. These systems are not contradictory to one another, but one is based on another, and there is a gradual unfolding of the theme which culminates in the Sutras of Vyasa. Then, between the Upanishads and the Sutras, which are the systematising of the marvellous truths of the Vedanta, comes in the Gitâ, the divine commentary on the Vedanta.

The Upanishads, the Vyasa Sutras, and the Gita, therefore, have been taken up by every sect in India that wants to claim authority for orthodoxy, whether dualist, or Vishishtâdvaitist, or Advaitist; the authorities of each of these are the three Prasthânas. We find that a Shankarâchârya, or a Râmânuja, or a Madhvâchârya, or a Vallabhâchârya, or a Chaitanya—any one who wanted to propound a new sect—had to take up these three systems and write only a new commentary on them. Therefore, it would be wrong to confine the word Vedanta only to one system which has arisen out of the Upanishads. All these are covered by the word Vedanta. The Vishishtadvaitist has as much right to be called a Vedantist as the Advaitist; in fact I will go a little further and say that what we really mean by the word Hindu is really the same as Vedantist. I want you to note that these three systems have been current in India almost from time immemorial—for you must not believe that Shankara was the inventor of the Advaita system; it existed ages before Shankara was born; he was one of its last representatives. So with the Vishishtadvaita system; it had existed ages before Ramanuja appeared, as we already know from the commentaries he has written. So with the dualistic systems that have existed side by side with the others. And with my little knowledge, I have come to the conclusion that they do not contradict each other. Just as in the case of the six Darshanas, we find they are a gradual unfolding of the grand principles, whose music beginning far back in the soft low notes ends in the triumphant blast of the Advaita, so also in these three systems we find the gradual working up of the human mind towards higher ideals, till everything is merged in that wonderful unity which is reached in the Advaita system. Therefore these three are not contradictory. On the other hand I am bound to tell you this has been a mistake committed by not a few. We find that an Advaitist teacher keeps intact those texts which especially teach Advaitism, and tries to interpret the dualistic or qualified non-dualistic texts into his own meaning. Similarly we find dualistic teachers trying to read their dualistic meaning into Advaitic texts. Our Gurus were great men, yet there is a saying, "Even the faults of Guru must be told." I am of opinion that in this only they were mistaken. We need not go into text-torturing, we need not go into any sort of religious dishonesty, we need not go into any sort of grammatical twaddle, we need not go about trying to put our own ideas into texts which were never meant for them, but the work is plain and becomes easier, once you understand the marvellous doctrine of Adhikârabheda.

It is true that the Upanishads have this one theme before them—कस्मिन्नु भगवो विज्ञाते सर्वमिदं विज्ञातं भवति—"What is that knowing which we know everything else?" In modern language, the theme of the Upanishads is to find an ultimate unity of things. Knowledge is nothing but finding unity in the midst of diversity. Every science is based upon this; all human knowledge is based upon the finding of unity in the midst of diversity; and if it is the task of small fragments of human knowledge, which we call our sciences, to find unity in the midst of a few different phenomena, the task becomes stupendous when the theme before us is to find unity in the midst of this marvellously diversified universe, where prevail unnumbered differences in name and form, in matter and spirit—each thought differing from every other thought, each form differing from every other form. Yet, to harmonise these many planes and unending Lokas, in the midst of this infinite variety to find unity, is the theme of the Upanishads. On the other hand, the old idea of Arundhati Nyâya applies. To show a man the fine star Arundhati, one takes the big brilliant star nearest to it, upon which he is asked to fix his eyes first, and then it becomes quite easy to direct his sight to Arundhati. This is the task before us, and to prove my idea I have simply to show you the Upanishads, and you will see it. Nearly every chapter begins with dualistic teaching, Upâsanâ. God is first taught as some one who is the Creator of this universe, its Preserver, and unto whom everything goes at last. He is one to be worshipped, the Ruler, the Guide of nature, external and internal, yet appearing as if He were outside of nature and external. One step further, and we find the same teacher teaching that this God is not outside of nature, but immanent in nature. And at last both ideas are discarded, and whatever is real is He; there is no difference. तत्त्वमसि श्वेतकेतो—"Shvetaketu, That thou art." That Immanent One is at last declared to be the same that is in the human soul. Here is no compromise; here is no fear of others' opinions. Truth, bold truth, has been taught in bold language, and we need not fear to preach the truth in the same bold language today, and, by the grace of God, I hope at least to be the one who dares to be that bold preacher.

To go back to our preliminaries. There are first two things to be understood—one, the psychological aspect common to all the Vedantic schools, and the other, the cosmological aspect. I will first take up the latter. Today we find wonderful discoveries of modern science coming upon us like bolts from the blue, opening our eyes to marvels we never dreamt of. But many of these are only re-discoveries of what had been found ages ago. It was only the other day that modern science found that even in the midst of the variety of forces there is unity. It has just discovered that what it calls heat, magnetism, electricity, and so forth, are all convertible into one unit force, and as such, it expresses all these by one name, whatever you may choose to call it. But this has been done even in the Samhita; old and ancient as it is, in it we meet with this very idea of force I was referring to. All the forces, whether you call them gravitation, or attraction, or repulsion, whether expressing themselves as heat, or electricity, or magnetism, are nothing but the variations of that unit energy. Whether they express themselves as thought, reflected from Antahkarana, the inner organ of man, or as action from an external organ, the unit from which they spring is what is called the Prâna. Again, what is Prana? Prana is Spandana, or vibration. When all this universe shall have resolved back into its primal state, what becomes of this infinite force? Do they think that it becomes extinct? Of course not. If it became extinct, what would be the cause of the next wave, because the motion is going in wave forms, rising, falling, rising again, falling again? Here is the word Srishti, which expresses the universe. Mark that the word does not mean creation. I am helpless in talking English; I have to translate the Sanskrit words as best as I can. It is Srishti, projection. At the end of a cycle, everything becomes finer and finer and is resolved back into the primal state from which it sprang, and there it remains for a time, quiescent, ready to spring forth again. That is Srishti, projection. And what becomes of all these forces, the Pranas? They are resolved back into the primal Prana, and this Prana becomes almost motionless—not entirely motionless—and that is what is described in the Vedic Sukta: "It vibrated without vibration"—Ânidavâtam. There are many technical phrases in the Upanishads difficult to understand. For instance, take this word Vâta; many times it means air and many times motion, and often people confuse one with the other. We must guard against that. And what becomes of what you call matter? The forces permeate all matter, which all dissolve into Akasha, from which they again come out; this Akasha is the primal matter. Whether you translate it as ether, or anything else, the idea is that this Akasha is the primal form of matter. This Akasha vibrates under the action of Prana, and when the next Srishti is coming up, as the vibration becomes quicker, the Akasha is lashed into all these wave forms which we call suns, and moons, and systems.

We read again: यदिदं किंच जगत् सर्वं प्राण एजति निःसृतम्—"Everything in this universe has been projected, Prana vibrating." You must mark the word Ejati, because it comes from Eja—to vibrate. Nihsritam—projected. Yadidam Kincha—whatever in this universe.

This is a part of the cosmological side. There are many details working into it. For instance, how the process takes place, how there is first ether, and how from the ether come other things, how that ether begins to vibrate, and from that Vâyu comes. But the one idea is here, that it is from the finer that the grosser has come. Gross matter is the last to emerge and the most external, and this gross matter had the finer matter before it. Yet we see that the whole thing has been resolved into two, but there is not yet a final unity. There is the unity of force, Prana, there is the unity of matter called Akasha. Is there any unity to be found among them again? Can they be melted into one? Our modern science is mute here, it has not yet found its way out; and if it is doing so, just as it has been slowly finding the same old Prana and the same ancient Akasha, it will have to move along the same lines.

The next unity is the omnipresent impersonal Being known by its old mythological name as Brahmâ, the fourheaded Brahma, and psychologically called Mahat. This is where the two unite. What is called your mind is only a bit of this Mahat caught in the trap of the brain, and the sum total of all minds caught in the meshes of brains is what you call Samashti, the aggregate, the universal. Analysis had to go further; it was not yet complete. Here we were each one of us, as it were, a microcosm, and the world taken altogether is the macrocosm. But whatever is in the Vyashti, the particular, we may safely conjecture that a similar thing is happening also outside. If we had the power to analyse our own minds we might safely conjecture that the same thing is happening in the cosmic mind. What is this mind, is the question. In modern times in Western countries, as physical science is making rapid progress, as physiology is step by step conquering stronghold after stronghold of old religions, the Western people do not know where to stand because, to their great despair, modern physiology at every step has identified the mind with the brain. But we in India have known that always. That is the first proposition the Hindu boy learns, that the mind is matter, only finer. The body is gross, and behind the body is what we call the Sukshma Sharira, the fine body, or mind. This is also material, only finer; and it is not the Âtman.

I will not translate this word to you in English, because the idea does not exist in Europe; it is untranslatable. The modern attempt of German philosophers is to translate the word Atman by the word "Self", and until that word is universally accepted it is impossible to use it. So, call it as Self or anything, it is our Atman. This Atman is the real man behind. It is the Atman that uses the material mind as its instrument, its Antahkarana, as is the phychological term for the mind. And the mind by means of a series of internal organs works the visible organs of the body. What is this mind? It was only the other day that Western philosophers have come to know that the eyes are not the real organs of vision, but that behind these are other organs, the Indriyas, and if these are destroyed, a man may have a thousand eyes, like Indra, but there will be no sight for him. Ay, your philosophy starts with this assumption, that by vision is not meant the external vision. The real vision belongs to the internal organs, the brain certres inside. You may call them what you like, but it is not that the Indriyas are the eyes, or the nose, or the ears. And the sum total of all these Indriyas plus the Manas, Buddhi, Chitta, Ahamkâra, etc. is what is called the mind, and if the modern physiologist comes to tell you that the brain is what is called the mind, and that the brain is formed of so many organs, you need not be afraid at all, tell him that your philosophers knew it always; it is one of the very first principles of your religion.

Well, then, we have to understand now what is meant by this Manas, Buddhi, Chitta, Ahamkara, etc. First of all, let us take Chitta. It is the mind-stuff—a part of the Mahat—it is the generic name for the mind itself, including all its various states. Suppose on a summer evening there is a lake, smooth and calm, without a ripple on its surface. And suppose some one throws a stone into this lake. What happens? First there is the action, the blow given to the water; next, the water rises and sends a reaction towards the stone, and that reaction takes the form of a wave. First the water vibrates a little, and immediately sends back a reaction in the form of a wave. The Chitta, let us compare to this lake, and the external objects are like the stones thrown into it. As soon as it comes in contact with any external object by means of these Indriyas—the Indriyas must be there to carry these external objects inside—there is a vibration, what is called the Manas, indecisive. Next there is a reaction, the determinative faculty, Buddhi, and along with this Buddhi flashes the idea of Aham and the external object. Suppose there is a mosquito sitting upon my hand. This sensation is carried to my Chitta and it vibrates a little; this is the psychological Manas. Then there is a reaction, and immediately comes the idea that I have a mosquito on my hand, and that I shall have to drive it off. Thus these stones are thrown into the lake, but in the case of the lake every blow that comes to it is from the external world, while in the case of the lake of the mind, the blows may either come from the external world, or the internal world. This whole series is what is called the Antahkarana.

Along with it, you ought to understand one thing more; that will help us in understanding the Advaita system later on. It is this. All of you must have seen pearls, and most of you know how pearls are formed. A grain of sand enters into the shell of a pearl oyster and sets up an irritation there, and the oyster's body reacts towards the irritation and covers the little particle with its own juice. That crystallises and forms the pearl. So the whole universe is like that, it is the pearl which is being formed by us. What we get from the external world is simply the blow. Even to be conscious of that blow we have to react, and as soon as we react, we really project a portion of our own mind towards the blow, and when we come to know of it, it is really our own mind as it has been shaped by the blow. Therefore, it is clear even to those who want to believe in a hard and fast realism of an external world, which they cannot but admit in these days of physiology—that supposing we represent the external world by "*x*", what we really know is "*x*" plus mind, and this mind-element is so great that it has covered the whole of that "*x*", which has remained unknown and unknowable throughout, and therefore, if there is an external world, it is always unknown and unknowable. What we know of it is as it is moulded, formed, fashioned by our own mind. So with the internal world. The same applies to our own soul, the Atman. In order to know the Atman we shall have to know it through the mind, and therefore what little we know of this Atman is simply the Atman plus the mind. That is to say, the Atman covered over, fashioned, and moulded by the mind, and nothing more. We shall return to this a little later, but we will remember what has been told here.

The next thing to understand is this. The question arose that this body is the name of one continuous stream of matter; every moment we are adding material to it, and every moment material is being thrown off by it, like a river continually flowing, vast masses of water always changing places; yet all the same, we take up the whole thing in imagination and call it the same river. What do we call the river? Every moment the water is changing, the shore is changing, every moment the environment is changing. What is the river, then? It is the name of this series of changes. So with the mind. That is the great Kshanika Vijnâna Vâda doctrine, most difficult to understand, but most rigorously and logically worked out in the Buddhistic philosophy, and this arose in India in opposition to some part of the Vedanta. That had to be answered and we shall see how, later on, it could only be answered by Advaitism and by nothing else. We will see also how, in spite of people's curious notions about Advaitism, people's fright about Advaitism, it is the salvation of the world, because therein alone is to be found the reason of things. Dualism and other *isms* are very good as means of worship, very satisfying to the mind, and may be, they have helped the mind onward; but if man wants to be rational and religious at the same time, Advaita is the one system in the world for him. Well, now, we shall regard the mind as a similar river, continually filling itself at one end and emptying itself at the other end. Where is that unity which we call the Atman? The idea is this, that in spite of this continuous change in the body, and in spite of this continuous change in the mind, there is in us something that is unchangeable, which makes our ideas of things appear unchangeable. When rays of light coming from different quarters fall upon a screen, or a wall, or upon something that is not changeable, then and then alone it is possible for them to form a unity, then and then alone it is possible for them to form one complete whole. Where is this unity in the human organs, falling upon which, as it were, the various ideas will come to unity and become one complete whole? This certainly cannot be the mind itself, seeing that it also changes. Therefore there must be something which is neither the body nor the mind, something which changes not, something permanent, upon which all our ideas, our sensations fall to form a unity and a complete whole, and this is the real soul, the Atman, of man. And seeing that everything material, whether you call it fine matter, or mind, must be changeful, seeing that what you call gross matter, the external world, must also be changeful in comparison to that—this unchangeable something cannot be of material substance, therefore it is spiritual, that is to say, it is not matter; it is indestructible, unchangeable.

Next will come another question: Apart from those old arguments which only rise in the external world, the arguments in support of design—who created this external world, who created matter, etc? The idea here is to know truth only from the inner nature of man, and the question arises just in the same way as it arose about the soul. Taking for granted that there is a soul, unchangeable, in each man, which is neither the mind, nor the body, there is still a unity of idea among the souls, a unity of feeling, of sympathy. How is it possible that my soul can act upon your soul, where is the medium through which it can work, where is the medium through which it can act? How is it I can feel anything about your soul? What is it that is in touch both with your soul and with my soul? Therefore there is a metaphysical necessity of admitting another soul, for it must be a soul which acts in contact with all the different souls, and in and through matter; one Soul which covers and interpenetrates all the infinite number of souls in the world, in and through which they live, in and through which they sympathise, and love, and work for one another. And this universal Soul is Paramâtman, the Lord God of the universe. Again, it follows that because the soul is not made of matter, since it is spiritual, it cannot obey the laws of matter, it cannot be judged by the laws of matter. It is therefore unconquerable, birthless, deathless, and changeless.

नैनं छिन्दन्ति शस्त्राणि नैनं दहति पावकः ।
न चैनं क्लेदयंत्यापो न शोषयति मारुतः ॥
नित्यः सर्वगतः स्थाणुरचलोऽयं सनातनः ॥

—"This Self weapons cannot pierce, nor fire can burn, water cannot wet, nor air can dry up. Changeless, all-pervading, unmoving, immovable, eternal is this Self of man." We learn according to the Gita and the Vedanta, that this individual Self is also Vibhu, and according to Kapila, is omnipresent. Of course there are sects in India which hold that the Self is

Anu, infinitely small; but what they mean is Anu in manifestation; its real nature is Vibhu, all-pervading.

There comes another idea, startling perhaps, yet a characteristically Indian idea, and if there is any idea that is common to all our sects, it is this. Therefore I beg you to pay attention to this one idea and to remember it, for this is the very foundation of everything that we have in India. The idea is this. You have heard of the doctrine of physical evolution preached in the Western world by the German and the English savants. It tells us that the bodies of the different animals are really one, the differences that we see are but different expressions of the same series, that from the lowest worm to the highest and the most saintly man it is but one, the one changing into the other, and so on, going up and up, higher and higher, until it attains perfection. We had that idea also. Declares our Yogi Patanjali—जात्यन्तरपरिणामः प्रकृत्यापूरात् । One species—the Jâti is species—changes into another species—evolution; Parinâma means one thing changing into another, just as one species changes into another. Where do we differ from the Europeans? Patanjali says, Prakrityâpurât—"By the infilling of nature." The European says, it is competition, natural and sexual selection, etc., that forces one body to take the form of another. But here is another idea, a still better analysis, going deeper into the thing, and saying—"By the infilling of nature." What is meant by this infilling of nature? We admit that the amoeba goes higher and higher until it becomes a Buddha; we admit that, but we are, at the same time, as much certain that you cannot get an amount of work out of a machine unless you have put it in in some shape or other. The sum total of the energy remains the same, whatever the forms it may take. If you want a mass of energy at one end, you have got to put it in at the other end, it may be in another form, but the amount of energy that should be produced out of it must be the same. Therefore, if a Buddha is the one end of the change, the very amoeba must have been the Buddha also. If the Buddha is the evolved amoeba, the amoeba was the involved Buddha also. If this universe is the manifestation of an almost infinite amount of energy, when this universe was in a state of Pralaya, it must have represented the same amount of involved energy. It cannot have been otherwise. As such it follows that every soul is infinite. From the lowest worm that crawls under our feet to the noblest and greatest saints, all have this infinite power, infinite purity, and infinite everything. Only the difference is in the degree of manifestation. The worm is only manifesting just a little bit of that energy, you have manifested more; another god-man has manifested still more: that is all the difference. But that infinite power is there all the same. Says Patanjali: ततः क्षेत्रिकवत्—"Like the peasant irrigating his field." Through a little corner of his field he brings water from a reservoir somewhere, and perhaps he has got a little lock that prevents the water from rushing into his field. When he wants water, he has simply to open the lock, and in rushes the water of its own power. The power has not to be added, it is already there in the reservoir. So every one of us, every being, has as his own background such a reservoir of strength, infinite power, infinite purity, infinite bliss, and existence infinite—only these locks, these bodies, are hindering us from expressing what we really are to the fullest.

And as these bodies become more and more finely organised, as the Tamoguna becomes the Rajoguna, and as the Rajoguna becomes Sattvaguna, more and more of this power and purity become manifest, and therefore it is that our people have been so careful about eating and drinking, and the food question. It may be that the original ideas have been lost, just as with our marriage—which, though not belonging to the subject, I may take as an example. If I have another opportunity, I will talk to you about these; but let me tell you now that the ideas behind our marriage system are the only ideas through which there can be a real civilisation. There cannot be anything else. If a man or a woman were allowed the freedom to take up any woman or man as wife or husband, if individual pleasure, if satisfaction of animal instincts, were to be allowed to run loose in society, the result must be evil, evil children, wicked and demoniacal. Ay, man in every country is, on the one hand, producing these brutal children, and on the other hand multiplying the police force to keep these brutes down. The question is not how to destroy evil that way, but how to prevent the very birth of evil, and so long as you live in society, your marriage certainly affects every member of it; and therefore society has the right to dictate whom you shall marry, and whom you shall not. And great ideas of this kind have been behind the system of marriage here, what they call the astrological Jâti of the bride and bridegroom. And in passing I may remark that according to Manu a child who is born of lust is not an Aryan. The child whose very conception and whose death are according to the rules of the Vedas, such is an Aryan. Yes, and less of these Aryan children are being produced in every country, and the result is the mass of evil which we call Kali Yuga. But we have lost all these ideals; it is true we cannot carry all these ideas to the fullest length now, it is perfectly true we have made almost a caricature of some of these great ideas. It is lamentably true that the fathers and mothers are not what they were in old times, neither is society so educated as it used to be, neither has society that love for individuals that it used to have. But, however faulty the working out may be, the principle is sound; and if its application has become defective, if one method has failed, take up the principle and work it out better; why kill the principle? The same applies to the food question. The work and details are bad, very bad indeed, but that does not hurt the principle. The principle is eternal and must be there. Work it out afresh, and make a re-formed application.

This is the one great idea of the Atman which every one of our sects in India has to believe. Only, as we shall find, the dualists preach that this Atman by evil works becomes Sankuchita, i.e. all its powers and its nature become contracted, and by good works again that nature expands. And the Advaitist says that the Atman never expands nor contracts, but seems to do so. It appears to have become contracted. That is all the difference, but all have the one idea that our Atman has all the powers already, not that anything will come to It from outside, not that anything will drop into It from the skies. Mark you, your Vedas are not inspired, but expired, not that they came from anywhere outside, but they are the eternal laws living in every soul. The Vedas are in the soul of the ant, in the soul of the god. The ant has only to evolve and get the body of a sage or a Rishi, and the Vedas will come out, eternal laws expressing themselves. This is the one great idea to understand, that our power is already ours, our salvation is already within us. Say either that it has become contracted, or say that it has been covered with the veil of Mâyâ, it matters little; the idea is there already; you must have to believe in that, believe in the possibility of everybody—even in the lowest man there is the same possibility as in the Buddha. This is the doctrine of the Atman.

But now comes a tremendous fight. Here are the Buddhists, who equally analyse the body into a material stream and as equally analyse the mind into another. And as for this Atman they state that it is unnecessary; so we need not assume the Atman at all. What use of a substance, and qualities adhering to the substance? We say, Gunas, qualities, and qualities alone. It is illogical to assume two causes where one will explain the whole thing. And the fight went on, and all the theories which held the doctrine of substance were thrown to the ground by the Buddhists. There was a break-up all along the line of those who held on to the doctrine of substance and qualities, that you have a soul, and I have a soul, and every one has a soul separate from the mind and body, and that each one is an individual.

So far we have seen that the idea of dualism is all right; for there is the body, there is then the fine body—the mind—there is this Atman, and in and through all the Atmans, is that Paramâtman, God. The difficulty is here, that this Atman and Paramatman are both called substance, to which the mind and body and so-called substances adhere like so many qualities. Nobody has ever seen a substance, none can ever conceive; what is the use of thinking of this substance? Why not become a Kshanikavâdi and say that whatever exists is this succession of mental currents and nothing more? They do not adhere to each other, they do not form a unit, one is chasing the other, like waves in the ocean, never complete, never forming one unit whole. Man is a succession of waves, and when one goes away, it generates another, and the cessation of these wave-forms is what is called Nirvâna. You see that dualism is mute before this; it is impossible that it can bring up any argument, and the dualistic God also cannot be retained here. The idea of a God that is omnipresent, and yet is a person who creates without hands, and moves without feet, and so on, and who has created the universe as a Kumbhakâra (potter) creates a Ghata (pot), the Buddhist declares, is childish, and that if this is God, he is going to fight this God and not worship Him. This universe is full of misery; if it is the work of a God, we are going to fight this God. And secondly, this God is illogical and impossible, as all of you are aware. We need not go into the defects of the "design theory", as all our Kshanikas have shown them full well; and so this Personal God fell to pieces.

Truth, and nothing but truth, is the watchword of the Advaitist. सत्यमेव जयते नानृतं । सत्येन पन्था विततो देवयान:—"Truth alone triumphs, and not untruth. Through truth alone lies Devayâna, the way to gods." Everybody marches forward under that banner; ay, but it is only to crush the weaker man's position by his own. You come with your dualistic idea of God to pick a quarrel with a poor man who is worshipping an image, and you think you are wonderfully rational, you can confound him, but if he turns round and shatters your own Personal God, and calls that an imaginary ideal, where are you? You fall back on faith and so on, or raise the cry of atheism, the old cry of a weak man—whosoever defeats him is an atheist. If you are to be rational, be rational all along the line, and if not, allow others the same privilege which you ask for yourselves. How can you prove the existence of this God? On the other hand it can be almost disproved. There is not a shadow of a proof as to His existence, and there are very strong arguments to the contrary. How will you prove His existence, with your God, and His Gunas, and an infinite number of souls which are substance, and each soul an individual? In what are you an individual? You are not as a body, for you know today better than even the Buddhists of old knew, that what may have been matter in the sun has just now become matter in you, and will go out and become matter in the plants; then where is your individuality, Mr. So-and-so? The same applies to the mind. Where is your individuality? You have one thought tonight and another tomorrow. You do not think the same way as you thought when you were a child, and old men do not think the same way as they did when they were young. Where is your individuality, then? Do not say it is in consciousness, this Ahamkara, because this only covers a small part of your existence. While I am talking to you, all my organs are working and I am not conscious of it. If consciousness is the proof of existence they do not exist then, because I am not conscious of them. Where are you then with your Personal God theories? How can you prove such a God?

Again, the Buddhists will stand up and declare—not only is it illogical, but immoral, for it teaches man to be a coward and to seek assistance outside, and nobody can give him such help. Here is the universe, man made it; why then depend on an imaginary being outside, whom nobody ever saw or felt, or got help from? Why then do you make cowards of yourselves, and teach your children that the highest state of man is to be like a dog, and go crawling before this imaginary being, saying that you are weak and impure, and that you are everything vile in this universe? On the other hand, the Buddhists may urge not only that you tell a lie, but that you bring a tremendous amount of evil upon your children; for, mark you, this world is one of hypnotisation. Whatever you tell yourself, that you become. Almost the first words the great Buddha uttered were: "What you think, that you are; what you will think, that you will be." If this is true, do not teach yourself that you are nothing, ay, that you cannot do anything unless you are helped by somebody who does not live here, but sits above the clouds. The result will be that you will be more and more weakened every day. By constantly repeating, "We are very impure, Lord, make us pure", the result will be that you will hypnotise yourselves into all sorts of vices. Ay, the Buddhists say that ninety per cent of these vices that you see in every society are on account of this idea of a Personal God; this is an awful idea of the human being that the end and aim of this expression of life, this wonderful expression of life, is to become like a dog. Says the Buddhist to the Vaishnava, if your ideal, your aim and goal is to go to the place called Vaikuntha where God lives, and there stand before Him with folded hands all through eternity, it is better to commit suicide than do that. The Buddhists may even urge that that is why he is going to create annihilation, Nirvana, to escape this. I am putting these ideas before you as a Buddhist just for the time being, because nowadays all these Advaitic ideas are said to make you immoral, and I am trying to tell you how the other side looks. Let us face both sides boldly and bravely.

We have seen first of all that this cannot be proved, this idea of a Personal God creating the world; is there any child that can believe this today? Because a Kumbhakara creates a Ghata, therefore a God created the world! If this is so, then your Kumbhakara is God also, and if any one tells you that he acts without head and hands, you may take him to a lunatic asylum.

Has ever your Personal God, the Creator of the world, to

whom you cry all your life, helped you?—is the next challenge from modern science. They will prove that any help you have had could have been got by your own exertions, and better still, you need not have spent your energy in that crying, you could have done it better without that weeping and crying. And we have seen that along with this idea of a Personal God comes tyranny and priestcraft. Tyranny and priestcraft have prevailed wherever this idea existed, and until the lie is knocked on the head, say the Buddhists, tyranny will not cease. So long as man thinks he has to cower before a supernatural being, so long there will be priests to claim rights and privileges and to make men cower before them, while these poor men will continue to ask some priest to act as interceder for them. You may do away with the Brahmin, but mark me, those who do so will put themselves in his place, and will be worse, because the Brahmin has a certain amount of generosity in him, but these upstarts are always the worst of tyrannisers. If a beggar gets wealth, he thinks the whole world is a bit of straw. So these priests there must be, so long as this Personal God idea persists, and it will be impossible to think of any great morality in society. Priestcraft and tyranny go hand in hand. Why was it invented? Because some strong men in old times got people into their hands and said, you must obey us or we will destroy you. That was the long and the short of it. महद्भयं वज्रमुद्यतम् । It is the idea of the thunderer, who kills every one who does not obey him.

Next the Buddhist says, you have been perfectly rational up to this point, that everything is the result of the law of Karma. You believe in an infinity of souls and that souls are without birth or death, and this infinity of souls and the belief in the law of Karma are perfectly logical no doubt. There cannot be a cause without an effect, the present must have had its cause in the past, and will have its effect in the future. The Hindu says that Karma is Jada (inert) and not Chaitanya (spirit), therefore some Chaitanya is necessary to bring this cause to fruition. Is it so, that Chaitanya is necessary to bring the plant to fruition? If I plant the seed and add water, no Chaitanya is necessary. You may say there was some original Chaitanya there, but the souls themselves were the Chaitanya, nothing else is necessary. If human souls have it too, what necessity is there for a God, as say the Jains, who, unlike the

Buddhists, believe in souls, and do not believe in God. Where are you logical, where are you moral? And when you criticise Advaitism and fear that it will make for immorality, just read a little of what has been done in India by dualistic sects. If there have been twenty thousand Advaitist blackguards, there have also been twenty thousand Dvaitist blackguards. Generally speaking, there will be more Dvaitist blackguards, because it takes a better type of mind to understand Advaitism, and Advaitists can scarcely be frightened into anything. What remains for you Hindus, then? There is no help for you out of the clutches of the Buddhists. You may quote the Vedas, but he does not believe in them. He will say, "My Tripitakas say otherwise, and they are without beginning or end, not even written by Buddha, for Buddha says he is only reciting them; they are eternal." And he adds, "Yours are wrong, ours are the true Vedas, yours are manufactured by the Brahmin priests, therefore out with them." How do you escape?

Here is the way to get out. Take up the first objection, the metaphysical one, that substance and qualities are different. Says the Advaitist, they are not. There is no difference between substance and qualities. You know the old illustration, how the rope is taken for the snake, and when you see the snake, you do not see the rope at all, the rope has vanished. Dividing the thing into substance and quality is a metaphysical something in the brains of philosophers, for never can they be in effect outside. You see qualities if you are an ordinary man, and substance if you are a great Yogi, but you never see both at the same time. So, Buddhists, your quarrel about substance and qualities has been but a miscalculation which does not stand in fact. But, if substance is unqualified, there can only be one. If you take qualities off from the soul, and show that these qualities are in the mind, really superimposed on the soul, then there can never be two souls, for it is qualification that makes the difference between one soul and another. How do you know that one soul is different from the other? Owing to certain differentiating marks, certain qualities. And where qualities do not exist how can there be differentiation? Therefore there are not two souls, there is but One, and your Paramatman is unnecessary, it is this very soul. That One is called Paramatman, that very One is called Jivâtman, and so on; and you dualists, such as the Sânkhyas and others, who say that the soul is Vibhu, omnipresent, how can you make two infinites? There can be only one. What else? This One is the one Infinite Atman, everything else is Its manifestation. There the Buddhist stops, but there it does not end.

The Advaitist position is not merely a weak one of criticism. The Advaitist criticises others when they come too near him, and just throws them away, that is all, but he propounds his own position. He is the only one that criticises and does not stop with criticism and showing books. Here you are. You say the universe is a thing of continuous motion. In Vyashti (the finite) everything is moving, you are moving, the table is moving, motion everywhere; it is Samsâra, continuous motion; it is Jagat. Therefore there cannot be an individuality in this Jagat, because individuality means that which does not change; there cannot be any changeful individuality, it is a contradiction in terms. There is no such thing as individuality in this little world of ours, the Jagat. Thought and feeling, mind and body, men and animals and plants are in a continuous state of flux. But suppose you take the universe as a unit whole; can it change or move? Certainly not. Motion is possible in comparison with something which is a little less in motion, or entirely motionless. The universe as a whole, therefore, is motionless, unchangeable. You are, therefore, an individual then and then alone, when you are the whole of it, when the realisation of "I am the universe" comes. That is why the Vedantist says that so long as there are two, fear does not cease. It is only when one does not see another, does not feel another, when it is all one—then alone fear ceases, then alone death vanishes, then alone Samsara vanishes. Advaita teaches us therefore that man is individual in being universal, and not in being particular. You are immortal only when you are the whole. You are fearless and deathless only when you are the universe; and then that which you call the universe is the same as that you call God, the same that you call existence, the same that you call the whole. It is the one undivided Existence which is taken to be the manifold world which we see, as also others who are in the same state of mind as we. People who have done a little better Karma and got a better state of mind, when they die, look upon it as Svarga, and see Indras and so forth. People still higher will see it, the very same thing, as Brahma-loka, and the perfect ones will neither see the earth nor the heaven, nor any Loka at all. This universe will have vanished, and Brahman will be in its stead.

Can we know this Brahman? I have told you of the painting of the Infinite in the Samhita. Here we shall find another side shown, the infinite internal. That was the infinite of the muscles. Here we shall have the Infinite of thought. There the Infinite was attempted to be painted in language positive; here that language failed and the attempt has been to paint it in language negative. Here is this universe, and even admitting that it is Brahman, can we know it? No! No! You must understand this one thing again very clearly. Again and again this doubt will come to you, if this is Brahman, how can we know it? विज्ञातारमरे केन विजानीयात्—"By what can the knower be known?" How can the knower be known? The eyes see everything; can they see themselves? They cannot. The very fact of knowledge is a degradation. Children of the Aryans, you must remember this, for herein lies a big story. All the Western temptations that come to you, have their metaphysical basis on that one thing—there is nothing higher than sense-knowledge. In the East, we say in our Vedas that this knowledge is lower than the thing itself, because it is always a limitation. When you want to know a thing it immediately becomes limited by your mind. They say, refer back to that instance of the oyster making a pearl and see how knowledge is limitation, gathering a thing, bringing it into consciousness, and not knowing it as a whole. This is true about all knowledge, and can it be less so about the Infinite? Can you thus limit Him who is the substance of all knowledge, Him who is the Sâkshi, the Witness, without whom you cannot have any knowledge, Him who has no qualities, who is the Witness of the whole universe, the Witness in our own souls? How can you know Him? By what means can you bind Him up? Everything, the whole universe, is such a false attempt. This Infinite Atman is, as it were, trying to see His own face, and all, from the lowest animals to the highest of gods, are like so many mirrors to reflect Himself in, and He is taking up still others, finding them insufficient, until in the human body He comes to know that it is the finite of the finite, all is finite, there cannot be any expression of the Infinite in the finite. Then comes the retrograde march, and this is what is called renunciation, Vairâgya. Back from the senses, back! Do not go to the senses is the watchword of

Vairagya. This is the watchword of all morality, this is the watchword of all well-being; for you must remember that with us the universe begins in Tapasyâ, in renunciation, and as you go back and back, all the forms are being manifested before you, and they are left aside one after the other until you remain what you really are. This is Moksha, or liberation.

This idea we have to understand: विज्ञातारमरे केन विजानीयात् —"How to know the knower?" The knower cannot be known, because if it were known, it will not be the knower. If you look at your eyes in a mirror, the reflection is no more your eyes, but something else, only a reflection. Then if this Soul, this Universal, Infinite Being which you are, is only a witness, what good is it? It cannot live, and move about, and enjoy the world, as we do. People cannot understand how the witness can enjoy. "Oh," they say, "you Hindus have become quiescent, and good for nothing, through this doctrine that you are witnesses!" First of all, it is only the witness that can enjoy. If there is a wrestling match, who enjoys it, those who take part in it, or those who are looking on, the outsiders? The more you are the witness of anything in life, the more you enjoy it. And this is Ânanda, and therefore infinite bliss can only be yours when you have become the witness of this universe, then alone you are a Mukta Purusha. It is the witness alone that can work without any desire, without any idea of going to heaven, without any idea of blame, without any idea of praise. The witness alone enjoys, and none else.

Coming to the moral aspect, there is one thing between the metaphysical and the moral aspect of Advaitism; it is the theory of Maya. Every one of these points in the Advaita system requires years to understand and months to explain. Therefore you will excuse me if I only just touch them *en passant*. This theory of Maya has been the most difficult thing to understand in all ages. Let me tell you in a few words that it is surely no theory, it is the combination of the three ideas Desha-Kâla-Nimitta—space, time, and causation—and this time and space and cause have been further reduced into Nâma-Rupa. Suppose there is a wave in the ocean. The wave is distinct from the ocean only in its form and name, and this form and this name cannot have any separate existence from the wave; they exist only with the wave. The wave may sub side, but the same amount of water remains, even if the name and form that were on the wave vanish for ever. So this Maya is what makes the difference between me and you, between all animals and man, between gods and men. In fact, it is this Maya that causes the Atman to be caught, as it were, in so many millions of beings, and these are distinguishable only through name and form. If you leave it alone, let name and form go, all this variety vanishes for ever, and you are what you really are. This is Maya. It is again no theory, but a statement of facts. When the realist states that this table exists, what he means is that this table has an independent existence of its own, that it does not depend on the existence of anything else in the universe, and if this whole universe be destroyed and annihilated, this table will remain just as it is now. A little thought will show you that it cannot be so. Everything here in the sense-world is dependent and interdependent, relative and correlative, the existence of one depending on the other. There are three steps, therefore, in our knowledge of things: the first is that each thing is individual, and separate from every other; and the next step is to find that there is a relation and correlation between all things; and the third is that there is only one thing which we see as many. The first idea of God with the ignorant is that this God is somewhere outside the universe, that is to say, the conception of God is extremely human; He does just what a man does, only on a bigger and higher scale. And we have seen how that idea of God is proved in a few words to be unreasonable and insufficient. And the next idea is the idea of a power we see manifested everywhere. This is the real Personal God we get in the *Chandi,* but, mark me, not a God that you make the reservoir of all good qualities only. You cannot have two Gods, God and Satan; you must have only one, and dare to call Him good and bad; have only one, and take the logical consequences. We read in the *Chandi*: "We salute Thee, O Divine Mother, who lives in every being as peace. We salute Thee, O Divine Mother, who lives in all beings as purity." At the same time we must take the whole consequence of calling Him the All-formed. "All this is bliss, O Gârgi; wherever there is bliss, there is a portion of the Divine." You may use it how you like. In this light before me, you may give a poor man a hundred rupees, and another man may forge your name, but the light will be the same for both. This is the second stage.

And the third is that God is neither outside nature nor inside nature, but God and nature and soul and universe are all convertible terms. You never see two things; it is your metaphysical words that have deluded you. You assume that you are a body and have a soul, and that you are both together. How can that be? Try in your own mind. If there is a Yogi among you, he knows himself as Chaitanya, for him the body has vanished. An ordinary man thinks of himself as a body; the idea of spirit has vanished from him; but because the metaphysical ideas exist that man has a body and a soul and all these things, you think they are all simultaneously there. One thing at a time. Do not talk of God when you see matter; you see the effect and the effect alone, and the cause you cannot see, and the moment you can see the cause the effect will have vanished. Where is this world then, and who has taken it off?

"One that is present always as consciousness, the bliss absolute, beyond all bounds, beyond all compare, beyond all qualities, ever-free, limitless as the sky, without parts, the absolute, the perfect—such a Brahman, O sage, O learned one, shines in the heart of the Jnâni in Samâdhi.

"Where all the changes of nature cease for ever, who is thought beyond all thoughts, who is equal to all yet having no equal, immeasurable, whom the Vedas declare, who is the essence in what we call our existence, the perfect—such a Brahman, O sage, O learned one, shines in the heart of the Jnani in Samadhi.

"Beyond all birth and death, the Infinite One, incomparable, like the whole universe deluged in water in Mahâpralaya—water above, water beneath, water on all sides, and on the face of that water not a wave, not a ripple—silent and calm, all visions have died out, all fights and quarrels and the war of fools and saints have ceased for ever—such a Brahman, O sage, O learned one, shines in the heart of the Jnani in Samadhi."

That also comes, and when that comes, the world has vanished.

We have seen, then, that this Brahman, this Reality, is unknown and unknowable, not in the sense of the agnostic, but because to know Him would be a blasphemy, because you are He already. We have also seen that this Brahman is not this table and yet is this table. Take off the name and form, and whatever is reality is He. He is the reality in everything.

"Thou art the woman, thou the man, thou art the boy, and the girl as well, thou the old man supportest thyself on a stick, thou art all in all in the Universe." That is the theme of Advaitism. A few words more. Herein lies, we find, the explanation of the essence of things. We have seen how here alone we can take a firm stand against all the onrush of logic and scientific knowledge. Here at last reason has a firm foundation, and, at the same time, the Indian Vedantist does not curse the preceding steps; he looks back and he blesses them, and he knows that they were true, only wrongly perceived, and wrongly stated. They were the same truth, only seen through the glass of Maya, distorted it may be—yet truth, and nothing but truth. The same God whom the ignorant man saw outside nature, the same whom the little-knowing man saw as interpenetrating the universe, and the same whom the sage realises as his own self, as the whole universe itself—all are One and the same Being, the same entity seen from different standpoints, seen through different glasses of Maya, perceived by different minds, and all the difference was caused by that. Not only so, but one view must lead to the other. What is the difference between science and common knowledge? Go out into the streets in the dark, and if something unusual is happening there, ask one of the passers-by what is the cause of it. It is ten to one that he will tell you it is a ghost causing the phenomenon. He is always going after ghosts and spirits outside, because it is the nature of ignorance to seek for causes outside of effects. If a stone falls, it has been thrown by a devil or a ghost, says the ignorant man, but the scientific man says it is the law of nature, the law of gravitation.

What is the fight between science and religion everywhere? Religions are encumbered with such a mass of explanations which come from outside—one angel is in charge of the sun, another of the moon, and so on *ad infinitum*; every change is caused by a spirit, the one common point of agreement being that they are all outside the thing; while science means that the cause of a thing is sought out by the nature of the thing itself. As step by step science is progressing, it has taken the explanation of natural phenomena out of the hands of spirits and angels. Because Advaitism has done likewise in spiritual matters, it is the most scientific religion. This universe has not been created by any extra-cosmic God, nor is it the work of any outside genius. It is self-creating, self-dissolving, self-manifesting, One Infinite Existence, the Brahman. Tattvamasi Shvetaketo—"That Thou art, O Shvetaketu!" Thus you see that this, and this alone, and none else, can be the only scientific religion. And with all the prattle about science that is going on daily at the present time in modern half-educated India, with all the talk about rationalism and reason that I hear every day, I expect that whole sects of you will come over and dare to be Advaitists, and dare to preach it to the world in the words of Buddha: बहुजनहिताय बहुजनसुखाय "For the good of many, for the happiness of many." If you do not, I take you for cowards. If you cannot get over your cowardice, if your fear is your excuse, allow the same liberty to others, do not try to break up the poor idol-worshipper, do not call him a devil, do not go about preaching to every man that does not agree entirely with you. Know first, that you are cowards yourselves, and if society frightens you, if your own superstitions of the past frighten you so much, how much more will these superstitions frighten and bind down those who are ignorant? That is the Advaita position. Have mercy on others. Would to God that the whole world were Advaitists tomorrow, not only in theory, but in realisation. But if that cannot be, let us do the next best thing; let us take the ignorant by the hand, lead them always step by step just as they can go, and know that every step in all religious growth in India has been progressive. It is not from bad to good, but from good to better.

Something more has to be told about the moral relation. Our boys blithely talk nowadays, they learn from somebody —the Lord knows from whom—that Advaita makes people immoral, because if we are all one and all God, what need of morality will there be at all! In the first place, that is the argument of the brute, who can only be kept down by the whip. If you are such brutes commit suicide, rather than pass for human beings, who have to be kept down by the whip. If the whip is taken away you will all be demons! You ought all to be killed, if such is the case; there is no help for you; you must always be living under this whip and rod, and there is no salvation, no escape for you. In the second place, Advaita and Advaita alone explains morality. Every religion preaches that the essence of all morality is to do good to others. And why? Be unselfish. And why should I? Some God has said it? He is not for me. Some texts have declared it? Let them; that is nothing to me; let them all tell it. And if they do, what is it to me? Each one for himself, and somebody take the hindmost; that is all the morality in the world, at least with many. What is the reason that I should be moral? You cannot explain it except when you come to know the truth as given in the Gita: "He who sees everyone in himself, and himself in everyone, thus seeing the same God living in all, he, the sage, no more kills the Self by the self." Know through Advaita that whomsoever you hurt, you hurt yourself; they are all you. Whether you know it or not, through all hands you work, through all feet you move, you are the king enjoying in the palace, you are the beggar leading that miserable existence in the street; you are in the ignorant as well as in the learned, you are in the man who is weak, and you are in the strong; know this and be sympathetic. And that is why we must not hurt others. That is why I do not even care whether I have to starve, because there will be millions of mouths eating at the same time, and they are all mine. Therefore I should not care what becomes of me and mine, for the whole universe is mine, I am enjoying all the bliss at the same time; and who can kill me, or the universe? Herein is morality. Here, in Advaita alone, is morality explained. The others teach it, but cannot give you its reason. Then, so far about explanation.

What is the gain? It is strength. Take off that veil of hypnotism which you have cast upon the world, send not out thoughts and words of weakness unto humanity. Know that all sins and all evils can be summed up in that one word, weakness. It is weakness that is the motive power in all evil doing; it is weakness that is the source of all selfishness; it is weakness that makes men injure others; it is weakness that makes them manifest what they are not in reality. Let them all know what they are; let them repeat day and night what they are. Soham. Let them suck it in with their mothers' milk, this idea of strength—I am He, I am He. This is to be heard first—श्रोतव्यो मन्तव्यो निदिध्यासितव्यः etc. And then let them think of it and out of that thought, out of that heart will proceed works such as the world has never seen. What has to be done? Ay, this Advaita is said by some to be impracticable;

that is to say, it is not yet manifesting itself on the material plane. To a certain extent that is true, for, remember the saying of the Vedas:

ओमित्येकाक्षरं ब्रह्म ओमित्येकाक्षरं परम् ।
ओमित्येकाक्षरं ज्ञात्वा यो यदिच्छति तस्य तत् ॥

—"Om, this is the Brahman; Om, this is the greatest reality; he who knows the secret of this Om, whatever he desires that he gets." Ay, therefore, first know the secret of this Om, that you are the Om; know the secret of this Tattvamasi, and then and then alone whatever you want shall come to you. If you want to be great materially, believe that you are so. I may be a little bubble, and you may be a wave mountain-high, but know that for both of us the infinite ocean is the background, the infinite Brahman is our magazine of power and strength, and we can draw as much as we like, both of us, I the bubble and you the mountain-high wave. Believe therefore in yourselves. The secret of Advaita is: Believe in yourselves first, and then believe in anything else. In the history of the world, you will find that only those nations that have believed in themselves have become great and strong. In the history of each nation, you will always find that only those individuals who have believed in themselves have become great and strong. Here, to India, came an Englishman who was only a clerk, and for want of funds and other reasons he twice tried to blow his brains out, and when he failed, he believed in himself, he believed that he was born to do great things, and that man became Lord Clive, the founder of the Empire. If he had believed the Padres and gone crawling all his life—"O Lord, I am weak, and I am low"—where would he have been? In a lunatic asylum. You also are made lunatics by these evil teachings. I have seen all the world over the bad effects of these weak teachings of humility destroying the human race. Our children are brought up in this way, and is it a wonder that they become semi-lunatics?

This is teaching on the practical side. Believe, therefore, in yourselves, and if you want material wealth, work it out; it will come to you. If you want to be intellectual, work it out on the intellectual plane, and intellectual giants you shall be. And if you want to attain to freedom, work it out on the spiritual plane, and free you shall be, and shall enter into

Nirvana, the Eternal Bliss. But one defect which lay in the Advaita was its being worked out so long on the spiritual plane only, and nowhere else; now the time has come when you have to make it practical. It shall no more be a Rahasya, a secret, it shall no more live with monks in caves and forests, and in the Himalayas; it must come down to the daily, everyday life of the people; it shall be worked out in the palace of the king, in the cave of the recluse, it shall be worked out in the cottage of the poor, by the beggar in the secret, everywhere, anywhere it can be worked out. Therefore do not fear whether you are a woman or a Shudra, for this religion is so great, says Lord Krishna, that even a little of it brings a great amount of good. Therefore, children of the Aryans, do not sit idle; awake, arise, and stop not till the goal is reached. The time has come when this Advaita is to be worked out practically. Let us bring it down from heaven unto the earth; this is the present dispensation. Ay, the voices of our forefathers of old are telling us to bring it down from heaven to the earth. Let your teachings permeate the world, till they have entered into every pore of society, till they have become the common property of everybody, till they have become part and parcel of our lives, till they have entered into our veins and tingle with every drop of blood there.

Ay, you may be astonished to hear that as practical Vedantists the Americans are better than we are. I used to stand on the seashore at New York, and look at the emigrants coming from different countries, crushed, down-trodden, hopeless, unable to look a man in the face, with a little bundle of clothes as all their possession, and these all in rags; if they saw a policeman, they were afraid and tried to get to the other side of the foot-path. And, mark you, in six months those very men were walking erect, well-clothed, looking everybody in the face; and what made this wonderful difference? Say, this man comes from Armenia, or somewhere else where he was crushed down beyond all recognition, where everybody told him he was a born slave, and born to remain in a low state all his life, and where at the least move on his part he was trodden upon. There everything told him as it were, "Slave! you are a slave, remain so. Hopeless you were born, hopeless you must remain." Even the very air murmured round him as it were, "There is no hope for you, hopeless and a slave you must remain", while the strong man crushed the life out of him. And when he landed in the streets of New York, he found a gentleman, well dressed, shaking him by the hand; it made no difference that the one was in rags and the other well clad. He went a step further and saw a restaurant, that there were gentlemen dining at a table, and he was asked to take a seat at the corner of the same table. He went about, and found a new life, that there was a place where he was a man among men. Perhaps he went to Washington, shook hands with the President of the United States, and perhaps there he saw men coming from distant villages, peasants, and ill clad, all shaking hands with the President. Then the veil of Maya slipped away from him. He is Brahman, he who has been hypnotised into slavery and weakness, is once more awake, and he rises up and finds himself a man, in a world of men. Ay, in this country of ours, the very birthplace of the Vedanta, our masses have been hypnotised for ages into that state. To touch them is pollution, to sit with them is pollution! Hopeless they were born, hopeless they must remain! And the result is that they have been sinking, sinking, sinking, and have come to the last stage to which a human being can come. For what country is there in the world where man has to sleep with the cattle? And for this, blame nobody else, do not commit the mistake of the ignorant. The effect is here and the cause is here too. We are to blame. Stand up, be bold and take the blame on your own shoulders. Do not go about throwing mud at others; for all the faults you suffer from, you are the sole and only cause.

Young men of Lahore, understand this, therefore, this great sin, hereditary and national, is on our shoulders. There is no hope for us. You may make thousands of societies, twenty thousand political assemblages, fifty thousand institutions. These will be of no use until there is that sympathy, that love, that heart, that thinks for all; until Buddha's heart comes once more into India, until the words of Lord Krishna are brought to their practical use, there is no hope for us. You go on imitating the Europeans and their societies and their assemblages, but let me tell you a story, a fact that I saw with my own eyes. A company of Burmans was taken over to London by some persons here, who turned out to be Eurasians. They exhibited these people in London, took all the money, and then took these Burmans over to the Continent, and left them there for good or evil. These poor people did not know a word of any European language, but the English Consul in Austria sent them over to London. They were helpless in London, without knowing any one. But an English lady got to know of them, took these foreigners from Burma into her own house, gave them her own clothes, her bed, and everything, and then sent the news to the papers. And, mark you, the next day the whole nation was, as it were, roused. Money poured in, and these people were helped out and sent back to Burma. On this sort of sympathy are based all their political and other institutions; it is the rock-foundation of love, for themselves at least. They may not love the world; and the Burmans may be their enemies, but in England, it goes without saying, there is this great love for their own people, for truth and justice and charity to the stranger at the door. I should be the most ungrateful man if I did not tell you how wonderfully and how hospitably I was received in every country in the West. Where is the heart here to build upon? No sooner do we start a little joint-stock company than we try to cheat each other, and the whole thing comes down with a crash. You talk of imitating the English, and building up as big a nation as they are. But where are the foundations? Ours are only sand, and therefore the building comes down with a crash in no time.

Therefore, young men of Lahore, raise once more that mighty banner of Advaita, for on no other ground can you have that wonderful love, until you see that the same Lord is present everywhere. Unfurl that banner of love! Arise, awake, and stop not till the goal is reached. Arise, arise once more, for nothing can be done without renunciation. If you want to help others, your little self must go. In the words of the Christians—you cannot serve God and Mammon at the same time. Have Vairagya—your ancestors gave up the world for doing great things. At the present time there are men who give up the world to help their own salvation. Throw away everything, even your own salvation, and go and help others. Ay, you are always talking bold words, but here is practical Vedanta before you. Give up this little life of yours. What matters it if you die of starvation, you and I and thousands like us, so long as this nation lives? The nation is sinking, the curse of unnumbered millions is on our heads—those to whom we have been giving ditch-water to drink when they have been dying of thirst and while the perennial river of water was flowing past, the unnumbered millions whom we have allowed to starve in sight of plenty, the unnumbered millions to whom we have talked of Advaita and whom we have hated with all our strength, the unnumbered millions for whom we have invented the doctrine of Lokâchâra (usage), to whom we have talked theoretically that we are all the same and all are one with the same Lord, without even an ounce of practice. "Yet, my friends, it must be only in the mind and never in practice!" Wipe off this blot. Arise and awake. What matters it if this little life goes? Everyone has to die, the saint or the sinner, the rich or the poor. The body never remains for anyone. Arise and awake and be perfectly sincere. Our insincerity in India is awful; what we want is character, that steadiness and character that make a man cling on to a thing like grim death.

"Let the sages blame or let them praise, let Lakshmi come today or let her go away, let death come just now, or in a hundred years; he indeed is the sage who does not make one false step from the right path." Arise and awake, for the time is passing and all our energies will be frittered away in vain talking. Arise and awake, let minor things, and quarrels over little details, and fights over little doctrines be thrown aside, for here is the greatest of all works, here are the sinking millions. When the Mohammedans first came into India, what a great number of Hindus were here; but mark, how today they have dwindled down. Every day they will become less and less till they wholly disappear. Let them disappear, but with them will disappear the marvellous ideas, of which, with all their defects and all their misrepresentations, they still stand as representatives. And with them will disappear this marvellous Advaita, the crest-jewel of all spiritual thought. Therefore, arise, awake, with your hands stretched out to protect the spirituality of the world. And first of all, work it out for your own country. What we want is not so much spirituality as a little of the bringing down of the Advaita into the material world. First bread and then religion. We stuff them too much with religion, when the poor fellows have been starving. No dogmas will satisfy the cravings of hunger. There are two curses here, first our weakness, secondly, our hatred, our dried-up hearts. You may talk doctrines by the millions, you may have sects by the hundreds of millions; ay, but it is nothing until you have the heart to feel. Feel for them as your Veda teaches you, till you find they are parts of your own bodies, till you realise that you and they, the poor and the rich, the saint and the sinner, are all parts of One Infinite Whole, which you call Brahman.

Gentlemen, I have tried to place before you a few of the most brilliant points of the Advaita system, and now the time has come when it should be carried into practice, not only in this country but everywhere. Modern science and its sledge-hammer blows are pulverising the porcelain foundations of all dualistic religions everywhere. Not only here are the dualists torturing texts till they will extend no longer—for texts are not India-rubber—it is not only here that they are trying to get into the nooks and corners to protect themselves; it is still more so in Europe and America. And even there something of this idea will have to go from India. It has already got there. It will have to grow and increase, and save their civilisations too. For, in the West, the old order of things is vanishing, giving way to a new order of things, which is the worship of gold, the worship of Mammon. Thus, this old crude system of religion was better than the modern system, namely competition and gold. No nation, however strong, can stand on such foundations, and the history of the world tells us that all that had such foundations are dead and gone. In the first place we have to stop the incoming of such a wave in India. Therefore, preach the Advaita to every one, so that religion may withstand the shock of modern science. Not only so, you will have to help others; your thought will help out Europe and America. But, above all, let me once more remind you that here is need of practical work, and the first part of that is that you should go to the sinking millions of India, and take them by the hand, remembering the words of the Lord Krishna:

इहैव तैर्जितः सर्गो येषां साम्ये स्थितं मनः ।
निर्दोषं हि समं ब्रह्म तस्मात् ब्रह्मणि ते स्थिताः ॥

—"Even in this life they have conquered relative existence whose minds are firm-fixed on the sameness of everything, for God is pure and the same to all; therefore, such are said to be living in God."

THE FUTURE OF INDIA

This is the ancient land where wisdom made its home before it went into any other country, the same India whose influx of spirituality is represented, as it were, on the material plane, by rolling rivers like oceans, where the eternal Himalayas, rising tier above tier with their snow-caps, look as it were into the very mysteries of heaven. Here is the same India whose soil has been trodden by the feet of the greatest sages that ever lived. Here first sprang up inquiries into the nature of man, and into the internal world. Here first arose the doctrines of the immortality of the soul, the existence of a supervising God, an immanent God in nature and in man, and here the highest ideals of religion and philosophy have attained their culminating points. This is the land from whence, like the tidal waves, spirituality and philosophy have again and again rushed out and deluged the world, and this is the land from whence once more such tides must proceed in order to bring life and vigour into the decaying races of mankind. It is the same India which has withstood the shocks of centuries, of hundreds of foreign invasions, of hundreds of upheavals of manners and customs. It is the same land which stands firmer than any rock in the world, with its undying vigour, indestructible life. Its life is of the same nature as the soul, without beginning and without end, immortal, and we are the children of such a country.

Children of India, I am here to speak to you today about some practical things, and my object in reminding you about the glories of the past is simply this. Many times have I been told that looking into the past only degenerates and leads to nothing, and that we should look to the future. That is true. But out of the past is built the future. Look back, therefore, as far as you can, drink deep of the eternal fountains that are behind, and after that, look forward, march forward and make India brighter, greater, much higher than she ever was. Our ancestors were great. We must first recall that. We must learn the elements of our being, the blood that courses in our veins; we must have faith in that blood, and what it did in the past; and out of that faith, and consciousness of past greatness, we must build an India yet greater than what she has been. There have been periods of decay and degradation. I do not attach much importance to them; we all know that. Such periods have been necessary. A mighty tree produces a beautiful ripe fruit. That fruit falls on the ground, it decays and rots, and out of that decay springs the root and the future tree, perhaps mightier than the first one. This period of decay through which we have passed was all the more necessary. Out of this decay is coming the India of the future; it is sprouting, its first leaves are already out, and a mighty, gigantic tree, the "Urdhvamulam," is here, already beginning to appear, and it is about that that I am going to speak to you.

The problems in India are more complicated, more momentous, than the problems in any other country. Race, religion, language, governent—all these together make a nation. The elements which compose the nations of the world are indeed very few, taking race after race, compared to this country. Here have been the Aryan, the Dravidian, the Tartar, the Turk, the Mogul, the European—all the nations of the world, as it were, pouring their blood into this land. Of languages the most wonderful conglomeration is here; of manners and customs there is more difference between two Indian races than between the European and the Eastern races.

The one common ground that we have is our sacred traditions, our religion. That is the only common ground, and upon that we shall have to build. In Europe, political ideas form the national unity. In Asia, religious ideals form the national unity. The unity in religion, therefore, is absolutely necessary as the first condition of the future of India. There must be the recognition of one religion throughout the length and breadth of this land. What do I mean by one religion? Not in the sense of one religion as held among the Christians, or the Mohammedans, or the Buddhists. We know that our religion has certain common grounds, common to all our sects, however varying their conclusions may be, however different their claims may be. So there are certain common grounds, and within their limitation this religion of ours admits of a marvellous variation, an infinite amount of liberty to think, and live our own lives. We all know that, at least those of us who have thought, and what we want is to bring out these life-giving common principles of our religion, and let every man, woman and child throughout the length and breadth of this country, understand them, know them, and try to bring them out in their lives. This is the first step, and therefore it has to be taken.

We see how in Asia, and especially in India, race difficulties, linguistic difficulties, social difficulties, national difficulties, all melt away before this unifying power of religion. We know that to the Indian mind there is nothing higher than religious ideals, that this is the keynote of Indian life, and we can only work in the line of least resistance. It is not only true that the ideal of religion is the highest ideal. In the case of India it is the only possible means of work; work in any other line, without first strengthening this, would be disastrous. Therefore, the first plank in the making of a future India, the first step that is to be hewn out of that rock of ages, is this unification of religion. All of us have to be taught that we Hindus —dualists, qualified monists, or monists, Shaivas, Vaishnavas, or Pâshupatas—to whatever denomination we may belong, have certain common ideas behind us, and that the time has come when for the well-being of ourselves, for the well-being of our race, we must give up all our little quarrels and differences. Be sure these quarrels are entirely wrong; they are condemned by our scriptures, forbidden by our forefathers; and those great men from whom we claim our descent, whose blood is in our veins, look down with contempt on their children quarrelling about minute differences.

With the giving up of quarrels all other improvements will come. When the life-blood is strong and pure no disease germ can live in that body. Our life-blood is spirituality. If it flows clear, if it flows strong and pure and vigorous, everything is right; political, social, any other material defects, even the poverty of the land, will all be cured if that blood is pure. For if the disease germ be thrown out, nothing will be able to enter into the blood. To take a simile from modern medicine, we know that there must be two causes to produce a disease, some poison germ outside and the state of the body. Until the body is in a state to admit the germs, until the body is degraded to a lower vitality so that the germs may enter and thrive and multiply, there is no power in any germ in the world to produce a disease in the body. In fact, millions of germs are continually passing through everyone's body; but so long as it is vigorous it never is conscious of them. It is only when the body is weak that these germs take possession of it and produce disease. Just so with the national life. It is when the national body is weak that all sorts of disease germs, in the political state of the race or in its social state, in its educational or intellectual state, crowd into the system and produce disease. To remedy it, therefore, we must go to the root of this disease and cleanse the blood of all impurities. The one tendency will be to strengthen the man, to make the blood pure, the body vigorous, so that it will be able to resist and throw off all external poisons.

We have seen that our vigour, our strength, nay, our national life is in our religion. I am not going to discuss now whether it is right or not, whether it is correct or not, whether it is beneficial or not in the long run, to have this vitality in religion, but for good or evil it is there; you cannot get out of it, you have it now and for ever, and you have to stand by it, even if you have not the same faith that I have in our religion. You are bound by it, and if you give it up you are smashed to pieces. That is the life of our race and that must be strengthened. You have withstood the shocks of centuries simply because you took great care of it, you sacrificed everything else for it. Your forefathers underwent everything boldly, even death itself, but preserved their religion. Temple after temple was broken down by the foreign conqueror, but no sooner had the wave passed than the spire of the temple rose up again. Some of these old temples of Southern India, and those like Somnâth of Gujarat, will teach you volumes of wisdom, will give you a keener insight into the history of the race than any amount of books. Mark how these temples bear the marks of a hundred attacks and a hundred regenerations, continually destroyed and continually springing up out of the ruins, rejuvenated and strong as ever! That is the national mind, that is the national life-current. Follow it and it leads to glory. Give it up and you die; death will be the only result, annihilation the only effect, the moment you step beyond that life-current. I do not mean to say that other things are not necessary. I do not mean to say that political or social improvements are not necessary, but what I mean is this, and I want you to bear it in mind, that they are secondary here, and that religion is primary. The Indian mind is first religious, then anything else. So this is to be strengthened, and how to do it? I will lay before you my ideas. They have been in my mind for a long time, even years before I left the shores of Madras for America, and that I went to America and England was simply for propagating those ideas. I did not care at all for the Parliament of Religions or anything else; it was simply an opportunity; for it was really those ideas of mine that took me all over the world.

My idea is first of all to bring out the gems of spirituality that are stored up in our books, and in the possession of a few only, hidden, as it were, in monasteries and in forests—to bring them out; to bring the knowledge out of them, not only from the hands where it is hidden, but from the still more inaccessible chest, the language in which it is preserved, the incrustation of centuries of Sanskrit words. In one word, I want to make them popular. I want to bring out these ideas and let them be the common property of all, of every man in India, whether he knows the Sanskrit language or not. The great difficulty in the way is the Sanskrit language, this glorious language of ours, and this difficulty cannot be removed until, if it is possible, the whole of our nation are good Sanskrit scholars. You will understand the difficulty when I tell you that I have been studying this language all my life, and yet every new book is new to me. How much more difficult would it then be for people who never had time to study the language thoroughly! Therefore the ideas must be taught in the language of the people; at the same time, Sanskrit education must go on along with it, because the very sound of Sanskrit words gives a prestige and a power and a strength to the race. The attempts of the great Râmânuja and of Chaitanya and of Kabir to raise the lower classes of India, show that marvellous results were attained during the lifetime of those great prophets; yet the later failures have to be explained, and cause shown why the effect of their teachings stopped almost within a century of the passing away of these great Masters. The secret is here. They raised the lower classes; they had all the wish that these should come up, but they did not apply their energies to the spreading of the Sanskrit language among the masses. Even the great Buddha made one false step when he stopped the Sanskrit language from being studied by the masses. He wanted rapid and immediate results, and translated and preached in the language of the day, Pâli. That was grand, he spoke in the language of the people, and the people understood him. That was great; it spread the ideas quickly and made them reach far and wide, but, along with that, Sanskrit ought to have spread. Knowledge came but the prestige was not there, culture was not there. It is culture that withstands shocks, not a simple mass of knowledge. You can put a mass of knowledge into the world, but that will not do it much good. There must come culture into the blood. We all know in modern times of nations which have masses of knowledge, but what of them? They are like tigers, they are like savages, because culture is not there. Knowledge is only skin-deep, as civilisation is, and a little scratch brings out the old savage. Such things happen; this is the danger. Teach the masses in the vernaculars, give them ideas. They will get information, but something more is necessary; give them culture. Until you give them that, there can be no permanence in the raised condition of the masses. There will be another caste created, having the advantage of the Sanskrit language, which will quickly get above the rest and rule them all the same. The only safety, I tell you men who belong to the lower castes, the only way to raise your condition, is to study Sanskrit, and this fighting and writing and frothing against the higher castes is in vain, it does no good, and it creates fight and quarrel, and this race, unfortunately already divided, is going to be divided more and more. The only way to bring about the levelling of caste is to appropriate the culture, the education, which is the strength of the higher castes. That done, you have what you want.

In connection with this I want to discuss one question which has a particular bearing with regard to Madras. There is a theory that there was a race of mankind in Southern India called Dravidians, entirely differing from another race in Northern India called the Aryans, and that the Southern India Brahmins are the only Aryans that came from the North, the other men of Southern India belong to an entirely different caste and race to those of Southern India Brahmins. Now I beg your pardon, Mr. Philologist, this is entirely unfounded. The only proof of it is that there is a difference of language between the North and the South. I do not see any other difference. We are so many Northern men here, and I ask my European friends to pick out the Northern and Southern men from this assembly. Where is the difference? A little difference of language. But the Brahmins are a race that came here speaking the Sanskrit language! Well then, they took up

Dravidian language and forgot their Sanskrit. Why should not the other castes have done the same? Why should not all the other castes have come one after the other from Northern India, taken up the Dravidian language, and so forgotten their own? That is an argument working both ways. Do not believe in such silly things. There may have been a Dravidian people who vanished from here, and the few who remained lived in forests and other places. It is quite possible that the language may have been taken up, but all these are Aryans who came from the North. The whole of India is Aryan, nothing else.

Then there is the other idea that the Shudra caste are surely the aborigines. What are they? They are slaves. They say history repeats itself. The Americans, English, Dutch, and the Portuguese got hold of the poor Africans, and made them work hard while they lived, and their children of mixed birth were born in slavery and kept in that condition for a long period. From that wonderful example, the mind jumps back several thousand years and fancies that the same thing happened here, and our archaeologist dreams of India being full of dark-eyed aborigines, and the bright Aryan came from—the Lord knows where. According to some, they came from Central Tibet, others will have it that they came from Central Asia. There are patriotic Englishmen who think that the Aryans were all red-haired. Others, according to their idea, think that they were all black-haired. If the writer happens to be a black-haired man, the Aryans were all black-haired. Of late, there was an attempt made to prove that the Aryans lived on the Swiss lakes. I should not be sorry if they had been all drowned there, theory and all. Some say now that they lived at the North Pole. Lord bless the Aryans and their habitations! As for the truth of these theories, there is not one word in our scriptures, not one, to prove that the Aryan ever came from anywhere outside of India, and in ancient India was included Afghanistan. There it ends. And the theory that the Shudra caste were all non-Aryans and they were a multitude, is equally illogical and equally irrational. It could not have been possible in those days that a few Aryans settled and lived there with a hundred thousand slaves at their command. These slaves would have eaten them up, made "chutney" of them in five minutes. The only explanation is to be found in the Mahâbhârata, which says that in the beginning of the Satya

Yuga there was one caste, the Brahmins, and then by difference of occupations they went on dividing themselves into different castes, and that is the only true and rational explanation that has been given. And in the coming Satya Yuga all the other castes will have to go back to the same condition. The solution of the caste problem in India, therefore, assumes this form, not to degrade the higher castes, not to crush out the Brahmin.

The Brahminhood is the ideal of humanity in India, as wonderfully put forward by Shankarâchârya at the beginning of his commentary on the Gita, where he speaks about the reason for Krishna's coming as a preacher for the preservation of Brahminhood, of Brahminness. That was the great end. This Brahmin, the man of God, he who has known Brahman, the ideal man, the perfect man, must remain; he must not go. And with all the defects of the caste now, we know that we must all be ready to give to the Brahmins this credit, that from them have come more men with real Brahminness in them than from all the other castes. That is true. That is the credit due to them from all the other castes. We must be bold enough, must be brave enough to speak of their defects, but at the same time we must give the credit that is due to them. Remember the old English proverb, "Give every man his due."

Therefore, my friends, it is no use fighting among the castes. What good will it do? It will divide us all the more, weaken us all the more, degrade us all the more. The days of exclusive privileges and exclusive claims are gone, gone for ever from the soil of India, and it is one of the great blessings of the British Rule in India. Even to the Mohammedan Rule we owe that great blessing, the destruction of exclusive privilege. That Rule was, after all, not all bad; nothing is all bad, and nothing is all good. The Mohammedan conquest of India came as salvation to the down-trodden, to the poor. That is why one-fifth of our people have become Mohammedans. It was not the sword that did it all. It would be the height of madness to think it was all the work of sword and fire. And one-fifth—one half—of your Madras people will become Christians if you do not take care. Was there ever a sillier thing before in the world than what I saw in Malabar country? The poor Pariah is not allowed to pass through the same street as the high-caste man, but if he changes his name to a hodge-podge English name, it is all right; or to a Mohammedan name, it is all right. What inference would you draw except that these Malabaris are all lunatics, their homes so many lunatic asylums, and that they are to be treated with derision by every race in India until they mend their manners and know better. Shame upon them that such wicked and diabolical customs are allowed; their own children are allowed to die of starvation, but as soon as they take up some other religion they are well fed. There ought to be no more fight between the castes.

The solution is not by bringing down the higher, but by raising the lower up to the level of the higher. And that is the line of work that is found in all our books, in spite of what you may hear from some people whose knowledge of their own scriptures and whose capacity to understand the mighty plans of the ancients are only zero. They do not understand, but those do that have brains, that have the intellect to grasp the whole scope of the work. They stand aside and follow the wonderful procession of national life through the ages. They can trace it step by step through all the books, ancient and modern. What is the plan? The ideal at one end is the Brahmin and the ideal at the other end is the Chandâla, and the whole work is to raise the Chandala up to the Brahmin. Slowly and slowly you find more and more privileges granted to them. There are books where you read such fierce words as these: "If the Shudra hears the Vedas, fill his ears with molten lead, and if he remembers a line, cut his tongue out. If he says to the Brahmin, 'You Brahmin,' cut his tongue out." This is diabolical old barbarism, no doubt, that goes without saying; but do not blame the law-givers, who simply record the customs of some section of the community. Such devils sometimes arose among the ancients. There have been devils everywhere more or less in all ages. Accordingly, you will find that later on, this tone is modified a little, as for instance—"Do not disturb the Shudras but do not teach them higher things." Then gradually we find in other Smritis, especially in those that have full power now, that if the Shudras imitate the manners and customs of the Brahmins they do well, they ought to be encouraged. Thus it is going on. I have no time to place before you all these workings, nor how they can be traced in detail; but coming to plain facts, we find that all the castes are to rise slowly and slowly; however, there are thousands of castes and some are even getting admission into Brahminhood, for what prevents any caste from declaring they are Brahmins? Thus caste, with all its vigour, has been created in that manner. Let us suppose that there are castes here with ten thousand people in each. If these put their heads together and say, we will call ourselves Brahmins, nothing can stop them; I have seen it in my own life. Some castes become strong, and as soon as they all agree, who is to say nay? Because whatever it was, each caste was exclusive of the other. It did not meddle with others' affairs; even the several divisions of one caste did not meddle with the other divisions, and those powerful epoch-makers, Shankaracharya and others, were the great caste-makers. I cannot tell you all the wonderful things they fabricated, and some of you may resent what I have to say. But in my travels and experiences I have traced them out, and have arrived at most wonderful results. They would sometimes get hordes of Baluchis and at once make them Kshatriyas, also get hold of hordes of fishermen and make them Brahmins forthwith. They were all Rishis and sages and we have to bow down to their memory. So, be you all Rishis and sages; that is the secret. More or less we shall all be Rishis. What is meant by a Rishi? The pure one. Be pure first, and you will have power. Simply saying, "I am a Rishi," will not do, but when you are a Rishi you will find that others obey you instinctively. Something mysterious emanates from you which makes them follow you, makes them hear you, makes them unconsciously, even against their will, carry out your plans. That is Rishihood.

Now, as to the details, they, of course, have to be worked out through generations. But this is merely a suggestion in order to show you that these quarrels should cease. Especially do I regret that in modern times there should be so much dissension between the castes. This must stop. It is useless on both sides, especially on the side of the higher caste, the Brahmin, because the day for these privileges and exclusive claims is gone. The duty of every aristocracy is to dig its own grave, and the sooner it does so, the better. The more it delays, the more it will fester and the worse death it will die. It is the duty of the Brahmin, therefore, to work for the salvation of the rest of mankind, in India. If he does that and so long as he does that, he is a Brahmin, but he is no Brahmin when he goes about making money. You on the other hand should give help only to the real Brahmin, who deserves it;

that leads to heaven, but sometimes a gift to another person who does not deserve it, leads to the other place, says our scripture. You must be on your guard about that. He only is the Brahmin who has no secular employment. Secular employment is not for the Brahmin, but for the other castes. To the Brahmins I appeal, that they must work hard to raise the Indian people by teaching them what they know, by giving out the culture that they have accumulated for centuries. It is clearly the duty of the Brahmins of India to remember what real Brahminhood is. As Manu says, all these privileges and honours are given to the Brahmin because, "with him is the treasury of virtue." He must open that treasury and distribute its valuables to the world. It is true that he was the earliest preacher to the Indian races, he was the first to renounce everything in order to attain to the higher realisation of life, before others could reach to the idea. It was not his fault that he marched ahead of the other castes. Why did not the other castes so understand and do as he did? Why did they sit down and be lazy, and let the Brahmins win the race?

But it is one thing to gain an advantage, and another thing to preserve it for evil use. Whenever power is used for evil it becomes diabolical; it must be used for good only. So this accumulated culture of ages of which the Brahmin has been the trustee, he must now give to the people at large, and it was because he did not give it to the people that the Mohammedan invasion was possible. It was because he did not open this treasury to the people from the beginning that for a thousand years we have been trodden under the heels of every one who chose to come to India. It was through that we have become degraded, and the first task must be to break open the cells that hide the wonderful treasures which our common ancestors accumulated; bring them out, and give them to everybody, and the Brahmin must be the first to do it. There is an old superstition in Bengal that if the cobra that bites, sucks out his own poison from the patient, the man must survive. Well then, the Brahmin must suck out his own poison. To the non-Brahmin castes I say, wait, be not in a hurry. Do not seize every opportunity of fighting the Brahmin, because, as I have shown, you are suffering from your own fault. Who told you to neglect spirituality and Sanskrit learning? What have you been doing all this time? Why have you been indifferent?

Why do you now fret and fume because somebody else had more brains, more energy, more pluck and go, than you? Instead of wasting your energies in vain discussions and quarrels in the newspapers, instead of fighting and quarrelling in your own homes—which is sinful—use all your energies in acquiring the culture which the Brahmin has, and the thing is done. Why do you not become Sanskrit scholars? Why do you not spend millions to bring Sanskrit education to all the castes of India? That is the question. The moment you do these things, you are equal to the Brahmin. That is the secret of power in India.

Sanskrit and prestige go together in India. As soon as you have that, none dares say anything against you. That is the one secret; take that up. The whole universe, to use the ancient Advaitist's simile, is in a state of self-hypnotism. It is will that is the power. It is the man of strong will that throws, as it were, a halo round him and brings all other people to the same state of vibration as he has in his own mind. Such gigantic men do appear. And what is the idea? When a powerful individual appears, his personality infuses his thoughts into us, and many of us come to have the same thoughts and thus we become powerful. Why is it that organisations are so powerful? Do not say organisation is material. Why is it, to take a case in point, that forty millions of Englishmen rule three hundred millions of people here? What is the psychological explanation? These forty millions put their will together and that means infinite power, and you three hundred millions have a will each separate from the other. Therefore to make a great future India, the whole secret lies in organisation, accumulation of power, co-ordination of wills. Already before my mind rises one of the marvellous verses of the Rig-Veda Samhitâ which says: "Be thou all of one mind, be thou all of one thought, for in the days of yore, the gods being of one mind were enabled to receive oblations. That the gods can be worshipped by men is because they are of one mind." Being of one mind is the secret of society. And the more you go on fighting and quarrelling about all trivialities such as "Dravidian" and "Aryan," and the question of Brahmins and non-Brahmins and all that, the further you are off from that accumulation of energy and power which is going to make the future India. For, mark you, the future India depends entirely upon that. This is the secret, accumulation of will-power, co-ordination, bringing them all, as it were, into one focus. Each Chinaman thinks in his own way, and a handful of Japanese all think in the same way, and you know the result. That is how it goes throughout the history of the world. You find in every case compact little nations always governing and ruling huge unwieldy nations, and this is natural, because it is easier for the little compact nations to bring their ideas into the same focus, and thus they become developed. And the bigger the nation, the more unwieldy it is. Born as it were, a disorganised mob, they cannot combine. All these dissensions must stop.

There is yet another defect in us. Ladies, excuse me, but through centuries of slavery, we have become like a nation of women. You scarcely can get three women together for five minutes in this country, or any other country but they quarrel. Women make big societies in European countries, and make tremendous declarations of women's power and so on; then they quarrel, and some man comes and rules them all. All over the world they still require some man to rule them. We are like them. Women we are. If a woman comes to lead women they all begin immediately to criticise her, tear her to pieces, and make her sit down. If a man comes and gives them a little harsh treatment, scolds them now and then, it is all right, they have been used to that sort of mesmerism. The whole world is full of such mesmerists and hypnotists. In the same way, if one of our countrymen stands up and tries to become great, we all try to hold him down, but if a foreigner comes and tries to kick us, it is all right. We have been used to it, have we not? And slaves must become great masters! So give up being a slave. For the next fifty years this alone shall be our keynote—this, our great Mother India. Let all other vain gods disappear for the time from our minds. This is the only God that is awake, our own race, everywhere His hands, everywere His feet, everywhere His ears, He covers everything. All other gods are sleeping. What vain gods shall we go after and yet cannot worship the God that we see all round us, the Virât? When we have worshipped this, we shall be able to worship all other gods. Before we can crawl half a mile, we want to cross the ocean like Hanumân! It cannot be. Everyone going to be a Yogi, everyone going to meditate! It cannot be. The whole day mixing with the world, with Karma-kânda, and in the evening sitting down and blowing through your nose! Is it so easy? Should Rishis come flying through the air, because you have blown three times through the nose? Is it a joke? It is all nonsense. What is needed is Chittashuddhi, purification of the heart. And how does that come? The first of all worship is the worship of the Virat—of those all around us. Worship it. Worship is the exact equivalent of the Sanskrit word, and no other English word will do. These are all our gods—men and animals, and the first gods we have to worship are our own countrymen. That is what we have to worship, instead of being jealous of each other and fighting each other. It is the most terrible Karma for which we are suffering, and yet it does not open our eyes!

Well, the subject is so great that I do not know where to stop, and I must bring my lecture to a close by placing before you in a few words the plans I want to carry out in Madras. We must have a hold on the spiritual and secular education of the nation. Do you understand that? You must dream it, you must talk it, you must think it, and you must work it out. Till then there is no salvation for the race. The education that you are getting now has some good points, but it has a tremendous disadvantage which is so great that the good things are all weighed down. In the first place it is not a man-making education, it is merely and entirely a negative education. A negative education, or any training that is based on negation, is worse than death. The child is taken to school, and the first thing he learns is that his father is a fool, the second thing, that his grandfather is a lunatic, the third thing, that all his teachers are hypocrites, the fourth, that all the sacred books are lies! By the time he is sixteen he is a mass of negation, lifeless and boneless. And the result is that fifty years of such education has not produced one original man in the three Presidencies. Every man of originality that has been produced has been educated elsewhere, and not in this country, or they have gone to the old universities once more to cleanse themselves of superstitions. Education is not the amount of information that is put into your brain and runs riot there, undigested, all your life. We must have life-building, man-making, character-making assimilation of ideas. If you have assimilated five ideas and made them your life and character, you have more education than any man who has got by heart a whole library. यथा खरश्चन्दनभारवाही

भारस्य वेत्ता न तु चन्दनस्य—"The ass carrying its load of sandalwood knows only the weight and not the value of the sandalwood." If education is identical with information, the libraries are the greatest sages in the world, and encyclopaedias are the Rishis. The ideal therefore is that we must have the whole education of our country, spiritual and secular, in our own hands, and it must be on national lines, through national methods, as far as practicable.

Of course this is a very big scheme, a very big plan. I do not know whether it will ever work out. But we must begin the work. But how? Take Madras, for instance. We must have a temple; for, with Hindus religion must come first. Then, you may say, all sects will quarrel about it. But we will make it a non-sectarian temple, having only "Om" as the symbol, the greatest symbol of any sect. If there is any sect here which believes that "Om" ought not to be the symbol, it has no right to call itself Hindu. All will have the right to interpret Hinduism, each one according to his own sect ideas, but we must have a common temple. You can have your own images and symbols in other places, but do not quarrel here with those who differ from you. Here should be taught the common grounds of our different sects, and at the same time the different sects should have perfect liberty to come and teach their doctrines, with only one restriction, that is, not to quarrel with other sects. Say what you have to say, the world wants it, but the world has no time to hear what you think about other people; you can keep that to yourselves.

Secondly, in connection with this temple there should be an institution to train teachers who must go about preaching religion and giving secular education to our people; they must carry both. As we have been already carrying religion from door to door, let us along with it carry secular education also. That can be easily done. Then the work will extend through these bands of teachers and preachers, and gradually we shall have similar temples in other places, until we have covered the whole of India. That is my plan. It may appear gigantic, but it is much needed. You may ask, where is the money? Money is not needed. Money is nothing. For the last twelve years of my life, I did not know where the next meal would come from; but money and everything else I want must come, because they are my slaves, and not I theirs; money and everything else must come. Must—that is the word. Where are the men? That is the question. Young men of Madras, my hope is in you. Will you respond to the call of your nation? Each one of you has a glorious future if you dare—believe me. Have a tremendous faith in yourselves, like the faith I had when I was a child, and which I am working out now. Have that faith, each one of you, in yourself—that eternal power is lodged in every soul—and you will revive the whole of India. Ay, we will then go to every country under the sun, and our ideas will before long be a component of the many forces that are working to make up every nation in the world. We must enter into the life of every race in India and abroad; we shall have to *work* to bring this about. Now for that I want young men. "It is the young, the strong, and healthy, of sharp intellect, that will reach the Lord," say the Vedas. This is the time to decide your future—while you possess the energy of youth, not when you are worn out and jaded, but in the freshness and vigour of youth. Work; this is the time, for the freshest, the untouched and unsmelled flowers alone are to be laid at the feet of the Lord, and such He receives. Rouse yourselves, therefore, for life is short. There are greater works to be done than aspiring to become lawyers, and picking quarrels, and such things. A far greater work is this sacrifice of yourselves for the benefit of your race, for the welfare of humanity. What is in this life? You are Hindus, and there is the instinctive belief in you that life is eternal. Sometimes I have young men come and talk to me about atheism; I do not believe a Hindu can become an atheist. He may read European books, and persuade himself he is a materialist, but it is only for a time. It is not in your blood. You cannot believe what is not in your constitution; it would be a hopeless task for you. Do not attempt that sort of thing. I once attempted it when I was a boy, but it could not be. Life is short, but the soul is immortal and eternal, and one thing being certain, death, let us therefore take up a great ideal, and give up our whole life to it. Let this be our determination, and may He, the Lord, who "comes again and again for the salvation of His own people," to quote from our scriptures—may the great Krishna bless us, and lead us all to the fulfilment of our aims!

REPLY TO THE CALCUTTA ADDRESS

One wants to lose the individual in the universal, one renounces, flies off, and tries to cut himself off from all associations of the body, of the past, one works hard to forget even that he is a man; yet, in the heart of his heart, there is a soft sound, one string vibrating, one whisper, which tells him, East or West, home is best. Citizens of the capital of this Empire, before you I stand, not as a Sannyâsin, no, not even as a preacher, but I come before you the same Calcutta boy to talk to you as I used to do. Ay, I would like to sit in the dust of the streets of this city, and, with the freedom of childhood, open my mind to you, my brothers. Accept, therefore, my heartfelt thanks for this unique word that you have used, "Brother". Yes, I am your brother, and you are my brothers. I was asked by an English friend on the eve of my departure, "Swami, how do you like now your motherland after four years' experience of the luxurious, glorious, powerful West?" I could only answer: "India I loved before I came away. Now the very dust of India has become holy to me, the very air is now to me holy, it is now the holy land, the place of pilgrimage, the Tirtha." Citizens of Calcutta—my brothers—I cannot express my gratitude to you for the kindness you have shown, or rather I should not thank you at all, for you are my brothers, you have done only a brother's duty, ay, only a Hindu brother's duty, for such family ties, such relationships, such love, exist nowhere beyond the bounds of this motherland of ours.

The Parliament of Religions was a great affair, no doubt. From various cities of this land, we have thanked the gentlemen who organised the meeting, and they deserved all our thanks for the kindness that has been shown to us, but yet allow me to construe for you the history of the Parliament of Religions. They wanted a horse, and they wanted to ride it. There were people there who wanted to make it a heathen show, but it was ordained otherwise; it could not help being so. Most of them were kind, but we have thanked them enough.

On the other hand, my mission in America was not to the Parliament of Religions. That was only something by the way, it was only an opening, an opportunity, and for that we are very thankful to the members of the Parliament; but really, our thanks are due to the great people of the United States, the American nation, the warm-hearted, hospitable, great nation of America, where more than anywhere else the feeling of brotherhood has been developed. An American meets you for five minutes on board a train, and you are his friend, and the next moment he invites you as a guest to his home, and opens the secret of his whole living there. That is the character of the American race, and we highly appreciate it. Their kindness to me is past all narration, it would take me years yet to tell you how I have been treated by them, most kindly and most wonderfully. So are our thanks due to the other nation on the other side of the Atlantic. No one ever landed on English soil with more hatred in his heart for a race than I did for the English, and on this platform are present English friends who can bear witness to the fact; but the more I lived among them, and saw how the machine was working—the English national life—and mixed with them, I found where the heartbeat of the nation was, and the more I loved them. There is none among you here present, my brothers, who loves the English people more than I do now. You have to see what is going on there, and you have to mix with them. As the philosophy, our national philosophy of the Vedanta, has summarised all misfortune, all misery, as coming from that one cause, ignorance, herein also we must understand that the difficulties that arise between us and the English people are mostly due to that ignorance; we do not know them, they do not know us.

Unfortunately, to the Western mind, spirituality, nay, even morality, is eternally connected with worldly prosperity, and as soon as an Englishman or any other Western man lands on our soil, and finds a land of poverty and of misery, he forthwith concludes that there cannot be any religion here, there cannot be any morality even. His own experience is true. In Europe, owing to the inclemency of the climate and many other circumstances, poverty and sin go together, but not so in India. In India, on the other hand, my experience is that the poorer the man the better he is in point of morality. Now this takes time to understand, and how many foreign people are there who will stop to understand this, the very secret of national existence in India? Few are there who will have the patience to study the nation and understand. Here, and here alone, is the only race where poverty does not mean crime, poverty does not mean sin, and here is the only race where not only poverty does not mean crime, but poverty has been deified, and the beggar's garb is the garb of the highest in the land. On the other hand, we have also similarly, patiently to study the social institutions of the West, and not rush into mad judgments about them. Their intermingling of the sexes, their different customs, their manners, have all their meaning, have all their grand sides, if you have the patience to study them. Not that I mean that we are going to borrow their manners and customs, not that they are going to borrow ours, for the manners and customs of each race are the outcome of centuries of patient growth in that race and each one has a deep meaning behind it, and therefore neither are they to ridicule our manners and customs, nor we theirs.

Again, I want to make another statement before this assembly. My work in England has been more satisfactory to me than my work in America. The bold, brave, and steady Englishman, if I may use the expression, with his skull a little thicker than those of other people—if he has once an idea put into his brain, it never comes out, and the immense practicality and energy of the race makes it sprout up and immediately bear fruit. It is not so in any other country. That immense practicality, that immense vitality of the race, you do not see anywhere else. There is less of imagination, but more of work, and who knows the well-spring, the mainspring of the English heart? How much of imagination and of feeling is there! They are a nation of heroes, they are the true Kshatriyas; their education is to hide their feelings and never to show them. From their childhood they have been educated up to that. Seldom will you find an Englishman manifesting feeling, nay, even an Englishwoman. I have seen Englishwomen go to work and do deeds which would stagger the bravest of Bengalis to follow. But with all this heroic superstructure, behind this covering of the fighter, there is a deep spring of feeling in the English heart. If you once know how to reach it, if you get there, if you have personal contact and mix with him, he will open his heart, he is your friend for ever, he is your servant. Therefore, in my opinion, my work in England has been more satisfactory than anywhere else. I firmly believe that if I should die tomorrow, the work in England would not die, but would go on expanding all the time.

Brothers, you have touched another chord in my heart, the deepest of all, and that is the mention of my teacher, my Master, my hero, my ideal, my God in life—Shri Ramakrishna Paramahamsa. If there has been anything achieved by me, by thoughts, or words, or deeds, if from my lips has ever fallen one word that has helped any one in the world, I lay no claim to it, it was his. But if there have been curses falling from my lips, if there has been hatred coming out of me, it is all mine, and not his. All that has been weak has been mine, and all that has been life-giving, strengthening, pure, and holy has been his inspiration, his words, and he himself. Yes, my friends, the world has yet to know that man. We read in the history of the world about prophets and their lives, and these come down to us through centuries of writings and workings by their disciples. Through thousands of years of chiselling and modelling the lives of the great prophets of yore come down to us: and yet, in my opinion, not one stands so high in brilliance as that life which I saw with my own eyes, under whose shadow I have lived, at whose feet I have learnt everything—the life of Ramakrishna Paramahamsa. Ay, friends, you all know the celebrated saying of the Gita:

यदा यदा हि धर्मस्य ग्लानिर्भवति भारत ।
अभ्युत्थानमधर्मस्य तदात्मानं सृजाम्यहम् ॥
परित्राणाय साधूनां विनाशाय च दुष्कृताम् ।
धर्मसंस्थापनार्थाय संभवामि युगे युगे ॥

"Whenever, O descendant of Bharata, there is decline of Dharma, and rise of Adharma, then I body Myself forth. For the protection of the good, for the destruction of the wicked, and for the establishment of Dharma, I come into being in every age."

Along with it you have to understand one thing more. Such a thing is before us today. Before one of these tidal waves of spirituality comes, there are whirlpools of lesser manifestation all over society. One of these comes up, at first unknown, unperceived, and unthought of, assuming proportion, swallowing, as it were, and assimilating all the other little whirlpools, becoming immense, becoming a tidal wave, and falling upon society with a power which none can resist. Such is happening before us. If you have eyes, you will see it. If your heart is open, you will receive it. If you are truth-seekers, you will find it. Blind, blind indeed is the man who does not see the signs of the day! Ay, this boy born of poor Brahmin parents in an out-of-the-way village, of which very few of you have even heard, is literally being worshipped in lands which have been fulminating against heathen worship for centuries. Whose power is it? Is it mine, or yours? It is none else than the power which was manifested here as Ramakrishna Paramahamsa. For, you and I, and sages and prophets, nay, even Incarnations, the whole universe, are but manifestations of power more or less individualised, more or less concentrated. Here has been a manifestation of an immense power, just the very beginning of whose workings we are seeing, and before this generation passes away, you will see more wonderful workings of that power. It has come just in time for the regeneration of India, for we forget from time to time the vital power that must always work in India.

Each nation has its own peculiar method of work. Some work through politics, some through social reforms, some through other lines. With us, religion is the only ground along which we can move. The Englishman can understand religion even through politics. Perhaps, the American can understand religion even through social reforms. But the Hindu can understand even politics when it is given through religion; sociology must come through religion, everything must come through religion. For that is the theme, the rest are the variations in the national life-music. And that was in danger. It seemed that we were going to change this theme in our national life, that we were going to exchange the backbone of our existence, as it were, that we were trying to replace a spiritual by a political backbone. And if we could have succeeded, the result would have been annihilation. But it was not to be. So this power became manifest. I do not care in what light you understand this great sage, it matters not how much respect you pay to him, but I challenge you face to face with the fact, that here is a manifestation of the most marvellous power that has been for several centuries in India, and it is your duty, as Hindus, to study this power, to find what has been done for the regeneration, for the good of India, and for the good of the whole human race through it. Ay, long before ideas of universal religion and brotherly feeling between different sects were mooted and discussed in any country in the world, here, in sight of this city, had been living a man whose whole life was a Parliament of Religions, as it should be.

The highest ideal in our scriptures is the Impersonal, and would to God everyone of us here were high enough to realise that Impersonal ideal: but as that cannot be, it is absolutely necessary for the vast majority of human beings to have a Personal ideal; and no nation can rise, can become great, can work at all, without enthusiastically coming under the banner of one of these great ideals in life. Political ideals, personages representing political ideals, even social ideals, commercial ideals, would have no power in India. We want spiritual ideals before us, we want enthusiastically to gather round grand spiritual names. Our heroes must be spiritual. Such a hero has been given to us in the person of Ramakrishna Paramahamsa. If this nation wants to rise, take my word for it, it will have to rally enthusiastically round this name. It does not matter who preaches Ramakrishna Paramahamsa, whether I, or you, or anybody else. But him I place before you, and it is for you to judge, and for the good of our race, for the good of our nation, to judge now, what you shall do with this great ideal of life. One thing we are to remember, that it was the purest of all lives that you have ever seen, or let me tell you distinctly, that you have ever read of. And before you is the fact that it is the most marvellous manifestation of soul-power that you can read of, much less expect to see. Within ten years of his passing away, this power has encircled the globe; that fact is before you. In duty bound therefore for the good of our race, for the good of our religion, I place this great spiritual ideal before you. Judge him not through me. I am only a weak instrument. Let not his character be judged by seeing me. It was so great that if I, or any other of his disciples, spent hundreds of lives, we could not do justice to a millionth part of what he really was. Judge for yourselves; in the heart of your hearts is the Eternal Witness, and may He, the same Ramakrishna Paramahamsa, for the good of our nation, for the welfare of our country, and for the good of humanity, open your hearts, make you true and steady to work for the immense change which must come, whether we exert ourselves or not. For the work of the Lord does not wait for the like of you or me. He can raise His workers from the dust by hundreds and by thousands. It is a glory and a privilege that we are allowed to work at all under Him.

From this the idea expands. As you have pointed out to me, we have to conquer the world. That we have to! India must conquer the world, and nothing less than that is my ideal. It may be very big, it may astonish many of you, but it is so. We must conquer the world or die. There is no other alternative. The sign of life is expansion; we must go out, expand, show life, or degrade, fester, and die. There is no other alternative. Take either of these, either live or die. Now, we all know about the petty jealousies and quarrels that we have in our country. Take my word, it is the same everywhere. The other nations with their political lives have foreign policies. When they find too much quarrelling at home, they look for somebody abroad to quarrel with, and the quarrel at home stops. We have these quarrels, without any foreign policy to stop them. This must be our eternal foreign policy, preaching the truths of our Shâstras to the nations of the world. I ask you who are politically minded, do you require any other proof that this will unite us as a race? This very assembly is a sufficient witness.

Secondly, apart from these selfish considerations, there are the unselfish, the noble, the living examples behind us. One of the great causes of India's misery and downfall has been that she narrowed herself, went into her shell, as the oyster does, and refused to give her jewels and her treasures to the other races of mankind, refused to give the life-giving truths to thirsting nations outside the Aryan fold. That has been the one great cause, that we did not go out, that we did not compare notes with other nations—that has been the one great cause of our downfall, and every one of you knows that the little stir, the little life that you see in India, begins from the day when Raja Rammohun Roy broke through the walls of that exclusiveness. Since that day, history in India has taken another turn, and now it is growing with accelerated motion. If we have had little rivulets in the past, deluges are coming, and none can resist them. Therefore we must go out, and the secret of life is to give and take. Are we to take always, to sit at the feet of the Westerners to learn everything, even religion? We can learn mechanism from them. We can learn many other things. But we have to teach them something, and that is our religion, that is our spirituality. For a complete civilisation the world is waiting, waiting for the treasures to come out of India, waiting for the marvellous spiritual inheritance of the race, which, through decades of degradation and misery, the nation has still clutched to her breast. The world is waiting for that treasure; little do you know how much of hunger and of thirst there is outside of India for these wonderful treasures of our forefathers. We talk here, we quarrel with each other, we laugh at and we ridicule everything sacred, till it has become almost a national vice to ridicule everything holy. Little do we understand the heartpangs of millions waiting outside the walls, stretching forth their hands for a little sip of that nectar which our forefathers have preserved in this land of India. Therefore we must go out, exchange our spirituality for anything they have to give us; for the marvels of the region of spirit we will exchange the marvels of the region of matter. We will not be students always, but teachers also. There cannot be friendship without equality, and there cannot be equality when one party is always the teacher and the other party sits always at his feet. If you want to become equal with the Englishman or the American, you will have to teach as well as to learn, and you have plenty yet to teach to the world for centuries to come. This has to be done. Fire and enthusiasm must be in our blood. We Bengalis have been credited with imagination, and I believe we have it. We have been ridiculed as an imaginative race, as men with a good deal of feeling. Let me tell you, my friends, intellect is great indeed, but it stops within certain bounds. It is through the heart, and the heart alone, that inspiration comes. It is through the feelings that the highest secrets are reached, and therefore, it is the Bengali, the man of feeling, that has to do this work.

उत्तिष्ठत जाग्रत प्राप्य वरान्निबोधत ।—Awake, arise and stop not till the desired end is reached. Young men of Calcutta, arise, awake, for the time is propitious. Already everything is opening out before us. Be bold and fear not. It is only in our scriptures that this adjective is given unto the Lord—Abhih, Abhih. We have to become Abhih, fearless and our task will be done. Arise, awake, for your country needs this tremendous sacrifice. It is the young men that will do it. "The young, the energetic, the strong, the well-built, the intellectual"—for them is the task. And we have hundreds and thousands of such young men in Calcutta. If, as you say, I have done something, remember that I was that good-for-nothing boy playing in the streets of Calcutta. If I have done so much how much more will you do? Arise and awake, the world is calling upon you. In other parts of India, there is intellect, there is money, but enthusiasm is only in my motherland. That must come out; therefore arise, young men of Calcutta, with enthusiasm in your blood. Think not that you are poor, that you have no friends. Ay, who ever saw money make the man? It is man that always makes money. The whole world has been made by the energy of man, by the power of enthusiasm, by the power of faith.

Those of you who have studied that most beautiful of all the Upanishads, the Katha, will remember how the king was going to make a great sacrifice, and instead of giving away things that were of any worth, he was giving away cows and horses that were not of any use, and the book says that at that time Shraddhâ entered into the heart of his son Nachiketâ. I would not translate this word Shraddha to you, it would be a mistake; it is a wonderful word to understand, and much depends on it; we will see how it works, for immediately we find Nachiketa telling himself, "I am superior to many, I am inferior to a few, but nowhere am I the last, I can also do something." And this boldness increased, and the boy wanted to solve the problem, which was in his mind, the problem of death. The solution could only be got by going to the house of Death, and the boy went. There he was, brave Nachiketa, waiting at the house of Death for three days and you know how he obtained what he desired. What we want is this Shraddha. Unfortunately, it has nearly vanished from India, and this is why we are in our present state. What makes the difference between man and man is the difference in the Shraddha and nothing else. What makes one man great and another weak and low is this Shraddha. My Master used to say, he who thinks himself weak will become weak, and that is true. This Shraddha must enter into you. Whatever of material power you see manifested by the Western races is the outcome of this Shraddha, because they believe in their muscles, and if you believe in your spirit, how much more will it work! Believe in that Infinite Soul, the Infinite Power, which with consensus of opinion, your books and sages preach. That Atman which nothing can destroy, in it is Infinite Power, only waiting to be called out. For here is the great difference between all other philosophies and the Indian philosophy. Whether dualistic, qualified monistic, or monistic, they all firmly believe that everything is in the soul itself; it has only to come out and manifest itself. Therefore, this Shraddha is what I want, and what all of us here want, this faith in ourselves, and before you is the great task to get that faith. Give up the awful disease that is creeping into our national blood, that idea of ridiculing everything, that loss of seriousness. Give that up. Be strong and have this Shraddha, and everything else is bound to follow.

I have done nothing as yet; you have to do the task. If I die tomorrow the work will not die. I sincerely believe that there will be thousands coming up from the ranks to take up the work and carry it further and further, beyond all my most hopeful imagination ever painted. I have faith in my country, and especially in the youth of my country. The youth of Bengal have the greatest of all tasks that have ever been placed on the shoulders of young men. I have travelled for the last ten years or so over the whole of India, and my conviction is that from the youth of Bengal will come the power which will raise India once more to her proper spiritual place. Ay, from the youth of Bengal, with this immense amount of feeling and enthusiasm in the blood, will come those heroes who will march from one corner of the earth to the other, preaching and teaching the eternal spiritual truth of our forefathers. And this is the great work before you. Therefore, let me conclude by reminding you once more, "Arise, awake, and stop not till the desired end is reached." Be not afraid, for all great power, throughout the history of humanity, has been with the people. From out of their ranks have come all the greatest geniuses of the world, and history can only repeat itself. Be not afraid of anything. You will do marvellous work. The moment you fear, you are nobody. It is fear that is the great cause of misery in the world. It is fear that is the greatest of all superstitions. It is fear that is the cause of our woes, and it is fearlessness that brings heaven even in a moment. Therefore, "Arise, awake, and stop not till the goal is reached."

Gentlemen, allow me to thank you once more for all the kindness that I have received at your hands. It is my wish—my intense, sincere wish—to be even of the least service to the world, and above all to my own country and countrymen.

THE SAGES OF INDIA

In speaking of the sages of India, my mind goes back to those periods of which history has no record, and tradition tries in vain to bring the secrets out of the gloom of the past. The sages of India have been almost innumerable, for what has the Hindu nation been doing for thousands of years except producing sages? I will take, therefore, the lives of a few of the most brilliant ones, the epoch-makers, and present them before you, that is to say, my study of them.

In the first place, we have to understand a little about our scriptures. Two ideals of truth are in our scriptures, the one is what we call the eternal, and the other is not so authoritative yet binding under particular circumstances, times, and places. The eternal relations which deal with the nature of the soul, and of God, and the relations between souls and God, are embodied in what we call the Shrutis, the Vedas. The next set of truths is what we call the Smritis, as embodied in the works of Manu, Yâjnavalkya, and other writers, and also in the Purânas, down to the Tantras. This second class of books and teachings is subordinate to the Shrutis, inasmuch as whenever any one of these contradicts anything in the Shrutis, the Shrutis must prevail. This is the law. The idea is that the framework of the destiny and goal of man has been all delineated in the Vedas, the details have been left to be worked out in the Smritis and Puranas. As for general directions, the Shrutis are enough; for spiritual life, nothing more can be said, nothing more can be known. All that is necessary has been known, all the advice that is necessary to lead the soul to perfection has been completed in the Shrutis; the details alone were left out, and these the Smritis have supplied from time to time.

Another peculiarity is that these Shrutis have many sages as the recorders of the truths in them, mostly men, even some women. Very little is known of their personalities, the dates of their birth, and so forth, but their best thoughts, their best discoveries, I should say, are preserved there, embodied in the sacred literature of our country, the Vedas. In the Smritis, on the other hand, personalities are more in evidence. Startling, gigantic, impressive, world-moving persons stand before us, as it were, for the first time, sometimes of more magnitude even than their teachings.

This is a peculiarity which we have to understand—that our religion preaches an Impersonal Personal God. It preaches any amount of impersonal laws *plus* any amount of personality, but the very fountain-head of our religion is in the Shrutis, the Vedas, which are perfectly impersonal; the persons all come in the Smritis and Puranas, the great Avatâras, Incarnations of God, Prophets, and so forth. And this ought also to be observed, that except our religion, every other religion in the world depends upon the life or lives of some personal founder or founders. Christianity is built upon the life of Jesus Christ, Mohammedanism, upon Mohammed, Buddhism, upon Buddha, Jainism, upon the Jinas, and so on. It naturally follows that there must be in all these religions a good deal of fight about what they call the historical evidences of these great personalities. If at any time the historical evidences about the existence of these personages in ancient times become weak, the whole building of the religion tumbles down and is broken to pieces. We escaped this fate because our religion is not based upon persons but on principles. That you obey your religion is not because it came through the authority of a sage, no, not even of an Incarnation. Krishna is not the authority of the Vedas, but the Vedas are the authority of Krishna himself. His glory is that he is the greatest preacher of the Vedas that ever existed. So with the other Incarnations; so with all our sages. Our first principle is that all that is necessary for the perfection of man, and for attaining unto freedom is there, in the Vedas. You cannot find anything new. You cannot go beyond a perfect unity, which is the goal of all knowledge; this has been already reached there, and it is impossible to go beyond the unity. Religious knowledge became complete when Tat Tvam Asi was discovered, and that was in the Vedas. What remained was the guidance of people from time to time, according to different times and places, according to different circumstances and environments; people had to be guided along the old, old path, and for this these great teachers came, these great sages. Nothing can bear out more clearly this position than the celebrated saying of Shri Krishna in the Gita: "Whenever virtue subsides and irreligion prevails, I create Myself for the protection of the good; for the destruction of all immorality I am coming from time to time." This is the idea in India.

What follows? That on the one hand, there are these eternal principles which stand upon their own foundations, without depending on any reasoning even, much less on the authority of sages however great, of Incarnations however brilliant they may have been. We may remark that as this is the unique position in India, our claim is that the Vedanta only can be the universal religion, that it is already the existing universal religion in the world, because it teaches principles and not persons. No religion built upon a person can be taken up as a type by all the races of mankind. In our own country we find that there have been so many grand characters; in even a small city many persons are taken up as types by the different minds in that one city. How is it possible that one person, as Mohammed or Buddha or Christ, can be taken up as the one type for the whole world, nay, that the whole of morality, ethics, spirituality, and religion can be true only from the sanction of that one person, and one person alone? Now, the Vedantic religion does not require any such personal authority. Its sanction is the eternal nature of man, its ethics are based upon the eternal spiritual solidarity of man, already existing, already attained and not to be attained. On the other hand, from the very earliest times, our sages have been feeling conscious of this fact that the vast majority of mankind require a personality. They must have a Personal God, in some form or other. The very Buddha who declared against the existence of a Personal God had not died fifty years before his disciples manufactured a Personal God out of him. This Personal God is necessary, and at the same time we know that instead of, and better than, vain imaginations of a Personal God, which in ninety-nine cases out of a hundred are unworthy of human worship, we have in this world, living and walking in our midst, living Gods, now and then. These are more worthy of worship than any imaginary God, any creation of our imagination, that is to say, any idea of God which we can form. Shri Krishna is much greater than any idea of God you or I can have. Buddha is a much higher idea, a more living and idolised idea, than the ideal you or I can conceive of in our minds, and therefore it is that they always command the worship of mankind, even to the exclusion of all imaginary deities.

This our sages knew, and therefore left it open to all Indian people to worship such great personages, such Incarnations. Nay, the greatest of these Incarnations goes further: "Wherever an extraordinary spiritual power is manifested by external man, know that I am there; it is from Me that that manifestation comes." That leaves the door open for the Hindu to worship the Incarnations of all the countries in the world. The Hindu can worship any sage and any saint from any country whatsoever, and as a fact we know that we go and worship many times in the churches of the Christians, and many, many times in the Mohammedan mosques, and that is good. Why not? Ours, as I have said, is the universal religion. It is inclusive enough, it is broad enough to include all the ideals. All the ideals of religion that already exist in the world can be immediately included, and we can patiently wait for all the ideals that are to come in the future, to be taken in the same fashion, embraced in the infinite arms of the religion of the Vedanta.

This, more or less, is our position with regard to the great sages, the Incarnations of God. There are also secondary characters. We find the word Rishi again and again mentioned in the Vedas, it has become a common word at the present time. The Rishi is the great authority. We have to understand that idea. The definition is that the Rishi is the Mantra-drashtâ, the seer of thought. What is the proof of religion?—this was asked in very ancient times. There is no proof in the senses, was the declaration. यतो वाचो निवर्तन्ते अप्राप्य मनसा सह —"From whence words reflect back with thought without reaching the goal." न तत्र चक्षुर्गच्छति न वाग्‌गच्छति नो मनः—"There the eyes cannot reach, neither can speech, nor the mind"—that has been the declaration for ages and ages. Nature outside cannot give us any answer as to the existence of the soul, the existence of God, the eternal life, the goal of man, and all that. This mind is continually changing, always in a state of flux; it is finite, it is broken into pieces. How can nature tell of the Infinite, the Unchangeable, the Unbroken, the Indivisible, the Eternal? It never can. And whenever mankind has striven to get an answer from dull dead matter, history shows how disastrous the results have been. How comes, then, the knowledge which the Vedas declare? It comes through being a Rishi. This knowledge is not in the senses; but are the senses the be-all and the end-all of the human being? Who dares say that the senses are the all-in-all of man? Even in our lives, in the life of every one of us here, there come moments of calmness, perhaps when we see before us the death of one we loved, when some shock comes to us, or when extreme blessedness comes to us. Many other occasions there are when the mind, as it were, becomes calm, feels for the moment its real nature, and a glimpse of the Infinite beyond, where words cannot reach nor the mind go, is revealed to us. This happens in ordinary life, but it has to be heightened, practised, perfected. Men found out ages ago that the soul is not bound or limited by the senses, no, not even by consciousness. We have to understand that this consciousness is only the name of one link in the infinite chain. Being is not identical with consciousness, but consciousness is only one part of Being. Beyond consciousness is where the bold search. Consciousness is bound by the senses. Beyond that, beyond the senses, men must go, in order to arrive at truths of the spiritual world, and there are even now persons who succeed in going beyond the bounds of the senses. These are called Rishis, because they come face to face with spiritual truths.

The proof, therefore, of the Vedas is just the same as the proof of this table before me, Pratyaksha, direct perception. This I see with the senses, and the truths of spirituality we also see in a superconscious state of the human soul. This Rishi state is not limited by time or place, by sex or race. Vâtsyâyana boldly declares that this Rishihood is the common property of the descendants of the sage, of the Aryan, of the non-Aryan, of even the Mlechchha. This is the sageship of the Vedas and constantly we ought to remember this ideal of religion in India, which I wish other nations of the world would also remember and learn, so that there may be less fight and less quarrel. Religion is not in books, nor in theories, nor in dogmas, nor in talking, not even in reasoning. It is being and becoming. Ay, my friends, until each one of you has become a Rishi and come face to face with spiritual facts, religious life has not begun for you. Until the superconscious opens for you, religion is mere talk, it is nothing but preparation. You are talking second-hand, third-hand, and here applies that beautiful saying of Buddha when he had a discussion with some Brahmins! They came discussing about the nature of Brahman, and the great sage asked, "Have you seen Brahman?" "No," said the Brahmin; "Or your father?" "No, neither has he"; "Or your grandfather?" "I don't think even he saw Him." "My friend, how can you discuss about a person whom your father and grandfather never saw, and try to put each other down?" That is what the whole world is doing. Let us say in the language of the Vedanta, "This Atman is not to be reached by too much talk, no, not even by the highest intellect, no, not even by the study of the Vedas themselves."

Let us speak to all the nations of the world in the language of the Vedas: Vain are your fights and your quarrels; have you seen God whom you want to preach? If you have not seen, vain is your preaching; you do not know what you say, and if you have seen God, you will not quarrel, your very face will shine. An ancient sage of the Upanishads sent his son out to learn about Brahman, and the child came back, and the father asked, "What have you learnt?" The child replied he had learnt so many sciences. But the father said, "That is nothing, go back". And the son went back and when he returned again the father asked the same question, and the same answer came from the child. Once more he had to go back, and the next time he came, his whole face was shining, and his father stood up and declared, "Ay, today, my child, your face shines like a knower of Brahman". When you have known God your very face will be changed, your voice will be changed, your whole appearance will be changed. You will be a blessing to mankind; none will be able to resist the Rishi. This is the Rishihood, the ideal in our religion. The rest, all these talks, and reasonings and philosophies, and dualisms, and monisms, and even the Vedas themselves, are but preparations, secondary things. The other is primary. The Vedas, Grammar, Astronomy, etc., all these are secondary; that is supreme knowledge which makes us realise the Unchangeable One. Those who realised are the sages whom we find in the Vedas, and we understand how this Rishi is the name of a type, of a class, which every one of us, as true Hindus, is expected to become at some period of our life, and becoming which, to the Hindu, means salvation. Not belief in doctrines, not going to thousands of temples, nor bathing in all the rivers in the world, but becoming the Rishi, the Mantra-drashta, that is freedom, that is salvation.

Coming down to later times, there have been great world-moving sages, great Incarnations, of whom there have been many, and according to the Bhâgavata they also are infinite in number, and those that are worshipped most in India are Râma and Krishna. Rama, the ancient idol of the heroic ages, the embodiment of truth, of morality, the ideal son, the ideal husband, the ideal father, and above all, the ideal king, this Rama has been presented before us by the great sage Vâlmiki. No language can be purer, none chaster, none more beautiful, and at the same time simpler, than the language in which the great poet has depicted that life of Rama. And what to speak of Sita? You may exhaust the literature of the world that is past, and I may assure you that you will have to exhaust the literature of the world of the future, before finding another Sita. Sita is unique; that character was depicted once and for all. There may have been several Ramas, perhaps, but never more than one Sita! She is the very type of the true Indian woman, for all the Indian ideals of a perfected woman have grown out of that one life of Sita; and here she stands these thousands of years, commanding the worship of every man, woman, and child, throughout the length and breadth of the land of Âryâvarta. There she will always be, this glorious Sita, purer than purity itself, all patience, and all suffering. She who suffered that life of suffering without a murmur, she the ever-chaste and ever-pure wife, she, the ideal of the people, the ideal of the gods, the great Sita, our national God, she must always remain. And every one of us knows her too well to require much delineation. All our mythology may vanish, even our Vedas may depart, and our Sanskrit language may vanish for ever, but so long as there will be five Hindus living here, even if only speaking the most vulgar *patois,* there will be the story of Sita present, mark my words. Sita has gone into the very vitals of our race. She is there in the blood of every Hindu man and woman; we are all children of Sita. Any attempt to modernise our women, if it tries to take our women away from that ideal of Sita, is immediately a failure, as we see every day. The women of India must grow and develop in the footprints of Sita, and that is the only way.

The next is He who is worshipped in various forms, the favourite ideal of men as well as of women, the ideal of children, as well as of grown-up men. I mean He whom the writer of the Bhagavata was not content to call an Incarnation but says, "The other Incarnations were but parts of the Lord. He, Krishna was the Lord Himself." And it is not strange that such adjectives are applied to him when we marvel at the many-sidedness of his character. He was the most wonderful Sannyâsin, and the most wonderful householder in one; he had the most wonderful amount of Rajas, power, and was at the same time living in the midst of the most wonderful renunciation. Krishna can never be understood until you have studied the Gita, for he was the embodiment of his own teaching. Every one of these Incarnations came as a living illustration of what they came to preach. Krishna, the preacher of the Gita, was all his life the embodiment of that Song Celestial; he was the great illustration of non-attachment. He gives up his throne and never cares for it. He, the leader of India, at whose word kings come down from their thrones, never wants to be a king. He is the simple Krishna, ever the same Krishna who played with the Gopis. Ah, that most marvellous passage of his life, the most difficult to understand, and which none ought to attempt to understand until he has become perfectly chaste and pure, that most marvellous expansion of love, allegorised and expressed in that beautiful play at Vrindaban, which none can understand but he who has become mad with love, drunk deep of the cup of love! Who can understand the throes of the love of the Gopis—the very ideal of love, love that wants nothing, love that even does not care for heaven, love that does not care for anything in this world, or the world to come?

And here, my friends, through this love of the Gopis, has been found the only solution of the conflict between the Personal and the Impersonal God. We know how the Personal God is the highest point of human life; we know that it is philosophical to believe in an Impersonal God, immanent in the universe, of whom everything is but a manifestation. At the same time our souls hanker after something concrete, something which we want to grasp, at whose feet we can pour out our soul, and so on. The Personal God is therefore the highest conception of human nature. Yet reason stands aghast at such an idea. It is the same old, old question which you find discussed in the Brahma-Sutras, which you find Draupadi discussing with Yudhisthira in the forest—if there is a Personal God, all-merciful, all-powerful, why is the hell of an earth here, why did He create this?—He must be a partial God. There was no solution, and the only solution that can be found is what you read about the love of the Gopis. They hated every adjective that was applied to Krishna; they did not care to know that he was the Lord of creation, they did not care to know that he was almighty, they did not care to know that he was omnipotent, and so forth. The only thing they understood was that he was infinite Love, that was all. The Gopis understood Krishna only as the Krishna of Vrindaban. He, the leader of the hosts, the King of kings, to them was the shepherd, and the shepherd for ever. "I do not want wealth, nor many people, nor do I want learning; no, not even do I want to go to heaven. Let me be born again and again, but Lord, grant me this, that I may have love for Thee, and that for love's sake." A great landmark in the history of religion is here, the ideal of love for love's sake, work for work's sake, duty for duty's sake, and it for the first time fell from the lips of the greatest of Incarnations, Krishna, and for the first time in the history of humanity, upon the soil of India. The religions of fear and of temptations were gone for ever, and in spite of the fear of hell, and temptation of enjoyment in heaven, came the grandest of ideals, love for love's sake, duty for duty's sake, work for work's sake.

And what a love! I have told you just now that it is very difficult to understand the love of the Gopis. There are not wanting fools, even in the midst of us, who cannot understand the marvellous significance of that most marvellous of all episodes. There are, let me repeat, impure fools, even born of our blood, who try to shrink from that as if from something impure. To them I have only to say, first make yourselves pure; and you must remember that he who tells the history of the love of the Gopis is none else but Shuka Deva. The historian who records this marvellous love of the Gopis is one who was born pure, the eternally pure Shuka, the son of Vyâsa. So long as there is selfishness in the heart, so long is love of God impossible; it is nothing but shopkeeping. I give you something, O Lord, you give me something in return. And says the Lord—if you do not do this, I will take good care of you when you die. I will roast you all the rest of your lives, perhaps, and so on. So long as such ideas are in the brain, how can one understand the mad throes of the Gopis' love? "O for one, one kiss of those lips! One who has been kissed by Thee, his thirst for Thee increases for ever, all sorrows vanish, and he forgets love for everything else but for Thee and Thee alone." Ay, forget first the love for gold, and name and fame, and for this little trumpery world of ours. Then, only then, you will understand the love of the Gopis, too holy to be attempted without giving up everything, too sacred to be understood until the soul has become perfectly pure. People with ideas of sex, and of money, and of fame, bubbling up every minute in the heart, daring to criticise and understand the love of the Gopis! That is the very essence of the Krishna Incarnation. Even the Gita, the great philosophy itself, does not compare with that madness, for in the Gita the disciple is taught slowly how to walk towards the goal, but here is the madness of enjoyment, the drunkenness of love, where disciples and teachers and teachings and books and all these things have become one, even the ideas of fear, and God, and heaven. Everything has been thrown away. What remains is the madness of love. It is forgetfulness of everything, and the lover sees nothing in the world except that Krishna, and Krishna alone, when the face of every being becomes a Krishna, when his own face looks like Krishna, when his own soul has become tinged with the Krishna colour. That was the great Krishna!

Do not waste your time upon little details. Take up the framework, the essence of the life. There may be many historical discrepancies, there may be interpolations in the life of Krishna. All these things may be true, but, at the same time, there must have been a basis, a foundation for this new and tremendous departure. Taking the life of any other sage or prophet, we find that that prophet is only the evolution of what had gone before him, we find that that prophet is only preaching the ideas that had been scattered about his own country even in his own times. Great doubts may exist even as to whether that prophet existed or not. But here, I challenge any one to show whether these things, these ideals—work for work's sake, love for love's sake, duty for duty's sake, were not original ideas with Krishna, and as such, there must have been someone with whom these ideas originated. They could not have been borrowed from anybody else. They were not floating about in the atmosphere when Krishna was born. But the Lord Krishna was the first preacher of this; his disciple Vyasa took it up and preached it unto mankind. This is the highest idea to picture. The highest thing we can get out of him is

Gopijanavallabha, the Beloved of the Gopis of Vrindaban. When that madness comes in your brain, when you understand the blessed Gopis, then you will understand what love is. When the whole world will vanish, when all other considerations will have died out, when you will become pure-hearted with no other aim, not even the search after truth, then and then alone will come to you the madness of that love, the strength and the power of that infinite love which the Gopis had, that love for love's sake. That is the goal. When you have got that, you have got everything.

To come down to the lower stratum—Krishna, the preacher of the Gita. Ay, there is an attempt in India now which is like putting the cart before the horse. Many of our people think that Krishna as the lover of the Gopis is something rather uncanny, and the Europeans do not like it much. Dr. So-and-so does not like it. Certainly then, the Gopis have to go! Without the sanction of Europeans how can Krishna live? He cannot! In the Mahâbhârata there is no mention of the Gopis except in one or two places, and those not very remarkable places. In the prayer of Draupadi there is mention of a Vrindaban life, and in the speech of Shishupâla there is again mention of this Vrindaban. All these are interpolations! What the Europeans do not want must be thrown off! They are interpolations, the mention of the Gopis and of Krishna too! Well, with these men, steeped in commercialism, where even the ideal of religion has become commercial, they are all trying to go to heaven by doing something here; the Buniya wants compound interest, wants to lay by something here and enjoy it there. Certainly the Gopis have no place in such a system of thought. From that ideal lover we come down to the lower stratum of Krishna, the preacher of the Gita.

Than the Gita no better commentary on the Vedas has been written or can be written. The essence of the Shrutis, or of the Upanishads, is hard to be understood, seeing that there are so many commentators, each one trying to interpret in his own way. Then the Lord Himself comes, He who is the inspirer of the Shrutis, to show us the meaning of them, as the preacher of the Gita, and today India wants nothing better, the world wants nothing better than that method of interpretation. It is a wonder that subsequent interpreters of the scriptures, even commenting upon the Gita, many times could not catch the meaning, many times could not catch the drift. For what do you find in the Gita, and what in modern commentators? One non-dualistic commentator takes up an Upanishad; there are so many dualistic passages, and he twists and tortures them into some meaning, and wants to bring them all into a meaning of his own. If a dualistic commentator comes, there are so many non-dualistic texts which he begins to torture, to bring them all round to dualistic meaning. But you find in the Gita there is no attempt at torturing any one of them. They are all right, says the Lord; for slowly and gradually the human soul rises up and up, step after step, from the gross to the fine, from the fine to the finer, until it reaches the Absolute, the goal.

That is what is in the Gita. Even the Karma-kânda is taken up, and it is shown that although it cannot give salvation direct, but only indirectly, yet that is also valid; images are valid indirectly; ceremonies, forms, everything is valid, only with one condition, purity of the heart. For worship is valid, and leads to the goal, if the heart is pure and the heart is sincere; and all these various modes of worship are necessary, else why should they be there? Religions and sects are not the work of hypocrites and wicked people, who invented all these to get a little money, as some of our modern men want to think. However reasonable that explanation may seem, it is not true, and they were not invented that way at all. They are the outcome of the necessity of the human soul. They are all here to satisfy the hankering and thirst of different classes of human minds, and you need not preach against them. The day when that necessity will cease they will vanish along with the cessation of that necessity, and so long as that necessity remains they must be there, in spite of your preaching, in spite of your criticisms. You may bring the sword or the gun into play, you may deluge the world with human blood, but so long as there is a necessity for idols, they must remain. These forms, and all the various steps in religion will remain, and we understand from the Lord Shri Krishna why they should.

A rather sad chapter of India's history comes now. In the Gita we already hear the distant sound of the conflicts of sects, and the Lord comes in the middle to harmonise them all; He, the great preacher of harmony, the greatest teacher of harmony, Lord Shri Krishna. He says, "In Me they are all strung like pearls upon a thread". We already hear the distant sounds, the murmurs of the conflict, and possibly there was a period of harmony and calmness, when it broke out anew, not only on religious grounds, but most possibly on caste grounds —the fight between the two powerful factors in our community, the kings and the priests. And from the topmost crest of the wave that deluged India for nearly a thousand years, we see another glorious figure, and that was our Gautama Shâkyamuni. You all know about his teachings and preachings. We worship him as God incarnate, the greatest, the boldest preacher of morality that the world ever saw, the greatest Karma-Yogi; as a disciple of himself, as it were, the same Krishna came to show how to make his theories practical. There came once again the same voice that in the Gita preached, "Even the least bit done of this religion saves from great fear." "Women, or Vaishyas, or even Shudras, all reach the highest goal." Breaking the bondages of all, the chains of all, declaring liberty to all to reach the highest goal, come the words of the Gita, rolls like thunder the mighty voice of Krishna: "Even in this life they have conquered relativity whose minds are firmly fixed upon the sameness, for God is pure and the same to all, therefore such are said to be living in God." "Thus seeing the same Lord equally present everywhere, the sage does not injure the Self by the self, and thus reaches the highest goal." As it were to give a living example of this preaching, as it were to make at least one part of it practical, the preacher himself came in another form, and this was Shakyamuni, the preacher to the poor and the miserable, he who rejected even the language of the gods to speak in the language of the people, so that he might reach the hearts of the people; he who gave up a throne to live with beggars, and the poor, and the downcast, he who pressed the Pariah to his breast like a second Rama.

You all know about his great work, his grand character. But the work had one great defect, and for that we are suffering even today. No blame attaches to the Lord. He is pure and glorious, but unfortunately such high ideals could not be well assimilated by the different uncivilised and uncultured races of mankind who flocked within the fold of the Aryans. These races, with varieties of superstition and hideous worship, rushed within the fold of the Aryans, and for a time appeared as if they had become civilised, but before a century had passed they brought out their snakes, their ghosts, and all the other things their ancestors used to worship, and thus the whole of India became one degraded mass of superstition. The earlier Buddhists in their rage against the killing of animals had denounced the sacrifices of the Vedas; and these sacrifices used to be held in every house. There was a fire burning, and that was all the paraphernalia of worship. These sacrifices were obliterated, and in their place came gorgeous temples, gorgeous ceremonies, and gorgeous priests, and all that you see in India in modern times. I smile when I read books written by some modern people who ought to have known better, that the Buddha was the destroyer of Brahminical idolatry. Little do they know that Buddhism created Brahminism and idolatry in India.

There was a book written a year or two ago by a Russian gentleman, who claimed to have found out a very curious life of Jesus Christ, and in one part of the book he says that Christ went to the Temple of Jagannâtha to study with the Brahmins, but became disgusted with their exclusiveness and their idols, and so he went to the Lamas of Tibet instead, became perfect, and went home. To any man who knows anything about Indian history, that very statement proves that the whole thing was a fraud, because the Temple of Jagannatha is an old Buddhistic Temple. We took this and others over and re-Hinduised them. We shall have to do many things like that yet. That is Jagannatha, and there was not one Brahmin there then, and yet we are told that Jesus Christ came to study with the Brahmins there. So says our great Russian archaeologist.

Thus, in spite of the preaching of mercy to animals, in spite of the sublime ethical religion, in spite of the hair-splitting discussions about the existence or non-existence of a permanent soul, the whole building of Buddhism tumbled down piecemeal; and the ruin was simply hideous. I have neither the time nor the inclination to describe to you the hideousness that came in the wake of Buddhism. The most hideous ceremonies, the most horrible, the most obscene books that human hands ever wrote, or the human brain ever conceived, the most bestial forms that ever passed under the name of religion, have all been the creation of degraded Buddhism.

But India has to live, and the spirit of the Lord descended again. He who declared, "I will come whenever virtue subsides," came again, and this time the manifestation was in the South, and up rose that young Brahmin of whom it has been declared that at the age of sixteen he had completed all his writings; the marvellous boy Shankarâchârya arose. The writings of this boy of sixteen are the wonders of the modern world, and so was the boy. He wanted to bring back the Indian world to its pristine purity, but think of the amount of the task before him. I have told you a few points about the state of things that existed in India. All these horrors that you are trying to reform are the outcome of that reign of degradation. The Tartars and the Baluchis and all the hideous races of mankind came to India and became Buddhists, and assimilated with us, and brought their national customs, and the whole of our national life became a huge page of the most horrible and the most bestial customs. That was the inheritance which that boy got from the Buddhists, and from that time to this, the whole work in India is a reconquest of this Buddhistic degradation, by the Vedanta. It is still going on, it is not yet finished. Shankara came, a great philosopher, and showed that the real essence of Buddhism and that of the Vedanta are not very different, but that the disciples did not understand the Master and have degraded themselves, denied the existence of the soul and of God, and have become atheists. That was what Shankara showed, and all the Buddhists began to come back to the old religion. But then they had become accustomed to all these forms; what could be done?

Then came the brilliant Râmânuja. Shankara, with his great intellect, I am afraid, had not as great a heart. Ramanuja's heart was greater. He felt for the downtrodden, he sympathised with them. He took up the ceremonies, the accretions that had gathered, made them pure so far as they could be, and instituted new ceremonies, new methods of worship, for the people who absolutely required them. At the same time he opened the door to the highest spiritual worship from the Brahmin to the Pariah. That was Ramanuja's work. That work rolled on, invaded the North, was taken up by some great leaders there, but that was much later, during the Mohammedan rule, and the brightest of these prophets of comparatively modern times in the North was Chaitanya.

You may mark one characteristic since the time of Ramanuja—the opening of the door of spirituality to everyone. That has been the watchword of all prophets succeeding Ramanuja, as it had been the watchword of all the prophets before Shankara. I do not know why Shankara should be represented as rather exclusive; I do not find anything in his writings which is exclusive. As in the case of the declarations of the Lord Buddha, this exclusiveness that has been attributed to Shankara's teachings is most possibly not due to his teachings, but to the incapacity of his disciples. This one great northern sage, Chaitanya, represented the mad love of the Gopis. Himself a Brahmin, born of one of the most rationalistic families of the day, himself a professor of logic fighting and gaining a word-victory—for, this he had learnt from his childhood as the highest ideal of life—and yet through the mercy of some sage the whole life of that man became changed; he gave up his fight, his quarrels, his professorship of logic and became one of the greatest teachers of Bhakti the world has ever known—mad Chaitanya. His Bhakti rolled over the whole land of Bengal, bringing solace to every one. His love knew no bounds. The saint or the sinner, the Hindu or the Mohammedan, the pure or the impure, the prostitute, the streetwalker—all had a share in his love, all had a share in his mercy, and even to the present day, although greatly degenerated, as everything does become in time, his sect is the refuge of the poor, of the downtrodden, of the outcast, of the weak, of those who have been rejected by all society. But at the same time I must remark for truth's sake that we find this: In the philosophic sects we find wonderful liberalism. There is not a man who follows Shankara who will say that all the different sects of India are really different. At the same time he was a tremendous upholder of exclusiveness as regards caste. But with every Vaishnavite preacher we find a wonderful liberalism as to the teaching of caste questions, but exclusiveness as regards religious questions.

The one had a great head, the other a large heart, and the time was ripe for one to be born, the embodiment of both this head and heart; the time was ripe for one to be born, who in one body would have the brilliant intellect of Shankara and the wonderfully expansive, infinite heart of Chaitanya; one who would see in every sect the same spirit working, the same God; one who would see God in every being, one whose heart would weep for the poor, for the weak, for the outcast, for the downtrodden, for every one in this world, inside India or outside India; and at the same time whose grand brilliant intellect would conceive of such noble thoughts as would harmonise all conflicting sects, not only in India but outside of India, and bring a marvellous harmony, the universal religion of head and heart, into existence. Such a man was born, and I had the good fortune to sit at his feet for years. The time was ripe, it was necessary that such a man should be born, and he came; and the most wonderful part of it was that his life's work was just near a city which was full of Western thought, a city which had run mad after these Occidental ideas, a city which had become more Europeanised than any other city in India. There he lived, without any book-learning whatsoever; this great intellect never learnt even to write his own name,[1] but the most brilliant graduates of our university found in him an intellectual giant. He was a strange man, this Shri Ramakrishna Paramahamsa. It is a long, long story, and I have no time to tell anything about him tonight. Let me now only mention the great Shri Ramakrishna, the fulfilment of the Indian sages, the sage for the time, one whose teaching is just now, in the present time, most beneficial. And mark the Divine power working behind the man. The son of a poor priest, born in an out-of-the-way village, unknown and unthought of today, is worshipped literally by thousands in Europe and America, and tomorrow will be worshipped by thousands more. Who knows the plans of the Lord! Now, my brothers, if you do not see the hand, the finger of Providence, it is because you are blind, born blind indeed. If time comes, and another opportunity, I will speak to you more fully about him. Only let me say now that if I have told you one word of truth, it was his and his alone, and if I have told you many things which were not true, which were not correct, which were not beneficial to the human race, they were all mine, and on me is the responsibility.

[1] Subsequent research has shown that he could read and write Bengali, though he was illiterate in the Western sense.

CHRIST, THE MESSENGER

(A lecture delivered at Los Angeles, California, 1900)

The wave rises on the ocean, and there is a hollow. Again another wave rises, perhaps bigger than the former, to fall down again; similarly, again to rise—driving onward. In the march of events, we notice the rise and fall, and we generally look towards the rise, forgetting the fall. But both are necessary, and both are great. This is the nature of the universe. Whether in the world of our thoughts, the world of our relations in society, or in our spiritual affairs, the same movement of succession, of rises and falls, is going on. Hence great predominances in the march of events, the liberal ideals, are marshalled ahead, to sink down, to digest, as it were, to ruminate over the past—to adjust, to conserve, to gather strength once more for a rise and a bigger rise.

The history of nations, also, has ever been like that. The great soul, the Messenger we are to study this afternoon, came at a period of the history of his race which we may well designate as a great fall. We catch only little glimpses here and there of the stray records that have been kept of his sayings and doings; for, verily it has been well said that the doings and sayings of that great soul would fill the world if they had all been written down. And the three years of his ministry were like one compressed, concentrated age, which it has taken nineteen hundred years to unfold, and who knows how much longer it will yet take! Little men like you and me are simply the recipients of just a little energy. A few minutes, a few hours, a few years at best, are enough to spend it all, to stretch it out, as it were, to its fullest strength, and then we are gone for ever. But mark this giant that came; centuries and ages pass, yet the energy that he left upon the world is not yet stretched, nor yet expended to its full. It goes on adding new vigour as the ages roll on.

Now what you see in the life of Christ is the life of all the past. The life of every man is, in a manner, the life of the past. It comes to him through heredity, through surroundings, through education, through his own reincarnation

—the past of the race. In a manner, the past of the earth, the past of the whole world is there, upon every soul. What are we, in the present, but a result, an effect, in the hands of that infinite past? What are we but floating wavelets in the eternal current of events, irresistibly moved forward and onward and incapable of rest? But you and I are only little things, bubbles. There are always some giant waves in the ocean of affairs; and in you and me the life of the past race has been embodied only a little; but there are giants who embody, as it were, almost the whole of the past and who stretch out their hands for the future. These are the sign-posts here and there, which point to the march of humanity; these are verily gigantic, their shadows covering the earth—they stand undying, eternal! As it has been said by the same Messenger, "No man hath seen God at any time, but through the Son." And that is true. And where shall we see God but in the Son? It is true that you and I, and the poorest of us, the meanest even, embody that God, reflect that God. The vibration of light is everywhere, omnipresent, but we have to strike the light of the lamp before we can see the light. The Omnipresent God of the universe cannot be seen until He is reflected by these giant lamps of the earth—the Prophets, the man-Gods, the Incarnations, the embodiments of God.

We all know that God exists, and yet we do not see Him, we do not understand Him. Take one of these great Messengers of light, compare his character with the highest ideal of God that you ever formed, and you will find that your God falls short of the ideal, and that the character of the Prophet exceeds your conceptions. You cannot even form a higher ideal of God than what the actually embodied have practically realised, and set before us as an example. Is it wrong, therefore, to worship these as God? Is it a sin to fall at the feet of these man-Gods, and worship them as the only divine beings in the world? If they are really, actually, higher than all our conceptions of God, what harm is there in worshipping them? Not only is there no harm, but it is the only possible and positive way of worship. However much you may try, by struggle, by abstraction, by whatsoever method you like, still so long as you are a man in the world of men, your world is human, your religion is human and your God is human. And that must be so. Who is not practical enough to take up an actually existing thing, and give up an idea which is only an abstraction, which he cannot grasp, and is difficult of approach except through a concrete medium? Therefore, these Incarnations of God have been worshipped in all ages and in all countries.

We are now going to study a little of the life of Christ, the Incarnation of the Jews. When Christ was born, the Jews were in that state which I call a state of fall between two waves; a state of conservatism, a state where the human mind is, as it were, tired for the time being of moving forward and is taking care only of what it has already; a state when the attention is more bent upon particulars, upon details, than upon the great, general, and bigger problems of life; a state of stagnation, rather than a towing ahead; a state of suffiering more than of doing. Mark you, I do not blame this state of things. We have no right to criticise it—because had it not been for this fall, the next rise, which was embodied in Jesus of Nazareth, would have been impossible. The Pharisees and Sadducees might have been insincere, they might have been doing things which they ought not to have done; they might have been even hypocrites; but whatever they were, these factors were the very cause, of which the Messenger was the effect. The Pharisees and Sadducees at one end were the very impetus which came out at the other end as the gigantic brain of Jesus of Nazareth.

The attention to forms, to formulas, to the everyday details of religion, and to rituals, may sometimes be laughed at, but nevertheless within them is strength. Many times in the rushing forward we lose much strength. As a fact the fanatic is stronger than the liberal man. Even the fanatic therefore, has one great virtue, he conserves energy, a tremendous amount of it. As with the individual, so with the race, energy is gathered to be conserved. Hemmed in all around by external enemies, driven to focus in a centre by the Romans, by the Hellenic tendencies in the world of intellect, by waves from Persia, India, and Alexandria—hemmed in physically, mentally, and morally—there stood the race with an inherent, conservative, tremendous strength, which their descendants have not lost even today. And the race was forced to concentrate, and focus all its energies upon Jerusalem and Judaism. But all power when once gathered cannot remain collected; it must expend and expand itself. There is no power on earth which can be kept long confined within a narrow limit. It cannot be kept compressed too long to allow of expansion at a subsequent period.

This concentrated energy amongst the Jewish race found its expression at the next period, in the rise of Christianity. The gathered streams collected into a body. Gradually, all the little streams joined together, and became a surging wave on the top of which we find standing out the character of Jesus of Nazareth. Thus, every Prophet is a creation of his own times, the creation of the past of his race; he, himself, is the creator of the future. The cause of today is the effect of of the past and the cause for the future. In this position stands the Messenger. In him is embodied all that is the best and greatest in his own race, the meaning, the life, for which that race has struggled for ages; and he, himself, is the impetus for the future, not only to his own race but to unnumbered other races of the world.

We must bear another fact in mind: that my view of the great Prophet of Nazareth would be from the standpoint of the Orient. Many times you forget, also, that the Nazarene himself was an Oriental of Orientals. With all your attempts to paint him with blue eyes and yellow hair, the Nazarene was still an Oriental. All the similes, the imageries, in which the Bible is written—the scenes, and locations, the attitudes, the groups, the poetry and symbol—speak to you of the Orient: of the bright sky, of the heat, of the sun of the desert, of the thirsty men and animals; of men and women coming with pitchers on their heads to fill them at the wells; of the flocks, of the ploughmen, of the cultivation that is going on around; of the water-mill and wheel, of the millpond, of the millstones—all these are to be seen today in Asia.

The voice of Asia has been the voice of religion. The voice of Europe is the voice of politics. Each is great in its own sphere. The voice of Europe is the voice of ancient Greece. To the Greek mind, his immediate society was all in all. Beyond that, it is Barbarian—none but the Greek has the right to live. Whatever the Greeks do is right and correct; whatever else there exists in the world is neither right nor correct, nor should be allowed to live. It is intensely human in its sympathies, intensely natural, intensely artistic, therefore. The Greek lives entirely in this world. He does not care to dream.

Even his poetry is practical. His gods and goddesses are not only human beings, but intensely human, with all human passions and feelings, almost the same as with any of us. He loves what is beautiful, but, mind you, it is always external nature: the beauty of the hills, of the snows, of the flowers; the beauty of forms and of figures; the beauty in the human face, and, more often, in the human form—that is what the Greeks liked. And the Greeks being the teachers of all subsequent Europeanism, the voice of Europe is Greek.

There is another type in Asia. Think of that vast, huge continent, whose mountain-tops go beyond the clouds, almost touching the canopy of heaven's blue; a rolling desert of miles upon miles, where a drop of water cannot be found, neither will a blade of grass grow; interminable forests and gigantic rivers rushing down into the sea. In the midst of all these surroundings, the Oriental love of the beautiful and of the sublime developed itself in another direction. It looked inside, and not outside. There is also the thirst for Nature, and there is also the same thirst for power; there is also the same thirst for excellence, the same idea of the Greek and Barbarian; but it has extended over a larger circle. In Asia, even today, birth or colour or language never makes a race. That which makes a race is its religion. We are all Christians; we are all Mohammedans; we are all Hindus, or all Buddhists. No matter if a Buddhist is a Chinaman, or is a man from Persia, they think that they are brothers, because of their professing the same religion. Religion is the tie, the unity of humanity. And then again, the Oriental, for the same reason, is a visionary, is a born dreamer. The ripples of the waterfalls, the songs of the birds, the beauties of the sun and moon and the stars and the whole earth, are pleasant enough; but they are not sufficient for the Oriental mind. He wants to dream a dream beyond. He wants to go beyond the present. The present, as it were, is nothing to him. The Orient has been the cradle of the human race for ages, and all the vicissitudes of fortune are there. Kingdoms succeeding kingdoms; empires succeeding empires; human power, glory, and wealth, all rolling down there: a Golgotha of power and learning. That is the Orient: a Golgotha of power, of kingdoms, of learning. No wonder, the Oriental mind looks with contempt upon the things of this world and naturally wants to see something that changeth not, something which dieth not, something which in the midst of this world of misery and death is eternal, blissful, undying. An Oriental Prophet never tires of insisting upon these ideas; and, as for Prophets, you may also remember that without one exception, all the Messengers were Orientals.

We see, therefore, in the life of this great Messenger of life, the first watchword: "Not this life, but something higher"; and, like the true son of the Orient, he is practical in that. You people of the West are practical in your own department, in military affairs, and in managing political circles and other things. Perhaps, the Oriental is not practical in those ways, but he is practical in his own field: he is practical in religion. If one preaches a philosophy, tomorrow there are hundreds who will struggle their best to make it practical in their lives. If a man preaches that standing on one foot would lead to salvation, he will immediately get five hundred to stand on one foot. You may call it ludicrous; but, mark you, beneath that is their philosophy—that intense practicality. In the West, plans of salvation mean intellectual gymnastics, plans which are never worked out, never brought into practical life. In the West, the preacher who talks the best is the greatest preacher.

So, we find Jesus of Nazareth, in the first place, the true son of the Orient, intensely practical. He has no faith in this evanescent world and all its belongings. No need of text-torturing, as is the fashion in the West in modern times, no need of stretching out texts until they will not stretch any more. Texts are not India-rubber, and even that has its limits. Now, no making of religion to pander to the sense vanity of the present day! Mark you, let us all be honest. If we cannot follow the ideal, let us confess our weakness, but not degrade it; let not any try to pull it down. One gets sick at heart at the different accounts of the life of the Christ that Western people give. I do not know what he was or what he was not! One would make him a great politician; another perhaps, would make of him a great military general; another, a great patriotic Jew, and so on. Is there any warrant in the books for all such assumptions? The best commentary on the life of a great teacher is his own life. "The foxes have holes, and the birds of the air have nests, but the Son of man hath not where to lay his head." That is what Christ says as the only way to salvation; he lays down no other way . Let us confess in sackcloth and ashes that we cannot do that. We still have fondness for "me" and "mine". We want property, money, wealth. Woe unto us! Let us confess and not put to shame that great Teacher of Humanity! He had no family ties. But do you think that that Man had any physical ideas in him? Do you think that this mass of light, this God and not-man, came down to earth, to be the brother of animals? And yet, people make him preach all sorts of things. He had no sex ideas! He was a soul! Nothing but a soul, just working a body for the good of humanity; and that was all his relation to the body. In the soul there is no sex. The disembodied soul has no relationship to the animal, no relationship to the body. The ideal may be far away beyond us. But never mind, keep to the ideal. Let us confess that it is our ideal, but we cannot approach it yet.

He had no other occupation in life; no other thought except that one, that he was a Spirit. He was a disembodied, unfettered, unbound Spirit. And not only so, but he, with his marvellous vision, had found that every man and woman, whether Jew or Gentile, whether rich or poor, whether saint or sinner, was the embodiment of the same undying Spirit as himself. Therefore, the one work his whole life showed, was calling upon them to realise their own spiritual nature. Give up, he says, these superstitious dreams that you are low and that you are poor. Think not that you are trampled upon and tyrannised over as if you were slaves, for within you is something that can never be tyrannised over, never be trampled upon, never be troubled, never be killed. You are all Sons of God, Immortal Spirit. "Know," he declared, "the Kingdom of Heaven is within you." "I and my Father are one." Dare you stand up and say, not only that "I am the Son of God" but I shall also find in my heart of hearts that "I and my Father are one." That was what Jesus of Nazareth said. He never talks of this world and of this life. He has nothing to do with it, except that he wants to get hold of the world as it is, give it a push and drive it forward and onward until the whole world has reached to the effulgent Light of God, until everyone has realised his spiritual nature, until death is vanquished and misery banished.

We have read the different stories that have been written about him; we know the scholars and their writings, and the higher criticism, and we know all that has been done by study. We are not here to discuss how much of the New Testament is true, we are not here to discuss how much of that life is historical. It does not matter at all whether the New Testament was written within five hundred years of his birth, nor does it matter, even, how much of that life is true. But there is something behind it, something we want to imitate. To tell a lie, you have to imitate a truth, and that truth is a fact. You cannot imitate that which never existed. You cannot imitate that which you never perceived. But there must have been a nucleus, a tremendous power that came down, a marvellous manifestation of spiritual power—and of that we are speaking. It stands there. Therefore, we are not afraid of all the criticism of the scholars. If I, as an Oriental, have to worship Jesus of Nazareth, there is only one way left to me, that is, to worship him as God and nothing else. Have we no right to worship him in that way, do you mean to say? If we bring him down to our own level and simply pay him a little respect as a great man, why should we worship at all? Our scriptures say, "These great children of Light, who manifest the Light themselves, who are Light themselves, they being worshipped, become, as it were, one with us and we become one with them."

For, you see, in three ways man perceives God. At first the undeveloped intellect of the uneducated man sees God as far away, up in the heavens somewhere, sitting on a throne, as a great Judge. He looks upon Him as a fire, as a terror. Now, that is good, for there is nothing bad in it. You must remember that humanity travels not from error to truth, but from truth to truth; it may be, if you like it better, from lower truth to higher truth, but never from error to truth. Suppose you start from here and travel towards the sun in a straight line. From here the sun looks only small in size. Suppose you go forward a million miles, the sun will be much bigger. At every stage the sun will become bigger and bigger. Suppose twenty thousand photographs have been taken of the same sun, from different standpoints; these twenty thousand photographs will all certainly differ from one another. But can you deny that each is a photograph of the same sun? So all forms of religion, high or low, are just different stages towards that eternal state of Light which is God Himself. Some embody a lower view, some a higher, and that is all the difference. Therefore, the religions of the unthinking masses all over the world must be, and have always been, of a God who is outside of the universe, who lives in heaven, who governs from that place, who is a punisher of the bad and a rewarder of the good, and so on. As man advanced spiritually, he began to feel that God was omnipresent, that He must be in him, that He must be everywhere, that He was not a distant God, but clearly the Soul of all souls. As my soul moves my body, even so is God the mover of my soul. Soul within soul. And a few individuals who had developed enough and were pure enough, went still further, and at last found God. As the New Testament says, "Blessed are the pure in heart, for they shall see God" And they found at last that they and the Father were one.

You find that all these three stages are taught by the Great Teacher in the New Testament. Note the Common Prayer he taught: "Our Father which art in Heaven, hallowed be Thy name," and so on—a simple prayer, a child's prayer. Mark you, it is the "Common Prayer" because it is intended for the uneducated masses. To a higher circle, to those who had advanced a little more, he gave a more elevated teaching: "I am in my Father, and ye in me, and I in you." Do you remember that? And then, when the Jews asked him who he was, he declared that he and his Father were one, and the Jews thought that that was blasphemy. What did he mean by that? This has been also told by your old Prophets. "You are gods and all of you are children of the Most High." Mark the same three stages. You will find that it is easier for you to begin with the first and end with the last.

The Messenger came to show the path: that the Spirit is not in forms, that it is not through all sorts of vexatious and knotty problems of philosophy that you know the Spirit. Better that you had no learning, better that you never read a book in your life. These are not at all necessary for salvation—neither wealth, nor position, nor power, not even learning—but what is necessary is that one thing, purity: "Blessed are the pure in heart," for the Spirit in its own nature is pure. How can it be otherwise? It is of God, it has come from God. In the language of the Bible, "It is the breath of God". In the language of the Koran, "It is the soul of God". Do you mean to say that the Spirit of God can ever be impure? But, alas, it has been, as it were, covered over with the dust and dirt of ages, through our own actions, good and evil. Various works which were not correct, which were not true, have covered the same Spirit with the dust and dirt of the ignorance of ages. It is only necessary to clear away the dust and dirt, and then the Spirit shines immediately. "Blessed are the pure in heart, for they shall see God." "The Kingdom of Heaven is within you." Where goest thou to seek for the Kingdom of God, asks Jesus of Nazareth, when it is there, within you? Cleanse the Spirit, and it is there. It is already yours. How can you get what is not yours? It is yours by right. You are the heirs of immortality, sons of the Eternal Father.

This is the great lesson of the Messenger, and another, which is the basis of all religions, is renunciation. How can you make the Spirit pure? By renunciation. A rich young man asked Jesus, "Good Master, what shall I do that I may inherit eternal life?" And Jesus said unto him, "One thing thou lackest: go thy way, sell whatsoever thou hast, and give to the poor, and thou shalt have treasures in heaven: and come, take up thy cross, and follow Me." And he was sad at that saying, and went away grieved: for he had great possessions. We are all more or less like that. The Voice is ringing in our ears day and night. In the midst of our pleasures and joys, in the midst of worldly things, we think that we have forgotten everything else. Then comes a moment's pause and the Voice rings in our ears: "Give up all that thou hast and follow me." "Whosoever will save his life shall lose it; and whosoever shall lose his life for My sake shall find it." For whoever gives up this life for His sake, finds the life immortal. In the midst of all our weakness there is a moment of pause and the Voice rings: "Give up all that thou hast; give it to the poor and follow Me." This is the one ideal he preaches, and this has been the ideal preached by all the great Prophets of the world: renunciation. What is meant by renunciation? That there is only one ideal in morality: unselfishness. Be selfless. The ideal is perfect unselfishness. When a man is struck on the right cheek, he turns the left also. When a man's coat is carried off, he gives away his cloak also.

We should work in the best way we can, without dragging the ideal down. Here is the ideal. When a man has no more self in him, no possession, nothing to call "me" or "mine", has given himself up entirely, destroyed himself as it were—in that man is God Himself; for in him self-will is gone, crushed out, annihilated. That is the ideal man. We cannot reach that state yet; yet, let us worship the ideal, and slowly struggle to reach the ideal, though maybe with faltering steps. It may be tomorrow, or it may be a thousand years hence, but that ideal has to be reached. For it is not only the end, but also the means. To be unselfish, perfectly selfless, is salvation itself, for the man within dies, and God alone remains.

One more point. All the teachers of humanity are unselfish. Suppose Jesus of Nazareth was teaching, and a man came and told him: "What you teach is beautiful. I believe that it is the way to perfection and I am ready to follow it; but I do not care to worship you as the only begotten Son of God." What would be the answer of Jesus of Nazareth? "Very well, brother, follow the ideal and advance in your own way. I do not care whether you give me the credit for the teaching or not. I am not a shopkeeper. I do not trade in religion. I only teach truth, and truth is nobody's property. Nobody can patent truth. Truth is God Himself. Go forward." But what the disciples say nowadays is: "No matter whether you practise the teachings or not, do you give credit to the Man? If you credit the Master, you will be saved; if not, there is no salvation for you." And thus the whole teaching of the Master is degenerated and all the struggle and fight is for the personality of the Man. They do not know that in imposing that difference they are, in a manner, bringing shame to the very Man they want to honour—the very Man that would have shrunk with shame from such an idea. What did he care if there was one man in the world that remembered him or not? He had to deliver his message, and he gave it. And if he had twenty thousand lives he would give them all up for the poorest man in the world. If he had to be tortured millions of times, for a million despised Samaritans, and if for each one of them the sacrifice of his own life would be the only condition of salvation, he would have given his life. And all this without wishing to have his name known even to a single person. Quiet, unknown, silent, would he work, just as the Lord works. Now, what would the disciple say? He will tell you that you may be a perfect man, perfectly unselfish, but unless you give the credit to our Teacher, to our Saint, it is of no avail. Why? What is the origin of this superstition, this ignorance? The disciple thinks that the Lord can manifest Himself only once. There lies the whole mistake. God manifests Himself to you in man. But throughout nature, what happens once must have happened before, and must happen in future. There is nothing in nature which is not bound by law, and that means that whatever happens once, must go on and must have been going on.

In India they have the same idea of the incarnations of God. One of their great Incarnations, Krishna, whose grand Sermon, the Bhagavad-Gita, some of you might have read, says, "Though I am unborn, of changeless nature, and Lord of beings, yet subjugating My Prakriti, I come into being by My own Mâyâ. Whenever virtue subsides and immorality prevails, I body Myself forth. For the protection of the good, for the destruction of the wicked, and for the establishment of Dharma, I come into being, in every age." Whenever the world goes down, the Lord comes to help it forward; and so He does from time to time and place to place. In another passage He speaks to this effect: Wherever thou findest a great soul of immense power and purity struggling to raise humanity, know that he is born of My splendour, that I am there working through him.

Let us, therefore, find God not only in Jesus of Nazareth but in all the great Ones that have preceded him, in all that came after him, and all that are yet to come. Our worship is unbounded and free. They are all manifestations of the same Infinite God. They are all pure and unselfish; they struggled, and gave up their lives for us, poor human beings. They each and all suffer vicarious atonement for every one of us, and also for all that are to come hereafter.

In a sense you are all Prophets; every one of you is a Prophet, bearing the burden of the world on your own shoulders. Have you ever seen a man, have you ever seen a woman, who is not quietly, patiently, bearing his or her little burden of life? The great Prophets were giants—they bore a gigantic world on their shoulders. Compared with them we are pigmies, no doubt, yet we are doing the same task; in our little circles, in our little homes, we are bearing our little crosses. There is no one so evil, no one so worthless, but he has to bear his own cross. But with all our mistakes, with all our evil thoughts and evil deeds, there is a bright spot somewhere, there is still somewhere the golden thread through which we are always in touch with the divine. For, know for certain, that the moment the touch of the divine is lost, there would be annihilation. And because none can be annihilated, there is always somewhere in our heart of hearts, however low and degraded we may be, a little circle of light which is in constant touch with the divine.

Our salutations go to all the past Prophets whose teachings and lives we have inherited, whatever might have been their race, clime, or creed! Our salutations go to all those Godlike men and women who are working to help humanity, whatever be their birth, colour, or race! Our salutations to those who are coming in the future—living Gods—to work unselfishly for our descendants!

MY MASTER[1]

"Whenever virtue subsides and vice prevails, I come down to help mankind," declares Krishna, in the Bhagavad-Gitâ. Whenever this world of ours, on account of growth, on account of added circumstances, requires a new adjustment, a wave of power comes; and as a man is acting on two planes, the spiritual and the material, waves of adjustment come on both planes. On the one side, of the adjustment on the material plane, Europe has mainly been the basis during modern times; and of the adjustment on the other, the spiritual plane, Asia has been the basis throughout the history of the world. Today, man requires one more adjustment on the spiritual plane; today when material ideas are at the height of their glory and power, today when man is likely to forget his divine nature, through his growing dependence on matter, and is likely to be reduced to a mere money-making machine, an adjustment is necessary; the voice has spoken, and the power is coming to drive away the clouds of gathering materialism. The power has been set in motion which, at no distant date, will bring unto mankind once more the memory of its real nature; and again the place from which this power will start will be Asia.

This world of ours is on the plan of the division of labour. It is vain to say that one man shall possess everything. Yet how childish we are! The baby in its ignorance thinks that its doll is the only possession that is to be coveted in this whole universe. So a nation which is great in the possession of material power thinks that that is all that is to be coveted, that that is all that is meant by progress, that that is all that is meant by civilisation, and if there are other nations which do not care for possession, and do not possess that power, they are not fit to live, their whole existence is useless! On the other hand, another nation may think that mere material civilisation is utterly useless. From the Orient came the voice which once told the world that if a man possesses everything that is under the sun and does not possess spirituality, what avails it? This is the oriental type; the other is the occidental type.

[1] Two lectures delivered in New York and England in 1896 were combined subsequently under the present heading.

Each of these types has its grandeur, each has its glory. The present adjustment will be the harmonising, the mingling of these two ideals. To the Oriental, the world of spirit is as real as to the Occidental is the world of senses. In the spiritual, the Oriental finds everything he wants or hopes for; in it he finds all that makes life real to him. To the Occidental he is a dreamer; to the Oriental the Occidental is a dreamer playing with ephemeral toys, and he laughs to think that grown-up men and women should make so much of a handful of matter which they will have to leave sooner or later. Each calls the other a dreamer. But the oriental ideal is as necessary for the progress of the human race as is the occidental, and I think it is more necessary. Machines never made mankind happy and never will make. He who is trying to make us believe this will claim that happiness is in the machine; but it is always in the mind. That man alone who is the lord of his mind can become happy, and none else. And what, after all, is this power of machinery? Why should a man who can send a current of electricity through a wire be called a very great man and a very intelligent man? Does not nature do a million times more than that every moment? Why not then fall down and worship nature? What avails it if you have power over the whole of the world, if you have mastered every atom in the universe? That will not make you happy unless you have the power of happiness in yourself, until you have conquered yourself. Man is born to conquer nature, it is true, but the Occidental means by "nature" only physical or external nature. It is true that external nature is majestic, with its mountains, and oceans, and rivers, and with its infinite powers and varieties. Yet there is a more majestic internal nature of man, higher than the sun, moon, and stars, higher than this earth of ours, higher than the physical universe, transcending these little lives of ours; and it affords another field of study. There the Orientals excel, just as the Occidentals excel in the other. Therefore it is fitting that, whenever there is a spiritual adjustment, it should come from the Orient. It is also fitting that when the Oriental wants to learn about machine-making, he should sit at the feet of the Occidental and learn from him. When the Occident wants to learn about the spirit, about God, about the soul, about the meaning and the mystery of this universe, he must sit at the feet of the Orient to learn.

I am going to present before you the life of one man who has put in motion such a wave in India. But before going into the life of this man, I will try to present before you the secret of India, what India means. If those whose eyes have been blinded by the glamour of material things, whose whole dedication of life is to eating and drinking and enjoying, whose ideal of possession is lands and gold, whose ideal of pleasure is that of the senses, whose God is money, and whose goal is a life of ease and comfort in this world and death after that, whose minds never look forward, and who rarely think of anything higher than the sense-objects in the midst of which they live—if such as these go to India, what do they see? Poverty, squalor, superstition, darkness, hideousness everywhere. Why? Because in their minds enlightenment means dress, education, social politeness. Whereas occidental nations have used every effort to improve their material position, India has done differently. There live the only men in the world who, in the whole history of humanity, never went beyond their frontiers to conquer anyone, who never coveted that which belonged to anyone else, whose only fault was that their lands were so fertile, and they accumulated wealth by the hard labour of their hands, and so tempted other nations to come and despoil them. They are contented to be despoiled, and to be called barbarians; and in return they want to send to this world visions of the Supreme, to lay bare for the world the secrets of human nature, to rend the veil that conceals the real man, because they know the dream, because they know that behind this materialism lives the real, divine nature of man which no sin can tarnish, no crime can spoil, no lust can taint, which fire cannot burn, nor water wet, which heat cannot dry nor death kill. And to them this true nature of man is as real as is any material object to the senses of an Occidental.

Just as you are brave to jump at the mouth of a cannon with a hurrah, just as you are brave in the name of patriotism to stand up and give up your lives for your country, so are they brave in the name of God. There it is that when a man declares that this is a world of ideas, that it is all a dream, he casts off clothes and property to demonstrate that what he believes and thinks is true. There it is that a man sits on the bank of a river, when he has known that life is eternal, and wants to give up his body just as nothing, just as you can give up a bit of straw. Therein lies their heroism, that they are ready to face death as a brother, because they are convinced that there is no death for them. Therein lies the strength that has made them invincible through hundreds of years of oppression and foreign invasion and tyranny. The nation lives today, and in that nation even in the days of the direst disaster, spiritual giants have never failed to arise. Asia produces giants in spirituality, just as the Occident produces giants in politics, giants in science. In the beginning of the present century, when Western influence began to pour into India, when Western conquerors, sword in hand, came to demonstrate to the children of the sages that they were mere barbarians, a race of dreamers, that their religion was but mythology, and god and soul and everything they had been struggling for were mere words without meaning, that the thousands of years of struggle, the thousands of years of endless renunciation, had all been in vain, the question began to be agitated among young men at the universities whether the whole national existence up to then had been a failure, whether they must begin anew on the occidental plan, tear up their old books, burn their philosophies, drive away their preachers, and break down their temples. Did not the occidental conqueror, the man who demonstrated his religion with sword and gun, say that all the old ways were mere superstition and idolatry? Children brought up and educated in the new schools started on the occidental plan, drank in these ideas, from their childhood; and it is not to be wondered at that doubts arose. But instead of throwing away superstition and making a real search after truth, the test of truth became, "What does the West say?" The priests must go, the Vedas must be burned, because the West has said so. Out of the feeling of unrest thus produced, there arose a wave of so-called reform in India.

If you wish to be a true reformer, three things are necessary. The first is to feel. Do you really feel for your brothers? Do you really feel that there is so much misery in the world, so much ignorance and superstition? Do you really feel that men are your brothers? Does this idea come into your whole being? Does it run with your blood? Does it tingle in your veins? Does it course through every nerve and filament of your body? Are you full of that idea of sympathy? If you are, that is only the first step. You must think next if you have found any remedy. The old ideas may be all superstition, but in and round these masses of superstition are nuggets of gold and truth. Have you discovered means by which to keep that gold alone, without any of the dross? If you have done that, that is only the second step; one more thing is necessary. What is your motive? Are you sure that you are not actuated by greed of gold, by thirst for fame or power? Are you really sure that you can stand to your ideals and work on, even if the whole world wants to crush you down? Are you sure you know what you want and will perform your duty, and that alone, even if your life is at stake? Are you sure that you will persevere so long as life endures, so long as there is one pulsation left in the heart? Then you are a real reformer, you are a teacher, a Master, a blessing to mankind. But man is so impatient, so short-sighted! He has not the patience to wait, he has not the power to see. He wants to rule, he wants results immediately. Why? He wants to reap the fruits himself, and does not really care for others. Duty for duty's sake is not what he wants. "To work you have the right, but not to the fruits thereof," says Krishna. Why cling to results? Ours are the duties. Let the fruits take care of themselves. But man has no patience. He takes up any scheme. The larger number of would-be reformers all over the world can be classed under this heading.

As I have said, the idea of reform came to India when it seemed as if the wave of materialism that had invaded her shores would sweep away the teachings of the sages. But the nation had borne the shocks of a thousand such waves of change. This one was mild in comparison. Wave after wave had flooded the land, breaking and crushing everything for hundreds of years. The sword had flashed, and "Victory unto Allah" had rent the skies of India; but these floods subsided, leaving the national ideals unchanged.

The Indian nation cannot be killed. Deathless it stands, and it will stand so long as that spirit shall remain as the background, so long as her people do not give up their spirituality. Beggars they may remain, poor and poverty-stricken, dirt and squalor may surround them perhaps throughout all time, but let them not give up their God, let them not forget that they are the children of the sages. Just as in the West, even the man in the street wants to trace his descent from some robber-baron of the Middle Ages, so in India, even an Emperor on the throne wants to trace his descent from some beggar-sage in the forest, from a man who wore the bark of a tree, lived upon the fruits of the forest and communed with God. That is the type of descent we want; and so long as holiness is thus supremely venerated, India cannot die.

Many of you perhaps have read the article by Prof. Max Müller in a recent issue of the *Nineteenth Century,* headed "A Real Mahâtman". The life of Shri Ramakrishna is interesting, as it was a living illustration of the ideas that he preached. Perhaps it will be a little romantic for you who live in the West in an atmosphere entirely different from that of India. For the methods and manners in the busy rush of life in the West vary entirely from those of India. Yet perhaps it will be of all the more interest for that, because it will bring into a newer light, things about which many have already heard.

It was while reforms of various kinds were being inaugurated in India that a child was born of poor Brâhmin parents on the eighteenth of February, 1836, in one of the remote villages of Bengal. The father and mother were very orthodox people. The life of a really orthodox Brahmin is one of continuous renunciation. Very few things can he do; and over and beyond them the orthodox Brahmin must not occupy himself with any secular business. At the same time he must not receive gifts from everybody. You may imagine how rigorous that life becomes. You have heard of the Brahmins and their priestcraft many times, but very few of you have ever stopped to ask what makes this wonderful band of men the rulers of their fellows. They are the poorest of all the classes in the country; and the secret of their power lies in their renunciation. They never covet wealth. Theirs is the poorest priesthood in the world, and therefore the most powerful. Even in this poverty, a Brahmin's wife will never allow a poor man to pass through the village without giving him something to eat. That is considered the highest duty of the mother in India; and because she is the mother it is her duty to be served last; she must see that everyone is served before her turn comes. That is why the mother is regarded as God in India. This particular woman, the mother of our subject, was the very type of a Hindu mother. The higher the caste, the greater the restrictions. The lowest caste people can eat and drink anything they like. But as men rise in the social scale, more and more restrictions come; and when they reach the highest caste, the Brahmin, the hereditary priesthood of India, their lives, as I have said, are very much circumscribed. Compared to Western manners, their lives are of continuous asceticism. The Hindus are perhaps the most exclusive nation in the world. They have the same great steadiness as the English, but much more amplified. When they get hold of an idea they carry it out to its very conclusion, and they keep hold of it generation after generation until they make something out of it. Once give them an idea, and it is not easy to take it back; but it is hard to make them grasp a new idea.

The orthodox Hindus, therefore, are very exclusive, living entirely within their own horizon of thought and feeling. Their lives are laid down in our old books in every little detail, and the least detail is grasped with almost adamantine firmness by them. They would starve rather than eat a meal cooked by the hands of a man not belonging to their own small section of caste. But withal, they have intensity and tremendous earnestness. That force of intense faith and religious life occurs often among the orthodox Hindus, because their very orthodoxy comes from a tremendous conviction that it is right. We may not all think that what they hold on to with such perseverance is right; but to them it is. Now, it is written in our books that a man should always be charitable even to the extreme. If a man starves himself to death to help another man, to save that man's life, it is all right; it is even held that a man ought to do that. And it is expected of a Brahmin to carry this idea out to the very extreme. Those who are acquainted with the literature of India will remember a beautiful old story about this extreme charity, how a whole family, as related in the Mahâbhârata, starved themselves to death and gave their last meal to a beggar. This is not an exaggeration, for such things still happen. The character of the father and the mother of my Master was very much like that. Very poor they were, and yet many a time the mother would starve herself a whole day to help a poor man. Of them this child was born; and he was a peculiar child from very boyhood. He remembered his past from his birth and was conscious for what purpose he came into the world, and every power was devoted to the fulfilment of that purpose.

While he was quite young, his father died; and the boy was sent to school. A Brahmin's boy must go to school; the caste restricts him to a learned profession only. The old system of education in India, still prevalent in many parts of the country, especially in connection with Sannyâsins, is very different from the modern system. The students had not to pay. It was thought that knowledge is so sacred that no man ought to sell it. Knowledge must be given freely and without any price. The teachers used to take students without charge, and not only so,. most of them gave their students food and clothes. To support these teachers the wealthy families on certain occasions, such as a marriage festival, or at the ceremonies for the dead, made gifts to them. They were considered the first and foremost claimants to certain gifts; and they in their turn had to maintain their students. So whenever there is a marriage, especially in a rich family, these professors are invited, and they attend and discuss various subjects. This boy went to one of these gatherings of professors, and the professors were discussing various topics, such as logic or astronomy, subjects much beyond his age. The boy was peculiar, as I have said, and he gathered this moral out of it: "This is the outcome of all their knowledge. Why are they fighting so hard? It is simply for money; the man who can show the highest learning here will get the best pair of cloth, and that is all these people are struggling for. I will not go to school any more." And he did not; that was the end of his going to school. But this boy had an elder brother, a learned professor, who took him to Calcutta, however, to study with him. After a short time the boy became fully convinced that the aim of all secular learning was mere material advancement, and nothing more, and he resolved to give up study and devote himself solely to the pursuit of spiritual knowledge. The father being dead, the family was very poor; and this boy had to make his own living. He went to a place near Calcutta and became a temple priest. To become a temple priest is thought very degrading to a Brahmin. Our temples are not churches in your sense of the word, they are not places for public worship; for, properly speaking, there is no such thing as public worship in India. Temples are erected mostly by rich persons as a meritorious religious act.

If a man has much property, he wants to build a temple. In that he puts a symbol or an image of an Incarnation of God, and dedicates it to worship in the name of God. The worship is akin to that which is conducted in Roman Catholic churches, very much like the mass, reading certain sentences from the sacred books, waving a light before the image, and treating the image in every respect as we treat a great man. This is all that is done in the temple. The man who goes to a temple is not considered thereby a better man than he who never goes. More properly, the latter is considered the more religious man, for religion in India is to each man his own private affair. In the house of every man there is either a little chapel, or a room set apart, and there he goes morning and evening, sits down in a corner, and there does his worship. And this worship is entirely mental, for another man does not hear or know what he is doing. He sees him only sitting there, and perhaps moving his fingers in a peculiar fashion, or closing his nostrils and breathing in a peculiar manner. Beyond that, he does not know what his brother is doing; even his wife, perhaps, will not know. Thus, all worship is conducted in the privacy of his own home. Those who cannot afford to have a chapel go to the banks of a river, or a lake, or the sea if they live at the seaside, but people sometimes go to worship in a temple by making salutation to the image. There their duty to the temple ends. Therefore, you see, it has been held from the most ancient times in our country, legislated upon by Manu, that it is a degenerating occupation to become a temple priest. Some of the books say it is so degrading as to make a Brahmin worthy of reproach. Just as with education, but in a far more intense sense with religion, there is the other idea behind it that the temple priests who take fees for their work are making merchandise of sacred things. So you may imagine the feelings of that boy when he was forced through poverty to take up the only occupation open to him, that of a temple priest.

There have been various poets in Bengal whose songs have passed down to the people; they are sung in the streets of Calcutta and in every village. Most of these are religious songs, and their one central idea, which is perhaps peculiar to the religions of India, is the idea of realisation. There is not a book in India on religion which does not breathe this idea. Man must realise God, feel God, see God, talk to God. That is religion. The Indian atmosphere is full of stories of saintly persons having visions of God. Such doctrines form the basis of their religion; and all these ancient books and scriptures are the writings of persons who came into direct contact with spiritual facts. These books were not written for the intellect, nor can any reasoning understand them, because they were written by men who saw the things of which they wrote, and they can be understood only by men who have raised themselves to the same height. They say there is such a thing as realisation even in this life, and it is open to everyone, and religion begins with the opening of this faculty, if I may call it so. This is the central idea in all religions, and this is why we may find one man with the most finished oratorical powers, or the most convincing logic, preaching the highest doctrines and yet unable to get people to listen to him, while we may find another, a poor man, who scarcely can speak the language of his own motherland, yet half the nation worships him in his own lifetime as God. When in India the idea somehow or other gets abroad that a man has raised himself to that state of realisation, that religion is no more a matter of conjecture to him, that he is no more groping in the dark in such momentous questions as religion, the immortality of the soul, and God, people come from all quarters to see him and gradually they begin to worship him.

In the temple was an image of the "Blissful Mother". This boy had to conduct the worship morning and evening, and by degrees this one idea filled his mind: "Is there anything behind this image? Is it true that there is a Mother of Bliss in the universe? Is it true that She lives and guides the universe, or is it all a dream? Is there any reality in religion?"

This scepticism comes to the Hindu child. It is the scepticism of our country: Is this that we are doing real? And theories will not satisfy us, although there are ready at hand almost all the theories that have ever been made with regard to God and soul. Neither books nor theories can satisfy us, the one idea that gets hold of thousands of our people is this idea of realisation. Is it true that there is a God, If it be true, can I see Him? Can I realise the truth? The Western mind may think all this very impracticable, but to us it is intensely practical. For this idea men will give up their lives. You have just heard how from the earliest times there have been persons who have given up all comforts and luxuries to live in caves, and hundreds have given up their homes to weep bitter tears of misery, on the banks of sacred rivers, in order to realise this idea—not to know in the ordinary sense of the word, not intellectual understanding, not a mere rationalistic comprehension of the real thing, not mere groping in the dark, but intense realisation, much more real than this world is to our senses. That is the idea. I do not advance any proposition as to that just now, but that is the one fact that is impressed upon them. Thousands will be killed, other thousands will be ready. So upon this one idea the whole nation for thousands of years have been denying and sacrificing themselves. For this idea thousands of Hindus every year give up their homes, and many of them die through the hardships they have to undergo. To the Western mind this must seem most visionary, and I can see the reason for this point of view. But though I have resided in the West, I still think this idea the most practical thing in life.

Every moment I think of anything else is so much loss to me—even the marvels of earthly sciences; everything is vain if it takes me away from that thought. Life is but momentary, whether you have the knowledge of an angel or the ignorance of an animal. Life is but momentary, whether you have the poverty of the poorest man in rags or the wealth of the richest living person. Life is but momentary, whether you are a downtrodden man living in one of the big streets of the big cities of the West or a crowned Emperor ruling over millions. Life is but momentary, whether you have the best of health or the worst. Life is but momentary, whether you have the most poetical temperament or the most cruel. There is but one solution of life, says the Hindu, and that solution is what they call God and religion. If these be true, life becomes explained, life becomes bearable, becomes enjoyable. Otherwise, life is but a useless burden. That is our idea, but no amount of reasoning can demonstrate it; it can only make it probable, and there it rests. The highest demonstration of reasoning that we have in any branch of knowledge can only make a fact probable, and nothing further. The most demonstrable facts of physical science are only probabilities, not facts yet. Facts are only in the senses. Facts have to be perceived, and we have to perceive religion to demonstrate it to ourselves. We have to sense God to be convinced that there is a God. We must sense the facts of religion to know that they are facts. Nothing else, and no amount of reasoning, but our own perception can make these things real to us, can make my belief firm as a rock. That is my idea, and that is the Indian idea.

This idea took possession of the boy and his whole life became concentrated upon that. Day after day he would weep and say, "Mother, is it true that Thou existest, or is it all poetry? Is the Blissful Mother an imagination of poets and misguided people, or is there such a Reality?" We have seen that of books, of education in our sense of the word, he had none, and so much the more natural, so much the more healthy, was his mind, so much the purer his thoughts, undiluted by drinking in the thoughts of others. Because he did not go to the university, therefore he thought for himself. Because we have spent half our lives in the university we are filled with a collection of other people's thoughts. Well has Prof. Max Müller said in the article I have just referred to that this was a clean, original man; and the secret of that originality was that he was not brought up within the precincts of a university. However, this thought—whether God can be seen—which was uppermost in his mind gained in strength every day until he could think of nothing else. He could no more conduct the worship properly, could no more attend to the various details in all their minuteness. Often he would forget to place the food-offering before the image, sometimes he would forget to wave the light; at other times he would wave it for hours, and forget everything else.

And that one idea was in his mind every day: "Is it true that Thou existest, O Mother? Why dost Thou not speak? Art Thou dead?" Perhaps some of us here will remember that there are moments in our lives when, tired of all these ratiocinations of dull and dead logic, tired of plodding through books—which after all teach us nothing, become nothing but a sort of intellectual opium-eating—we must have it at stated times or we die—tired with all this, the heart of our hearts sends out a wail: "Is there no one in this universe who can show me the light? If Thou art, show the light unto me. Why dost Thou not speak? Why dost Thou make Thyself so scarce, why send so many Messengers and not Thyself come to me? In this world of fights and factions whom am I to follow and believe? If Thou art the God of every man and woman alike, why comest Thou not to speak to Thy child and see if he is not ready?" Well, to us all come such thoughts in moments of great depression; but such are the temptations surrounding us, that the next moment we forget. For the moment it seemed that the doors of the heavens were going to be opened, for the moment it seemed as if we were going to plunge into the light effulgent; but the animal man again shakes off all these angelic visions. Down we go, animal man once more, eating and drinking and dying, and dying and drinking and eating again and again. But there are exceptional minds which are not turned away so easily, which once attracted can never be turned back, whatever may be the temptation in the way, which want to see the Truth, knowing that life must go. They say, let it go in a noble conquest, and what conquest is nobler than the conquest of the lower man, than this solution of the problem of life and death, of good and evil?

At last it became impossible for him to serve in the temple. He left it and entered into a little wood that was near and lived there. About this part of his life, he told me many times that he could not tell when the sun rose or set, or how he lived. He lost all thought of himself and forgot to eat. During this period he was lovingly watched over by a relative who put into his mouth food which he mechanically swallowed.

Days and nights thus passed with the boy. When a whole day would pass, towards the evening when the peal of bells in the temples, and the voices singing, would reach the wood, it would make the boy very sad, and he would cry, "Another day is gone in vain, Mother, and Thou hast not come. Another day of this short life has gone, and I have not known the Truth." In the agony of his soul, sometimes he would rub his face against the ground and weep, and this one prayer burst forth: "Do Thou manifest Thyself in me, Thou Mother of the universe! See that I need Thee and nothing else!" Verily, he wanted to be true to his own ideal. He had heard that the Mother never came until everything had been given up for Her. He had heard that the Mother wanted to come to everyone, but they would not have Her, that people wanted all sorts of foolish little idols to pray to, that they wanted their own enjoyments, and not the Mother, and that the moment they really wanted Her with their whole soul, and nothing else, that moment She would come. So he began to break himself into that idea; he wanted to be exact, even on the plane of matter. He threw away all the little property he had, and took a vow that he would never touch money, and this one idea, "I will not touch money", became a part of him. It may appear to be something occult, but even in after-life when he was sleeping, if I touched him with a piece of money his hand would become bent, and his whole body would become, as it were, paralysed. The other idea that came into his mind was that lust was the other enemy. Man is a soul, and soul is sexless, neither man nor woman. The idea of sex and the idea of money were the two things, he thought, that prevented him from seeing the Mother. This whole universe is the manifestation of the Mother, and She lives in every woman's body. "Every woman represents the Mother; how can I think of woman in mere sex relation?" That was the idea: Every woman was his Mother, he must bring himself to the state when he would see nothing but Mother in every woman. And he carried it out in his life.

This is the tremendous thirst that seizes the human heart. Later on, this very man said to me, "My child, suppose there is a bag of gold in one room, and a robber in the next room; do you think that the robber can sleep? He cannot. His mind will be always thinking how to get into that room and obtain possession of that gold. Do you think then that a man, firmly persuaded that there is a Reality behind all these appearances, that there is a God, that there is One who never dies, One who is infinite bliss, a bliss compared with which these pleasures of the senses are simply playthings, can rest contended without struggling to attain It? Can he cease his efforts for a moment? No. He will become mad with longing." This divine madness seized the boy. At that time he had no teacher, nobody to tell him anything, and everyone thought that he was out of his mind. This is the ordinary condition of things. If a man throws aside the vanities of the world, we hear him called mad. But such men are the salt of the earth. Out of such madness have come the powers that have moved this world of ours, and out of such madness alone will come the powers of the future that are going to move the world.

So days, weeks, months passed in continuous struggle of the soul to arrive at truth. The boy began to see visions, to see wonderful things; the secrets of his nature were beginning to open to him. Veil after veil was, as it were, being taken off. Mother Herself became the teacher and initiated the boy into the truths he sought. At this time there came to this place a woman of beautiful appearance, learned beyond compare. Later on, this saint used to say about her that she was not learned, but was the embodiment of learning; she was learning itself, in human form. There, too, you find the peculiarity of the Indian nation. In the midst of the ignorance in which the average Hindu woman lives, in the midst of what is called in Western countries her lack of freedom, there could arise a woman of supreme spirituality. She was a Sannyâsini; for women also give up the world, throw away their property, do not marry, and devote themselves to the worship of the Lord. She came; and when she heard of this boy in the grove, she offered to go and see him; and hers was the first help he received. At once she recognised what his trouble was, and she said to him. "My son, blessed is the man upon whom such madness comes. The whole of this universe is mad—some for wealth, some for pleasure, some for fame, some for a hundred other things. They are mad for gold, or husbands, or wives, for little trifles, mad to tyrannise over somebody, mad to become rich, mad for every foolish thing except God. And they can understand only their own madness. When another man is mad after gold, they have fellow-feeling and sympathy for him, and they say he is the right man, as lunatics think that lunatics alone are sane. But if a man is mad after the Beloved, after the Lord, how can they understand? They think he has gone crazy; and they say, 'Have nothing to do with him.' That is why they call you mad; but yours is the right kind of madness. Blessed is the man who is mad after God. Such men are very few." This woman remained near the boy for years, taught him the forms of the religions of India, initiated him into the different practices of Yoga, and, as it were, guided and brought into harmony this tremendous river of spirituality.

Later, there came to the same grove a Sannyasin, one of the begging friars of India, a learned man, a philosopher. He was a peculiar man, he was an idealist. He did not believe that this world existed in reality; and to demonstrate that, he would never go under a roof, he would always live out of doors, in storm and sunshine alike. This man began to teach the boy the philosophy of the Vedas; and he found very soon, to his astonishment, that the pupil was in some respects wiser than the master. He spent several months with the boy, after which he initiated him into the order of Sannyasins, and took his departure.

When as a temple priest his extraordinary worship made people think him deranged in his head, his relatives took him home and married him to a little girl, thinking that that would turn his thoughts and restore the balance of his mind. But he came back and, as we have seen, merged deeper in his madness. Sometimes, in our country, boys are married as children and have no voice in the matter; their parents marry them. Of course such a marriage is little more than a betrothal. When they are married they still continue to live with their parents, and the real marriage takes place when the wife grows older, when it is customary for the husband to go and bring his bride to his own home. In this case, however, the husband had entirely forgotten that he had a wife. In her far off home the girl had heard that her husband had become a religious enthusiast, and that he was even considered insane by many. She resolved to learn the truth for herself, so she set out and walked to the place where her husband was. When at last she stood in her husband's presence, he at once admitted her right to his life, although in India any person, man or woman, who embraces a religious life, is thereby freed from all other obligations. The young man fell at the feet of his wife and said, "As for me, the Mother has shown me that She resides in every woman, and so I have learnt to look upon every woman as Mother. That is the one idea I can have about you; but if you wish to drag me into the world, as I have been married to you, I am at your service."

The maiden was a pure and noble soul and was able to understand her husband's aspirations and sympathise with them. She quickly told him that she had no wish to drag him down to a life of worldliness; but that all she desired was to remain near him, to serve him, and to learn of him. She became one of his most devoted disciples, always revering him as a divine being. Thus through his wife's consent the last barrier was removed, and he was free to lead the life he had chosen.

The next desire that seized upon the soul of this man was to know the truth about the various religions. Up to that time he had not known any religion but his own. He wanted to understand what other religions were like. So he sought teachers of other religions. By teachers you must always remember what we mean in India, not a bookworm, but a man of realisation, one who knows truth at first hand and not through an intermediary. He found a Mohammedan saint and placed himself under him; he underwent the disciplines prescribed by him, and to his astonishment found that when faithfully carried out, these devotional methods led him to the same goal he had already attained. He gathered similar experience from following the true religion of Jesus the Christ. He went to all the sects he could find, and whatever he took up he went into with his whole heart. He did exactly as he was told, and in every instance he arrived at the same result. Thus from actual experience, he came to know that the goal of every religion is the same, that each is trying to teach the same thing, the difference being largely in method and still more in language. At the core, all sects and all religions have the same aim; and they were only quarrelling for their own selfish purposes—they were not anxious about the truth, but about "my name" and "your name". Two of them preached the same truth, but one of them said, "That cannot be true, because I have not put upon it the seal of my name. Therefore do not listen to him." And the other man said, "Do not hear him, although he is preaching very much the same thing, yet it is not true because he does not preach it in my name."

That is what my Master found, and he then set about to learn humility, because he had found that the one idea in all religions is, "not me, but Thou", and he who says, "not me", the Lord fills his heart. The less of this little "I" the more of God there is in him. That he found to be the truth in every religion in the world, and he set himself to accomplish this. As I have told you, whenever he wanted to do anything he never confined himself to fine theories, but would enter into the practice immediately. We see many persons talking the most wonderfully fine things about charity and about equality and the rights of other people and all that, but it is only in theory. I was so fortunate as to find one who was able to carry theory into practice. He had the most wonderful faculty of carrying everything into practice which he thought was right.

Now, there was a family of Pariahs living near the place. The Pariahs number several millions in the whole of India and are a sect of people so low that some of our books say that if a Brahmin coming out from his house sees the face of a Pariah, he has to fast that day and recite certain prayers before he becomes holy again. In some Hindu cities when a Pariah enters, he has to put a crow's feather on his head as a sign that he is a Pariah, and he has to cry aloud, "Save yourselves, the Pariah is passing through the street", and you will find people flying off from him as if by magic, because if they touch him by chance, they will have to change their clothes, bathe, and do other things. And the Pariah for thousands of years has believed that it is perfectly right; that his touch will make everybody unholy. Now my Master would go to a Pariah and ask to be allowed to clean his house. The business of the Pariah is to clean the streets of the cities and to keep houses clean. He cannot enter the house by the front door; by the back door he enters; and as soon as he has gone, the whole place over which he has passed is sprinkled with and made holy by a little Gangâ water. By birth the Brahmin stands for holiness, and the Pariah for the very reverse. And this Brahmin asked to be allowed to do the menial services in the house of the Pariah. The Pariah of course could not allow that, for they all think that if they allow a Brahmin to do such menial work it will be an awful sin, and they will become extinct. The Pariah would not permit it; so in the dead of night, when all were sleeping, Ramakrishna would enter the house. He had long hair, and with his hair he would wipe the place, saying, "Oh, my Mother, make me the servant of the Pariah, make me feel that I am even lower than the Pariah." "They worship Me best who worship My worshippers. These are all My children and your privilege is to serve them"—is the teaching of Hindu scriptures.

There were various other preparations which would take a long time to relate, and I want to give you just a sketch of his life. For years he thus educated himself. One of the Sâdhanâs was to root out the sex idea. Soul has no sex, it is neither male nor female. It is only in the body that sex exists, and the man who desires to reach the spirit cannot at the same time hold to sex distinctions. Having been born in a masculine body, this man wanted to bring the feminine idea into everything. He began to think that he was a woman, he dressed like a woman, spoke like a woman, gave up the occupations of men, and lived in the household among the women of a good family, until, after years of this discipline, his mind became changed, and he entirely forgot the idea of sex; thus the whole view of life became changed to him.

We hear in the West about worshipping woman, but this is usually for her youth and beauty. This man meant by worshipping woman, that to him every woman's face was that of the Blissful Mother, and nothing but that. I myself have seen this man standing before those women whom society would not touch, and falling at their feet bathed in tears, saying, "Mother, in one form Thou art in the street, and in another form Thou art the universe. I salute Thee, Mother, I salute Thee." Think of the blessedness of that life from which all carnality has vanished, which can look upon every woman with that love and reverence when every woman's face becomes transfigured, and only the face of the Divine Mother, the Blissful one, the Protectress of the human race, shines upon it! That is what we want. Do you mean to say that the divinity back of a woman can ever be cheated? It never was and never will be. It always asserts itself. Unfailingly it detects fraud, it detects hypocrisy, unerringly it feels the warmth of truth, the light of spirituality, the holiness of purity. Such purity is absolutely necessary if real spirituality is to be attained.

This rigorous, unsullied purity came into the life of that man. All the struggles which we have in our lives were past for him. His hard-earned jewels of spirituality, for which he had given three-quarters of his life, were now ready to be given to humanity, and then began his mission. His teaching and preaching were peculiar. In our country a teacher is a most highly venerated person, he is regarded as God Himself. We have not even the same respect for our father and mother. Father and mother give us our body, but the teacher shows us the way to salvation. We are his children, we are born in the spiritual line of the teacher. All Hindus come to pay respect to an extraordinary teacher, they crowd around him. And here was such a teacher, but the teacher had not thought whether he was to be respected or not, he had not the least idea that he was a great teacher, he thought that it was Mother who was doing everything and not he. He always said, "If any good comes from my lips, it is the Mother who speaks; what have I to do with it?" That was his one idea about his work, and to the day of his death he never gave it up. This man sought no one. His principle was, first form character, first earn spirituality and results will come of themselves. His favourite illustration was, "When the lotus opens, the bees come of their own accord to seek the honey; so let the lotus of your character be full-blown, and the results will follow." This is a great lesson to learn.

My Master taught me this lesson hundreds of times, yet I often forget it. Few understand the power of thought. If a man goes into a cave, shuts himself in, and thinks one really great thought and dies, that thought will penetrate the walls of that cave, vibrate through space, and at last permeate the whole human race. Such is the power of thought; be in no hurry therefore to give your thoughts to others. First have something to give. He alone teaches who has something to give, for teaching is not talking, teaching is not imparting doctrines, it is communicating. Spirituality can be communicated just as really as I can give you a flower. This is true in the most literal sense. This idea is very old in India and finds illustration in the West in the theory, in the belief, of apostolic succession. Therefore first make character—that is the highest duty you can perform. Know Truth for yourself, and there will be many to whom you can teach it afterwards; they will all come. This was the attitude of my Master. He criticised no one. For years I lived with that man, but never did I hear those lips utter one word of condemnation for any sect. He had the same sympathy for all sects; he had found the harmony between them. A man may be intellectual, or devotional, or mystic, or active; the various religions represent one or the other of these types. Yet it is possible to combine all the four in one man, and this is what future humanity is going to do. That was his idea. He condemned no one, but saw the good in all.

People came by thousands to see and hear this wonderful man who spoke in a *patois* every word of which was forceful and instinct with light. For it is not what is spoken, much less the language in which it is spoken, but it is the personality of the speaker which dwells in everything he says that carries weight. Every one of us feels this at times. We hear most splendid orations, most wonderfully reasoned-out discourses, and we go home and forget them all. At other times we hear a few words in the simplest language, and they enter into our lives, become part and parcel of ourselves and produce lasting results. The words of a man who can put his personality into them take effect, but he must have tremendous personality. All teaching implies giving and taking, the teacher gives and the taught receives, but the one must have something to give, and the other must be open to receive.

This man came to live near Calcutta, the capital of India, the most important university town in our country which was sending out sceptics and materialists by the hundreds every year. Yet many of these university men—sceptics and agnostics—used to come and listen to him. I heard of this man, and I went to hear him. He looked just like an ordinary man, with nothing remarkable about him. He used the most simple language, and I thought "Can this man be a great teacher?"—crept near to him and asked him the question which I had been asking others all my life: "Do you believe in God, Sir?" "Yes," he replied. "Can you prove it, Sir?" "Yes." "How?" "Because I see Him just as I see you here, only in a much intenser sense." That impressed me at once. For the first time I found a man who dared to say that he saw God, that religion was a reality to be felt, to be sensed in an infinitely more intense way than we can sense the world. I began to go to that man, day after day, and I actually saw that religion could be given. One touch, one glance, can change a whole life. I have read about Buddha and Christ and Mohammed, about all those different luminaries of ancient times, how they would stand up and say, "Be thou whole", and the man became whole. I now found it to be true, and when I myself saw this man, all scepticism was brushed aside. It could be done; and my Master used to say, "Religion can be given and taken more tangibly, more really than anything else in the world." Be therefore spiritual first; have something to give and then stand before the world and give it. Religion is not talk, or doctrines, or theories; nor is it sectarianism. Religion cannot live in sects and societies. It is the relation between the soul and God; how can it be made into a society? It would then degenerate into business, and wherever there are business and business principles in religion, spirituality dies. Religion does not consist in erecting temples, or building churches, or attending public worship. It is not to be found in books, or in words, or in lectures, or in organisations. Religion consists in realisation. As a fact, we all know that nothing will satisfy us until we know the truth for ourselves. However we may argue, however much we may hear, but one thing will satisfy us, and that is our own realisation; and such an experience is possible for every one of us if we will only try. The first ideal of this attempt to realise religion is that of renunciation. As far as we can, we must give up. Darkness and light, enjoyment of the world and enjoyment of God will never go together. "Ye cannot serve God and Mammon." Let people try it if they will, and I have seen millions in every country who have tried; but after all, it comes to nothing. If one word remains true in the saying, it is, give up everything for the sake of the Lord. This is a hard and long task, but you can begin it here and now. Bit by bit we must go towards it.

The second idea that I learnt from my Master, and which is perhaps the most vital, is the wonderful truth that the religions of the world are not contradictory or antagonistic. They are but various phases of one eternal religion. That one eternal religion is applied to different planes of existence, is applied to the opinions of various minds and various races. There never was my religion or yours, my national religion or your national religion; there never existed many religions, there is only the one. One infinite religion existed all through eternity and will ever exist, and this religion is expressing itself in various countries in various ways. Therefore we must respect all religions and we must try to accept them all as far as we can. Religions manifest themselves not only according to race and geographical position, but according to individual powers. In one man religion is manifesting itself as intense activity, as work. In another it is manifesting itself as intense devotion, in yet another, as mysticism, in others as philosophy, and so forth. It is wrong when we say to others, "Your methods are not right." Perhaps a man, whose nature is that of love, thinks that the man who does good to others is not on the right road to religion, because it is not his own way, and is therefore wrong. If the philosopher thinks, "Oh, the poor ignorant people, what do they know about a God of Love, and loving Him? They do not know what they mean," he is wrong, because they may be right and he also.

To learn this central secret that the truth may be one and yet many at the same time, that we may have different visions of the same truth from different standpoints, is exactly what must be done. Then, instead of antagonism to anyone, we shall have infinite sympathy with all. Knowing that as long as there are different natures born in this world, the same religious truth will require different adaptations, we shall understand that we are bound to have forbearance with each other. Just as nature is unity in variety—an infinite variation in the phenomenal—as in and through all these variations of the phenomenal runs the Infinite, the Unchangeable, the Absolute Unity, so it is with every man; the microcosm is but a miniature repetition of the macrocosm; in spite of all these variations, in and through them all runs this eternal harmony, and we have to recognise this. This idea, above all other ideas, I find to be the crying necessity of the day. Coming from a country which is a hotbed of religious sects—and to which, through its good fortune or ill fortune, everyone who has a religious idea wants to send an advanced-guard—I have been acquainted from my childhood with the various sects of the world. Even the Mormons come to preach in India. Welcome them all! That is the soil on which to preach religion. There it takes root more than in any other country. If you come and teach politics to the Hindus, they do not understand; but if you come to preach religion, however curious it may be, you will have hundreds and thousands of followers in no time, and you have every chance of becoming a living God in your lifetime. I am glad it is so, it is the one thing we want in India.

The sects among the Hindus are various, a great many in number, and some of them apparently hopelessly contradictory. Yet they all tell you they are but different manifestations of religion. "As different rivers, taking their start from different mountains, running crooked or straight, all come and mingle their waters in the ocean, so the different sects, with their different points of view, at last all come unto Thee." This is not a theory, it has to be recognised, but not in that patronising way which we see with some people: "Oh yes, there are some very good things in it. These are what we call the ethnical religions. These ethnical religions have some good in them." Some even have the most wonderfully liberal idea that other religions are all little bits of a prehistoric evolution, but "ours is the fulfilment of things". One man says, because his is the oldest religion, it is the best; another makes the same claim, because his is the latest.

We have to recognise that each one of them has the same

saving power as the other. What you have heard about their difference, whether in the temple or in the church, is a mass of superstition. The same God answers all; and it is not you, or I, or any body of men that is responsible for the safety and salvation of the least little bit of the soul; the same Almighty God is responsible for all. I do not understand how people declare themselves to be believers in God, and at the same time think that God has handed over to a little body of men all truth, and that they are the guardians of the rest of humanity. How can you call that religion? Religion is realisation; but mere talk—mere trying to believe, mere groping in darkness, mere parroting the words of ancestors and thinking it is religion, mere making a political something out of the truths of religion—is not religion at all. In every sect—even among the Mohammedans whom we always regard as the most exclusive—even among them we find that wherever there was a man trying to realise religion, from his lips have come the fiery words: "Thou art the Lord of all, Thou art in the heart of all, Thou art the guide of all, Thou art the Teacher of all, and Thou carest infinitely more for the land of Thy children than we can ever do." Do not try to disturb the faith of any man. If you can, give him something better; if you can, get hold of a man where he stands and give him a push upwards; do so, but do not destroy what he has. The only true teacher is he who can convert himself, as it were, into a thousand persons at a moment's notice. The only true teacher is he who can immediately come down to the level of the student, and transfer his soul to the student's soul and see through the student's eyes and hear through his ears and understand through his mind. Such a teacher can really teach and none else. All these negative, breaking-down, destructive teachers that are in the world can never do any good.

In the presence of my Master I found out that man could be perfect, even in this body. Those lips never cursed anyone, never even criticised anyone. Those eyes were beyond the possibility of seeing evil, that mind had lost the power of thinking evil. He saw nothing but good. That tremendous purity, that tremendous renunciation is the one secret of spirituality. "Neither through wealth, nor through progeny, but through renunciation alone, is immortality to be reached", say the Vedas. "Sell all that thou hast and give to the poor, and follow me", says the Christ. So all great saints and Prophets have expressed it, and have carried it out in their lives. How can great spirituality come without that renunciation? Renunciation is the background of all religious thought wherever it be, and you will always find that as this idea of renunciation lessens, the more will the senses creep into the field of religion, and spirituality will decrease in the same ratio.

That man was the embodiment of renunciation. In our country it is necessary for a man who becomes a Sannyasin to give up all worldly wealth and position, and this my Master carried out literally. There were many who would have felt themselves blest if he would only have accepted a present from their hands, who would gladly have given him thousands of rupees if he would have taken them, but these were the only men from whom he would turn away. He was a triumphant example, a living realisation of the complete conquest of lust and of desire for money. He was beyond all ideas of either, and such men are necessary for this century. Such renunciation is necessary in these days when men have begun to think that they cannot live a month without what they call their "necessities", and which they are increasing out of all proportion. It is necessary in a time like this that a man should arise to demonstrate to the sceptics of the world that there yet breathes a man who does not care a straw for all the gold or all the fame that is in the universe. Yet there are such men.

The other idea of his life was intense love for others. The first part of my Master's life was spent in acquiring spirituality, and the remaining years in distributing it. People in our country have not the same customs as you have in visiting a religious teacher or a Sannyasin. Somebody would come to ask him about something, some perhaps would come hundreds of miles, walking all the way, just to ask one question, to hear one word from him, "Tell me one word for my salvation." That is the way they come. They come in numbers, unceremoniously, to the place where he is mostly to be found; they may find him under a tree and question him; and before one set of people has gone, others have arrived. So if a man is greatly revered, he will sometimes have no rest day or night. He will have to talk constantly. For hours people will come pouring in, and this man will be teaching them.

So men came in crowds to hear him, and he would talk

twenty hours in the twenty-four, and that not for one day, but for months and months until at last the body broke down under the pressure of this tremendous strain. His intense love for mankind would not let him refuse to help even the humblest of the thousands who sought his aid. Gradually, there developed a vital throat disorder, and yet he could not be persuaded to refrain from these exertions. As soon as he heard that people were asking to see him, he would insist upon having them admitted, and would answer all their questions. When expostulated with, he replied, "I do not care. I will give up twenty thousand such bodies to help one man. It is glorious to help even one man." There was no rest for him. Once a man asked him, "Sir, you are a great Yogi. Why do you not put your mind a little on your body and cure your disease?" At first he did not answer, but when the question had been repeated, he gently said, "My friend, I thought you were a sage, but you talk like other men of the world. This mind has been given to the Lord. Do you mean to say that I should take it back and put it upon the body which is but a mere cage of the soul? "

So he went on preaching to the people, and the news spread that his body was about to pass away, and the people began to flock to him in greater crowds than ever. You cannot imagine the way they come to these great religious teachers in India, how they crowd round them and make gods of them while they are yet living. Thousands wait simply to touch the hem of their garments. It is through this appreciation of spirituality in others that spirituality is produced. Whatever man wants and appreciates, he will get; and it is the same with nations. If you go to India and deliver a political lecture, however grand it may be, you will scarcely find people to listen to you; but just go and teach religion, *live* it, not merely talk it, and hundreds will crowd just to look at you, to touch your feet. When the people heard that this holy man was likely to go from them soon, they began to come round him more than ever, and my Master went on teaching them without the least regard for his health. We could not prevent this. Many of the people came from long distances, and he would not rest until he had answered their questions. "While I can speak, I must teach them," he would say, and he was as good as his word. One day, he told us that he would lay down the body that day, and repeating the most sacred word of the Vedas he entered into Samâdhi and passed away.

His thoughts and his message were known to very few capable of giving them out. Among others, he left a few young boys who had renounced the world, and were ready to carry on his work. Attempts were made to crush them. But they stood firm, having the inspiration of that great life before them. Having had the contact of that blessed life for years,, they stood their ground. These young men, living as Sannyasins, begged through the streets of the city where they were born, although some of them came from high families. At first they met with great antagonism, but they persevered and went on from day to day spreading all over India the message of that great man, until the whole country was filled with the ideas he had preached. This man, from a remote village of Bengal, without education, by the sheer force of his own determination, realised the truth and gave it to others, leaving only a few young boys to keep it alive.

Today the name of Shri Ramakrishna Paramahamsa is known all over India to its millions of people. Nay, the power of that man has spread beyond India; and if there has ever been a word of truth, a word of spirituality, that I have spoken anywhere in the world, I owe it to my Master; only the mistakes are mine.

This is the message of Shri Ramakrishna to the modern world: "Do not care for doctrines, do not care for dogmas, or sects, or churches, or temples; they count for little compared with the essence of existence in each man, which is spirituality; and the more this is developed in a man, the more powerful is he for good. Earn that first, acquire that, and criticise no one, for all doctrines and creeds have some good in them. Show by your lives that religion does not mean words, or names, or sects, but that it means spiritual realisation. Only those can understand who have felt. Only those who have attained to spirituality can communicate it to others, can be great teachers of mankind. They alone are the powers of light."

The more such men are produced in a country, the more that country will be raised; and that country where such men absolutely do not exist is simply doomed, nothing can save it. Therefore my Master's message to mankind is: "Be spiritual and realise truth for yourself." He would have you give up for the sake of your fellowbeings. He would have you cease talking about love for your brother, and set to work to prove your words. The time has come for renunciation, for realisation; and then you will see the harmony in all the religions of the world. You will know that there is no need of any quarrel. And then only will you be ready to help humanity. To proclaim and make clear the fundamental unity underlying all religions was the mission of my Master. Other teachers have taught special religions which bear their names, but this great teacher of the nineteenth century made no claim for himself. He left every religion undisturbed because he had realised that in reality they are all part and parcel of the one eternal religion.

NOTES FROM LECTURES AND DISCOURSES

LORD BUDDHA

(Delivered in Detroit)

In every religion we find one type of self-devotion particularly developed. The type of working without a motive is most highly developed in Buddhism. Do not mistake Buddhism and Brâhminism. In this country you are very apt to do so. Buddhism is one of our sects. It was founded by a great man called Gautama, who became disgusted with the eternal metaphysical discussions of his day, and the cumbrous rituals and more especially with the caste system. Some people say that we are born to a certain state, and therefore we are superior to others who are not thus born. He was against this as also against the tremendous priesteraft. He preached a religion in which there was no motive power, and was perfectly agnostic about metaphysics or theories about God. He was often asked if there was a God, and he answered he did not know. When asked about right conduct, he would reply—Do good and be good. There came five Brahmins who asked him to settle their discussion. One said, "Sir, my Book says that God is such and such, and that this is the way to come to God". Another said, "That is wrong for my Book says such and such, and this is the way to come to God"; and so did the others. He listened calmly to all of them, and then asked them one by one, "Does any one of your Books say that God becomes angry, that He ever injures any one, that He is impure?" "No, sir, they all teach that God is pure and good" "Then, my friends, why do you not become pure and good first, that you may know what God is?"

Of course I do not endorse all his philosophy. I want a good deal of metaphysics for myself. I entirely differ in many respects, but because I differ, is that any reason why I should not see the beauty of the man? He was the only man who was bereft of all motive power. There were other great men who all said they were the Incarnations of God Himself, and that those who would believe in them would go to heaven. But what did Buddha say with his dying breath? "None can help you; help yourself; work out your own salvation." He said about himself, "Buddha is the name of infinite knowledge, infinite as the sky; I, Gautama, have reached that state; you will all reach that too if you struggle for it." Bereft of all motive power, he did not want to go to heaven, did not want money; he gave up his throne and everything else, and went about begging his bread through the streets of India, preaching for the good of men and animals with a heart as wide as the ocean. He was the only man who was ever ready to give up his life for animals, to stop a sacrifice. He once said to a king, "If the sacrifice of a lamb help you to go to heaven, sacrificing a man will help you better, so sacrifice me." The king was astonished. And yet this man was without any motive. He stands as the perfection of the active type, and the very height to which he attained shows that through the power of work we can also attain to the highest spirituality.

To many the path becomes easier if they believe in God. But the life of Buddha shows that even a man who does not believe in God, has no metaphysics, belongs to no sect, and does not go to any church, or temple, and is a confessed materialist, even he can attain to the highest. We have no right to judge him. I wish I had one infinitesimal part of Buddha's heart. Buddha may or may not have believed in God; that does not matter to me. He reached the same state of perfection to which others come by Bhakti—love of God, Yoga, or Jnâna. Perfection does not come from belief or faith. Talk does not count for anything. Parrots can do that. Perfection comes through the disinterested performance of action.

THE SYMBOL OM

Every idea that you have in the mind has a counterpart in a word; the word and the thought are inseparable. The external part of one and the same thing is what we call word, and the internal part is what we call thought. No man can, by analysis, separate thought from word. The idea that language was created by men—certain men sitting together and deciding upon words—has been proved to be wrong. So long as man has existed there have been words and language. What is the connection between an idea and a word? Although we see that there must always be a word with a thought, it is not necessary that the same thought requires the same word. The thought may be the same in twenty different countries, yet the language is different. We must have a word to express each thought, but these words need not necessarily have the same sound. Sounds will vary in different nations. One commentator says, "Although the relation between thought and word is perfectly natural, yet it does not mean a rigid connection between one sound and one idea." These sounds vary, yet the relation between the sounds and the thoughts is a natural one. The connection between thoughts and sounds is good only if there be a real connection between the thing signified and the symbol; until then that symbol will never come into general use. A symbol is the manifestor of the thing signified, and if the thing signified has already an existence, and if, by experience, we know that the symbol has expressed that thing many times, then we are sure that there is a real relation between them. Even if the things are not present, there will be thousands who will know them by their symbols. There must be a natural connection between the symbol and the thing signified; then, when that symbol is pronounced, it recalls the thing signified. The commentator says the manifesting word of God is Om. Why does he emphasise this word? There are hundreds of words for God. One thought is connected with a thousand words; the idea, God, is connected with hundreds of words, and each one stands as a symbol for God. Very good. But there must be a generalisation among all these words, some substratum, some common ground of all these symbols, and that which is the common symbol will be the best, and will really represent them all. In making a sound we use the larynx and the palate as a sounding board. Is there any material sound of which all other sounds must be manifestations, one which is the most natural sound? Om (Aum) is such a sound, the basis of all sounds. The first letter, *A*, is the root sound, the key, pronounced without touching any part of the tongue or palate; *M* represents the last sound in the series, being produced by the closed lips, and the *U* rolls from the very root to the end of the sounding board of the mouth. Thus, Om represents the whole phenomena of sound-producing. As such, it must be the natural symbol, the matrix of all the various sounds. It denotes the whole range and possibility of all the words that can be made. Apart from these speculations we see that around this word Om are centred all the different religious ideas in India; all the various religious ideas of the Vedas have gathered themselves round this word Om. What has that to do with America and England, or any other country? Simply this, that the word has been retained at every stage of religious growth in India, and it has been manipulated to mean all the various ideas about God. Monists, dualists, mono-dualists, separatists, and even atheists took up this Om. Om has become the one symbol for the religious aspiration of the vast majority of human beings. Take, for instance, the English word God. It covers only a limited function, and if you go beyond it, you have to add adjectives, to make it Personal, or Impersonal, or Absolute God. So with the words for God in every other language their signification is very small. This word Om, however, has around it all the various significances. As such it should be accepted by everyone.

SANNYASA: ITS IDEAL AND PRACTICE[1]

This is not the time for a long lecture. But I shall speak to you in brief about a few things which I should like you to carry into practice. First, we have to understand the ideal, and then the methods by which we can make it practical. Those of you who are Sannyasins must try to do good to others, for Sannyasa means that. There is no time to deliver a long discourse on "Renunciation", but I shall very briefly characterise it as *"the love of death"*. Worldly people love life. The Sannyasin is to love death. Are we to commit suicide then? Far from it. For suicides are not lovers of death, as it is often seen that when a man trying to commit suicide fails, he never attempts it for a second time. What is the love of death, then? We must die, that is certain; let us die then for a good cause. Let all our actions—eating, drinking, and everything that we do—tend towards the sacrifice of our self. You nourish your body by eating. What good is there in doing that if you do not hold it as a sacrifice to the well-being of others? You nourish your minds by reading books. There is no good in

[1] Summary of his reply to the Address given on June 19, 1899, by the junior Sannyâsins of the Belur Math, on the eve of his leaving for the West for the second time.

doing that unless you hold it also as a sacrifice to the whole world. . . . It is right for you that you should serve your millions of brothers rather than aggrandise this little self. . . . Thus you must die a gradual death. In such a death is heaven, all good is stored therein—and in its opposite is all that is diabolical and evil.

Then as to the methods of carrying the ideal into practical life. First, we have to understand that we must not have any impossible ideal. An ideal which is too high makes a nation weak and degraded. This happened after the Buddhistic and the Jain reforms. On the other hand, too much practicality is also wrong. If you have not even a little imagination, if you have no ideal to guide you, you are simply a brute. So we must not lower our ideal, neither are we to lose sight of practicality. We must avoid the two extremes. In our country the old idea is to sit in a cave and meditate and die. To go ahead of others in salvation is wrong. One must learn sooner or later that one cannot get salvation if one does not try to seek the salvation of his brothers. You must try to combine in your life immense idealism with immense practicality. You must be prepared to go into deep meditation now, and the next moment you must be ready to go and cultivate these fields. You must be prepared to explain the difficult intricacies of the Shâstras now, and the next moment to go and sell the produce of the fields in the market. You must be prepared for all menial services, not only here, but elsewhere also.

The next thing to remember is that the aim of this institution is to make men. You must not merely learn what the Rishis taught. Those Rishis are gone, and their opinions are also gone with them. You must be Rishis yourselves. You are also men as much as the greatest men that were ever born—even our Incarnations. What can mere book-learning do? What can meditation do, even? What can the Mantras and Tantras do? You must stand on your own feet. You must have this new method—the method of man-making. The true *man* is he who is strong as strength itself and yet possesses a woman's heart. You must feel for the millions of beings around you, and yet you must be strong and inflexible, and you must also possess obedience; though it may seem a little paradoxical—you must possess these apparently conflicting virtues. If your superior orders you to throw yourself into a river and catch a crocodile, you must first obey and then reason with him. Even if the order be wrong, first obey and then contradict it. The bane of sects, especially in Bengal, is that if any one happens to have a different opinion, he immediately starts a new sect, he has no patience to wait. So you must have a deep regard for your Sangha. There is no place for disobedience here. Crush it out without mercy. No disobedient members here, you must turn them out. There must not be any traitors in the camp. You must be as free as the air, and as obedient as the plant and the dog.

THOUGHTS ON THE GITA*

(A class-talk given at the Alambazar Math in 1897)

The book known as the Gitâ forms a part of the Mahâbhârata. To understand the Gita properly several things are very important to know. First, whether it formed a part of the Mahabharata, that is, whether the authorship attributed to Veda-Vyâsa was true, or if it was merely interpolated within the great epic; secondly, whether there was any historical personality of the name of Krishna; thirdly, whether the great war of Kurukshetra as mentioned in the Gita actually took place; and fourthly, whether Arjuna and others were real historical persons.

In the first place, let us see what grounds there are for such inquiry. We know that there were many who went by the name of Veda-Vyasa; among them who was the real author of the Gita—Bâdarâyana Vyasa or Dvaipâyana Vyasa? "Vyasa" was only a title. Any one who composed a new Purâna was known by the name of Vyasa, like the word Vikramâditya, which was also a general name. Another point is, the book, Gita, was not much known to the generality of people before Shankarâchârya made it famous by writing his great commentary on it. Long before that, there was current, according to many, the commentary on it by Bodhâyana. If this could be proved, it would go a long way, no doubt, to establish the antiquity of the Gita and the authorship of Vyasa. But the Bodhayana Bhâshya on the Vedanta Sutras—from which Râmânuja compiled his Shri-Bhâshya, which Shankaracharya mentions and even quotes in part here and there in his own commentary, and which was so greatly discussed by Swami Dayânanda—not a copy of that Bodhayana Bhashya could I find while travelling throughout India. It is said that even Ramanuja compiled his Bhashya from a worm-eaten manuscript which he happened to find. When even this great Bodhayana Bhashya on the Vedanta Sutras is so much shrouded in uncertainty, it is simply useless to try to establish the existence of the Bodhayana Bhashya on the Gita. Some infer that Shankaracharya was the author of the Gita, and that it was he who foisted it into the body of the Mahabharata.

Then as to the second point in question, much doubt exists about the personality of Krishna. In one place in the Chhândogya Upanishad we find mention of Krishna, the son of Devaki, who received spiritual instruction from one Ghora, a Yogi. In the Mahabharata, Krishna is the king of Dwârakâ; and in the Vishnu Purâna we find a description of Krishna playing with the Gopis. Again, in the *Bhâgavata,* the account of his Râsalilâ is detailed at length. In very ancient times in our country, there was in vogue an Utsava called Madanotsava (celebration in honour of Cupid). That very thing was transformed into Dola (Holi) and thrust upon the shoulders of Krishna. Who can be so bold as to assert that the Rasalila and other things connected with him were not similarly fastened upon him? In ancient times, there was very little tendency in our country to find out truths by historical research. So any one could say what he thought best without substantiating it with proper facts and evidence. Another thing: In those ancient times there was very little hankering after name and fame in men. So it often happened that one man composed a book and made it pass current in the name of his Guru or of some one else. In such cases it is very hazardous for the investigator of historical facts to get at the truth. In ancient times, they had no knowledge whatever of geography—imagination ran riot, and so we meet with such fantastic creations of the brain as sweet ocean, milk ocean, clarified butter ocean, curd ocean, etc.! In the Puranas, we find one living ten thousand years, another a hundred thousand years! But the Vedas say, शतायुर्वै पुरुषः —"Man lives a hundred years." Whom shall we follow here? So, to reach a correct conclusion in the case of Krishna is well-nigh impossible.

It is human nature to build round the real character of a great man all sorts of imaginary superhuman attributes. As regards Krishna the same must have happened, but it seems quite probable that he was a king. Quite probable I say, because in ancient times in our country it was chiefly the kings who exerted themselves most in the preaching of Brahma-Jnâna. Another point to be especially noted here is that whoever might have been the author of the Gita, we find its teachings the same as those in the whole of the Mahabharata. From this we can safely infer that in the age of the Mahabharata some great man rose and preached the Brahma-Jnana in this new garb to the then existing society. Another fact comes to the fore, that in the olden days, as one sect after another arose, there also came into existence and use among them one new scripture or another. It happened, too, that in the lapse of time both the sect and its scripture died out, or the sect ceased to exist, but its scripture remained. Similarly it was quite probable that the Gita was the scripture of such a sect, which had embodied its high and noble ideas in this sacred book.

Now to the third point, bearing on the subject of the Kurukshetra War: No special evidence in support of it can be adduced. But there is no doubt that there was a war fought between the Kurus and the Panchâlas. Another thing: How could there be so much discussion about Jnana, Bhakti, and Yoga on the battle-field, where the huge army stood in battle array ready to fight, just waiting for the last signal? And was any shorthand writer present there to note down every word spoken between Krishna and Arjuna, in the din and turmoil of the battle-field? According to some, this Kurukshetra War is only an allegory. When we sum up its esoteric significance, it means the war which is constantly going on within man between the tendencies of good and evil. This meaning too, may not be irrational.

About the fourth point, there is enough ground for doubt as regards the historicity of Arjuna and others, and it is this: Shatapatha Brâhmana is a very ancient book. In it are mentioned somewhere all the names of those who were the performers of the Ashvamedha Yajna, but in those places there is not only no mention but no hint even of the names of Arjuna and others, though it speaks of Janamejaya, the son of Parikshit who was a grandson of Arjuna. Yet in the Mahabharata and other books it is stated that Yudhishthira, Arjuna, and others celebrated the Ashvamedha sacrifice.

One thing should be especially remembered here, that there is no connection between these historical researches and our real aim, which is, the knowledge that leads to the acquirement of Dharma. Even if the historicity of the whole thing is proved to be absolutely false today, it will not in the least be any loss to us. Then what is the use of so much historical research, you may ask. It has its use, because we have to get at the truth; it will not do for us to remain bound by wrong ideas due to ignorance. In this country people think very little of the importance of such inquiries. Many of the sects believe that in order to preach a good thing which may be beneficial to many, there is no harm in telling an untruth, if that helps such preaching, or in other words, the end justifies the means. Hence we find many of our Tantras beginning with, "Mahâdeva said to Pârvati" But our duty should be to convince ourselves of the truth, to believe in truth only. Such is the power of superstition, or faith in old traditions without inquiry into its truth, that it keeps men bound hand and foot, so much so, that even Jesus the Christ, Mohammed and other great men believed in many such superstitions and could not shake them off. You have to keep your eye always fixed on truth only, and shun all superstitions completely.

Now it is for us to see what there is in the Gita. If we study the Upanishads we notice, in wandering through the mazes of many irrelevant subjects, the sudden introduction of the discussion of a great truth, just as in the midst of a huge wilderness a traveller unexpectedly comes across here and there an exquisitely beautiful rose, with its leaves, thorns, roots all entangled. Compared with that, the Gita is like these truths beautifully arranged together in their proper places—like a fine garland or a bouquet of the choicest flowers. The Upanishads deal elaborately with Shraddhâ in many places, but hardly mention Bhakti. In the Gita, on the other hand, the subject of Bhakti is not only again and again dealt with, but in it, the innate spirit of Bhakti has attained its culmination.

Now let us see some of the main points discussed in the Gita. Wherein lies the originality of the Gita, which distinguishes it from all preceding scriptures? It is this: Though before its advent, Yoga, Jnana, Bhakti, etc. had each its strong adherents, they all quarrelled among themselves, each claiming superiority for his own chosen path; no one ever tried to seek for reconciliation among these different paths. It was the author of the Gita who for the first time tried to harmonise these. He took the best from what all the sects then existing had to offer, and threaded them in the Gita. But even where Krishna failed to show a complete reconciliation (Samanvaya) among these warring sects, it was fully accomplished by Ramakrishna Paramahamsa in this nineteenth century.

The next is, Nishkâma Karma, or work without desire or attachment. People nowadays understand what is meant by this in various ways. Some say, what is implied by being unattached is to become purposeless. If that were its real meaning, then heartless brutes and the walls would be the best exponents of the performance of Nishkama Karma. Many others, again, give the example of Janaka, and wish themselves to be equally recognised as past masters in the practice of Nishkama Karma!. Janaka did not acquire that distinction by bringing forth children, but these people all want to be Janakas, with the sole qualification of being the fathers of a brood of children! No! The true Nishkama Karmi (performer of work without desire) is neither to be like a brute, nor to be inert, nor heartless. He is not Tâmasika, but of pure Sattva. His heart is so full of love and sympathy that he can embrace the whole world with his love. The world at large cannot generally comprehend his all-embracing love and sympathy.

The reconciliation of the different paths of Dharma, and work without desire or attachment—these are the two special characteristics of the Gita.

Let us now read a little from the second chapter.

संजय उवाच ॥

तं तथा कृपयाविष्टमश्रुपूर्णाकुलेक्षणम् ।
विषीदन्तमिदं वाक्यमुवाच मधुसूदनः ॥१॥

श्रीभगवानुवाच ॥

कुतस्त्वा कश्मलमिदं विषमे समुपस्थितम् ।
अनार्यजुष्टमस्वर्ग्यमकीर्तिकरमर्जुन ॥२॥
क्लैब्यं मा स्म गमः पार्थ नैतत्त्वय्युपपद्यते ।
क्षुद्रं हृदयदौर्बल्यं त्यक्त्वोत्तिष्ठ परंतप ॥३॥

Sanjaya said:

"To him who was thus overwhelmed with pity and sorrowing, and whose eyes were dimmed with tears, Madhusudana spoke these words:

"The Blessed Lord said:

'In such a strait, whence comes upon thee, O Arjuna, this dejection, un-Arya-like, disgraceful, and contrary to the attainment of heaven?

'Yield not to unmanliness, O son of Prithâ! Ill doth it become thee. Cast off this mean faint-heartedness and arise, O scorcher of thine enemies!'"

In the Shlokas beginning with तं तथा कृपयाविष्टं, how poetically, how beautifully, has Arjuna's real position been painted! Then Shri Krishna advises Arjuna; and in the words क्लैब्यं मा स्म गमः पार्थ etc., why is he goading Arjuna to fight? Because it was not that Arjuna's disinclination to fight arose out of the overwhelming predominance of pure Sattva Guna; it was all Tamas that brought on this unwillingness. The nature of a man of Sattva Guna is that he is equally calm in all situations in life—whether it be prosperity or adversity. But Arjuna was afraid, he was overwhelmed with pity. That he had the instinct and the inclination to fight is proved by the simple fact that he came to the battle-field with no other purpose than that. Frequently in our lives also such things are seen to happen. Many people think they are Sâttvika by nature, but they are really nothing but Tâmasika. Many living in an uncleanly way regard themselves as Paramahamsas! Why? Because the Shâstras say that Paramahamsas live like one inert, or mad, or like an unclean spirit. Paramahamsas are compared to children, but here it should be understood that the comparison is one-sided. The Paramahamsa and the child are not one and the same. They only appear similar, being the two extreme poles, as it were. One has reached a state beyond Jnana, and the other has not got even an inkling of Jnana. The quickest and the gentlest vibrations of light are both beyond the reach of our vision; but in the one case it is intense heat, and in the other it may be said to be almost without any heat. So it is with opposite qualities of Sattva and Tamas. They seem in some respects no doubt to be the same, but there is a world of difference between them. The Tamoguna loves very much to array itself in the garb of the Sattva. Here, in Arjuna, the mighty warrior, it has come under the guise of Dayâ (pity).

In order to remove this delusion which had overtaken Arjuna, what did the Bhagavân say? As I always preach that you should not decry a man by calling him a sinner, but that you should draw his attention to the omnipotent power that is in him, in the same way docs the Bhagavan speak to Arjuna, "नैतत्त्वय्युपपद्यते" —It doth not befit thee! Thou art that Âtman imperishable, beyond all evil. Having forgotten thy real nature, thou hast, by thinking thyself a sinner, as one afflicted with bodily evils and mental grief, thou hast made thyself so—this doth not befit thee! So says the Bhagavan: "क्लैब्यं मा स्म गमः पार्थ" —Yield not to unmanliness, O son of Prithâ. There is in the world neither sin nor misery, neither disease nor grief; if there is anything in the world which can be called sin, it is this—"fear"; know that any work which brings out the latent power in thee is Punya (virtue); and that which makes thy body and mind weak is, verily, sin. Shake off this weakness, this faintheartedness! "क्लैब्यं मा स्म गमः पार्थ"। Thou art a hero, a Vira; "this is unbecoming of thee."

If you, my sons, can proclaim this message to the world, "क्लैब्यं मा स्म गमः पार्थ नैतत्त्वय्युपपद्यते", then all this disease, grief, sin, and sorrow will vanish from the face of the earth in three days. All these ideas of weakness will be nowhere. Now it is everywhere—this current of the vibration of fear. Reverse the current; bring in the opposite vibration, and behold the magical transformation! You are omnipotent—go, go to the mouth of the cannon, fear not.

Hate not the most abject sinner, look not to his exterior Turn your gaze inward, where resides the Paramâtman. Proclaim to the whole world with trumpet voice, "There is no sin in thee, there is no misery in thee; thou art the reservoir of omnipotent power. Arise, awake, and manifest the Divinity within!"

If one reads this one Shloka, क्लैब्यं मा स्म गमः पार्थ नैतत्त्वय्युपपद्यते। क्षुद्रं हृदयदौर्बल्यं त्यक्त्वोत्तिष्ठ परंतप॥—he gets all the merits of reading the entire Gita; for in this one Shloka lies imbedded the whole message of the Gita.

INTERVIEWS

I

INDIA'S MISSION

(*Sunday Times, London, 1896*)

English people are well acquainted with the fact that they send missionaries to India's "coral strands". Indeed, so thoroughly do they obey the behest: "Go ye forth into all the world and preach the Gospel," that none of the chief British sects are behindhand in obedience to the call to spread Christ's teaching. People are not so well aware that India also sends missionaries to England.

By accident, if the term may be allowed, I fell across Swami Vivekananda in his temporary home at 63, St. George's Road, S. W., and as he did not object to discuss the nature of his work and visit to England, I sought him there, and began our talk with an expression of surprise at his assent to my request.

"I got thoroughly used to the interviewer in America. Because it is not the fashion in my country, that is no reason why I should not use means existing in any country I visit, for spreading what I desire to be known. There I was representative of the Hindu religion at the World's Parliament of Religions at Chicago in 1893. The Raja of Mysore and some other friends sent me there. I think I may lay claim to having had some success in America. I had many invitations to other great American cities besides Chicago; my visit was a very long one, for, with the exception of a visit to England last summer, repeated as you see this year, I remained about three years in America. The American civilisation is, in my opinion, a very great one. I find the American mind peculiarly susceptible to new ideas; nothing is rejected because it is new. It is examined on its own merits, and stands or falls by these alone."

"Whereas in England—you mean to imply something?"

"Yes, in England, civilisation is older, it has gathered many accretions as the centuries have rolled on. In particular, you have many prejudices that need to be broken through, and whoever deals with you in ideas must lay this to his account."

"So they say. I gather that you did not found anything like a church or a new religion in America."

"That is true. It is contrary to our principles to multiply organisations, since, in all conscience, there are enough of them. And when organisations are created, they need individuals to look after them. Now, those who have made Sannyâsa—that is, renunciation of all worldly position, property, and name—whose aim is to seek spiritual knowledge, cannot undertake this work, which is, besides, in other hands."

"Is your teaching a system of comparative religion?"

"It might convey a more definite idea to call it the kernel of all forms of religion, stripping from them the nonessential, and laying stress on that which is the real basis. I am a disciple of Ramakrishna Paramahamsa, a perfect Sannyâsin whose influence and ideas I fell under. This great Sannyasin never assumed the negative or critical attitude towards other religions, but showed their positive side—how they could be carried into life and practised. To fight, to assume the antagonistic attitude, is the exact contrary of his teaching, which dwells on the truth that the world is moved by love. You know that the Hindu religion never persecutes. It is the land where all sects may live in peace and amity. The Mohammedans brought murder and slaughter in their train, but until their arrival peace prevailed. Thus the Jains, who do not believe in a God and who regard such belief as a delusion, were tolerated, and still are there today. India sets the example of real strength, that is meekness. Dash, pluck, fight, all these things are weakness."

"It sounds very like Tolstoy's doctrine; it may do for individuals, though personally I doubt it. But how will it answer for nations?"

"Admirably for them also. It was India's Karma, her fate, to be conquered, and in her turn, to conquer her conqueror. She has already done so with her Mohammedan victors: Educated Mohammedans are Sufis, scarcely to be distinguished from Hindus. Hindu thought has permeated their civilisation; they assumed the position of learners. The great Akbar, the Mogul Emperor, was practically a Hindu. And England will be conquered in her turn. Today she has the sword, but it is worse than useless in the world of ideas. You know what Schopenhauer said of Indian thought. He foretold that its influence would be as momentous in Europe, when it became well known, as the revival of Greek and Latin culture after the Dark Ages."

"Excuse me saying that there do not seem many signs of it just now."

"Perhaps not," said the Swami, gravely. "I dare say a good many people saw no signs of the old Renaissance, and did not know it was there, even after it had come. But there is a great movement, which can be discerned by those who know the signs of the times. Oriental research has of recent years made great progress. At present it is in the hands of scholars, and it seems dry and heavy in the work they have achieved. But gradually the light of comprehension will break."

"And India is to be the great conqueror of the future? Yet she does not send out many missionaries to preach her ideas. I presume she will wait until the world comes to her feet?"

"India was once a great missionary power. Hundreds of years before England was converted to Christianity, Buddha sent out missionaries to convert the world of Asia to his doctrine. The world of thought is being converted. We are only at the beginning as yet. The number of those who decline to adopt any special form of religion is greatly increasing, and this movement is among the educated classes. In a recent American census, a large number of persons declined to class themselves as belonging to any form of religion. All religions are different expressions of the same truth; all march on or die out. They are the radii of the same truth, the expression that variety of minds requires."

"Now we are getting near it. What is that central truth?"

"The Divine within; every being, however degraded, is the expression of the Divine. The Divinity becomes covered, hidden from view. I call to mind an incident of the Indian Mutiny. A Swami, who for years had fulfilled a vow of eternal silence, was stabbed by a Mohammedan. They dragged the murderer before his victim and cried out, 'Speak the word, Swami, and he shall die.' After many years of silence, he broke it to say with his last breath: 'My children, you are all mistaken. That man is God Himself.' The great lesson is, that unity is behind all. Call it God, Love, Spirit, Allah, Jehovah—it is the same unity that animates all life from the lowest animal to the noblest man. Picture to yourself an ocean ice-bound, pierced with many different holes. Each of these is a soul, a man, emancipated according to his degree of intelligence, essaying to break through the ice."

"I think I see one difference between the wisdom of the East and that of the West. You aim at producing very perfect individuals by Sannyasa, concentration, and so forth. Now the ideal of the West seems to be the perfecting of the social state; and so we work at political and social questions, since we think that the permanence of our civilisation depends upon the well-being of the people."

"But the basis of all systems, social or political," said the Swami with great earnestness, "rests upon the goodness of men. No nation is great or good because Parliament enacts this or that, but because its men are great and good. I have visited China, which had the most admirable organisation of all nations. Yet today China is like a disorganised mob, because her men are not equal to the system contrived in the olden days. Religion goes to the root of the matter. If it is right, all is right."

"It sounds just a little vague and remote from practical life, that the Divine is within everything but covered. One can't be looking for it all the time."

"People often work for the same ends but fail to recognise the fact. One must admit that law, government, politics are phases not final in any way. There is a goal beyond them where law is not needed. And by the way, the very word Sannyasin means the divine outlaw, one might say, divine Nihilist, but that miscomprehension pursues those that use such a word. All great Masters teach the same thing. Christ saw that the basis is not law, that morality and purity are the only strength. As for your statement that the East aims at higher self-development and the West at the perfecting of the social state, you do not of course forget that there is an apparent self and a real self."

"The inference, of course, being that we work for the apparent, you for the real?"

"The mind works through various stages to attain its fuller development. First, it lays hold of the concrete, and only gradually deals with abstractions. Look, too, how the idea of universal brotherhood is reached. First it is grasped as brotherhood within a sect—hard, narrow, and exclusive. Step by step we reach broad generalisations and the world of abstract ideas."

"So you think that those sects, of which we English are so fond, will die out. You know what the Frenchman said, 'England, that land of a thousand sects and but one sauce'."

"I am sure that they are bound to disappear. Their existence is founded on non-essentials: the essential part of them will remain, and be built up into another edifice. You know the old saying that it is good to be born in a church, but not to die in it."

"Perhaps you will say how your work is progressing in England?"

"Slowly, for the reasons I have already named. When you deal with roots and foundations, all real progress must be slow. Of course, I need not say that these ideas are bound to spread by one means or another, and to many of us the right moment for their dissemination seems now to have come."

Then I listened to an explanation of how the work is carried on. Like many an old doctrine, this new one is offered without money and without price, depending entirely upon the voluntary efforts of those who embrace it.

The Swami is a picturesque figure in his Eastern dress. His simple and cordial manner, savouring of anything but the popular idea of asceticism, an unusual command of English and great conversational powers add not a little to an interesting personality. . . . His vow of Sannyasa implies renunciation of position, property, and name, as well as the persistent search for spiritual knowledge.

II

THE ABROAD AND THE PROBLEMS AT HOME

(*The Hindu, Madras, February, 1897*)

Our representative met Swami Vivekananda in the train at the Chingleput Station and travelled with him to Madras. The following is the report of the interview:

"What made you go to America, Swamiji?"

"Rather a serious question to answer in brief. I can only answer it partly now. Because I travelled all over India, I wanted to go over to other countries. I went to America by the Far East."

"What did you see in Japan, and is there any chance of India following in the progressive steps of Japan?"

"None whatever, until all the three hundred millions of India combine together as a whole nation. The world has never seen such a patriotic and artistic race as the Japanese, and one special feature about them is this: that while in Europe and elsewhere Art generally goes with dirt, Japanese Art is Art *plus* absolute cleanliness. I would wish that every one of our young men could visit Japan once at least in his lifetime. It is very easy to go there. The Japanese think that everything Hindu is great, and believe that India is a holy land. Japanese Buddhism is entirely different from what you see in Ceylon. It is the same as the Vedanta. It is positive and theistic Buddhism, not the negative atheistic Buddhism of Ceylon."

"What is the key to Japan's sudden greatness?"

"The faith of the Japanese in themselves, and their love for their country. When you have men who are ready to sacrifice their everything for their country, sincere to the backbone —when such men arise, India will become great in every respect. It is the men that make the country! What is there in the country? If you catch the social morality and the political morality of the Japanese, you will be as great as they are. The Japanese are ready to sacrifice everything for their country, and they have become a great people. But you are not; you cannot be, you sacrifice everything only for your own families and possessions."

"Is it your wish that India should become like Japan?"

"Decidedly not. India should continue to be what she is. How could India ever become like Japan, or any nation for the matter of that? In each nation, as in music, there is a main note, a central theme, upon which all others turn. Each nation has a theme: everything else is secondary. India's theme is religion. Social reform and everything else are secondary. Therefore, India cannot be like Japan. It is said that when 'the heart breaks', then the flow of thought comes. India's heart must break, and the flow of spirituality will come out. India is India. We are not like the Japanese, we are Hindus. India's very atmosphere is soothing. I have been working incessantly here, and amidst this work I am getting rest. It is only from spiritual work that we can get rest in India. If your work is material here, you die of—diabetes!"

"So much for Japan. What was your first experience of America, Swamiji?"

"From first to last it was very good. With the exception

of the missionaries and 'Church-women' the Americans are most hospitable, kind-hearted, generous and good-natured."

"Who are these 'Church-women' that you speak of, Swamiji?"

"When a woman tries her best to find a husband, she goes to all the fashionable seaside resorts and tries all sorts of tricks to catch a man. When she fails in her attempts, she becomes what they call in America an 'old maid', and joins the Church. Some of them become very 'Churchy'. These 'Church-women' are awful fanatics. They are under the thumb of the priests there. Between them and the priests they make hell of earth and make a mess of religion. With the exception of these, the Americans are a very good people. They loved me, and I love them a great deal. I felt as if I was one of them."

"What is your idea about the results of the Parliament of Religions?"

"The Parliament of Religions, as it seems to me, was intended for a 'heathen show' before the world; but it turned out that the heathens had the upper hand, and made it a Christian show all around. So the Parliament of Religions was a failure from the Christian standpoint, seeing that the Roman Catholics, who were the organisers of that Parliament, are, when there is a talk of another Parliament at Paris, now steadily opposing it. But the Chicago Parliament was a tremendous success for India and Indian thought. It helped on the tide of Vedanta, which is flooding the world. The American people—of course, *minus* the fanatical priests and Church-women—are very glad of the results of the Parliament."

"What prospects have you, Swamiji, for the spread of your mission in England?"

"There is every prospect. Before many years elapse a vast majority of the English people will be Vedantins. There is a greater prospect of this in England than there is in America. You see, Americans make a fanfaronade of everything, which is not the case with Englishmen. Even Christians cannot understand their New Testament without understanding the Vedanta. The Vedanta is the rationale of all religions. Without the Vedanta every religion is superstition; with it everything becomes religion."

"What is the special trait you noticed in the English character?"

"The Englishman goes to practical work as soon as he believes in something. He has tremendous energy for practical work. There is in the whole world no human being superior to the English gentleman or lady. That is really the reason of my faith in them. John Bull is rather a thick-headed gentleman to deal with. You must push and push an ideal till it reaches his brain, but once there, it does not get out. In England, there was not one missionary or anybody who said anything against me; not one who tried to make a scandal about me. To my astonishment, many of my friends belong to the Church of England. I learn, these missionaries do not come from the higher classes in England. Caste is as rigorous there as it is here, and the English churchmen belong to the class of gentlemen. They may differ in opinion from you, but that is no bar to their being friends with you; therefore, I would give a word of advice to my countrymen, which is, not to take notice of the vituperative missionaries, now that I have known what they are. We have 'sized' them, as the Americans say. Non-recognition is the only attitude to assume towards them."

"Will you kindly enlighten me, Swamiji, on the social reform movements in America and England?"

"Yes. All the social upheavalists, at least the leaders of them, are trying to find that all their communistic or equalising theories must have a spiritual basis, and that spiritual basis is in the Vedanta only. I have been told by several leaders, who used to attend my lectures, that they required the Vedanta as the basis of the new order of things."

"What are your views with regard to the Indian masses?"

"Oh, we are awfully poor, and our masses are very ignorant about secular things. Our masses are very good because poverty here is not a crime. Our masses are not violent. Many times I was near being mobbed in America and England, only on account of my dress. But I never heard of such a thing in India as a man being mobbed because of peculiar dress. In every other respect, our masses are much more civilised than the European masses."

"What will you propose for the improvement of our masses?"

"We have to give them secular education. We have to follow the plan laid down by our ancestors, that is, to bring all the ideals slowly down among the masses. Raise them slowly up, raise them to equality. Impart even secular knowledge through religion."

"But do you think, Swamiji, it is a task that can be easily accomplished?"

"It will, of course, have gradually to be worked out. But if there are enough self-sacrificing young fellows, who I hope will work with me, it can be done tomorrow. It all depends upon the zeal and the self-sacrifice brought to the task."

"But if the present degraded condition is due to their past Karma, Swamiji, how do you think they could get out of it easily, and how do you propose to help them?"

The Swamiji readily answered, "Karma is the eternal assertion of human freedom. If we can bring ourselves down by our Karma, surely it is in our power to raise ourselves by it. The masses, besides, have not brought themselves down altogether by their own Karma; so we should give them better environments to work in. I do not propose any levelling of castes. Caste is a very good thing. Caste is the plan we want to follow. What caste really is, not one in a million understands. There is no country in the world without caste. In India, from caste we reach to the point where there is no caste Caste is based throughout on that principle. The plan in India is to make everybody Brahmin, the Brahmin being the ideal of humanity. If you read the history of India you will find that attempts have always been made to raise the lower classes. Many are the classes that have been raised. Many more will follow, till the whole will become Brahmin. That is the plan. We have only to raise them without bringing down anybody. And this has mostly to be done by the Brahmins themselves, because it is the duty of every aristocracy to dig its own grave; and the sooner it does so, the better for all. No time should be lost. Indian caste is better than the caste which prevails in Europe or America. I do not say it is absolutely good. Where would you be if there were no caste? Where would be our learning, and other things, if there were no caste? There would be nothing left for the Europeans to study if caste had never existed! The Mohammedans would have smashed everything to pieces. Where do you find the Indian society standing still? It is always on the move. Sometimes, as in the times of foreign invasions, the movement has been slow, at other times quicker. This is what I say to my countrymen. I do not condemn them. I look into their past. I find that under the circumstances no nation could do more glorious work. I tell them that they have done well. I only ask them to do better."

"What are your views, Swamiji, in regard to the relation of caste to rituals?"

"Caste is continually changing, rituals are continually changing, so are forms. It is the substance, the principle, that does not change. It is in the Vedas that we have to study our religion. With the exception of the Vedas every book must change. The authority of the Vedas is for all time to come; the authority of every one of our other books is for the time being. For instance, one Smriti is powerful for one age, another for another age. Great prophets are always coming and pointing the way to work. Some prophets worked for the lower classes, others like Madhva gave to women the right to study the Vedas. Caste should not go; but should only be readjusted occasionally. Within the old structure is to be found life enough for the building of two hundred thousand new ones. It is sheer nonsense to desire the abolition of caste. The new method is—evolution of the old."

"Do not Hindus stand in need of social reform?"

"We do stand in need of social reform. At times great men would evolve new ideas of progress, and kings would give them the sanction of law. Thus social improvements had been in the past made in India, and in modern times to effect such progressive reforms, we will have first to build up such an authoritative power. Kings having gone, the power is the people's. We have, therefore, to wait till the people are educated, till they understand their needs and are ready and able to solve their problems. The tyranny of the minority is the worst tyranny in the world. Therefore, instead of frittering away our energies on ideal reforms, which will never become practical, we had better go to the root of the evil and make a legislative body, that is to say, educate our people, so that they may be able to solve their own problems. Until that is done all these ideal reforms will remain ideals only. The new order of things is the salvation of the people by the people, and it takes time to make it workable, especially in India, which has always in the past been governed by kings."

"Do you think Hindu society can successfully adopt European social laws?"

"No, not wholly. I would say, the combination of the Greek mind represented by the external European energy added to the Hindu spirituality would be an ideal society for India. For instance, it is absolutely necessary for you, instead of frittering away your energy and often talking of ideal nonsense, to learn from the Englishman the idea of prompt obedience to leaders, the absence of jealousy, the indomitable perseverance, and the undying faith in himself. As soon as he selects a leader for a work, the Englishman sticks to him through thick and thin and obeys him. Here in India, everybody wants to become a leader, and there is nobody to obey. Every one should learn to obey before he can command. There is no end to our jealousies; and the more important the Hindu, the more jealous he is. Until this absence of jealousy and obedience to leaders are learnt by the Hindu, there will be no power of organisation. We shall have to remain the hopelessly confused mob that we are now, hoping and doing nothing. India has to learn from Europe the conquest of external nature, and Europe has to learn from India the conquest of internal nature. Then there will be neither Hindus nor Europeans—there will be the ideal humanity which has conquered both the natures, the external and the internal. We have developed one phase of humanity, and they another. It is the union of the two that is wanted. The word freedom, which is the watchword of our religion, really means freedom physically, mentally, and spiritually."

"What relation, Swamiji, does ritual bear to religion?"

"Rituals are the kindergarten of religion. They are absolutely necessary for the world as it is now; only we shall have to give people newer and fresher rituals. A party of thinkers must undertake to do this. Old rituals must be rejected and new ones substituted."

"Then you advocate the abolition of rituals, don't you?"

"No, my watchword is construction, not destruction. Out of the existing rituals, new ones will have to be evolved. There is infinite power of development in everything; that is my belief. One atom has the power of the whole universe at its back. All along in the history of the Hindu race, there never was any attempt at destruction, only construction. One sect wanted to destroy, and they were thrown out of India; they were the Buddhists. We have had a host of reformers—Shankara, Râmânuja, Madhva, and Chaitanya. These were great reformers, who always were constructive, and built according to the circumstances of their time. This is our peculiar method of work. All the modern reformers take to European destructive reformation, which will never do good to anyone and never did. Only once was a modern reformer mostly constructive, and that one was Raja Ram Mohun Roy. The progress of the Hindu race has been towards the realisation of the Vedantic ideals. All history of Indian life is the struggle for the realisation of the ideal of the Vedanta through good or bad fortune. Whenever there was any reforming sect or religion which rejected the Vedantic ideal, it was smashed into nothing."

"What is your programme of work here?"

"I want to start two institutions, one in Madras and one in Calcutta, to carry out my plan; and that plan briefly is to bring the Vedantic ideals into the everyday practical life of the saint or the sinner, of the sage or the ignoramus, of the Brahmin or the Pariah."

III

ON THE BOUNDS OF HINDUISM

(*Prabuddha Bharata, April, 1899*)

Having been directed by the Editor (writes our representative) to interview Swami Vivekananda on the question of converts to Hinduism, I found an opportunity one evening on the roof of a Ganga houseboat. It was after nightfall, and we had stopped at the embankment of the Ramakrishna Math, and there the Swami came down to speak with me.

Time and place were alike delightful. Overhead the stars, and around—the rolling Ganga; and on one side stood the dimly lighted building, with its background of palms and lofty shade-trees.

"I want to see you, Swami," I began, "on this matter of receiving back into Hinduism those who have been perverted from it. Is it your opinion that they should be received?"

"Certainly," said the Swami, "they can and ought to be taken."

He sat gravely for a moment, thinking, and then resumed. "Besides," he said, "we shall otherwise decrease in numbers.

When the Mohammedans first came, we are said—I think on the authority of Ferishta, the oldest Mohammedan historian—to have been six hundred millions of Hindus. Now we are about two hundred millions. And then every man going out of the Hindu pale is not only a man less, but an enemy the more.

"Again, the vast majority of Hindu perverts to Islam and Christianity are perverts by the sword, or the descendants of these. It would be obviously unfair to subject these to disabilities of any kind. As to the case of born aliens, did you say? Why, born aliens have been converted in the past by crowds, and the process is still going on.

"In my own opinion, this statement not only applies to aboriginal tribes, to outlying nations, and to almost all our conquerors before the Mohammedan conquest, but also to all those castes who find a special origin in the Purânas. I hold that they have been aliens thus adopted.

"Ceremonies of expiation are no doubt suitable in the case of willing converts, returning to their Mother-Church, as it were; but on those who were alienated by conquest—as in Kashmir and Nepal—or on strangers wishing to join us, no penance should be imposed."

"But of what caste would these people be, Swamiji?" I ventured to ask. "They must have some, or they can never be assimilated into the great body of Hindus. Where shall we look for their rightful place?"

"Returning converts," said the Swami quietly, "will gain their own castes, of course. And new people will make theirs." "You will remember," he added, "that this has already been done in the case of Vaishnavism. Converts from different castes and aliens were all able to combine under that flag and form a caste by themselves—and a very respectable one too. From Râmânuja down to Chaitanya of Bengal, all great Vaishnava Teachers have done the same."

"And where should these new people expect to marry?" I asked.

"Amongst themselves, as they do now," said the Swami quietly.

"Then as to names," I inquired, "I suppose aliens and perverts who have adopted non-Hindu names should be named newly. Would you give them caste-names, or what?"

"Certainly," said the Swami, thoughtfully, "there is a great deal in a name!" and on this question he would say no more.

But my next inquiry drew blood. "Would you leave these new-comers, Swamiji, to choose their own form of religious belief out of many-visaged Hinduism, or would you chalk out a religion for them?"

"Can you ask that?" he said. "They will choose for themselves. For unless a man chooses for himself, the very spirit of Hinduism is destroyed. The essence of our Faith consists simply in this freedom of the Ishta."

QUESTIONS AND ANSWERS AT THE BELUR MATH

(*Selections from the Math Diary*)

Q.—Whom can we call a Guru?

A.—He who can tell your past and future is your Guru.

Q.—How can one have Bhakti?

A.—There is Bhakti within you, only the veil of lust and wealth covers it, and as soon as that is removed Bhakti will manifest by itself.

Q.—What is the true meaning of the assertion that we should depend on ourselves?

A.—Here self means the eternal Self. But even dependence on the non-eternal self may lead gradually to the right goal, as the individual self is really the eternal Self under delusion.

Q.—If unity is the only reality, how could duality which is perceived by all every moment have arisen?

A.—Perception is never dual; it is only the representation of perception that involves duality. If perception were dual, the known could have existed independently of the knower, and vice versa.

Q.—How is harmonious development of character to be best effected?

A.—By association with persons whose character has been so developed.

Q.—What should be our attitude to the Vedas?

A.—The Vedas, that is only those portions of them which agree with reason, are to be accepted as authority. Other Shâstras, such as the Purânas, are only to be accepted so far as they do not go against the Vedas. All the religious thoughts that have come subsequent to the Vedas, in the world, in whatever part of it, have been derived from the Vedas.

Q.—Is the division of time into four Yugas astronomical or arbitrary calculation?

A.—There is no mention of such divisions in the Vedas. They are arbitrary assumptions of Paurânika times.

Q.—Is the relation between concepts and words necessary and immutable, or accidental and conventional?

A.—The point is exceedingly debatable. It seems that there is a necessary relation, but not absolutely so, as appears from the diversity of language. There may be some subtle relation which we are not yet able to detect.

Q.—What should be the principle to be followed in working within India?

A.—First of all, men should be taught to be practical and physically strong. A dozen of such lions will conquer the world, and not millions of sheep can do so. Secondly, men should not be taught to imitate a personal ideal, however great.

Q.—What part will the Ramakrishna Mission take in the regenerating work of India?

A.—From this Math will go out men of character who will deluge the world with spirituality. This will be followed by revivals in other lines. Thus Brahmins, Kshatriyas, and Vaishyas will be produced. The Shudra caste will exist no longer—their work being done by machinery. The present want of India is the Kshatriya force.

Q.—Is retrograde reincarnation from the human stage possible?

A.—Yes. Reincarnation depends on Karma. If a man accumulates Karma akin to the beastly nature, he will be drawn thereto.

Q.—Does the Kundalini really exist in the physical body?

A.—Shri Ramakrishna used to say that the so-called lotuses of the Yogi do not really exist in the human body, but that they are created within oneself by Yoga powers.

Q.—Can a man attain Mukti by image-worship?

A.—Image-worship cannot directly give Mukti; it may be an indirect cause, a help on the way. Image-worship should not be condemned, for, with many, it prepares the mind for the realisation of the Advaita, which alone makes man perfect.

Q.—What should be our highest ideal of character?

A.—Renunciation.

Q.—How did Buddhism leave the legacy of corruption in India?

A.—The Bauddhas tried to make everyone in India a monk or a nun. We cannot expect that from everyone. This led to gradual relaxation among monks and nuns. It was also caused by their imitating Tibetan and other barbarous customs in the name of religion. They went to preach in those places and assimilated their corruptions, and then introduced them into India.

Q.—Is Mâyâ without beginning and end?

A.—Maya is eternal both ways, taken universally, as genus; but it is non-eternal individually.

Q.—Brahman and Maya cannot be cognised simultaneously. How could the absolute reality of either be proved as arising out of the one or the other?

A.—It could be proved only by realisation. When one realises Brahman, for him Maya exists no longer, just as once the identity of the rope is found out, the illusion of the serpent comes no more.

Q.—What is Maya?

A.—There is only one thing, call it by any name—matter or spirit. It is difficult, or rather impossible, to think of the one independently of the other. This is Maya, or ignorance.

Q.—What is Mukti?

A.—Mukti means entire freedom—freedom from the bondages of good and evil. A gold chain is as much a chain as an iron one. Shri Ramakrishna used to say that to pick out one thorn which has struck into the foot, another thorn is requisitioned, and when the thorn is taken out, both are thrown away. So the bad tendencies are to be counteracted by the good ones, but after that, the good tendencies have also to be conquered.

Q.—Can Mukti be obtained without the grace of God?

A.—Mukti has nothing to do with God. Freedom already *is*.

Q.—What is the proof of the Self in us not being the product of the body etc.?

A.—The "ego", like its correlative, "non-ego", is the product of the body, mind, etc. The only proof of the existence of the real Self is realisation.

Q.—Who is a true Jnâni, and who is a true Bhakta?

A.—The true Jnani (man of wisdom) is he who has the deepest love within his heart and at the same time is a practical seer of Advaita in his outward relations. And the true Bhakta (lover) is he who, realising his own soul as identified with the universal Soul, and thus possessed of the true Jnâna within, feels for and loves everyone. Of Jnana and Bhakti, he who advocates one and denounces the other cannot be either a Jnani or a Bhakta, but he is a thief and a cheat.

Q.—Why should a man serve Ishvara?

A.—If you once admit that there is such a thing as Ishvara (God), you have numberless occasions to serve Him. Service of the Lord means, according to all the scriptural authorities, remembrance (Smarana). If you believe in the existence of God, you will be reminded of Him at every step of your life.

Q.—Is Mâyâvada different from Advaitavada?

A.—No. They are identical. There is absolutely no other explanation of Advaitavada except Mayavada.

Q.—How it is possible for God who is infinite to be limited in the form of a man (as an Avatâra)?

A.—It is true that God is infinite, but not in the sense in which you comprehend it. You have confounded your idea of infinity with the materialistic idea of vastness. When you say that God cannot take the form of a man, you understand that a very, very large substance or form (as if material in nature), cannot be compressed into a very, very small compass. God's infinitude refers to the unlimitedness of a purely spiritual entity, and as such, does not suffer in the least by expressing itself in a human form.

Q.—Some say, "First of all become a Siddha (one who has realised the Truth), and then you have the right to Karma, or work for others," while others say that one should work for others even from the beginning. How can both these views be reconciled?

A.—You are confusing one thing with the other. Karma means either service to humanity or preaching. To real preaching, no doubt, none has the right except the Siddha Purusha, that is, one who has realised the Truth. But to service every one has the right, and not only so, but every one is under obligation to serve others, so long as he is accepting service from others.

INSPIRED TALKS[1]

TUESDAY, *June 25, 1895.*

After every happiness comes misery; they may be far apart or near. The more advanced the soul, the more quickly does one follow the other. *What we want is neither happiness nor misery.* Both make us forget our true nature; both are chains, one iron, another gold; behind both is the Âtman, who knows neither happiness nor misery. These are *states* and states must ever change; but the nature of the soul is bliss, peace, unchanging. We have not to get it, we have it; only wash away the dross and see it.

Stand upon the Self, then only can we truly love the world. Take a very, very high stand; knowing our universal nature, we must look with perfect calmness upon all the *panorama* of the world. It is but baby's play, and we know that, so cannot be disturbed by it. If the mind is pleased with praise, it will be displeased with blame. All pleasures of the senses or even of the mind are evanescent, but within ourselves is the one true unrelated pleasure, dependent upon nothing. It is perfectly free, it is bliss. *The more our bliss is within, the more spiritual we are.* The pleasure of the Self is what the world calls religion.

The internal universe, the *real,* is infinitely greater than the external, which is only a shadowy projection of the true one. This world is neither true nor untrue, it is the shadow of truth. "Imagination is the gilded shadow of truth," says the poet.

We enter into creation, and then for us it becomes living. Things are dead in themselves; only we give them life, and then, like fools, we turn around and are afraid of them, or enjoy them. But be not like certain fisherwomen, who, caught in a storm on their way home from market, took refuge in the house of a florist. They were lodged for the night in a room next to the garden, where the air was full of the fragrance of flowers. In vain did they try to rest, until one of their number suggested

[1] From the teachings given to a group of select disciples at Thousand Island Park, New York State, in the summer of 1895. Recorded by Miss S. E. Waldo, a disciple.

that they wet their fish baskets and place them near their heads. Then they all fell into a sound sleep.

The world is our fish basket, we must not depend upon it for enjoyment. Those who do are the Tâmasas, or the bound. Then there are the Râjasas, or the egotistical, who talk always about "I", "I". They do good work sometimes and may become spiritual. But the highest are the Sâttvikas, the introspective, those who live only in the Self. These three qualities, Tamas, Rajas, and Sattva, are in everyone, and different ones predominate at different times.

Creation is not a "making" of something, it is the struggle to regain the equilibrium, as when atoms of cork are thrown to the bottom of a pail of water and rush to rise to the top, singly or in clusters. *Life is and must be accompanied by evil.* A little evil is the source of life; the little wickedness that is in the world is very good, for when the balance is regained, the world will end, because sameness and destruction are one. When this world goes, good and evil go with it; but when we can transcend this world we get rid of both good and evil and have bliss.

There is no possibility of ever having pleasure without pain, good without evil, for living itself is just the lost equilibrium. What we want is freedom, not life, nor pleasure, nor good. Creation is infinite, without beginning and without end, the ever-moving ripple in an infinite lake. There are yet unreached depths and others where the equilibrium has been regained, but the ripple is always progressing, the struggle to regain the balance is eternal. Life and death are only different names for the same fact, the two sides of the one coin. Both are Maya, the inexplicable state of striving at one time to live, and a moment later to die. Beyond this is the true nature, the Atman. While we recognise a God, it is really only the Self, which we have separated ourselves from and worship as outside of us; but it is our true Self all the time, the one and only God.

To regain the balance we must counteract Tamas by Rajas, then conquer Rajas by Sattva, the calm beautiful state that will grow and grow until all else is gone. Give up bondage, become a son, be free, and then you can "see the Father," as did Jesus. Infinite strength is religion and God. Avoid weakness and slavery. You are only a soul, *if* you are free; there is immortality for you, *if* you are free; there is a God, *if* He is free. . . .

The world for me, not I for the world. Good and evil are our slaves, not we theirs. It is the nature of the brute to remain where he is (not to progress); it is the nature of man to seek good and avoid evil; it is the nature of God to seek neither, but just to be eternally blissful. Let us be God! Make the heart like an ocean, go beyond all the trifles of the world, be mad with joy even at evil, see the world as a picture and then enjoy its beauty, knowing that nothing affects you. Children finding glass beads in a mud puddle, that is the good of the world. Look at it with calm complacency; see good and evil as the same, both are merely "God's play"; enjoy all. . . .

My Master used to say, "All is God, but tiger-God is to be shunned. All water is water, but we avoid dirty water for drinking."

The whole sky is the censer of God and the sun and moon are the lamps. What temple is needed? All eyes are Thine, yet Thou hast not an eye; all hands are Thine, yet Thou hast not a hand.

Neither seek nor avoid, take what comes. It is liberty to be affected by nothing; do not merely endure, be unattached. Remember the story of the bull. A mosquito sat long on the horn of a certain bull. Then his conscience troubled him and he said, "Mr. Bull, I have been sitting here a long time, perhaps I annoy you. I am sorry, I will go away." But the bull replied: "Oh no, not at all! Bring your whole family and live on my horn; what can you do to me?"

WEDNESDAY, *June 26*.

Our best work is done, our greatest influence is exerted when we are without thought of self. All great geniuses know this. Let us open ourselves to the one Divine Actor and let Him act, and do nothing ourselves. *"O Arjuna! I have no duty in the whole world,"* says Krishna. Be perfectly resigned, perfectly unconcerned; then alone can you do any true work. No eyes can see the real forces, we can only see the results. Put out self, lose it, forget it; just let God work, it is His business. We have nothing to do but stand aside and let God work. The more we go away, the more God comes in. Get rid of the little "I" and let only the great "I" live.

We are what our thoughts have made us; so take care of what you think. Words are secondary. Thoughts live, they travel far. Each thought we think is tinged with our own character, so that for the pure and holy man, even his jests or abuses will have the twist of his own love and purity and do good.

Desire nothing; think of God and look for no return; it is the desireless who bring results. The begging monks carry religion to every man's door; but they think that they do nothing, they claim nothing, their work is unconsciously done. If they should eat of the tree of knowledge, they would become egoists and all the good they do would fly away. As soon as we say "I" we are humbugged all the time, and we call it "knowable", but it is only going round and round like a bullock tied to a tree. The Lord has hidden himself best and His work is best; so he who hides himself best, accomplishes most. Conquer *yourself* and the whole universe is yours.

In the state of Sattva we see the very nature of things, we go beyond the senses and beyond reason. The adamantine wall that shuts us in is egoism; we refer everything to ourselves, thinking I do this, that and the other. Get rid of this puny "I"; kill this diabolism in us; "not I, but Thou"—say it, feel it, live it. Until we give up the world manufactured by the ego, never can we enter the kingdom of heaven. None ever did, none ever will. To give up the world is to forget the ego, to know it not at all, living *in* the body but not *of* it. This rascal ego must be obliterated. Bless men when they revile you. Think how much good they are doing you; they can only hurt themselves. Go where people hate you, let them thrash the ego out of you and you will get nearer to the Lord. Like the mother-monkey,[1] we hug our "baby", the world, as long as we can, but at last when we are driven to put it under our feet and step on it, then we are ready to come to God. Blessed it is to be persecuted for the sake of righteousness. Blessed are we if we cannot read, we have less to take us away from God.

Enjoyment is the million-headed serpent that we must tread underfoot. We renounce, and go on, then find nothing and despair; but hold on, *hold on*. The world is a demon.

[1] The mother-monkey is very fond of her young in time of safety but when danger comes, she does not scruple to throw it down and trample on it, if necessary, to save herself.

It is a kingdom of which the puny ego is king. Put it away and stand firm. Give up lust and gold and fame and hold fast to the Lord, and at last we shall reach a state of perfect indifference. The idea that the gratification of the senses constitutes enjoyment is purely materialistic. There is not one spark of real enjoyment there: all the joy there is, is a mere reflection of the true bliss.

Those who give themselves up to the Lord do more for the world than all the so-called workers. One man who has purified himself thoroughly accomplishes more than a regiment of preachers. *Out of purity and silence comes the word of power.*

"Be like a lily, stay in one place and expand your petals and the bees will come of themselves." There was a great contrast between Keshab Chandra Sen and Shri Ramakrishna. The second never recognised any sin or misery in the world, no evil to fight against. The first was a great ethical reformer, leader, and founder of the Brahmo Samaj. After twelve years the quiet prophet of Dakshineswar had worked a revolution not only in India, but in the world. The power is with the silent ones, who only live and love and then withdraw their personality. They never say "me" and "mine"; they are only blessed in being instruments. Such men are the makers of Christ and Buddhas, ever living, fully identified with God, ideal existences, asking nothing and not consciously doing anything. They are the real movers, the Jivanmuktas,[1] absolutely selfless, the little personality entirely blown away, ambition non-existent. They are all principle, no personality.

MONDAY, *July 1.* (*Shri Ramakrishna Deva*)

Shri Ramakrishna was the son of a very orthodox Brahmin, who would refuse even a gift from any but a special caste of Brahmins; neither might he work, nor even be a priest in a temple, nor sell books nor serve anyone. He could only have "what fell from the skies" (alms) and even then it must not come through a "fallen" Brahmin. Temples have no hold on the Hindu religion; if they were all destroyed, religion would not be affected a grain. A man must only build a house for "God and guests", to build for himself would be selfish; therefore he erects temples as dwelling places for God.

Owing to the extreme poverty of his family, Shri Rama-

[1] Literally, free even while living.

krishna was obliged to become in his boyhood a priest in a temple dedicated to Divine Mother, also called Prakriti, or Kâli, represented by a female figure standing with feet on a male figure, indicating that until Mâyâ lifts, we can know nothing. Brahman is neuter, unknown and unknowable, but to be objectified. He covers Himself with a veil of Maya, becomes the Mother of the Universe and so brings forth the creation. The prostrate figure (Shiva, or God) has become Shava (dead, or lifeless) by being covered by Maya. The Jnani says, "I will uncover God by force" (Advaitism); but the dualist says, "We will uncover God by praying to Mother, begging Her to open the door to which She alone has the key."

The daily service of the Mother Kali gradually awakened such intense devotion in the heart of the young priest that he could no longer carry on the regular temple worship, so he abandoned his duties and retired to a small woodland in the temple compound, where he gave himself up entirely to meditation. These woods were on the bank of the river Ganga, and one day the swift current bore to his very feet just the necessary materials to build him a little enclosure. In this enclosure he stayed and wept and prayed, taking no thought for the care of his body or for aught except his Divine Mother. A relative fed him once a day and watched over him. Later came a Sannyâsini, or ascetic woman, to help him find his "Mother". Whatever teachers he needed came to him unsought; from every sect some holy saint would come and offer to teach him, and to each he listened eagerly. But he worshipped only Mother; all to him was Mother.

Shri Ramakrishna never spoke a harsh word against anyone. So beautifully tolerant was he that every sect thought that he belonged to them. He loved everyone. To him all religions were true. He found a place for each one. He was free, but free in love, not in "thunder". The mild type creates, the thundering type spreads. Paul was the thundering type to spread the light.[1]

The age of St. Paul, however, is gone; we are to be the new lights for this day. A self-adjusting organisation is the great need of our time. When we can get one, that will be the last

[1] And it has been said by many that Swami Vivekananda himself was a kind of St. Paul to Shri Ramakrishna.

religion of the world. The wheel must turn, and we should help it, not hinder. The waves of religious thought rise and fall, and on the topmost one stands the "prophet of the period". Ramakrishna came to teach the religion of today, constructive, not destructive. He had to go afresh to Nature to ask for facts and he got a scientific religion, which never says "believe" but "see"; "I see, and you too can see." Use the same means and you will reach the same vision. God will come to every-one, harmony is within the reach of all. Shri Ramakrishna's teachings are "the gist of Hinduism"; they were not peculiar to him. Nor did he claim that they were; he cared naught for name or fame.

He began to preach when he was about forty; but he never went out to do it. He waited for those who wanted his teach-ings to come to him. In accordance with Hindu custom, he was married by his parents in early youth to a little girl of five, who remained at home with her family in a distant village, unconscious of the great struggle through which her young hus-band was passing. When she reached maturity, he was already deeply absorbed in religious devotion. She travelled on foot from her home to the temple at Dakshineswar, where he was then living, and as soon as she saw him she recognised what he was, for she herself was a great soul, pure and holy, who only desired to help his work, never to drag him down to the level of the Grihastha (householder).

Shri Ramakrishna is worshipped in India as one of the great Incarnations, and his birthday is celebrated there as a religious festival.

TUESDAY, *July* 2. (*The Divine Mother.*)

Shâktas worship the Universal Energy as Mother, the sweetest name they know; for the mother is the highest ideal of womanhood in India. When God is worshipped as "Mother", as Love, the Hindus call it the "right-handed" way, and it leads to spirituality, but never to material prosperity. When God is worshipped on His terrible side, that is, in the "left-handed" way, it leads usually to great material prosperity, but rarely to spirituality; and eventually it leads to degeneration and the obliteration of the race that practises it.

Mother is the first manifestation of power and is considered a higher idea than father. With the name of Mother comes the idea of Shakti, Divine Energy and omnipotence, just as the baby believes its mother to be all-powerful, able to do anything. The Divine Mother is the Kundalini ("coiled up" power) sleeping in us; without worshipping Her we can never know ourselves. All-merciful, all-powerful, omni-present are attributes of Divine Mother. She is the sum total of the energy in the universe. Every manifestation of power in the universe is "Mother". She is life, She is Intelligence, She is Love. She is in the universe, yet separate from it. She is a person and can be seen and known (as Shri Ramakrishna saw and knew Her). Established in the idea of Mother, we can do anything. She quickly answers prayer.

She can show Herself to us in any form at any moment. Divine Mother can have form (Rupa) and name (Nama), or name without form, and as we worship Her in these various aspects we can rise to pure Being, having neither form nor name.

The sum total of all the cells in an organism is one person; so each soul is like one cell and the sum of them is God, and beyond that is the Absolute. The sea calm is the Absolute; the same sea in waves is Divine Mother. She is time, space, and causation. God is Mother and has two natures, the conditioned and the unconditioned. As the former, She is God, Nature, and soul (man). As the latter, She is unknown and unknowable. Out of the Unconditioned came the trinity, God, Nature, and soul, the triangle of existence. This is the Vishishtâdvaitist idea.

A bit of Mother, a drop, was Krishna, another was Buddha, another was Christ. The worship of even one spark of Mother in our earthly mother leads to greatness. Worship Her if you want love and wisdom.

SATURDAY, *July 20.*

Perception is our only real knowledge or religion. Talking about it for ages will never make us know our soul. There is no difference between theories and atheism. In fact, the atheist is the truer man. Every step I take in the light is mine for ever. When you go to a country and see it, then it is yours. We have each to see for ourselves; teachers can only "bring the food", we must eat it to be nourished. Argument can never prove God save as a logical conclusion.

It is impossible to find God outside of ourselves. Our own

souls contribute all the divinity that is outside of us. We are the greatest temple. The objectification is only a faint imitation of what we see within ourselves.

Concentration of the powers of the mind is our only instrument to help us see God. If you know one soul (your own), you know all souls, past, present, and to come. The will concentrates the mind; certain things excite and control this will, such as reason, love, devotion, breathing. The concentrated mind is a lamp that shows us every corner of the soul.

No one method can suit all. These different methods are not steps necessary to be taken one after another. Ceremonials are the lowest form; next God external and after that God internal. In some cases gradation may be needed, but in many only one way is required. It would be the height of folly to say to everyone, "You must pass through Karma and Bhakti before you can reach Jnana".

Stick to your reason until you reach something higher and you will know it to be higher because it will not jar with reason. The stage beyond consciousness is inspiration (Samâdhi); but never mistake hysterical trances for the real thing. It is a terrible thing to claim this inspiration falsely, to mistake instinct for inspiration. There is no external test for inspiration, we know it ourselves; our guardian against mistake is negative—the voice of reason. All religion is going beyond reason, but reason is the only guide to get there. Instinct is like ice, reason is the water, and inspiration is the subtlest form or vapour; one follows the other. Everywhere is this eternal sequence—unconsciousness, consciousness, intelligence—matter, body, mind, and to us it seems as if the chain began with the particular link we first lay hold of. Arguments on both sides are of equal weight and both are true. We must reach beyond both, to where there is neither the one nor the other. These successions are all Maya.

Religion is above reason, supernatural. Faith is not belief, it is the grasp on the Ultimate, an illumination. First hear, then reason and find out all that reason can give about the Atman; let the flood of reason flow over It, then take what remains. If nothing remains, thank God you have escaped a superstition. When you have determined that nothing *can* take away the Atman, that It stands every test, hold fast to this and teach it to all. Truth cannot be partial; it is for the good of all. Finally, in perfect rest and peace meditate upon It, concentrate your mind upon It, make yourself one with It. Then no speech is needed; silence will carry the truth. Do not spend your energy in talking, but meditate in silence; and do not let the rush of the outside world disturb you. When your mind is in the highest state, you are unconscious of it. Accumulate power in silence and become a dynamo of spirituality. What can a beggar give? Only a king can give, and he only when he wants nothing himself.

Hold your money merely as custodian for what is God's. Have no attachment for it. Let name and fame and money go; they are a terrible bondage. Feel the wonderful atmosphere of freedom. You are free, free! Oh, blessed am I! Freedom am I! I am the Infinite! In my soul I can find no beginning and no end. All is my Self. Say this unceasingly.

MONDAY, *July 29.*

We sometimes indicate a thing by describing its surroundings. When we say "Sachchidânanda" (Existence-Knowledge-Bliss), we are merely indicating the shores of an indescribable Beyond. Not even can we say "is" about it, for that too is relative. Any imagination, any concept, is in vain. Neti, Neti "not this, not this" is all that can be said, for even to think is to limit and so to lose.

The senses cheat you day and night. The Vedanta found that out ages ago; modern science is just discovering the same fact. A picture has only length and breadth, and the painter copies Nature in her cheating by artificially giving the appearance of depth. No two people see the same world. The highest knowledge will show you that there is no motion, no change, in anything; that the very idea of it is all Maya. Study Nature as a whole, that is, study motion. Mind and body are not our real Self; both belong to Nature, but eventually we can know the *ding an sich*. Then mind and body being transcended, all that they conceive goes. When you cease utterly to know and see the world, then you realise Atman. The superseding of relative knowledge is what we want. There is no infinite mind or infinite knowledge, because both mind and knowledge are limited. We are now seeing through a veil; then we reach the "x", which is the Reality of all our knowing.

If we look at a picture through a pin-hole in a cardboard,

we get an utterly mistaken notion; yet what we see is really the picture. As we enlarge the hole, we get a clearer and clearer idea. Out of the reality we manufacture the different views in conformity with our mistaken perceptions of name and form. When we throw away the cardboard, we see the same picture, but we see it as it is. We put in all the attributes, all the errors, the picture itself is unaltered thereby. That is because Atman is the reality of all; all we see is Atman, but not as we see It, as name and form; they are all in our veil, in Maya.

They are like spots in the object-glass of a telescope, yet it is the light of the sun that shows us the spots; we could not even see the illusion save for the background of reality which is Brahman. Swami Vivekananda is just the speck on the object-glass; I am Atman, real, unchangeable, and that reality alone enables me to see Swami Vivekananda. Atman is the essence of every hallucination; but the sun is never identified with the spots on the glass, it only shows them to us. Our actions, as they are evil or good, increase or decrease the "spots", but they never affect the God within us. Perfectly cleanse the mind of spots and instantly we see, "I and my Father are one".

We first perceive, then reason later. We must have this perception as a fact, and it is called religion, realisation. No matter if one never heard of creed or prophet or book, let him get this realisation and he needs no more. Cleanse the mind, this is all of religion; and until we ourselves clear off the spots, we cannot see the Reality as it is. The baby sees no sin; he has not yet the measure of it in himself. Get rid of the defects within yourself, and you will not be able to see any without. A baby sees robbery done and it means nothing to him. Once you find the hidden object in a puzzle picture, you see it ever more; so when once you are free and stainless, you see only freedom and purity in the world around. That moment all the knots of the heart are cut asunder, all crooked places are made straight and this world vanishes as a dream. And when we awake, we wonder how we ever came to dream such trash!

"Getting whom, misery mountain high has no power to move the soul."

With the axe of knowledge cut the wheels asunder and the Atman stands free, even though the old momentum carries on the wheel of mind and body. The wheel can now only go straight, can only do good. If that body does anything bad, know that the man is not Jivanmukta; he lies if he makes that claim. But it is only when the wheels have got a good straight motion (from cleansing the mind) that the axe can be applied. All purifying action deals conscious or unconscious blows on delusion. To call another a sinner is the worst thing you can do. Good action done ignorantly produces the same result and helps to break the bondage.

To identify the sun with the spots on the object-glass is the fundamental error. Know the sun, the "I", to be ever unaffected by anything, and devote yourself to cleansing the spots. Man is the greatest being that ever can be. The highest worship there is, is to worship man as Krishna, Buddha, Christ. What you want, you create. Get rid of desire.

• • • •

The angels and the departed are all here, seeing this world as heaven. The same "x" is seen by all according to their mental attitude. The best vision to be had of the "x" is here on this earth. Never want to go to heaven, that is the worst delusion. Even here, too much wealth and grinding poverty are both bondages and hold us back from religion. Three great gifts we have—first, a human body. (The human mind is the nearest reflection of God, we are "His own image".) Second, the desire to be free. Third, the help of a noble soul who has crossed the ocean of delusion, as a teacher. When you have these three, bless the Lord; you are sure to be free.

What you only grasp intellectually may be overthrown by a new argument, but what you realise is yours for ever. Talking, talking religion is but little good. Put God behind everything, man, animal, food, work; make this a habit.

Ingersoll once said to me: "I believe in making the most out of this world, in squeezing the orange dry, because this world is all we are sure of." I replied: "I know a better way to squeeze the orange of this world than you do and I get more out of it. I *know* I cannot die, so I am not in a hurry; I know there is no fear, so I enjoy the squeezing. I have no duty, no bondage of wife and children and property; I can love all men and women. Everyone is God to me. Think of the joy of loving man as God! Squeeze your orange this way and get ten thousandfold more out of it. Get every single drop."

That which seems to be the will is the Atman behind, it is really free.

MONDAY AFTERNOON.

Jesus was imperfect, because he did not live up fully to his own ideal, and, above all, because he did not give woman a place equal to man. Women did everything for him and yet he was so bound by the Jewish custom that not one was made an apostle. Still he was the greatest character next to Buddha, who in his turn was not fully perfect. Buddha, however, recognised woman's right to an equal place in religion, and his first and one of his greatest disciples was his own wife, who became the head of the whole Buddhistic movement among the women of India. But we ought not to criticise these great ones, we should only look upon them as far above ourselves. Nonetheless we must not pin our faith to any man, however great; we too must become Buddhas and Christs.

No man should be judged by his defects. The great virtues a man has are his especially, his errors are the common weakness of humanity and should never be counted in estimating his character.

. . . .

Vira, the Sanskrit word for "heroic", is the origin of our word "virtue", because in ancient times the best fighter was regarded as the most virtuous man.

TUESDAY, *July 30.*

Christs and Buddhas are simply occasions upon which to objectify our own inner powers. We really answer our own prayers.

It is blasphemy to think that if Jesus had never been born, humanity would not have been saved. It is horrible to forget thus the divinity in human nature, a divinity that must come out. Never forget the glory of human nature. We are the greatest God that ever was or ever will be. Christs and Buddhas are but waves on the boundless ocean which *I am.* Bow down to nothing but your own higher Self. Until you know that you are that very God of gods, there will never be any freedom for you.

All our past actions are really good, because they lead us to what we ultimately become. Of whom to beg? I am the real existence and all else is a dream save as it is I. I am the whole ocean; do not call the little wave you have made

"I"; know it for nothing but a wave. Satyakâma (lover of truth) heard the inner voice telling him, "You are the infinite, the universal is in you. Control yourself and listen to the voice of your true Self."

The great prophets who do the fighting have to be less perfect than those who live silent lives of holiness, thinking great thoughts and so helping the world. These men, passing out one after another, produce as final outcome the man of power who preaches.

• • • •

Knowledge exists, man only discovers it. The Vedas are the eternal knowledge through which God created the world. They talk high philosophy—the highest—and make this tremendous claim.

• • • •

Tell the truth boldly, whether it hurts or not. Never pander to weakness. If truth is too much for intelligent people and sweeps them away, let them go; the sooner the better. Childish ideas are for babies and savages; and these are not all in the nursery and the forests, some of them have fallen into the pulpits.

It is bad to stay in the church after you are grown up spiritually. Come out and die in the open air of freedom.

All progression is in the relative world. The human form is the highest and man the greatest being, because here and now we can get rid of the relative world entirely, can actually attain freedom, and this is the goal. Not only we can, but some have reached perfection; so no matter what finer bodies come, they could only be on the relative plane and could do no more than we, for to attain freedom is all that can be done.

The angels never do wicked deeds, so they never get punished and never get saved. Blows are what awaken us and help to break the dream. They show us the insufficiency of this world and make us long to escape, to have freedom.

• • • •

A thing dimly perceived we call by one name; the same thing when fully perceived we call by another. The higher the moral nature, the higher the perception and the stronger the will.

TUESDAY AFTERNOON.

The reason of the harmony between thought and matter is that they are two sides of one thing, call it "x", which divides itself into the internal and the external.

The English word "paradise" comes from the Sanskrit Para-desha, which was taken over into the Persian language and means literally "the land beyond", or the other world. The old Aryans always believed in a soul, never that man was the body. Their heavens and hells were all temporary, because no effect can outlast its cause and no cause is eternal; therefore all effects must come to an end.

The whole of the Vedanta Philosophy is in this story: Two birds of golden plumage sat on the same tree. The one above, serene, majestic, immersed in his own glory; the one below restless and eating the fruits of the tree, now sweet, now bitter. Once he ate an exceptionally bitter fruit, then he paused and looked up at the majestic bird above; but he soon forgot about the other bird and went on eating the fruits of the tree as before. Again he ate a bitter fruit and this time he hopped up a few boughs nearer to the bird at the top. This happened many times until at last the lower bird came to the place of the upper bird and lost himself. He found all at once that there had never been two birds, but that he was all the time that upper bird, serene, majestic, and immersed in his own glory.

THURSDAY AFTERNOON, *August 1.*

There are endless series of manifestations, like "merry-go-rounds", in which the souls ride, so to speak. The series are eternal; individual souls get out, but the events repeat themselves eternally and that is how one's past and future can be read, because all is really present. When the soul is in a certain chain, it has to go through the experiences of that chain. From one series souls go to other series; from some series they escape for ever by realising that they are Brahman By getting hold of one prominent event in a chain and holding on to it, the whole chain can be dragged in and read. This power is easily acquired, but it is of no real value and to practise it takes just so much from our spiritual forces. Go not after these things, worship God.

FRIDAY, *August 2.*

Nishthâ (devotion to one Ideal) is the beginning of realisation. "Take the honey out of all flowers: sit and be friendly with all, pay reverence to all, say to all, 'Yes, brother, yes, brother,' but keep firm in your own way." A higher stage is actually to take the position of the other. If I am all, why can I not really and actively sympathise with my brother and see with his eyes? While I am weak, I must stick to one course (Nishtha), but when I am strong, I can feel with every other and perfectly sympathise with his ideas.

The old idea was: "Develop one idea at the expense of all the rest." The modern way is "harmonious development". A third way is to "develop the mind and control it", then put it where you will; the result will come quickly. This is developing yourself in the truest way. Learn concentration and use it in any direction. Thus you lose nothing. He who gets the whole must have the parts too. Dualism is included in Advaitism (monism).

"I first saw him and he saw me,

"There was a flash of eye from me to him and from him to me."

This went on until the two souls became so closely united that they actually became one.

• • • •

There are two kinds of Samadhi: I concentrate on myself, then I concentrate and there is a unity of subject and object.

You must be able to sympathise fully with each particular, then at once to jump back to the highest monism. After having perfected yourself, you limit yourself voluntarily. Take the whole power into each action. Be able to become a dualist for the time being and forget Advaita, yet be able to take it up again at will.

• • • •

Cause and effect are all Maya, and we shall grow to understand that all we see is as disconnected as the child's fairy tales now seem to us. There is really no such thing as cause and effect and we shall come to know it. Then if you can, lower your intellect to let any allegory pass through your mind without questioning about connection. Develop love of imagery and beautiful poetry and then enjoy all mythologies as poetry. Come not to mythology with ideas of history and reasoning. Let it flow as a current through your mind, let it be whirled as a candle before your eyes, without asking who holds the candle, and you will get the circle; the residuum of truth will remain in your mind.

The writers of all mythologies wrote in symbols of what they saw and heard, they painted flowing pictures. Do not try to pick out the themes and so destroy the pictures; take them as they are and let them act on you. Judge them only by the effect and get the good out of them.

Your own will is all that answers prayer, only it appears under the guise of different religious conceptions to each mind. We may call it Buddha, Jesus, Krishna, Jehovah, Allah, Agni, but it is only the Self, the "I".

• • • •

Concepts grow, but there is no historical value in the allegories which present them. Moses' visions are more likely to be wrong than ours are, because we have more knowledge and are less likely to be deceived by illusions.

Books are useless to us until our own book opens; then all other books are good so far as they confirm our book. It is the strong that understand strength, it is the elephant that understands the lion, not the rat. How can we understand Jesus until we are his equals? It is all in the dream to feed five thousand with two loaves, or to feed two with five loaves; neither is real and neither affects the other. Only grandeur appreciates grandeur, only God realises God. The dream is only the dreamer, it has no other basis. It is not one thing and the dreamer another. The keynote running through the music is—"I am He, I am He," all other notes are but variations and do not affect the real theme. We are the living books and books are but the words we have spoken. Everything is the living God, the living Christ; see it as such. Read man, he is the living poem. We are the light that illumines all the Bibles and Christs and Buddhas that ever were. Without that, these would be dead to us, not living.

Stand on your own Self.

The dead body resents nothing; let us make our bodies dead and cease to identify ourselves with them.

SATURDAY, *August 3.*

Individuals who are to get freedom in this life have to live thousands of years in one lifetime. They have to be ahead of their times, but the masses can only crawl. Thus we have Christs and Buddhas.

• • • •

There was once a Hindu queen, who so much desired that all her children should attain freedom in this life that she herself took all the care of them; and as she rocked them to sleep, she sang always the one song to them: "Tat tvam asi, Tat tvam asi" (That thou art, That thou art). Three of them became Sannyasins, but the fourth was taken away to be brought up elsewhere to become a king. As he was leaving home, the mother gave him a piece of paper which he was to read when he grew to manhood. On that piece of paper was written, "God alone is true. All else is false. The soul never kills or is killed. Live alone or in the company of holy ones." When the young prince read this, he too at once renounced the world and became a Sannyasin.

Give up, renounce the world. Now we are like dogs strayed into a kitchen and eating a piece of meat, looking round in fear lest at any moment some one may come and drive them out. Instead of that, be a king and know you own the world This never comes until you give it up and it ceases to bind. Give up mentally, if you do not physically. Give up from the heart of your hearts. Have Vairâgya (renunciation). This is the real sacrifice, and without it, it is impossible to attain spirituality. Do not desire, for what you desire you get and with it comes terrible bondage. It is nothing but bringing "noses on us", as in the case of the man who had three boons to ask.[1] We never get freedom until we are self-contained. "Self is the Saviour of self, none else."

[1] A poor man was once able to propitiate a certain god who gave him three boons to ask along with three throws of dice. The happy man communicated this news to his wife, who at once told him to cast for wealth first. To this the man said, "We both have very ugly little noses,

Learn to feel yourself in other bodies, to know that we are all one. Throw all other nonsense to the winds. Spit out your actions, good or bad, and never think of them again. What is done is done. Throw off superstition. Have no weakness even in the face of death. Do not repent, do not brood over past deeds, and do not remember your good deeds; be *azad* (free). The weak, the fearful, the ignorant will never reach the Atman. You cannot undo, the effect must come; face it, but be careful never to do the same thing again. Give up the burden of all deeds to the Lord; give all, both good and bad. Do not keep the good and give only the bad. God helps those who do *not* help themselves.

"Drinking the cup of desire, the world becomes mad." Day and night never come together, so desire and the Lord can never come together. Give up desire.

• • • •

There is a vast difference between saying "food, food" and eating it, between saying "water, water" and drinking it. So by merely repeating the words "God, God," we cannot hope to attain realisation. We must strive and practise.

Only by the wave falling back into the sea can it become unlimited, never as a wave can it be so. Then after it has become the sea, it can become the wave again and as big a one as it pleases. Break the identification of yourself with the current and know that you are free.

True philosophy is the systematising of certain perceptions. Intellect ends where religion begins. Inspiration is much higher than reason, but it must not contradict it. Reason

for which people laugh at us. Let us first cast for beautiful aquiline noses." But the wife was for wealth first and so she caught hold of his hand to prevent him from throwing the dice. The man hastily snatched his hand away and at once threw the dice, exclaiming, "Let us both have beautiful noses and nothing but noses." All at once both their bodies were covered over with many beautiful noses, but they proved such a great nuisance to them that both of them agreed to throw for the second time asking for their removal. It was done, but they also lost their own little ones by that! There was only one boon more to ask. Having lost their noses, they looked uglier than before. They wanted to have two beautiful noses, but they feared to be questioned about their transformation, lest they should be regarded by all to be two big fools who could not mend their circumstances even with the help of three boons. So both of them agreed to get back their ugly little noses and the dice were accordingly cast.

is the rough tool to do the hard work; inspiration is the bright light which shows us all truth. The will to do a thing is not necessarily inspiration.

. . . .

Progression in Maya is a circle that brings you back to the starting point; but you start ignorant and come to the end with all knowledge. Worship of God, worship of the holy ones, concentration and meditation, and unselfish work, these are the ways of breaking away from Maya's net; but we must first have the strong desire to get free. The flash of light that will illumine the darkness for us is in us; it is the knowledge that freedom is our nature—there is no "birthright," we were never born. All that we have to do is to drive away the clouds that cover it.

Give up all desire for enjoyment in earth or heaven. Control the organs of the senses and control the mind. Bear every misery without even knowing that you are miserable. Think of nothing but liberation. Have faith in the Guru, in his teachings, and in the surety that you can get free. Say "Soham, Soham" whatever comes. Tell yourself this even in eating, walking, suffering; tell the mind this incessantly—that what we see never existed—that there is only "I". Flash—the dream will break! Think day and night, this universe is zero, only God is. Have intense desire to get free.

All relatives and friends are but "old dry wells"; we fall into them and get dreams of duty and bondage, and there is no end. Do not create illusion by *helping* anyone. It is like a banyan tree that spreads on and on. If you are a dualist, you are a fool to try to help God. If you are a monist, you know that you are God; where find duty? You have no duty to husband, child, friend. Take things as they come, lie still and when your body floats, go; rise with the rising tide, fall with the falling tide. Let the body die; this idea of body is but a worn-out fable. "Be still and know that you are God."

The present only is existent. There is no past or future even in thought, because to think it you have to make it the present. Give up everything and let it float where it will. This world is all a delusion, do not let it fool you again. You have known it for what it is not, now know it for what it is. If the body is dragged anywhere, let it go; do not care where the body is. This tyrannical idea of duty is a terrible poison and is destroying the world.

Do not wait to have a harp and rest by degrees; why not take a harp and begin here? Why wait for heaven? Make it here. In heaven there is no marrying or giving in marriage; why not begin at once and have none here? The yellow robe of the Sannyasin is the sign of the free.. Give up the beggar's dress of the world; wear the flag of freedom, the ochre robe.

SUNDAY AFTERNOON, *August 4.*

Mind is an instrument in the hand of the Atman just as the body is an instrument in the hand of mind. Matter is motion outside, mind is motion inside. All change begins and ends in time. If the Atman is unchangeable, It must be perfect; if perfect, It must be infinite; and if It be infinite, It must be only One; there cannot be two infinites. So the Atman, the Self, can be only One. Though It seems to be various, It is really only One. If a man were to go toward the sun, at every step he would see a different sun, and yet it would be the same sun after all.

Asti, "isness", is the basis of all unity and as soon as the basis is found, perfection ensues. If all colour could be resolved into one colour, painting would cease. The perfect oneness is rest; we refer all manifestations to one Being. Taoists, Confucianists, Buddhists, Hindus, Jews, Mohammedans, Christians, and Zoroastrians, all preached the golden rule and in almost the same words; but only the Hindus have given the rationale, because they saw the reason. Man must love others because those others are himself. There is but One.

Of all the great religious teachers the world has known, only Lao-tze, Buddha, and Jesus transcended the golden rule and said, "Do good to your enemies," "Love them that hate you."

Principles exist; we do not create them, we only discover them. Religion consists solely in realisation. Doctrines are methods, not religion. All the different religions are but applications of the one religion adapted to suit the requirements of different nations. Theories only lead to fighting; thus the Name of God that ought to bring peace has been the cause of half the bloodshed of the world. Go to the direct source. Ask God what He is. Unless He answers, He is not; but every religion teaches that He does answer.

Have something to say for yourself, else how can you have any idea of what others have said? Do not cling to old superstitions; be ever ready for new truths. "Fools are they who would drink brackish water from a well that their forefathers have dug and would not drink pure water from a well that others have dug." Until we realise God for ourselves, we can know nothing about Him. Each man is perfect by his nature; prophets have manifested this perfection, but it is potential in us. How can we understand that Moses saw God unless we too see Him? If God ever came to anyone, He will come to me. I will go to God direct; let Him talk to me, I cannot take belief as a basis, that is atheism and blasphemy. If God spake to a man in the deserts of Arabia two thousand years ago, He can also speak to me today, else how can I know that He has not died? Come to God any way you can; only come. But in coming do not push anyone down.

The knowing ones must have pity on the ignorant. One who knows is willing to give up his body even for an ant, because he knows that the body is nothing.

MONDAY, *August 5.*

The question is: Is it necessary to pass through all the lower stages to reach the highest, or can a plunge be taken at once? The modern American boy takes twenty-five years to attain that which his forefathers took hundreds of years to do. The present-day Hindu gets in twenty years to the height reached in eight thousand years by his ancestors. On the physical side, the embryo goes from the amoeba to man in the womb. These are the teachings of modern science. The Vedanta goes further and tells us that we not only have to live the life of all past humanity, but also the future life of all humanity. The man who does the first is the educated man, the second is the Jivanmukta, for ever free.

Time is merely the measure of our thoughts, and thought being inconceivably swift, there is no limit to the speed with which we can live the life ahead. So it cannot be stated how long it would take to live all future life. It might be in a second, or it might take fifty lifetimes. It depends on the intensity of the desire. The teaching must therefore be modified according to the needs of the taught. The consuming fire is ready for all, even water and chunks of ice quickly consume. Fire a mass of bird-shot, one at least will strike; give a man a whole museum of truths, he will at once take what is suited to him. Past lives have moulded our tendencies; give to the taught in accordance with his tendency. Intellectual, mystical, devotional, practical—make one the basis, but teach the others with it. Intellect must be balanced with love, the mystical nature with reason, while practice must form part of every method. Take every one where he stands and push him forward. Religious teaching must always be constructive, not destructive.

Each tendency shows the life-work of the past, the line or radius along which that man must move. All radii lead to the centre. Never even attempt to disturb anyone's tendencies; to do that puts back both teacher and taught. When you teach Jnana, you must become a Jnani and stand mentally exactly where the taught stands. Similarly in every other Yoga. Develop every faculty as if it were the only one possessed, this is the true secret of so-called harmonious development. That is, get extensity with intensity, but not at its expense. We are infinite. There is no limitation in us, we can be as intense as the most devoted Mohammedan and as broad as the most roaring atheist.

The way to do this is not to put the mind on any one subject, but to develop and control the mind itself; then you can turn it on any side you choose. Thus you keep the intensity and extensity. Feel Jnana as if it were all there was, then do the same with Bhakti, with Râja, with Karma. Give up the waves and go to the ocean, then you can have the waves as you please. Control the "lake" of your own mind, else you cannot understand the lake of another's mind.

The true teacher is one who can throw his whole force into the tendency of the taught. Without real sympathy we can never teach well. Give up the notion that man is a responsible being, only the perfect man is responsible. The ignorant have drunk deep of the cup of delusion and are not sane. You, who *know,* must have infinite patience with these. Have nothing but love for them and find out the disease that has made them see the world in a wrong light, then help them to cure it and see aright. Remember always that only the free have free will; all the rest are in bondage, and are not responsible for what they do. Will as will is bound. The water when melting on the top of the Himalayas is free, but becoming the river, it is bound by the banks; yet the original impetus carries it to the sea and it regains its freedom. The first is the "fall of man", the second is the "resurrection". Not one atom can rest until it finds its freedom.

Some imaginations help to break the bondage of the rest. The whole universe is imagination, but one set of imaginations will cure another set. Those which tell us that there is sin and sorrow and death in the world are terrible; but the other set which says ever, "I am holy, there is God, there is no pain," these are good and help to break the bondage of the others. The highest imagination that can break all the links of the chain is that of Personal God.

"Om tat sat" is the only thing beyond Maya, but God exists eternally. As long as the Niagara Falls exist, the rainbow will exist; but the water continually flows away. The falls are the universe and the rainbow is Personal God, and both are eternal. While the universe exists, God must exist. God creates the universe and the universe creates God and both are eternal. Maya is neither existence nor non-existence. Both the Niagara Falls and the rainbow are eternally changeable—Brahman seen through Maya. Persians and Christians split Maya into two and call the good half "God" and the bad half the "devil". The Vedanta takes Maya as a whole and recognises a unity beyond it—Brahman.

Mohammed found that Christianity was straying out from the Semitic fold and his teachings were to show what Christianity ought to be as a Semitic religion, that it should hold to one God. The Aryan idea that "I and my Father are one", disgusted and terrified him. In reality the conception of the Trinity was a great advance over the dualistic idea of Jehovah, who was for ever separate from man. The theory of incarnation is the first link in the chain of ideas leading to the recognition of the oneness of God and man. God appearing first in one human form, then reappearing at different times in other human forms, is at last recognised as being in every human form, or in all men. Monistic is the highest stage, monotheistic is a lower stage. Imagination will lead you to the highest even more rapidly and easily than reasoning.

Let a few stand out and live for God alone and save religion for the world. Do not pretend to be like Janaka when you are only the "progenitor" of delusions. (The name Janaka means "progenitor" and belonged to a king who, although he still held his kingdom for the sake of his people, had given up everything mentally). Be honest and say, "I see the ideal but I cannot yet approach it"; but do not pretend to give up when you do not. If you give up, stand fast. If a hundred fall in the fight, seize the flag and carry it on. God is true for all that, no matter who falls. Let him who falls hand on the flag to another to carry on; it can never fall.

When I am washed and clean why shall impurity be added on to me? Seek first the kingdom of Heaven and let everything else go. Do not want anything "added unto you"; be only glad to get rid of it. Give up and know that success will follow, even if you never see it. Jesus left twelve fishermen and yet those few blew up the Roman Empire.

Sacrifice on God's altar earth's purest and best. He who struggles is better than he who never attempts. Even to look on one who has given up has a purifying effect. Stand up for God; let the world go. Have no compromise. Give up the world, then alone you are loosened from the body. When it dies, you are *azad,* free. Be free. Death alone can never free us. Freedom must be attained by our own efforts during life; then, when the body falls, there will be no rebirth for the free.

Truth is to be judged by truth and by nothing else. Doing good is not the test of truth; the sun needs no torch by which to see it. Even if truth destroys the whole universe, still it is truth: stand by it.

Practising the concrete forms of religion is easy and attracts the masses; but really there is nothing in the external.

"As the spider throws her web out of herself and draws it in, even so this universe is thrown out and drawn in by God."

TUESDAY, *August 6.*

Without the "I" there can be no "you" outside. From this some philosophers came to the conclusion that the external world did not exist save in the subject; that the "you" existed only in the "I". Others have argued that the "I" can only be known through the "you" and with equal logic. These two views are partial truths, each wrong in part and each right in part. Thought is as much material and as much in nature as body is. Both matter and mind exist in a third, a unity which divides itself into the two. This unity is the Atman, the real Self.

There is Being, "x", which is manifesting itself as both mind and matter. Its movements in the seen are along certain fixed lines called law. As a unity, it is free; as many, it is bound by law. Still, with all this bondage, an idea of freedom is ever present, and this is Nivritti or the "dragging (withdrawal) from attachment". The materialising forces which through desire lead us to take an active part in worldly affairs are called Pravritti.

That action is moral which frees us from the bondage of matter and vice versa. This world appears infinite because everything is in a circle; it returns to whence it came. The circle meets, so there is no rest or peace here in any place. We must get out. Mukti is the one end to be attained.

• • • •

Evil changes in form, but remains the same in quality. In ancient times force ruled, today it is cunning. Misery in India is not so bad as in America, because the poor man here sees the greater contrast to his own bad condition.

Good and evil are inextricably combined, and one cannot be had without the other. The sum total of energy in this universe is like a lake, every wave inevitably leads to a corresponding depression. The sum total is absolutely the same; so to make one man happy is to make another unhappy. External happiness is material and the supply is fixed; so that not one grain can be had by one person without taking from another. Only bliss beyond the material world can be had without loss to any. Material happiness is but a transformation of material sorrow.

Those who are born in the wave and keep in it, do not see the depression and what is there. Never think you can make the world better and happier. The bullock in the oil-mill never reaches the wisp of hay tied in front of him, he only grinds out the oil. So we chase the will-o'-the-wisp of happiness that always eludes us and we only grind Nature's mill, then die merely to begin again. If we could get rid of evil, we should never catch a glimpse of anything higher; we would be satisfied and never struggle to get free. When man finds that all search for happiness in matter is nonsense, then religion begins. All human knowledge is but a part of religion.

In the human body the balance between good and evil is so even that there is a chance for man to wish to free himself from both.

The free never became bound; to ask how he did, is an illogical question. Where no bondage is, there is no cause and effect. "I became a fox in a dream and a dog chased me." Now how can I ask why the dog chased me? The fox was a part of the dream and the dog followed as a matter of course; but both belong to the dream and have no existence outside. Science and religion are both attempts to help us out of the bondage; only religion is the more ancient and we have the superstition that it is the more holy. In a way it is, because it makes morality a vital point and science does not.

"Blessed are the pure in heart, for they shall see God." This sentence alone would save mankind, if all books and prophets were lost. This purity of heart will bring the vision of God. It is the theme of the whole music of this universe. In purity is no bondage. Remove the veils of ignorance by purity, then we manifest ourselves as we really are and know that we were never in bondage. The seeing of many is the great sin of all the world. See all as Self and love all; let all idea of separateness go.

The diabolical man is a part of my body as a wound or a burn is. We have to nurse it and get it better; so continually nurse and help the diabolical man until he "heals" and is once more happy and healthy.

While we think on the relative plane, we have the right to believe that as bodies we can be hurt by relative things and equally that we can be helped by them. This idea of help, abstracted, is what we call God. The sum total of all ideas of help is God.

God is the abstract compound of all that is merciful and good and helpful; that should be the sole idea. As Atman we have no body; so to say, "I am God and poison does not hurt me", is an absurdity. While there is a body and we see it, we have not realised God. Can the little whirlpool remain after the river vanishes? Cry for help and you will get it, and at last you will find that the one crying for help has vanished and so has the Helper, and the play is over; only the Self remains.

This once done, come back and play as you will. This

body can then do no evil, because it is not until the evil forces are all burnt out that liberation comes. All dross has been burnt out and there remains "flame without heat and without smoke"

The past momentum carries on the body, but it can only do good, because the bad was all gone before freedom came. The dying thief on the cross reaped the effects of his past actions He had been a Yogi and had slipped; then he had to be born again; again he slipped and became a thief; but the past good he had done bore fruit, and he met Jesus in the moment when liberation could come and one word made him free.

Buddha set his greatest enemy free because he, by hating him (Buddha) so much, kept constantly thinking of him; that thought purified his mind and he became ready for freedom. Therefore think of God all the time and that will purify you.

CONVERSATIONS

I[1]

STARTING THE RAMAKRISHNA MISSION—DID SWAMI VIVEKANANDA DIFFER FROM SHRI RAMAKRISHNA—SWAMI VIVEKANANDA'S ATTITUDE TOWARDS SHRI RAMAKRISHNA—THE LAW OF GRACE—GIRISH CHANDRA GHOSH

[Place: *Baghbazar, Calcutta. May 1, 1897*]

Swami Vivekananda has been staying for some days at the house of the late Balaram Bose. At his wish, a large number of devotees of Shri Ramakrishna have assembled at the house at 3 p.m. Swami Yogananda is amongst those present here. The object of Swamiji is to form an association. When all present had taken their seats, Swamiji proceeded to speak as follows:

"The conviction has grown in my mind after all my travels in various lands that no great cause can succeed without an organisation. In a country like ours, however, it does not seem quite practicable to me to start an organisation at once with a democratic basis or work by general voting. People in the West are more educated in this respect, and less jealous of one another than ourselves. They have learnt to respect merit. Take for instance my case. I was just an insignificant man there, and yet see how cordially they received and entertained me. When with the spread of education the masses in our country grow more sympathetic and liberal, when they learn to have their thoughts expanded beyond the limits of sect or party, then it will be possible to work on the democratic basis of organisation. For this reason it is necessary to have a dictator for this society. Everybody should obey him, and then in time we may work on the principle of general voting.

"Let this association be named after him in whose name, indeed, we have embraced the monastic life, with whom as your ideal in life you all toil on the field of work from your station in family-life, within twenty years of whose passing away a wonderful diffusion of his holy name and extraordinary life

[1] Sections I—V recorded by Sharat Chandra Chakravarty, a disciple of Swami Vivekananda.

has taken place both in the East and the West. We are the servants of the Lord. Be you all helpers in this cause."

When Srijut Girish Chandra Ghosh and all other householder disciples present had approved of the above proposal, the future programme of this Society of Shri Ramakrishna was taken up for discussion. The Society was named the Ramakrishna Mission.

Swamiji himself became the general President of the Mission and other office-bearers also were elected. The rule was laid down that the association should hold meetings at the house of Balaram Babu every Sunday at 4 p.m. Needless to say that Swamiji used to attend these meetings whenever convenient.

When the meeting had broken up and the members departed, addressing Swami Yogananda Swamiji said, "So the work is now begun this way; let us see how far it succeeds by the will of Shri Ramakrishna."

Swami Yogananda: You are doing these things with Western methods. Should you say Shri Ramakrishna left us any such instructions?

Swamiji: Well, how do you know that all this is not on Shri Ramakrishna's lines? He had an infinite breadth of feeling, and dare you shut him up within your own limited views of life? I will break down these limits and scatter broadcast over the earth his boundless inspiration. He never instructed me to introduce any rites of his own worship. We have to realise the teachings he has left us about religious practice and devotion, concentration and meditation and such higher ideas and truths, and then preach these to all men. The infinite number of faiths are only so many paths. I haven't been born to found one more sect in a world already teeming with sects. We have been blessed with obtaining refuge at the feet of the Master, and we are born to carry his message to the dwellers of the three worlds.

Swami Yogananda uttered no word of dissent and so Swamiji continued: Time and again have I received in this life marks of his grace. He stands behind and gets all this work done by me. When lying helpless under a tree in an agony of hunger, when I had not even a scrap of cloth for Kaupin, when I was resolved on travelling penniless round the world, even then help came in all ways by the grace of Shri Ramakrishna. And again when crowds jostled with one another in the streets of Chicago to have a sight of this Vivekananda, then also I could digest without difficulty all that honour—a hundredth part of which would have been enough to turn mad any ordinary man—because I had his grace, and by his will, victory followed me everywhere. Now I must conclude by doing something in this country. So casting all doubt away, please help my work; and you will find everything fulfilled by his will.

Swami Yogananda: Yes, whatever you will, shall be fulfilled; and are we not all ever obedient to you? Now and then I do clearly see how Shri Ramakrishna is getting all these things done through you. And yet, to speak plainly, some misgiving rises at intervals, for as we saw it, his way of doing things was different. So I question myself: Are we sure that we are not going astray from Shri Ramakrishna's teachings?—and so I take the opposing attitude and warn you.

Swamiji: You see, the fact is that Shri Ramakrishna is not exactly what the ordinary followers have comprehended him to be. He had infinite moods and phases. Even if you might form an idea of the limits of Brahmajnâna, the knowledge of the Absolute, you could not do the same with the unfathomable depths of his mind! Thousands of Vivekanandas may spring forth through one gracious glance of his eyes! But instead of doing that, he has chosen to get things done this time through me as his single instrument, and what can I do in this matter, you see?

Saying this, Swamiji left to attend to something else waiting for him, and Swami Yogananda went on praising Swamiji's versatile gifts.

Meanwhile Swamiji returned and asked the disciple, "Do the people in your part of the country know much of Shri Ramakrishna?"

Disciple: Only one man, Nag Mahâshaya, came to Shri Ramakrishna from our part of Bengal; it is from him that many came to hear of him and had their curiosity excited to know more. But that Shri Ramakrishna was the Incarnation of God, the people there have not yet come to know, and some would not believe it even if told so.

Swamiji: Do you think it is an easy matter to believe so? We who had actual dealings with him in every respect, we who heard of that fact again and again from his own lips, we who lived and stayed with him for twenty-four hours of the day—even we off and on have doubts about it coming over us! So what to speak of others!

Disciple: Did Shri Ramakrishna out of his own lips ever say that he was God, the all-perfect Brahman?

Swamiji: Yes, he did so many times. And he said this to all of us. One day while he was staying at the Cossipore garden, his body in imminent danger of falling off for ever, by the side of his bed I was saying in my mind: 'Well, now if you can declare that you are God, then only will I believe you are really God Himself". It was only two days before he passed away. Immediately, he looked up towards me all on a sudden and said, "He who was Râma, He who was Krishna, verily is now Ramakrishna in this body. And that not merely from the standpoint of your Vedanta!"[1] At this I was struck dumb. Even we haven't yet had perfect faith, after hearing it again and again from the holy lips of our Lord himself—our minds still get disturbed now and then with doubt and despair—and so, what shall we speak of others being slow to believe? It is indeed a very difficult thing to be able to declare and believe a man with a body like ours to be God Himself. We may just go to the length of declaring him to be a "perfected one", or a "knower of Brahman". Well, it matters little what you may call him or think of him—a saint or a knower of Brahman, or anything. But take it from me, never did come to this earth such an all-perfect man as Shri Ramakrishna! In the utter darkness of the world this great man is like the shining pillar of illumination in this age! And by his light alone will man now cross the ocean of Samsâra!

Disciple: To me it seems, sir, that true faith comes only after actually seeing or hearing something. Mathur Babu,[2] I have heard, actually saw so many things about Shri Ramakrishna, and thus had that wonderful faith in him.

Swamiji: He who believes not, believes not even after seeing, and thinks that it is all hallucination, or dream and so on. The great transfiguration of Krishna, the Vishvarupa (form universal), was seen alike by Duryodhana and by Arjuna. But only Arjuna believed, while Duryodhana took it to be

[1] By realising the Brahman, sages may declare their identity with any being, such as Manu and so forth. Vide the *Vedanta-Sutras*, I. i. 30.

[2] Son-in-law of Rani Rashmani, the foundress of the Temple at Dakshineswar.

magic! Unless He makes us understand, nothing can be stated or understood. Somebody comes to the fullest faith even without seeing or hearing, while somebody else remains plunged in doubt even after witnessing various extraordinary powers for twelve years, with his own eyes! The secret of it all is His grace! But then one must persevere, so that the grace may be received.

Disciple: Is there, sir, any law of grace.

Swamiji: Yes and no.

Disciple: How is that?

Swamiji: Those who are pure always in body, mind, and speech, who have strong devotion, who discriminate between the real and the unreal, who persevere in meditation and contemplation—upon them alone the grace of the Lord descends. The Lord, however, is beyond all natural laws—is not under any rules and regulations, or, just as Shri Ramakrishna used to say, He has the child's nature—and that's why we find some failing to get any response even after calling on Him for millions of births, while some one else whom we regard as a sinful man, or a disbeliever, would have illumination in a flash! On the latter the Lord perhaps lavishes His grace quite unsolicited! You may argue that this man had good merits stored up from previous life, but the mystery is really difficult to understand. Shri Ramakrishna used to say sometimes, "Do rely on Him; be like the dry leaf at the mercy of the wind"; and again he would say, "The wind of His grace is always blowing, what you need to do is to unfurl your sail."

Disciple: But, sir, this is a most tremendous statement. No reasoning, I see, can stand here.

Swamiji: Ah, the limit of all reasoning and arguing is in the realm of Mâyâ; it lies within the categories of time, space, and causation. But He is beyond these categories. We speak of His law, still He is beyond all law. He creates, or becomes, all that we speak of as laws of nature, and yet He is outside of them all. He on whom His grace descends, in a moment goes beyond all law. For this reason there is no condition in grace. It is as His play or sport. All this creation of the universe is like His Play—लोकवत्तु लीलाकैवल्यम्—"It is the pure delight of sport, as in the case of men."[1] Is it not possible

[1] *Vedanta-Sutras,* II. i. 33.

for Him who creates and destroys the universe, as if in play, to grant salvation by grace to the greatest sinner? But then it is just His pleasure, His play, to get somebody through the practice of spiritual discipline and somebody else without it.

Disciple: Sir, I can't understand this.

Swamiji: And you needn't. Only get your mind to cling to Him as far as you can. For then only the great magic of this world will break of itself. But then, you must persevere. You must take off your mind from lust and lucre, must discriminate always between the real and the unreal—must settle down into the mood of bodilessness with the brooding thought that you are not this body, and must always have the realisation that you are the all-pervading Atman. This persevering practice is called Purushakâra (self-exertion—as distinguished from grace). By such self-exertion will come true reliance on Him, and that is the goal of human achievement.

After a pause Swamiji resumed: Had you not been receiving His grace, how else would you come here at all? Shri Ramakrishna used to say, "Those who have had the grace of God cannot but come here. Wherever they might be, whatever they might be doing, they are sure to be affected by words or sentiments uttered from here."[1] Just take your own case—do you think it is possible without the grace of God to have the blessed company of Nag Mahashaya, a man who rose to spiritual perfection through the strength of divine grace and came to know fully what this grace really means? अनेकजन्मसंसिद्ध-स्ततो याति परां गतिम्—"One attains the highest goal after being perfected by the practice of repeated births" (Gita). It is only by virtue of great religious merit acquired through many births that one comes across a great soul like him. All the characteristics of the highest type of Bhakti, spoken of in the scriptures, have manifested themselves in Nag Mahashaya. It is only in him that we actually see fulfilled the widely quoted text, तृणादपि सुनीचेन ।[2] Blessed indeed is your East Bengal to have been hallowed by the touch of Nag Mahashaya's feet!

While speaking thus, Swamiji rose to pay a visit to the

[1] With his egoism perfectly merged in the consciousness of the Mother, the use of the word "here" by Shri Ramakrishna would often stand for the ordinary reference to self. By "here" is evidently meant the centre of the Mother's self-revelation.

[2] "Lowlier far than the lowly stalk of grass."

great poet, Babu Girish Chandra Ghosh. Swami Yogananda and the disciple followed him. Reaching Girish Babu's place, Swamiji seated himself and said: You see, G. C., the impulse is constantly coming nowadays to my mind to do this and to do that, to scatter broadcast on earth the message of Shri Ramakrishna and so on. But I pause again to reflect, lest all this give rise to another sect in India. So I have to work with a good deal of caution. Sometimes I think: What if a sect does grow up? But again the thought comes—No. Shri Ramakrishna never disturbed anybody's own spiritual outlook; he always looked at the inner sameness. Often do I restrain myself with this thought. Now, what do you say?

Girish Babu: What can I say to this? You are the instrument in his hand. You have to do just what he would have you do. I don't trouble myself over the detail. But I see that the power of the Lord is getting things done by you. I see it clear as daylight.

Swamiji: But I think we do things according to our own will. Yet, that in misfortunes and adversities, in times of want and poverty, he reveals himself to us and guides us along the true path—this I have been able to realise. But alas, I still fail to comprehend in any way the greatness of his power.

Girish Babu: Yes, he said, "If you understand it to the full, everything will at once vanish. Who will work then, or who will be made to work?"

After this the talk drifted on to America. And Swamiji grew warm on his subject and went on describing the wonderful wealth of the country, the virtues and defects of men and women there, their luxury and so on.

II

INDIA WANTS NOT LECTURING BUT WORK—THE CRYING PROBLEM IN INDIA IS POVERTY—YOUNG SANNYASINS TO BE TRAINED BOTH AS SECULAR AND SPIRITUAL TEACHERS AND WORKERS FOR THE MASSES—EXHORTATION TO YOUNG MEN TO WORK FOR OTHERS

[PLACE: *The Belur Math while under construction.* YEAR: *1898.*]

Disciple: How is it, Swamiji, that you do not lecture in this country? You have stirred Europe and America with your lectures, but coming back here you have kept silence.

Swamiji: In this country, the ground should be prepared first; then if the seed is sown, the plant will come out best. The ground in the West, in Europe and America, is very fertile and fit for sowing seeds. There, they have reached the climax of Bhoga (enjoyment). Being satiated with Bhoga to the full, their minds are not getting peace now, even in those enjoyments, and they feel as if they wanted something else. In this country you have neither Bhoga nor Yoga (renunciation). When one is satiated with Bhoga, then it is that one will listen to and understand the teachings on Yoga. What good will lectures do in a country like India which has become the birthplace of disease, sorrow, and affliction, and where men are emaciated through starvation, and weak in mind?

Disciple: How is that? Do you not say that ours is the land of religion and that here the people understand religion as they do nowhere else? Why then will not this country be animated by your inspiring eloquence and reap to the full the fruits thereof?

Swamiji: Now understand what religion means. The first thing required is the worship of the Kurma (tortoise) Incarnation, and the belly-god is this Kurma, as it were. Until you pacify this, no one will welcome your words about religion. India is restless with the thought of how to face this spectre of hunger. The draining of the best resources of the country by the foreigners, the unrestricted exports of merchandise, and, above all, the abominable jealousy natural to slaves, are eating into the vitals of India. First of all, you must remove this evil of hunger and starvation, this constant anxiety for bare existence, from those to whom you want to preach religion; otherwise, lectures and such things will be of no benefit.

Disciple: What should we do then to remove that evil?

Swamiji: First, some young men full of the spirit of renunciation are needed—those who will be ready to sacrifice their lives for others, instead of devoting themselves to their own happiness. With this object in view I shall establish a Math to train young Sannyâsins, who will go from door to door and make the people realise their pitiable condition by means of facts and reasoning, and instruct them in the ways and means for their welfare, and at the same time will explain to them as clearly as possible, in very simple and easy language, the higher truths of religion. The masses in our country are like the sleeping Leviathan. The education imparted by the present university system reaches one or two per cent of the masses only. And even those who get that do not succeed in their endeavours of doing any good to their country. But it is not their fault, poor fellows! As soon as they come out of their college, they find themselves fathers of several children! Somehow or other they manage to secure the position of a clerk, or at the most, a deputy magistrate. This is the finale of education! With the burden of a family on their backs, they find no time to do anything great or think anything high. They do not find means enough to fulfil their personal wants and interests; so what can be expected of them in the way of doing anything for others?

Disciple: Is there then no way out for us?

Swamiji: Certainly there is. This is the land of Religion Eternal. The country has fallen, no doubt, but will as surely rise again, and that upheaval will astound the world. The lower the hollows the billows make, the higher and with greater force will they rise again.

Disciple: How will India rise again?

Swamiji: Do you not see? The dawn has already appeared in the eastern sky, and there is little delay in the sun's rising. You all set your shoulders to the wheel! What is there in making the world all in all and thinking of "My Samsâra, my Samsara"? Your duty at present is to go from one part of the country to another, from village to village, and make the people understand that mere sitting idly won't do any more. Make them understand their real condition and say, "O ye brothers, arise! awake! How much longer would you remain asleep!" Go and advise them how to improve their own condition, and make them comprehend the sublime truths of the Shâstras, by presenting them in a lucid and popular way. So long the Brahmins have monopolised religion; but since they cannot hold their ground against the strong tide of time, go and take steps so that one and all in the land may get that religion. Impress upon their minds that they have the same right to religion as the Brahmins. Initiate all, even down to the Chandâlas, in these fiery Mantras. Also instruct them, in simple words, about the necessities of life, and in trade, commerce, agriculture, etc. If you cannot do this, then fie upon your education and culture, and fie upon your studying the Vedas and Vedanta!

Disciple: But where is that strength in us? I should have felt myself blessed if I had a hundredth part of your powers, Swamiji.

Swamiji: How foolish! Power and things like that will come by themselves. Put yourself to work, and you will find such tremendous power coming to you that you will feel it hard to bear. Even the least work done for others awakens the power within; even thinking the least good of others gradually instils into the heart the strength of a lion. I love you all ever so much, but I wish you all to die working for others—I should rather be glad to see you do that!

Disciple: What will become of those, then, who depend on me?

Swamiji: If you are ready to sacrifice your life for others, God will certainly provide some means for them. Have you not read in the Gita the words of Shri Krishna, न हि, कल्याणकृत्कश्चित् दुर्गतिं तात गच्छति—"Never does a doer of good, O my beloved, come to grief"?

Disciple: I see, sir.

Swamiji: The essential thing is renunciation. Without renunciation none can pour out his whole heart in working for others. The man of renunciation sees all with an equal eye and devotes himself to the service of all. Does not our Vedanta also teach us to see all with an equal eye? Why then do you cherish the idea that the wife and children are your own, more than others? At your very threshold, Nârâyana Himself, in the form of a poor beggar, is dying of starvation! Instead of giving him anything, would you only satisfy the appetites of your wife and children with delicacies? Why, that is beastly!

Disciple: To work for others requires a good deal of money at times, and where shall I get that?

Swamiji: Why not do as much as lies within your power? Even if you cannot give to others for want of money, surely you can at least breathe into their ears some good words or impart some good instruction, can't you? Or does that also require money?

Disciple: Yes, sir, that I can do.

Swamiji: But saying, "I can", won't do. Show me through action what you can do, and then only I shall know that your coming to me is turned to some good account. Get up, and put your shoulders to the wheel—how long is this life for? As you have come into this world, leave some mark behind. Otherwise, where is the difference between you and the trees and stones? They, too, come into existence, decay, and die. If you like to be born and to die like them you are at liberty to do so. Show me by your actions that your reading the Vedanta has been fruitful of the highest good. Go and tell all, "In every one of you lies that Eternal Power", and try to wake It up. What will you do with individual salvation? That is sheer selfishness. Throw aside your meditation, throw away your salvation and such things! Put your whole heart and soul in the work to which I have consecrated myself.

With bated breath the disciple heard these inspiring words, and Swamiji went on with his usual fire and eloquence.

Swamiji: First of all, make the soil ready, and thousands of Vivekanandas will in time be born into this world to deliver lectures on religion. You needn't worry yourself about that! Don't you see why I am starting orphanages, famine-relief works, etc? Don't you see how Sister Nivedita, a British lady, has learnt to serve Indians so well, by doing even menial work for them? And can't you, being Indians, similarly serve your own fellow-countrymen? Go, all of you, wherever there is an outbreak of plague or famine, or wherever the people are in distress, and mitigate their sufferings. At the most you may die in the attempt—what of that? How many like you are being born and dying like worms every day? What difference does that make to the world at large? Die you must, but have a great ideal to die for, and it is better to die with a great ideal in life. Preach this ideal from door to door, and you will yourselves be benefited by it at the same time that you are doing good to your country. On you lie the future hopes of our country. I feel extreme pain to see you leading a life of inaction. Set yourselves to work—to work! Do not tarry—the time of death is approaching day by day: Do not sit idle, thinking that everything will be done in time, later on! Mind—nothing will be done that way!

III

THE DOCTRINE OF AHIMSA AND MEAT-EATING—THE SATTVA, RAJAS, AND TAMAS IN MAN—DISCRIMINATION OF FOOD AND SPIRITUALITY —'AHARA'—THE THREE DEFECTS IN FOOD—DON'T-TOUCHISM AND CASTE-PREJUDICES—PLAN OF RESTORING THE OLD CHATURVARNYA AND THE LAWS OF THE RISHIS

[PLACE: *The Belur Math while under construction.* YEAR: *1898.*]

Disciple: Pray, Swamiji, do tell me if there is any relation between the discrimination of food taken and the development of spirituality in man.

Swamiji: Yes, there is, more or less.

Disciple: Is it proper or necessary to take fish and meat?

Swamiji: Ay, take them, my boy! And if there be any harm in doing so, I will take care of that. Look at the masses of our country! What a look of sadness on their faces and want of courage and enthusiasm in their hearts, with large stomachs and no strength in their hands and feet—a set of cowards frightened at every trifle!

Disciple: Does the taking of fish and meat give strength? Why do Buddhism and Vaishnavism preach —अहिंसा परमो धर्मः —"Non-killing is the highest virtue"?

Swamiji: Buddhism and Vaishnavism are not two different things. During the decline of Buddhism in India, Hinduism took from her a few cardinal tenets of conduct and made them her own, and these have now come to be known as Vaishnavism. The Buddhist tenet, "Non-killing is supreme virtue," is very good, but in trying to enforce it upon all by legislation without paying any heed to the capacities of the people at large, Buddhism has brought ruin upon India. I have come across many a "religious heron"[1] in India, who feed ants with sugar, and at the same time would not hesitate to bring ruin on his own brother for the sake of "filthy lucre"!

Disciple: But in the Vedas as well as in the laws of Manu, there are injunctions to take fish and meat.

[1] Meaning, religious hypocrite. The heron, so the story goes, gave it out to the fishes that he had forsaken his old habit of catching fish and turned highly religious. So he took his stand by the brink of the water and feigned to be meditating, while in reality he was always watching his opportunity to catch the unwary fish.

Swamiji: Ay, and injunctions to abstain from killing as well. For the Vedas enjoin—मा हिंस्यात् सर्वभूतानि—"Cause no injury to any being," and Manu also has said— निवृत्तिस्तु महाफला —"Cessation of desire brings great results." Killing and non-killing have both been enjoined, according to the individual capacity, or fitness and adaptability, of those who will observe the one practice or the other.

Disciple: It is the fashion here nowadays to give up fish and meat as soon as one takes to religion, and to many it is more sinful not to do so than to commit such great sins as adultery. How, do you think, such notions came into existence?

Swamiji: What's the use of your knowing how they came, when you see clearly, do you not, that such notions are working ruin to our country and our society? Just see—the people of East Bengal eat much fish, meat and turtle, and they are much healthier than those of this part of Bengal. Even the rich men of East Bengal have not yet taken to Loochis or Chapatis at night, and they do not suffer from acidity and dyspepsia like us. I have heard that in the villages of East Bengal the people have not the slightest idea of what dyspepsia means!

Disciple: Quite so, Swamiji. We never complain of dyspepsia in our part of the country. I first heard of it after coming to these parts. We take fish with rice, mornings and evenings.

Swamiji: Yes, take as much of that as you can, without fearing criticism. The country has been flooded with dyspeptic Babajis living on vegetables only. That is no sign of Sattva, but of deep Tamas—the shadow of death. Brightness in the face, undaunted enthusiasm in the heart, and tremendous activity—these result from Sattva; whereas idleness, lethargy, inordinate attachment and sleep are the signs of Tamas.

Disciple: But do not fish and meat increase Rajas in man?

Swamiji: That is what I want you to have. Rajas is badly needed just now! More than ninety per cent of those whom you now take to be men with the Sattva quality are only steeped in the deepest Tamas. Enough if you find one-sixteenth of them to be really Sâttvika! What we want now is an immense awakening of Râjasika energy, for the whole country is wrapped in the shroud of Tamas. The people of this land must be fed and clothed, must be awakened, must be made more fully active. Otherwise they will become inert, as inert as trees and stones. So, I say, eat large quantities of fish and meat, my boy!

Disciple: Does a liking for fish and meat remain when one has fully developed the Sattva quality?

Swamiji: No, it does not. All liking for fish and meat disappears when pure Sattva is highly developed, and these are the signs of its manifestation in a soul—sacrifice of everything for others, perfect non-attachment to lust and wealth, want of pride and egoism. The desire for animal food goes when these things are seen in a man. And where such indications are absent, and yet you find men siding with the non-killing party, know it for a certainty that here there is either hypocrisy or a show of religion. When you yourself come to that state of pure Sattva, give up fish and meat, by all means.

Disciple: But in the Chhândogya Upanishad there is the passage, आहारशुद्धौ सत्त्वशुद्धिः —"Through pure food the Sattva quality in a man becomes pure."

Swamiji: Yes, I know. Shankarâchârya has said that the word Âhâra there means "objects of the senses", whereas Shri Râmânuja has taken the meaning of Ahara to be "food". In my opinion we should take that meaning of the word which reconciles both these points of view. Are we to pass our lives discussing all the time about the purity and impurity of food only, or are we to practise the restraining of our senses? Surely, the restraining of the senses is the main object; and the discrimination of good and bad, pure and impure foods, only helps one, to a certain extent, in gaining that end. There are, according to our scriptures, three things which make food impure: (1) Jâti-dosha, or natural defects of a certain class of food, like onions, garlic, etc.; (2) Nimitta-dosha, or defects arising from the presence of external impurities in it, such as dead insects, dust, etc., that attach to sweetmeats bought in shops; (3) Âshraya-dosha or defects that arise by the food coming from evil sources, as when it has been touched and handled by wicked persons. Special care should be taken to avoid the first and second classes of defects. But in this country men pay no regard just to these two, and go on fighting for the third alone, the very one that none but a Yogi could really discriminate! The country from end to end is being bored to extinction by the cry, "Don't touch", "Don't touch" of the non-touchism party. In that exclusive circle of theirs, too, there is no discrimination of good and bad men, for their food may be taken from the hands of anyone who wears a thread round his neck and calls himself a Brahmin! Shri Ramakrishna was quite unable to take food in this indiscriminate way from the hands of any and all. It happened many a time that he would not accept food touched by a certain person or persons, and on rigorous investigation it would turn out that these had some particular stain to hide. Your religion seems nowadays to be confined to the cooking-pot alone. You put on one side the sublime truths of religion and fight, as they say, for the skin of the fruit and not for the fruit itself!

Disciple: Do you mean, then, that we should eat the food handled by anyone and everyone?

Swamiji: Why so? Look here. You being a Brahmin of a certain class, say, of the Bhattâchârya class, why should you not eat rice cooked by Brahmins of all classes? Why should you, who belong to the Râhri section, object to taking rice cooked by a Brahmin of the Vârendra section or why should a Varendra object to taking your rice? Again, why should not the other sub-castes in the west and south of India, e.g. the Mahratti, Telingi, Kanouji, do the same? Do you not see that hundreds of Brahmins and Kâyasthas in Bengal now go secretly to eat dainties in public restaurants, and, when they come out of those places, pose as leaders of society and frame rules to support don't-touchism? Must our society really be guided by laws dictated by such hypocrites? No, I say. On the contrary we must turn them out. The laws laid down by the great Rishis of old must be brought back and be made to rule supreme once more. Then alone can national well-being be ours.

Disciple: Then, do not the laws laid down by the Rishis rule and guide our present society?

Swamiji: Vain delusion! Where indeed is that the case nowadays? Nowhere have I found the laws of the Rishis current in India, even when during my travels I searched carefully and thoroughly. The blind and, not unoften, meaningless, customs sanctioned by the people, local prejudices and ideas, and the usages and ceremonials prevalent amongst women, are what really govern society everywhere! How many care to read the Shâstras or to lead society according to their ordinances after careful study?

Disciple: What are we to do, then?

Swamiji: We must revive the old laws of the Rishis. We must initiate the whole people into the codes of our old Manu and Yâjnavalkya with a few modifications here and there to adjust them to the changed circumstances of the time. Do you not see that nowhere in India now are the original four castes (Châturvarnya) to be found? We have to redivide the whole Hindu population, grouping it under the four main castes of Brahmins, Kshatriyas, Vaishyas, and Shudras, as of old. The numberless modern subdivisions of the Brahmins that split them up into so many castes, as it were, have to be abolished and a single Brahmin caste to be made by uniting them all. Each of the three remaining castes also will have to be brought similarly into single groups, as was the case in Vedic times. Without this will the Motherland be really benefited by your simply crying, as you do nowadays, "We won't touch you!"; "We won't take him back into our caste!"? Never, my boy!

IV

BRAHMAN, ISHVARA, JIVA, AND AVIDYA—RENUNCIATION AND SELF-REALISATION—HOW TO CONTROL THE MIND—ATMAN AS THE OBJECT OF MEDITATION—JNANA, BHAKTI, KARMA, AND YOGA—THE DOCTRINE OF INCARNATION OF GOD—EXHORTATION FOR SELF-REALISATION—WORKS OF A JNANI

[PLACE: *Belur Math*. YEAR: *1899*.]

Swamiji is now in very good health. The disciple has come to the Math on a Sunday morning. After visiting Swamiji he has come downstairs and is discussing the Vedantic scriptures with Swami Nirmalananda. At this moment Swamiji himself came downstairs and, addressing the disciple, said, "What were you discussing with Nirmalananda?"

Disciple: Sir, he was saying, "The Brahman of the Vedanta is only known to you and your Swamiji. We on the contrary know, कृष्णस्तु भगवान् स्वयं—that Shri Krishna is the Lord incarnate."

Swamiji: What did you say?

Disciple: I said that the Âtman is the one Truth, and that Krishna was merely a person who had realised this Atman. Swami Nirmalananda is at heart a beliver in the Advaita Vedanta, but outwardly he takes up the dualistic side. His first idea seems to be to moot the personal aspect of the Ishvara and then by a gradual process of reasoning to strengthen the foundations of Vedanta. But as soon as he calls me a "Vaishnava" I forget his real intention and begin a heated discussion with him.

Swamiji: He loves you and so enjoys the fun of teasing you. But why should you be upset by his words? You will also answer, "You, sir, are an atheist, a believer in nihility".

Disciple: Sir, is there any such statement in the Upanishads that Ishvara is an all-powerful Person? But people generally believe in such an Ishvara.

Swamiji: The highest principle, the Lord of all, cannot be a Person. The Jiva is an individual and the sum total of all Jivas is the Ishvara. In the Jiva, Avidyâ or Nescience is predominant, but Ishvara controls Maya composed of Avidya and Vidyâ and independently projects this world of moving and immovable things out of Himself. But Brahman transcends both the individual and collective aspects, the Jiva and Ishvara. In Brahman there is no part. It is for the sake of easy comprehension that parts have been imagined in It. That part of Brahman in which there is the superimposition of creation, maintenance, and dissolution of the universe, has been spoken of as Ishvara in the scriptures. While the other unchangeable portion, with reference to which there is no thought of duality, is indicated as Brahman. But do not on that account think that Brahman is a distinct and separate substance from the Jivas and the universe. The qualified monists hold that it is Brahman that has transformed Itself into Jivas and the universe. The Advaitins, on the contrary, maintain that jivas and the universe have been merely superimposed on Brahman. But in reality there has been no modification in Brahman. The Advaitin says that the universe consists only in name and form. It endures only so long as there are name and form. When through meditation and other practices name and form are dissolved then only the transcendent Brahman remains. Then the separate reality of Jivas and the universe is felt no longer. Then it is realised that one is the Eternal, Pure Essence of Intelligence, or Brahman. The real nature of the Jiva is Brahman. When the veil of name and form vanishes through meditation etc., then that idea is simply realised. This is the substance of pure Advaita. The Vedas, the Vedanta, and all other scriptures only explain this idea in different ways.

Disciple: How, then, is it true that Ishvara is an almighty Person?

Swamiji: Man is man in so far as he is qualified by the limiting adjunct of mind. Through the mind he has to understand and grasp everything, and therefore whatever he thinks must be limited by the mind. Hence it is the natural tendency of man to argue, from the analogy of his own personality, the personality of Ishvara (God). Man can only think of his ideal as a human being. When, buffeted by sorrows in this world of disease and death, he is driven to desperation and helplessness, then he seeks refuge with someone, relying on whom he may feel safe. But where is that refuge to be found? The omnipresent Atman which depends on nothing else to support It, is the only Refuge. At first man does not find that. When discrimination and dispassion arise in the course of meditation and spiritual practices, he comes to know it. But in whatever way he may progress on the path of spirituality, everyone is unconsciously awakening the Brahman within him. But the means may be different in different cases. Those who have faith in the Personal God, have to undergo spiritual practices holding on to that idea. If there is sincerity, through that will come the awakening of the lion of Brahman within. The knowledge of Brahman is the one goal of all beings, but the various ideas are the various paths to it. Although the real nature of the Jiva is Brahman, still as he has identification with the qualifying adjunct of mind, he suffers from all sorts of doubts and difficulties, pleasure and pain. But everyone from Brahmâ down to a blade of grass is advancing towards the realisation of his real nature. And none can escape the round of births and deaths until he realises his identity with Brahman. Getting the human birth, when the desire for freedom becomes very strong, and along with it comes the grace of a person of realisation, then man's desire for Self-knowledge becomes intensified. Otherwise the mind of men given to lust and greed never inclines that way. How should the desire to know Brahman arise in one who has the hankering in his mind for the pleasures of family life, for wealth, and for fame? He who is prepared to renounce all, who amid the strong current of the duality of good and evil, happiness and misery, is calm, steady, balanced, and awake to his Ideal, alone endeavours to attain to Self-knowledge. He alone by the might of his own power tears asunder the net of the world, and breaking the barriers of Maya emerges like a mighty lion—निर्गच्छति जगज्जालात् पिञ्जरादिव केशरी ।

Disciple: Well, then, is it true that without Sannyâsa, there can be no knowledge of Brahman?

Swamiji: That is true, a thousand times. One must have both internal and external Sannyasa—renunciation in spirit as also formal renunciation. Shankarâchârya, in commenting on the Upanishadic text, "Neither by Tapas (spiritual practice) devoid of the necessary accompaniments", has said that by practising Sâdhanâ without the external badge of Sannyasa (the Gerua-robe, the staff, Kamandalu, etc.), Brahman, which is difficult to attain, is not realised. Without dispassion for the world, without renunciation, without giving up the desire for enjoyment absolutely, nothing can be accomplished in the spiritual life. "It is not like a sweetmeat in the hands of a child which you can snatch by a trick."[1]

Disciple: But, sir, in the course of spiritual practices, that renunciation may come.

Swamiji: Let those to whom it will come gradually, have it in that way. But why should you sit and wait for that? At once begin to dig the channel which will bring the waters of spirituality to your life. Shri Ramakrishna used to deprecate lukewarmness in spiritual practices, as, for instance, saying that religion would come gradually, and that there was no hurry for it. When one is thirsty, can one sit idle? Does he not run about for water? Because your thirst for spirituality has not come, therefore you are sitting idly. The desire for knowledge has not grown strong, therefore you are satisfied with the little pleasures of family life.

Disciple: Really I do not understand why I don't get that idea of renouncing everything. Do make some way for that, please.

Swamiji: The end and the means are all in your hands. I can only stimulate them. You have read so many scriptures and are serving and associating with such Brahmajnâni Sâdhus—if even this does not bring the idea of renunciation, then your life is in vain. But it will not be altogether vain—the effects of this will manifest some way or other in time.

The disciple was much dejected and again said to Swamiji,

[1] Song of Ramprasad.

"Sir, I have come under your refuge, do open the path of Mukti for me—that I may realise the Truth in this body."

Swamiji: What fear is there? Always discriminate—your body, your house, these Jivas, and the world are all absolutely unreal like a dream. Always think that this body is only an inert instrument. And the self-contained Purusha within is your real nature. The adjunct of mind is His first and subtle covering; then there is this body which is His gross, outer covering. The indivisible, changeless, self-effulgent Purusha is lying hidden under these delusive veils, therefore your real nature is unknown to you. The direction of the mind which always runs after the senses has to be turned within. The mind has to be killed. The body is but gross—it dies and dissolves in the five elements. But the bundle of mental impressions which is the mind, does not die soon. It remains for some time in seed-form and then sprouts and grows in the form of a tree—it takes on another physical body and goes the round of birth and death, until Self-knowledge arises. Therefore I say, by meditation and concentration and by the power of philosophical discrimination plunge this mind in the Ocean of Existence-Knowledge-Bliss Absolute. When the mind dies, all limiting adjuncts vanish and you are established in Brahman.

Disciple: Sir, it is so difficult to direct this uncontrollable mind towards Brahman.

Swamiji: Is there anything difficult for the hero? Only men of faint hearts speak so. वीराणामेव करतलगता मुक्तिः, न पुनः कापुरुषाणाम् —"Mukti is easy of attainment only to the hero—but not to cowards." Says the Gita, अभ्यासेन तु कौन्तेय वैराग्येण च गृह्यते —"By renunciation and by practice is the mind brought under control, O Arjuna." The Chitta or mindstuff is like a transparent lake, and the waves which rise in it by the impact of sense-impressions constitute Manas or the mind. Therefore the mind consists of a succession of thought-waves. From these mental waves arises desire. Then that desire transforms itself into will and works through its gross instrument, the body. Again, as work is endless, so its fruits also are endless. Hence the mind is always being tossed by countless myriads of waves—the fruits of work. This mind has to be divested of all modifications (Vrittis) and reconverted into the transparent lake, so that there remains not a single wave of modification in it. Then will Brahman manifest Itself. The scriptures give a glimpse of this state in such passages as: "Then all the knots of the heart are cut asunder," etc. Do you understand?

Disciple: Yes, sir, but meditation must base itself on some object?

Swamiji: You yourself will be the object of your meditation. Think and meditate that you are the omnipresent Atman. "I am neither the body, nor the mind, nor the Buddhi (determinative faculty), neither the gross nor the subtle body"—by this process of elimination, immerse your mind in the transcendent knowledge which is your real nature. Kill the mind by thus plunging it repeatedly in this. Then only you will realise the Essence of Intelligence, or be established in your real nature. Knower and known, meditator and the object meditated upon, will then become one, and the cessation of all phenomenal superimpositions will follow. This is styled in the Shâstras as the transcendence of the triad of relative knowledge (Triputibheda). There is no relative or conditioned knowledge in this state. When the Atman is the only knower, by what means can you possibly know it? The Atman is knowledge, the Atman is Intelligence, the Atman is Sacchidânanda. It is through the inscrutable power of Maya, which cannot be indicated as either existent or non-existent, that the relative consciousness has come upon the Jiva, who is none other than Brahman. This is generally known as the conscious state. And the state in which this duality of relative existence becomes one in the pure Brahman is called in the scriptures the superconscious state and described in such words as, स्तिमितसलिलराशिप्रख्यमाख्याविहीनं—"It is like an ocean perfectly at rest and without a name."

Swamiji spoke these words as if from the profound depths of realisation of Brahman.

Swamiji: All philosophy and scriptures have come from the plane of relative knowledge of subject and object. But no thought or language of the human mind can fully express the Reality which lies beyond the plane of relative knowledge! Science, philosophy, etc. are only partial truths. So they can never be the adequate channels of expression for the transcendent reality. Hence viewed from the transcendent standpoint, everything appears to be unreal—religious creeds, and works, I and thou, and the universe—everything is unreal! Then only it is perceived: I am the only reality; I am the all-pervading

Atman, and I am the proof of my own existence. Where is the room for a separate proof to establish the reality of my existence? I am, as the scriptures say, नित्यमस्मत्-प्रसिद्धम् —"always known to myself as the eternal subject." I have actually seen that state, realised it. You also see and realise it and preach this truth of Brahman to all. Then only will you attain to peace.

While speaking these words, Swamiji's face wore a serious expression and he was lost in thought. After some time he continued: "Realise in your own life this knowledge of Brahman which comprehends all theories and is the rationale of all truths, and preach it to the world. This will conduce to your own good and the good of others as well. I have told you today the essence of all truths; there is nothing higher than this."

Disciple: Sir, now you are speaking of Jnana; but sometimes you proclaim the superiority of Bhakti, sometimes of Karma, and sometimes of Yoga. This confuses our understanding.

Swamiji: Well, the truth is this, the knowledge of Brahman is the ultimate goal—the highest destiny of man. But man cannot remain absorbed in Brahman all the time. When he comes out of It, he must have something to engage himself. At that time he should do such work as will contribute to the real well-being of people. Therefore do I urge you in the service of Jivas in a spirit of oneness. But, my son, such are the intricacies of work, that even great saints are caught in them and become attached. Therefore work has to be done without any desire for results. This is the teaching of the Gita. But know that in the knowledge of Brahman there is no touch of any relation to work. Good works, at the most, purify the mind. Therefore has the commentator Shankara so sharply criticised the doctrine of the combination of Jnana and Karma. Some attain to the knowledge of Brahman by means of unselfish work. This is also a means, but the end is the realisation of Brahman. Know this thoroughly that the goal of the path of discrimination and of all other modes of practice is the realisation of Brahman.

Disciple: Now, sir, please tell me about the utility of Raja-Yoga and Bhakti-Yoga.

Swamiji: Striving in these paths also some attain to the realisation of Brahman. The path of Bhakti, or devotion to God, is a slow process, but is easy of practice. In the path of Yoga there are many obstacles; perhaps the mind runs after psychic powers and thus draws you away from attaining your real nature. Only the path of Jnana is of quick fruition and the rationale of all other creeds; hence it is equally esteemed in all countries and all ages. But even in the path of discrimination there is the chance of the mind getting stuck in the interminable net of vain argumentation. Therefore along with it meditation should be practised. By means of discrimination and meditation, the goal, or Brahman, has to be reached. One is sure to reach the goal by practising in this way. This, in my opinion, is the easy path ensuring quick success.

Disciple: Now please tell me something about the doctrine of Incarnation of God.

Swamiji: You want to master everything in a day, it seems!

Disciple: Sir, if the doubts and difficulties of the mind be solved in one day, then I shall not have to trouble you time and again.

Swamiji: Those by whose grace the knowledge of this Atman, which is extolled so much in the scriptures, is attained in a minute, are the moving Tirthas (seats of holiness)—the Incarnations. From their very birth they are knowers of Brahman, and between Brahman and the knower of Brahman there is not the least difference. ब्रह्म वेद ब्रह्मैव भवति —"He who knows Brahman becomes Brahman." The Atman cannot be known by the mind, for It is Itself the Knower—this I have already said. Therefore man's relative knowledge reaches up to the Avatâras—those who are always established in the Atman. The highest ideal of Ishvara which the human mind can grasp is the Avatara. Beyond this there is no relative knowledge. Such knowers of Brahman are rarely born in the world. And very few people can understand them. They alone are the proof of the truths of the scriptures—the towers of light in the ocean of the world. By the company of such Avataras and by their grace, the darkness of the mind disappears in a trice—and realisation flashes immediately in the heart. Why or by what process it comes, it cannot be ascertained. But it does come. I have seen it happen like that. Shri Krishna spoke the Gita, establishing Himself in the Atman. Those passages of the Gita where references to the word "I" occur, invariably indicate the Atman: "Take refuge in Me alone" means, "Be established in the Atman." This knowledge of the Atman is the highest aim of the Gita. The references to Yoga etc. are but incidental to this realisation of the Atman. Those who have not this knowledge of the Atman are "suicides" "They kill themselves by the clinging to the unreal"—they lose their life in the noose of sense pleasures. You are also men, and can't you ignore this trash of sensual enjoyment that won't last for two days? Should you also swell the ranks of those who are born and die in utter ignorance? Accept the "beneficial" and discard the "pleasant". Speak of this Atman to all, even to the lowest. By continued speaking your own intelligence also will clear up. And always repeat the great Mantras —तत्त्वमसि, "Thou art That," सोऽहमस्मि, "I am That", सर्वं खल्विदं ब्रह्म, "All this is verily Brahman"—and have the courage of a lion in the heart. What is there to fear? Fear is death—fear is the greatest sin. The human soul, represented by Arjuna was touched with fear. Therefore Bhagavân Shri Krishna, established in the Atman, spoke to him the teachings of the Gita. Still his fear would not leave him. Later, when Arjuna saw the Universal Form of the Lord and became established in the Atman, then, with all bondages of Karma burnt by the fire of knowledge, he fought the battle.

Disciple: Sir, can a man do work even after realisation?

Swamiji: After realisation, what is ordinarily called work does not persist. It changes its character. The work which the Jnani does only conduces to the well-being of the world. Whatever a man of realisation says or does contributes to the welfare of all. We have observed Shri Ramakrishna—he was, as it were, देहस्थोऽपि न देहस्थः —"in the body, but not of it!" About the motive of the actions of such personages only this can be said—लोकवत्तु लीलाकैवल्यम् —"Everything they do like men, simply by way of sport."

V

PLAN OF THE FUTURE MATH FOR WOMEN—SOUL HAS NO SEX—WOMEN HAVE EQUAL OPPORTUNITY FOR REALISING THE BRAHMAN—RELIGION TO BE THE CENTRE OF FEMALE EDUCATION—DEFINITION OF GOOD WORK—WORK AND KNOWLEDGE

[PLACE: *Belur Math.* YEAR: *1901.*]

Swamiji is in indifferent health since his return to the Math from the Shillong hills. His feet have swollen. All this has made his brother-disciples very anxious. At the request of

Swami Niranjanananda, Swamiji has agreed to take Ayurvedic medicine. He is to begin this treatment from next Tuesday and entirely give up taking water and salt. Today is Sunday. The disciple asked him, "Sir, it is terribly hot now and you drink water very frequently; it will be unbearable for you now to stop taking water altogether for this treatment."

Swamiji: What do you say? I shall make a firm resolve, on the morning of the day I shall begin this treatment, not to take any water. After that no water shall pass down the throat any more. For three weeks not a drop of water shall be able to go down the throat. The body is but an outer covering of the mind and whatever the mind will dictate to it, it will have to carry out. So there is nothing to be afraid of. At the request of Niranjan I have to undergo this treatment. Well, I cannot be indifferent to the request of my brother-disciples.

It is now about ten o'clock. Swamiji cheerfully raised the topic of his future Math for women, saying, "With the Holy Mother as the centre of inspiration, a Math is to be established on the eastern bank of the Ganga. As Brahmachârins and Sâdhus will be trained in this Math here, so in the other Math also, Brahmachârinis and Sâdhvis will be trained."

Disciple: Sir, history does not tell us of any Maths for women in India in ancient times. Only during the Buddhistic period one hears of Maths for women; but from it in course of time many corruptions arose. The whole country was overrun by great evil practices.

Swamiji: It is very difficult to understand why in this country so much difference is made between men and women, whereas the Vedanta declares that one and the same conscious Self is present in all beings. You always criticise the women, but say, what have you done for their uplift? Writing down Smritis etc., and binding them by hard rules, the men have turned the women into mere manufacturing machines! If you do not raise the women, who are the living embodiment of the Divine Mother, don't think that you have any other way to rise.

Disciple: Women are a bondage and a snare to men. By their Maya they cover the knowledge and dispassion of men. It is for this, I suppose, that scriptural writers hint that knowledge and devotion are difficult of attainment to them.

Swamiji: In what scriptures do you find statements that women are not competent for knowledge and devotion? In the period of degradation, when the priests made the other castes incompetent for the study of the Vedas, they deprived the women also of all their rights. Otherwise you will find that in the Vedic or Upanishadic age Maitreyi, Gârgi, and other ladies of revered memory have taken the places of Rishis through their skill in discussing about Brahman. In an assembly of a thousand Brahmins who were all erudite in the Vedas, Gargi boldly challenged Yâjnavalkya in a discussion about Brahman. When such ideal women were entitled to spiritual knowledge, then why shall not the women have the same privilege now? What has happened once can certainly happen again. History repeats itself. All nations have attained greatness by paying proper respect to the women. That country and that nation which do not respect the women have never become great, nor will ever be in future. The principal reason why your race has so much degenerated is that you had no respect for these living images of Shakti. Manu says, "Where women are respected, there the gods delight; and where they are not, there all works and efforts come to naught."[1] There is no hope of rise for that family or country where there is no estimation of women, where they live in sadness. For this reason, they have to be raised first; and an ideal Math has to be started for them.

Disciple: Sir, when you first returned from the West, in your lecture at the Star Theatre, you sharply criticised the Tantras. Now by your supporting the worship of women, as taught in the Tantras, you are contradicting yourself.

Swamiji: I denounced only the present corrupted form of Vâmâchara of the Tantras. I did not denounce the Mother-worship of the Tantras, or even the real Vamachara. The purport of the Tantras is to worship women in a spirit of Divinity. During the downfall of Buddhism, the Vamachara became very much corrupted, and that corrupted form obtains to the present day. Even now the Tantra literature of India is influenced by those ideas. I denounced only these corrupt and horrible practices—which I do even now. I never objected to the worship of women, who are the living embodiments of Divine Mother, whose external manifestations, appealing to the senses, have maddened men, but whose internal manifestations, such as knowledge, devotion, discrimination, and dispassion make

[1] *Manu Samhita,* III. 56.

man omniscient, of unfailing purpose, and a knower of Brahman. सैषा प्रसन्ना वरदा नृणां भवात मुक्तये—"She, when pleased, becomes propitious and the cause of the freedom of man." Without propitiating the Mother by worship and obeisance, not even Brahmâ and Vishnu have the power to elude Her grasp and attain to freedom. Therefore for the worship of these family goddesses, in order to manifest the Brahman within them, I shall establish the women's Math.

Disciple: It may be a good idea, but where will you get the women inmates? With the present hard restrictions of society, who will permit the ladies of their household to join your Math?

Swamiji: Why so? Even now there are women disciples of Shri Ramakrishna. With their help I shall start this Math. The Holy Mother will be their central figure, and the wives and daughters of devotees of Shri Ramakrishna will be its first inmates. For they will easily appreciate the usefulness of such a Math. After that, following their example, many householders will help in this noble work.

Disciple: The devotees of Shri Ramakrishna will certainly join this work. But I don't think the general public will help in this work.

Swamiji: No great work has been done in the world without sacrifice. Who on seeing the tiny sprout of the banyan can imagine that in course of time it will develop into a gigantic banyan tree? At present I shall start the Math in this way. Later on you will see that after a generation or two people of the country will appreciate the worth of this Math. My women disciples will lay down their lives for it. Casting off fear and cowardice, you also be helpers in this noble mission, and hold this high ideal before all. You will see, it will shed its lustre over the whole country in time.

Disciple: Sir, please tell me all about your plan of this Math for women.

Swamiji: On the other side of the Ganga a big plot of land will be acquired, where unmarried girls or Brahmacharini widows will live; devout married women will also be allowed to stay now and then. Men will have no concern with this Math. The elderly Sâdhus of the Math will manage the affairs of this Math from a distance. There shall be a girls' school attached to this women's Math, in which religious scriptures, literature, Sanskrit, grammar, and even some amount of English should be taught. Other matters, such as sewing, culinary art, rules of domestic work, and upbringing of children, will also be taught, while Japa, worship, meditation, etc. shall form an indispensable part of the teaching. Those who will be able to live here permanently, renouncing home and family ties, will be provided with food and clothing from this Math. Those who will not be able to do that will be allowed to study in this Math as day-scholars. With the permission of the head of the Math, the latter will be allowed even to stay in the Math occassionally, and during such stay will be maintained by the Math. The older Brahmacharinis will take charge of the training of the girl students in Brahmacharya. After five or six years' training in this Math, the guardians of the girls may marry them. If deemed fit for Yoga and religious life, with the permission of their guardians they will be allowed to stay in this Math, taking the vow of celibacy. These celibate nuns will in time be the teachers and preachers of the Math. In villages and towns they will open centres and strive for the spread of female education. Through such devout preachers of character there will be the real spread of female education in the country. So long as the students will remain in association with this Math, they must observe Brahmacharya as the basic idea of this Math.

Spirituality, sacrifice, and self-control will be the motto of the pupils of this Math, and service or Sevadharma the vow of their life. In view of such ideal lives, who will not respect and have faith in them? If the life of the women of this country be moulded in such fashion, then only will there be the reappearance of such ideal characters as Sitâ, Sâvitri, and Gârgi. To what straits the strictures of local usages have reduced the women of this country, rendering them lifeless and inert, you could understand if only you visited the Western countries. You alone are responsible for this miserable condition of the women, and it rests with you also to raise them again. Therefore I say, set to work. What will it do to memorise a few religious books like the Vedas and so on?

Disciple: Sir, if the girl students, after being trained in this Math, marry, how will one find ideal characters in them? Will it not be better if the rule is made that those who will be educated in this Math shall not marry?

Swamiji: Can that be brought about all at once? They must be given education and left to themselves. After that they will act as they think best. Even after marriage and entering the world, the girls educated as above will inspire their husbands with noble ideals and be the mothers of heroic sons. But there must be this rule that the guardians of the students in the women's Math must not even think of marrying them before they attain the age of fifteen.

Disciple: Sir, then those girls will not command reputation in society. Nobody will like to marry them.

Swamiji: Why will not they be wanted in marriage? You have not yet understood the trend of society. These learned and accomplished girls will never be in want of bridegrooms. Society nowadays does not follow the texts recommending child-marriage nor will do so in future. Even now don't you see?

Disciple: But there is sure to be a violent opposition against this in the beginning.

Swamiji: Let it be. What is there to be afraid of in that? Opposition to a righteous work initiated with moral courage will only awaken the moral power of the initiators the more. That which meets with no obstruction, no opposition, only takes men to the path of moral death. Struggle is the sign of life.

Disciple: Yes, sir.

Swamiji: In the highest reality of the Parabrahman, there is no distinction of sex. We notice this only in the relative plane. And the more the mind becomes introspective, the more that idea of difference vanishes. Ultimately, when the mind is wholly merged in the homogeneous and undifferentiated Brahman, such ideas as this is a man or that a woman do not remain at all. We have actually seen this in the life of Shri Ramakrishna. Therefore do I say that though outwardly there may be difference between men and women, in their real nature there is none. Hence, if a man can be a knower of Brahman why cannot a woman attain to the same knowledge? Therefore I was saying that if even one amongst the women became a knower of Brahman, then by the radiance of her personality thousands of women would be inspired and awakened to truth, and great well-being of the country and society would ensue. Do you understand?

Disciple: Sir, your teachings have opened my eyes today.

Swamiji: Not fully yet. When you will realise that all-illuminating reality of the Atman, then you will see that this idea of sex-distinction has vanished altogether; then only will you look upon all women as the veritable manifestation of Brahman. We have seen in Shri Ramakrishna how he had this idea of divine motherhood in every woman, of whatever caste she might be, or whatever might be her worth. It is because I have seen this that I ask you all so earnestly to do likewise and open girls' schools in every village and try to uplift them. If the women are raised, then their children will by their noble actions glorify the name of the country—then will culture, knowledge, power, and devotion awaken in the land.

Disciple: But, sir, contrary results appear to have come out of the present female education. With just a smattering of education, they take merely to the Western modes of living, but it is not clear how far they are advancing in the spirit of renunciation, self-control, austerity, Brahmacharya, and other qualities conducive to Brahmajnâna.

Swamiji: In the beginning a few mistakes like that are unavoidable. When a new idea is preached in the country, some, failing to grasp it properly, go wrong in that way. But what matters it to the well-being of society at large? Well, those who are pioneers of the little bit of female education that now obtains in the country, were undoubtedly very great-hearted. But the truth is that some defect or other must creep into that learning or culture which is not founded on a religious basis. But now female education is to be spread with religion as its centre. All other training should be secondary to religion. Religious training, the formation of character, and observance of the vow of celibacy—these should be attended to. In the female education which has obtained up till now in India, it is religion that has been made a secondary concern; hence those defects you were speaking of have crept in. But no blame attaches therefore to the women. Reformers having proceeded to start female education without being Brahmacharins themselves have stumbled like that. Founders of all good undertakings, before they launch on their desired work, must attain to the knowledge of the Atman through rigorous self-discipline. Otherwise defects are bound to occur in their work.

Disciple: Yes, sir, it is observed that many educated

women spend their time in reading novels and so on; but in East Bengal even with education women have not given up their religious observances. Is it so here in this part?

Swamiji: In every country, nations have their good and bad sides. Ours is to do good works in our lives and hold an example before others. No work succeeds by condemnation. It only repels people. Let anybody say what he likes, don't contradict him. In this world of Maya, whatever work you will take up will be attended with some defects: सर्वारम्भा हि दोषेण धूमेनाग्निरिवावृताः—"All works are covered with defects, as fire is with smoke." Every fire has a chance of being attended with smoke. But will you, on that account, sit inactive? As far as you can, you must go on doing good work.

Disciple: What is this good work?

Swamiji: Whatever helps the manifestation of Brahman is good work. Any work can be done so as to help, if not directly, at least indirectly, the manifestation of the Atman. But following the path laid down by the Rishis, that knowledge of the Atman manifests quickly; on the contrary, the doing of works which have been indicated by the scriptural writers as wrong, brings only bondage of the soul, and sometimes this bondage of delusion does not vanish even in many lives. But in all ages and climes, freedom is sure to be attained by Jivas ultimately. For the Atman is the real nature of the Jiva. Can anybody give up his own nature? If you fight with your shadow for a thousand years, can you drive it away from you?—it will always remain with you.

Disciple: But sir, according to Shankara, Karma is antagonistic to Jnâna. He has variously refuted the intermingling of Jnana and Karma. So how can Karma be helpful to the manifestation of Jnana?

Swamiji: Shankara after saying so has again described Karma as indirect help to the manifestation of Jnana and the means for the purification of the mind. But I do not contradict his conclusion that in transcendent knowledge there is no touch of any work whatsoever. So long as man is within the realm of the consciousness of action, agent, and the result of action, he is powerless to sit idle without doing some work. So, as work is thus ingrained in the very nature of man, why don't you go on doing such works as are helpful to the manifestation of the knowledge of the Atman? That all work is the effect of ignorance may be true from the absolute standpoint, but within the sphere of relative consciousness it has a great utility. When you will realise the Atman, the doing or non-doing of work will be within your control, and whatever you will do in that state will be good work, conducive to the well-being of Jivas and the world. With the manifestation of Brahman, even the breath you draw will be to the good of Jivas. Then you will no longer have to work by means of conscious planning. Do you understand?

Disciple: Yes, it is a beautiful conclusion reconciling Karma and Jnana from the Vedantic standpoint.

At this time, the bell for supper rang, and the disciple, before going to partake of it, prayed with folded hands, "Bless me, sir, that I may attain to the knowledge of Brahman in this very life". Swamiji placing his hand on the disciple's head said, "Have no fear, my son. You are not like ordinary worldly men—neither householders, nor exactly Sannyâsins—but quite a new type."

VI[1]

THE OLD INSTITUTION OF LIVING WITH THE GURU—THE PRESENT UNIVERSITY SYSTEM—LACK OF SHRADDHA—WE HAVE A NATIONAL HISTORY—WESTERN SCIENCE COUPLED WITH VEDANTA—THE SO-CALLED HIGHER EDUCATION—THE NEED OF TECHNICAL EDUCATION AND EDUCATION ON NATIONAL LINES—THE STORY OF SATYAKAMA—MERE BOOK-LEARNING AND EDUCATION UNDER TYAGIS—SHRI RAMAKRISHNA AND THE PANDITS—ESTABLISHMENT OF MATHS WITH SADHUS IN CHARGE OF COLLEGES—TEXT-BOOKS FOR BOYS TO BE COMPILED—STOP EARLY MARRIAGE—PLAN OF SENDING UNMARRIED GRADUATES TO JAPAN—THE SECRET OF JAPAN'S GREATNESS—ART: ASIATIC AND EUROPEAN—ART AND UTILITY—STYLES OF DRESS—THE FOOD QUESTION AND POVERTY

It was about two years after the new Math had been constructed and while all the Swamis were living there that I came one morning to pay a visit to my Guru. Seeing me, Swamiji smiled and after inquiring of my welfare etc., said, "You are going to stay today, are you not?"

"Certainly," I said, and after various inquiries I asked, "Well, Mahârâj, what is your idea of educating our boys?"

[1] Recorded by Priya Nath Sinha, a schoolmate of Swamiji.

Swamiji: गुरुगृहवासः—living with the Guru.

Question: How?

Swamiji: In the same way as of old. But with this education has to be combined modern Western science. Both these are necessary.

Q.: Why, what is the defect in the present university system?

Swamiji: It is almost wholly one of defects. Why, it is nothing but a perfect machine for turning out clerks. I would even thank my stars if that were all. But no! See how men are becoming destitute of Shraddhâ and faith. They assert that the Gita is only an interpolation, and that the Vedas are but rustic songs! They like to master every detail concerning things and nations outside of India; but if you ask them, they do not know even the names of their own forefathers up to the seventh generation, not to speak of the fourteenth!

Q.: But what does that matter? What if they do not know the names of their forefathers?

Swamiji: Don't think so. A nation that has no history of its own has nothing in this world. Do you believe that one who has such faith and pride as to feel, "I come of noble descent," can ever turn out to be bad? How could that be? That faith in himself would curb his actions and feelings, so much so that he would rather die than commit wrong. So a national history keeps a nation well-restrained and does not allow it to sink so low. Oh, I know you will say, "But we have not such a history!" No, there is not any, according to those who think like you. Neither is there any, according to your big university scholars; and so also think those who, having travelled through the West in one great rush, come back dressed in European style and assert, "We have nothing, we are barbarians". Of course, we have no history exactly like that of other countries. Suppose we take rice, and the Englishmen do not. Would you for that reason imagine that they all die of starvation, and are going to be exterminated? They live quite well on what they can easily procure or produce in their own country and what is suited to them. Similarly, we have our own history exactly as it ought to have been for us. Will that history be made extinct by shutting your eyes and crying, "Alas! we have no history"? Those who have eyes to see, find a luminous history there, and on the strength of that they know the nation is still alive. But that history has to be rewritten. It should be restated and suited to the understanding and ways of thinking which our men have acquired in the present age through Western education.

Q.: How has that to be done?

Swamiji: That is too big a subject for a talk now, However, to bring that about, the old institution of "living with the Guru" and similar systems of imparting education are needed. What we want are Western science coupled with the Vedanta, Brahmacharya as the guiding motto, and also Shraddha and faith in one's own Self. Another thing that we want is the abolition of that system which aims at educating our boys in the same manner as that of the man who battered his ass, being advised that it could thereby be turned into a horse.

Q.: What do you mean by that?

Swamiji: You see, no one can teach anybody. The teacher spoils everything by thinking that he is teaching. Thus the Vedanta says that within man is all knowledge—even in a boy it is so—and it requires only an awakening, and that much is the work of a teacher. We have to do only so much for the boys that they may learn to apply their own intellect to the proper use of their hands, legs, ears, eyes, etc., and finally everything will become easy. But the root is religion. Religion is as the rice, and everything else, like the curries. Taking only curries causes indigestion, and so is the case with taking rice alone. Our pedagogues are making parrots of our boys, and ruining their brains by cramming a lot of subjects into them. Looking from one standpoint, you should rather be grateful to the Viceroy[1] for his proposal of reforming the university system, which means practically abolishing higher education—the country will, at least, feel some relief by having breathing time. Goodness gracious! what a fuss and fury about graduating and after a few days all cools down! And after all that, what is it they learn but that what religion and customs we have are all bad, and what the Westerners have are all good? At last, they cannot keep the wolf from the door? What does it matter if this higher education remains or goes? It would be better if the people got a little technical education

[1] Lord Curzon, who took steps to raise the standard of University education so high as to make it very expensive and hence almost inaccessible to boys of the middle classes.

so that they might find work and earn their bread, instead of dawdling about and crying for service.

Q.: Yes, the Marwaris are wiser, since they do not accept service and most of them engage themselves in some trade.

Swamiji: Nonsense! They are on the way to bringing ruin on the country. They have little understanding of their own interests. You are much better, because you have more of an eye towards manufactures. If the money that they lay out in their business and with which they make only a small percentage of profit were utilised in conducting a few factories and workshops, instead of filling the pockets of Europeans by letting them reap the benefit of most of the transactions, then it would not only conduce to the well-being of the country but bring by far the greater amount of profit to them as well. It is only the Kabulis who do not care for service—the spirit of independence is in their very bone and marrow. Propose to anyone of them to take service, and you will see what follows!

Q.: Well, Maharaj, in case higher education is abolished, will not the men become as stupid as cows, as they were before?

Swamiji: What nonsense! Can ever a lion become a jackal? What do you mean? Is it ever possible for the sons of the land that has nourished the whole world with knowledge from time immemorial to turn as stupid as cows, because of the abolition of higher education by Lord Curzon?

Q.: But think what our people were before the advent of the English, and what they are now.

Swamiji: Does higher education mean mere study of material sciences and turning out things of everyday use by machinery? The use of higher education is to find out how to solve the problems of life, and this is what is engaging the profound thought of the modern civilised world, but it was solved in our country thousands of years ago.

Q.: But your Vedanta also was about to disappear?

Swamiji: It might be so. In the efflux of time the light of Vedanta now and then seems as if about to be extinguished, and when that happens, the Lord has to incarnate Himself in the human body; He then infuses such life and strength into religion that it goes on again for some time with irresistible vigour. That life and strength has come into it again.

Q.: What proof is there, Maharaj, that India has freely contributed her knowledge to the rest of the world?

Swamiji: History itself bears testimony to the fact. All the soul-elevating ideas and the different branches of knowledge that exist in the world are found on proper investigation to have their roots in India.

Aglow with enthusiasm, Swamiji dwelt at length on this topic. His health was very bad at the time, and moreover, owing to the intense heat of summer he was feeling thirsty and drinking water too often. At last he said, "Dear Singhi, get a glass of iced water for me please, I shall explain everything to you clearly." After drinking the iced water he began afresh.

Swamiji: What we need, you know, is to study, independent of foreign control, different branches of the knowledge that is our own, and with it the English language and Western science; we need technical education and all else that may develop industries, so that men, instead of seeking for service, may earn enough to provide for themselves, and save something against a rainy day.

Q.: What were you going to say the other day about the Tol (Sanskrit boarding school) system?

Swamiji: Haven't you read the stories from the Upanishads? I will tell you one. Satyakâma went to live the life of a Brahmachârin with his Guru. The Guru gave into his charge some cows and sent him away to the forest with them. Many months passed by and when Satyakama saw that the number of cows was doubled he thought of returning to his Guru. On his way back, one of the bulls, the fire, and some other animals gave him instructions about the Highest Brahman. When the disciple came back, the Guru saw by a mere glance at his face that the disciple had learnt the knowledge of the Supreme Brahman. Now, the moral this story is meant to teach is that true education is gained by constant living in communion with Nature.

Knowledge should be acquired in that way; otherwise by educating yourself in the Tol of a Pandit you will be only a human ape all your life. One should live from his very boyhood with one whose character is like a blazing fire, and should have before him a living example of the highest teaching. Mere reading that it is a sin to tell a lie will be of no use. Every boy should be trained to practise absolute Brahmacharya, and then, and then only, faith—Shraddha—will come. Otherwise, why will not one who has no Shraddha speak an untruth? In our country, the imparting of knowledge has always been through men of renunciation. Later, the Pandits, by monopolising all knowledge and restricting it to the Tols, have only brought the country to the brink of ruin. India had all good prospects so long as Tyâgis (men of renunciation) used to impart knowledge.

Q.: What do you mean, Maharaj? There are no Sannyâsins in other countries, but see how by dint of their knowledge India is laid prostrate at their feet!

Swamiji: Don't talk nonsense, my dear, hear what I say. India will have to carry others' shoes for ever on her head if the charge of imparting knowledge to her sons does not again fall upon the shoulders of Tyagis. Don't you know how an illiterate boy, possessed of renunciation, turned the heads of your great old Pandits? Once at the Dakshineswar Temple the Brahmin who was in charge of the worship of Vishnu broke a leg of the image. Pandits were brought together at a meeting to give their opinions, and they after consulting old books and manuscripts, declared that the worship of this broken image could not be sanctioned according to the Shâstras and a new image would have to be consecrated. There was, consequently, a great stir. Shri Ramakrishna was called at last. He heard and asked, "Does a wife forsake her husband in case he becomes lame?" What followed? The Pandits were struck dumb, all their Shâstric commentaries and erudition could not withstand the force of this simple statement. If what you say was true, why should Shri Ramakrishna come down to this earth, and why should he discourage mere book-learning so much? That new life-force which he brought with him has to be instilled into learning and education, and then the real work will be done.

Q.: But that is easier said than done.

Swamiji: Had it been easy, it would not have been necessary for him to come. What you have to do now is to establish a Math in every town and in every village. Can you do that? Do something at least. Start a big Math in the heart of Calcutta. A well-educated Sâdhu should be at the head of that centre, and under him there should be departments for teaching practical science and arts, with a specialist Sannyasin in charge of each of these departments.

Q.: Where will you get such Sâdhus?

Swamiji: We shall have to manufacture them. Therefore I always say that some young men with burning patriotism and renunciation are needed. None can master a thing perfectly in so short a time as the Tyagis will.

After a short silence Swamiji said, "Singhi, there are so many things left to be done for our country that thousands like you and me are needed. What will mere talk do? See to what a miserable condition the country is reduced; now do something. We haven't even got a single book well suited for the little boys."

Q.: Why, there are so many books of Ishvar Chandra Vidyâsâgar for the boys!

No sooner had I said this than he laughed out and said: Yes, there you read, "Ishvar nirâkâr chaitanya svarup"—God is without form and of the essence of pure knowledge; "Subal ati subodh Bâlak"—Subal is a very good boy, and so on. That won't do. We must compose some books in Bengali as also in English with short stories from the Ramayana, the Mahabharata, the Upanishads etc., in very easy and simple language, and these are to be given to our little boys to read.

It was about eleven o'clock by this time. The sky became suddenly overcast, and a cold wind began to blow. Swamiji was greatly delighted at the prospect of rain. He got up and said, "Let us, Singhi, have a stroll by the side of the Ganga." We did so, and he recited many stanzas from the *Meghaduta* of Kâlidâsa, but the one under-current of thought that was all the time running through his mind was the good of India. He exclaimed, "Look here, Singhi, can you do one thing? Can you put a stop to the marriage of our boys for some time?"

I said, "Well, Maharaj, how can we think of that, when the Babus are trying, on the other hand, all sorts of means to make marriage cheaper?"

Swamiji: Don't trouble your head on that score; who can stem the tide of time! All such agitations will end in empty sound, that is all. The dearer the marriages become, the better for the country. What a hury-scurry of passing examinations and marrying right off! It seems as if no one was to be left a bachelor, but it is just the same thing again, next year!

After a short silence, Swamiji again said:

"If I can get some unmarried graduates, I may try to send them over to Japan and make arrangements for their technical education there, so that when they come back, they may turn their knowledge to the best account for India. What a good thing that would be!"

Q.: Why, Maharaj, is it better for us to go to Japan than to England?

Swamiji: Certainly! In my opinion, if all our rich and educated men once go and see Japan, their eyes will be opened.

Q.: How?

Swamiji: There, in Japan, you find a fine assimilation of knowledge, and not its indigestion, as we have here. They have taken everything from the Europeans, but they remain Japanese all the same, and have not turned European; while in our country, the terrible mania of becoming Westernised has seized upon us like a plague.

I said: "Maharaj, I have seen some Japanese paintings; one cannot but marvel at their art. Its inspiration seems to be something which is their own and beyond imitation."

Swamiji: Quite so. They are great as a nation because of their art. Don't you see they are Asiatics, as we are? And though we have lost almost everything, yet what we still have is wonderful. The very soul of the Asiatic is interwoven with art. The Asiatic never uses a thing unless there be art in it. Don't you know that art is with us a part of religion? How greatly is a lady admired among us, who can nicely paint the floors and walls, on auspicious occasions, with the paste of rice-powder! How great an artist was Shri Ramakrishna himself!

Q.: The English art is also good, is it not?

Swamiji: What a stupid fool you are! But what is the use of blaming you, when that seems to be the prevailing way of thinking! Alas, to such a state is our country reduced! The people will look upon their own gold as brass, while the brass of the foreigner is gold to them! This is, indeed, the magic wrought by modern education! Know that since the time the Europeans have come into contact with Asia, they are trying to infuse art into their own life.

Myself: If others hear you talk like this, Maharaj, they will think that you take a pessimistic view of things.

Swamiji: Naturally! What else can they think who move

in a rut! How I wish I could show you everything through my eyes! Look at their buildings—how commonplace, how meaningless, they are! Look at those big government buildings; can you, just by seeing their outside, make out any meaning for which each of them stands? No, because they are all so unsymbolical. Take again the dress of Westerners: their stiff coats and straight pants, fitting almost tightly to the body, are, in our estimation, hardly decent, is it not so? And oh, what beauty, indeed, in that! Now, go all over our motherland and see if you cannot read aright, from their very appearance, the meaning for which our buildings stand, and how much art there is in them! The glass is their drinking vessel, and ours is the metal Ghati (pitcher-shaped); which of the two is artistic? Have you seen the farmers' homes in our villages?

Myself: Yes, I have, of course.

Swamiji: What have you seen of them?

I did not know what to say. However, I replied, "Maharaj they are faultlessly neat and clean, the yards and floors being daily well plastered over."

Swamiji: Have you seen their granaries for keeping paddy? What an art is there in them! What a variety of paintings even on their mud walls! And then, if you go and see how the lower classes live in the West, you would at once mark the difference. Their ideal is utility, ours, art. The Westerner looks for utility in everything, whereas with us art is everywhere. With the Western education, those beautiful Ghatis of ours have been discarded, and enamel glasses have usurped their place in our homes! Thus, the ideal of utility has been imbibed by us to such an extent as to make it look little short of the ridiculous. Now what we need is the combination of art and utility. Japan has done that very quickly, and so she has advanced by giant strides. Now, in their turn, the Japanese are going to teach the Westerners.

Q.: Maharaj, which nation in the world dresses best?

Swamiji: The Aryans do; even the Europeans admit that. How picturesquely their dresses hang in folds! The royal costumes of most nations are, to some extent, a sort of imitation of the Aryans'—the same attempt is made there to keep them in folds, and those costumes bear a marked difference to their national style.

By the by, Singhi, leave off that wretched habit of wearing those European shirts.

Q.: Why, Maharaj?

Swamiji: For the reason that they are used by the Westerners only as underwear. They never like to see them worn outside. How mistaken of the Bengali to do so! As if one should wear anything and everything, as if there was no unwritten law about dress, as if there was no ancestral style to follow! Our people are outcasted by taking the food touched by the lower classes; it would have been very well if the same law applied to their wearing any irregular style of dress. Why can't you adapt your dress in some way to our own style? What sense is there in your adopting European shirts and coats?

It began to rain now, and the dinner-bell also rang. So we went in to partake of the Prasâda with others. During the meal, Swamiji said, addressing me: "Concentrated food should be taken. To fill the stomach with a large quantity of rice is the root of laziness." A little while after he said again, "Look at the Japanese, they take rice with the soup of split peas, twice or thrice a day. But even the strongly-built take a little at a time, though the number of meals may be more. Those who are well-to-do among them take meat daily. While we stuff ourselves twice a day up to the throat, as it were, and the whole of our energy is exhausted in digesting such a quantity of rice!"

Q.: Is it feasible for us Bengalis, poor as we are, to take meat?

Swamiji: Why not? You can afford to have it in small quantities. Half a pound a day is quite enough. The real evil is idleness, which is the principal cause of our poverty. Suppose the head of a firm gets displeased with someone and decreases his pay; or, out of three or four bread-winning sons in a family one suddenly dies; what do they do? Why, they at once curtail the quantity of milk for the children, or live on one meal a day, having a little popped rice or so at night!

Q: But what else can they do under the circumstances?

Swamiji: Why can't they exert themselves and earn more, to keep up their standard of food? But no! They must go to their local Addas (rendezvous) and idle hours away! Oh, if they only knew how they wasted their time!

VII[1]

INTERMARRIAGE AMONG SUBDIVISIONS OF A VARNA—AGAINST EARLY MARRIAGE—THE EDUCATION THAT INDIA NEEDS—BRAHMACHARYA

Monday, the 24th January, 1898.

The same gentleman who was asking questions of Swamiji on Saturday last came again. He raised again the topic of intermarriage and inquired, "How should intermarriage be introduced between different nationalities?"

Swamiji: I do not advise our intermarriage with nations professing an alien religion. At least for the present, that will, of a certainty, slacken the ties of society and be a cause of manifold mischief. It is the intermarriage between people of the same religion that I advocate.

Q.: Even then, it will involve much perplexity. Suppose I have a daughter who is born and brought up in Bengal, and I marry her to a Mahratti or a Madrasi. Neither will the girl understand her husband's language nor the husband the girl's. Again, the difference in their individual habits and customs is so great. Such are a few of the troubles in the case of the married couple. Then as regards society, it will make confusion worse confounded.

Swamiji: The time is yet very long in coming when marriages of that kind will be widely possible. Besides it is not judicious now to go in for that all of a sudden. One of the secrets of work is to go along the line of least resistance. So, first of all, let there be marriages within the sphere of one's own caste-people. Take, for instance, the Kâyasthas of Bengal. They have several subdivisions amongst them, such as, the Uttar-rârhi, Dakshin-rârhi, Bangaja, etc., and they do not intermarry with each other. Now, let there be intermarriages between the Uttar-rarhis and the Dakshin-rarhis; and if that is not possible at present, let it be between the Bangajas and the Dakshin-rarhis. Thus we are to build up that which is already existing, and which is in our hands to reduce into practice—reform does not mean wholesale breaking down.

Q.: Very well, let it be as you say; but what corresponding good can come of it?

[1] Recorded by Surendra Nath Sen, a disciple of Swamiji.

Swamiji: Don't you see how in our society, marriage being restricted for several hundreds of years within the same subdivisions of each caste, has come to such a pass nowadays as virtually to mean marital alliance between cousins and near relations; and how for this very reason the race is getting deteriorated physically, and consequently all sorts of disease and other evils are finding a ready entrance into it? The blood having had to circulate within the narrow circle of a limited number of individuals has become vitiated; so the new-born children inherit from their very birth the constitutional diseases of their fathers. Thus, born with poor blood, their bodies have very little power to resist the microbes of any disease, which are ever ready to prey upon them. It is only by widening the circle of marriage that we can infuse a new and a different kind of blood into our progeny, so that they may be saved from the clutches of many of our present-day diseases and other consequent evils.

Q.: May I ask you, sir, what is your opinion about early marriage?

Swamiji: Amongst the educated classes in Bengal, the custom of marrying their boys too early is dying out gradually. The girls are also given in marriage a year or two older than before, but that has been under compulsion—from pecuniary want. Whatever might be the reason for it, the age of marrying girls should be raised still higher. But what will the poor father do? As soon as the girl grows up a little, every one of the female sex, beginning with the mother down to the relatives and neighbours even, will begin to cry out that he must find a bridegroom for her, and will not leave him in peace until he does so! And, about your religious hypocrites, the less said the better. In these days no one hears them, but still they will take up the role of leaders themselves. The rulers passed the Age of Consent Bill prohibiting a man under the threat of penalty to live with a girl of twelve years, and at once all these so-called leaders of your religion raised a tremendous hue and cry against it, sounding the alarm, "Alas, our religion is lost!" As if religion consisted in making a girl a mother at the age of twelve or thirteen! So the rulers also naturally think, "Goodness gracious! What a religion is theirs! And these people lead political agitations and demand political rights!"

Q.: Then, in your opinion, both men and women should be married at an advanced age?

Swamiji: Certainly. But education should be imparted along with it, otherwise irregularity and corruption will ensue. By education I do not mean the present system, but something in the line of positive teaching. Mere book-learning won't do. We want that education by which character is formed, strength of mind is increased, the intellect is expanded, and by which one can stand on one's own feet.

Q.: We have to reform our women in many ways.

Swamiji: With such an education women will solve their own problems. They have all the time been trained in helplessness, servile dependence on others, and so they are good only to weep their eyes out at the slightest approach of a mishap or danger. Along with other things they should acquire the spirit of valour and heroism. In the present day it has become necessary for them also to learn self-defence. See how grand was the Queen of Jhansi!

Q.: What you advise is quite a new departure, and it will, I am afraid, take a very long time yet to train our women in that way.

Swamiji: Anyhow, we have to try our best. We have not only to teach them but to teach ourselves also. Mere begetting children does not make a father; a great many responsibilities have to be taken upon one's shoulders as well. To make a beginning in woman's education: our Hindu women easily understand what chastity means, because it is their heritage. Now, first of all, intensify that ideal within them above everything else, so that they may develop a strong character by the force of which, in every stage of their life, whether married or single, if they prefer to remain so, they will not be in the least afraid even to give up their lives rather than flinch an inch from their chastity. Is it little heroism to be able to sacrifice one's life for the sake of one's ideal, whatever that ideal may be? Studying the present needs of the age, it seems imperative to train some women up in the ideal of renunciation, so that they will take up the vow of lifelong virginity, fired with the strength of that virtue of chastity which is innate in their life-blood from hoary antiquity. Along with that they should be taught sciences and other things which would be of benefit not only to them but to others as well, and knowing this they would easily learn these things and feel pleasure in doing so. Our motherland requires for her well-being some of her children to become such pure-souled Brahmachârins and Brahmachârinis.

Q.: In what way will that conduce to her well-being?

Swamiji: By their example and through their endeavours to hold the national ideal before the eyes of the people, a revolution in thoughts and aspirations will take place. How do matters stand now? Somehow, the parents must dispose of a girl in marriage, if she be nine or ten years of age! And what a rejoicing of the whole family if a child is born to her at the age of thirteen! If the trend of such ideas is reversed, then only there is some hope for the ancient Shraddhâ to return. And what to talk of those who will practise Brahmacharya as defined above—think how much faith in themselves will be theirs! And what a power for good they will be!

The questioner now saluted Swamiji and was ready to take leave. Swamiji asked him to come now and then. "Certainly, sir", replied the gentleman. "I feel so much benefited; I have heard from you many new things, which I have not been told anywhere before." I also went home, as it was about time for dinner.

WRITINGS

INDIA: THE LAND OF RELIGION[1]

"Whenever virtue subsides, and wickedness raises its head, I manifest Myself to restore the glory of religion"—are the words, noble Prince, of the Eternal One, in the holy Gita, striking the keynote of the pulsating ebb and flow of the spiritual energy in the universe.

These changes are manifesting themselves again and again in rhythms peculiar to themselves, and like every other tremendous change, though affecting, more or less, every particle within their sphere of action, they show their effects more intensely upon those particles which are naturally susceptible to their power.

As, in a universal sense, the primal state is a state of sameness of the qualitative forces, a disturbance of this equilibrium and all succeeding struggles to regain it, composing what we call the manifestation of nature, this universe—which state of things remains as long as the primitive sameness is not reached—so, in a restricted sense on our own earth, differentiation and its inevitable counterpart, this struggle towards homogeneity, must remain as long as the human race shall remain as such, creating strongly marked peculiarities in ethnic divisions, sub-races, and even down to individuals in all parts of the world.

In this world of impartial division and balance, therefore, each nation represents, as it were, a wonderful dynamo for the storage and distribution of a particular species of energy, and amidst all other possessions that particular property shines forth as the special characteristic of that race. And as any upheaval in any particular part of human nature, though affecting others more or less, stirs to its very depth that nation of which it is a special characteristic, and from which as a centre it generally starts, so any commotion in the religious world is sure to produce momentous changes in India, that land which again and again has had to furnish the centre of the widespread religious upheavals, for, above all, India is the land of religion.

[1] This was the reply to an Address, dated March 4, 1895, sent him in America by the Maharaja of Khetri (Rajputana).

Each man calls that alone real which helps him to realise his ideal. To the worldly-minded, everything that can be converted into money is real, that which cannot be so converted is unreal. To the man of a domineering spirit, anything that will conduce to his ambition of ruling over his fellowmen is real—the rest is naught, and man finds nothing in that which does not echo back the heartbeats of his special love in life.

Those whose only aim is to barter the energies of life for gold, or name, or any other enjoyment; those to whom the tramp of embattled cohorts is the only manifestation of power; those to whom the enjoyments of the senses are the only bliss that life can give—to these, India will ever appear as an immense desert whose every blast is deadly to the development of life, as it is known by them.

But to those whose thirst for life has been quenched for ever by drinking from the stream of immortality that flows from far away beyond the world of the senses; whose souls have cast away—as a serpent its slough—the threefold bondages of lust, gold, and fame; who, from their height of calmness, look with love and compassion upon the petty quarrels and jealousies and fights for little gilded puff-balls, filled with dust, called "enjoyment" by those under a sense-bondage; to those whose accumulated force of past good deeds has caused the scales of ignorance to fall off from their eyes, making them see through the vanity of name and fame—to such wheresoever they be, India, the motherland and eternal mine of spirituality, stands transfigured, a beacon of hope to every one in search of Him who is the only real Existence in a universe of vanishing shadows.

The majority of mankind can only understand power when it is presented to them in a concrete form, fitted to their perceptions. To them, the rush and excitement of war, with its power and spell, is something very tangible, and any manifestation of life that does not come like a whirlwind, bearing down everything before it, is to them as death. And India, for centuries at the feet of foreign conquerors, without any idea or hope of resistance, without the least solidarity among its masses, without the least idea of patriotism, must needs appear to such, as a land of rotten bones, a lifeless putrescent mass.

It is said—the fittest alone survive. How is it, then, that this most unfitted of all races, according to commonly accepted ideas, could bear the most awful misfortunes that ever befell a race, and yet not show the least signs of decay? How is it that, while the multiplying powers of the so-called vigorous and active races are dwindling every day, the immoral (?) Hindu shows a power of increase beyond them all? Great laurels are due, no doubt, to those who can deluge the world with blood at a moment's notice; great indeed is the glory of those who, to keep up a population of a few millions in plenty, have to starve half the population of the earth; but is no credit due to those who can keep hundreds of millions in peace and plenty, without snatching the bread from the mouth of any one else? Is there no power displayed in bringing up and guiding the destinies of countless millions of human beings, through hundreds of centuries, without the least violence to others?

The mythologies of all ancient races supply us with fables of heroes whose life was concentrated in a certain small portion of their bodies, and until that was touched they remained invulnerable. It seems as if each nation also has such a peculiar centre of life, and so long as that remains untouched, no amount of misery and misfortune can destroy it.

In religion lies the vitality of India, and so long as the Hindu race do not forget the great inheritance of their forefathers, there is no power on earth to destroy them.

Nowadays everybody blames those who constantly look back to their past. It is said that so much looking back to the past is the cause of all India's woes. To me, on the contrary, it seems that the opposite is true. So long as they forgot the past, the Hindu nation remained in a state of stupor; and as soon as they have begun to look into their past, there is on every side a fresh manifestation of life. It is out of this past that the future has to be moulded, this past will become the future.

The more, therefore, the Hindus study the past, the more glorious will be their future, and whoever tries to bring the past to the door of every one, is a great benefactor to his nation. The degeneration of India came not because the laws and customs of the ancients were bad, but because they were not allowed to be carried to their legitimate conclusions.

Every critical student knows that the social laws of India have always been subject to great periodic changes. At their inception, these laws were the embodiment of a gigantic plan, which was to unfold itself slowly through time. The great seers of ancient India saw so far ahead of their time that the world has to wait centuries yet to appreciate their wisdom, and it is this very inability on the part of their own descendants to appreciate the full scope of this wonderful plan, that is the one and only cause of the degeneration of India.

Ancient India had for centuries been the battle-field for the ambitious projects of two of her foremost classes—the Brahmins and the Kshatriyas.

On the one hand, the priesthood stood between the lawless social tyranny of the princes over the masses, whom the Kshatriyas declared to be their legal food. On the other hand, the Kshatriya power was the one potent force which struggled with any success against the spiritual tyranny of the priesthood, and the ever-increasing chain of ceremonials, which they were forging to bind down the people with.

The tug of war began in the earliest periods of the history of our race, and throughout the Shrutis it can be distinctly traced. A momentary lull came when Shri Krishna, leading the faction of Kshatriya power and of Jnâna, showed the way to reconciliation. The result was the teachings of the Gita—the essence of philosophy, of liberality, of religion. Yet the causes were there, and the effect must follow.

The ambition of these two classes to be the masters of the poor and ignorant was there, and the strife once more became fierce. The meagre literature that has come down to us from that period brings to us but faint echoes of that mighty past strife, but at last it broke out as a victory for the Kshatriyas, a victory for Jnana, for liberty—and ceremonial had to go down, much of it for ever. This upheaval was what is known as the Buddhistic reformation. On the religious side, it represented freedom from ceremonial; on the political side, overthrow of the priesthood by the Kshatriyas.

It is a significant fact that the two greatest men ancient India produced—Krishna and Buddha—were both Kshatriyas, and still more significant is the fact that both of these Godmen threw open the door of knowledge to every one, irrespective of birth or sex.

In spite of its wonderful moral strength, Buddhism was extremely iconoclastic and much of its force being spent in merely negative attempts, it had to die out in the land of its birth, and what remained of it became full of superstitions and ceremonials, a hundred times cruder than those it was intended to suppress. Although it partially succeeded in putting down the animal sacrifices of the Vedas, it filled the land with temples, images, symbols, and bones of saints.

Above all, in the medley of Aryans, Mongols, and aborigines which it created, it unconsciously led the way to some of the hideous Vâmâchâras. This was especially the reason why this travesty of the teaching of the great Master had to be driven out of India by Shri Shankara and his band of Sannyâsins.

Thus, even the current of life set in motion by the greatest soul that ever wore a human form, the Bhagavân Buddha himself, became a miasmatic pool, and India had to wait for centuries until Shankara arose, followed in quick succession by Râmânuja and Madhva.

By this time, an entirely new chapter had opened in the history of India. The ancient Kshatriyas and the Brahmins had disappeared. The land between the Himalayas and the Vindhyas, the home of the Aryas, the land which gave birth to Krishna and Buddha, the cradle of great Râjarshis and Brahmarshis, became silent, and from the very furthest end of the Indian Peninsula, from races alien in speech and form, from families claiming descent from the ancient Brahmins, came the reaction against the corrupted Buddhism.

What had become of the Brahmins and Kshatriyas of Âryâvarta? They had entirely disappeared, except here and there a few mongrel clans claiming to be Brahmins and Kshatriyas and in spite of their inflated, self-laudatory assertions, that the whole world ought to learn from एतद्देशप्रसूतस्य सकाशादग्रजन्मनः,[1] they had to sit in sackcloth and ashes, in all humility, to learn at the feet of the Southerners. The result was the bringing back of the Vedas to India—a revival of the Vedanta, such as India never before had seen; even the householders began to study the Âranyakas.

In the Buddhistic movement, the Kshatriyas were the real leaders, and whole masses of them became Buddhists. In the zeal of reform and conversion, the popular dialects had been almost exclusively cultivated, to the neglect of Sanskrit, and the larger portion of Kshatriyas had become disjointed from the Vedic literature and Sanskrit learning. Thus this wave of reform, which came from the South, benefited to a certain extent

[1] From the Brahmin born in this part of the land.

the priesthood, and the priests only. For the rest of India's millions, it forged more chains than they had ever known before.

The Kshatriyas have always been the backbone of India, so also they had been the supporters of science and liberty, and their voices had rung out again and again to clear the land from superstitions, and throughout the history of India they ever formed the invulnerable barrier to aggressive priestly tyranny.

When the greater part of their number sank into ignorance, and another portion mixed their blood with savages from Central Asia and lent their swords to establish the rules of priests in India, her cup became full to the brim, and down sank the land of Bharata, not to rise again, until the Kshatriya rouses himself, and making himself free, strikes the chains from the feet of the rest. Priestcraft is the bane of India. Can man degrade his brother, and himself escape degradation?

Know, Rajaji, the greatest of all truths, discovered by your ancestors, is that the universe is one. Can one injure any one without injuring himself? The mass of Brahmin and Kshatriya tyranny has recoiled upon their own heads with compound interest; and a thousand years of slavery and degradation is what the inexorable law of Karma is visiting upon them.

This is what one of our ancestors said, "Even in this life they have conquered relativity, whose mind is fixed in sameness", one who is believed to be God incarnate. We all believe it. Are his words then vain, and without meaning? If not, and we know they are not, any attempt against this perfect equality of all creation, irrespective of birth, sex, or even qualification, is a terrible mistake, and no one can be saved until he has attained to this idea of sameness.

Follow, therefore, noble Prince, the teachings of the Vedanta, not as explained by this or that commentator, but as the Lord within you understands them. Above all, follow this great doctrine seeing the same God in all.

This is the way to freedom; inequality, the way to bondage. No man and no nation can attempt to gain physical freedom without physical equality, nor mental freedom without mental equality.

Ignorance, inequality, and desire, are the three causes of human misery, and each follows the other in inevitable union. Why should a man think himself above any other man, or even an animal? It is the same throughout:

त्वं स्त्री त्वं पुमानसि त्वं कुमार उत वा कुमारी ।

—"Thou art the man, thou the woman, thou art the young man, thou the young woman."

Many will say, "That is all right for the Sannyasins, but we are householders". No doubt, a householder having many other duties to perform, cannot as fully attain to this sameness; yet this should be also their ideal, for it is the ideal of all societies, of all mankind, all animals, and all nature, to attain to this sameness. But alas! they think inequality is the way to attain equality, as if they could come to right by doing wrong!

This is the bane of human nature, the curse upon mankind, the root of all misery—this inequality. This is the source of all bondage, physical, mental, and spiritual.

समं पश्यन् हि सर्वत्र समवस्थितमीश्वरम् ।
न हिनस्त्यात्मनात्मानं ततो याति परां गतिम् ॥

—"Since seeing the Lord equally existent everywhere, he injures not Self by self, and so goes to the Highest Goal." This one saying contains, in a few words, the universal way to salvation.

You, Rajputs, have been the glories of ancient India. With your degradation came national decay, and India can only be raised if the descendants of the Kshatriyas co-operate with the descendants of the Brahmins, not to share the spoils of pelf and power, but to help the weak, to enlighten the ignorant, and to restore the lost glory of the holy land of their forefathers.

And who can say but that the time is propitious? Once more the wheel is turning up, once more vibrations have been set in motion from India, which are destined at no distant day to reach the farthest limits of the earth. One voice has spoken, whose echoes are rolling on and gathering strength every day, a voice even mightier than those which have preceded it, for it is the summation of them all. Once more the voice that spoke to the sages on the banks of the Sarasvati, the voice whose echoes reverberated from peak to peak of the "Father of Mountains", and descended upon the plains through Krishna, Buddha, and Chaitanya, in all-carrying floods, has spoken again. Once more the doors have opened. Enter ye into the realms of light, the gates have been opened wide once more.

And you, my beloved Prince, you the scion of a race who

are the living pillars upon which rests the religion eternal, its sworn defenders and helpers, the descendants of Râma and Krishna, will you remain outside? I know this cannot be. Yours, I am sure, will be the first hand that will be stretched forth to help religion once more. And when I think of you, Raja Ajit Singh, one in whom the well-known scientific attainments of your house have been joined to a purity of character of which a saint ought to be proud, to an unbounded love for humanity, I cannot help believing in the glorious renaissance of the religion eternal, when such hands are willing to rebuild it again.

May the blessings of Ramakrishna be on you and yours for ever and ever, and that you may live long for the good of many and for the spread of truth, is the constant prayer of—

VIVEKANANDA.

IN DEFENCE OF HINDUISM[1]

FRIENDS, FELLOW-COUNTRYMEN, AND CO-RELIGIONISTS OF MADRAS:

It is most gratifying to me to find that my insignificant service to the cause of our religion has been acceptable to you, not because it is a personal appreciation of me and my work in a foreign and distant land, but as a sure sign that, though whirlwind after whirlwind of foreign invasion has passed over the devoted head of India, though centuries of neglect on our part, and contempt on the part of our conquerors, have visibly dimmed the glories of ancient Âryâvarta, though many a stately column on which it rested, many a beautiful arch and many a marvellous corner, have been washed away by the inundations that deluged the land for centuries—the centre is all sound, the keystone is unimpaired. The spiritual foundation upon which the marvellous monument of glory to God and charity to all beings has been reared, stands unshaken, strong as ever. Generous is your appreciation of Him whose message to India and to the whole world, I, the most unworthy of His servants, had the privilege to bear. It is your innate spiritual instinct which saw in Him and His message the first murmurs of that tidal wave of spirituality which is destined at no distant future to break upon India in all its irresistible powers, carrying away in its omnipotent flood all that is weak and defective, and raising the Hindu race to the platform it is destined to occupy in the providence of God, crowned with more glory than it ever had even in the past, the reward of centuries of silent suffering, and fulfilling its mission amongst the races of the world—the evolution of spiritual humanity.

The people of Northern India are especially grateful to you of the South, as the great source to which most of the impulses that are working in India today can be traced. The great Bhâshyakâras, epoch-making Âchâryas—Shankara, Râmânuja, and Madhva—were born in Southern India. Great

[1] When the success of the Swami in America became well known in India, several meetings were held and addresses of thanks and congratulations were forwarded to him. The first reply which he wrote in September 1894 was that to the Address of the Hindus of Madras.

Shankara to whom every Advaitavâdin in the world owes allegiance; great Ramanuja whose heavenly touch converted the downtrodden pariahs into Alwars; great Madhva whose leadership was recognised even by the followers of the only Northern Prophet whose power has been felt all over the length and breadth of India—Shri Krishna Chaitanya. Even at the present day it is the South that carries the palm in the glories of Varanasi; your renunciation controls the sacred shrines on the farthest peaks of the Himalayas; and what wonder that with the blood of prophets running in your veins, with your lives blessed by such Acharyas, you are the first and foremost to appreciate and hold on to the message of Bhagavân Shri Ramakrishna?

The South has been the repository of Vedic learning, and you will understand me when I state that, in spite of the reiterated assertions of aggressive ignorance, it is the Shruti that is still the backbone of all the different divisions of the Hindu religion.

However great may be the merits of the Samhitâ and the Brâhmana portions of the Vedas to the ethnologists or the philologists, however desirable may be the results that the अग्निमीले[1] or इषेत्वोर्ज्त्वा[2] or शन्नो देवीरभीष्टये[3] in conjunction with the different Vedis and sacrifices and libations produce—it was all in the way of Bhoga; and no one ever contended that it could produce Moksha. As such, the Jnânakânda, the Âranyakas, the Shrutis *par excellence* which teach the way to spirituality, the Moksha-Mârga, have always ruled and will always rule in India.

Lost in the mazes and divisions of the "Religion Eternal", by prepossession and prejudice unable to grasp the meaning of the only religion whose universal adaptation is the exact shadow of the अणोरणीयान् महतो महीयान्[4] God it preaches, groping in the

[1] ओं अग्निमीले पुरोहितं यज्ञस्य देवमृत्विजम्। होतारं रत्नधातमम्॥ ऋग्वेदः १।१।१।

[2] ओं इषेत्वोर्ज्त्वा वायवः स्थोपायवः स्थ देवो वः सविता प्रार्पयतु श्रेष्ठतमाय कर्मणे॥ शुक्लयजुर्वेदः।१।१ १।

[3] ओं शन्नो देवीरभीष्टये आपो भवन्तु पीतये शंयोरभिस्रवन्तु नः॥ अथर्ववेदः १।१।१।

[4] "Smaller than the smallest, greater than the greatest." (Katha, II.20)

dark with a standard of spiritual truth borrowed second-hand from nations who never knew anything but rank materialism, the modern young Hindu struggles in vain to understand the religion of his forefathers, and gives up the quest altogether, and becomes a hopeless wreck of an agnostic, or else, unable to vegetate on account of the promptings of his innate religious nature, drinks carelessly of some of those different decoctions of Western materialism with an Eastern flavour, and thus fulfils the prophecy of the Shruti:

दंद्रम्यमाणाः परियन्ति मूढा अन्धेनैव नीयमाना यथान्धाः ।

—"Fools go staggering to and fro, like blind men led by the blind" (Katha, II. 5).

They alone escape whose spiritual nature has been touched and vivified by the life-giving touch of the "Sadguru".

Well has it been said by Bhagavân Bhâshyakâra:

दुर्लभं त्रयमेवैतत् देवानुग्रहहेतुकम् ।
मनुष्यत्वं मुमुक्षुत्वं महापुरुषसंश्रयः ॥

—"These three are difficult to obtain in this world, and depend on the mercy of the gods—the human birth, the desire for salvation, and the company of the great-souled ones."

Either in the sharp analysis of the Vaisheshikas, resulting in the wonderful theories about the Paramânus, Dvyanus, and Trasarenus[1] or the still more wonderful analysis displayed in the discussions of the Jâti, Dravya, Guna, Samavâya,[2] and the various categories of the Naiyâyikas, rising to the solemn march of thought of the Sânkhyas, the fathers of the theories of evolution, ending with the ripe fruit, the result of all these researches, the Sutras of Vyâsa—the one background to all these different analyses and syntheses of the human mind is still the Shrutis. Even in the philosophical writings of the Buddhists or Jains, the help of the Shrutis is never rejected, and at least in some of the Buddhistic schools, and in the majority of the Jain writings, the authority of the Shrutis is fully admitted, excepting what they call the Himsaka Shrutis, which they hold to be interpolations of the Brahmins. In recent

[1] Atoms, entities composed of two atoms, entities composed of three atoms.

[2] Genus, substance, quality, inherence.

times, such a view has been held by the late great Swami Dayananda Sarasvati.

If one is asked to point out the system of thought towards which as a centre all the ancient and modern Indian thoughts have converged, if one wants to see the real backbone of Hinduism in all its various manifestations, the Sutras of Vyasa will unquestionably be pointed out as constituting all that.

Whether one hears the Advaita-Keshari roaring in peals of thunder the Asti, Bhâti, and Priya[1] amidst the heartstopping solemnities of the Himalayan forests, mixing with the solemn cadence of the river of heaven, or listens to the cooing of the Piyâ, Pitam[2] in the beautiful bowers of the grove of Vrindâ; whether one mingles with the sedate meditations of the monasteries of Varanasi, or the ecstatic dances of the followers of the Prophet of Nadia; whether one sits at the feet of the teacher of the Vishishtâdvaita system with its Vadakale, Tenkale,[3] and all the other subdivisions, or listens with reverence to the Acharyas of the Madhva school; whether one hears the martial "Wâh Guru Ki Fateh"[4] of the secular Sikhs, or the sermons on the Grantha Sâhib of the Udâsis and Nirmalâs; whether he salutes the Sannyâsin disciples of Kabir with "Sat Sâhib", or listens with joy to the Sâkhis (Bhajans); whether he pores upon the wonderful lore of that reformer of Rajputana, Dâdu, or the works of his royal disciple, Sundaradâsa, down to the great Nishchaladâsa, the celebrated author of *Vichârasâgara*—which book has more influence in India than any that has been written in any language within the last three centuries; if even one asks the Bhangi Mehtar of Northern India to sit down and give an account of the teachings of his Lâlguru—one will find that all these various teachers and schools have as their basis that system whose authority is the Shruti, Gita its divine commentary, the *Shâriraka-Sutras* its organised system, and all the different sects in India, from the Paramahamsa Parivrâjakâchâryas to the poor despised Mehtar disples of Lalguru, are different manifestations.

These three Prasthânas,[5] then, in their different explana-

[1] Exists (Sat), Shines (Chit), is beloved (Ananda)—the three predicates of Brahman.

[2] Darling, beloved.

[3] The two divisions of the Ramanuja sect.

[4] Victory to the Guru.

[5] "Courses", viz the Upanishads, the Gita, and the *Shariraka-Sutras*.

tions, as Dvaita, Vishishtadvaita, or Advaita with a few minor recensions, form the "authorities" of the Hindu religion. The Purânas, the modern representations of the ancient Nârāsamsi (anecdote portion of the Vedas), supply the mythology, and the Tantras, the modern representations of the Brâhmanas (ritual and explanatory portion of the Vedas), supply the ritual. Thus the three Prasthanas, as authorities, are common to all the sects; but as to the Puranas and Tantras, each sect has its own.

The Tantras, as we have said, represent the Vedic rituals, in a modified form, and before any one jumps to the most absurd conclusions about them, I will advise him to read the Tantras in conjunction with the Brahmanas, especially the Adhvaryu portion. And most of the Mantras used in the Tantras will be found taken verbatim from their Brahmanas. As to their influence, apart from the Shrauta and Smârta rituals, all the forms of rituals in vogue from the Himalayas to Cape Comorin have been taken from the Tantras, and they direct the worship of the Shâkta or Shaiva or Vaishnava and all the others alike.

Of course, I do not pretend that all the Hindus are thoroughly acquainted with these sources of their religion. Many especially in lower Bengal, have not heard of the names of these sects and these great systems; but consciously or unconsciously, it is the plan laid down in the three Prasthanas, that they are all working out.

Wherever, on the other hand, the Hindi language is spoken, even the lowest classes have more knowledge of the Vedantic religion than many of the highest in lower Bengal.

And why so?

Transported from the soil of Mithilâ to Navadvipa, nurtured and developed by the fostering genius of Shiromani, Gadâdhara, Jagadisha, and a host of other great names, an analysis of the laws of reasoning, in some points superior to every other system in the whole world, expressed in a wonderful and precise mosaic of language, stands the Nyâya of Bengal, respected and studied throughout the length and breadth of Hindusthan. But alas, the Vedic study was sadly neglected, and until within the last few years, scarcely any one could be found in Bengal to teach the *Mahâbhâshya* of Patanjali. Once only a mighty genius rose above the never-ending Avachchhinnas and Avachchhedakas[1]—Bhagavan Shri Krishna Chaitanya. For once the religious lethargy of Bengal was shaken, and for a time it entered into communion with the religious life of other parts of India.

It is curious to note that though Shri Chaitanya obtained his Sannyasa from a Bhârati, and as such was a Bharati himself, it was through Mâdhavendra Puri that his religious genius was first awakened.

The Puris seem to have a peculiar mission in rousing the spirituality of Bengal. Bhagavan Shri Ramakrishna got his Sannyâsâshrama from Totâ Puri.

The commentary that Shri Chaitanya wrote on the *Vyâsa-Sutras* has either been lost or not found yet. His disciples joined themselves to the Mâdhvas of the South, and gradually the mantles of such giants as Rupa and Sanâtana and Jiva Goswâmi, fell on the shoulders of Bâbâjis, and the great movement of Shri Chaitanya was decaying fast, till of late years there is a sign of revival. Hope that it will regain its lost splendour.

The influence of Shri Chaitanya is all over India. Wherever the Bhakti-Mârga is known, there he is appreciated, studied and worshipped. I have every reason to believe that the whole of the Vallabhâchârya recension is only a branch of the sect founded by Shri Chaitanya. But most of his so-called disciples in Bengal do not know how his power is still working all over India; and how can they? The disciples have become Gadiâns (rich abbots), while he was preaching barefooted from door to door in India, begging Âchandâlas (all down to the lowest) to love God.

The curious and unorthodox custom of hereditary Gurus that prevails in Bengal, and for the most part in Bengal alone, is another cause of its being cut off from the religious life of the rest of India.

The greatest cause of all is that the life of Bengal never received an influx from that of the great brotherhood of Sannyasins who are the representatives and repositories of the highest Indian spiritual culture, even at the present day.

Tyâga (renunciation) is never liked by the higher classes of Bengal. Their tendency is for Bhoga (enjoyment). How can they get a deep insight into spiritual things? त्यागेनैके

[1] In Nyaya, "determined", and "determining attribute".

अमृतत्वमानशुः —"By renunciation (alone) immortality was reached." How can it be otherwise?

On the other hand, throughout the Hindi-speaking world, a succession of brilliant Tyagi teachers of far-reaching influence have brought the doctrines of the Vedanta to every door. Especially the impetus given to Tyaga during the reign of Ranjit Singh of the Punjab, has made the highest teachings of the Vedantic philosophy available for the very lowest of the low. With true pride, the Punjabi peasant girl says that even her spinning wheel repeats: "Soham," "Soham." And I have seen Mehtar Tyagis in the forest of Hrishikesh, wearing the garb of the Sannyasin, studying the Vedanta. And many a proud high-class man would be glad to sit at their feet and learn. And why not? अन्त्यादपि परं धर्मं—"Supreme knowledge (can be learnt) even from the man of low birth."

Thus it is that the North-West and the Punjab have a religious education which is far ahead of that of Bengal, Bombay, or Madras. The ever-travelling Tyagis of the various orders —Dashanâmis or Vairâgis or Panthis—bring religion to everybody's door, and the cost is only a bit of bread. And how noble and disinterested most of them are! There is one Sannyasin belonging to the Kachu Panthis, or independents (who do not identify themselves with any sect), who has been instrumental in the establishing of hundreds of schools and charitable asylums all over Rajputana. He has opened hospitals in forests, and thrown iron bridges over the gorges in the Himalayas, and this man never touches a coin with his hands, has no earthly possession except a blanket, which has given him the nick-name of the "Blanket Swami", and begs his bread from door to door. I have never known him taking a whole dinner from one house, lest it should be a tax on the householder. And he is only one amongst many. Do you think that so long as these gods on earth live in India, and protect the "Religion Eternal" with the impenetrable rampart of such godly characters, the old religion will die?

In this country,[1] the clergymen sometimes receive as high salaries as rupees thirty thousand, forty thousand, fifty thousand, even ninety thousand a year, for preaching two hours on Sunday only, and that only six months in a year. Look at the millions upon millions they spend for the support of their religion, and

[1] United States of America.

young Bengal has been taught that these Godlike, absolutely unselfish men like Kambli-Swami are idle vagabonds. मद्भक्तानाञ्च ये भक्तास्ते मे भक्ततमा मताः। —"Those who are devoted to My worshippers are regarded as the best of devotees."

Take an extreme case, that of an extremely ignorant Vairâgi. Even he, when he goes into a village, tries his best to impart to the villagers whatever he knows, from Tulasidâsa, or *Chaitanya-Charitâmrita* or the Âlwârs in Southern India. Is that not doing some good? And all this for only a bit of bread and a rag of cloth. Before unmercifully criticising them, think how much you do, my brother, for your poor fellow-countrymen, at whose expense you have got your education, and by grinding whose face you maintain your position and pay your teachers, for teaching you that the Babajis are only vagabonds.

A few of your fellow-countrymen in Bengal have criticised what they call—a new development of Hinduism. And well they may. For Hinduism is only just now penetrating into Bengal, where so long the whole idea of religion was a bundle of Deshâchâras (local customs) as to eating and drinking and marriage.

This short paper has not space for the discussion of such a big subject as to whether the view of Hinduism which the disciples of Ramakrishna have been preaching all over India, was according to the "Sad-Shâstras" or not. But I will give a few hints to our critics, which may help them in understanding our position better.

In the first place, I never contended that a correct idea of Hinduism can be gathered from the writings of Kâshidâsa or Krittivâsa, though their words are "Amrita Samâna" (like nectar), and those that hear them are "Punyavâns" (virtuous). But we must go to Vedic and Dârshanika authorities, and to the great Acharyas and their disciples all over India.

If, brethren, you begin with the Sutras of Gautama, and read his theories about the "Âptas" (inspired) in the light of the commentaries of Vâtsyâyana, and go up to the Mimâmsakas with Shabara and other commentators, you will find out what they say about अलौकिकप्रत्यक्षम् (supersensuous realisation), and who are the "Aptas", and whether every being can become an "Apta" or not, and that the proof of the Vedas is in their being the words of such "Aptas". If you have time to look into the introduction of Mahidhara to the Yajur-Veda, you will find a still more lucid discussion as to the Vedas being laws of the inner life of man, and as such they are eternal.

As to the eternity of Creation—this doctrine is the corner-stone not only of the Hindu religion but of the Buddhists and Jains also.

Now all the sects in India can be grouped roughly as following the Jnana-Marga or the Bhakti-Marga. If you will kindly look into the introduction to the *Shariraka-Bhashya* of Shri Shankaracharya, you will find there the Nirapekshatâ (transcendence) of Jnana is thoroughly discussed, and the conclusion is that realisation of Brahman or the attainment of Moksha does not depend upon ceremonial, creed, caste, colour, or doctrine. It will come to any being who has the four Sâdhanas, which are the most perfect moral culture.

As to the Bhaktas, even Bengali critics know very well that some of their authorities even declared that caste or nationality or sex, or, as to that, even the human birth, was never necessary to Moksha. Bhakti is the one and only thing necessary.

Both Jnana and Bhakti are everywhere preached to be unconditioned, and as such there is not one authority who lays down the conditions of caste or creed or nationality in attaining Moksha. See the discussion on the Sutra of Vyasa अन्तरा चापि तु तद्दृष्टे[1] by Shankara, Ramanuja, and Madhva.

Go through all the Upanishads, and even in the Samhitas, nowhere you will find the limited ideas of Moksha which every other religion has. As to toleration, it is everywhere; even in the Samhita of the Adhvaryu Veda, in the third or fourth verse of the fortieth chapter, if my memory does not fail, it begins with न बुद्धिभेदं जनयेदज्ञानां कर्मसंगिनाम् ।[2] This is running through everywhere. Was anybody persecuted in India for choosing his Ishta Devatâ (favourite deity), or becoming an atheist or agnostic even, so long as he obeyed the social regulations?

[1] "But also (persons standing) between (are qualified for knowledge); for that is seen (in scripture)."—III. iv. 36. A person, even if he does not belong to an Ashrama (not possessing the means to entitle him to one or other of the Ashramas) and thus stands between, as it were, is qualified for the knowledge of Brahman; for we meet scriptural passages declaring that even such persons possessed it. *Vide* Chh. Upa. IV. I; Bri. Upa. III. vi. & viii.

[2] "(The wise one) should not unsettle the understanding of the ignorant, attached to action." The line also occurs in the Gita.

Society may punish anybody by its disapprobation for breaking any of its regulations, but no man, the lowest Patita (fallen), is ever shut out from Moksha. You must not mix up the two together. As to that, in Malabar a Chandâla is not allowed to pass through the same street as a high-caste man, but let him become a Mohammedan or a Christian, he will be immediately allowed to go anywhere, and this rule has prevailed in the dominion of a Hindu sovereign for centuries. It may be queer, but it shows the idea of toleration for other religions even in the most untoward circumstances.

The one idea the Hindu religions differ in from every other in the world, the one idea to express which the sages almost exhaust the vocabulary of the Sanskrit language, is that man must realise God even in this life. And the Advaita texts very logically add, "To know God is to become God"

And here comes as a necessary consequence the broadest and most glorious idea of inspiration—not only as asserted and declared by the Rishis of the Vedas, not only by Vidura and Dharmavyâdha and a number of others, but even the other day Nishchaladasa, a Tyagi of the Dadupanthi sect, boldly declared in his *Vicharasagara*: "He who has known Brahman has become Brahman. His words are Vedas, and they will dispel the darkness of ignorance, either expressed in Sanskrit or any popular dialect."

Thus to realise God or Brahman, as the Dvaitins say, or to become Brahman, as the Advaitins say—is the aim and end of the whole teachings of the Vedas, and every other teaching therein contained represents a stage in the course of our progress thereto. And the great glory of Bhagavan Bhashyakara Shankaracharya is that it was his genius that gave the most wonderful expression to the ideas of Vyasa.

As absolute, Brahman alone is true; as relative truth, all the different sects, standing upon different manifestations of the same Brahman, either in India or elsewhere, are true. Only some are higher than others. Suppose a man starts straight towards the sun. At every step of his journey he will see newer and newer visions of the sun—the size, the view, and light will every moment be new until he reaches the real sun. He saw the sun at first like a big ball, and then it began to increase in size. The sun was never small like the ball he saw; nor was it ever like all the succession of suns he saw in his journey. Still is it not true that our traveller always saw the sun, and nothing but the sun? Similarly, all these various sects are true—some nearer, some further off from the real Sun —which is our एकमेवाद्वितीयम्—One without a second.

And as the Vedas are the only scriptures which teach this real absolute God, of which all other ideas of God are but minimised and limited visions; as the सर्वलोकहितैषिणी[1] Shruti takes the devotee gently by the hand, and leads him from one stage to another, through all the stages that are necessary for him to travel to reach the Absolute; and as all other religions represent one or other of these stages in an unprogressive and crystallised form—all the other religions of the world are included in the nameless, limitless, eternal Vedic religion.

Work hundreds of lives out, search every corner of your mind for ages, and still you will not find one noble religious idea that is not already imbedded in that infinite mine of spirituality.

As to the so-called Hindu idolatry, first go and learn the forms they are going through, and where it is that the worshippers are really worshipping—whether in the temple, in the image, or in the temple of their own bodies. First know for certain what they are doing—which more than ninety per cent of the revilers are thoroughly ignorant of—and then it will explain itself in the light of the Vedantic philosophy.

Still these Karmas are not compulsory; on the other hand, open your Manu, and see where it orders every old man to embrace the fourth Âshrama, and whether he embraces it or not, he must give up all Karma.

It is reiterated everywhere that all these Karmas ज्ञाने परिसमाप्यते—"finally end in Jnana".

As to the matter of that, a Hindu peasant has more religious education than many a gentleman in other countries. A friend criticised the use of European terms of philosophy and religion in my addresses. I would have been very glad to use Sanskrit terms; it would have been much more easy, as being the only perfect vehicle of religious thought. But the friend forgot that I was addressing an audience of Western people; and although a certain Indian missionary declared that the Hindus had forgotten the meaning of their Sanskrit books, and that it was the missionaries who unearthed the meaning,

[1] The well-wisher to all the world.

I could not find one in that large concourse of missionaries who could understand a line in Sanskrit—and yet some of them read learned papers criticising the Vedas, and all the sacred sources of the Hindu religion!

It is not true that I am against any religion. It is equally untrue that I am hostile to the Christian missionaries in India. But I protest against certain of their methods of raising money in America. What is meant by those pictures in the school-books for children where the Hindu mother is painted as throwing her children to the crocodiles in the Ganga? The mother is black, but the baby is painted white, to arouse more sympathy, and get more money. What is meant by those pictures which paint a man burning his wife at a stake with his own hands, so that she may become a ghost, and torment the husband's enemy? What is meant by the pictures of huge cars crushing over human beings? The other day a book was published for children in this country, where one of these gentlemen tells a narrative of his visit to Calcutta. He says he saw a car running over fanatics in the streets of Calcutta. I have heard one of these gentlemen preach in Memphis that in every village of India there is a pond full of the bones of little babies.

What have the Hindus done to these disciples of Christ that every Christian child is taught to call the Hindus "vile" and "wretches", and the most horrible devils on earth? Part of the Sunday School education for children here consists in teaching them to hate everybody who is not a Christian, and the Hindus especially, so that from their very childhood they may subscribe their pennies to the missions. If not for truth's sake, for the sake of the morality of their own children, the Christian missionaries ought not to allow such things going on. Is it any wonder that such children grow up to be ruthless and cruel men and women? The greater a preacher can paint the tortures of eternal hell—the fire that is burning there, the brimstone—the higher is his position among the orthodox. A servant-girl in the employ of a friend of mine had to be sent to a lunatic asylum as a result of her attending what they call here the revivalist preaching. The dose of hell-fire and brimstone was too much for her. Look again at the books published in Madras against the Hindu religion. If a Hindu writes one such line against the Christian religion, the missionaries will cry fire and vengeance.

My countrymen, I have been more than a year in this country. I have seen almost every corner of the society; and after comparing notes, let me tell you that neither are we devils, as the missionaries tell the world we are, nor are they angels, as they claim to be. The less the missionaries talk of immorality, infanticide, and the evils of the Hindu marriage system, the better for them. There may be actual pictures of some countries before which all the imaginary missionary pictures of the Hindu society will fade away into light. But my mission in life is not to be a paid reviler. I will be the last man to claim perfection for the Hindu society. No man is more conscious of the defects that are therein, or the evils that have grown up under centuries of misfortunes. If, foreign friends, you come with genuine sympathy to help and not to destroy, Godspeed to you. But if by abuses incessantly hurled against the head of a prostrate race, in season and out of season, you mean only the triumphant assertion of the moral superiority of your own nation, let me tell you plainly, if such a comparison be instituted with any amount of justice, the Hindu will be found head and shoulders above all other nations in the world as a moral race.

In India religion was never shackled. No man was ever challenged in the selection of his Ishta Devatâ, or his sect, or his preceptor, and religion grew, as it grew nowhere else. On the other hand, a fixed point was necessary to allow this infinite variation to religion, and society was chosen as that point in India. As a result, society became rigid and almost immovable. For liberty is the only condition of growth.

On the other hand, in the West, the field of variation was society, and the constant point was religion. Conformity was the watchword and even now is the watchword of European religion, and each new departure had to gain the least advantage only by wading through a river of blood. The result is a splendid social organisation, with a religion that never rose beyond the grossest materialistic conceptions.

Today the West is awakening to its wants, and the "true self of man" and "spirit" is the watchword of the advanced school of Western theologians. The student of Sanskrit philosophy knows where the wind is blowing from, but it matters not whence the power comes so long as it brings new life.

In India, new circumstances at the same time are persistently demanding a new adjustment of social organisations. For the last three-quarters of a century, India has been bubbling over with reform societies and reformers. But, alas, every one of them has proved a failure. They did not know the secret. They had not learnt the great lesson to be learnt. In their haste, they laid all the evils in our society at the door of religion, and, like the man in the story, wanting to kill the mosquito that sat on a friend's forehead, they were trying to deal such heavy blows as would have killed man and mosquito together. But in this case, fortunately, they only dashed themselves against immovable rocks, and were crushed out of existence in the shock of recoil. Glory unto those noble and unselfish souls who have struggled and failed in their misdirected attempts. Those galvanic shocks of reformatory zeal were necessary to rouse the sleeping leviathan. But they were entirely destructive, and not constructive, and as such they were mortal and therefore died.

Let us bless them, and profit by their experience. They had not learnt the lesson that all is a growth from inside out, that all evolution is only a manifestation of a preceding involution. They did not know that the seed can only assimilate the surrounding elements, but grows a tree in its own nature. Until all the Hindu race becomes extinct, and a new race takes possession of the land, such a thing can never be—try East or West, India can never be Europe until she dies.

And will she die—this old Mother of all that is noble or moral or spiritual, the land which the sages trod, the land in which Godlike men still live and breathe? I will borrow the lantern of the Athenian sage, and follow you, my brother, through the cities and villages, plains and forests, of this broad world—show me such men in other lands if you can. Truly have they said, the tree is known by its fruits. Go under every mango tree in India; pick up bushels of the worm-eaten, unripe, fallen ones from the ground, and write hundreds of the most learned volumes on each one of them—still you have not described a single mango. Pluck a luscious, full-grown, juicy one from the tree, and now you have known all that the mango is.

Similarly, these Man-Gods show what the Hindu religion is. They show the character, the power and the possibilities of that racial tree which counts culture by centuries, and has borne the buffets of a thousand years of hurricane, and still stands with the unimpaired vigour of eternal youth.

Shall India die? Then from the world all spirituality will be extinct; all moral perfection will be extinct; all sweet-souled sympathy for religion will be extinct; all ideality will be extinct; and in its place will reign the duality of lust and luxury as the male and female deities, with money as its priest; fraud, force, and competition its ceremonies; and the human soul its sacrifice. Such a thing can never be. The power of suffering is infinitely greater than the power of doing; the power of love is infinitely of greater potency than the power of hatred. Those that think that the present revival of Hinduism is only a manifestation of patriotic impulse are deluded.

First, let us study the quaint phenomenon.

Is it not curious that, whilst under the terrific onset of modern scientific research, all the old forts of Western dogmatic religions are crumbling into dust; whilst the sledge-hammer blows of modern science are pulverising the porcelain mass of systems whose foundation is either in faith or in belief, or in the majority of votes of church synods; whilst Western theology is at its wit's end to accommodate itself to the ever-rising tide of aggressive modern thought; whilst in all other sacred books the texts have been stretched to their utmost tension, under the ever-increasing pressure of modern thought, and the majority of them are broken and have been stored away in lumber rooms; whilst the vast majority of thoughtful Western humanity have broken asunder all their ties with the church, and are drifting about in a sea of unrest—the religions which have drunk the water of life at that fountain of light, the Vedas—Hinduism and Buddhism—alone are reviving?

The restless Western atheist or agnostic finds in the Gita or in the *Dhammapada* the only place where his soul can anchor.

The tables have been turned, and the Hindu, who saw through tears of despair his ancient homestead covered with incendiary fire, ignited by unfriendly hands, now sees, when the search-light of modern thought has dispersed the smoke, that his home is the one that is standing in all its strength, and all the rest have either vanished or are building their houses anew after the Hindu plan. He has wiped away his tears, and has found that the axe that tried to cut down to the roots the ऊर्ध्वमूलमधःशाखं अश्वत्थं प्राहुरव्ययम्[1] has proved the merciful knife of the surgeon.

He has found that he has neither to torture texts nor commit any other form of intellectual dishonesty to save his religion. Nay, he may call all that is weak in his scriptures weak, because they were meant to be so by the ancient sages, to help the weak, under the theory of—अरुन्धतीदर्शनन्याय ।[2] Thanks to the ancient sages who have discovered such an all-pervading, ever-expanding system of religion that can accommodate all that has been discovered in the realm of matter, and all that is to be known; he has begun to appreciate them anew, and discover anew that those discoveries which have proved so disastrous to every limited little scheme of religion, are but rediscoveries, in the plane of intellect and sense-consciousness, of truths which his ancestors discovered ages ago in the higher plane of intuition and superconsciousness.

He has not therefore to give up anything nor go about seeking for anything anywhere, but it will be enough for him if he can utilise only a little from the infinite store he has inherited, and apply it to his needs. And that he has begun to do, and will do more and more. Is this not the real cause of this revival?

Young men of Bengal, to you I especially appeal. Brethren, we know to our shame that most of the real evils for which the foreign races abuse the Hindu nation are only owing to us. We have been the cause of bringing many undeserved calumnies on the head of the other races in India. But glory unto God,

[1] "They speak of an eternal Ashvattha, rooted above and branching below, whose leaves are the Vedas." (Gita XV. i).

[2] When a bride is brought to the house of her husband for the first time, he shows her a tiny star called Arundhati. To do this, he has to direct her gaze the right way, which he does by asking her to look at something near and big in the direction of the star, e.g. a branch of a tree. Next he draws her attention to a large bright star observed beyond this branch and so on, till by several steps, he succeeds in leading her eyes to the right thing. This method of leading to a subtle object through easy and gradual steps is called Arundhati Nyaya.

we have been fully awakened to it, and with His blessings, we will not only cleanse ourselves, but help the whole of India to attain the ideals preached in the religion eternal.

Let us wipe off first that mark which nature always puts on the forehead of a slave—the stain of jealousy. Be jealous of none. Be ready to lend a hand to every worker of good. Send a good thought for every being in the three worlds.

Let us take our stand on the one central truth in our religion, the common heritage of the Hindus, the Buddhists, and Jains alike—the Spirit of man, the Atman of man, the immortal, birthless, all-pervading, eternal Soul of man, whose glories the Vedas cannot themselves express, before whose majesty the universe with its galaxy upon galaxy of suns and stars and nebulae is as a drop. Every man or woman, nay, from the highest Devas to the worm that crawls under your feet, is such a Spirit evoluted or involuted. The difference is not in kind, but in degree.

This infinite power of the Spirit, brought to bear upon matter evolves material development, made to act upon thought evolves intellectuality, and made to act upon Itself makes of man a God.

First, let us be gods, and then help others to be gods. "Be and make." Let this be our motto. Say not man is a sinner. Tell him that he is a god. Even if there were a devil, it would be our duty to remember God always, and not the devil.

If the room is dark, the constant feeling and repeating of darkness will not take it away, but bring in the light. Let us know that all that is negative, all that is destructive, all that is mere criticism, is bound to pass away; it is the positive, the affirmative, the constructive, that is immortal, that will remain for ever. Let us say, "We are" and "God is", and "We are God", "Shivoham, Shivoham", and march on. Not matter, but Spirit. All that has name and form is subject to all that has none. This is the eternal truth the Shrutis preach. Bring in the light; the darkness will vanish of itself. Let the lion of Vedanta roar; the foxes will fly to their holes. Throw the ideas broadcast, and let the result take care of itself. Let us put the chemicals together; the crystallisation will take its own course. Bring forth the power of the Spirit, and pour it over the length and breadth of India, and all that is necessary will come by itself.

Manifest the divinity within you, and everything will be harmoniously arranged around it. Remember the illustration of Indra and Virochana in the Vedas; both were taught their divinity. But the Asura, Virochana, took his body for his God. Indra, being a Deva, understood that the Atman was meant. You are the children of Indra. You are the descendants of the Devas. Matter can never be your God; body can never be your God.

India will be raised, not with the power of the flesh, but with the power of the Spirit; not with the flag of destruction, but with the flag of peace and love, the garb of the Sannyasin; not by the power of wealth, but by the power of the begging-bowl. Say not that you are weak. The Spirit is omnipotent. Look at that handful of young men called into existence by the divine touch of Ramakrishna's feet. They have preached the message from Assam to Sind, from the Himalayas to Cape Comorin. They have crossed the Himalayas at a height of twenty thousand feet over snow and ice on foot, and penetrated into the mysteries of Tibet. They have begged their bread, covered themselves with rags; they have been persecuted, followed by the police, kept in prison, and at last set free when the Government was convinced of their innocence.

They are now twenty. Make them two thousand tomorrow. Young men of Bengal, your country requires it. The world requires it. Call up the divinity within you, which will enable you to bear hunger and thirst, heat and cold. Sitting in luxurious homes, surrounded with all the comforts of life, and doling out a little amateur religion may be good for other lands, but India has a truer instinct. It intuitively detects the mask. You must give up. Be great. No great work can be done without sacrifice. The Purusha Himself sacrificed Himself to create this world. Lay down your comforts, your pleasures, your names, fame, or position, nay even your lives, and make a bridge of human chains over which millions will cross this ocean of life. Bring all the forces of good together. Do not care under what banner you march. Do not care what be your colour—green, blue, or red—but mix up all the colours and produce that intense glow of white, the colour of love. Ours is to work; the results will take care of themselves. If any social institution stands in your way of becoming God, it will give way before the power of Spirit. I do not see into the future, nor do I care to see. But one vision I see clear as life before me: that the ancient Mother has awakened once more, sitting on Her throne rejuvenated, more glorious than ever. Proclaim Her to all the world with the voice of peace and benediction.

Yours ever in love and labour,

VIVEKANANDA.

AN APPEAL TO HIS COUNTRYMEN*

(From *Modern India*)

On one side, New India is saying, "If we only adopt Western ideas, Western language, Western food, Western dress and Western manners, we shall be as strong and powerful as the Western nations"; on the other, Old India is saying, "Fools! By imitation, other's ideas never become one's own—nothing, unless earned, is your own. Does the ass in lion's skin become the lion?"

On one side, New India is saying, "What the Western nations do is surely good, otherwise how did they become so great?" On the other side, Old India is saying, "The flash of lightning is intensely bright, but only for a moment; look out, boys, it is dazzling your eyes. Beware!"

Have we not then to learn anything from the West? Must we not needs try and exert ourselves for better things? Are we perfect? Is our society entirely spotless, without any flaw? There are many things to learn, we must struggle for new and higher things till we die; struggle is the end of human life. Shri Ramakrishna used to say, "As long as I live, so long do I learn". That man or that society which has nothing to learn, is already in the jaws of death. Yes, learn we must many things from the West—but there are fears as well.

A certain young man of little understanding used always to blame the Hindu Shâstras before Shri Ramakrishna. One day he praised the Bhagavad-Gitâ, on which Shri Ramakrishna said, "Methinks some European Pandit has praised the Gita, and so he has also followed suit".

O India, this is your terrible danger. The spell of imitating the West is getting such a strong hold upon you that what is good or what is bad is no longer decided by reason, judgment, discrimination, or reference to the Shastras. Whatever ideas, whatever manners the white men praise or like, are good; whatever things they dislike or censure, are bad! Alas! what can be a more tangible proof of foolishness than this?

Western ladies move freely everywhere, therefore that is good; they choose for themselves their husbands, therefore that is the highest step of advancement; the Westerners disapprove of our dress, decorations, food, and ways of living, therefore they must be very bad; the Westerners condemn image-worship as sinful, surely, then, image-worship is the greatest sin, there is no doubt of it!

The Westerners say that worshipping a single Deity is fruitful of the highest spiritual good, therefore let us throw our gods and goddesses into the river Gangâ! The Westerners hold caste distinctions to be obnoxious, therefore let all the different castes be jumbled into one! The Westerners say that child-marriage is the root of all evils, therefore that is also very bad, of a certainty it is!

We are not discussing here whether these customs deserve continuance or rejection; but if the mere disapproval of the Westerners be the measure of the abominableness of our manners and customs, then it is our duty to raise our emphatic protest against it.

The present writer has, to some extent, personal experience of Western society. His conviction resulting from such experience has been that there is such a wide divergence between Western society and Indian, as regards the main course and goal of each, that any sect in India, framed after the Western model, will miss the aim. We have not the least sympathy for those who, never having lived in Western society and, therefore, utterly ignorant of the rules and prohibitions regarding the association of men and women that obtain there, and which act as safeguards to preserve the purity of the Western women, allow an unrestricted intermingling of men and women in our society.

I have observed in the West also that the children of weaker nations, if born in England, give themselves out as Englishmen, instead of Greek, Portuguese, Spaniard, etc. as the case may be. All drift towards the strong; that the light which shines in the glorious, may somehow fall and reflect on one's own body, i.e. to shine in the borrowed light of the great, is the one desire of the weak. When I see Indians dressed in European costume, the thought comes to my mind, perhaps they feel ashamed to own their nationality and kinship with the ignorant, poor, illiterate, downtrodden people of India! Nourished by the blood of the Hindu for the last fourteen centuries, the Parsee is no longer a "native"! Before the arrogance of the casteless, who pretend to be and glorify themselves in being Brahmins, the true nobility of the old, heroic, high-class Brahmin melts into nothingness! Again, the Westerners have now taught us that those stupid, ignorant low-caste millions of India, clad only in loin cloths, are non-Aryans. They are therefore no more our kith and kin!

O India! With this mere echoing of others, with this base imitation of others, with this dependence on others, this slavish weakness, this vile, detestable cruelty—wouldst thou, with these provisions only, scale the highest pinnacle of civilisation and greatness? Wouldst thou attain, by means of thy disgraceful cowardice, that freedom deserved only by the brave and the heroic? O India, forget not that the ideal of thy womanhood is Sitâ, Sâvitri, Damayanti; forget not that the God thou worshippest is the great Ascetic of ascetics, the all-renouncing Shankara, the Lord of Umâ; forget not that thy marriage, thy wealth, thy life are not for sense pleasure, are not for thy individual personal happiness; forget not that thou art born as a sacrifice to the Mother's altar; forget not that thy social order is but the reflex of the Infinite Universal Motherhood; forget not that the lower classes, the ignorant, the poor, the illiterate, the cobbler, the sweeper, are thy flesh and blood, thy brothers. Thou brave one, be bold, take courage, be proud that thou art an Indian, and proudly proclaim, "I am an Indian, every Indian is my brother". Say, "The ignorant Indian, the poor and destitute Indian, the Brahmin Indian, the Pariah Indian, is my brother". Thou, too, clad with but a rag round thy loins, proudly proclaim at the top of thy voice, "The Indian is my brother, the Indian is my life, India's gods and goddesses are my God, India's society is the cradle of my infancy, the pleasure-garden of my youth, the sacred heaven, the Vârânasi of my old age." Say, brother, "The soil of India is my highest heaven, the good of India is my good," and repeat and pray day and night, "O thou Lord of Gauri, O Thou Mother of the Universe, vouchsafe manliness unto me! O Thou Mother of Strength, take away my weakness, take away my unmanliness, and make me a Man!"

HINDUISM AND SHRI RAMAKRISHNA*

By the word "Shâstras" the Vedas without beginning or end are meant. In matters of religious duty the Vedas are the only competent authority.

The Purânas and other religious scriptures are all denoted by the word "Smriti". And their authority goes so far as they follow the Vedas and do not contradict them.

Truth is of two kinds: (1) that which is cognisable by the five ordinary senses of man, and by reasonings based thereon; (2) that which is cognisable by the subtle, supersensuous power of Yoga.

Knowledge acquired by the first means is called science; and knowledge acquired by the second is called the Vedas.

The whole body of supersensuous truths, having no beginning or end, and called by the name of the Vedas, is eternal. The Creator Himself is creating, preserving, and destroying the universe with the help of these truths.

The person in whom this supersensuous power is manifested is called Rishi, and the supersensuous truths which he realises by this power are called the Vedas.

This Rishihood, this power of supersensuous preception of the Vedas, is real religion. And so long as this does not develop in the life of an initiate, so long is religion a mere empty word to him, and it is to be understood that he has not yet taken the first step in religion.

The authority of the Vedas extends to all ages, climes, and persons; that is to say, their application is not confined to any particular place, time, and persons.

The Vedas are the only exponent of the Universal Religion.

Although the supersensuous vision of truths is to be met with in some measure in our Puranas and Itihâsas and in the religious scriptures of other races, still the fourfold scripture known among the Aryan race as the Vedas being the first, the most complete, and the most undistorted collection of spiritual truths, deserve to occupy the highest place among all scriptures, command the respect of all nations of the earth, and furnish the rationale of all their respective scriptures.

With regard to the whole Vedic collection of truths discovered by the Aryan race, this also has to be understood that those portions alone which do not refer to purely secular matters and which do not merely record tradition or history, or merely provide incentives to duty, form the Vedas in the real sense.

The Vedas are divided into two portions, the Jnâna-kânda (knowledge-portion) and the Karma-kânda (ritual portion). The ceremonies and the fruits of the Karma-kanda are confined within the limits of the world of Mâyâ, and therefore they have been undergoing and will undergo transformation according to the law of change which operates through time, space, and personality.

Social laws and customs likewise, being based on this Karma-kanda, have been changing and will continue to change hereafter. Minor social usages also will be recognised and accepted when they are compatible with the spirit of the true scriptures and the conduct of holy sages. But blind allegiance only to usages, such as are repugnant to the spirit of the Shastras and the conduct of holy sages, has been one of the main causes of the downfall of the Aryan race.

It is the Jnana-kanda or the Vedanta only that has for all time commanded recognition for leading men across Maya and bestowing salvation on them through the practice of Yoga, Bhakti, Jnana, or selfless work; and as its authority remains unaffected by any limitations of time, place, or person, it is the only exponent of the universal and eternal religion for all mankind.

The Samhitâs of Manu and other sages, following the lines laid down in the Karma-kanda, have mainly ordained rules of conduct conducive to social welfare, according to the exigencies of time, place, and person. The Puranas etc. have taken up the truths imbedded in the Vedanta and have explained them in detail by way of describing the exalted life and deeds of Avatâras and others. They have each emphasised, besides, some out of the infinite aspects of the Divine Lord to teach men about them.

But when by the process of time, fallen from the true ideals and rules of conduct, devoid of the spirit of renunciation, addicted only to blind usages and degraded in intellect, the descendants of the Aryans failed to appreciate even the spirit of these Puranas etc., which taught men of ordinary intelligence the abstruse truths of the Vedanta in concrete form and diffuse language and appeared antagonistic to one another on the surface, because of each inculcating with special emphasis only particular aspects of the Spiritual Ideal—

And when, as a consequence, they reduced India, the fair land of religion to a scene of almost infernal confusion by breaking up into fragments the one Eternal Religion of the Vedas (Sanâtana Dharma), the grand synthesis of all the aspects of the Spiritual Ideal, into conflicting sects and by seeking to sacrifice one another in the flames of sectarian hatred and intolerance—

Then it was that Shri Bhagavân Ramakrishna incarnated himself in India, to demonstrate what the true religion of the Aryan race is; to show where amidst all its many divisions and offshoots, scattered over the land in the course of its immemorial history, lies the true unity of the Hindu religion, which by its overwhelming number of sects, discordant to superficial view, quarrelling constantly with one another and abounding in customs divergent in every way, has constituted itself a misleading enigma for our countrymen and the butt of contempt for foreigners; and, above all, to hold up before men, for their lasting welfare, as a living embodiment of the Sanatana Dharma, his own wonderful life, into which he infused the universal and eternal spirit of this Dharma, so long cast into oblivion by the process of time.

In order to show how the Vedic truths, eternally existent as the instrument with the Creator in His work of creation, preservation, and dissolution, reveal themselves spontaneously in the minds of the Rishis purified of all impressions of worldly attachment, and because such verification of the scriptural truths will help the revival, reinstatement, and spread of Religion, the Lord, though the very embodiment of the Vedas, has, in this new incarnation of His, thoroughly discarded all external forms of learning.

That the Lord incarnates Himself again and again in human form for the protection of the Vedas or the true religion, and of Brahminhood or the ministry of that religion, is a doctrine well established in the Puranas etc.

The waters of a river falling in a cataract acquire greater velocity, the rising wave after a hollow swells higher; so after every spell of decline, the Aryan society, recovering from all the evils by the merciful dispensation of Providence, has risen the more glorious and powerful—such is the testimony of history.

After rising from every fall, our revived society is expressing more and more its innate eternal perfection, and so also the omnipresent Lord, in each successive incarnation, is manifesting Himself more and more.

Again and again has our country fallen into a swoon, as it were, and again and again has India's Lord, by the manifestation of Himself, revivified her.

But no pall of darkness greater than the present deep, dismal night, now almost over, had ever before enveloped this holy land of ours. And compared with the depth of this fall, all previous falls appear like little hoof-marks.

Therefore, before the effulgence of this new awakening, the glory of all past revivals in her history will pale like stars before the rising sun, and compared with this mighty manifestation of renewed strength, many past epochs of such restoration will all be as child's play.

The various constituent ideals of the Religion Eternal during its present state of decline, have been lying scattered here and there for want of competent men to realise them—some being partially preserved among small sects, and some completely lost.

But strong in the strength of this new spiritual renaissance, men, after reorganising these scattered and disconnected spiritual ideals, will be able to comprehend and practise them in their own lives and also to recover from oblivion those that are lost. And as the sure pledge of this glorious future, the all-merciful Lord has manifested in the present age, as stated above, an incarnation which, in point of completeness in revelation, its harmonising of all ideals and its promoting of every sphere of spiritual culture, surpasses the manifestations of all past ages.

So, at the very dawn of this momentous epoch, the reconciliation of all aspects and ideals of religious thought and worship is being proclaimed; this boundless, all-embracing idea had been lying inherent, but so long concealed, in the Religion Eternal and its scriptures, and now rediscovered, it is being declared to humanity in a trumpet voice.

This epochal new dispensation is the harbinger of great good to the whole world, specially to India; and the inspirer of this dispensation, Shri Bhagavan Ramakrishna, is the reformed and remodelled manifestation of all the past great epoch-makers in religion. O man, have faith in this, and lay it to heart.

The dead never return; the past night does not reappear; a spent-up tidal wave does not rise anew; neither does man inhabit the same body over again. So from the worship of the dead past, O man, we invite you to the worship of the living present; from the regretful brooding over bygones, we invite you to the activities of the present; from the waste of energy in retracing lost and demolished pathway, we call you to broad new-laid highways lying very near. He that is wise, let him understand.

Of that power which at the very first impulse has roused echoes from all the four quarters of the globe, conceive in your mind the manifestation in its fullness; and discarding all idle misgivings, weaknesses, and jealousies characteristic of enslaved peoples, come and help in the turning of this mighty wheel of new dispensation!

With the conviction firmly rooted in your heart that you are the servants of the Lord, His children, and helpers in the fulfilment of His purpose, enter the arena of work.

ON THE UPPER CASTES OF INDIA*

However much you may parade your descent from Aryan ancestors and sing the glories of ancient India day and night, and however much you may be strutting in the pride of your birth, you, the upper classes of India, do you think you are alive? You are but mummies ten thousand years old! It is among those whom your ancestors despised as "walking carrion", that the little of vitality there is still in India is to be found; and it is you who are the real "walking corpses". Your houses, your furniture, look like museum specimens, so lifeless and antiquated they are; and even an eye-witness of your manners and customs, your movements and modes of life, is inclined to think that he is listening to a grandmother's tale! When, even after making a personal acquaintance with you, one returns home, one seems to think one had been to visit the paintings in an art gallery! In this world of Mâyâ, you are the real illusions, the mystery, the real mirage in the desert, you, the upper classes of India! You represent the past tense, with all its varieties of form jumbled into one. That one still seems to see you at the present time, is nothing but a nightmare brought on by indigestion. You are the void, the unsubstantial nonentities of the future. Denizens of the dreamland, why are you loitering any longer? Fleshless and bloodless skeletons of the dead body of Past India that you are, why do you not quickly reduce yourselves into dust and disappear in the air? Ay, on your bony fingers are some priceless rings of jewel, treasured up by your ancestors, and within the embrace of your stinking corpses are preserved a good many ancient treasure-chests. Up to now you have not had the opportunity to hand them over. Now under the British rule, in these days of free education and enlightenment, pass them on to your heirs, ay, do it as quickly as you can. You merge yourselves in the void and disappear, and let New India arise in your place.

Let her arise—out of the peasants' cottage, grasping the plough; out of the huts of the fisherman, the cobbler, and the sweeper. Let her spring from the grocer's shop, from beside the oven of the fritter-seller. Let her emanate from the factory, from marts and from markets Let her emerge from groves and forests, from hills and mountains. These common people have suffered oppression for thousands of years—suffered it without murmur, and as a result have got wonderful fortitude. They have suffered eternal misery, which has given them unflinching vitality. Living on a handful of gram, they can convulse the world; give them only half a piece of bread, and the whole world will not be big enough to contain their energy; they are endowed with the inexhaustible vitality of a Raktabija.[1] And besides, they have got the wonderful strength that comes of a pure and moral life, which is not to be found anywhere else in the world. Such peacefulness, such contentment, such love, such power of silent and incessant work, and such manifestation of lion's strength in times of action—where else will you find these! Skeletons of the Past, there, before you, are your successors, the India that is to be. Throw those treasure-chests of yours and those jewelled rings among them, as soon as you can; and you vanish into the air, and be seen no more—only keep your ears open. No sooner will you disappear than you will hear the inaugural shout of renascent India, ringing with the voice of a million thunders and reverberating throughout the universe, "Wah Guru Ki Fateh"—victory to the Guru!

[1] A powerful demon mentioned in the Durgâ-Saptashati, every drop of whose blood falling to the ground produced another demon like him.

(12)

ALMORA,
29th July, 1897.

MY DEAR MISS NOBLE,[1]

A letter from Sturdy reached me yesterday, informing me that you are determined to come to India and see things with your own eyes. I replied to that yesterday; but what I learnt from Miss Müller about your plans makes this further note necessary, and it is better that it should be direct.

Let me tell you frankly that I am now convinced that you have a great future in the work for India. What was wanted was not a man, but a woman; a real lioness, to work for the Indians, women specially.

India cannot yet produce great women, she must borrow them from other nations. Your education, sincerity, purity, immense love, determination, and above all, the Celtic blood make you just the woman wanted.

Yet the difficulties are many. You cannot form any idea of the misery, the superstition, and the slavery that are here. You will be in the midst of a mass of half-naked men and women with quaint ideas of caste and isolation, shunning the white skin through fear or hatred and hated by them intensely. On the other hand, you will be looked upon by the white as a crank, and every one of your movements will be watched with suspicion.

Then the climate is fearfully hot; our winter in most places being like your summer, and in the South it is always blazing.

Not one European comfort is to be had in places out of the cities. If in spite of all this you dare venture into the work, you are welcome, a hundred times welcome. As for me, I am nobody here as elsewhere, but what little influence I have, shall be devoted to your service.

You must think well before you plunge in; and after work, if you fail in this or get disgusted, on my part I promise you I *will stand by you unto death* whether you work for India or not, whether you give up Vedanta or remain in it. "The tusks of the elephant come out, but never go back"; so are the words of a man never retracted. I promise you that. Again, I must

[1] Miss Margaret E. Noble—later Sister Nivedita.

give you a bit of warning. You must stand on your own feet and not be under the wings of Miss Müller or anybody else. Miss Müller is a good lady in her own way, but unfortunately it got into her head, when she was a girl, that she was a born leader and that no other qualifications were necessary to move the world but money! This idea is coming on the surface again and again in spite of herself and you will find it impossible to pull on with her in a few days. She now intends to take a house in Calcutta for herself and yourself and other European or American friends who may come.

It is very kind and good of her, but her Lady Abbess plan will never be carried out for two reasons—her violent temper and overbearing conduct, and her awfully vacillating mind. Friendship with many is best at a distance and everything goes well with the person who stands on his own feet.

Mrs. Sevier is a jewel of a lady, so good, so kind. The Seviers are the *only* English people who do not hate the *natives,* Sturdy not excepted. Mr. and Mrs. Sevier are the only persons who *did not come* to patronise us, but they have no fixed plans yet. When you come, you may get them to work with you and that will be really helpful to them and to you. But after all it is absolutely necessary to stand on one's own feet.

I learn from America two friends of mine, Mrs. Ole Bull of Boston and Miss MacLeod, are coming on a visit to India this autumn. Miss MacLeod you already know in London, the Paris-dressed young American lady; Mrs. Ole Bull is about fifty and has been a kind friend to me in America.

I may suggest that your joining the party may while away the tedium of the journey, as they also are coming by way of Europe.

I am glad to receive a note at last from Sturdy after long. But it was so stiff and cold. It seems he is disappointed at the collapse of the London work.

With everlasting love.

Yours ever in the Lord,
VIVENANANDA.

(13)

ALMORA,
10th June, 1898.

MY DEAR FRIEND,[1]

I appreciate your letter very much and am extremely happy to learn that the Lord is silently preparing wonderful things for our motherland.

Whether we call it Vedantism or any *ism,* the truth is that Advaitism is the last word of religion and thought and the only position from which one can look upon all religions and sects with love. We believe it is the religion of the future enlightened humanity. The Hindus may get the credit of arriving at it earlier than other races, they being an older race than either the Hebrew or the Arab; yet practical Advaitism, which looks upon and behaves to all mankind as one's own soul, is yet to be developed among the Hindus universally.

On the other hand our experience is that if ever the followers of any religion approach to this equality in an appreciable degree on the plane of practical workaday life —it may be quite unconscious generally of the deeper meaning and the underlying principle of such conduct, which the Hindus as a rule so clearly perceive—it is those of Islam and Islam alone.

Therefore we are firmly persuaded that without the help of practical Islam, theories of Vedantism, however fine and wonderful they may be, are entirely valueless to the vast mass of mankind. We want to lead mankind to the place where there is neither the Vedas nor the Bible nor the Koran; yet this has to be done by harmonising the Vedas, the Bible, and the Koran. Mankind ought to be taught that religions are but the varied expressions of THE RELIGION, which is Oneness, so that each may choose the path that suits him best.

For our own motherland a junction of the two great systems, Hinduism and Islam—Vedanta brain and Islam body —is the only hope.

I see in my mind's eye the future perfect India rising out of this chaos and strife, glorious and invincible, with Vedanta brain and Islam body.

[1] Mohammed Sarfaraz Husain of Naini Tal.

Ever praying that the Lord may make of you a great instrument for the help of mankind, and especially of our poor, poor motherland.

Yours with love,
VIVEKANANDA.

(14)*

C/o BABU PRIYANATH MOOKHERJI,
DEOGHAR, VAIDYANATH,
23rd Dec., 1898.

DEAR MOTHER,[1]

I am very glad to receive your letter. What you have understood is right. स ईशोऽनिर्वचनीयप्रेमस्वरूप: —"The Lord is identical with unspeakable love." That this characteristic of God mentioned by Nârada is manifest and admitted on all hands is the firm conviction of my life. The aggregate of many individuals is called Samashti (the whole), and each individual is called Vyashti (a part). You and I—each is Vyashti, society is Samashti. You, I, an animal, a bird, a worm, an insect, a tree, a creeper, the earth, a planet, a star—each is Vyashti, while this universe is Samashti, which is called Virât, Hiranyagarbha, or Ishvara in the Vedanta, and Brahmâ, Vishnu, Devi, etc. in the Puranas. Whether or not Vyashti has individual freedom, and if it has, what should be its measure, whether or not Vyashti should completely sacrifice its own will, its own happiness for Samashti—are the perennial problems before every society. Society everywhere is busy finding the solution of these problems. These, like big waves, are agitating modern Western society. The doctrine which demands the sacrifice of individual freedom to social supremacy is called socialism, while that which advocates the cause of the individual is called individualism.

Our motherland is a glowing example of the consequences of the eternal subjection of the individual to society and forced self-sacrifice by dint of institution and discipline. In this country men are born according to Shâstric injunctions, they eat and drink by prescribed rules throughout life, they go through marriage and kindred functions in the same way; in short, they

[1] Sm. Mrinalini Bose, distant relative and disciple of Swamiji.

even die according to Shastric injunctions. This hard discipline, with the exception of one great good point, is fraught with evil. The good point is that men can do one or two things well with very little effort, having practised them every day through generations. The delicious rice and curry which a cook of this country prepares with the aid of three lumps of earth and a few sticks can be had nowhere else. With the simple mechanism of an antediluvian loom worth one rupee, and the feet put in a pit, it is possible to make kincobs worth twenty rupees a yard, in this country alone. A torn mat, an earthen lamp, and that fed by castor oil—with the aid of such materials as these, wonderful *savants* are produced in this country alone. An all-forbearing attachment to an ugly and deformed wife, and a lifelong devotion to a worthless and villainous husband, are possible in this country alone. Thus far the bright side.

But all these things are done by people guided like lifeless machines—there is no mental activity, no unfoldment of the heart, no vibration of life, no flux of hope; there is no strong stimulation of the will, no experience of keen pleasure, nor the contact of intense sorrow; there is no stir of inventive genius, no desire for novelty, no appreciation of new things. Clouds never pass away from this mind, the radiant picture of the morning sun never charms this heart. It never even occurs to the mind to inquire if there is any better state than this; where it does, it cannot convince; in the event of conviction, effort is lacking; and even where there is effort, lack of enthusiasm kills it out.

If living by rule alone ensures excellence, if it be virtue strictly to follow the rules and customs handed down through generations, say then, who is more virtuous than a tree, who is a greater devotee, a holier saint, than a railway train? Who has ever seen a piece of stone transgress a natural law? Who has ever known cattle to commit sin?

The huge steamer, the mighty railway engine—they are non-intelligent; they move, turn, and run; but they are without intelligence. And yonder tiny worm which moved away from the railway line to save its life, why is it intelligent? There is no manifestation of will in the machine: it never wishes to transgress law; the worm wants to oppose law, rises against law whether it succeeds or not; therefore it is intelligent. Greater is the happiness, higher is the Jiva, in proportion as this will is more successfully manifest. The will of God is perfectly fruitful; therefore He is the highest.

What is education? Is it book-learning? No. Is it diverse knowledge? Not even that. The training by which the current and expression of will are brought under control and become fruitful is called education. Now consider, is that education as a result of which the will, being continuously choked by force through generations, is well-nigh killed out; is that education under whose sway, even the old ideas, let alone the new ones, are disappearing one by one; is that education which is slowly making man a machine? It is more blessed, in my opinion, even to go wrong impelled by one's free will and intelligence than to be good as an automaton. Again, can that be called society which is formed by an aggregate of men who are like lumps of clay, like lifeless machines, like heaped up pebbles? How can such society fare well? Were good possible, then, instead of being slaves for hundreds of years, we should have been the greatest nations on earth, and this soil of India, instead of being a mine of stupidity, would have been the eternal fountain-head of learning.

Is not self-sacrifice, then, a virtue? Is it not the most virtuous deed to sacrifice the happiness of one, the welfare of one, for the sake of the many? Exactly, but as the Bengali adage goes, "Can beauty be manufactured by rubbing and scrubbing? Can love be generated under compulsion?" What glory is there in the renunciation of an eternal beggar? What virtue is there in the sense-control of one devoid of sense-power? What, again, is the self-sacrifice of one devoid of ideas, devoid of heart, devoid of ambition, and devoid of the conception of what constitutes society? What expression of devotedness to a husband is there in forcing a widow to commit Sati? Why make people do virtuous deeds by teaching superstitions? I say, liberate, undo the shackles of people as much as you can. Can dirt be washed by dirt? Can bondage be removed by bondage? Where is the instance? When you will be able to sacrifice all desire for happiness for the sake of society, then you will be the Buddha, then you will be free; that is far off. Again, do you think the way to do it lies through oppression? "Oh, what an example of self-denial are our widows! Oh, how sweet is child-marriage! Is another such custom possible!

Can there be anything but love between husband and wife in such a marriage!"—such is the whine going round nowadays. But as to the men, the masters of the situation, there is no need of self-denial for them! Is there a virtue higher than serving others? But the same does not apply to Brahmins—you others do it! The truth is that in this country parents and relatives can ruthlessly sacrifice the best interests of their children and others for their own selfish ends, to save themselves by a compromise to society, and the teaching of generations, rendering the mind callous, has made it perfectly easy. The brave alone can deny self. The coward, afraid of the lash, with one hand wipes his eyes and gives with the other. What avail such gifts? It is a far cry to love universal. The young plant should be hedged in and taken care of. One can hope gradually to attain to universal love if one can learn to love one object unselfishly. If devotion to one particular Ishtadeva (favourite deity) is attained, devotion to the universal Virat is gradually possible.

Therefore, when one has been able to deny self for an individual, one may talk of self-sacrifice for the sake of society, not before. It is action with desire that leads to action without desire. Is the renunciation of desire possible if desire did not exist in the beginning? And what could it mean? Can light have any meaning if there is no darkness?

Worship with desire, with attachment, comes first. Begin with the worship of the little, then the greater will come of itself.

Mother, be not anxious. It is against the big tree that a great wind strikes. "Poking a fire makes it burn better"; "A snake struck on the head raises its hood"; and so on. When affliction seizes the heart, when the storm of sorrow blows all around, and it seems light will be seen no more, when hope and courage are almost gone, it is then, in the midst of this great spiritual tempest, that the light of the Brahman within gleams. Brought up in the lap of luxury, lying on a bed of roses, and never shedding a tear, who has ever become great, who has ever unfolded the Brahman within? Why do you fear to weep? Weep! Weeping clears the eyes and brings about intuition. Then the vision of diversity—man, animal, tree—slowly melts away and makes room for the infinite realisation of Brahman everywhere and in everything. Then—

समं पश्यन् हि सर्वत्र समवस्थितमीश्वरम् ।
न हिनस्त्यात्मनात्मानं ततो याति परां गतिम् ॥

—"Verily, seeing the same God equally existent everywhere, he does not injure the self by the self, and so goes to the Supreme Goal."

Ever your well-wisher,
VIVEKANANDA.

(15)*

DEOGHAR, VAIDYANATH,
3rd January, 1899.

DEAR MOTHER,[1]

Some very important questions have been raised in your letter. It is not possible to answer them fully in a short note, still I reply to them as briefly as possible.

(1) Rishi, Muni, or God—none has power to force an institution on society. When the needs of the times press hard on it, society adopts certain customs for self-preservation. Rishis have only recorded those customs. As a man often resorts even to such means as are good for immediate self-protection, but which are very injurious in the future, similarly, society also not unfrequently saves itself for the time being, but these immediate means which contributed to its preservation turn out to be terrible in the long run.

For example, take the prohibition of widow-marriage in our country. Don't think that Rishis or wicked men introduced the law pertaining to it. Notwithstanding the desire of men to keep women completely under their control, they never could succeed in introducing those laws without betaking themselves to the aid of a social necessity of the time. Of this custom two points should be specially observed:

(*a*) Widow-marriage takes place among the lower classes.

(*b*) Among the higher classes the number of women is greater than that of men.

Now, if it be the rule to marry every girl, it is difficult enough to get one husband apiece; then how to get, in succession, two or three for each? Therefore has society put one party under disadvantage, i.e. it does not let her have a second husband, who has had one; if it did, one maid would have to go without a husband. On the other hand, widow-marriage obtains in communities having a greater number of

[1] Shrimati Mrinalini Bose.

men than women, as in their case the objection stated above does not exist. It is becoming more and more difficult in the West, too, for unmarried girls to get husbands.

Similar is the case with the caste system and other social customs.

So, if it be necessary to change any social custom, the *necessity* underlying it should be found out first of all, and by altering it the custom will die of itself. Otherwise no good will be done by condemnation or praise.

(2) Now the question is: Is it for the good of the public at large that social rules are framed, or society is formed? Many reply to this in the affirmative; some, again, may hold that it is not so. Some men, being comparatively powerful, slowly bring all others under their control and by stratagem, force, or adroitness gain their own objects. If this be true, what can be the meaning of the statement that there is danger in giving liberty to the ignorant? What, again, is the meaning of liberty?

Liberty does not certainly mean the absence of obstacles in the path of misappropriation of wealth etc. by you and me, but it is our natural right to be allowed to use our own body, intelligence, or wealth according to our will, without doing any harm to others; and all the members of a society ought to have the same opportunity for obtaining wealth, education, or knowledge. The second question is: Those who say that if the ignorant and the poor be given liberty, i.e. full right to their body, wealth, etc. and if their children have the same opportunity to better their condition and acquire knowledge as those of the rich and the highly situated, they would be perverse—do they say this for the good of society, or blinded by their selfishness? In England, too, I have heard, "Who will serve us, if the lower classes get education?"

For the luxury of a handful of the rich, let millions of men and women remain submerged in the hell of want and abysmal depth of ignorance; for if they get wealth and education, society will be upset!

Who constitute society? The millions—or you, I, and a few others of the upper classes?

Again, even if the latter be true, what ground is there for our vanity that we lead others? Are we omniscient? उद्धरेदात्मनात्मानम् —"One should raise the self by the self." Let each work out his own salvation. It is freedom in every way, i.e. advance towards Mukti, the worthiest gain of man. To advance oneself towards freedom, physical, mental, and spiritual, and help others to do so is the supreme prize of man. Those social rules which stand in the way of unfoldment of this freedom are injurious, and steps should be taken to destroy them speedily. Those institutions should be encouraged by which men advance in the path of freedom.

That in this life we feel a deep love at first sight towards a particular person who may not be endowed with extraordinary qualities, is explained by the thinkers of our country as due to the association of a past incarnation.

Your question regarding the will is very interesting: it is the subject to know. The essence of all religions is the annihilation of desire, along with which comes, of a certainty, the annihilation of the will as well, for desire is only the name of a particular mode of the will. Why, again, is this world? Or why are these manifestations of the will? Some religions hold that the evil will should be destroyed and not the good. The denial of desire here would be compensated by enjoyments hereafter. This reply does not of course satisfy the wise. The Buddhists, on the other hand, say that desire is the cause of misery, its annihilation is quite desirable. But like killing a man in the effort to kill the mosquito on his cheek, they have gone to the length of annihilating their own selves in their efforts to destroy misery according to the Buddhist doctrine.

The fact is, what we call will is an inferior modification of something higher. Desirelessness means the disappearance of the inferior modification in the form of will and the appearance of that superior state. That state is beyond the range of mind and intellect. But though the look of the gold mohur is quite different from that of the rupee and the pice, yet as we know for certain that the gold mohur is greater than either, so that highest state, Mukti, or Nirvâna, call it what you like, though out of the reach of the mind and intellect, is greater than the will and all other powers. It is no power, but power is its modification, therefore, it is higher. Now you will see that the result of the proper exercise of the will, first with motive for an object, and then without motive, is that the will-power will attain a much higher state.

In the preliminary state, the form of the Guru is to be

meditated upon by the disciple. Gradually it is to be merged in the Ishta. By Ishta is meant the object of love and devotion. . . .

It is very difficult to superimpose divinity on man, but one is sure to succeed by repeated efforts. God is in every man, whether man knows it or not; your loving devotion is bound to call up the divinity in him.

Ever your well-wisher,
VIVEKANANDA

(16)*

CALIFORNIA,
21st February, 1900.

MY DEAR AKHANDANANDA,

I am very glad to receive your letter and go through the details of news. Learning and wisdom are superfluities, the surface glitter merely, but it is the heart that is the seat of all power. It is not in the brain, but in the heart that the Atman, possessed of knowledge, power, and activity, has Its seat. शतं चैका च हृदयस्य नाड्यः —"The nerves of the heart are a hundred and one," etc. The chief nerve-centre near the heart, called the sympathetic ganglia, is where the Atman has Its citadel. The more heart you will be able to manifest, the greater will be the victory you achieve. It is only a few that understand the language of the brain, but everyone, from the Creator down to a clump of grass, understands the language that comes from the heart. But then, in our country, it is a case of rousing men that are, as it were, dead. It will take time, but if you have infinite patience and perseverance, success is bound to come. No mistake in that.

How are the English officials to blame? Is the family of whose unnatural cruelty you have written an isolated one in India? Or are there plenty of such? It is the same story all the country over. But then, it is not as a result of pure wickedness that the selfishness commonly met with in our country has come. This bestial selfishness is the outcome of centuries of failure and repression. It is not real selfishness, but deep-rooted despair. It will be cured at the first inkling of success. It is only this that the English officials are noticing all round; so how can they have faith at the very outset? But tell me, do they not sympathise with any real work that they meet with?

In these days of dire famine, flood, disease, and pestilence, tell me where your Congressmen are! Will it do merely to say, "Hand the government of the country over to us"? And who is there to listen to them? If a man does work, has he to open his mouth to ask for anything? If there be two thousand people like you working in several districts, won't it be the turn of the English themselves to consult you in matters of political moment? स्वकार्यमुद्धरेत्प्राज्ञः—"The wise man should achieve his object." . . . A——was not allowed to open a centre, but what of that? Has not Kishengarh allowed it? —Let him work on without ever opening his lips, there is no use of their telling anything to anybody, or quarrelling with any. Whoever will assist in this work of the Divine Mother of the universe will have Her grace, and whoever will oppose it will not only be अकारणाविष्कृतवैरदारुणः–"raising a deadly enemy for nothing," but also laying the axe to his own prospects. शनैः पन्थाः etc.—all in good time. Many a little makes a mickle. When a great work is being done, when the foundations are laid or a road is constructed, when superhuman energy is needed —it is one or two extraordinary men who silently and noiselessly work through a world of obstacles and difficulties. When thousands of people are benefited, there is a great hue and cry, and the whole country is loud in notes of praise. But, then the machine has already been set a-going and even a boy can work it, or a fool add to it some impetus. Grasp this, that that benefit done to a village or two, that orphanage with its twenty orphans, those ten or twenty workers—all these are enough, that they form the nucleus, never to be destroyed. From these, hundreds of thousands of people will be benefited in time. Now we want half a dozen lions, then excellent work will be turned out by even hundreds of jackals.

If orphan girls happen to come to your hands for shelter, you must take them up above all else. Otherwise, Christian missionaries will take them, poor things, away! What matters it that you have no particular arrangements for them? Through the Divine Mother's will, they will be provided for. When you get a horse, never you worry about the whip. . . . Get together whomsoever you can lay your hands on, no picking and choosing now—everything will be set right in course of time. In every attempt there are many obstacles to cope with, but gradually the path becomes smooth.

Convey to the European officer many thanks from me. Work on fearlessly—there is a hero! Bravo! Thrice well done! The starting of a centre at Bhagalpur that you have written about is no doubt a good idea—enlightening the school-boys and suchlike things. But our mission is for the destitute, the poor, and the illiterate peasantry and labouring classes, and if after everything has been done for them first, there is spare time, then only for the gentry. Those peasants and labouring people will be won over by love. Afterwards it will be they who will collect small sums and start missions at their own villages, and gradually, among those very men teachers will spring.

Teach some boys and girls of the peasant classes the rudiments of learning and infuse a number of ideas into their brains. Afterwards the peasants of each village will collect funds and have one of these in their village. उद्धरेदात्मनात्मानम् —"One must raise oneself by one's own exertions"—this holds good in all spheres. We help them to help themselves. That they are supplying you with your daily bread, is a real bit of work done. The moment they will come to understand their own condition, and feel the necessity of help and improvement, know that your work is taking effect and is in the right direction, while the little good that the moneyed classes, out of pity, do to the poor, does not last, and ultimately it does nothing but harm to both parties. The peasants and labouring classes are in a moribund condition; so what is needed is that the moneyed people will only help them to regain their vitality, and nothing more. Then leave the peasants and labourers to look to their own problem, to grapple with and solve it. But then you must take care not to set up class-strife between the poor peasants, the labouring people and wealthy classes. Make it a point not to abuse the moneyed classes; स्वकार्यमुद्धरेत्प्राज्ञः—"The wise man should achieve his own object."

Victory to the Guru! Victory to the Mother of the Universe! What fear! Opportunity, remedy, and its application—will present themselves. I do not care about the results, good or bad, I shall be happy if only you do this much of work. Wordy warfares, texts and scriptures, doctrines and dogmas—all these I am coming to loathe as poison in this my advanced age. Know this for certain that he who will work will be the crown on my head. Useless bandying of words and making noise is taking away our time, is consuming our life-energy, without pushing the cause of humanitarianism a step farther. माभैः —"Away with fear!" Bravo! There is a hero indeed! May the blessed Guru be enthroned in your heart, and the Divine Mother guide your hands!

Yours affectionately,
VIVEKANANDA.

(17)

(*Written to an American friend*)

ALAMEDA, CALIFORNIA,
12th April, 1900.

Mother is becoming propitious once more. Things are looking up. They must.

Work always brings evil with it. I have paid for the accumulated evil with bad health. I am glad. My mind is all the better for it. There is a mellowness and a calmness in life now, which was never there before. I am learning now how to be detached as well as attached, and mentally becoming my own master.

Mother is doing Her own work; I do not worry much now. Moths like me die by the thousand every instant. Her work goes on all the same. Glory unto Mother! . . . Alone and drifting about in the will-current of the Mother, has been my whole life. The moment I have tried to break this, that moment I have been hurt. Her will be done!

I am happy, at peace with myself, and more of the Sannyâsin than I ever was before. The love for my own kith and kin is growing less every day, and that for Mother increasing. Memories of long nights of vigil with Shri Ramakrishna under the Dakshineswar Banyan are waking up once more. And work? What is work? Whose work? Whom shall I work for?

I am free. I am Mother's child. She works, She plays. Why should I plan? What should I plan? Things came and went, just as She liked, without my planning. We are Her automata. She is the wire-puller.

(18)

ALAMEDA, CALIFORNIA,
18th April, 1900.

MY DEAR JOE,[1]

Just now I received yours and Mrs. Bull's welcome letter. I direct this to London. I am so glad Mrs. Leggett is on the sure way to recovery. I am so sorry Mr. Leggett resigned the presidentship.

Well, I keep quiet for fear of making further trouble. You know my methods are extremely harsh, and once roused I may rattle A—— too much for his peace of mind.

I wrote to him only to tell him that his notions about Mrs. Bull are entirely wrong.

Work is always difficult; pray for me, Joe, that my work may stop for ever, and my whole soul be absorbed in Mother. Her works She knows.

You must be glad to be in London once more; the old friends—give them all my love and gratitude.

I am well, very well mentally. I feel the rest of the soul more than that of the body. The battles are lost and won. I have bundled my things and am waiting for the great deliverer. "Shiva, O Shiva, carry my boat to the other shore."

After all, Joe, I am only the boy who used to listen with rapt wonderment to the wonderful words of Ramakrishna under the Banyan at Dakshineswar. That is my true nature; works and activities, doing good and so forth are all superimpositions. Now I again hear his voice; the same old voice thrilling my soul. Bonds are breaking, love dying, work becoming tasteless, the glamour is off life. Now only the voice of the Master calling. "I come Lord, I come". "Let the dead bury the dead, follow thou Me." "I come, my beloved Lord, I come."

Yes, I come. Nirvâna is before me. I feel it at times, the same infinite ocean of peace, without a ripple, a breath.

I am glad I was born, glad I suffered so, glad I did make big blunders, glad to enter peace. I leave none bound. I take no bonds. Whether this body will fall and release me or I enter into freedom in the body, the old man is gone, gone for ever, never to come back again!

[1] Miss Josephine MacLeod.

The guide, the Guru, the leader, the teacher, has passed away; the boy, the student, the servant, is left behind.

You understand why I do not want to meddle with A—. Who am I to meddle with any, Joe? I have long given up my place as a leader—I have no right to raise my voice. Since the beginning of this year I have not dictated anything in India. You know that. Many thanks for what you and Mrs. Bull have been to me in the past. All blessings follow you ever. The sweetest moments of my life have been when I was drifting; I am drifting again, with the bright, warm sun ahead and masses of vegetation around, and in the heat everything is so still, so calm, and I am drifting languidly, in the warm heart of the river. I dare not make a splash with my hands or feet—for fear of breaking the wonderful stillness, stillness that makes you feel sure it is an illusion!

Behind my work was ambition, behind my love was personality, behind my purity was fear, behind my guidance the thirst of power. Now they are vanishing and I drift. I come, Mother, I come; in Thy warm bosom, floating wheresoever Thou takest me, in the voiceless, in the strange, in the wonderland, I come—a spectator, no more an actor.

Oh, it is so calm! My thoughts seem to come from a great, great distance in the interior of my own heart. They seem like faint, distant whispers, and peace is upon everything, sweet, sweet peace, like that one feels for a few moments just before falling into sleep, when things are seen and felt like shadows—without fear, without love, without emotion. Peace that one feels alone, surrounded with statues and pictures. I come, Lord, I come.

The world *is,* but not beautiful nor ugly, but as sensations without exciting any emotion. Oh, Joe, the blessedness of it! Everything is good and beautiful; for things are all losing their relative proportions to me—my body among the first. Om That Existence!

I hope great things to come to you all in London and Paris. Fresh joy—fresh benefits to mind and body.

With love as ever to you and Mrs. Bull.

Yours faithfully,
VIVEKANANDA.

POEMS

THE SONG OF THE SANNYASIN[1]

Wake up the note! the song that had its birth
Far off, where worldly taint could never reach;
In mountain caves, and glades of forest deep;
Whose calm no sigh for lust or wealth or fame
Could ever dare to break; where rolled the stream
Of knowledge, truth, and bliss that follows both.
Sing high that note, Sannyâsin bold! Say—
"Om Tat Sat, Om!"

Strike off thy fetters! Bonds that bind thee down,
Of shining gold, or darker, baser ore;
Love, hate—good, bad—and all the dual throng.
Know, slave is slave, caressed or whipped, not free;
For fetters though of gold, are not less strong to bind;
Then, off with them, Sannyasin bold! Say—
"Om Tat Sat, Om!"

Let darkness go; the will-o'-the-wisp that leads
With blinking light to pile more gloom on gloom.
This thirst for life, for ever quench; it drags
From birth to death, and death to birth, the soul.
He conquers all who conquers self. Know this
And never yield, Sannyasin bold! Say—
"Om Tat Sat, Om!"

"Who sows must reap," they say, "and cause must bring
The sure effect; good, good; bad, bad; and none
Escape the law. But whoso wears a form
Must wear the chain." Too true; but far beyond
Both name and form is Âtman, ever free.
Know thou art That, Sannyasin bold! Say—
"Om Tat Sat, Om!"

[1] Composed at Thousand Island Park, U.S.A., in July 1895.

They know not truth, who dream such vacant dreams
As father, mother, children, wife, and friend.
The sexless Self! whose father He? whose child?
Whose friend, whose foe is He who is but One?
The Self is all in all, none else exists;
And thou art That, Sannyasin bold! Say—
"Om Tat Sat, Om!"

There is but One—The Free—The Knower—Self!
Without a name, without a form or stain.
In Him is Mâyâ, dreaming all this dream.
The Witness, He appears as nature, soul.
Know thou art That, Sannyasin bold! Say—
"Om Tat Sat, Om!"

Where seekest thou? That freedom, friend, this world
Nor that can give. In books and temples vain
Thy search. Thine only is the hand that holds
The rope that drags thee on. Then cease lament,
Let go thy hold, Sannyasin bold! Say—
"Om Tat Sat, Om!"

Say, "Peace to all: From me no danger be
To aught that lives. In those that dwell on high,
In those that lowly creep, I am the Self in all!
All life both here and there, do I renounce,
All heavens, and earths and hells, all hopes and fears."
Thus cut thy bonds, Sannyasin bold! Say—
"Om Tat Sat, Om!"

Heed then no more how body lives or goes:
Its task is done. Let Karma float it down;
Let one put garlands on, another kick,
This frame; say naught. No praise or blame can be
Where praiser, praised, and blamer, blamed are—one.
Thus be thou calm, Sannyasin bold! Say—
"Om Tat Sat, Om!"

Truth never comes where lust and fame and greed
Of gain reside. No man who thinks of woman
As his wife can ever perfect be;
Nor he who owns the least of things, nor he
Whom anger chains, can ever pass thro' Maya's gates.
So, give these up, Sannyasin bold! Say—
"Om Tat Sat, Om!"

Have thou no home. What home can hold thee, friend?
The sky thy roof, the grass thy bed; and food,
What chance may bring—well cooked or ill, judge not.
No food or drink can taint that noble Self
Which knows Itself. Like rolling river free
Thou ever be, Sannyasin bold! Say—
"Om Tat Sat, Om!"

Few only know the truth. The rest will hate
And laugh at thee, great one; but pay no heed.
Go thou, the free, from place to place, and help
Them out of darkness, Maya's veil. Without
The fear of pain or search for pleasure, go
Beyond them both, Sannyasin bold! Say—
"Om Tat Sat, Om!"

Thus, day by day, till Karma's powers spent
Release the soul for ever. No more is birth,
Nor I, nor thou, nor God, nor man. The "I"
Has All become, the All is "I" and Bliss.
Know thou art That, Sannyasin bold! Say—
"Om Tat Sat, Om!"

KALI THE MOTHER[1]

The stars are blotted out,
    The clouds are covering clouds,
It is darkness vibrant, sonant.
    In the roaring, whirling wind
Are the souls of a million lunatics
    Just loosed from the prison-house,
Wrenching trees by the roots,
    Sweeping all from the path.

The sea has joined the fray,
    And swirls up mountain-waves,
To reach the pitchy sky.
    The flash of lurid light
Reveals on every side
    A thousand, thousand shades
Of Death begrimed and black—
    Scattering plagues and sorrows,
Dancing mad with joy.
    Come, Mother, come!

For Terror is Thy name,
    Death is in Thy breath,
And every shaking step
    Destroys a world for e'er.
Thou "Time,"[2] the All-Destroyer!
    Come, O Mother, come!

Who dares misery love,
    And hug the form of Death,
Dance in Destruction's dance,
    To him the Mother comes.

[1] Composed at Kashmir in 1898.
[2] Kali.

THE CUP

This is your cup—the cup assigned to you from the beginning.
Nay, My child, I know how much of that dark drink is your own brew
Of fault and passion, ages long ago,
In the deep years of yesterday, I know.

This is your road—a painful road and drear.
I made the stones that never give you rest.
I set your friend in pleasant ways and clear,
And he shall come like you, unto My breast.

But you, My child, must travel here.
This is your task. It has no joy nor grace,
But it is not meant for any other hand,
And in My universe hath measured place,
Take it. I do not bid you understand.
I bid you close your eyes to see My face.

PEACE[1]

Behold, it comes in might,
The power that is not power,
The light that is in darkness,
The shade in dazzling light.

It is joy that never spoke,
And grief unfelt, profound,
Immortal life unlived,
Eternal death unmourned.

It is not joy nor sorrow,
But that which is between,
It is not night nor morrow,
But that which joins them in.

[1] Composed at Ridgely Manor, New York, on 21st September, 1899.

It is sweet rest in music,
And pause in sacred art;
The silence between speaking;
Between two fits of passion—
It is the calm of heart.

It is beauty never seen,
And love that stands alone,
It is song that lives un-sung,
And knowledge never known.

It is death between two lives,
And lull between two storms,
The void whence rose creation,
And that where it returns.

To it the tear-drop goes,
To spread the smiling form.
It is the Goal of Life,
And Peace—its only home!

A SONG ON SAMADHI[1]

Lo! The sun is not, nor the comely moon,
All light extinct; in the great void of space
Floats shadow-like the image-universe.

In the void of mind involute, there floats
The fleeting universe, rises and floats,
Sinks again, ceaseless, in the current "I".

Slowly, slowly, the shadow-multitude
Entered the primal womb, and flowed ceaseless,
The only current, "I am", "I am".

[1] Rendered from a Bengali song, composed by Swamiji.

Lo! 'Tis stopped, ev'n that current flows no more,
Void merged into void—beyond speech and mind!
Whose heart understands, he verily does.

TO THE FOURTH OF JULY[1]

Behold, the dark clouds melt away
That gathered thick at night, and hung
So like a gloomy pall above the earth!
Before thy magic touch, the world
Awakes. The birds in chorus sing.
The flowers raise their star-like crowns,
Dew-set, and wave thee welcome fair.
The lakes are opening wide in love
Their hundred thousand lotus-eyes
To welcome thee, with all their depth.
All hail to thee, thou Lord of Light!
A welcome new to thee, today,
O Sun! Today thou sheddest *Liberty*!

Bethink thee how the world did wait,
And search for thee, through time and clime.
Some gave up home and love of friends,
And went in quest of thee, self-banished,
Through dreary oceans, through primeval forests,
Each step a struggle for their life or death;
Then came the day when work bore fruit,
And worship, love, and sacrifice,
Fulfilled, accepted, and complete.
Then thou, propitious, rose to shed
The light of *Freedom* on mankind.

Move on, O Lord, in thy resistless path!
Till thy high noon o'erspreads the world,
Till every land reflects thy light,
Till men and women, with uplifted head,
Behold their shackles broken, and
Know, in springing joy, their life renewed!

[1] Written in Kashmir on the 4th of July, 1898, the anniversary of the American Declaration of Independence.

MY PLAY IS DONE[1]

Ever rising ever falling with the waves of time, still rolling on I go
From fleeting scene to scene ephemeral, with life's currents' ebb and flow,
Oh! I am sick of this unending farce; these shows they please no more,
This ever running, never reaching, nor e'en a distant glimpse of shore!

From life to life I'm waiting at the gates, alas, they open not.
Dim are my eyes with vain attempt to catch one ray long sought.
On little life's high, narrow bridge I stand and see below
The struggling, crying, laughing throng. For what? No one can know.

In front yon gates stand frowning dark, and say: "No farther way,
This is the limit; tempt not, Fate, bear it as best you may;
Go, mix with them and drink this cup and be as mad as they.
Who dares to know but comes to grief, stop then, and with them stay."

Alas for me, I cannot rest. This floating bubble, earth—
Its hollow form, its hollow name, its hollow death and birth—
For me is nothing. How I long to get beyond the crust
Of name and form! Ah, ope the gates, to me they open must.

[1] Written in the spring of 1895 in New York.

Open the gates of light, O Mother, to me Thy tired son.
I long, oh, long to return home! Mother, my play is done.

You sent me out in the dark to play, and wore a frightful mask;
Then hope departed, terror came, and play became a task.
Tossed to and fro, from wave to wave in this seething surging sea
Of passions strong and sorrows deep, grief is, and joy *to be*.

Where life is living death, alas! and death—who knows but 'tis
Another start, another round of this old wheel of grief and bliss?
Where children dream bright, golden dreams, too soon to find them dust,
And aye look back to hope long lost and life a mass of rust!
Too late, the knowledge age doth gain, scarce from the wheel we're gone.

When fresh, young lives put their strength to the wheel, which thus goes on
From day to day and year to year. 'Tis but delusion's toy,
False hope its motor; desire nave, its spokes are grief and joy.

I go adrift and know not whither. Save me from this fire!
Rescue me, merciful Mother, from floating with desire!
Turn not to me Thy awful face, 'tis more than I can bear,
Be merciful and kind to me, to chide my faults forbear.

Take me, O Mother, to those shores where strifes
for ever cease;
Beyond all sorrows, beyond tears, beyond e'en
earthly bliss;
Whose glory neither sun, nor moon, nor stars that
twinkle bright,
Nor flash of lightning can express. They but reflect
its light.

Let never more delusive dreams veil off Thy face
from me
My play is done; O Mother, break my chains and
make me free!

A BLESSING[1]

The Mother's heart, the hero's will,
The softest flowers' sweetest feel;
The charm and force that ever sway
The altar-fire's flaming play;
The strength that leads, in love obeys;
Far-reaching dreams, and patient ways,
Eternal faith in Self, in all,
The light Divine in great, in small;
All these and more than I could see,
Today may "Mother" grant to thee!

[1] Written to Miss Alberta Sturges from Perrors Guirec, Brittany, France, on September 22, 1900.

INDEX

BOOKS ON AND BY
SWAMI VIVEKANANDA

WHAT RELIGION IS: IN THE WORDS OF SWAMI VIVEKANANDA

Edited by Swami Vidyatmananda.
Introduction by Christopher Isherwood.

Pages: 372 Rs. 55

RAJA YOGA

Explains union of the individual soul with the universal soul through the 'control of the modifications of the mind'.

Pages: 296 Rs. 36

KARMA YOGA

Tells how the individual soul realizes oneness with the universal soul by doing one's duty without attachment to the fruits thereof.

Pages: 136 Rs. 18

BHAKTI YOGA

Deals with the method of realizing the Lord through divine love unassociated with mundane cravings.

Pages: 120 Rs. 16

JNANA YOGA

Discusses the way of realization of truth through discrimination that Brahman alone is real and all else is illusory.

Pages: 412 Rs. 50

LECTURES FROM COLOMBO TO ALMORA

All the thirty lectures delivered in India from 1897 to 1901.

Pages: 444 Rs. 70

TEACHINGS OF SWAMI VIVEKANANDA

A choice collection with an introduction by Christopher Isherwood.

Pages: 338 Rs. 42

THE LIFE OF SWAMI VIVEKANANDA

By His Eastern and Western Disciples

In Two Volumes each about 650 pages. (With a Glossary, Bibliography, Index and many Illustrations.)

The most exhaustive and reliable biography in English, collating accounts provided by friends, admirers, and disciples. A vivid narration of events in the making of a Prophet and a World Teacher.

Sri C. Rajagopalachari, the noted statesman-philosopher, wrote thus about the tremendous contribution Swami Vivekananda has made to India: 'Swami Vivekananda saved Hinduism and saved India. But for him, we would have lost our religion and would not have gained our freedom. We, therefore, owe everything to Swami Vivekananda.'

He was a man of original thoughts and numerous moods. Efforts have been made in this work to present the Swami in all his moods and varied illumination so as to reveal the man *as he was*.

Paperback Set (2 vols.) Subsidized		Rs. 200
De luxe	Vol. I	Rs. 155
	Vol. II	Rs. 140

REMINISCENCES OF SWAMI VIVEKANANDA

By His Eastern and Western Admirers

(Enlarged edition)

Swami Vivekananda's towering personality influenced numerous persons in India and abroad in various ways. The impress which his life and character made on those who were around him, reveals the multiple facets of Swamiji's personality.

Pages: 472 Rs. 100